I dedicate this book to my wife, Tricia. I've not had a bad day since the day I met her.

About the Author

Roger A. Grimes has been fighting malicious computer hackers and malware for more than three decades (since 1987). He's earned dozens of computer certifications (including CISSP, CISA, MCSE, CEH, and Security+). He even passed the very tough Certified Public Accountant (CPA) exam, although it has nothing to do with computer security and he is the (self-proclaimed) world's worst accountant. He's been a professional penetration tester breaking into companies and their websites and devices for over 20 years. Roger has been on nearly a dozen project teams tasked with hacking various multifactor authentication (MFA) solutions over his career.

He has created and updated dozens of computer security classes and taught thousands of students how to hack or defend. Roger is a frequent presenter at national computer security conferences, including RSA and Black Hat. He's previously written or cowritten 11 books on computer security and more than a thousand magazine articles. He was the weekly computer security columnist for *InfoWorld* and *CSO* magazines for nearly 15 years, and he's been working as a full-time computer security consultant for more than two decades. Roger is frequently interviewed by newspapers, including the Wall Street Journal, magazines, including *Newsweek*, and he has been a guest on radio shows, such as NPR's "All Things Considered." Roger currently advises companies, large and small, around the world on how to stop malicious hackers and malware quickest and most efficiently.

You can contact and read more from Roger at:

- Email: roger@banneretcs.com
- LinkedIn: www.linkedin.com/in/rogeragrimes
- Twitter: @rogeragrimes
- CSOOnline: www.csoonline.com/author/Roger-A.-Grimes

Acknowledgments

I would like to thank Wiley and Jim Minatel for greenlighting this book. I have been giving presentations on this topic for almost two years to enthusiastic crowds, and I'm glad they also saw the enthusiasm it generated. Wiley really is a great place to work with to write a book. Thanks to Kim Wimpsett for her project management. I think this is the third or fourth time Kim and I have worked together on a book. Thanks to Barath Kumar Rajasekaran for his editorial guidance, Pete Gaughan, copyeditor Elizabeth Welch, and proofreader Nancy Carrasco, in helping to prepare this book for publication.

Thanks to my employer, KnowBe4, Inc., and awesome CEO Stu Sjouwerman, Kathy Wattman, Kendra Irmie, and Mary Owens for letting me develop the original Hacking MFA presentation and go around the country presenting it. I truly love working for KnowBe4. It's been my favorite job of my career. Thanks to my friend and KnowBe4's Chief Hacking Officer, Kevin Mitnick, for showing me and the world many ways to hack what they thought was unhackable MFA solutions. Thanks to Erich Kron, my coworker, for the many discussions we had about MFA, for his MFA device demonstrations, and for many of the pictures in this book. I was lucky to have found and work elbow to elbow with a good friend and knowledgeable coworker. My wife, Tricia, frequently says she prefers Erich's presentation style over mine. . .so there's also that. Thanks to Corey Nachreiner and Alexandre Cagnoni of WatchGuard Technologies for agreeing to be this book's technical editors and for providing hours of discussion on the best MFA solutions and how to hack them. I think both of them have forgotten more than I know about MFA. My special thanks to Rolf Lindemann of Nok Nok for MitM classifications and FIDO defense information.

I want to thank all the MFA developers and vendors who have befriended me over the last two years and challenged me to see how secure their particular MFA solution was. It was only by looking at and reviewing well over a hundred solutions that I felt comfortable enough to write a book like this. Thanks to the hundreds of article writers and YouTube posters showing how they hacked various MFA solutions. Lastly, I have strived to be technically accurate at all times. If, however, I said something technically wrong, I apologize. I'm only human and I tried my best.

Contents at a Glance

Contents

Introduction

This book came about through an interesting happenstance. Arguably, the world's most infamous hacker, Kevin Mitnick, co-owner and Chief Hacking Officer at KnowBe4, Inc., did a public presentation that included showing how he could easily "hack around" two-factor authentication using a simple phishing email. Kevin is a lot more famous than I am, and his demonstration hack was viewed by thousands of people. And about that many wrote to him to get more details.

So many people wrote and requested interviews that the KnowBe4 (who I also work for) public relations team asked if I could help answer queries Kevin couldn't get to. I was glad to. I've got decades of experience in hacking different MFA solutions. Reporters accustomed to covering computer security topics frequently asked if we had yet reported the exploit Kevin used to the MITRE list of Common Vulnerabilities and Exposures (cve.mitre.org). The CVE is where most cybersecurity vulnerabilities, new or old, are listed and tracked. When a brand-new exploit is discovered, it's customary to report it to the CVE, along with relevant details. Most of us in the cybersecurity world follow it to check out what new exploits have been found and to see if we really need to be worried about them.

I laughed. The hack Kevin demonstrated (which is called *session cookie hijacking* and is covered in Chapter 6, "Access Control Token Tricks" of this book) has been around for decades. It's not new at all. In fact, it's one of the most common forms of network hacking. Dozens of free hacking tools are available that help hackers to do it, and it's likely been used to take over millions of user accounts over three decades. It's been used to take over thousands of accounts protected by two-factor authentication, at least since the late 1990s. It's the opposite of new.

I was surprised that when I talked to the beat reporters and computer security people I knew, most thought it was a new attack. So, not only did everyone's mom and dad and regular people not know that it wasn't new, but knowledgeable, experienced computer security people—who you would *expect* to know—didn't know that. It was surprising to me.

I was also surprised that many of the people I spoke to thought the attack was due to a vulnerability in LinkedIn, the website Kevin used in his demonstration. It wasn't. What Kevin showed could be used against hundreds to thousands of popular sites, and LinkedIn, in particular, didn't have a flaw that they were going to have to close. It was an attack against a very common form of multifactor authentication and how it worked in general. No patch was coming to fix some flaw. And you could update the multifactor authentication solution that was used with it to prevent the particular type of attack Kevin demonstrated, but it could be attacked at least another five different ways, as can any multifactor authentication method.

To many of the people I talked with, I shared that I knew of at least 10 ways (as I quickly counted) to hack different forms of multifactor authentication. They were all shocked. As a result, I decided to write a column about it in CSOOnline (www.csoonline.com), where I was a writer at the time. By the time I finished the column (www.csoonline.com/article/3272425/authentication/11-ways-to-hack-2fa.html) in May 2018 I had come up with 11 ways.

I was sharing the news of my column with the CEO of KnowBe4, Stu Sjouwerman, the next morning when he wisely suggested I create a presentation on the topic and start giving it. Within a few days, I had created a new presentation called 12 Ways to Defeat Multi-Factor Authentication (info.knowbe4.com/webinar-12-ways-to-defeat-mfa). As I did more research and thinking, I quickly came up with new ways to hack MFA nearly every week.

I'm up to over 50 ways now, all of which I share in this book. The presentation turned into a long whitepaper. At KnowBe4, the average whitepaper is three to five pages long; mine was 20 pages. It was the longest whitepaper in the history of KnowBe4, and it quickly became a running joke around the office and one that still follows me around. I shared that I had originally created a rough draft double that size and that the 20 pages was my trimmed-down version after their chiding. That then led it into becoming a short e-book (www.knowbe4.com/how-to-hack-multi-factor-authentication) at 40 pages.

I began to give my presentation around the country and world, including at the biggest computer security conferences, RSA and Black Hat. In both places I had standing room–only crowds and long lines of attendees trying to get in to see some of the hack discussions. My original 12 Ways to Defeat Multi-Factor Authentication presentation grew to be so long that I now have to choose which fifth of the hacks I'm going to share with audiences, although Kevin's original MFA hacking demo is still clearly a crowd favorite (and I provide the URL for it in this book).

Jim Minatel, my longtime friend and acquisitions editor at Wiley, came to see me give the presentation at RSA and saw the enthusiastic crowds. I was sick as a dog when I gave the presentation. In fact, I was hospitalized for a week the day after the presentation with an acute, life-threatening illness. I felt like I had done a terrible job at presenting the material. I certainly would love a future do-over. But Jim saw the crowds and the energy the material generated and asked if I would write a book on the subject. I said yes over lunch, and this is that book. The best part is that now I've given hundreds and hundreds of pages to share everything I know on the subject. Even then I'm sure several more books of the same size could be written on the subject. Multifactor authentication and its weaknesses are many. In truth, even this book is just scratching the surface. It's 500-plus pages of summary material. But I hope all readers will better understand the strengths and weaknesses of multifactor authentication and that MFA developers will create better, more secure, solutions.

The ultimate objective of this book is to appropriately frame the security and weaknesses of all MFA solutions. If you know only the benefits and none of the risks, you're more likely to implement an MFA solution without the appropriate policies, controls, and education. This book is a push-back against the overzealous marketing messages broadcast by some MFA vendors. MFA solutions can significantly reduce many forms of cybersecurity risk, but they aren't a perfect panacea and it doesn't mean we can throw away all the previous computer security lessons learned. If you come away with a suitable understanding of what MFA can and can't do, and change your practices and controls appropriately, then I've done my job.

Who This Book Is For

This book is primarily aimed at anyone who is in charge of or managing their organization's computer security and, in particular, logon authentication. It is for anyone who is considering reviewing, buying, or using multifactor authentication for the first or the tenth time. It's for developers and vendors who make multifactor authentication solutions. Prior to this book there has not been a single place where anyone, customer or vendor, could go to learn about all the common ways multifactor authentication can be hacked. Now there is that source, although I'm sure I haven't covered every hacking method, defense, and caveat. But I tried.

It's mostly for all the people who have heard the great security promises that multifactor authentication will give and somehow equate those vendor promises with a larger falsehood, that using MFA means "I can't get hacked!" Nothing could be further from the truth. This book is your counterargument any time someone tries to convince you that using MFA means you don't have to worry about hacking anymore. That isn't true and will never be true.

It also dispels the naive notion that we really want a 100 percent secure solution. We don't. Society wants a security solution that impacts them the least and provides "just OK" protection. This is a hard reality that both administrators and developers learn in the marketplace of computer security products. Some of the best, really secure computer products never get purchased by more than a few companies, and they end up on the tall heap of unused products.

In that respect, this book reminds me of the famous quote delivered by Jack Nicholson's character, Colonel Nathan Jessup, in the 1992 movie *A Few Good Men*: "You can't handle the truth!" You may not like to hear that we don't want the best security, but ignore what the user wants at your own peril. So, the purpose of this book is not only about developers and customers learning all the ways to hack MFA, but also about when layered security is just *too much* security.

What Is Covered in This Book?

Hacking Multifactor Authentication contains 25 chapters separated into three parts:

Part I: Introduction   Part I discusses authentication basics and the problems that MFA is trying to solve. It includes the background facts you'll need to know to understand why MFA is a favored authentication solution and how it is hacked.

Chapter 1: Logon Problems   Chapter 1 covers the central problems that MFA is trying to solve. MFA didn't come out of the blue. Password and single-factor solutions failed so often that better and improved authentication solutions were invented. Learn about the problems MFA is trying to solve.

Chapter 2: Authentication Basics   Authentication isn't one process—it's a series of connected processes with a multitude of different components. Any of the steps and components can be hacked. To understand how MFA can be hacked, you first have to understand how authentication works with or without MFA involved. Chapter 2 provides that foundation.

Chapter 3: Types of Authentication   Chapter 3 covers dozens of types of authentication, describes how they differ from one another, and examines the inherent strengths and weaknesses of each type of solution.

Chapter 4: Usability vs. Security   Security is always a trade-off between user-friendliness and security. MFA is no exception. The most secure options will often not be tolerated by end users. Chapter 4 covers the fundamental challenges of good security and when good security actually becomes so onerous that it becomes bad security. The best security options are good trade-offs between usability and security. Find out when that line is crossed.

Part II: Hacking MFA   This part of the book covers the various ways to hack and attack various MFA solutions. Mitigations and defenses for each of the attacks are detailed in each chapter.

Chapter 5: Hacking MFA in General   Chapter 5 begins by explaining the very high-level ways that MFA can be hacked, with a summary of the various techniques. Every MFA solution is susceptible to multiple hacking attacks and are covered in the rest of the chapters of this section.

Chapter 6: Access Control Token Tricks   Chapter 6 starts off by discussing, in detail, one of the most popular, decades-long, MFA hacking methods: that of compromising the resulting access control token. Chapter 6 shows multiple ways in which access control tokens can be compromised.

Chapter 7: Endpoint Attacks   A compromised device or computer can be attacked in hundreds of different ways, including bypassing or hijacking MFA solutions. A compromised endpoint cannot be trusted. Chapter 7 discusses several popular endpoint attacks.

Chapter 8: SMS Attacks   Chapter 8 covers multiple Short Message Service (SMS) attacks, including subscriber identity module (SIM) hacks. For years now, the U.S. government has said that SMS should not be used for strong authentication and yet the most common MFA solutions on the Internet involve SMS. Learn why that shouldn't be the case.

Chapter 9: One-Time Password Attacks   One-time password (OTP) solutions are among the most popular MFA solutions, and they are good but not unhackable. Chapter 9 covers the various types of OTP solutions and how to hack them.

Chapter 10: Subject Hjack Attacks   Unlike most of the other MFA attacks described in this book, subject hijack attacks are not very popular. In fact, they have not been knowingly accomplished in a single public attack. Still, they can be done, and simply knowing about them and how they can be accomplished is an important lesson. Chapter 10 covers one specific type of subject hijack attack on the world's most popular corporate authentication platform, in enough detail, that you will likely be worried about them forever.

Chapter 11: Fake Authentication Attacks   Chapter 11 covers a type of MFA attack that can be used successfully against most MFA solutions. It involves taking the end user to a bogus web page and faking the entire authentication transaction, accepting anything the end user types in or provides, as successful. Learn how fake authentication attacks can be prevented.

Chapter 12: Social Engineering Attacks   Social engineering attacks are responsible for the most malicious breaches of any of the hacker attack methods. Social engineering can be used to get around any MFA solution. Chapter 12 covers many of the popular social engineering attack methods against popular MFA solutions.

Chapter 13: Downgrade/Recovery Attacks   Most of the popular MFA solutions allow a lesser secure method to be used to recover the associated account in the event of a problem with the primary MFA method. Chapter 13 covers how to use downgrade/recovery attacks to bypass and disable legitimate MFA solutions.

Chapter 14: Brute-Force Attacks   Many MFA solutions require users to type in PINs and other codes and do not have a mitigating "account lockout" feature enabled to prevent an attacker from guessing over and over until they find that information. In fact, it is so common for relatively new MFA solutions to forget this important safety feature, as Chapter 14 shows, that it is almost more commonplace than not.

Chapter 15: Buggy Software   Security software is as buggy as any other software. MFA solutions are no exception. Chapter 15 discusses why we have buggy software and gives dozens of examples of buggy MFA solutions, including a single bug that led to tens of millions of MFA devices being immediately vulnerable.

Chapter 16: Attacks Against Biometrics   There is not a biometric MFA solution that cannot be hacked or a biometric trait that cannot be mimicked. Chapter 16 describes many such attacks, including attacks against facial and fingerprint recognition, and discusses mitigations against copying and reuse attacks.

Chapter 17: Physical Attacks   A common security dogma says that if an attacker has physical access of your device, it's game over. This is especially true of MFA devices. Chapter 17 will cover multiple physical attacks, ranging from using a multimillion-dollar electron microscope to using a $5 can of compressed air.

Chapter 18: DNS Hijacking   Chapter 18 discusses how hijacking the name resolution service attached to an MFA solution can lead to the whole solution failing. Some MFA solution providers dispute whether this sort of attack should be considered a real attack against the MFA solution since it doesn't attack the MFA solution directly but allows MFA compromises.

Chapter 19: API Abuses   Many MFA solutions have application programming interfaces (APIs). Chapter 19 shows how APIs can be used to compromise a single MFA scenario or a million victims at the same time.

Chapter 20: Miscellaneous MFA Hacks Chapter 20 details several other MFA attacks that don't fit neatly in the other chapters or that made it in this book at the last second.

Chapter 21: Test: Can You Spot the Vulnerabilities? I'm going to test you. This chapter introduces a real-world, very secure MFA solution that is used by one of the largest companies in the world. After I describe how it works, most readers will think that it is pretty unhackable. But it is hackable, and I want you to use what you've learned in the previous chapters to find those potential vulnerabilities.

Part III: Looking Forward This last part of the book discusses how to better design MFA solutions and what the future of authentication may look like.

Chapter 22: Designing a Secure Solution Perhaps one of the most important tasks facing the world today is how to allow voters to remotely securely cast votes online in free elections. Chapter 22 discusses the ways remote voting can go wrong and what a secure, remote MFA voting solution might look like.

Chapter 23: Selecting the Right MFA Solution Chapter 23 covers how you and your organization can pick the right MFA solution, one that appropriately balances usability and security and that works in most of your critical security scenarios. There is no one perfect MFA solution, but Chapter 23 helps you pick the best solution for you and your organization.

Chapter 24: The Future of Authentication The authentication of the future is probably going to look a lot different than the choices we have today. It's likely to look a lot different than the perfect MFA solutions we designed in Chapter 22 and the one you picked in Chapter 23. Find out why the future is different from what we have today.

Chapter 25: Takeaway Lessons Chapter 25 closes the book by summarizing the most important lessons learned in the previous chapters, all tidied up in one place for easy referencing.

Appendix: List of MFA Vendors Appendix lists over 115 different MFA vendors and includes a link to a Microsoft Excel spreadsheet which lists the different MFA vendors which lists their basic features to help you explore and choose an MFA solution.

MFA Is Good

Before we get into the meat of the book, I want to dispel the myth that I think MFA is terrible or useless. I've been presenting at least some of this material for over two years now. The whole goal has always been to share that although MFA does, sometimes significantly so, decrease some forms of authentication attacks, it does not mean MFA is unhackable. And anyone can send you a normal looking phishing email and take over your account even though it is protected by MFA. Believing that MFA is unhackable or can't be easily hacked can lead to weak controls, bad education, and higher-than-necessary cybersecurity risk. At the same time, some readers, after reading the dozens of ways that MFA can be hacked, sometimes easily so, can come away feeling that using MFA is useless or even bad. This is not true.

Every person should use MFA, where it makes sense and they are able, until we come up with some better authentication solutions. Every one of us will be required to use passwords in places, and in some places using passwords is even better and/or more appropriate than using MFA. But where it makes sense to use MFA, and where you can, you should strive to use it. Just be aware that MFA can be hacked, will always be hackable, and in some cases, easily. Adjust your thinking and security controls to accept that reality.

How to Contact Wiley or the Author

Wiley strives to keep you supplied with the latest tools and information you need for your work. Please check the website at wiley.com/go/hackingmultifactor, where I'll post additional content and updates that supplement this book should the need arise.

If you have any questions, suggestions, or corrections, feel free to email me at roger@banneretcs .com.

Introduction

1

Logon Problems

Authentication is the process of something (e.g., a user or a device) proving ownership of an identity account by providing one or more proofs of ownership and control (authentication factors) of that identity account. Weaknesses or compromises of the various authentication methods are responsible for a large amount of malicious hacking.

Chapter 1 will cover logon problems and, in particular, authentication issues due to the widespread use of password authentication. I'll begin by discussing the state of malicious hacking today, followed by password authentication basics and a broader discussion of password-based weaknesses and attacks. I'll explain why multifactor authentication (MFA) is being promoted and becoming increasingly popular.

It's Bad Out There

We clearly have a very serious problem, and it is getting steadily and consistently worse without a hint that it will abate any time soon. Malicious hacking is as bad as it has ever been after more than three decades of struggling to make computer use significantly more secure. Without a doubt, the problem will be worse yet again next year and the year after that. We are in what seems like a perpetual, never-ending up cycle of maliciousness.

How do I know? Because as a practicing computer security professional and columnist for more than three decades, I'm asked at the end of every year if computer attacks will get better or worse in the coming year. And for 32 years I've answered that they will become worse, and my prediction has never been wrong. Even knowing that, each new year comes, and somehow I'm still truly astounded by how much worse malicious hacking has gotten. Despite my experience, I keep secretly hoping each year that we must have finally hit the peak.

After all, how could it possibly get worse? Hackers are breaking into nearly any place they want at will. Pretty high numbers of end users can still be easily tricked into opening a malicious email and clicking on a rogue file attachment. There are hundreds of millions of unique-looking, malware variants created and put into our online ecosystem every year. Large cities, like Baltimore and Atlanta, have been brought to their knees by ransomware. Cyberattacked businesses in operation for decades are closing doors and laying off all employees after just one attack. Nations think nothing of cyberattacking each other, destroying infrastructure more thoroughly than any physical bomb would be capable of. Many nations not only don't stop malicious hacking but actually rely on the billions in funding and stolen secrets that the cyberattacks provide. Thousands of company-like entities exist solely to cyberattack others. They have employees, org charts, human resource departments, weekly paychecks, and benefits. People are being killed because of cyberattacks, and the number of deaths due to them will only keep rising.

It didn't used to be this way. Two decades ago, the worst we had to worry about was a mischievous malware program playing Yankee Doodle on a PC speaker (`malware.wikia.org/wiki/Yankeedoodle`) or a boot sector virus admonishing us to decriminalize pot (`en.wikipedia.org/wiki/Stoned_(computer_virus)`) with its "Legalise Marijuana" message. The fastest-spreading malware program to date, the 2003 SQL Slammer worm (`en.wikipedia.org/wiki/SQL_Slammer`), which exploited every unpatched Microsoft SQL instance reachable from the Internet in minutes, didn't do anything malicious beyond spreading too quickly. Yes, there were the occasional malware programs that did something intentionally malicious, like the 1992 Michelangelo virus (`en.wikipedia.org/wiki/Michelangelo_%28computer_virus%29`), which formatted hard drives, but they were the rare exception and not the rule.

Today, we wish we only had to worry about prank viruses and script kiddies out to prove their programming mettle to their peers. Today's cyber incident world is crowded with full-time, professional criminals out to steal money, identities, and secrets. The mischievous script kiddie hackers have all but been squeezed out of the hacking world, or they've ended up being offered high-paying jobs on both sides of the cybersecurity world. Almost no one gets arrested—it's so rare that it's almost a freak occurrence. Most crimes are happening across global borders where one country doesn't recognize another country's jurisdictional boundaries or subpoenas, assuming the victimized could gather anything appearing like real evidence anyway.

The hacking methods used are not new. For more than two decades, just two root causes have been behind 90 to 99 percent of all successful hacking attacks: social engineering and unpatched software. Seventy to ninety percent of all malicious data breaches happen because of social engineering and phishing (`blog.knowbe4.com/70-to-90-of-all-malicious-breaches-are-due-to-social-engineering-and-phishing-attacks`). Usually it occurs because people have been phished out of their passwords or tricked into running a trojan horse program. Unpatched software accounts for 20 to 40 percent of all malicious data breaches. Every other possible root hacking cause (e.g., eavesdropping, misconfiguration, human error, insider attacks) added all together accounts for only 1 to 10 percent of all successful compromises.

And there have been lots of data breaches. We almost don't bother to pay attention when the latest 100 million plus record data breach occurs. Meh. It barely makes the news. The Privacy Rights Clearinghouse Data Breach database shows that more than 11.6 billion records breached from nearly 10,000 separate public data breaches since 2005 (`www.privacyrights.org/data-breaches`) have been publicly reported. And those are only the ones we know about. Most data breaches go unnoticed and/or unreported. And many of those breaches are due to password issues.

The Problem with Passwords

The move to MFA and away from passwords didn't happen without a significant reason. Hacked passwords play an oversized role in malicious hacking and are the internationally accepted currency of the hacker world. So many passwords have been hacked and are available for unauthorized use that hackers have a hard time selling them for decent money. Just a decade or so ago, a single compromised password could earn a hacker many tens of dollars, and collections of compromised passwords were guarded like gold at the end of a digital rainbow. But today most hackers have so many of them sitting around that buyers aren't willing to pay much at all, if anything. It's not that compromised passwords aren't being used to hack people and organizations—they still are in very large numbers. There are just so, so many publicly available compromised passwords that illegal hackers can't even begin to use them all. There are only so many minutes in a day. It's an embarrassment of riches.

Instead, compromised logons end up being placed on the Internet where anyone can see and use them. Single password *dumps* contain billions of previously compromised logon names and passwords. In 2019, a single password archived dump, named Collection#1, contained more than 770 million logon names and passwords. It made all the major news channels—one of those cybersecurity events that goes far beyond just the IT-centric world. It was to be surpassed a few days later by related Collections#2-5 with 2.2 billion passwords. Altogether they contained nearly 3 billion compromised logon names and passwords that anyone, including you, could download and use. Read about it here: www.forbes.com/sites/daveywinder/2019/02/01/2-2-billion-accounts-found-in-big-gest-ever-data-dump-how-to-check-if-youre-a-victim. Another hacker released another almost 1 billion newly obtained accounts in 2019 (www.zdnet.com/article/a-hacker-has-dumped-nearly-one-billion-user-records-over-the-past-two-months). So, that's more than 4 billion logon accounts within a few months of each other alone available on the web. There is a good chance that at least one of your logon accounts, with your password, is available on the web for anyone to view and use.

Multiple websites are dedicated to telling you if your passwords end up in one of these many password dumps. The most used and famous one is Troy Hunt's HaveIBeenPwned (haveibeenpwned.com). Started as a hobby, it now contains more than 8.5 billion logon names and passwords from copied password dumps found on the Internet and dark web. You simply type in your email address, and the website will tell you how many times your logon name and password appears in its database from all the collected password breaches it knows about. Figure 1.1 shows examples of my business and personal email accounts and whether they have been noted as having been previously breached. The first example, using my business email address of rogerg@knowbe4.com, shows it is connected with zero breaches. The second, my personal email address that I've had for more than 20 years, roger@banneretcs.com, has been included in at least 10 breaches. That's up two since the last time I checked it a few months ago. In my anecdotal experience, when I introduce people to Troy's site and they check using their email address, they usually find out that their logon information has been compromised in at least five places. Usually two or three of the logons contain no longer used passwords, but not all of them. Almost always the user was unaware of most of the data breaches and is currently using at least one of the previously compromised passwords, if not several.

Figure 1.1: Examples of compromised logon names and password checks from Troy Hunt's HaveIBeenPwned website

The website not only tells you how many times your logon name and password has been compromised but also gives you the websites that were compromised to get it or the password dumps it was found in. Most of the time, as in the case of my personal passwords getting compromised, it had nothing to do with any action I performed. It was due to other websites, where I had legitimate logon accounts (like Adobe.com when I registered to download a paid version of Adobe Acrobat), getting compromised, but, yes, instances may also include times when a computer I was on was compromised or when I got socially engineered out of it.

Troy's site offers an *application programming interface* (API) that anyone can use to submit multiple names to check at one time. It's mostly available so concerned corporate IT people can query Troy's database to find out how many of their users' passwords are out on the Internet and to sign up to be alerted if an employee's password suddenly appears due to a newly reported breach.

NOTE Another site similar to HaveIBeenPwned is HPI Identity Leak Checker (`sec.hpi.de/ilc/?`). You enter your email address and it sends you a report listing where your email address and other personal information has been compromised that it knows about. It will tell you if information beyond your logon information has been compromised, such as Social Security number, telephone number, and banking details.

Many other free and commercial tools and services are available that will notify you if your password ends up on one of the dumps or data breaches. For example, I use a password manager program called 1Password (`1password.com`), which notifies me when a website on my personal logon list gets compromised. In 2018, it proactively notified me when a data breach was documented involving Facebook (see Figure 1.2). When it first alerted me, I was so shocked that it included Facebook that I thought something was wrong with the password manager program. I looked around on various IT security news websites and nothing was out yet about a Facebook data breach. About three hours later the news confirming the breach began to pour into every major news media website. My password manager product was on to it hours earlier, and I had already changed my password before the news broke.

Figure 1.2: Real-world example of my password manager notifying me of a new password data breach involving Facebook

There are many ways for hackers to locate your password if it is already in an existing breach. One way is for them just to use the API that attaches to Troy Hunt's website. Troy doesn't know who is or isn't checking his website for password breach checks, plus he doesn't store the user's password in a way that anyone, hacker or not, can just pull up individual plaintext passwords. But his site can be used to see if a particular user's or company's passwords exist in a known password dump. If it is, then the hacker can try some of the more popular, larger, dump sites and get the full logon information, including the password.

Dozens of free and commercial tools exist that allow anyone, including hackers, not only to look up inclusions of people's logon names and passwords in the various password dumps, but also to readily return the associated password in plaintext. When a malicious hacker wants to attack a target, they can just pull up one of their favorite hacking open source intelligence (OSINT) tools and type in a name or domain URL, and the tool will do the searching and return everything it finds. One popular OSINT tool for researching password dump databases is recon-ng (see Figure 1.3).

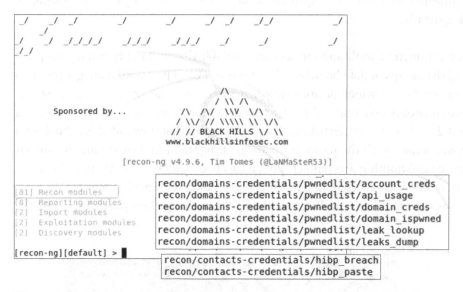

Figure 1.3: The recon-ng OSINT tool, which contains many modules for doing mass searches of password dump databases

The recon-ng OSINT tool is one of the most popular tools for researching password dump databases, but there are dozens. One great central collection site of OSINT tools is Awesome OSINT (github.com/jivoi/awesome-osint); see Figure 1.4. It contains more than one hundred OSINT tools, including many that search for password dumps.

In summary, there are billions of people's passwords out on the Internet, possibly including yours, and finding and using them just isn't that hard. This is just one of the big problems with using passwords for authentication. We will cover several more in the section "Password Problems and Attacks," later in this chapter.

NOTE   My advice is to use these password dump checking sites and tools to see if your or your organization's logon name and passwords are out on the Internet or dark web. Don't let hackers be the only ones checking. If you find any compromised logon accounts, make the associated users change their compromised passwords unless they know for sure that the passwords they are using now are not the same ones at the time of the associated compromises.

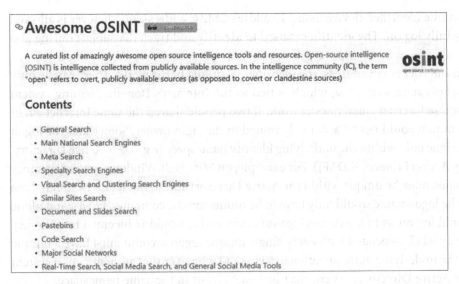

Figure 1.4: Awesome OSINT website

Passwords are not inherently evil, but they do contain built-in weaknesses that lead them to being one of the top causes of compromises and are responsible for the push to use MFA to get us beyond passwords into a password-less world. To understand MFA and MFA hacks better, it's good to have an understanding of the strengths and weaknesses of password authentication.

Password Basics

Password authentication is usually more involved than most people new to computer security initially suspect. Many pieces and parts are involved with setting up a password, storing it, and using it in the future to authenticate a logon.

> **NOTE**   A *subject* is any security principal associated with a logon account, be it a user, computer, service, application program, device, or anything else that must log on and be authenticated. When authentication is performed, the subject may be involved in manually submitting the needed information, or a process or application on their behalf may do so.

Identity

First, all passwords must be associated with a logon name or some other sort of identity label, which is unique in the associated authentication database. The "logon name" can be any text label associated with the logon mechanism. It can be an email address, logon name, application/service name or identifier, global unique identifier, device name, IP address, MAC address, or whatever is allowed or required to successfully log on. The identifier is used to identify and track the subject during and after the logon.

Sometimes, like an Internet email address, the identifier is unique in the world. There can be only one person using `roger@banneretcs.com`, which is tied to the Internet's Domain Naming System (DNS), at one time, or else Internet email doesn't work. If two people shared the same Internet email address, any email sent to it could not be accurately routed to the right owner. Sometimes the logon identity needs to be unique only within the underlying identity namespace (e.g., DNS, Active Directory, Lightweight Directory Access Protocol [LDAP]). For example, on Microsoft Windows Active Directory networks, the logon name must be unique within the Active Directory forest. But if I had a stand-alone Windows computer, the logon name would only have to be unique on the computer. On a stand-alone computer, anyone could log on as `billgates@microsoft.com` and it wouldn't hiccup a bit. The key point is that the identity label associated with every single unique logon account must have a unique identity label within the underlying authentication system (and whatever that authentication system relies on, like DNS or Active Directory). There can't be two `rogergs` in the same namespace.

The Password

The subject (or their representative) provides a password during the initial setup registration and during subsequent authentication events. The password can be temporary or permanent. Passwords can usually be made up of any allowed combination of characters, with a certain minimum and maximum number of characters, and sometimes other required constituent components. The allowed characters may be alphabetic (say letters *a* to *z* in the American alphabet), may or may not allow capitalized letters (say letters *A* to *Z*), may or may not allow numbers (0–9), may or may not allow other nonalphabetic characters (such as !@#$%^&*()-), and may or may not allow other characters not even represented on a standard 93-character keyboard. For example, Microsoft Windows allows any Unicode character you can create from a computer keyboard or application, which includes more than 65,000 different characters. Further, passwords are constrained to whatever language is installed and allowed. Most computer systems natively support English-based passwords, but not all systems natively support other foreign languages. For example, Chinese-language passwords may be supported only on systems that understand and support Simplified Chinese.

> **NOTE** Passwords are constrained, at the very least, to what characters are possible on a particular computer system. Different types of computer systems use different allowed character sets. Popular character sets are known as ASCII (7- and 8-bit), ANSI, UTF, and Unicode. Many times, what characters are allowed to be used are restricted far below all possible allowable characters, but the maximum number of characters allowed to be used in a password will be equal to or less than the total number of characters that can be represented with the computer system. Many available characters are restricted because they are used internally in the operating system to indicate "control characters" or are unprintable. For example, although Windows allows and uses up to 65,000 different characters, several dozen are not allowed to be used in passwords.

A minimum or maximum password size may be enforced. A common minimum password size is six characters, but that has been slowly creeping upward over the last decade or two. Today, many companies require a minimum of 8-to-12 characters for a regular end user's password and may require 16-character (or longer) passwords for elevated administrator accounts. Usually spaces are not allowed at the beginning or end of a password, and in any event they may be "stripped" out accidentally by the involved application or operating system. A space may be allowed in the middle of a password, but older systems often mistakenly truncated any supplied password containing a space at the space as if it were a control character signaling the end of the password. Most of today's password systems will handle spaces in the middle of a password, but many still will not allow or handle them correctly at the beginning or end.

Password Registration

During a user's initial password registration, which may or may not be initially accomplished by the actual end user (an admin could set up the initial account), the password is associated with the unique identity label. The logon account may require or allow additional information, such as the user's full name, alternate identifiers, and department.

The other information may or may not be verified. For example, if the full name is required, that information may be verified by checking the involved user's federal or state identification card (like a driver's license or passport) or may be automatically supplied by some other previous process that did the verification (e.g., human resources or payroll). The more information that is verified and included in the logon account the better, from a security viewpoint. Each piece of included information could be required during a logon event or included and passed along during an authentication or authorization event. If used in this way, these pieces of information are known as authentication *attributes*. Security-centric types want as many attributes to be included in an authentication event as it takes to be assured that the person is who they say they are and assures their uniqueness in the system. A privacy-centric security person wants to minimize the required attributes to the bare minimum needed to complete the authentication or authorization event. More on this in the next chapter.

Password Complexity

Usually the password is checked to make sure that it meets any requirements, such as minimum and maximum size, composition, and complexity, and may even be checked to make sure it is not a common password or has been used previously by the same identity account.

Some password authentication systems allow almost any combination of characters to be used. Others require that particular types of characters be used, such as lowercase alphabetic letters, uppercase alphabetic letters, numbers, and symbols. The password review process may even require something like "Must use three of the following five character sets." Sadly, what is included and required for password complexity is often different for different authentication systems. Password complexity, when required, is an attempt to prevent the password from being constructed of extremely popular and easy-to-guess or easy-to-crack passwords.

The "official" term to describe password randomness is covered by the term *entropy*. A password's entropy is a measure of its true randomness. A truly random password—as might be picked by a password manager program, say #kF&NBn1A—is considered to have high entropy. The passwords most humans pick, say Frogfrog1, are considered to have low entropy. Low-entropy passwords are easier to guess and hack than passwords with high entropy. High-entropy passwords are harder for humans to create, remember, and use. But if we all used only high-entropy passwords, password guessers and crackers would have a much harder time successfully compromising them.

> **NOTE** The longer a password is, even without any special characters, the higher entropy it has. Faced with a choice of using more special characters or using a longer password, use a longer password. It will provide more entropy protection and be easier to remember and use (for humans).

Password Storage

Passwords can be stored in their *plaintext* form exactly as typed in, but they can also be slightly modified in ways the user may be unaware of. For example, especially in older password systems, all alphabetic characters, whether typed in uppercase or lowercase, would be converted and stored in a single case. Or overly long passwords would be silently truncated. The user may think they are using a very long and hard-to-crack password, not aware that the system only cares about and stores the first six characters.

The location where the passwords are stored may be on a local file or database, stored in a network location, stored in one or more other cached locations (including on disk or in memory), other non-file locations (like the Windows registry or memory), or a combination of two or more. Passwords or their subsequent representations (covered more in a moment) can be stored in multiple separate databases, appear distinctly different, and be used in different ways in each location.

It's important that wherever any identity and password information (and all required attributes used in authentication and authorization) be stored in secure locations. If an attacker can access the authentication database, wherever it is stored, it's game over! Most authentication databases and storage locations can be accessed only by highly privileged administrators.

Password Hashes

In most of today's password authentication systems, any typed-in passwords are immediately converted to another non-plaintext representation. These representations are often the result of cryptographically hashing the plaintext password. Cryptographic hashing algorithms return a consistent, but unique, output for any unique input. For example, if I type in a password of **frog**, the (SHA2) hashed output is 74FA5327CC0F4E947789DD5E989A61A8242986A596F170640AC90337B1DA1EE4. And it will always be the same output any time I type in **frog** (without an additional salt).

A *salt* is a randomly generated set of characters that may be added to the password hash generation so that if the passwords of two different users are identical and somehow revealed in hashed form, one person's password and related hash would not immediately reveal the password of another user with an identical password hash. The additional salt ends up making the two hashes of the same password different. When a salt is used, the salt value or algorithm used must be stored along with the password hash or easily regenerated in some other way for use in subsequent authentication events.

The hashing (with or without the salt), when used, is done to provide some immediate protection if the password authentication database is compromised. That way, any attacker gaining access can see only the representative hash and not the original plaintext password. It doesn't stop all types of password attacks, but it does stop some and it makes others harder to accomplish. Some authentication systems use salts in their password hashing and others don't. The ones using salts are considered at least slightly more secure.

There are many cryptographic hash worldwide standards that have been commonly used as password hashing algorithms in the past and currently, including Message Digest 5 (MD5), Windows LANManager (LM), Windows NT (NT), Password-Based Key Derivation Function (PBKDF), Secure Hash Algorithm-1 (SHA-1), Secure Hash Algorithm-2 (SHA-2), Secure Hash Algorithm-3 (SHA-3), and Bcrypt. Today, the NT (non-salted) and PBKDF2 (salted) hashes are used by default for password hashing on Windows computers and SHA-2 or Bcrypt on Linux/BSD/Unix-style computers.

The output of the hashing algorithm (called the *hash*, *message digest*, and other things) is known as the *password hash* when passwords are hashed and often becomes the only representation of the password when stored and used. The plaintext version of the password is not stored anywhere on disk or in memory. As soon as the user types the plaintext password in, it is stored or used in its hashed form. Again, this is done for safety and security reasons. Even when MFA is used, authentication hashes of some sort may still be involved in authentication transactions, for similar reasons.

Password Authentication

When a password authentication event happens, it is typically a user (or some other type of subject) trying to successfully authenticate to a system, and/or vice versa. This is often known as *client-server* authentication, although the authentication may be taking place entirely on a single computer or device, may involve only a client operating system, or may be client-to-client or server-to-server. The phrase *client-server* (or client/server) indicates that one subject is authenticating itself to another and that one side is intentionally subjecting itself ("the client") to the other's ("the server") approval, which processes, evaluates, and approves or denies the authentication attempt. The client may be trying to access a protected resource on the server, or the server may be acting purely as an authentication provider and verifier.

When password authentication is performed, the subject, when prompted by the server, types in or otherwise submits the identity label and the password. Again, the password is usually immediately transformed to its representative password hash. The server accepts the submitted password or hash and compares it to the password or password hash associated with the submitted identity label.

If the passwords or password hashes agree, the subject is considered successfully authenticated. If the passwords or password hashes don't agree, the authentication attempt is considered a failed authentication. The subject may be allowed one or more additional authentication attempts, or they may be prevented from trying again (for a set period of time or until an admin "unlocks" the identity account) after a predetermined number of successive failed attempts.

The user may have to remember the password and/or write or document it in some way for future use. Some operating systems and applications may offer (or do automatically) to store and reuse the typed-in password if used successfully at least once previously by the user. The password may be stored in another additional location that is specified by the operating system or application. It may be stored on disk so that all subsequent future authentication events are handled automatically, or it may be just stored in memory so that only future authentications done before restarting the computer or device are automatically handled. Programs known as *password managers* are made to store multiple passwords and may be able to automatically submit the passwords on the user's behalf when instructed, along with other related helpful features. Password managers can be part of an operating system or may need to be installed as an additional *third-party program* by the user.

Challenge-Response Authentication

In some operating systems or applications, if an attacker obtains the password hash, the hash alone can be used to be successful in some forms of authentication hacking. To prevent attackers from stealing or eavesdropping on the hash during a password authentication event, a *challenge-response* authentication set of steps may be used. When used, not even the password hash appears outside of the password storage database (although it can always be derived or verified). Instead, the client and server use the hash to create another intermediate representation, which can be used to verify the hash that is used to verify the password. Here is a simplified representation of the steps involved in a challenge-response authentication event when a client wants to authenticate to a server using password authentication:

1. The client attempts to authenticate to a server.
2. The client provides or the server prompts the client for their identity.
3. The server generates a random set of characters known as the *challenge* and sends it to the client.
4. The client uses their password hash to manipulate the challenge into another intermediate form called the *response* and sends it back to the server.
5. The server takes the client's stored hash and performs the same calculation on the challenge to create what should be an identical response if authentication is to be successful.
6. The server compares the response sent back by the client to the response it generated using the client's stored password hash. If they are identical, the client is successfully authenticated.

Challenge-response authentication is often used on client-server authentication performed over a network. That way, if the attacker is eavesdropping, they will not get the password in plaintext or even the password hash. However, if the attacker can get both the challenge and the response, they can try to derive the involved password hash, because the only difference between the challenge and response is the password hash plus the algorithmic steps to generate the response (which are generally well-known).

Password Policies

Password authentication systems, or the people who control them, may have a recommended or enforced password policy. A *password policy* includes all the recommended or enforced characteristics required of any password used in a particular authentication system or for all managed authentication systems under a single sphere of control. A password policy may have both recommended and enforced provisions. It can contain a host of prescriptions, including, but not limited to, the following:

- Minimum password size
- Maximum password size
- Password composition and complexity
- Maximum number of time that a password can be used before expiring
- Minimum number of days a password must be used before it can be changed
- How many times a failed authentication event can happen successively before causing an account lockout
- Disallowance of previous used past passwords
- Determination of whether shared passwords are allowed
- Declaration of whether anyone, including an admin, can request or know someone else's password
- Who can reset someone's password
- What password hashes are allowed in a password hash system
- Whether salting is allowed or required
- How a password authentication database is encrypted or protected
- What password authentication is used locally and/or over the network

A written or declared password policy often can state recommendations and requirements that cannot easily be enforced using technical controls. For example, these can include, but are not limited to, the following:

- Passwords must be unique between all unrelated systems or applications.
- Passwords cannot be written down.
- Passwords cannot be shared.

A good password policy considers the totality of any password authentication system. It recognizes that all the components protecting the password authentication system can be used in an attack against the system, and so it strives to minimize weaknesses.

Common Password Policy

For decades, a common password policy looked like this:

- The password must be a minimum of eight characters long.
- The password must be complex, composed of at least one nonalphabetic symbol.
- The password must be changed every 90 days.
- Password lockout must happen after 3 successive failed logon attempts within 15 minutes and lock the account out until an administrator verifies what happened.
- A new password cannot be the same as the most recent 10 or more passwords used by the same subject in the past.
- Passwords should not be shared, stored, or reused between dissimilar systems not under the same sphere of control.

And it was thought that this password policy was a fairly good trade-off between security and usability (usability will be covered in Chapter 4, "Usability vs. Security"). Many organizations and operating systems adopted this password policy, or something similar, by default, including the National Institute of Standards and Technology (NIST) for government-controlled computers and Microsoft Corporation as Microsoft Windows operating system defaults. For two decades, if your password policy wasn't at least as strongly equivalent, you were seen as having a weak and insecure password policy.

NIST New Password Policy

Then in 2015, NIST released an authentication update, NIST Special Publication 800-63, titled the Digital Identity Guidelines (pages.nist.gov/800-63-3/sp800-63b.html). In it, NIST essentially said that the old password policy advice it had been recommending for decades was wrong. NIST recommended a nearly 180-degree turn in some of the components and essentially recommended that the world move from passwords on to something better altogether. But if you continued to use passwords, and we all have to, then it recommended that passwords no longer have minimum password sizes, no longer require complexity, and never have to be changed unless you think the password has been maliciously compromised. NIST proposed that following the old password policy guidelines, in practice, actually made an organization more likely, not less, to be compromised because of those password policies.

The primary argument was that the traditional previous requirement to have long, complex, and frequently changing passwords has led the average password user to more likely reuse the same password (or passwords with a discernable pattern, for example, Frogfrog$1, Frogfrog$2, Frogfrog$3. . .). And since the bigger password threat is from compromised websites as compared to password guessing or hash cracking, this is likely true (although I have not been able to independently view and verify the underlying data).

To say that it astounded the world is an understatement. So far, years later, not one of the world's major computer security compliance bodies (PCI-DSS, HIPAA, NERC, CIS, etc.) is recommending the new advice. All are still following the old advice. Microsoft, a major pusher of the old password policy recommendations, stopped recommending any particular password policy, which was essentially a passive nod to the new NIST recommendations.

For a year or two after NIST's new recommendation, I too strongly advocated for the new NIST password policy position. But after debating it with other security friends and practitioners and looking at subsequent password hacking incidents, I can't agree with all of what NIST now recommends. In particular, the part about not ever changing your passwords unless you think you are compromised seems dubious to me. You can't always be assured of knowing when your password was compromised. Most people and companies aren't aware that their passwords (or password hashes) have been compromised. The fact that we have many billions of logon accounts out there on the Internet, many of which contain actively used logon account information, is a strong rebuttal to what NIST is recommending, especially the "no need to change your password" part. Additionally, if users use a password manager program to create and use separate passwords on all different sites, the password reuse risk would diminish.

My Password Policy Advice

My new "official" password advice is this:

- Use multifactor authentication (MFA) when possible and when obviously needed for security (i.e., you don't need it for every site and logon).
- Where MFA is not an option, use password managers where you can, creating unique, long-as-possible, random passwords for each website or security domain.
- Where password managers aren't possible, use long, simple passphrases.
- Change all passwords at least once a year, and change business passwords every 90 to 180 days.
- In all cases, don't use common passwords (e.g., "password" or "qwerty") and never reuse any password between different sites.

If you don't want to use long passwords, it's okay to use simple, noncomplex passwords. Just don't reuse them between sites.

Password Managers

The average person has six to seven passwords that they reuse between all sites and services they use. This is just asking for trouble. Out of everything I've listed, the most important recommendation is not to reuse the same password (or password pattern) between multiple unrelated sites or services. Doing so increases your risk of being hacked significantly. And if you do use different passwords for every unrelated site and service, you're going to have to write them down somewhere. If you write them down somewhere, you'll need to protect that document so that it doesn't get compromised and reveal all your passwords. At this point, you are much better off using a password manager program. They are a convenient place to generate and store all your unique passwords, and you can use them to autofill your passwords when logging into most places. I use one and I love saying that I can't be phished out of my passwords because I don't know them. You can find dozens of good password managers out there, and I'm not going to recommend a specific one as the "best." Try one or three and choose the one you like the best. *Wired* magazine has a good article on the ones they liked for different use cases: www.wired.com/story/best-password-managers.

Passwords Will Be with Us for a While

You will constantly read stories about how passwords are horrible and will soon be gone. I've been hearing that story for more than 30 years. I now have more passwords than ever. Passwords have a ton of issues, many of which we will cover in the next section, but passwords are often the only authentication option for the vast majority of sites and services that require authentication. There is not a non-password option that works for all sites and services. Not even close. Even if you wanted to get rid of all your passwords, you couldn't.

Passwords are actually an okay to good option for many authentication scenarios. They are acceptable authentication on most sites and services (even when other options are allowed), and they are easy to implement and use. For low-security sites, not protecting personal or confidential information, they can even be the right authentication solution. For example, I use passwords on many chat and messaging websites. Sure, my passwords for those sites can get compromised, but even if they do, what's the worst harm that can happen? Someone can log on as me and write things that are contrary to my own interests. They can say horrible, terrible things, and some people might mistakenly believe I said them. That's the worst that can happen. It's not an uncommon occurrence. Apple, Google, Facebook, Microsoft. . .they've all had their far more popular media sites taken over by hacking groups that then said terrible fraudulent things posing as the legitimate brand. Almost everyone immediately recognized the accounts were compromised, and other than some short-term embarrassment and the effort it took to retake control of the accounts, no harm was done. I'm not saying that I would love any account I control to be taken over, but if they don't have my personal or financial information, there's only so much harm that can happen. Worse things in life occur. With that said, if you can implement something better than passwords and it makes sense for the situation, do it. Passwords have inherent weaknesses, some of which I covered earlier. Now I'm going to cover some more.

Password Problems and Attacks

Even though passwords are ubiquitous and easy to use, there's a reason why the world is trying to get rid of them as soon as possible. As I previously mentioned, one of the key problems is that everyone's passwords are all over the Internet. But how did they get there? What's the root cause that allows them to be so easily stolen? This section will answer that question.

Password Guessing

One of the simplest and easiest ways for an attacker to compromise someone's password is to simply guess it. Although there are literally billions to trillions of possible password combinations that anyone could select among if they used all possible allowed password characters, most people select among the same 30 characters, and the order they are in isn't that much of a mystery.

Humans, when making up their own passwords, like to use their default language and like to use words that they use and are comfortable with. When I was a full-time penetration tester and I was on-site physically at a location trying to guess someone's password, I would look around their office. I would often note what pictures were closest to their computers. If they had a picture of a child or children, I would guess password combinations that included the names of their children. If they had a boyfriend's/girlfriend's or spouse's picture nearest the computer, I would use that. If they had a picture of a hobby or favorite sports team, I tried that. I was often right. You'd be amazed how many CEOs have a golf-related word in their password.

Even if the password has to be supposedly "complex," most passwords really aren't complex. If an organization requires a "complex" password, that tells me that most of the passwords are going to begin with an uppercase consonant followed immediately by a lowercase vowel (usually an *a*, *i*, or *o*); if a number was required, it would be a 1 or a 2 located at the end; and if a symbol was required, it would be a !, @, #, $, or & and be located in place of a look-alike letter. If I've just described your password, don't worry—80 percent of your coworkers have a similarly formatted password.

Most passwords are fairly easy to guess. They aren't as easy to guess as Hollywood shows. You can't hold a gun to a hacker's head and get them to guess someone else's password in under a minute. It doesn't work that way, although I did once—just once in my over 30-year career—do such a thing. I was trying to log on to an old accounting system I was hired to replace with the company's new accounting system. The upgrade was scheduled for the weekend so that it would not disrupt the business. I was let into the building by a security guard and left alone to accomplish the upgrade. To do the upgrade, I had to run a year-end posting process to close out some accounts. I didn't know it before, but while trying to perform the action, it asked me for a "master password." I tried a few things, like password, Password, password, password123, and qwerty (these are always the top most-used passwords in any given year), but they didn't work. I was frustrated, and in frustration I typed "rosebud" because I had just recently watched one of the world's most treasured old films, *Citizen Kane*. In the movie, Orson Welles's character whispers that word as he dies, and the whole film is about the origin of that word. I won't be a plot spoiler; you'll have to watch the film. But apparently the creators of the old accounting software were fans of the movie, because when I typed it in, it worked! I was very proud of myself. And 30 years later, I've never again been so lucky.

Automated Password Guessing

Most password guessing is accomplished using automated tools built for just such a purpose. There are dozens, possibly over a hundred tools (names like Brutus, THC Hydra, Web Brute, Bert, SqlPing, Wfuzz, Aircrack-NG) all over the Internet that can be used to automate the process of guessing at passwords. You simply pick the right tool for the logon screen you are targeting, start it, load your favorite *password dictionary* (list of passwords to try), load a list of possible logon names, and point the tool toward a victim target. If your software has a logon screen asking for a password, there's a tool to take advantage of it. Figure 1.5 shows THC Hydra GUI version working in a demo.

```
C:\hydra>hydra -L userlist.txt -P password.txt -t 1 ftp://192.168.33.146
Hydra v9.0 (c) 2019 by van Hauser/THC - Please do not use in military or secret service organizations, or for illegal pu
rposes.

Hydra (https://github.com/vanhauser-thc/thc-hydra) starting at 2020-03-02 22:07:11
[DATA] max 1 task per 1 server, overall 1 task, 119 login tries (1:17/p:0), ~7 tries per task
[DATA] attacking ftp://192.168.33.146:21/
[21][ftp] host: 192.168.33.146   login: triciag   password: Colton5
[21][ftp] host: 192.168.33.146   login: taedison  password: Bonvoy2
```

Figure 1.5: THC Hydra GUI version password guessing tool in action

Brute-Force Guessing

The hardest and longest way is to *brute-force guess*. Brute-force guessing means that the guessing starts either very intended sequentially from the first entry to the last (say *a, aa, aaa. . .*to *z, zz, zzz. . .*) or absolutely randomly (e.g., a7$Rt1Sv, bb, NM^rR3#, frog). Brute-force guessing runs through all possible password dictionary entries without any sort of intelligence involving the likelihood of a particular password guess actually being the correct password. If you've got the luxury of time and as many guesses as possible without being stopped, then brute-force guessing will get you to the right password at some future point in time.

Dictionary Attacks

But brute-force guessing is almost always the highest cost in terms of number of guesses needed and time required to be successful. If the target password was created by a human, you're almost always better off using some sort of intelligence about the probabilities of what a human-created password most likely looks like (as discussed earlier). The average password creator uses a "root word" as at least part of their password. The average human's working vocabulary is 10,000 words on the upper side. That would be someone who is a prolific reader or a professional editor. Most people's vocabularies are closer to 3,000 to 4,000 words. So a good password guesser would start with trying the most 10,000 common words in the intended target's vocabulary before trying all the over 170,000 words you might find in the Oxford English dictionary.

And there are "popular password" dictionaries all over the Internet, which contain the passwords discovered and used by most people. For two decades I used to analyze every password dump I came across on the Internet. Lots of people have the same weird hobby. After you do it a few times, you're going to get very bored because the most popular passwords from three decades ago are still the same most popular passwords today. They are passwords containing the word *password*, easy key combinations on the keyboard, and common names of people. Most organizations have employees with passwords from a list of the thousand most common passwords.

Malware Password Guessing

Many malware programs contain password-guessing routines, which when they encounter an authentication logon—say to a website, remote logon service (e.g., RDP, SSH), or network drive share—will try many common passwords. Several popular malware programs will try a hundred or more common passwords and will often be successful in guessing the password.

NOTE Automated password guessing malware programs are also notorious for locking up large blocks of user accounts because the company network they are attacking has an account lockout feature enabled. The password guessing malware program is coded to guess a hundred or more different passwords, but they end up locking out the user account after three to five guesses. Many times, the main first sign of a password guessing malware program running loose on a network is nearly everyone's account being locked out all at the same time unexpectedly. Luckily, at least on Windows computers and networks, the one true Administrator account cannot be locked out, so it can be used to get back into the network, eradicate the malware program, and unlock everyone else's account. Unfortunately, because it cannot ever be locked out, it is also a favorite target of password guessing malware programs and hackers.

Password Spray Attacks

"Password spray" (or "credential stuffing") attacks are very, very popular these days. A typical automated password guessing attack will try to guess a thousand or ten thousand passwords against one known identity account. If a company enables account lockout or monitors failed logons, they might be alerted to a traditional password guessing attack. But a password spray attack tries a thousand or ten thousand guesses, one at a time, slowly, never fast enough to make the account lockout protection feature kick in, against every identity account they can find. So instead of trying to password guess against one account a thousand or ten thousand times, they guess a handful of times against a thousand or ten thousand identity accounts.

Password spray attacks have been highly successful. Both Google and Microsoft consider them one of the biggest threats against authentication systems. In September 2019, Akami reported that they saw 61 billion password spray attacks in just 18 months on the servers and services they monitor (www.cbronline.com/news/credential-stuffing-attempts-akamai). Within those tries were plenty of successful attacks.

Performing a password spray attack involves the following steps:

1. The attacker decides on a target.
2. The attacker uses OSINT tools to collect as many logon names as they can find and places them into a single file.
3. The attacker finds an accessible online victim logon portal (e.g., Outlook for Web Access, Gmail, Remote Desktop Protocol, Cisco VPN, Microsoft Active Directory Federated Services) that they can guess against.
4. The attacker determines what the victim's account lockout policy is.
5. The attacker downloads a password guessing dictionary.
6. The attacker downloads a password spray attack tool.
7. The attacker loads the target's logon portal location in the tool, loads the password dictionary, loads the logon identity list, and executes the tool.
8. The password spray guessing tool starts the credential stuffing attack and notifies the hacker of any successful logons.

They are many password spray tools available for free on the Internet. Figure 1.6 shows one of those tools, Spray, in action, with its command-line inputs shown here:

```
spray.sh -<typeoflogon> <targetIP> <usernameList> <passwordList>
<AttemptsPerLockoutPeriod> <LockoutPeriodInMinutes> <DOMAIN>
```

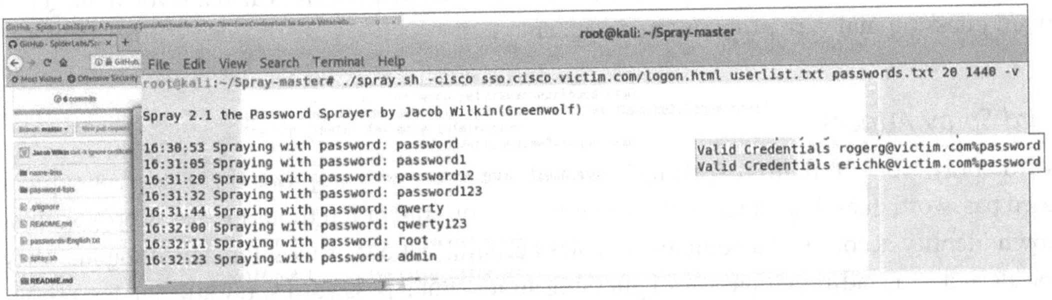

Figure 1.6: Spray password spray guessing tool

In addition to password guessing hackers and hacking tools, there is a myriad of automated malware that spends its time guessing and stealing passwords. For decades there have been worms that included the ability to guess at user passwords. They break into one node on a network and try to spread themselves by guessing at other logon prompts, often having up to one hundred popular passwords in their repertoire.

These days password guessing against Microsoft's Remote Desktop Protocol (RDP) implementations is popular. RDP is often enabled on Microsoft Windows computers and servers, and attackers and remote password guessing attack tools are common. In one study (nakedsecurity.sophos

`.com/2019/07/17/rdp-exposed-the-wolves-already-at-your-door`), the researchers set up 10 RDP "honeypot" computers to study how long it would take for them to be discovered and guessed against and how many password guesses would be taken. The first honeypot was discovered in less than 2 minutes; they averaged over 110,000 guesses a day and had more than 4 million guesses taken against them in a month. Wow! The same type of rampant guessing happens against Linux-based Secure Sockets Shell (SSH) remote logon portals.

Password Hash Cracking

Password hashes are nearly as valuable as the plaintext passwords they represent. Hackers can often use them in future authentication attacks that take advantage of processes and applications that will accept the hashes as valid as an otherwise typed-in plaintext password, or they can "crack" the password hash back to its plaintext equivalent. The former types of attacks, where the obtained hash itself is used in further attacks, are often known as *pass-the-hash* (PtH) attacks. They've been around for decades and are most popular on Microsoft Windows systems. However, having the actual plaintext password is even better, because it can be used to directly log on to authentication portals that accept only plaintext passwords. Many attackers, if they gain access to only the password hashes, will convert as many of them as possible to their plaintext equivalents. Plaintext passwords still rule!

Obtaining the password hashes in the first place takes another first-order root cause exploit. The attacker not only must break in past a computer's normal defenses but must usually obtain elevated privileges if they are to be successful in getting the hashes. Sometimes the initial root exploit gets the attack elevated access from the start, and other times they must initiate a second *privilege escalation* exploit. The harder part is in obtaining the initial access. Once inside an exploited computer, gaining privileged access, if not obtained immediately, is easier to accomplish.

If an attacker can gain local administrator access on a Microsoft Windows computer, they can then use one of a dozen or so free hacker utilities to obtain available hashes. These tools include Pwdump, Mimikatz, Metasploit, and the Empire PowerShell Toolkit, in increasing order of current popularity. All these tools require obtaining at least local admin access on the Windows computer; the attacker then has to install a second driver or software process that operates at the system level (which is higher than administrator) to get the hashes. Getting hashes from a Microsoft Active Directory domain controller—where all the hashes of all networked user and computer accounts are stored—requires a domain admin account to accomplish. Apparently, gaining this level of access isn't too hard because obtaining the Windows password hashes is among the most common successful attack outcomes there is in the computer world for corporate hackers.

Network Eavesdropping

If an attacker can insert themselves and eavesdrop on a network authentication session, they can usually capture any typed-in plaintext passwords, hashes, or challenge-response sessions. If all sides and transactions of a challenge-response session can be viewed, they can usually be converted back to the involved password hash and then eventually to the underlying plaintext password.

A challenge-response session makes it harder for an attacker, because they can't just "sniff" the network and get a plaintext password right away. But with a complete challenge-response session, the only unknown variable between the challenge and response is the password hash. So, if an attacker can get both sides, the involved password hash can usually be computed.

Email Hash Theft Trick

It's also possible to steal password hashes remotely one at a time in some uncommon edge cases. For example, one very interesting method involves sending a phishing email to an intended victim. The email contains an embedded Universal Name Convention (UNC) file moniker formatted link, `file:////<URL link>`. Email links normally contain Uniform Resource Locator (URL) links and file monikers like `http:` or `https:`. The fact that the email contains a UNC file moniker instead, which is normally associated with local NetBIOS connections, confuses many email clients, and they can be tricked into connecting to any referenced remote (often malicious) server and resource. The remote server can state to the connecting email client (which is often a browser) that it requires the client to authenticate to access the resource referred to in the UNC/URL link (example: `file:////www.badlink.com/anyfilename.html`).

The email or browser client, if it supports integrated Windows authentication (Windows, Mac, and Linux clients usually do if connected to Windows networks), will automatically, unbeknownst to most users and admins, attempt to authenticate with the server holding the remote resource. The client will participate in a challenge-response NTLM authentication connection session, and from that a remote rogue server can derive the user's password hash. Here's a great discussion on the overall technique: `www.securify.nl/blog/SFY20180501/living-off-the-land_-stealing-netntlm-hashes.html`.

To summarize, an attacker can send an email that the victim simply opens, or at most clicks on the embedded link, and the remote attacker gets the victim's Windows network password hash, which they then can convert to a plaintext password. Infamous hacker, boss, and my friend, Kevin Mitnick, has a great YouTube video demonstrating this attack method: `blog.knowbe4.com/kevin-mitnick-demos-password-hack-no-link-click-or-attachments-necessary`.

> **NOTE** In Kevin's video he demonstrates that simply "previewing" the email is enough to kick off the connection to the embedded UNC/URL link resource, but most of the time the user must be tricked into clicking on the embedded link (i.e., the connection doesn't just initiate automatically). Still, tricking people into clicking on malicious links isn't all that hard. In fact, it's how most phishing emails work.

Even without converting the hash to its plaintext equivalent, there is a lot a hacker can do. The attacker can create additional logon sessions, log on remotely to available RDP sessions, manipulate group memberships, connect to network drives and resources, and even create brand-new, temporary, rogue domain controllers (look up "golden ticket" attacks—they are vicious). In most operating systems, including Microsoft Windows and Linux, the ultimate authentication "secret" is the password hash. Once you have that, you have the keys to the kingdom.

Rainbow Tables

As mentioned, most password hackers want to convert any stolen password hashes to their plaintext equivalents. However, cryptographic hashes, if they are any good, are explicitly designed to prevent someone capturing the hash from easily figuring out what the related plaintext root password is. But hackers can take guesses at what the password might be, hash the guess, and compare the hashed outcome of the guess to the captured password hash, and if they match, conclude they have the equivalent password.

The hacking world is full of *password hash databases*. These databases contain every (or a very high percentage) of possible passwords along with their corresponding password hash, so once you have the password hash, you can simply search for the equivalent hash right away. But if a password is fairly long and/or complex, the number of possible passwords can be overwhelming. All the possible password choices for a relatively short eight-character password can be many, many billions to trillions (especially if the password can be made up of over 65,000 different characters, as they can in Microsoft Windows). A smart password hash guesser will start out with intelligent guesses using a dictionary attack, instead of just blindly brute-forcing all the possible guesses sequentially through the password hash database. If the captured password hash represents a password like most of us use (i.e., relatively low entropy), then far fewer of the password hashes have to be tried before a match is made than using a full sequential search of all possible password guesses.

But if the password is long and/or complex enough, even the dictionary-based attack still leaves millions, if not billions, of possible choices that have to be tried before a successful guess. It can be a lot of possible passwords and hashes to search through. A typical password hash can be 128-to-256 bits long. To find the right hashes when doing a very fast search, a password hash database search will start searching for the right hash using one bit at a time. For example, if the hash is 74FA5327CC0F4E947789DD5E989A61A8242986A596F170640AC90337B1DA1EE4 (from our SHA2-hashed frog password earlier), it will begin by first searching for every possible hash that starts with a 7 (the first character in the hash) and rule out every other hash that doesn't start with a 7. Then, out of all the hashes that begin with a 7, it will look for all the hashes that begin with 74 (the first two digits of the hash), and rule out all hashes that don't begin with 74. Then in the hashes still around in the possible pool of correct hashes, it will look for all the hashes that begin with 74F (the first three digits), and so on, adding one character at a time until it narrows down the exact equivalent hash through a sequential series of inclusion of additional hash digits and subsequent rule-outs. Eventually, it will find the one hash that contains all the identical characters. You might wonder why it doesn't just look for the correct whole hash from the start, but having to search for the correct hash using all digits of the hash at once is exponentially harder and takes longer to do than the sequential rule-out method. Searching through an extremely large database, like normal password hash databases with many millions to billions of hashes takes a very long time.

There are more efficient password hash databases called *rainbow tables*. Rainbow tables convert all the much longer password hashes ahead of time to an intermediate representative, to a much shorter form, and do the same for the captured target hash. For example, using the very long original hash (as shown earlier), the intermediate representation may look like D9DE7E9AA. Unlike a true cryptographic hash, the intermediate representative form may match for many different unique password hashes, but the correct hash is included in the list of password hashes represented by the shorter representative form. For example, perhaps a few thousand stored password hashes match the same intermediate form. When the rainbow table process converts the targeted password hash to its intermediate form, it still has to search a much smaller pool of possible password hashes. It can take all the password hashes with the same intermediate form as the targeted hash, and then calculate their full password hash form and find out which of those thousand actually matches the full password hash of the targeted password—and find it without having to search through billions of much longer password hashes.

So, a smart password hash cracker will use a rainbow table program that incorporates a dictionary attack. There are a handful to dozens of rainbow table programs for most password hash types. Figure 1.7 shows a popular rainbow table program called Ophcrack (ophcrack.sourceforge.io).

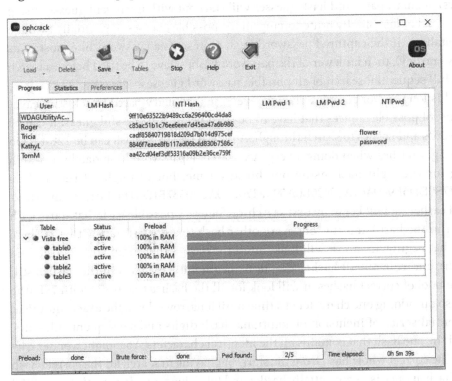

Figure 1.7: Ophcrack, a popular rainbow table program

Password Stealing

One of the most common ways a password attacker gets a password is to steal it. They steal it from the user's computer or device or from one of the many sites or services that store their password/hash. As I explained earlier, if an attacker can gain admin access to a user's computer or device, there are hundreds of hacking tools (such as Mimikatz) that will reveal a user's (and the system's) passwords, either in plaintext or in their hashed forms. Any hacker worth their weight uses one or more of these tools as soon as they gain admin access to a system.

Many automated malware programs, if they successfully exploit a computer or device, will go looking for passwords, either as their main objective or as one of their primary objectives. They will look for user and system passwords stored on disk and in memory and steal passwords from browser databases (when the user allows their browser to store their passwords for future auto-logons to websites and services requiring authentication).

Any hacker who gains admin access to a website or service that requires authentication for all users will immediately go looking for and steal any authentication databases that contain user logon information. This is how the passwords in most password dumps end up on the Internet. Why steal passwords one at a time when you can steal tens of thousands to millions of them for nearly the same effort?

Password Reuse Risk Is Huge

The biggest risk from any password theft is that even though a password may only be stolen from one website or service, it is often reused by the same user at more than one website (and sometimes every website they have). As I mentioned, the average user has six or seven passwords that they use among every website and service they use. So if I'm a password attacker and I compromise some rinky-dink, no-one-cares-about-website, and find that a logon name of roger@banneretcs.com has a password of frogfrog11, I'm going to start checking whether that same logon information works on a bunch of other more important websites, like Amazon, banks, and stock websites as well. And any good hacker will automate that checking process.

Password reuse is a huge risk. One compromise can lead to a bunch of other compromises. This makes those password dumps even more dangerous. Not only can they reveal currently, actively used logons, but they can also reveal patterns between passwords. Most people, if they don't use truly random passwords, and even if they do use different passwords for every website and service, use passwords with a pattern (such as Frog32, Frog33, Frog34. . .). An attacker seeing that pattern may figure out what the user likes to use and can break into additional sites.

Similarly, intentionally sharing passwords with or between other people is a bad, risky practice for several reasons. Many a person has shared their personal passwords with their one true love to learn that true love often doesn't last forever, and that previous love can sometimes access their accounts in an unauthorized way to make their life much harder than it needed to be. In the workplace, sharing passwords (and related identities) makes it difficult for IT to track who is doing what when looking at transactions in event logs. Every security compliance guideline in existence preaches against sharing passwords, but many companies do, especially when the same device is frequently accessed and used by multiple people. Password reuse and sharing makes password stealing and cracking even easier to accomplish.

Passwords in Plain View

And sometimes you don't have to guess or phish, because passwords are written down somewhere where anyone can see them. Developers are notorious for leaving "hard-coded" passwords left in development code that they then upload to a public, shared, repository, like github. Many large data breaches have occurred because of this single issue.

Many devices come with built-in, hard-coded, passwords which either can't be changed or are not forced to be changed. Either way, anyone can look up these built-in default passwords and attempt to use them. Many bot programs run around on the Internet looking for these devices and try using the built-in passwords. They are successful to the tunes of tens of millions of compromised devices.

It's not uncommon to see a public video where an easy to see password is typed in by the video-taped user. Here's a fairly recent 2019 example of a US congressman typing in his cellphone's password (a bunch of 7's): `mashable.com/article/congressman-lance-gooden-has-a-terrible-phone-passcode`.

There have been dozens of primetime news stories interviewing some interesting person of the day where some shared password is seen written down in the background and clearly seen in the video. We laugh, but it happens all the time. I was recently giving a lecture on password attacks and on the presentation laptop, in a large general conference room in a state legislature that was freely accessible by the general public. On the laptop was a paper sticky label (see Figure 1.8) that showed the logon name and password. I chuckled a bit, because I was there to speak about computer security and the laptop that I was to present from had the password printed for anyone to use and document. I said to the host in a kindly way, "You know that printing out a logon name and password and placing it where anyone can see it is the epitome of what you shouldn't do in computer security. I hope that at least it's a stand-alone logon and not a networked logon that works across your network." He responded, "If you want to tell yourself that to make yourself feel better, sure."

I hesitated putting this specific example in my book because I don't want to shame that particular customer. They obviously have a real need for that password to be there. They've done the cost–benefit analysis for that IT asset and figured that the laptop is in a place where malicious hacking is unlikely, or hopefully, they have the logon locked down to just that laptop and everything else besides presenting was disallowed by default. Of course, I'm just saying that to make myself feel better.

But more importantly, it happens all the time. That customer was far from unique. It points to an inherent issue with passwords and how easy they are to use, and at the same time, how inconvenient they can be for shared assets. I travel for a living, and if I could get a dollar for every hotel check-in lobby desk where I could physically see a documented password from the lobby, I'd have a nice house on the water in the Florida Keys.

Figure 1.8: Real-world example of a network logon printed out and attached to a laptop in plain view of anyone around it

Just Ask for It

Often the easiest way for a hacker to get someone's password is to just ask for it. *Phishing* is the process of maliciously masquerading as a trusted entity to acquire unauthorized information or to create a desired action that is contrary to the victim's or their company's self-interests. It can be accomplished using email, websites, Short Message Service (SMS) messaging, chat channels, written documents, and voice phone calls. Basically, any method used to communicate can be used to phish someone. Right now, email phishing is the number one way that most organizations are successfully hacked the most. Either the user is tricked into revealing their logon information or they get tricked into running a trojan horse program, which leads to the same result. Many of the password dumps contain collections of passwords that were obtained solely by phishing.

An attacker can simply ask for someone's password and you would be surprised how often you can get it from a complete stranger. Years ago when I was doing full-time penetration testing, I used to go to the CEO's executive assistants and say, "Hi, my name is Roger Grimes. I've been hired to test the password security of the company, including the CEO. What is the CEO's password?" Now, remember, they aren't even supposed to have the CEO's passwords—passwords are not to be shared. But want to know how many executive assistants gave me their CEO's passwords? All of them! In my 20 years of asking that question, not one assistant refused to give it to me. I had some hesitate a few seconds before giving it to me, but none who didn't comply and reveal the top executive's password.

I've participated in several studies and tests where we would offer people in a public place (e.g., street, subway system) small prizes like candy bars or pens if they would reveal their passwords to us. Our success rate was 30 to 60 percent, depending on the country and test. Don't believe me? There are videos all over the Internet showing the same thing. It's not like I have some special social engineering charm. You just have to ask.

Late-night talk show *Jimmy Kimmel Live* occasionally interviews real people walking down the street in Hollywood, California, and asks for their computer passwords. Here's an example: www .youtube.com/watch?v=RJJEyGkS9jA. It's hard to watch without not both laughing and sighing at the same time about how easy it is to get people to reveal their real passwords.

So, in summary, passwords are easy to use and easy to hack. Using a variety of methods, including guessing, cracking, stealing, eavesdropping, and asking, many billions of passwords have been stolen. And the problem isn't getting better after two decades—it's only getting worse. We didn't use to have billions of stolen passwords sitting on the Internet. It used to make the news when a hundred thousand of them ended up in a single password dump. Now I'm not even sure a billion stolen passwords will raise an eyebrow—hence, the constant push to get people off passwords and on to a better authentication method. Multifactor authentication is often touted as the panacea.

Password Hacking Defenses

I don't want to leave readers with the impression that password authentication can't be a safe authentication method. It can be, risks and all. And since passwords aren't going away anytime soon, here are the ways to make password authentication safer:

- Don't get phished into giving out your password to a malicious entity.
- Don't get phished into running a trojan horse program.
- Make sure your system are fully patched so the attacker can't use unpatched software to break into your computer and steal your passwords.
- Use a unique password per website or service.

- Passwords should have strong entropy.
- Don't share your password with anyone.
- Enable account lockout to prevent unrestrained password guessing.
- Change your passwords periodically, not to exceed 180 days for corporate passwords (90 days is better) and not to exceed 1 year for personal passwords.
- Consider using a password manager to create strong, unique passwords for each website and service.
- When typing passwords across networks, make sure the network channel is protected/encrypted to prevent eavesdropping.
- Only provide any critical personal or financial information to websites that need it and that you trust to protect your logon account and credentials.

If you follow just the first four recommendations in the previous list, your chances of getting maliciously hacked because of your password are significantly diminished.

MFA Riding to the Rescue?

Passwords aren't inherently evil, but they do, as discussed, have a lot of weaknesses and are hacked a lot—so much so that the entire world pretty much agrees they should not be relied on for serious authentication. We need to provide the world, everyone, with a significantly stronger and trustworthy authentication method that is fairly easy to use and that significantly diminishes the risk of compromise. And so far, the most often touted answer is multifactor authentication. Will MFA be that shining authentication knight that so many people are hoping for? Only time will tell. But we can say that MFA has its own security risk and issues, and that is what the rest of this book is all about.

What I can tell you for sure is that if all passwords go away and all we have is MFA, that authentication hacking will continue to occur. For one, it's what this entire book is about. MFA is harder to hack, but isn't impossible to hack, and there is a world of difference between the two statements. For decades I've seen system after system go from using passwords to MFA, thinking that all of a sudden they didn't have to worry about authentication hacking anymore. And all of those same systems (and their users) discovered that the hackers don't give up. MFA may slow hackers down, but it doesn't stop them. It's not like the hackers are going to see MFA, and knowing there are dozens of ways to hack it, and just call it a day, go home, and quit, because it might be harder to attack. The opposite is usually true. MFA may slow down the bulk, random attacks, but are far less likely to stop targeted attacks. And sometimes the other extreme is true. I've seen people's MFA so easily hacked that they gave up and went back to simple logon names and passwords (I'll cover this in future chapters).

Summary

Chapter 1 covered logon problems, particularly as they relate to passwords, explaining why MFA is needed to replace passwords. It discussed how billions of people's passwords are available all over the Internet and how they got there. It covered the password authentication process from account registration, authentication secret storage, and challenge-response authentication, which is used by most modern-day operating systems and applications. It then covered the basic password attacks including guessing, hash cracking, stealing, and social engineering; and ended with the various defenses against those attacks. Readers should have a very thorough understanding for why passwords are considered risky to use and why people are looking to MFA for improved security.

Chapter 2, "Authentication Basics" will cover authentication in general. You'll need a decent understanding of authentication, however it is done, to more easily grasp how MFA solutions work and how they are successfully attacked and hacked.

2 Authentication Basics

Chapter 1, "Logon Problems" covered logon problems and, in particular, the problems with password authentication. Chapter 2 will cover the basics of authentication in general. With that said, it's a pretty in-depth look at authentication from top to bottom, from beginning to end, from simple logons to complex mega-systems, and everything in between. If you ever wanted to know about authentication and what it entails, this is the chapter to read.

You will hear about the CIA (Confidentiality, Integrity, and Availability) triad used to summarize the major security control categories. And certainly, authentication includes all those components, but it also includes more. Here are the components and considerations of any authentication system, all of which will be covered in this book:

- Confidentiality
- Integrity
- Availability
- Identity management life cycle
- Scope of control/security domain
- Usability
- User control
- Privacy
- Protocols/standards/APIs
- Auditing/accounting/event logging

The primary reason for *authentication* is to confirm a subject's ability to access protected resources (e.g., security domains, files, folders, sites, services). The process determines whether the subject is who they say they are and whether they can prove it.

Not all things require authentication. For example, most of the web surfing we do requires no authentication. We don't want to have to authenticate to do an Internet search, download a public document, or read the news. But much of our online world requires that we authenticate to access private or stored personal information.

The authentication must have *integrity*, meaning that it accurately authenticates who or what should be successfully authenticated, and vice versa. The authentication secrets or factors used to authenticate a subject are kept secret by the authentication system and the subject. The authentication system should be resistant to malicious denial-of-service (DoS) attacks and be accessible with adequate performance to support its business function.

Authentication Life Cycle

Authentication is the set of system and processes, starting with establishing proof of ownership or control of an identity, followed by giving the person some sort of resulting digital content (often known as a *token* or *ticket*), which the authenticated subject can present during future access control checks. In a good system, the process of authentication and authorization is monitored, and critical events are logged to a file for potential future collecting, auditing, and evaluation. As Figure 2.1 shows, authentication is just one process in a series of progressive, linked steps.

The rest of this section will cover those steps in more detail.

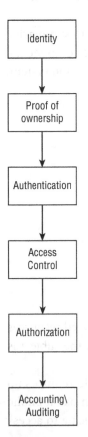

Figure 2.1: Basic authentication life cycle

Identity

Establishing control of a digital identity requires many cooperating components. In very early computer systems, there were no permissions or protected objects. The computer systems were large, monolithic machines, which we might refer to as "mainframes" or "big iron." Individual security settings and controls were not needed, because only the people who could physically access the computer system and flip switches, plug in cables, or feed it tabulating cards could interact with it. The access control was physical. And these systems ran only one program at a time. If another program was to be run, the people in charge of the computer would have to input it. The computer was dedicated to only one task.

Eventually these computers started to be accessed by multiple groups of people, more and more often remotely, and they could be running many different programs, each interacting with different files and resources, all at once. Some of these people probably accidentally interfered with another person's or group's program or resources, and someone realized that access control was needed. They couldn't have people associated with other programs and resources accidentally or intentionally interacting with the programs and resources of other groups. There needed to be some sort of logical separation. And that logical control within a computer became known as access control.

Access Control

Access control is a process that determines which subjects are allowed to access which protected resources. The *access control manager* process compares the rights, permissions, privileges, and group memberships of the supplied authenticated identity and compares them to a list of rules stating which subjects are allowed to access and manipulate which resources, and in which way (e.g., read-only or modify). Operating systems may also have default rules that describe how a specific access control operation should be performed if it's not explicitly defined. For example, if a subject can access a higher-level, "parent" object, then they can also access a lower-level, "child" object unless some specific change is made to the child object.

Every process or action in which a subject participates on an access-controlled computer system or device requires every access to be associated with a specific identity. An *identity* is a digital label that is uniquely tied to a subject. The identity must be unique within the participating namespace (e.g., DNS, Active Directory, LDAP) that the authentication system uses. Common identity identifiers include the following:

- Full name
- Logon name
- Email address
- User principal name (UPN)
- LDAP
- Digital certificate
- Global unique identifier (GUID) or universally unique identifier (UUID)
- Media Access Control (MAC) address

Essentially any predefined label that has been agreed on as the unique identifier can be used. Identity labels can be made up by registering users, or they can be automatically assigned by the system. A single subject may have multiple identities on the same system (also known as *personas*), and multiple subjects may share the same identities (although this is frowned upon in computer security circles) on the same system. Different identities, belonging to the same subject, may have different attributes, permissions, and privileges. For example, an administrator may have a regular user account for everyday, regular user–type computing tasks (such as reading email and browsing the Internet) as well as an elevated admin account for when they need to perform actions requiring privilege.

Many subjects may have different identities in different systems. In fact, for users that's highly common, since the average adult can easily have upward of a hundred separate systems that they log on to, each having a different identity system. Separate systems often have separate, isolated authentication systems, but they may share and interface with a common authentication system.

Although it is common for subjects to authenticate to a system to begin their computing experience, often after that initial logon the remaining interactions with the various future processes are done automatically using the subject's authenticated identifier or access control token (which we'll cover in a moment). The process of other software and processes using another subject's authenticated identifier is known as *impersonation* or *delegation*. The software or process that does the impersonation is known as the *user agent*.

For example, when the typical user browses the Internet, the user's Internet browser is often running in the context of the logged-on authenticated user. The browser is the user agent in that context. If the user is working in an email client, the email client is the user agent. When a user opens a word processing program and accesses their own previously stored document files, the word processor is considered the user agent, and the processes used to access the user's access-controlled documents are done by the word processor using impersonation of that user's subject identity.

It is common for a computer system running many different processes to be running different processes using different subject identities, some of which belong to the user and others that belong to the operating system or other previously installed applications. Figure 2.2 shows an example of the different identities belonging to various processes.

A single process can change which identities they use for particular actions. For example, when you browse to a website requiring authentication, an Internet browser, by default, will usually try to log on as an "anonymous" user three times and, only after rejection each time, try to log on as the subject identity that started the browser. And if the website and browser prompts you to manually supply logon credentials, it is possible for the user agent (i.e., the browser) to "spawn" another process using another identity. With operating systems, it is not unusual for a parent process to spawn a child process, and typically, by default, that new child process will have the same subject identifier (although it can be another separate identity).

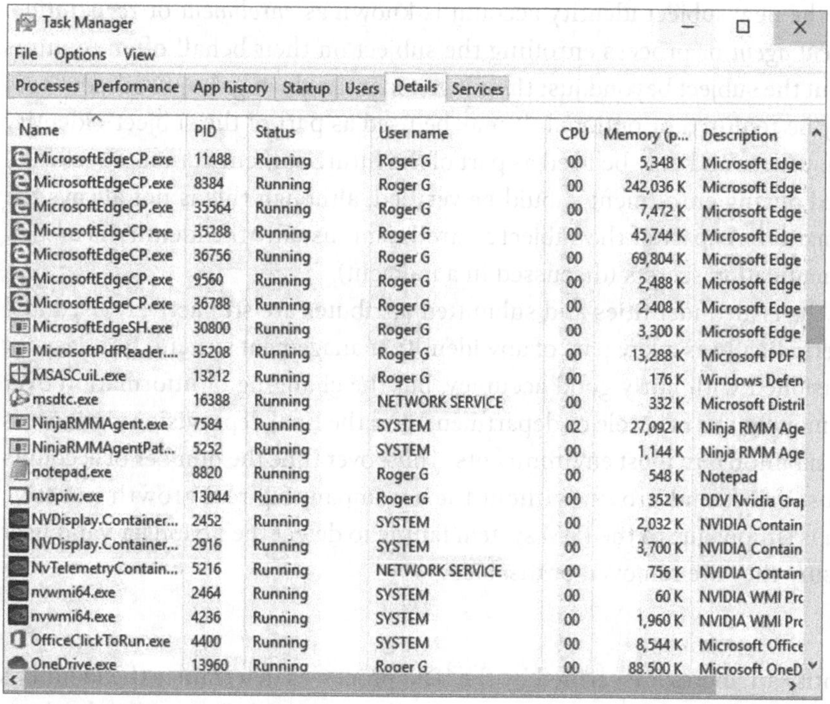

Task Manager

File Options View

Processes | Performance | App history | Startup | Users | Details | Services

Name	PID	Status	User name	CPU	Memory (p...	Description
MicrosoftEdgeCP.exe	11488	Running	Roger G	00	5,348 K	Microsoft Edge
MicrosoftEdgeCP.exe	8384	Running	Roger G	00	242,036 K	Microsoft Edge
MicrosoftEdgeCP.exe	35564	Running	Roger G	00	7,472 K	Microsoft Edge
MicrosoftEdgeCP.exe	35288	Running	Roger G	00	45,744 K	Microsoft Edge
MicrosoftEdgeCP.exe	36756	Running	Roger G	00	69,804 K	Microsoft Edge
MicrosoftEdgeCP.exe	9560	Running	Roger G	00	2,488 K	Microsoft Edge
MicrosoftEdgeCP.exe	36788	Running	Roger G	00	2,408 K	Microsoft Edge
MicrosoftEdgeSH.exe	30800	Running	Roger G	00	3,300 K	Microsoft Edge
MicrosoftPdfReader....	35208	Running	Roger G	00	13,288 K	Microsoft PDF R
MSASCuiL.exe	13212	Running	Roger G	00	176 K	Windows Defen
msdtc.exe	16388	Running	NETWORK SERVICE	00	332 K	Microsoft Distril
NinjaRMMAgent.exe	7584	Running	SYSTEM	02	27,092 K	Ninja RMM Age
NinjaRMMAgentPat...	5252	Running	SYSTEM	00	1,144 K	Ninja RMM Age
notepad.exe	8820	Running	Roger G	00	548 K	Notepad
nvapiw.exe	13044	Running	Roger G	00	352 K	DDV Nvidia Gra
NVDisplay.Container...	2452	Running	SYSTEM	00	2,032 K	NVIDIA Contain
NVDisplay.Container...	2916	Running	SYSTEM	00	3,700 K	NVIDIA Contain
NvTelemetryContain...	5216	Running	NETWORK SERVICE	00	756 K	NVIDIA Contain
nvwmi64.exe	2464	Running	SYSTEM	00	60 K	NVIDIA WMI Prc
nvwmi64.exe	4236	Running	SYSTEM	00	1,960 K	NVIDIA WMI Prc
OfficeClickToRun.exe	4400	Running	SYSTEM	00	8,544 K	Microsoft Office
OneDrive.exe	13960	Running	Roger G	00	88,500 K	Microsoft OneD

Figure 2.2: Microsoft Windows Task Manager with different processes and their associated subject identities (shown under the User Name column) all running at the same time

Identity Management

Most authentication systems depend on an underlying *identity management* (IDM) system, which handles all the possibly involved identities' "life cycle stages" from creation (i.e., *provisioning*) to removal/deletion (i.e., *deprovisioning*). The user or subject may create the new identity, or it may be assigned by another subject (i.e., admin) or through an automated process. For example, in an automated process a new employee added to the Human Resources systems may trigger a new logon identity in the rest of the environments in other computer systems. And if the employee has a separation-of-employment event, the employee's separation may result in the employee's computer accounts automatically being suspended, disabled, or removed. In fact, the process of automated, delegated user account creation and deletion is preferred by computer security professionals.

In a secure authentication system, it is critical that the person or process (known as *access governance*) initiating a new subject identity account verify the subject's need to be in the particular IDM system as well as verify their real-life identity before or during the new account's creation or setup. Without the validity of these steps, an authenticated identity cannot be considered valid or assured at all.

The process of creating the new subject identity account is known as *enrollment* or *registration*. The subject or the *enrollment agent* or process enrolling the subject on their behalf often requires additional information about the subject beyond just their logon identity during the enrollment process. This information may be required or optional. It may be used as part of the subject's identity attributes to determine uniqueness and may be used as part of the future authentication process. All information created or used during enrollment should be verified, although this is not always the case for all included information. As part of the subject's enrollment, usually the identity is associated with one or more authentication secrets (discussed in a moment).

A reaffirmation that all the issued identities and submitted attributes are still actively used and accurate should be done periodically as a key part of any identity management system. It is easy for logon accounts to be provisioned with fairly good accuracy, but the changing of information over time (such as an employee moving to a new role or department) and the final deprovisioning process are not nearly as accurately monitored in most environments. Thus, over time the number of accounts in an IDM system often just grows and grows, without the accompanying real growth in active physical users. The growth is simply due to the IDM system failing to detect the no longer valid user accounts and not making sure they are removed or disabled.

Assurance Levels

How well the subject's identity attributes are verified by the IDM processes determines the identity's *assurance*. Identities created with strong verification processes and protections are considered to have high assurance. Identities created with weak (or no) protections are considered to have low assurance. Most IDMs are somewhere in between. As examples, most websites that allow you to directly register a new logon account without verifying your identity are considered to have low assurance. Today, many website registrations require that you click on a verification link submitted to your supplied Internet email address so that at least your control of the registered email account is verified. This is some assurance, but it's still fairly low.

On the other end of the spectrum, the U.S. government digital multifactor authentication cards, known as Common Access Cards (CACs), are given only to federal government and military employees after significant identity verification (such as birth certificate, fingerprinting, picture ID, and in-personal interviews). A serviceperson's military-issued email account (ending in .mil) is tied to and requires successful authentication using that CAC. The CAC is a high-assurance IDM system and identity. It is possible for a .mil email account to be hacked (say from a local compromise on a computer or device that a legitimate user is logged into using it), but its association with a high-assurance CAC means it is more difficult to hack in many hacking scenarios. Thus, CACs are trusted by many relying agencies. If you show or use your CAC, "you are in."

A "middle of the road" assurance might be a regular corporate logon account that doesn't use MFA. The user of a corporate account has probably been identified by HR during the hiring process in order to be given use of a corporate account in the first place and has probably had to provide some sort of government ID (like a license or birth certificate). However, their account might be easier to compromise because they don't use MFA. Most authenticated identities fall in the low to medium assurance spectrum.

Trusts

All identity systems are based on trust. One security domain or IDM may *trust* another's identity system's operations and identities so that if a *foreign* subject shows up from the first, *trusted* domain and presents their identity for access to resources in the second, *trusting* domain, the *relying*, trusting security domain may automatically trust the submitted identity to be accurate. The relying domain may completely and automatically trust the identity label and its associated authentication, or it may also trust and use one or more other attributes related to the subject.

Note: *Foreign* means not from or directly managed by the local domain. It does not mean foreign as in foreign country.

The foreign identity system may be trusted so extensively that the authenticated identity is accepted on and used by the local system without further authentication. This is known as *federation*. Or the identity may be trusted but the subject is required to reauthenticate separately on the foreign system. In both cases, the local system is trusting the trusted domain but may not completely trust the authentication component without reauthentication.

One or more domains can also use the same identity and authentication information stored and authenticated in one place, or share the exact same information in two or more places (even if the information is identical). That information may be copied to or synchronized between the two or more locations, either on demand or automatically, or according to some other preset interval of time or specific event action.

If a single authenticated identity leads to automatically and seamlessly logging onto other domains, the logon may be known as *single-sign-on* (SSO). SSO systems often contain an intermediate database that stores the logon information for all the interfaced domains. The user may believe that one logon is working for all their relying resources, but behind the scenes, the SSO solution is actually using separate logons for each interfacing system. SSO may also be a single solution that is accepted by all participating sites and services (like Fast Identity Online [FIDO] authentication, covered in more detail in later chapters).

Real ID to Levels of Anonymity

Many identity services and web services advertise that they make sure that a particular identity is tied to the person whose name the identity appears to represent. For example, many celebrities will have @real Twitter accounts, where the @real label is a prefix to their whole (celebrity) name. Twitter users are supposed to feel confident that the celebrity's name after the @real portion actually represents the celebrity it logically appears to be. Some other services such as Twitter will put a check mark symbol along with the word "verified" if you hover over the check mark symbol (see an example in Figure 2.3).

Figure 2.3: Example of Twitter's real, verified identity

On the opposite end of the identity spectrum you have truly anonymous identities (i.e., *anonymity*), where no holder of an identity account is verified. In fact, it's an intended attribute that the real holder of the identity is never known. Many times, the anonymity simply happens because the requirements of the IDM system are not assured at all. Anyone can create nearly any identity label (within the scope of the acceptable identity label format) and are not required to submit any other qualifying information, and thus no submitted information is verified. The vast majority of Internet websites and services may fall under this category. But the anonymity is not necessarily required or intentional—it's more a fact that real identity was not needed or the IDM was intentionally lazy.

Other times the anonymity is guaranteed or near-guaranteed and is an advertised feature of the system. The Tor browser (`www.torproject.org`), for example, was intentionally made to maintain users' total anonymity. There are often still ways to track individual Tor users at times, depending on the scenario, but doing so isn't intentional.

Total and complete anonymity projects and services are trying to give their users as much identity anonymity as possible. Often they will not know the identity of the subject or any attribute about them. If they must store information about the subject, they will often store it encrypted in such a way that even they, the IDM service, cannot determine the real subject's identity or location. A law enforcement agency could serve a legal search warrant to obtain as much information as they could on the participating subjects and gain little to no useful information.

Total anonymity is often seen by many people, including this author, as a human right. If people want total anonymity to conduct particular actions or scenarios, they should be allowed to have it. There are many legitimate reasons to have and allow total anonymity, including political protests without fear of political reprisal, whistleblower reporting, and sensitive group meetings, such as for cancer, AIDs, and rape survivor groups.

NOTE These types of anonymity are not to be confused with generic, built-in anonymous accounts used in some operating systems. For example, Windows has a built-in, hard-coded "anonymous"

user account that is routinely used throughout the operating system for various normal operations. It is essentially a "stand-in" account to indicate that the logged-in user's authenticated identity is not being used during a particular action or transaction. As another example, most Internet browsers will attempt, by default, to connect to every website and service using an "anonymous" connection first before trying to use, or being prompted to have to use, authenticated user accounts. These types of anonymous accounts do not assure anonymity, and in fact, it can be relatively easy in some scenarios for a forensic investigator to figure out information that leads to the user's real identity or location. Just because you see the label *anonymous* used with an identity doesn't mean it is truly anonymous.

Conversely, I think it is okay for any service or site to reject total anonymous connections if they so choose. It is also true that many rogue bad players use total anonymity to conduct illegal and unethical actions with impunity. Any private group or service should be allowed to choose what level of anonymity or real identity they will allow along a spectrum of possible choices as long as they are not breaking any applicable laws.

Pseudo-anonymity is an interesting middle choice. With pseudo-anonymity, the subject registers their real identity with a trusted centralized identity service. The ID service verifies the subject's real identity and then assigns or allows the subject to pick a non-self-identifying identity label, which the subject can use on sites and services that trust the pseudo-anonymous service. So, the ultimate relying sites and services don't normally know the real identity of the subjects, but if a legal requirement comes up, they can serve a legal judicial document to the pseudo-anonymous service, which can find out relevant facts about the subject's real identity.

Of course, each real subject can have different levels of real identity to total anonymity for various identities that they use on different systems. One person may have decided to have a multitude of different IDs along the anonymity spectrum and even multiple identities on the same systems with various levels of identity assurance. For instance, I could have one Facebook or Twitter account with my real identity verified and still use another anonymously, or I could use a second one for my personal and family relationships instead of a public-facing one that anyone can interact with.

Privacy

I think most people in our society want some sort of basic, guaranteed level of privacy. I'm surprised it isn't in the U.S. Bill of Rights—yet. Dare to dream! Part of the reason why it's so hard to get and use anonymous identities is that it seems nearly the whole world is against us being anonymous. In fact, they want to identify us in every way. Advertisers want to track and target us. They want to know our utmost secrets so that they can market to us in specific ways. The world's websites want to make money and so they track us (using browser cookies and a thousand other ways). Most governments, even while claiming they want to protect your privacy (not all governments make this claim), really don't. It is in their best interests to know who you are and what you are up to all the time. Law enforcement wants to be able to see everything you are doing, although some are kind enough to note that they should have a valid, legal search warrant first.

It is this continuous tension between all the organizations who want to know everything about us and each individual's desire for privacy that most global identity systems face. How does a global IDM become the authentication choice for all users and at the same time let them know that their privacy could be invaded at any time by any legal source? It's the "sixty-four million-dollar question." Pseudo-anonymity may help with some of that contention, but it will probably not be the long-term answer.

Here's a quick global privacy story from my own experience. Years ago, I was working for a major company and we were asked to design and bid on a brand-new authentication system that would allow all people visiting Singapore to log on to the Internet. It was easily my biggest authentication design project. I was shaking in my proverbial boots. I was not experienced enough to be doing the project and was surely unqualified. But as I soon discovered, I was the best they had for the project at the time. I worked for many months to learn all I could about good mega-identity system design. And in the end, I turned in what I think was a very good, competitive design and bid. I surprised myself and in the process learned what it took to make a good global identity management system.

Just after I had handed it in, I realized that I had not included a section on privacy. At the time, privacy wasn't the household concern that it is today. There were no chief privacy officers, privacy policies, and worldwide organizations devoted to fighting for people's privacy. But there was just enough concern that I realized I had not included a section in our request for proposal (RFP) response dictating how we would protect users' privacy. I asked for the RFP response back. I told them I had forgotten to include the missing section but that I could quickly add it to the design.

What came back stunned me. They said, "We don't want people to have privacy. We want to track each person and where they go at all times!" I was blown away. They even wanted to ensure that visiting foreign guests to their hotels were tracked to the passports they had to hand over to the hotel front desk. It was the opposite of privacy. They wanted to know everything. I had not even considered that sort of requirement. It wasn't in the official requirements. I struggled with now having to design a country's Internet system with zero privacy. In the end, I withdrew our bid from consideration. I couldn't live with myself if something I designed intentionally removed privacy from everyone who used it. I'm glad to report that the company and my team supported my decision. After months of having to pay everyone's salary for working on the project, my company was fine with the decision after hearing what transpired. But it was a lesson learned. Not all countries value privacy.

It's been over a decade since that event, and in that time I've run into many countries (often in Asia and Europe) that do not value privacy or that even want the exact opposite. But now I realize that I can't have moral righteous indignation because every other country, including my own, the United States, doesn't want it either. Yes, perhaps they don't build the lack of anonymity into the design, but identifying who is who isn't that difficult in any country. Some countries are just more honest and blatant about it. I believe it is up to each individual to fight for the right to privacy, at least for the privacy expectations and rights I believe give us all human dignity—such as the ability to have truly private conservations when we want them and the ability to conduct anonymous transactions with others who want or respect anonymity. I run across people all the time who say they don't need privacy, that they "aren't watching child porn" or "breaking laws." To them I say, you don't understand the issues well enough. But writing all that needs to be said on the subject would require its own chapter or a complete book. Just know that reasonable (and sometimes complete) privacy is an expectation for many users of their authentication systems even if you don't believe you want or need it. Many people do.

Claims

Identities may be associated with one or more *claims* (aka *assertions* or *attributes*), which are other information or facts associated with the identity. For example, the claims could be the subject's real identity, name, work location, phone number, age, credit card information, group membership, roles, privileges, and permissions. During an authentication or authorization event, one or more claims may be involved. With a good IDM and authentication process, only the minimum number of claims needed to conduct its legitimate purpose are collected and/or used. An identity management service should not collect more identity attributes than the user gives permission to or is aware of, and the authentication process should not require more subject claims than is necessary to conduct the legitimate authentication or authorization transactions.

For example, in the real world when you go to buy alcohol in the United States, you must be at least 21 years of age at the time of the purchase. Store clerks, bars, restaurants, and other relying parties will usually ask the person attempting to buy the alcohol to show a government-issued ID like a driver's license. But they are only really asking to verify the user's identity (does the person buying the alcohol and using the license look like the person on the photo of the identification card?) and their age (are they at least 21 years old?). The driver's license includes lots of other unneeded information that is not needed for the transaction, such as last known home address and whether or not they are an organ donor. Although great information, it has no bearing on the relevant transaction on hand.

A good IDM, authentication, and authorization transaction would essentially only ask, "Is the buyer 21 years or older?" and the identity claim would vouch for the user's validity and would reply either "Yes" or "No" to the age query. No more and no less. You will hear these types of IDM, authentication, and authorization systems known as *claims-based*. Although many claims-based systems are still struggling to provide only the bare amount of information needed, most still supply too much unneeded information in every transaction. Often it is because the relying party is requesting too much information and doesn't realize that much of it is unneeded.

A claim can be made by the subject itself on behalf of itself or made by someone else on the subject's behalf. It may even be the result of an action that the subject or something else involved in the authentication transaction does. For example, when a user logs on to a Windows system at the desktop logon prompt, Windows will automatically assign that user multiple, built-in claims, which the user cannot prevent, deny, or remove (such as being placed in the Interactive and Everyone groups). A claim backed up by another authenticating entity is known as *attestation*.

Issuing Authorities

The entity that confirms the subject's identity before issuing them an authenticated logon is called the *issuing authority* (or *credential service provider [CSP]* or *identity provider*). The person or subject who is attempting to prove their identity to the issuing authority by undergoing *identity proofing* is known as the *applicant*.

Any organization that accepts the authenticated logon identity as valid is called the *relying party*. A relying party must trust the issuing authority to confirm the identity of the subject before they issue the authentication logon identity. There is essentially always a three-way trust (see Figure 2.4) established between the user, issuing party, and relying parties.

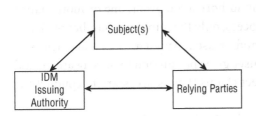

Figure 2.4: Basic three-way identity trust triad

The user must trust the issuing party to be a reliable issuer of authenticated identities (or anonymity), and be secure enough that the user can trust that other people will not be easily able to use their identity. The relying parties must trust the issuing authority to do their job of verifying the user's identity, at least according to the scope of registration, claims, and authentication. And both the user and the issuing authorities must trust that the participating relying parties will use the identities as the subject expects them to be used and in a secure way. If too many authenticated logons are determined to have been issued in error to fraudulent subjects or the authenticated identities are too easy to hack, none of the parties involved will trust and use each other.

When a subject is attempting to authenticate to a relying party, they are known as the *claimant*. The claimant presents their identity and proof of identity ownership as determined and controlled by the issuing authority. A relying party that verifies the claimant's identity is known as the *verifier* and may be the same as the subject's ultimate relying party, but they can also be separate entities. After a claimant is proven to own an identity, they are no longer "claiming" to be someone. They are an authenticated identity or a *subscriber* to the relying party or verifier.

> **NOTE**   All the terms associated with various phases of the authentication life cycle can be confusing. I would not get too hung up on the different terms unless you read authentication documents for interest, but if you do you'll see various sets of terms used with different documents and other sets of terms used with other documents. There isn't an agreed-on set of terms for the various phases of authentication, which is confusing, but there are only a few terms for each phase . . . so it's a pain, but not impossible to follow one document's description versus another. Just realize that different documents use different terms to describe the same thing.

Many issuing authorities will offer different assured identities with different levels of assurance. For example, many digital certificate issuers will offer digital certificates ranging from low level (little to no assurance) to very high levels of assurance (where the issue uses multiple different methods to confirm the digital certificate holder's identity).

The issuing authority can be local, centralized, or decentralized. If the identity is created solely on the local device, then it's considered a local authority. A local Windows logon and password is a good example of a local authority. A local account cannot automatically log on to any network-based asset.

Local issuing authorities can be proprietary or participate as part of a common standard. For example, the Information Card and FIDO authentication standards do not have a centralized or decentralized issuing authority. Each participating identity is created locally on the participating computer or device but can be used globally with any participating website or service.

A centralized authority is one where a single entity issues the identities and authentication. For example, for years Microsoft pushed an identity and authentication product called Microsoft Passport. It would work with any website or service that interfaced with Microsoft Passport, but the creation and control of every identity (and the entire life cycle) was under the sole control of Microsoft. Microsoft Password morphed into Live ID, which morphed into something called a Microsoft Account. Many authentication experts are critical of centralized issuing authorities because they "own" and control the identity and authentication standard. They may not always do what is in the user's best interest or improve the standard in a way that benefits competition.

A decentralized IDM system would be best represented by the Domain Name System (DNS). DNS is a hierarchical database that contains globally unique identities for subjects and resources, often tied to a unique Internet Protocol (IP) address. There is no single DNS database that contains every DNS identity entry. Instead, different databases contain different parts of the overall database and are referred to one another when necessary to resolve a particular identity. No authentication is associated with DNS, but a subject's DNS identity can be part of any participating identity system. For example, many websites and services use a user's email address as the identity of their authentication system.

Security Domain

Every IDM system is limited to a collection of subjects that is less than all possible subjects. In other words, there is no IDM system that includes all possible subjects, although the Internet's DNS is the largest list of unique identities in the world (so far). Most authentication systems relate to a much smaller set of authenticated users, such as the employees of one company or the digital certificate holder of a certification authority. For example, Microsoft Corporation and Alphabet, Inc. have authentication scopes full of hundreds of thousands to several millions of users. It's a lot of subjects, but not to the 7 billion users alive on planet Earth.

As another example, a Microsoft Active Directory forest cannot have duplicate UPNs within the same forest, but it can have people with the same logon name (as long as the UPN and DNS email addresses are different). You can have two user accounts named Roger Grimes, as long as the UPNs are something like rogerg@knowbe4.com and rogergrimes@knowbe4.com. You can even have two different forests with identical UPNs (say, roger@knowbe4.com for two different, unrelated people), as long as they belong to different forests and don't share the same DNS email address. Every IDM identity has to be unique within the scope of control.

Conversely, most digital users are members of dozens to well over a hundred different authentication accounts, and they can even be the exact same identity name as long as the scopes are different. Thus, I can have a logon name of rogeragrimes@banneretcs.com for hundreds of different websites, each of which has the same or different passwords. Unless the logon account is a shared logon account across multiple websites, the logon identities are not related, regardless of the identical identity names. A logon name of rogeragrimes@banneretcs.com for an Amazon logon and rogeragrimes@banneretcs.com for Twitter doesn't mean they are or aren't the same person. As long as the logon identity is unique for the particular IDM scope, that's all that matters.

Authentication

Authentication is the process of a subject proving ownership and/or control over a particular identity/ identity label. This is done by the subject providing "secrets" that only the subject trying to authenticate and the underlying authentication system know. Authentication secrets can include many things, such as passwords, PINs, knowledge of how to solve a particular puzzle, a digital secret, a device, or a physical attribute.

Some secrets may be stored in multiple forms. For example, in a Windows system, a user may provide a password as a secret, but Windows converts, stores, and uses that secret as a converted cryptographic hash. The authentication secret doesn't have to always be globally unique, although sometimes, as in the case of digital certificates and biometric attributes, it may be a requirement. Authentication secrets must be protected by both the subject using them and the underlying authentication system. If an attacker learns the secret, they can impersonate the legitimate subject.

The authentication secrets are usually stored within or referenced by the authentication system, typically within one of the following:

- Human mind
- Physical document (such as a piece of paper)
- File(s)
- Database
- Registry location
- Memory
- Storage device
- Or combinations of one or more of the above

All of those locations, other than the human mind, can be either local to the device being used to authenticate or remote, in which case physical access to or a network connection is required. Wherever the authentication secrets are stored, they need to be protected and secured. Each storage location becomes a potential attack point.

Authentication Factors

Proof of ownership of an identity is made by a subject supplying the identity and one or more associated authentication factors to the authentication service. An *authentication factor* (also known as a *bearer assertion*) is something supplied that only the subject knows or can supply and, by doing so, proves sole ownership of the authenticated identity. Authentication factors when supplied are known as *authenticators*, although the word *authenticator* may also refer to the digital package containing the authentication factors themselves.

In general, there are only three basic types of authentication factors, widely known as:

- Something you know
  - Examples include password, PIN, connect the dots
- Something you have
  - Examples include USB token, smartcard, cell phone number, RFID transmitter, dongle
- Something you are
  - Examples include biometrics, fingerprints, retina scan, smell

Traditionally, there are only three major types of authentication factors, as described here. Increasingly, authentication services are considering other types of factors known as *contextual* or *adaptive*. These factors include the device the user is using to authenticate, the location of the current authentication event as compared to past authentication events, how long it took the user to type a password, actions the user is currently taking, the sequence of actions, and a myriad of other factors. Some authentication services, such as those used by Microsoft and Google, can use over a hundred different types of assessment factors when considering whether a particular logon session is valid.

For example, many people don't realize it, but on many of the logon screens where they make you put in your logon name and then click the Next button to go to the next page to type in your password (versus just typing in your logon name and password on the same page without an intermediate step), it may be because the vendor is measuring how long it takes you to type in your password, and even possibly how long it takes you to type in the various individual characters. A vendor may think it's a bit strange that a person suddenly and dramatically changes how long they go from the first to the second letters of their password, and may conclude that person is an intruder. Conversely, if your password is being detected as being typed in extraordinarily fast, a vendor may be worried about an automated method being used, such as a malicious bot. They of course realize that people type in their passwords at different paces all of the time for normal reasons, but they may consider a sudden change from normal speed to be an additional risk factor.

When looking at many different risk factors, one measurement outcome may lead to additional inspection or even a denial. For instance, suppose that not only is the subject typing in their password at an unusual speed, but it's also done from a brand-new location and device that has never been detected before. At some point, the various weighted risk factors will create a risk profile and score that the vendor determines is too high to allow the user to log on and continue even though the user typed in all the right information. If the user is asked to reauthenticate or submit additional authentication factors based on their detected behaviors or actions, it is known as *step-up authentication*. Overall, it's pretty cool stuff, and it's likely to be a part of the future of authentication, similar to how you get credit card transactions approved or denied today.

There are discussions over whether these types of contextual factors can really be considered authentication factors. My feeling is that if they are being used as part of an authentication trust decision, then it is an authentication factor, traditional or not. Authentication is usually done before the user is admitted to a protected resource or site, but it can also be conducted afterward at any time. Many services will monitor what a user is doing and ask for reauthentication, or increasing levels of authentication assurance, for the user to be allowed to continue in their current or future actions. Any authentication factor verified and tied to a particular identity is known as a *binding* or *bounded*.

1FA vs. 2FA vs. MFA

A single-factor authentication (1FA) solution requires only a single authentication proof for a subject to successfully authenticate. A two-factor authentication (2FA) requires two authentication proofs, and a multifactor authentication (MFA) solution requires two or more factors. All other things being equal, MFA is usually (but not always) better than single-factor authentication for better security, although a single MFA solution is rarely universally allowed across all subject use scenarios, so 1FA or multiple MFA methods will usually be needed.

NOTE MFA includes 2FA, and many people will say MFA when speaking only about 2FA, and vice versa (even though MFA isn't always 2FA if it includes more than two factors).

In order for authentication factors to provide the best security protection in a multiauthentication process, they should be different types of factors. Using two or more of the same factor is still better than using a single factor when doing authentication but isn't as protective when using several different types of factors. The thinking is, for example, that an attacker will have a harder time both phishing what a user may know (e.g., password, PIN) and a physical device the user uses to log on at the same time. So, all things considered equally, multiple factors of different types is preferred over multiple instances of the same type of factor.

You will sometimes hear about MFA solutions that have more than three factors (e.g., five-factor), but what these solutions are usually referring to are multiple instances of the same three traditional factors. In order for the factors to be most protective in an MFA solution, they should be different.

NOTE Some single-factor hardware solutions that may look like MFA solutions (and people often assume they are) don't require an additional factor. For example, existing versions of Google Security Keys and YubiKeys can be used for one-factor or multifactor. In their one-factor implementations, simply inserting the physical authentication device into a USB slot (and perhaps pressing a button) successfully accomplishes the authentication. It also means that if an unauthorized user finds those hardware devices, they can use them and take over the digital identity associated with the token. It might be more difficult for a hacker to obtain another person's single-factor hardware token than phishing them out of a password online, but once the token is obtained, that would mean immediate compromise of that identity.

Bounded vs. Roaming Authenticators

Authenticators can be bound to only one logon location or device, or they can be used in multiple locations and/or on multiple devices. For a bounded example, most of the fingerprint scanners you find on laptops and phones only work on the laptop and phone where they were registered. So even though my wife and I both have cell phones that can be unlocked using our individual fingerprints, my wife's fingerprints don't unlock my phone, and vice versa, although they could be made to do so if we each registered again on each other's device. An example of a roaming authenticator might be a Windows Active Directory (AD) logon. I can register my AD logon credentials anywhere and readily use them at any device registered in the same AD domain/forest. And most logons involving a password are roaming. As long as I can remember my password, I can use it anywhere on any device that can access the website or service.

Some authenticators might be considered both bounded and roaming. For example, if I have a FIDO device, FIDO requires/allows a different authenticator for each website and service it is used with. Different authenticators can all be stored and used with the same FIDO device. In this sense, the FIDO ID is bound for each site and service. But I can use the FIDO device on any FIDO-participating host device to log on to those sites and services. The individual IDs are bound to the same FIDO device, but I can roam with it. In general, the FIDO device is going to be considered bounded, because the authenticators are absolutely bounded to a single FIDO device. And if you buy another FIDO device, you can't just easily (or at all) directly copy the authenticators to it.

Another similar term is *channel binding*. Channel binding refers to a unique authentication session being bound to a particular network channel. Without each authentication session being bound to a specific network channel, it is possible for an in-process authentication session to be maliciously redirected to another channel. In most cases, authentication involving channel binding (or not requiring channel binding because it's handled elsewhere in protection) is considered stronger than authentication not capable of channel binding or not capable of stopping channel misdirection.

Why isn't channel binding done all the time, every time? Well, sometimes it just isn't possible given the authentication solution as created or configured. Other times it's optional (such as in FIDO authentication) but isn't supported in most operational scenarios and, therefore, is not enabled by default.

One-Way vs. Mutual Authentication

Authentication is normally conducted between two or more parties, often referred (as covered in Chapter 1) to as the *server* (the object/application/process being authenticated to) and *client* (the object authentication to the server), and can be *one-way* or *two-way* (also known as *mutual* authentication).

NOTE   Many authenticating objects can act as both a server or a client depending on the reason for authenticating. This is to say, a physical server isn't always acting as a server and a client isn't always acting as a client. Additional servers may also be involved in the authentication process, and so there may be multiple authentications occurring during a single authentication event. A good example of that is Kerberos, where the client must authenticate to the Kerberos authentication server as well as the intended target server.

Most authentication is one-way, meaning the client authenticates to the server or the server authenticates to the client, but the opposite is not true, at least during the same authentication event. A common example of this is web servers using HTTPS. When HTTPS is involved, the web server has an HTTPS/TLS digital certificate, which is linked to and attests to the server or website's identity (usually by DNS address or computer hostname). When a client connects to the web server over HTTPS, the website sends its HTTPS digital certificate to the client to prove its identity and to secure an encrypted channel in which to generate symmetric keying material. The client receives the web server's HTTPS digital certificate and verifies its trustworthiness. If successful, the client will trust the website to be the website it says it is (based on the subject's identity). In one-way authentication, the client does *not* prove its identity to the server, at least not within the same authentication transaction.

With two-way, mutual authentication, both the client and server authenticate to each other as part of the same authentication process. If either side fails, the authentication fails regardless of the success of the other. Kerberos is a good example of two-way authentication. Two-way authentication is more secure than one-way authentication, but one-way authentication is significantly more commonly used (at least currently) because two-way authentication is more complex to set up and accomplish, and it's subject to increased failures. For that reason, most authentication mechanisms use only one-way authentication or rely on two, one-way, authentications.

For example, a banking website may authenticate itself to the user using a TLS digital certificate and the user might authenticate themselves to the website using a logon name and password after establishing the TLS trust. These are two one-way authentication events, and they are not, all other things considered equal, as secure as a simultaneous two-way authentication logon.

In-Band vs. Out-of-Band Authentication

Authentication factors can be considered in-band or out-of-band. *In-band* means that the authentication factor method being used is conducted over the same communications channel as the primary login method. *Out-of-band* is when the authentication factor is being sent over a channel different from the primary login channel.

For example, if you're trying to log in to an Internet service application and you are required to type in a password and a password recovery answer within the same browser, this is considered two instances of the same type of factor, both in-band. If, however, you are required to type in a password on your computer and also a second PIN code that was sent to your external cell phone, the second factor is considered out-of-band.

Even better, if you are required to respond to both separate band authentication factors *only* in those channels and they aren't "cross-channel" (i.e., an authentication factor sent to you out-of-band can be responded to only in the same band as the other factor), then it provides even more security assurance. Authentication factors sent on the same device, even if in different channels, are not considered as secure as authentication methods using different channels over different devices. Of course, this increases the complexity of the authentication process. In general, out-of-band authentication is usually considered more secure than in-band authentication.

As the number of separate authentication factors and communication bands increase, so too does security assurance. In most scenarios, using an MFA solution can only improve security, and MFA should be used where and when it makes sense to do so. Unfortunately, not all authentication scenarios allow MFA, or often not the same MFA solution. At least for now (2020 and the next few years), most users will still be required to use a single-factor authentication method in many scenarios.

No matter how it is done, successful authentication is the process of a subject providing a valid identity label and one or more required valid authentication factor proofs. If done successfully, the subject and their identity is considered authenticated.

Access Control Token

After a successful authentication, in most cases, the access control processes then associates an access control object (e.g., *token, ticket*) with the now verified, authenticated identity label. What this access control token contains varies by system and protocol. In nearly all systems, it will contain an unique identifier, such as a series of numbers or characters, which specifically identifies the identity label, either permanently or just for a particular logon session. In other systems, such as in Windows, it may also contain a list of group memberships, permissions, privileges, and other needed information. Figure 2.5 shows much of the information found in a Windows access control token.

The token may or may not have a predetermined maximum lifetime, which upon expiration forces the subject to reauthenticate to remain in an "active" session. In Windows, an access control token may arrive in the form of a Kerberos ticket or an New Technology LAN Manager (NTLM) or LAN Manager (LM) token. On websites and services, most access control tokens are represented by an

HTML cookie, which is a simple text file. Most web cookies contain a global unique identifier for the authenticated user and/or their session, followed by an expiration date (as shown in Figure 2.6).

```
USER INFORMATION
----------------

User Name                SID
======================== ================================================
desktop-oi9db93\roger g  S-1-5-21-1269248641-3246485367-2288545083-1002


GROUP INFORMATION
-----------------

Group Name                                                                Type               SID           Attributes
======================================================================    ================   ===========   ==============================
Everyone                                                                  Well-known group   S-1-1-0       Mandatory group, Enabled by
default, Enabled group
NT AUTHORITY\Local account and member of Administrators group             Well-known group   S-1-5-114     Mandatory group, Enabled by
default, Enabled group
BUILTIN\Administrators                                                    Alias              S-1-5-32-544  Mandatory group, Enabled by
default, Enabled group, Group owner
BUILTIN\Users                                                             Alias              S-1-5-32-545  Mandatory group, Enabled by
default, Enabled group
NT AUTHORITY\INTERACTIVE                                                   Well-known group   S-1-5-4       Mandatory group, Enabled by
default, Enabled group
CONSOLE LOGON                                                             Well-known group   S-1-2-1       Mandatory group, Enabled by
default, Enabled group
NT AUTHORITY\Authenticated Users                                          Well-known group   S-1-5-11      Mandatory group, Enabled by
default, Enabled group
NT AUTHORITY\This Organization                                            Well-known group   S-1-5-15      Mandatory group, Enabled by
default, Enabled group
NT AUTHORITY\Local account                                                Well-known group   S-1-5-113     Mandatory group, Enabled by
default, Enabled group
LOCAL                                                                     Well-known group   S-1-2-0       Mandatory group, Enabled by
default, Enabled group
NT AUTHORITY\NTLM Authentication                                          Well-known group   S-1-5-64-10   Mandatory group, Enabled by
default, Enabled group
Mandatory Label\High Mandatory Level                                      Label              S-1-16-12288


PRIVILEGES INFORMATION
----------------------

Privilege Name                  Description                                   State
==============================  ============================================  ========
SeIncreaseQuotaPrivilege        Adjust memory quotas for a process            Disabled
SeSecurityPrivilege             Manage auditing and security log              Disabled
SeTakeOwnershipPrivilege        Take ownership of files or other objects      Disabled
SeLoadDriverPrivilege           Load and unload device drivers                Disabled
SeSystemProfilePrivilege        Profile system performance                    Disabled
SeSystemtimePrivilege           Change the system time                        Disabled
SeProfileSingleProcessPrivilege Profile single process                        Disabled
SeIncreaseBasePriorityPrivilege Increase scheduling priority                  Disabled
```

Figure 2.5: Example of the type of information found inside a Windows access control token

```
TOKEN COOKIE: document.cookie =
"li_at=AQEDASYwnSMECG7oAAABbY50Kk6AAAAfjUlsXoE4agXEGoHz4Kv6onJ5hQBskTy6SSI8jjBPyPVgtk3Fu7T68BoTADYCa
en5N9EH4Xkx1P864BUY17coXGfVm66KezNMGoTaGU8DaGYXiphDdcxhh8MW; expires=2020-05-04 03:18:11"
```

Figure 2.6: Example HTML cookie access control token

The expiration date indicates for how long the cookie will be considered valid and that date may or may not indicate how long the user can reconnect to the same website without needing to reauthenticate. Procession of this token is often all that is needed to be successfully reauthenticated as a particular identity. In many cases, the token is seen as equivalent to the verified identity.

Get ready, important point ahead!

If you're reading along, blah, blah, blah, and not really comprehending, stop here to refocus your attention. What I'm getting ready to say is unknown to most people—even unknown to some computer security experts. Most computer security experts don't know this fact. And you reading this one fact makes you a far better computer security person. If you already know the fact in the next sentence, consider yourself one of the lucky ones.

Regardless of the method you used to authenticate, the resulting access control token is usually the same. It's formatted the same. It looks the same. It is treated the same. There are some edge cases where how you authenticated could impact the token, and maybe some of the contained claims are different because of how you authenticated, but most of the time there is very little or no difference.

Let me explain by giving an example. Suppose you log on to your Windows laptop using a logon name and password. When you do, you're given a Windows access control token. If you log on using a biometric fingerprint, you're given a Windows access control token. And both are either identical or close to identical. In most systems, the process of authenticating and the process of getting the authentication token are essentially unrelated events. The system component giving you the access control token doesn't really care how you authenticated, only that you successfully authenticated. And if you successfully authenticated, regardless of how you did it, here's your resulting access control token. In the access control system's view, both tokens are identical. Both are used the exact same way behind the scenes to access protected information.

Before I understood this correctly, I thought that different authentication methods created dramatically different access control tokens. For example, I believed that if you logged on using a fingerprint, somehow that fingerprint was being used in authentication and authorization comparisons behind the scenes. Suppose I wanted to access a database file that I had legitimate access to. I imagined that when I went to access that database file the access control process somehow took my submitted fingerprint and used it in an access control comparison to see if I could access the database. I imagined that there were some sort of "smarts" in the system that would look at my submitted fingerprint and go "Yeah, looks like the right guy, let's admit him!" But that's not at all what happens.

Instead, when I successfully authenticate using my fingerprint (or password or smartcard or FIDO key), what happens after I successfully authenticate is identical for all successfully authenticated users. And this is an important point, especially when added to the previous fact that possession of the token is usually treated the same as the subject had successfully authenticated. Regardless of how I authenticated, if my resulting access control token gets compromised, it's game over. We'll come back to this in Chapter 6, "Access Control Token Tricks."

Least Privilege Principle

One of the bedrock computer security principles is that subjects should have the least amount of permissions and privileges necessary to do their legitimate task. This holds true whether using passwords or for people using MFA solutions. You never want someone with and using the highest permissions and privileges all the time, especially if they are doing regular tasks (e.g., checking email, writing a document) that doesn't require those permissions and privileges.

On-Demand

Some authentication mechanisms allow a single real person to use multiple logons, one privileged and one nonprivileged, and the user picks which one they need at a single time. Other systems will allow a user to perform step-up authentication, say, moving from a regular user to an admin or root user (using sudo in Linux, for example) when the higher or different account is needed. Other systems require specific credential checkouts at the time of the need. All the highest privileged accounts may be stored in a centralized database, and any potential administrator has to successfully authenticate for that highest privilege account and "check out" the account. The checkout is tracked in an event log. The highly privileged account may be further limited by time duration, security domain scope, or allowed actions. These systems are generally known as *privileged account managers* (PAMs). Other types of access control systems act as SSO systems and will automatically elevate regular users to privileged status when needed and predefined.

Authorization

You've successfully authenticated your identity and obtained an access control token. Now you want to use it as a license to access protected objects (i.e., file, folders, websites, services). The process of an access control manager taking a submitted access control token and comparing it to a list of permissions associated with a protected resource is called *authorization*. Determining "can this person or device access that thing?" is the key function of an access control manager. How well it enforces the comparison between the identity and its access control token and what is allowed per the defined permissions and privileges stated attached to the protected object (often known as *access control lists*) tells us how secure the system is overall.

Accounting/Auditing

All the critical steps of the three previous steps (IDM, authentication, and authorization) should be noted and saved to an event log. In general, *accounting* refers to tracking how much of something (e.g., how many times they have logged on, time in the system) and *auditing* refers to a detailed analysis of the involved action. However, in today's world we usually just lump them into auditing or event log management. Any good authentication system will log all critical steps from provisioning to deprovisioning and everything in between.

Good auditing is crucial for good security. For example, without auditing I might not know that someone is trying to guess the password of a single user and is using over a million different password guesses in that attempt. An even better configured event log system would notice and alert on an attacker doing a "credential stuffing" attack where they are using all available user accounts to guess against tens of thousands of passwords, but never faster for any one user than the environment's account lockout policy.

These four major authentication components—identity, authentication, authorization, and accounting—are traditionally known as the *4A's* of authentication (ignoring the fact that identity can also be known as account management, but that is a fairly legacy term that does not encompass the full range of responsibilities).

Most of the MFA hacks that this book will cover are breaks in the individual components of these systems (identity, authentication, authorization, and accounting), or taking advantage of a weakness in between the steps. More on that in Chapter 5, "Hacking MFA in General."

All of these components we've discussed so far lead us to a more complete understanding of the authentication life cycle and all of its phases. Figure 2.7 shows a pictorial snapshot of the authentication life cycle in some of its more complicated glory and associated terms. In general, a subject enrolls with a credential service provider and undergoes identity proofing by successfully submitting one or more required authentication factors. If the subject successfully authenticates to the credential service provider, they become a subscriber of that identity provider. A subject trying to log on somewhere is known as a claimant. A claimant that successfully passes authentication to a verifier becomes a subscriber to the verifier and/or relying party. A subject/subscriber trying to access a relying party's protected resource(s) undergoes authorization using access control. Behind the scenes, every action is likely being audited to an event log.

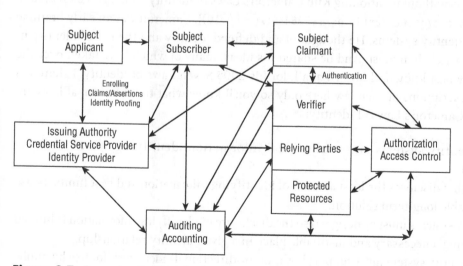

Figure 2.7: Example of authentication life cycle phases

It's a bit much to take in all at once, but you can use it to figure out where the various phases and components fit in the big picture. No doubt one of the first things you noticed was a lot of two-way interactions between many of the components and how they rely on each other. I don't think anyone who doesn't create authentication solutions memorizes every term and phase. Just understanding the general authentication life cycle process and everything that is involved will give you a step up.

Standards

The Internet has made it essential that any authentication credentials we share between systems use generally accepted protocol standards. A protocol is a predefined way of doing and communicating information between multiple, unrelated entities. Most of the time these standards need to be royalty free, not patented or copyrighted—that is, open. The digital world is full of open authentication standards (e.g., Security Assertion Markup Language [SAML], Open Authorization [oAuth], FIDO, and application programming interfaces [APIs]).

Open authentication standards come and go. Most fail. Some, like the ones mentioned here, are sticking around. And that's a good thing. Without open standards we would all be forced to work in a Tower of Babel mix of competing authentication standards and protocols. It would make a big mess of what is already a complex task. It might make it impossible. So, when you hear of another authentication open standard being adopted, celebrate. Your life just got that much easier.

Laws of Identity

All of us in the computer security world stand on the backs of previous giants. A book on authentication would be remiss without mentioning Kim Cameron's Laws of Identity [docs.microsoft.com/en-us/previous-versions/dotnet/articles/ms996456(v=msdn.10)]. Cameron was an early brainiac in the field of mega-identity systems. He thought of and defined identity and the use of identity in huge global systems better than most. And he shared his ideas, many of which have taken over the world. He is probably best known, if known at all, for his 2005 Seven Laws of Identity. I share his own one-sentence descriptions of each law here only so you'll know what those universal laws are or should be. Here's Cameron's Laws of Identity:

- Technical identity systems must only reveal information identifying a user with the user's consent.
- The solution that discloses the least amount of identifying information and best limits its use is the most stable long-term solution.
- Digital identity systems must be designed so the disclosure of identifying information is limited to parties having a necessary and justifiable place in a given identity relationship.
- A universal identity system must support both "omni-directional" identifiers for use by public entities and "unidirectional" identifiers for use by private entities, thus facilitating discovery while preventing unnecessary release of correlation handles.

- A universal identity system must channel and enable the inter-working of multiple identity technologies run by multiple identity providers.
- The universal identity metasystem must define the human user to be a component of the distributed system integrated through unambiguous human-machine communication mechanisms offering protection against identity attacks.
- The unifying identity metasystem must guarantee its users a simple, consistent experience while enabling separation of contexts through multiple operators and technologies.

Whenever I am looking at a new identity authentication system, these are the bare requirements I consider when trying to determine whether it is designed right from the ground up. Notice that the list doesn't mention protocols or technologies, only what Cameron thinks should be laws that any system should follow to be a good identity management system.

The security of any authentication system relies on how well all the pieces and parts of these components are protected, used, and audited, at every step of the way. It's not good enough to just do some of the parts well—all of the parts must be done as perfectly as possible. Because hackers are looking.

Authentication Problems in the Real World

We have all sorts of troubling authentication problems in the real world. Authentication hacks aren't just a problem for the Internet. Our world has long been filled with identity fraudsters who cash checks that aren't authorized, pretend to be people and organizations they aren't, and lead victims to performing actions harmful to themselves. Much of real-world crime is related to authentication issues, and we need to fix those as well.

Examples of these real-world authentication attacks abound and are very common. Among the most common are the fake "I'm with Microsoft and calling to help you with a virus on your computer" phone calls. Just as common are fake calls from the Internal Revenue Service telling the victim that they must pay several hundred or thousands of dollars for past tax return issues or they will go to jail. But somehow they will be happy to take that payment in Walmart gift cards.

As we start to fix the authentication issues in our online world, we should also focus on fixing those same issues in our real world. We need to update our telephone networks so that fraudsters can't fake caller origination telephone numbers, known as caller ID spoofing. In the United States, the new SHAKEN/STIR (Signature-based Handling of Asserted Information Using toKENs and the Secure Telephone Identity Revisited) protocols are supposed to minimize or even possibly stop all caller ID spoofing.

But people faking who they are happens in more places than just over the phone. We need ways to quickly and automatically identify whether someone interacting with me in the real world is really who they say they are. It is clear to me that as we fix the authentication issues in our online world the keys to fixing the authentication problems in the real world will also be found. When we fix one, we can fix the other.

With that said, we will always have crime and authentication issues in the digital and online worlds. You can't get rid of all crime. Getting rid of all crime would require draconian measures that few of us would want to tolerate, and even then, somehow crime would persist. Humanity and free choice essentially means that we will have some percentage of crime in our lives. But the goal shouldn't be to get rid of all authentication issues and crime, but to minimize it to a sustainable level where it is more background noise than a big problem.

For example, in the United States in the 1920s and 1930s Tommy machine gun–toting criminals crisscrossed the country robbing banks, merchants, and individuals. Many, like Bonnie and Clyde, John Dillinger, and mobsters like Al Capone were actually admired and almost a century later still have a strange celebrated mythology associated with them. Back in the 1920s and 1930s, it seemed as if the criminals might actually win. But steady improvements in law enforcement techniques and better defense tactics won out. Eventually it was harder to rob banks, and when someone did they got less money. Banks started keeping less cash on hand, hidden dye packs were put in the stolen money, and tellers were given easy access to an emergency alarm button. Coordination between different law enforcement agencies improved, and radios made it easier to report sightings and track fleeing criminals. Police got better weapons and bulletproof vests. So, it got significantly harder to rob banks and capture and punishment a lot more likely.

Today, banks are still being robbed and these incidents aren't rare (there were over 3,000 bank robberies in 2018), but for the most part they don't impact anyone significantly beyond the people directly involved. Robbers get even less money and, when caught, will spend a significant time behind bars. The same thing will eventually happen to authentication hacks in real life and online. Hacks will become less common and lead to less benefit, and being caught defrauding someone or a site will lead to stiffer penalties. We just have to get better authentication, completely along the life cycle. MFA and what may replace it eventually is part of the solution.

Summary

Chapter 2 covered the basics of the authentication life cycle in detail, including the registration of the identity, the authentication process, authorization, access control, and accounting/auditing. Identities were covered in detail including labels, assurance levels, anonymity levels, privacy, claims, and issuing authorities. Authentication was covered in detail including authentication factors, one-way versus mutual authentication, in-band versus out-of-band authentication, access control tokens, and bounded versus roaming authenticators. Chapter 2 finished with universal Laws of Identity that any authentication system should strive to meet and gave brief coverage to the idea that authentication isn't so secure even in our real world.

Chapter 3, "Types of Authentication" will explore the many different ways authentication can be accomplished by different solutions.

3 Types of Authentication

Humans have been performing authentication using one form or another for millennia. Authentication doesn't have to be digital. There are hundreds of different authentication solutions, human and digital, one-factor and multifactor, which can be divided between a dozen categories. This chapter will cover the major authentication solution types, along with advantages and disadvantages of each. It will also describe cryptography and how it applies to authentication. This is the longest chapter of this book because it takes a few inches to cover each type—and there are a lot of types. Still, I hope you find it an interesting summarization worth your time.

Personal Recognition

The most common form of authentication is personal recognition: we recognize one another. When spouses wake up together in the morning, as long as they recognize each other, no one screams. Most of us are allowed to walk into our day jobs, work all day, and get paychecks because everyone around us, from our boss to our coworkers, physically recognizes us. In the very early days of the computer, when it was a single, huge, supercomputer that took up an entire room, the computer technicians recognized one another. Early on there was no remote networking or connections. If you wanted to work on the computer, you had to show up in the computer room.

Personal recognition even works when we don't know one another. If I order a pizza from Dominos and a delivery person shows up in a Dominos uniform, we open the door and pay for the pizza. We recognize police in uniform or even in plain clothes if they have an official-looking badge.

The problem with personal recognition is that it doesn't scale well and has less and less accuracy as the direct relationship fades. Most of us meet many thousands of people in our lives, but we can only remember maybe 200 or so of them at once—and even then, we are better at remembering faces than names. Uniforms and badges "authenticate" people in roles, such as police officers, but it is fairly easy for anyone to fake being a police officer—all they need is an official-looking badge and uniform. Thousands of people are arrested each year for impersonating police officers. When you think about it, we put an awful lot of trust in a uniform, especially when someone impersonating a police officer could, if they wanted to, cause great personal harm to their intended victim. Personal recognition works only because most people don't take advantage of how easy it is fake more distant, less personal relationships.

And in authentication systems where tens of thousands of people are involved, most of whom don't have a direct, personal relationship, personal recognition doesn't work at all. Personal recognition, in the form of facial recognition, also works and doesn't work in the digital world. But more on that later in the section on biometrics.

Knowledge-Based Authentication

Most of today's authentication is based on the subject or user supplying information only they and the underlying authentication system knows. Most user and device authentication uses password-based authentication, the most popular form of knowledge-based authentication (KBA). KBA is often used to log on to computers, devices, networks, and websites, and to connect to wireless networks and join computers to domains.

The KBA secrets can be memorized by users, then stored in a database or in a document. Both sides of the client-server authentication have previously agreed on using a common KBA piece of information, such as providing a password or PIN, or solving some sort of puzzle.

Passwords

Passwords are generally a least a few characters long, but they can easily be a few tens of characters long. Passwords can be typed in by users, supplied by interfacing systems, or passed along by intermediate proxy programs. A single logon and password may be involved in multiple processes. For example, in a Windows system, users can log on to their computer using their password. That password can be used and stored locally (in the Security Account Manager [SAM] database on the local hard drive), or it can be a network-based logon (Active Directory or Azure Active Directory). The Windows operating system has dozens, if not well over a hundred, local logons going on as well between the various system operations. Those logon names and passwords are built in or stored and used by a process called the Local Security Authority Subsystem Service (LSASS). And users can connect to local area networks or to remote resources over the Internet using other logon names and processes (or have the operating system do it automatically on their behalf). Domain-joined Windows computers will log on to Active Directory or Azure Directory by using their own logon names and passwords. Though most of the time we talk about passwords, we are actually referring to users manually using password authentication.

Expected password sizes for systems varies greatly, from six to many hundred characters. Passwords for administrative accounts are typically on the longer side, 8 to 16 characters. Some people who care more than average about computer security will use passwords over 20 characters long. With that said, passwords for most user accounts are 6 to 20 characters long, with the vast majority in use today being between 6 to 8 characters long. Complexity is often required for today's passwords, but they aren't that complex and hard to guess in reality (i.e., they have low entropy).

Unless truly random, most human-selected passwords are composed entirely of alphabetic or numeric characters encompassing words, names, and dates in their chosen language. When complexity is required, passwords may include other keyboard symbols. Most human-chosen passwords are not very random; they do not contain much entropy. If humans are allowed to create their own passwords with no complexity requirements, they will be passwords like *password*, *Michael*, and *qwerty*. If humans are required to create supposedly "complex" passwords, they create passwords like *Frog33*, *P@ssw0rd*, and *qwerty123*. This makes them easy to remember and use—but also easy for password hackers to guess and hack.

Truly randomly generated passwords look more like this: *^2Vy6I}3zL#^.d!* and *46vavxTiWmLCQBZA*. These truly random passwords have high entropy and are harder for a password hacker to guess and crack. Unfortunately, as you can see, most humans would not like to have to memorize and type those sort of passwords over and over. I care a lot about computer security and even I don't want to memorize and type those sorts of passwords.

Some security-conscious password users instead use long passwords, looking more like sentences, such as *Thecowwalkedthroughthegate* or *ErichsThreeWolvesBayattheMoon*. These are known as *passphrases*. And although they can contain numbers and symbols, from their length alone, they have more entropy than the average shorter, "complex" password. Unfortunately, it's easy to make a typo with passwords that long, and many systems will not accept them. Many websites have a maximum password size of 8 to 12 characters, and many will not accept keyboard symbols at all.

Regardless of password composition, users can only remember so many passwords before they begin to forget old ones and even mistype in new ones, especially when forced password expiration is involved. As covered in Chapter 1, "Logon Problems," the average user has only six or seven passwords that they use for all their websites. When forced to update their password, they will use one of the other passwords they use all the time, or change the existing password just enough that the website accepts it (like going from *frog1* to *frog2*). Or if they actually use different passwords for every website, they usually choose a noticeable "base word" pattern such as *FrogFrogFB* for Facebook logons, *FrogFrogTW* for Twitter logons, and so forth. Also, as covered in Chapter 1, no matter what passwords are used or how complex they are, users' passwords are incredibly easy for hackers to learn—so much so that the world is trying to move to any other authentication method that doesn't involve passwords only.

The huge advantage of passwords is that they have, more or less, worked for nearly everyone fairly well since the beginning of computer authentication. They are readily understood and fairly easy to use (when not required to be complex). They are in use nearly everywhere. Failure rates for people using multifactor authentication is high. Not true for passwords. Nearly anyone, including a small child, can be easily instructed in how to successfully use passwords in a minute or two. I've seen children under the age of two type in passwords that a 60-year-old struggled with.

NOTE If you use a lot of passwords and don't use a password manager (which I'll discuss in a moment), *never* write your complete password in any document, password-protected or not, where a hacker could view it or steal it. Instead, write passwords using simple shorthand codes that only you know. For example, if your password is *FrogFrogFB* for Facebook and *FrogfrogTW33* for Twitter, only write down **FFFB** and **FfTW33**. If you never write down your complete password anywhere, no one can easily steal it. Of course, that means you have to remember what your shorthand codes stood for. Remember that it's best to avoid easy-to-recognize patterns.

PINS

PINs are essentially short KBA passwords, usually composed only of numerals (although they can contain additional types of character sets). They are most commonly used with building entry and exit control systems, smartcards, ATM/banking cards, credit cards, cell phones, and other portable computers. The average PIN is only four to six characters long.

Because PINs are short and consist of fewer possible characters than a password, PIN authentication solutions typically have strict "lockout" policies, where too many incorrect PIN attempts will invalidate the PIN or device trying to be used. Some devices accepting PINs, like a Windows PC with an enabled Trusted Platform Module (TPM) chip, will not completely lock out after a certain number of bad PIN attempts but will instead randomly make the user wait longer and longer between attempts. After more than a few bad PIN attempts, each additional bad attempt can have the subject waiting several minutes before being allowed to try again. This is known is *logon/login throttling*. Other devices will "brick" the device, meaning that the device is rendered inactive until an administrator or technician resets it.

On the good side, PINs are fairly easy for humans to remember and use. That's it for the good points. On the bad side, they are fairly easy to guess and hack. PINs are easy for other people to view "shoulder surfing" or when using hidden cameras and/or more easily figure out when viewing "wear patterns".

For example, Figure 3.1 shows a real-world PIN keypad I see nearly every day. You can see that the 1,3,6,0, and # keys have increased wear over the other keys. A reasonable person could easily assume that the PIN includes those numbers in one combination or another, and that submitting it likely requires a # keypress at the end of the sequence. Assuming no repeat characters, if the PIN is only four characters long, there are only 24 (4! = 24) possible solutions; if the PIN is five possible characters, then there are only 120 (5! = 120) possible solutions.

Note: The "!" mathematical symbol stands for factorial. Factorial means all numbers up to the number multiplied against each other. For example, $5! = 5 \times 4 \times 3 \times 2 \times 1 = 120$.

If you allow repeats, it definitely increases the number of possible solutions, but nothing compared to passwords with many more possible characters. A four-character password consisting only of 26 alphabetic characters has 456,976 (26^4) possibilities and a five-character password has 11,884,376

(26^5) possibilities. And if you allow numbers, as most passwords do, then the numbers really get big (36^4 and 36^5, respectively). PINs are so much easier to guess and hack compared to passwords.

Figure 3.1: Example PIN wear pattern

I also notice that the 2 is worn, but not as worn as the other keys. If I was a betting man, and I am, then I would guess that the 2 is part of some admin code with special privileges, that also possibly uses some of the other numbers. If the primary code I guessed correctly didn't allow me to my desired location, then I might start including the secondary wear numbers into my guessing.

I was in my brother's brand-new Tesla car recently and he was showing me how he activated the optional PIN so that thieves could not as easily steal his car just because he accidentally left the operating token (i.e., keys) in or near it or accidentally left it running. Not only is it easier to leave keyless cars running, but Tesla, in particular, leaves its mirrors extended out (at least temporarily) as one of the indications that the car is unlocked. Owners can require that drivers enter a PIN (called PIN to Drive) each time they want to use the car. As my brother was showing me this security feature, I could see which numbers on the PIN input pad had extra residual finger oil/grease left over from past keypresses compared to the other numbers. I asked him if the numbers I called out included the numbers in his PIN. He confirmed that they did.

Even if a hacker doesn't have wear patterns or finger oils to key off, PINs are fairly short and predictable. Most PINs are four characters; the longer ones are six characters. They usually don't expire, so they are used forever. Most are not randomly generated. Most are related to people's birthdates or significant dates of people they care about. A date like 0966 (representing September 1966, my birthdate) are far more common than 6699. A lot of PINs start with 0 for the same reason. Even worse, people reuse PINs even more than passwords. Many users have only one or two PINs that they reuse across all sites and devices requiring PINs.

Solving Puzzles

A growing number of authentication solutions require that the user solve some sort of puzzle: graphical, spatial, mathematical, or logical.

Connect the Dots

The most common types of puzzles involved in authentication include asking the user to "connect the dots" (see Figure 3.2). Dots are evenly placed on a tic-tac-toe grid, and the user selects or swipes the dots in a predefined, previously agreed-on, pattern.

Connect-the-dot puzzles suffer from many of the same problems as PINs, although probably the worst issue is how easy they are to figure out from shoulder surfing. It's easy for anyone watching it be done to re-create the pattern. I've seen many people, untrained for this type of skill in any way, re-create other people's patterns from across a room with the "target's" device turned 180 degrees away, obscuring direct viewing. The shoulder surfing hacker is able to tell from the target's hand movements and elbows what the target just did. I've seen and done this enough myself that I do not think connect-the-dot authentication is sufficient for anything beyond the merest suggestion of security.

Graphical Swiping

Another similar type of authentication puzzle asks the user to select a picture or graphic, or supply their own, and then determine a pattern that will be used for future authentication (see an example in Figure 3.3). Puzzle solutions like this usually allow the user to use a combination of distinction gestures, such as "points," swiping from one point to another without raising their finger, circles, or making other predefined gestures. These types of authentication solutions tend to be allowed on form factors larger than a few inches. On smaller form factors such as cell phones, it might be difficult to get enough movement area across the smaller representation of the figure to achieve the desired result.

The problems with these sorts of authentication solutions mimic the connect-the-dot puzzles, although not having stationary, fixed-positioned dots may help prevent easy shoulder surfing. Still, research has shown that people using these types of puzzle solutions have predictable locations they choose and gestures and motions they make depending on the patterns and shapes in the underlying photo.

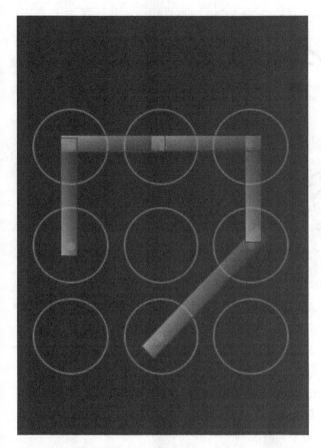

Figure 3.2: A connect-the-dot authentication solution

Solving Math Problems

Yes, some authentication solutions require users to solve a "math" problem. Usually the "math" problem is similar to a regular math problem where the user is asked to solve for some unknown answer value, known as "x" (i.e., solve for x). But instead of it simply being a matter of actually doing regular math, usually it's really a hint that leads to a predefined answer that no one else but the legitimate user should know or have access to.

Solving the problem may require that the user already have a preprinted "hint" sheet. For example, a few authentication solutions will show the user a simple math problem to solve, say 2 + 4 = ?, but instead of supplying the answer, 6, the user is asked to supply a color associated with the answer 6 as indicated on the previously issued "hint" sheet. So, the answer is 6, and 6 on the hint sheet points to the color blue. The user would type in blue as the answer instead of 6. Or maybe the answer 6 on the answer sheet points to the numeric value of 64, so the answer that successfully authenticates the user would be 64 and not 6. Anytime I see an authentication solution asking for math to be solved or for pre-printed sheets to be used I roll my eyes. They are not going to be used by very many people.

Figure 3.3: Example of graphical picture swipe authentication
Source: Courtesy of KnowBe4

Recovery Questions

One of the most popular KBA options are "recovery questions," so called because they are a popular alternative for users trying to recover an account after one of the other primary valid authentication methods have failed. With recovery questions, the user is given a list of questions to choose among, such as the following:

- What is your mother's maiden name?
- What was your first car?
- What is your favorite pet's name?
- What was the name of your fourth-grade teacher?

To each one selected, the user supplies an answer. In many recovery question setup scenarios, users are allowed to create their own questions and answers. The idea is that when a recovery event needs to happen (such as replacing a lost password), the system can prompt the user with one or more of their recovery questions (usually it's two or three of them) and ask for the user's answers. Answers normally have to be typed in exactly as given, although they are usually not case-sensitive. If the user correctly answers the questions, they are allowed to successfully perform the recovery action.

Recovery questions are easy to use, but they suffer from some big problems. Most notable is that the answers to the recovery questions may be public information or easy to glean from the victim by a hacker. There's a great Google paper called "Secrets, Lies, and Account Recovery: Lessons from the Use of Personal Knowledge Questions at Google" (www.a51.nl/sites/default/files/pdf/43783 .pdf). It contains many researched findings that conclusively argue against the safety of using recovery questions as an alternate authentication method. Some great examples:

- Some recovery questions can be guessed on the first try 20 percent of the time.
- Forty percent of people were unable to successfully recall their own recovery answers.
- Sixteen percent of answers could be found in the person's social media profile.

It's the wrong chapter to get into hacking attacks against MFA, but recovery questions are so easy to hack that they should be outlawed! Microsoft and Google have both banned recovery questions as a viable authentication solution. Guessing at recovery questions have been involved in many well-known, real-world attacks.

In 2008, when John McCain and his running mate, Sarah Palin, were unsuccessfully running against Barack Obama and Joe Biden for president of the United States, a young adult researched the answers for Sarah Palin's Yahoo email account in 45 minutes and successfully hijacked her account (www.washingtontimes.com/news/2008/sep/19/hacker-wanted-to-derail-palin). The "hacker" was identified after a federal investigation, arrested, found guilty, and served time in prison. They deserved to be arrested, but I'm not sure it's fair to call the perpetrators a "hacker" based on the crime. It would be fairer to call them a person who can use an Internet search engine. More on these types of attacks in Chapter 13, "Downgrade/Recovery Attacks."

CAPTCHAs

Completely Automated Public Turing test to tell Computers and Humans Apart (CAPTCHA) tests can be a simple KBA method. CAPTCHA tests come in all sorts of forms and are changing all the time, and are often required when signing up for a new account or posting a new message on a public bulletin board. They evolve to be more accurate and also to avoid hackers who are successfully compromising them in a variety of methods.

In the simplest common form, the user is asked to click a blank check box next to the words "I'm not a robot" (see Figure 3.4). The authentication system then reads the user's IP address and allowed cookies to determine whether the purported user's information is the same as used elsewhere before by a previously trusted user for whom they measured the same information (i.e., the same device and browser). With more advanced CAPTCHAs, the system analyzes how long it takes for the box to be clicked and enabled, as well as other behavior characteristics. The idea is that automated methods (i.e., "bots") would do it in a way that has a more predictable pattern, whereas humans have more entropy in their selections.

More involved CAPTCHA forms include showing a picture and asking the human to identify particular attributes. Examples include picking out particular objects, colors, and numbers. Figure 3.5 shows a common example of this CAPTCHA type, asking users to select the parts of the picture that contain pieces of a sign.

Figure 3.4: Example of a simple CAPTCHA

Figure 3.5: Example of a more complex CAPTCHA asking a user to select the portions of the picture containing a piece of the sign

These types of CAPTCHAs have started having increased failure rates because some users don't comprehend the instructions and some pictures are difficult to understand. For example, in Figure 3.5, the very bottom of the highway sign is intruding just a tiny bit into the second bottom row. Should that square be part of what the user picks, since the sign is indeed part of that square, or is the sliver of the sign so minute that the CAPTCHA creators didn't include it as a correct answer?

In any case, CAPTCHAs are weak authenticators. They only try to distinguish between automated malware programs and real human beings, and they don't have great accuracy once an attacker starts to concentrate on them. Attackers have even hired teams of people whose sole job is to analyze and respond to CAPTCHAs correctly. Their use does significantly slow down abusers, but it doesn't stop them. If you are interested in learning more about CAPTCHAs, check out the following site:

`www.256kilobytes.com/content/show/10414/busting-recaptcha-myths-reverse-engineering-anti-spam-algorithms-and-examining-existing-research-in-realistic-contexts`

Password Managers

As you learned in Chapter 1, a user should never use the same password on different systems, sites, or services. If they do, the compromise of one location could more easily lead to a compromise of additional locations. Unfortunately, most users share the same six or seven passwords across all sites and services they use. That's just asking for trouble. At the same time, every password should be as random and as long as possible to prevent easy guessing and cracking. Adding this requirement makes it more difficult for the average user to hold all their passwords in their head.

If users are going to try to meet both critical password requirements—unique and randomly complex—they will either need to write them down somewhere (a document, a database, etc.) or use a software program known as a *password manager*. A password manager is a program that not only securely stores multiple passwords, but also allows a user to call them up on demand (see Figure 3.6) while using their computer and have the password manager provide the site or service with the correct, agreed-on password. If the program is properly used to its full extent, the user doesn't pick the password; the password manager automatically generates long and complex, unique passwords. The user doesn't even need to know them! When a password is needed, the password manager pops up to automatically enter it, or the user calls up the password manager program and tells the program to type the password. It's hard to be phished or tricked out of your password if you don't know it.

Password managers have been around for decades, although they are getting more secure and feature-rich every year. Today, password managers not only store passwords, but may also act as MFA, act as virtual credit cards, and store other confidential information. There are dozens of different password managers, both free and commercial. *Wired* magazine reviewed seven password managers they liked here: www.wired.com/story/best-password-managers. One of my favorite "extra" features of my password manager is that it will notify users if websites associated with the password manager have been breached or use weak or vulnerable passwords (example shown in Figure 3.7).

Password managers can be used in conjunction with MFA, shared across supported devices, and shared with others. For example, my wife knows that if something happens to me, she can access my password manager and, with that, access every website I authenticate to, including retirement, financial, and insurance sites. It puts my online digital life into one neat place. This of course only works if you trust that additional person completely.

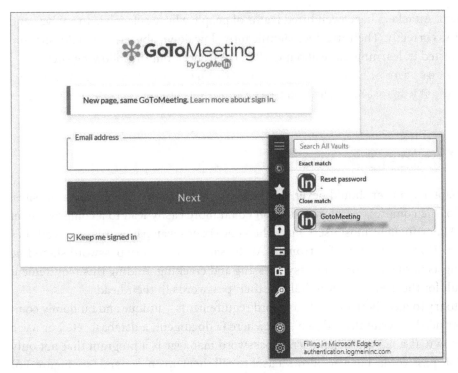

Figure 3.6: Example of Password Manager called up to type a website password

Figure 3.7: Example of password manager notifying a user of breaches or weak or vulnerable passwords the user is using across websites linked to the user's password manager use.

Password managers are great for managing lots of passwords. They easily beat storing all your passwords on a password-protected document or database. Still, they have their issues. First, none of them work with everything. Most won't allow you to log on to your laptop or device, and most don't work with corporate network logons. Most don't work with every website or service. Most don't support every possible device you would want to use it on. So, coverage can be spotty.

Second, if an attacker gains access to a device on which you have a password manager installed, they may be able to get all your passwords at once. An attacker who compromises your computer can get to all your passwords. They can sniff them out of memory, grab them from your browser (if you save passwords there), and get them from you using keylogging trojans. So, if an attacker has complete access to your device, they are going to get the passwords you use and store. But if you have a password manager, they can get them all, even the ones you haven't used in a long time, all in one place. Most password managers have protections against these sorts of attacks, but they are not perfect.

Third, all password managers have bugs. You can type your logon name and password all day long every day and never have a problem. But every password manager I've tested has had bugs. Most of the time they work; sometimes they don't.

Sometimes these bugs can be "fatal." I've read about many a password manager user who suddenly had their password manager program lock up or error out and the user was abruptly locked out and unable to use it. Because the user often doesn't know their logon information, they can't log on to a website they used the password manager with. They have effectively become locked out from all websites they were using the password manager with, until they either recover the password manager program or reset all their passwords, individually, one at a time. It is also not uncommon for a password manager to get a known security bug which attackers may be able to take advantage of until they get patched. My password manager is auto-updating all the time, so I'm assuming most of these publicly known bugs would be short-lived.

Overall, I trust password managers, occasional bugs and all. More importantly, if you have to have multiple passwords—and you do—then they are great for helping you use different long, complex, unique passwords per site and service. I think everyone should use one. Of course, if they became super popular and everyone used them, they would just become popular hacking magnets. All the password-stealing malware would target them. But until that happens, or even if that happens, using a password manager is a good thing, reducing risk for most of us.

NOTE Sometimes, OSs and browsers call the component that stores and reuses passwords on behalf of a user a "password manager". They do serve, very crudely, some of the basic features of a password program. One of the big distinctions is that most "real" password managers have tons of additional functionality beyond remembering and using passwords and can work with multiple OSs, browsers, and programs, whereas an OS or browser password manager only works with itself.

Single Sign-Ons and Proxies

Single-sign-On (SSO) and *proxy* programs are similar to password managers, but usually more complex. Unlike password managers, most of which run in a single local location on behalf of a single user, these programs run in a centralized, shared location on behalf of many users. The idea is that a user can log on once to the SSO program, and the SSO program will handle logging on to the rest of the programs the user needs to authenticate to (or as many as it can or will be allowed to). Most SSO solutions are installed and focused on helping one organization's user to connect to other resources the organization needs everyone to connect to.

Some SSO programs use APIs to programmatically interface with applications. Others use scripting to essentially "type" in what the user otherwise could, but faster than the user could do it. The logon information or passwords that the SSO program uses on behalf of the user may be supplied by the user or created and used without the user involved in the process. How they work depends on the SSO product. Proxies are technically different in that a user may be prompted for a different password or logon secret for each logon, but the actual logon used to log the user onto the remote location is different from what the user supplied.

NOTE   Privileged account managers (PAMs) and password "vaulting" solutions, which are usually very feature rich, are similar to SSO and proxies, though many people would not loop them into the same category. But in both cases, you have centralized shared repositories of logon credentials used by others. PAM and vaulting systems would probably require their own chapter to appropriately cover.

Although SSO programs and proxies are different from password managers, they suffer from many of the same problems. SSO and proxies are single points of failure. When they go down, the user may be unable log on to any websites and services. A hacker can also access all the logon information stored within the SSO/proxy database and compromise all users and their passwords at once. Essentially, you can take the good and bad of a password manager and just multiply their shared characteristics across the advantages and disadvantages.

Also, a centralized SSO or proxy often has one or more administrators to manage them. That way, the administrator can dictate appropriate policies, configure and troubleshoot them to work with the "foreign" systems, and reset logon information if needed. But it's a dual-edged sword—that admin also has access to everyone else's logon information, potentially acting as both an additional attack vector or an additional attacker themselves.

Cryptography

Cryptography is involved in nearly all digital authentication and is often the primary reason the authentication is able to be successful. And it's sometimes why it fails when poorly implemented. It is crucial that any reader wanting to understand digital authentication understand cryptography fairly well at least at a basic level. For that reason, this part of the chapter will be longer and go into more detail than the other sections.

Cryptography is the science, study, and practice of securing and authenticating people, data, transactions, and other objects between authorized parties. It is done by using encryption, integrity checks, and algorithmic implementations. Cryptography allows confidentiality and integrity of data, communications, and participants, to be maintained whenever desired between authorized, designated parties (or software or devices on their behalf). This will not be a thorough study of everything that is cryptography, but I will summarize the major components used in login authentication.

Encryption

Encryption is a popular method for subjects to keep something secret. Using encryption, *plaintext* content is rearranged to create a coded message that only the intended parties can later decode to understand. The process used to reverse an encrypted message back to its original, plaintext message form is called *decryption*. The documented process and steps used to encrypt or decrypt a message are referred to loosely as a *cipher*, or a *cipher algorithm*, which is usually represented mathematically. A single subject may want to keep something secret to their self, or the secret may be shared between a selected group of people or devices. The secret can be any type of content, including the identities of participating parties and any involved transactions and objects.

Key

Every cipher encrypts the plaintext content using a series of previously agreed-on characters or symbols known as the *key*. In the classical computer world, digital encryption keys are a long series of seemingly randomly generated 1s and 0s. A digital key looks something like 10101010101101000101 0101010101100111001010101, varying by composition and length. The key is applied to the plaintext message in a series of steps described by the mathematics of the cipher to create the encrypted message. The key must be kept secret to keep the encrypted text known only to the participating subjects.

If done correctly, both the key and the encrypted message appear like a random set of unpredictable bits. Today, digital encryption keys usually range in size from 128 to 4,096 bits, although they can be smaller and larger in less common scenarios. Whether a particular length of bits is considered secure depends on many factors, including the cipher algorithm, the speed at which all the possible key bit composition positions (called the *key space*) can be guessed, and any "tricks" that can be used to cut down the brute-force guessing methods. Strong cipher algorithms that are harder to "crack" can use smaller key bit sizes, whereas conversely, weaker algorithms often require longer key sizes for equal protection. Bit lengths for new keys using the same algorithms tend to grow over time to compensate for greater computational power and other cracking factors. Cryptographic attacks only get better over time, which weakens the protective power provided by the length of the key.

You can readily find and see cipher key examples by viewing any digital certificate on any computer or device. Figure 3.8 shows the 2,048-bit key extracted from a digital certificate.

NOTE   Nearly all digital cryptographic keys are shown converted to their hexadecimal representations (e.g., Base16 numbering system) on most computers and devices instead of their bits (i.e., 1s and 0s).

```
30 82 01 0a 02 82 01 01 00 ad 0c 9f 7d 67 bc
70 6d 79 ba 25 05 3a 64 60 a0 e2 23 f3 ec 17
3b 6e 75 9e 88 50 fb d9 de 9c 62 2b de 19 a8
52 57 f0 09 62 2c 5e 64 45 9c 60 39 b5 14 48
2e 27 a4 db 82 c8 02 da ba 1d 91 51 fb 90 fa
bf f7 55 65 f1 cc 98 1a 3f 6b 0f 74 18 8f d4
cc 3b 44 ca 4d 53 df 95 94 72 20 d1 45 1a a5
9b 3b a8 f2 71 79 0e 6e ad 5b 87 ca 9e d1 7f
72 b8 2b 93 e0 36 69 31 7b 60 9a 44 f8 f4 a5
45 de 15 62 01 93 cd b3 ea e6 d1 d5 3c 1a 6b
cd ea a2 fd 7d 56 35 d0 c5 aa 5f 0e 6f 6e b2
c7 fa 8c 57 10 58 d3 0a 14 b4 2a fd 09 c6 ac
17 8e 3a ba 2c e8 dc 51 9f 29 a8 cb 39 e2 5a
8a 60 96 62 d7 64 05 94 d1 d7 8c 5b e3 0f fd
01 ed b4 5f 32 de b9 b1 b3 ea 3e 4c 6e d0 90
c4 82 eb 58 dc 6c 14 f0 4e 9f 1f 74 a3 76 26
30 bc 9a 97 91 fd 7c c8 c6 5a fd f8 54 ae 09
48 5a 50 b3 0c 3b 8f 43 f6 5f 02 03 01 00 01
```

Figure 3.8: Example 2,048-bit key extracted from a digital certificate

A cipher key that is only known to and used by a single subject and that is not intentionally shared with anyone else is a *private* or *secret key*. A cipher key that is intentionally shared between multiple subjects is a *shared key*. A key that can be known and used by anyone is a *public key*. A key created to be used only temporarily is a *session key*.

If the same key is used to encrypt and decrypt the message, the cipher is *symmetric*. If one key is used to encrypt messages and another is used to decrypt messages, the cipher is *asymmetric*. Authentications often use multiple key types to accomplish their services, although asymmetric cryptography is more often directly responsible for the authentication.

NOTE You can see the general recommended minimum key sizes for popular ciphers by visiting www.keylength.com.

Symmetric Encryption

Symmetric keys are usually used for encrypting, and today's globally accepted symmetric ciphers are very good at it. Symmetric ciphers are stronger, faster, and easier to validate than asymmetric ciphers, and they require smaller key sizes. From a cryptographic viewpoint, good symmetric ciphers are easier to prove as strong and reliable. They have less complicated math. They require fewer assumptions and less guesswork. They are harder to attack. Accordingly, symmetric ciphers do most of the world's data encryption.

The world has used many different symmetric cipher standards since the 1970s, including Data Encryption Standard (DES), Triple DES (3DES), International Data Encryption Algorithm (IDEA), and Rivest Cipher 5 (RC5). All of these older symmetric ciphers are considered weak and broken today. Since 2001, the most popular symmetric cipher is Advanced Encryption Standard (AES). Currently, AES uses key sizes of 128-, 192- and 256-bit lengths, and its strength has held up very well under years of cryptographic scrutiny and attacks.

As good as symmetric ciphers are, they cannot be used alone to do authentication. This is because anyone involved with a single symmetric cipher transaction uses the same key. It's impossible, without some additional features and functions, to prove who encrypted or decrypted something. Tying a particular encryption implementation to a particular subject, which authentication explicitly does, requires asymmetric encryption and/or digital signing.

Asymmetric Encryption

Asymmetric ciphers, also known as *private/public key pair ciphers*, use one key to encrypt content and another cryptographically related key to decrypt. Each participating subject is given their own private/public key pair. The private key is known only to the subject and shared with no one else. The public key can be given out to anyone else. What one key in the key pair encrypts, the other cryptographically related key of the key pair can decrypt.

Even though both keys of the key pair can be used to encrypt a message to the other, and vice versa, the nature of who has the private and public key classifications is important. Remember, the private key is never shared with anyone else. Because of this, if someone wants to send a confidential message to another person, they must use the receiver's public key to encrypt the message. This will keep the message confidential until the receiver uses their related private key to decrypt it. Since no one else has the receiver's private key, no one else can decrypt the message. With asymmetric encryption, we must use the public key of the receiver to encrypt messages to them.

Key Exchange

Symmetric encryption is faster and stronger with small key sizes than asymmetric encryption. Because of this, asymmetric encryption is often used to securely communicate symmetric keys, which do most of the encryption, over possibly insecure network channels between two or more subjects. This process is known as *key exchange*. A very basic summary of the key exchange process looks similar to this:

1. The client and server connect to each other.
2. The server sends the client the server's public key of its asymmetric key pair.
3. The client uses the server's public key to encrypt the client's newly generated "session" symmetric key back to the server.
4. Both the server and the client now use the shared, session symmetric key to send encrypted content back and forth to each other.

In the real world, using asymmetric key exchange to securely transmit a shared symmetric key between the client and server has a few more steps and complexity, but this is a good summary of the basic steps of asymmetric key exchange. It is used billions of times a day to make our digital world run. When you connect to a HTTPS-enabled website, that's what is happening. When you pay using your credit card online, this is happening. And many times, when you use MFA, this is happening in the background somewhere.

Common types of asymmetric cryptography include Rivest–Shamir–Adleman (RSA), Diffie–Hellman (DH), Elliptic Curve Cryptography (ECC), and ElGamal. RSA is easily the most popularly used asymmetric encryption cipher, accounting for the supermajority of all asymmetric cipher uses. Although all asymmetric ciphers are used to perform key exchange, Diffie–Hellman (also known as Diffie–Hellman–Merkle) and Elliptic Curve Diffie–Hellman (ECDH) are more often associated with key exchange-only implementations, instead of being used as asymmetric encryption or authentication alone as is RSA. RSA and DH key sizes typically range from 2,048- to 4,096 bits and ECDH key sizes are smaller at 256-bits. Both provide comparative protection.

Digital Signing

Asymmetric cryptography users can also use their key pairs to authenticate and digitally sign content. *Digital signing* is the act of providing proof that the signed content is still as it was at the moment of the signing. To sign content, a user uses their private key to "encrypt" the content (or a hash result, covered later in a moment). We don't call the process "encryption" since anyone who has the related public key (which theoretically could be the entire world) could decrypt and read it. It can't be considered confidential or encrypted if everyone in the world can see it. Instead, we call it digital signing.

Any content signed by the private key can be revealed only by using the related public key. If the content can be verified ("decrypted") by the related public key, it must have been signed by the related private key because the only thing the related public key can "decrypt" is something signed by the related private key. Similar processes can be used to authenticate user identities involved in cryptographic operations, some of which will be covered later in this chapter. Common digital signature ciphers include Digital Signature Algorithm (DSA) and Elliptic Curve DSA (ECDSA). A message can be encrypted and signed if both protections are needed by using the appropriate keys during the associated process (i.e., private keys of the sender to sign, public keys of the receiver to encrypt).

Because each party has their own, unique key pair, and only that key pair can encrypt and decrypt messages between each other, asymmetric cryptography also allows subject and message authentication. Each involved key pair can be tied to a particular subject, which allows attribution and authentication. Usually, symmetric encryption, asymmetric encryption, and signing is used in authentication, but asymmetric and signing ciphers are more directly involved with and responsible for the authentication components.

Public Key Infrastructure

In order for asymmetric cipher systems to work with authentication, the people communicating using them must have trust that everyone's public key is valid and belongs to who they think it belongs to. In the early days of asymmetric cipher communications, it was enough for one person to send another person they already knew their public key, and the receiving person would trust that the person who sent it to them was the correct, valid person with the correct, valid private key.

But as the number of people in an asymmetric channel increases, not every participant may know and trust every other participant. One way to get public key trust in a person you don't know is to have someone you already trust vouch for the other person. For example, suppose Alice wanted to communicate asymmetrically with Bob but didn't know or trust Bob ahead of time. But she knew that Dan knew and trusted Bob and could vouch for Bob and Bob's valid public key. Dan could even sign Bob's public key with his own private key, which Alice could then validate using Dan's public key. This is called a *peer-to-peer trust* (or *web trust*). Many asymmetric cipher programs on the Internet work this way.

But peer-to-peer trust systems don't work as well as the number of participants scale, particularly in global asymmetric systems where most of the participants don't know one another. Enter public key infrastructure. *Public key infrastructure* (PKI) is a commonly used cryptographic framework and family of protocols used in the computer world to provide identity trust between unrelated parties. You may read or hear about many different descriptions of what PKI is and why it is needed, but at its base requirement, PKI primarily exists to authenticate subject identities and their asymmetric cryptographic keys involved in cryptographic transactions. Without this requirement, you would not need PKI.

PKIs issue verified subject's *digital certificates*, which are cryptographically protected documents attesting to the validity of a subject's identity and their associated asymmetric key pair. In practice, the subject (or something on their behalf) generates an asymmetric key pair for the subject to use. The subject submits their public key to the PKI (remember, we don't share private keys). The PKI's *certification authority* service process is then supposed to verify the identity of the subject submitting the public key.

NOTE Many times the PKI is creating and issuing the entire key pair, both the private and public portions, to the user. And when doing so, even though the PKI could know the private key, the key is still considered private as long as no one else outside the PKI (and PKI admins) can possibly see it.

The level of identity proof required of the subject by the PKI determines the level of assurance (or trust) the PKI can attest to. In any case, the primary job of a PKI is to verify the identity of the subject submitting their public key. If the subject's identity is validated, the PKI adds some additional information (such as validity dates, subject name[s], certificate serial number, and the certification authority's name and identifier) and signs the subject's public key (and other information) with the PKI's private key. This creates a digital certificate. Figure 3.9 shows a partial example of a digital certificate highlighting the public key field.

Theoretically, any entity who trusts the PKI (who issued a particular digital certificate) will trust any digital certificate created by the PKI and presented by the subject. The subject presenting the digital certificate is essentially saying, "I am who I say I am and an entity you trust verified it." A PKI can be likened to the Department of Motor Vehicles (DMV) used in the United States. DMV license holders must substantially prove their identity to the DMV in order to get a driver's license with their legal name, address, and birth date, on it. After the driver's (i.e., subject's) identity is successfully verified (assured), the DMV will take the subject's picture, add other information, and issue a DMV license, sealed along with the state emblem (somewhat like a real-world digital certificate). If the driver is stopped by law enforcement or goes to purchase something requiring age verification, they will often be required to present their DMV license. The officer and sales clerk trust the DMV license to be accurate and thus will rely on the information printed on the license during their verification process.

Figure 3.9: Example of partial details of a public certificate

Much of the Internet works on PKI. For example, every time you connect to a website using HTTPS, that website has an Hypertext Transport Protocol Secured/Transport Layer Security (HTTPS/TLS) digital certificate signed and issued by a trusted PKI. You may not personally trust that PKI, but your operating system or software does. When you connect to the website with your browser using the HTTPS protocol, the website sends you (or actually your browser) a copy of its digital certificate. The digital certificate, signed by a PKI, attests to the website's name (often by URL), the website's public key, and other related important information.

If by chance your browser or operating system didn't immediately know of and trust a particularly PKI, most of the time the involved application would present the PKI's own name and/or digital certificate, and ask you if you want to trust it (before trusting anything it signed). You could then select yes or no. If you select yes, the new PKI is added to a list of stored trusted PKIs that you or your software trusts, so you won't be prompted again the next time.

Once verified, your browser will generate a brand-new shared session symmetric key, which it then securely sends to the website (using the website's public key). Finally, both the server and client can begin communicating securely using symmetric key communications. Figure 3.10 summarizes the basic HTTPS authentication scenario.

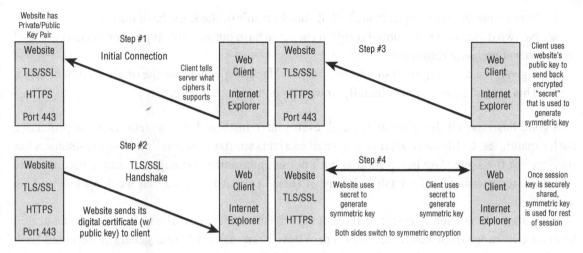

Figure 3.10: Example of the basic HTTPS authentication and encryption scenario

In another popular example of PKI use, when you're downloading new software from popular vendors, the software will come with a digital certificate validating who signed the software (or the related integrity hash, covered in more detail later) that allows the downloader (or more realistically usually a browser on their behalf) to validate that the software has not changed since the signer signed the software or hash. It doesn't matter where that software traveled between the signer and the receiver, whether it traveled over trusted or untrusted channels, how many intermediaries were involved, or how long ago the signing occurred (within reason). If validated, the digital certificate and accompanying validated hash tells users they can rely on the software to be as it was the moment it was signed and to be from who it says signed it.

Hashing

Another integral major cryptographic function is *integrity hashing*. Hash algorithms (also known as *hash functions* or simply *hashes*) are used to create unique output results for unique content inputs. They use "one-way" cryptographic functions, which create and output a unique representative set of characters or bits (the *hash*, *hash result*, or *message digest*) for unique content. Hash functions create cryptographic *digital fingerprints* of the content that they hash. Hashing functions can be used to cryptographically sign and verify the integrity of content, subjects, and other cryptographic objects. When the integrity hash result (often known simply as a hash or message digest) is cryptographically tied to a particular cryptographic subject identity (e.g., user, device, or service), it is known as a *digital signature*. A verified digital signature allows the receiver of signed content to have confidence that the signed contents have not been altered since the signing of the content by the authenticated signer. Secure, trusted hash functions have four important traits:

- For every unique input, a unique output result must be generated. This type of protection is called *collision resistance*.

- Every time the same input is hashed, it should result in the same hash output.
- No two different inputs should result in the same hash output. This type of protection is called *second preimage resistance*.
- If given the hash output, it should be nontrivial for anyone to derive the original content input. This type of protection is officially known as *preimage resistance*.

A good hash has all these attributes and, even under sustained attack, retains these protective hash capabilities. Collision resistance is related to and is similar to second-preimage resistance, but they are not the same. And being good at both doesn't guarantee preimage resistance because they are unrelated attributes. If a hash fails any of these tests, it is considered weak and should no longer be used.

Hash algorithms usually result in fixed-length hash results regardless of the input. Common hash lengths range from 128 to 256 bits. There have been many different generally accepted hash standards over the years, including Message Digest 5 (MD5), Windows LANManager (LM), Windows NT (NT), and Secure Hash Algorithm-1 (SHA-1). All of these previous standards, except for NT, are considered weak and broken. Today, the most popular hashing algorithm is Secure Hash Algorithm-2 (SHA-2 or SHA2), although in 2015 NIST recommended that SHA-2's successor, Secure Hash Algorithm-3 (SHA-3 or SHA3), be used instead because SHA-2 is being weakened over time from cryptographic attack improvements. So far, most people are still using SHA-2. SHA-2 has many different output sizes including 224, 384, 256, and 512 bits. Hashing is often used as part of an authentication solution. Table 3.1 shows some hash outputs for the word "frog" using common example hashes.

Table 3.1: Hash outputs for the word "frog" using common example hashes

Hash algorithm	Hash result for "frog"
MD5	938C2CC0DCC05F2B68C4287040CFCF71
SHA-1	B3E0F62FA1046AC6A8559C68D231B6BD11345F36
SHA-2	74FA5327CC0F4E947789DD5E989A61A8242986A596F170640AC90337B1DA1EE4
SHA-3 (512)	6EB693784D6128476291A3BBBF799d287F77E1816b05C611CE114AF239BE2DEE734B5Df71B21AC74A36BE12CD629890CE63EE87E0F53BE987D938D39E8D52B62

Hashes play a big part in authentication and many MFA solutions. Hashes are often used to digitally sign other authentication messages that need to be verified later on and to encode passwords and other secrets against easy eavesdropping.

Asymmetric encryption, key exchange, digital signing, symmetric encryption, and hashing play heavily into many forms of digital authentication. And if appropriately implemented, cryptography is usually not a weak link in most MFA solutions. If poorly implemented, it can create a critical error that undermines the whole solution. There are some huge cryptographic programming bugs that led to hundreds of millions of previously trusted authentication devices being rendered worthless upon discovery (more on this in Chapter 15, "Buggy Software").

Hardware Tokens

A common type of MFA solution is a hardware device or physical token of some sort. It uses the "Something You Have" factor as its core benefit. Usually they are piggybacked with "Something You Know," but can be used with "Something You Are" (biometrics) or alone (1FA). They are so popular that most of the general public equates MFA with a hardware device of some type. The hardware devices may simply display an authentication factor that the user views and retypes into another device's console, or the user may need to interact with the device in some way and that interaction is an integral part of the authentication input process. Some MFA hardware devices are stand-alone, and some require and work using networks. MFA hardware devices can require physical connections, such as plugging the device into a USB port or smartcard slot or using a wireless connection. The wireless and network connection distances can be local and very limited (i.e., a maximum of a few centimeters) or able to connect to and participate with other authentication resources around the globe.

One-Time Password Devices

Stand-alone hardware-based authenticators, which do not need an outside network connection, are very popular, and have been popular for decades. The most popular of these are *one-time-password* (OTP) devices. OTP devices automatically generate a seemingly "random" code (which is usually not random at all), which can be typed in an MFA logon screen that is synchronized with a similar process associated with the authentication check.

Usually the user types in a logon name or identity code, then provides a code generated by the OTP device as sort of a password. Depending on the OTP solution, another more permanent code may also be needed along with the changing code to make a resulting larger code. Whatever changing code is generated, it is good only for a preset amount of time, will supposedly never repeat, and often is not regenerated within a reasonable period of time. OTP devices may involve a hash function and, if so, are known as *HMAC-OTP* or *hash-based OTP* (HOTP) devices.

The security theory behind an OTP device is that if an attacker learns the automatically generated code, that code can only be used for a preset period of time and will never be used or generated again. Thus, it time-limits the amount of damage that can be done because of a single compromise. Most OTP devices generate new code changes on a preset time schedule (every 30 seconds, once a minute, every 5 or 10 minutes, once an hour, etc.). When an OTP device generates a new code based on or involving the current time, it is known as a *time-based-one-time-password* (TOTP) device. The key difference is that an HOTP device will change the code at a preset period of time or event but doesn't actually use the current time in the calculation, whereas a TOTP actually uses the current time value in the calculation to generate a new code.

Some OTP devices key off a particular event or action occurring and are known as *event-one-time-password* (EOTP) devices. Most EOTP devices have a button that the user clicks. The button click generates a new number, which is used in the OTP code generation. Often the button click serially advances a counter in the EOTP device. In these instances, the counter itself is used in the OTP calculation.

OTP devices usually have globally unique identifiers (i.e., serial numbers) that are hard-coded into the device and also stored in the backend authentication database. A seed value is randomly generated by the device and/or database and shared with the other. Then the seed value and other supplied information (possibly including the unique identifier) are used with a documented algorithm to generate all future codes. Internet Engineering Task Force (IETF) Request for Comment (RFC) 6238 (tools.ietf.org/html/rfc6238) is an open standard for OTP devices. Figure 3.11 shows a sampling of popular OTP devices.

Figure 3.11: Popular OTP devices
Source: Photo by Mateusz Adamowski, taken with Canon EOS. Own work, CC BY-SA 1.0, commons.wikimedia.org/w/index.php?curid=142232

TOTPs are very popular and have been in use for decades. Probably their number one usability drawback is the limited time a user has to access and view the code on the TOTP device before another code must be used. Every TOTP user has experienced the anxiety of hoping to be able to type in the current code and hoping it stays valid long enough to be authenticated before the next one appears. Every TOTP user understands the slight feeling of failure when they are too late and the authentication is rejected as the next code pops up.

Other downsides include that TOTPs can be relatively expensive versus other MFA solutions and they can become unsynchronized from the server-side authentication source. Most TOTP devices are designed to tolerate some small amount of time skew, but if the device goes beyond the threshold limits, the device will stop allowing successful authenticating.

To fight the time skewing issue, some OTP devices work purely on "asynchronous" challenge-response solutions. In these scenarios, the server usually generates a "challenge," which is then input into the stand-alone OTP device, which in turn generates a resulting, related, "response." The response is sent to the server and compared to the server's self-generated expected response value. If they match, the client is authenticated. RFC 6287 covers asynchronous OTP devices.

NOTE The Initiative for Open Authentication, or OAuth (`en.wikipedia.org/wiki/Initiative_for_Open_Authentication`), is involved with setting open standards for OTP devices. OAuth (or OAUTH) should not be confused with oAuth, which is another unrelated standard called Open Authorization, covered more in Chapter 19, "API Abuses."

OTP MFA devices are very popular, and for a while they seemed likely to become the future MFA solution of choice. But the wide availability of cell phones being used as MFA hardware devices and software-based OTP solutions have diminished their exponential rate of growth. More on OTP solutions and how to hack them in Chapter 9, "One-Time Password Attacks."

Physical Connection Devices

Another very popular hardware-based authentication device type is one that requires physical connections to the devices it is being used to authenticate to or from.

Dongles

Early examples of physical connection devices included devices a user had to connect to their computer's serial or parallel port to run software. Back in the 1980s and 1990s, to prevent illegal software copying, an antitheft device was a popular choice; the software had to check for the presence of this device before it ran. The device usually contained a serial number or some other code that could be queried and, if matched, the device would successfully authenticate the software and allow it to run. Related to these were illegal cable box "descramblers" or signal baluns, which allowed cable customers to access cable channels they had not subscribed to.

USB Devices

In more modern times, many MFA solutions involve plugging an authentication device into the base computing device's USB port. Nearly every computer and laptop has multiple USB ports, and USB-based authentication devices have been popular for at least two decades. USB-based authentication devices may need to be plugged in to boot up a device, to unlock an encrypted hard drive, or to authenticate to participating sites and services.

Today, some of the most popular USB MFA options come from a company called Yubico (www
.yubico.com) and are known as YubiKeys (see Figure 3.12 for USB-C, USB-A-Nano, and USB-A examples). USB-C devices are often used on Apple Mac devices and smartphones. Some USB devices
authenticate simply by plugging them in; others require pressing a button on the hardware device,
and some require additional factors and actions.

Figure 3.12: Examples of USB-C, USB-A-Nano, and USB-A YubiKeys

Smartcards

Smartcards are plastic credit card–sized authentication devices with an integrated cryptographic circuit chip (see Figure 3.13 for an example). The integrated chip contains an operating system, memory,
and storage space. If you look closely at the smartcard's physical integrated circuit chip, you will see
that it is divided into eight distinct areas known as "pins." Some of the pins are involved in powering
up the chip and others are input/output data areas.

When the integrated circuit chip comes into contact with a smartcard reader (smartcards that
require physical connections are also known as a *contact card*), the chip and operating system are
energized and begin to operate. Smartcards also come in wireless varieties, known as *contactless
cards*, where a hidden embedded metallic induction coil running along the outside perimeter of the
card (you can often see it if you look for it on contactless cards) get energized when brought within
range of the appropriate radio signals.

Smartcards contain a digital certificate with an Object Identifier (OID) field containing the following information: Smart Card Logon (1.3.6.1.4.1.311.20.2.2). Applications allowing smartcard
authentication look for that specific OID to be present in the digital certificate. If this specific OID
is missing on the digital certificate, the smartcard probably won't work.

Figure 3.13: Example smartcard

The smartcard usually contains both the public and private keys of each digital certificate. Smartcards are "smart" because the integrated circuit chip cryptographically protects the private key from being accessed by external programs or intruders. The private key is stored on the card and remains there, even when used. Smartcards make it difficult to impossible for a private key associated with a digital certificate and public key to be accessed. All private key operations occur within the secure confines of the smartcard chip. Most smartcards require a user PIN to be input as a second factor whenever the digital certificates on the card are to be used.

Smartcards are tamper resistant and may be permanently disabled if someone tries to hack them or physically access them in an unauthorized way. This is not to say that they can't be hacked, especially if the attacker has physical access. Smartcard hackers have used specialized electronic tools, acid, and other specialized techniques to compromise smartcards.

Disadvantages of smartcards include a fairly high cost of initialization and operation (e.g., initial purchase cost of the cards, readers, and solution; support personnel; and ongoing operational costs). The flexible plastic makes them fairly easy to damage and to lose. All of these issues have led some organizations to use *virtual smartcards* instead. With virtual smartcards, the smartcard certificate is stored on a specialized cryptographic chip on the primary computing device where the smartcard authentication is mostly used. The base computing device, in a sense, is the smartcard. However, it could be argued that a true smartcard is always separate from the computing device, giving it an "extra" factor of authentication protection. The virtual smartcard, because it is always a part of the base computing device, isn't separate. Virtual smartcards have become more popular over the last few years, since the overall support costs are significantly lower. All smartcard-based MFA solutions seem to be losing favor compared to other types of MFA solutions, particularly ones that use USB devices or cell phones. I'll describe an interesting smartcard-related hack in Chapter 10, "Subject Hijack Attacks."

EMV

A common hardware authentication standard, similar to smartcards, are EMV-enabled credit cards. EMV chips look like smartcard chips because they are smartcard chips with a specific application. EMV stands for Europay, Mastercard, and Visa, the three credit card companies that created the standard (although the standard is now managed by a larger group of related financial companies known as EMVCo). EMV-enabled credit cards, which come in both contact and contactless varieties, protect critical credit card information (which used to be stored on the unprotected magnetic stripe) so that the credit card cannot easily be duplicated. Before EMV chips were included, a malicious attacker could buy a cheap credit card reader and swipe anyone's credit card to get all the critical information about the card from the magnetic stripe on back of the card. Physical credit card duplication theft was rampant.

EMV (also known as *chip and pin* cards) put some of the most critical information within the secure confines of the EMV chip, where it cannot easily be read or duplicated. EMV credit cards also hold information that helps conduct each transaction it is involved in. Today, a credit card's magnetic stripe alone does not contain enough information to completely duplicate the card, although it is possible to get the credit card number and some other limited credit card holder information. Neither the EMV and magnetic stripe hold the credit card's CVV number (that three- or four-digit code you are often asked to provide when using a credit card remotely or on the Internet). Theoretically, anyone trying to duplicate the card will not be able to get enough information to conduct future credit card fraud unless the vendor accepts the limited information found on the magnetic stripe. This goal of EMV has been realized, as evidenced by the fact that credit card theft and duplication from physical (or wireless) reading has significantly diminished since its introduction.

One big area of contention is that in order to use EMV cards in Europe and most non-U.S. countries, users must not only insert the card into the EMV chip reader, but also type in a PIN (Something You Know). This requirement has significantly reduced credit card transaction fraud overall, in both physical and remote scenarios. The United States was a latecomer to the EMV scene, adopting the security standard only in the last half decade or so, and merchants in mass decided not to require the PIN. Because the U.S. has far more credit card–accepting vendors and users than most other countries, requiring PINs would cause issues with a non-minor percentage of those users who didn't set up their PINs or later forgot them. So, American vendors decided that it was fine to require less security as a trade-off for happier users. More on this sort of decision making in the next chapter.

Wireless

Many hardware tokens come in wireless forms. The wireless transmission methods include radio frequencies (RF), infrared light (IR), visible light, sound, near-field communications (NFC), radio-frequency identification (RFID), Bluetooth, Wi-Fi, cellular, TV, and many other methods. Figure 3.14 shows a Google Titan device that uses Bluetooth. With these types of devices, you only need to be within the defined range, from mere centimeters to the entire globe, to allow the authentication device to interact with your authentication mechanism. Wireless authentication devices are used in almost everything, including computer and user authentication, credit cards, building-entry proximity cards, and employee badges.

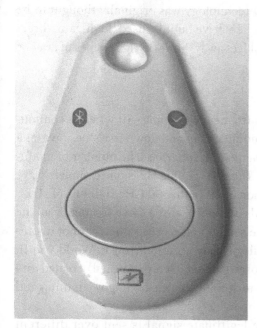

Figure 3.14: Google Titan Bluetooth authentication device

The security of the wireless authentication depends on the wireless transmission medium, as a base starting point, added to or subtracted by the device involved and its implementation. For example, NFC has very little physical protection. The founders of NFC thought NFC's limited useful distance range of a few centimeters would be its main physical defense (and to a great extent they have been proven correct). Bluetooth ranges can be from several feet to several tens of feet, and the Bluetooth protocol itself has built-in encryption modes. Some of the modes are fairly weak, but several are fairly strong. Which mode your Bluetooth device is using is up to the authentication device vendor, and the user is usually unaware of what cryptography is being used and may not even be able to easily learn. You can bet that most of the popular implementations by the biggest vendors, like YubiKeys and Google, are fairly well thought out and protected, beyond the security provided by the built-in wireless transmission channel protections.

The biggest advantage of wireless authentication is that the devices must be held only in the *general area* of the needed authentication. They don't need to be inserted, tethered, or in many cases, held. Ease of use is pretty high with wireless authentication devices.

One of the weaknesses of wireless authentication devices is signal eavesdropping and hijacking. Some wireless technologies like RFID have had a host of demonstrated eavesdropping hacks performed against them. And in general, the distances from which wireless devices can be read and intercepted only improves over time. For example, RFID technology was originally thought to be interceptable only within a few centimeters or inches. Hackers have built focused, high-gain, directional antennas to pick up RFID signals from many tens of feet away. More on these types of attacks in Chapter 20, "Miscellaneous MFA Hacks."

Frequency Hopping

One common defense for all wireless communications is frequency hopping. All wireless communications use modulating waves of energy. These waves modulate, up and down in a sine wave, at a particular frequency across what is called the *electromagnetic wave spectrum*. The number of modulating waves per second within a transmission signal is a *Hertz* (Hz). One Hz is one complete wave modulation per second. Radio and wireless signals function at 30 Hz to 300 GHz (billions of Hz).

Attackers have long tried to transmit erroneous signals and noise at the same frequency as the legitimate sender. Doing so "jams" the signal because the sender and receiver often cannot distinguish between the legitimate information signal and the illegitimate noise. Starting in World War II, famous Hollywood actress Hedy Lamarr (and her composer partner, George Antheil) created and patented the *frequency-hopping spread spectrum* wireless technology defense to fight jamming and eavesdropping, although it was not widely adopted until many decades later.

Frequency hopping works as a defense because the legitimate signal is sent over different frequencies (very quickly) that only the sender and receiver have agreed on (or computed) ahead of time. Anyone wishing to disrupt the signal would need to know what frequencies were being hopped to when, or would have to jam a wide set of the spectrum for a long time. Even then it would be fairly easy for the sender and receiver to figure out what is a legitimate signal and what is noise.

Frequency hopping prevents eavesdropping and jamming and makes most of today's wireless technologies possible. Not all wireless technologies use it. For example, NFC, Bluetooth, and RFID do not, because it is believed their limited range is enough of a defense. But most wider range wireless technologies, like cell phones and Wi-Fi, do.

NOTE My favorite book dedicated to Hedy Lamarr's discovery is *Hedy's Folly*, by Richard Rhodes (Vintage, 2011).

Phone-Based

A very popular and growing authentication method is to use cell phones either as part of the authentication solution or by letting it receive the authentication check.

Voice Authentication

Phones can be used for authentication in their base mode of a phone—taking a voice phone call. The caller or receiver involved in the authentication transaction can verify the other's identity and/or account information before performing a critical action. A common example is a call from a bank or credit card company to verify a particular suspicious transaction. Voice phone authentication can be performed by a human or automated system. An example of the latter method could be a credit card using an automated system to call the user's predefined cell phone number and asking the user to "Say or press 1 to confirm the transaction. Say or press 2 to decline the transaction and report it as fraudulent."

Your voice can even be recognized by voice-recognition systems to verify your identity (Something You Are). Financial companies will often recognize a caller's phone number and automatically pull up the correct account, and then ask the user to speak to authenticate their identity. Voice-recognition authentications are not super accurate and are usually not trusted for the most critical, highest-risk transactions. A lot of voice recognition accuracy depends on familiarity and the closeness of the relationship. Your family, friends, and coworkers may hear your voice and immediately trust that it is you. Your bank may require that you prove additional account information (Something You Know authentication step up) before moving money.

Phone Apps

Today's smartphones are basically computers. Many MFA solutions rely on custom-built or shared authentication applications. The user must install the phone app ahead of using it and often has to provide additional identity and authentication information to get the application running the first time. Thereafter, phone-based authentication apps usually work with less prompting, although some will ask for strong authentication proofs each time they start (such as the Bank of America phone app shown in Figure 3.15). Others will take the initial successful application installation and authentication and never ask the user to authenticate directly to the app again (e.g., the Google Authenticator phone app shown in Figure 3.16).

Figure 3.15: The Bank of America phone application asks for a biometric fingerprint on every startup.

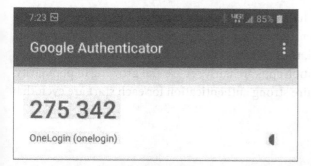

Figure 3.16: The Google Authenticator application displays OTP without any additional authentication needed.

The Bank of America app requires a logon name and password each time it starts, or a biometric fingerprint (if it has been enabled). Google Authenticator, a software-based TOTP solution, requires that the user get a QR (Quick Response) code (see Figure 3.17 for an example) from each participating corporate account, website, or service. Once the Google Authenticator app is enabled on a cell phone, it can be started and restarted to get new TOTP codes without the user being prompted to authenticate again.

Figure 3.17: Example QR code

Phone apps are very convenient. It seems everyone not only has a cell phone, but is also carrying it with or near them at all times. Phone apps, in general, are fairly secure MFA options. They are tied to a person's cell phone and must be installed and authenticated to at least once. If the user's cell phone is automatically locked after a preset number of minutes of inactivity, then the user has to authenticate to the phone before they can access the application. Even if an attacker is successful in stealing the user's cell phone number, the application doesn't automatically move to the attacker's phone using the phone number, and if the attacker tried to install and use the authentication app, they would have to authenticate at least once as the legitimate user.

On the negative side, any application can be hacked and attacked, and that includes phone apps. They are buggy like anything else. And if the user does not protect their cell phone with a lock screen, or if their locked screen can be easily bypassed, then the authentication app becomes a juicy target for an attacker. But, in general, phone authentication apps are fairly secure and growing in popularity. And phone apps like Bank of America that require strong authentication for each start are even that much more secure.

SMS

Short Message Service (SMS) allows systems and users to send messages to one another. Many popular MFA solutions use SMS, which is limited to 140 characters per message, to send users "out-of-band" codes to be used during MFA logons. Figure 3.18 shows several legitimate instances of SMS being used to send MFA codes, including from Bank of America, Microsoft, Google, Facebook, Marriott, and MyIDCare (a credit monitoring service).

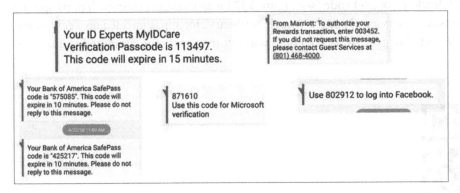

Figure 3.18: Examples of SMS MFA codes

The most commonly used MFA solutions on the Internet are SMS based. However, they are considered to be weak authenticators—so weak and potentially vulnerable that in 2017 the U.S. National Institute of Standards and Technology (NIST) stated, in NIST Special Publication 800-63, Revision 3, the Digital Identity Guidelines (`pages.nist.gov/800-63-3/sp800-63-3.html`), that SMS should not be used as an authenticator. Despite this recommendation, SMS continues to be one of the most popular MFA solution factors used in the world. More on this in Chapter 8, "SMS Attacks."

Biometrics

Biometrics (Something You Are) are seen by many people as the Holy Grail of the MFA world. I mean, how can you fake an authentication attribute that is based on the global uniqueness of DNA of humans? Biometric measurements include fingerprints, fingers, hands, retinas, irises, voice, and faces. In extreme and less popular cases, I've seen bodies, DNA, ears, and even smell used as biometric attributes. The user scans in or records the requested biometric attribute, and when they go to log in, they resubmit the same biometric attribute for comparison. If the originally recorded attribute matches the newly submitted one, the user is authenticated. In theory, it works as long as the biometric attribute is globally unique. And so far, there is no conclusive evidence that the most popular attributes used (fingers, hands, eyes, and even the faces of identical twins) are not globally unique.

Biometrics are fairly easy to use. We always have our fingers, face, eyes, and the rest of our body parts with us even more often than our cell phones. On the downside, biometric authentication is not nearly as accurate as the underlying body attribute is. Biometric authentication is full of false negatives and false positives. For every biometric measurement you can make, there are people in our population whose individual metric varies every day and cannot be relied on. For example, if your organization uses fingerprints for biometric analysis, in any large group (several thousands to tens of thousands), there will be at least one person, if not more, where for whatever reason, their biometric measurement does not match day to day.

I'm not a fan of biometrics—I'm the opposite of that. They are way too easy to hack. I only support biometrics with specific preconditions and limited reliance. Biometric hacks will be covered in Chapter 16, "Attacks Against Biometrics."

FIDO

The Fast Identity Online (FIDO) Alliance (fidoalliance.org) is a set of popular MFA open standards that relies on public–private key cryptography. Formed in late 2012–early 2013 and supported by many of the world's largest digital companies, the FIDO Alliance made it their mission to create open "password-less" authentication standards that could be used by a wide range of websites, services, software, and devices. And they appear to be achieving that goal better than any previous attempts by other open standards bodies. Some of the world's most popular OSs, websites, and services support it. FIDO supports a wide range of 1FA and MFA devices (computers, USB tokens, mobile phones, wired and wireless, etc.) and biometrics.

Currently, FIDO (now named FIDO2) has two main authentication parts and four (version 1.2) specifications. Any FIDO2-participating software (OS, browsers, websites, services, etc.) must use the World Wide Web Consortium's (W3C's) Web Authentication standard (WebAuthn) and APIs. Most of the major browsers support WebAuthn, although not all. The Client to Authenticator Protocol (CTAP) specification covers how wireless devices, including mobile devices, interact with FIDO2. The Universal Authentication Framework (UAF) specification is a password-less method, which can be 1FA or MFA, but does not necessarily have to involve a separate physical device. The Universal 2nd Factor (U2F) specification, as the name implies, covers MFA and requires a second factor and device of some type.

With U2F, the user registers their device with the participating site or service and chooses to implement an authentication factor, such as a PIN or biometric ID. When connecting to the site or service, or conducting a transaction that requires strong authentication, the device performs local authentication (verifying the PIN or biometric identity) and passes along the success or failure to the remote site or service. With U2F, an additional security device (such as a cell phone or USB dongle) is used as the second factor after the password or PIN has been provided.

The public–private key cryptography used behind the scenes is reminiscent of other types of TLS negotiations. Both the server and the client have a private–public key pair, and they share the public key only with each other to facilitate authentication over a protected transmission method. The relying party's public key is used to send randomly created "challenge" information back and forth between the server and client. The client's private key never leaves the client device and can be used only when the user physically interacts with the device.

Traditional TLS guarantees server authentication only to the client. FIDO2 authentication goes much further by linking "registered" devices to their users and those devices to the eventual websites or services. One authentication device can be linked to many (or all) websites and services. The pre-registration prevents many, but not all, types of authentication attacks. For more information on the FIDO2 standard and specifications, look here: `fidoalliance.org/specifications/download`.

Federated Identities and APIs

Many authentication open standards not only define the protocols for each participating subject, client, and server, but also allow a single authenticated logon and the resulting access control token to be shared so that additional logons are not needed for additional participating sites and services. It's SSO, but instead of being focused on a single corporate environment, it's intended to connect completely different sites and services.

One popular federated option many people are familiar with is the Facebook logon. As you may know, if you log in to a new website or service, the site may let you create a brand-new logon or just use Facebook, Twitter, or some other account type you may already have. That website or service has been coded to participate in a *federated identity service*. There have been many federated identity services over the years, including Microsoft Passport, and for corporate customers, Microsoft Active Directory Federated Services (ADFS).

OAuth

In the consumer space, the most recent and most popular federated authentication service is Open Authorization (OAuth). I'm going to cover it here in more detail because OAuth is the most popular open standard of its type, and understanding how it works will help explain how the others work and can be possibly hacked.

OAuth is an open standard authorization protocol or framework that describes how unrelated servers and services can safely allow authenticated access to their assets without actually sharing the initial single logon credential. In official authentication parlance, this is known as secure, third-party, user agent delegated authorization.

Created and strongly supported from the start by Twitter, Google, and other companies, OAuth was released as an open standard in 2010 as RFC 5849 (`tools.ietf.org/html/rfc5849`) and quickly became widely adopted. Over the next two years, it underwent substantial revision, and version 2.0 of OAuth was released in 2012 as RFC 5849 (`tools.ietf.org/html/rfc5849`). Today, you can add Amazon, Facebook, Instagram, LinkedIn, Microsoft, Netflix, PayPal, and a list of other Internet Who's-Who's (`en.wikipedia.org/wiki/List_of_OAuth_providers`) as adopters.

An early proponent (`oauth.net/about/introduction/`) describes OAuth as similar to a car's "valet key." Some luxury cars come with special, limited keys, which can be used to allow a valet to temporarily drive and park a car but that doesn't allow the holder full, unlimited access like a regular key. Instead, the car can only be driven a few miles, the key can't access the trunk or locked glove box, and many other limitations. OAuth essentially allows the user, via an authentication provider that they have previously successfully authenticated with, to give another website or service a limited-access authentication token for authorization to additional resources.

Additionally, OAuth 2.0 is a framework, not a protocol (like version 1.0). It would be like all the car manufacturers agreeing on how valets would automatically request, receive, and use the keys and how those valet keys would generally look, more than anything else. What the valet keys could do as compared to the full function keys would be up to each car manufacturer. Just as in real life, valets and car owners don't need to care about how it all works. They just want it all to work as seamlessly as possible. Here's how OAuth works behind the scenes, step-by-step. Let's assume a user has already signed into one website or service (OAuth only works using HTTP/S). The user then initiates a feature or transaction that has to access another unrelated site or service. The following happens (greatly simplified):

1. The first website connects to the second site on behalf of the user, using OAuth, providing the user's verified identity.
2. The second site generates a one-time token and a one-time secret unique to the transaction and parties involved.
3. The first site gives this token and secret to the initiating user's client software.
4. The client's software presents the request token and secret to their authorization provider (which may or may not be the second site).
5. If not already authenticated to the authorization provider, the client may be asked to authenticate. Once authenticated (or if already authenticated), the client is asked to approve the authorization transaction to the second website.
6. The user approves (or their software silently approves) a particular transaction type at the first website.

7. The user is given an approved access token (notice it's no longer a request token).

8. The user gives the approved access token to the first website.

9. The first site gives the access token to the second site as proof of authentication on behalf of the user.

10. The second site lets the first one access their site on behalf of the user.

11. The user sees a successfully completed transaction occurring.

There have been a lot of federated authentication schemes, like Microsoft Passport, that have tried to take over the online world. All before OAuth have failed after a few years; OAuth seems to be the one that finally made it. For more information on OAuth, visit `oauth.net`.

NOTE Josh Fruhlinger and I wrote an article for CSOOnline, and much of this chapter's information on OAuth comes from that September 2019 article: `www.csoonline.com/article/3216404/what-is-oauth-how-the-open-authorization-framework-works.html`.

The biggest advantage is that OAuth gives the user an SSO-like experience across multiple, distinctly different sites and services. The biggest risk is, as is the case with SSO, that a single compromise could lead to easier or even immediate compromise of the other participating sites and services.

APIs

Application programming interfaces (API) are created by developers of their underlying technologies to allow other developers and users to programmatically interface with their product. APIs allow other people to quickly interact with a product and to easily extend its functionality. APIs are a staple of the computer world, especially if you want your product to be widely adopted and used.

APIs can be abused by bad people. APIs allow malicious hackers to do bad things involving the underlying technology faster and more destructively across a wide group of people. APIs have been used to rob people of hundreds of thousands of dollars in seconds and to compromise millions of accounts of very popular websites and services. These types of attacks will be covered in more detail in Chapter 19, "API Abuses."

Contextual/Adaptive

As you'll recall from Chapter 2, "Authentication Basics," authentication services are increasingly considering many other additional types of authentication factors known as *contextual* or *adaptive*. These factors include the device the user is using to authenticate, the location of the current authentication as compared to past authentication events, how long it took the user to type a password, actions the user is actively taking, sequence of actions. and numerous other factors. Some authentication services can use over a hundred different types of contextual assessment factors to determine whether someone is authenticated.

The reason I'm including it here again is because not only are these types of factors used by themselves to determine authentication, but they are increasingly likely to be an important part of future authentication solutions. They already are for many authentication scenarios.

A great example is how your bank or credit card vendor determines whether to approve or deny any particular transaction you are performing in real time. Both of these services look at your current transaction to see if fits into a pattern that is usual and customary for you.

For example, if you always use taxis, why are you suddenly using an Uber? If you never travel and live in Florida, should it be strange that your credit card is being used to buy airline tickets from Texas to Malaysia? If you normally watch all your television on an iPad, would it be strange for you to suddenly buy an 80-inch TV? Is it possible for you to buy something in Boston, Massachusetts at 10 a.m. and then something in Spokane, Washington at 11 a.m.?

Banks and credit card companies are comparing your current transaction to your past behavior all the time. And overall, after decades of experience, they are pretty good at it. Most of the time we aren't prevented from buying stuff we want to buy, and most of the time the bank or credit card company proactively catches and stops the fraud (faster than most of the legitimate card holders). Contextual and behavioral authentication attributes are becoming an increasingly popular way authentication decisions are made, even if we aren't often aware of it. The only disadvantage is that these comparisons aren't perfect. Sometimes they do stop legitimate transactions and sometimes fraud is allowed. But there is an entire cottage industry dedicated to improving accuracy. We will talk more about this in Chapter 24, "The Future of Authentication."

Less Popular Methods

The authentication methods discussed in this section are far less popular today but are still used in specialized scenarios.

Voiceover Radio

Good authentication is key in any communication's scenario where the two parties do not know each other. One of the earliest forms of communication was the radio (invented in 1885 by Italian Guglielmo Marconi). And nearly as quickly as radio was used to communicate confidential information, it was being used by malicious people to eavesdrop and block. Analog radio signals have been replaced by digital signals in most places, but radio communications still exist in many specialized scenarios. For example, radio communications are used in military operations, on the ground, at sea, and in the air, to communicate between participants.

During military operations, most participants will communicate with each other using radio (or other types of wireless waves). They communicate to coordinate actions, update each other on key accomplishments, discuss new plans, call in airstrikes, and so forth. Today, the radio equipment they use has authentication and encryption built-in so that everything communicated using it is automatically protected. But back in the days of World War II, the Korean War, and the Vietnam War, they did not. During those wars, sometimes the enemy would intentionally seek out the main radio communications specialist, kill or kidnap them, and then use their radio to listen to current communications or to call in fraudulent, harmful, battle changes. There are many stories of adversaries faking strong American accents, such as a Texas drawl, to mimic the accent of the communications soldier they captured and call in fake strikes against the wrong locations.

To fight this before the days of cryptographic radios, the soldiers would each have call names to identify themselves, as well as codes (i.e., knowledge-based authentication) to confirm their participation or to call in battlefield actions. These verbal clues and codes helped the allies keep the communication lines free of adversarial fake instructions.

Paper-Based

Before the days of computers and pervasive digital cryptography, most cryptography was done by hand. The encryption and decryption codes were written down and copied between participating subjects. This method persisted for over a thousand years. History is replete with failed murderous pacts and royal assassinations because the written-down secret codes and related messages were discovered and deciphered. Starting about World War II, paper-based codes and cryptography diminished as machines, and later on, computers became the preferred way to do cryptography.

Still, paper-based cryptography persists. There are even digital authentication and encryption solutions that rely on printed, paper-based codes. Many times the printed codes are simply an alternative backup option for the online digital option in case the digital option gets lost or damaged. For example, many password managers generate printed codes that users may need in order to recover their implementation of the password manager program if it gets lost or corrupted. Lose those printed codes, and you risk losing all your stored passwords at once. It can be a real pain. It's also a pain because you have to securely store that piece of paper containing the printed code. The theory is that you should place it in a fireproof safe, bank deposit box, or something like that, and it should be stored in two distinctly separate physical locations that cannot be compromised by a single disaster event (fire, flood, hurricane, tornado, earthquake, etc.). Many people keep a single copy in their house in a paper file or desk drawer. For solutions that use paper-based components, the thinking is that since the MFA solution uses a paper component it is far harder to hack. Unfortunately, that also makes the solution harder to use.

Summary

As you can read there are a ton of different authentication options ranging from a person's physical presence and voice (and other biometric factors) to advanced MFA solutions involving external devices or cellphones, and everything in between. We covered the following categories: personal recognition, knowledge-based authentication, password managers, proxies, cryptography, hardware tokens, phone-based authentication, biometrics, federated solutions, contextual/adaptive, and radio- and paper-based solutions. If I missed your favorite authentication solution type, I apologize in advance. I covered every type I could remember, but I'm only human. Picking the right one for the authentication scenario is key to maintaining the right amount of security versus usability, which is discussed in the next chapter.

4

Usability vs. Security

Security has always been a struggle between usability and safety, and that struggle is definitely involved in deciding which MFA solution to use. Admins and IT are moving to MFA precisely to improve security. Many users really don't want the best security when it impacts usability. This chapter explores many of the main points of usability versus security. It contains lots of "hard truths" that can be surprising for some readers to learn. It might even seem a bit out of place for a book dedicated to MFA.

This chapter will start with a brief discussion of usability, and more detail on usability will be discussed in Chapter 23, "Selecting the Right MFA Solution." The bulk of this chapter is dedicated to the value of usability when it's competing with security.

What Does Usability Mean?

MFA must be sufficiently user-friendly that people won't mind using it and thus management feels they can require it. It must work with the organization's critical applications and fit within the culture. Not all MFA solutions meet both criteria. No MFA solution works with everything. Organizations always have to pick which critical applications they will end up protecting with MFA.

And different organizational cultures seem more inclined to particular types of MFA. For example, an organization whose employees already use physical building entry cards are more likely to be open to smartcards. Companies that are "Google shops" are more likely to be open to Google security keys and/or the Google Authenticator time-based-one-time-password (TOTP) app. Organizations with high-end security needs are probably better candidates for biometrics, since employees (mistakenly) relate biometrics to strong security. Companies with lots of remote employees are probably more open to hardware keys, like Fast Identity Online (FIDO) devices, or phone apps.

Any MFA solution must have a low number of *false negatives* (legitimate logons incorrectly rejected) and *false positives* (illegitimate logons incorrectly accepted). It must be relatively easy to install and integrate with the applications the organization desires MFA support for. The MFA solution must, of course, be affordable, both in purchasing and ongoing operations. Training support staff and end users is required. Troubleshooting costs need to be considered. How much will it cost to replace or reinstall the MFA solution if it breaks for a particular user? How much will tech support cost? It is not unusual for various MFA support calls to cost the supporting entity upward of $200 per call in labor and other related solution costs (replacement tokens, help desk software, training, corporate space, overhead, etc.). The organization must create supporting policies, training documentation, and recovery steps ahead of time.

Training and the ability of end users to understand and correctly use MFA solutions should not be overstated, especially as your end-user environment gets larger, more global, and more diverse. A fantastic representative presentation to see or hear about MFA training challenges is Studies of 2FA's "Why Johhny Can't Use 2FA and How We Can Change That" (`www.rsaconference.com/industry-topics/presentation/studies-of-2fa-why-johhny-cant-use-2fa-and-how-we-can-change-that`). You can download the slide deck here: `published-prd.lanyonevents.com/published/rsaus19/sessionsFiles/13259/IDY-T07-Studies-of-2FA-Why-Johhny-Can't-Use-2FA-and-How-We-Can-Change-That.pdf`. If you are interested in security versus usability, this presentation and slide deck, including notes, is worth its weight in gold.

The talk was related to a university study looking to see how well regular end users could understand and use instructions for basic MFA solutions. In their study, the researchers gave the participants a popular and simple MFA device. The users had to plug the device into their computer's USB port and press one button to activate the device. Each user was given instructions on how to register and use their device. Plug in something to a USB port and push a button. How hard could that be?

The failure rate was over 70 percent—a 70 percent failure rate for something that simple. Many of the participants plugged the device in upside down (not unthinkable with a USB device), harming either the device or the port. Another set of users thought the button was a biometric fingerprint reader and would swipe their finger over it instead of simply pressing it. Many times, the device was not working at all, but the users thought they had successfully performed all actions and were using an MFA device. Just as many had successfully installed it but were not sure and didn't use it.

After the study was over, the researchers told all participants that they could keep their MFA devices and use them. They waited a month and contacted all the participants to see if they had decided to keep their device. Not a single participant was still using it! Worse, many participants had given their device, which was tied to their identity, to other people or had placed the device in a lost-and-found box for others to use. They seemed unaware that any user placing their relinquished device into a computer and pressing a button would enable able that user to successfully authenticate as them.

In a similar study (`www.blackhat.com/html/webcast/11292018-two-factor-authentication-usable-or-not.html`), researchers wanted to see how many people could enroll in and use a popular 2FA token that most of us in the computer security world would not consider difficult to use. They found the same thing the first study did: a large percentage of users unable to appropriately use MFA devices and many who were able to use them but didn't want to. Here's the presentation outline if you don't have time to listen to the longer webcast: `i.blackhat.com/us-18/Thu-August-9/us-18-Das-Two-Factor-Authentication-Usable-Or-Not-A-Two-Phase-Usability.pdf`.

Here are some other MFA usability studies in case you are interested:

- www.usenix.org/system/files/soups2019-reese.pdf
- www.archive.ece.cmu.edu/~lbauer/papers/2018/chi2018-2fa.pdf
- ueaeprints.uea.ac.uk/id/eprint/61540/1/MahaAlthobaiti.pdf
- scholarsarchive.byu.edu/cgi/viewcontent.cgi?article=7869&context=etd

The studies communicate two things. First, no matter how easy you think your selected MFA solution is, there is a certain percentage of users who will struggle with it, at least initially. Second, and just as important, users really don't like to use MFA solutions even when they are free. And that leads us to the next and main part of this chapter.

We Don't Really Want the Best Security

Every computer security person understands the challenge of implementing good security controls without annoying users or making them more inefficient at their job or tasks. Make a control too secure and you risk doing both. Computer security experts are always trying to improve computer security and lower cybersecurity risk, and sometimes they (especially people new to the field) can get caught up in thinking that making security stronger is the only goal that matters. That's far from the case.

Any experienced computer security person will tell you that if you left it up to most end users they would want little to no computer security if it actually makes them do a single additional thing that slows them down in the slightest. Many employees want the least amount of "friction" possible to the point that they would prefer little to no security if it meant slowing them down from doing what they want to do. Well, they want everyone else to have what's needed as far as security is needed, but they feel that they, themselves, don't really need too many "cumbersome and onerous" computer security controls. They feel that they know what they are doing and that computer security only slows them down.

They reluctantly put up with what security controls management tells them they have to. They want the bare essential controls that it takes to perform their job relatively safely and effectively, and they don't even want those. They do what they have to because someone else higher up the chain said they have to. They see computer security as a necessary evil, and perhaps even a hinderance, until something goes very wrong, and then computer security gets blamed for not doing enough. For most computer security professionals, it's a dual-edged sword with all of the responsibility and accountability without any authority to get the job done correctly.

It's not like computer security professionals can't design very secure solutions that prevent most to all cybersecurity incidents. Most of us can design computer security controls that would stop most hackers and malware. It's designing them without an added burden to end users and keeping management's support that's the tricky part.

Every computer security person can repeat the well-worn computer security manta, "The only secure computer is one locked in a closet, not connected to a network, encased in concrete" or some similar hyperbolic attestation. But the truth is most people really don't want the best security that keeps them as safe as possible. This applies to nearly every security scenario, not just computer security.

For example, car crashes are the leading killer of people ages 2 to 34. In the United States, there are over 36,000 deaths a year, or around 99 per day, day after day, on top of the over 2 million injuries. Car crashes are one of the leading causes of death for people of all age groups. Your odds of dying in a car crash in a given year is higher than one in 8,000. There are only two risks higher, and both of those are medical conditions: cancer and heart disease. The odds of you dying in a car crash in your lifetime is one in 100 or higher! I think seeing those statistics shocks most people. Not only do we lose tens of thousands of people a year to car accidents, but we lose tens of billions of dollars due to insurance claims, damaged vehicles, and lost productivity.

We could prevent all of the deaths by getting rid of cars. That's not practical, but we could do it. And if we have to have cars, we could significantly reduce injuries and death by not allowing any car to go faster than 5 mph and require all drivers and riders to use five-point seat belt harnesses and safety helmets. We could make it against the law to have radios, cell phones, and anything else that might possibly distract a driver in a car powered up. It's ridiculous sounding. It's draconian. But it would work. We could significantly reduce car injuries and deaths. We know how to do it.

But instead, we have decided as a society to allow cars to be capable of going well over 120 mph (even though no speed limit in the US allows it), and we've essentially left it up to drivers (even though it is required by law in most places) to determine whether they should wear seat belts all the time. Car drivers can wear any type of headgear they want, many of which would protect against most head injuries. But drivers certainly aren't wearing helmets because that would mess up their hair and make them look silly (to other drivers and viewers). Heck, only 20 U.S. states require that all motorcycle riders wear helmets, and the odds of a helmetless motorcycle driver or passenger dying in a crash triple. There are all sorts of security situations in which we as a society allow substantially more deaths and injuries to occur because we value other things, such as usability and freedom, over greater safety. And that isn't necessarily a bad thing. Who wants to live in a society so utterly encumbered to prevent all possible accidents? We couldn't use ladders, bathtubs, or showers (which account for a huge amount of serious accidents). Gas-powered lawn mowers? Fuhgeddaboudit.

Instead, we knowingly allow a certain percentage of injuries and deaths to occur while trying to moderately mitigate the worst and biggest threats. Computers and authentication follow the same rules. We allow computers to be far more insecure than they could be because we also strongly value personal freedom and the ability to run and operate a PC or device almost any way the user wants. If we really cared about computer security as much as we claim, every computer would be able to run only a very limited set of computer programs and go to a very limited list of websites and services preapproved by IT.

Authentication would be overly cumbersome, but very secure. We could make computers far more secure than they are today without locking them in closets and putting them in concrete. But we don't want to do that. We want computers to be "kinda" secure, with the least amount of security interference in our life. We will gladly live with just okay security as long as we can do whatever we want on our computers and as long as the level of malicious hacking and badness stays to an acceptable level of essentially background noise. As long as our computers and sites are not hacked *most* of the time, we'll tolerate them being hacked *some* of the time.

Many new MFA vendors and creators don't understand this. They mistakenly believe that the previous MFA vendors over decades apparently didn't know how to design truly secure authentication solutions. This is ridiculous. Lots of MFA vendors understand how to design very secure solutions. It's designing a very secure solution that most of the general public *will use* that's the tricky part. Anyone can do one of the two things (i.e., make a truly secure solution or make a solution users actually don't mind using). It's creating an authentication solution that does both at the same time that has been the central challenge for decades.

I have seen many new MFA vendors make very secure solutions that no one wanted. When I've told them this—that they'd designed a too secure solution that no one will use—they've always attacked me, the messenger. I've never been wrong. To MFA vendors who might be reading this: Your seven-factor solution will be used by no one. You want to make a lot of money and get rich making a new MFA solution? Try designing a two- or three-factor solution that will be used by hundreds of millions of people. But no one is going to buy your five-, six-, or seven-factor, "very secure" MFA solution. Designing good security isn't hard—what's hard is designing good security the general public wants to use every day.

Security Isn't Usually Binary

Computer security is rarely binary—on or off, black or white. Computer security is along a continuum from no security to absolute, total security, and everything in between. Although in an ideal world we want to stop *all* malicious hackers (and criminals), what we really want to do is stop *most* of them most of the time with a reasonable amount of effort and resources.

There are many things that are better being binary. Is the airplane's engine working or not while you're flying? Is his heart beating or not? Did the bulletproof vest stop the bullet? Are the car's brakes working? Are the building iron beams strong enough to support the building's weight? Does the parachute's ripcord work? There are lots of life and death decisions in the real world that need to be binary. Computer security is rarely one of them. It can be. We want the very best computer security protecting our nuclear secrets and military weapons. We don't want just anyone manipulating or using them in an unauthorized manner. And so, the physical and computer security surrounding our nuclear and military weapons arsenal is appropriately pretty strong. We don't want to tolerate even one hack.

For almost everything else, okay security is good enough. We want most of our personal and business transactions protected by pretty good, but not perfect, security. We want it to be good enough to work most of the time. It is possible for security to be too secure.

Too Secure

In the years that I've been actively teaching about MFA and how to hack it, I've had dozens of MFA vendors and developers come up to me after my presentations to tell me why their particular MFA solution is unhackable or better than what's out there on the market. In most cases, with just casual review, I can easily hack the solution they have created or proposed. Most of the time, I can hack it seven to ten ways within 15 minutes of modeling. I'm constantly amazed by how many developers think they've created something new and "unhackable" that I've already seen proposed and debunked for decades. It's true that the more things change, the more they stay the same. I started telling anyone approaching me to "review" their solution that I charged $40,000. It wasn't that I wanted the $40,000—I just didn't want to do another "rinse and repeat" security review of something the developers should be able to figure out themselves just by looking at what I just had taught. But if they persisted with wanting me to seriously review their product, I should at least make it worth my while. For the record, I've been able to easily hack them all.

Seven-Factor MFA

I did have one very persistent, notable MFA creator. He had come to one of my "Hacking MFA" presentations and contacted me by email to see and review his newly created MFA solution. At the time I was still doing reviews for free if they didn't take too long. I was able to hack his solution 10 different ways fairly quickly, and I sent him an email summarizing the attacks. He wrote back a few days later that I should check out his new, updated version that was less hackable. I was able to hack it 11 ways (minus one way he had closed and two more new issues he had opened up with his change). He wrote me back several times, and each time he would close one or two holes with new updates, and sometimes I would find new issues.

He eventually asked if he could come in person to show me his latest update. I hesitated, but it turned out he lived in the same city as I did, so I decided to say okay. When he appeared in person the next week and showed me his slightly updated MFA product, I went a little crazy on him. I expected that it would be a major update with most of the holes I had found several times before fixed. But I could still hack it 10 different ways, and I was tired of all the previous effort I had put into helping him without him even fixing what I had previously found. I was angry at him for wasting my time.

Much to my surprise, after he left that day, he kept pursuing me like nothing had happened. I had given him my worse attitude, and he just kept on smiling and asking for help. And he started to fix the older issues I had found. I could only admire his persistence and passion. Something changed in me; I began to like him personally, and I decided to help him perfect his MFA solution as much as possible. I spent hours telling him all the defenses he would need to implement (all of which I share in this book) to make his MFA solution as "unhackable" as possible. And to his credit, he followed my advice and made what I think was the least likely to be hacked MFA solution I've ever seen.

It was seven-factor authentication. It required that the user authenticate to the MFA device. The MFA device authenticated to the computer. And the user used it to authenticate to the application with multiple factors. The user could initiate access to a website or service only from the MFA device. They could not just open up their normal browser and go to a website willy-nilly. Only participating websites and services implementing his API could use the MFA option. Not only did users have to satisfy a total of seven factors, but they had to actually solve a math problem that was only possible if they printed out and kept a solution sheet that was generated during the installation process. I'm not making this up; the user had to look at a three-variable quadratic equation and solve fairly complex math involving the solution sheet.

I was amazed. Not only had the creator actually developed a solution that I thought was fairly hard to hack (I could not think of an easy way to hack it at the time, although I have thought of a few ways since), but I couldn't believe that he thought his solution would work for anyone. I responded, "Congratulations, you've made a very secure solution that no one will use!" He, of course, did not believe me. He was lost in his MFA inventor dream of where he would build the "perfect" secure MFA solution and the world would beat a path to his door and make him rich. He was angry with me. He said he disagreed. I told him, "No one wanting to go on Amazon to shop or log into a work network is going to put in seven factors and solve quadratic equations just to log on!" He disagreed.

He said that he believed that normal users caring about computer security would want to use his solution because it was so secure, but that he would start off by promoting it to very high-security organizations like the National Security Agency (NSA). Although he did not know it at the time, I had taught hundreds of NSA personnel how to hack for years when I taught Ultimate Hacking courses for Foundstone. I had been in the NSA Fort Meade building and I knew a fair number of senior NSA people. I replied, "Not even the NSA is going to buy your solution. They don't use seven-factor solutions and don't need to. A good MFA solution doesn't need more than three or four factors to be truly secure." It's like crypto; good crypto doesn't need overly large key sizes, like a million bits big. When you need or advertise overly large key sizes, you're essentially saying your crypto isn't that great. He disagreed and said he was disappointed that I didn't see the same vision. And then, we mutually agreed to part ways.

After a year went by, I emailed him to ask how things were going. Turns out the NSA and Amazon did not want his product. He said two organizations were using his product. When I asked who was using it, he volunteered that both companies were using it for free in a limited beta testing program. I pressed for their names and contact information. He refused to give me names so that I could interview the users to get their thoughts on what it was like to use a seven-factor solution. I've heard this story before. I've interviewed small and new computer security businesses for a living for over 20 years. Likely, his two "demonstration projects" means he's using it at whatever company he works at full-time, in a very limited way, and one of his friends is doing the same thing as a personal favor.

Ultimately, he will never sell his product to anyone. I don't mean to be a negative person, crushing dreams. I'm not always right. I probably wouldn't have seen the genius of Instagram. But I've been doing computer security for 32 years and have 20 years' experience as a computer security columnist who reviewed hundreds of security products. I got 15 to 20 product pitches a day that claim they are going to take over the world. I've seen what does and doesn't take over the computer security world. I've got a fairly good feel on what does and doesn't make it. There isn't a lack of very good, truly secure computer products. There is a lack of very good, truly secure computer technologies and solutions that people care enough about to actually buy and use. The former are a dime a dozen. The latter is the utopian gold mine. FIDO and Google security key devices are skyrocketing in popularity, and they don't even use three factors. It is easy to get lost in the belief that what the world is looking for is a better security solution without regard to user friendliness.

Moving ATM Keypad Numbers

A lot of MFA developers who write me are surprised to learn that users don't want to be inconvenienced in the slightest by computer security. If your MFA solution is asking users to change their normal behavior and actions, it's going to be a long, uphill battle for that solution. If it's good enough and easy enough to use, it might win. But you would be amazed about even the little changes in user behavior that will kill a good MFA idea.

For example, over the years I've had at least a dozen authentication developers write me with their new, "perfect" scheme to protect ATM users from shoulder-surfing and hidden camera "skimmers," which record the numbers ATM users type when using an ATM.

> **NOTE**   If you are interested in learning more about ATM skimming, you can't do better than to visit Brian Krebs's blog: `krebsonsecurity.com`. Brian is a world authority on skimmers, and he keeps up with the latest skimming equipment and the arrests of skimming gangs. He covers many other topics, and his blog is a must-read for many of us in the computer security world.

The creator's "perfect" scheme is often to create a virtual keypad overlay for the ATM instead of using a traditional, fixed, permanently printed keypad. Instead of having the numbers on the keypad in a predictable, sequential order—1, 2, 3, 4, . . . —the virtual keypad will randomly rearrange the numbers in a different order for each user session. The idea is that any secreted cameras or people looking over shoulders would not be as easily able to see which PIN numbers were pressed by the user operating the ATM. A lot of designers have this same design "epiphany."

Ignoring for the moment that most ATM "keyhole"-skimming cameras and surreptitiously placed malicious keypad components would have no problem recording the correct numbers no matter how they were arranged, most users would simply not tolerate having to think about where their normal ATM PIN numbers are located when trying to perform their normal ATM operations. They want to type their PIN in as fast as they can and get it over with as quickly as possible. Anything the user has to manually do with their authentication solution is known as *user friction*. And increased user friction is usually a bad thing in the computer security world.

If a bank or ATM tried to force their users to use a keypad with randomly changing number placement, a sizable percentage of users would end up typing in their PIN wrong over and over, and eventually simply start doing business with other banks and ATMs that use traditional keypads. And that means that banks and ATM vendors aren't going to tolerate it.

The sooner you understand that users want the least amount of user friction possible to do their job or task, with as little interruption as possible, the sooner you can start designing better MFA solutions.

Not as Worried as You Think About Hacking

If you live in the computer security world, you can be forgiven for thinking that everyone cares as much as you do about getting better computer security. Most people don't. It's not part of their daily thought process. When people think about computer security they are thinking about how annoying it is. They see it as the foe, not as the desired solution. Welcome to the real world! As covered in Chapter 1, "Logon Problems," some non-minor percentage of our population will give out their password to strangers on a street. Most users, if allowed, would use the same short, simple password on all sites and services and never change it. Many of those users would not change it even if they learned it was compromised on one website or service. It's a strange world we live in.

It might surprise you to learn that many vendors and industries don't fear hackers nearly as much as they fear pissed-off customers. A good example of this is the credit card industry. The credit card industry is rife with financial fraud. Credit card fraud accounts for over $20 billion annually and that figure is growing. We all know that credit card companies are trying their best to defeat fraud and credit card criminals.

Would it surprise you to know that credit card companies are far more worried about causing issues with legitimate transactions than with catching or stopping hackers? There is a cottage industry of companies that help banks and credit card vendors deny fraudulent transactions. They are actually pretty good at it. Only 11 cents of every $100 spent on credit cards is fraudulent. So even though it's growing (it used to only be 5 to 6 cents), it's still very small in comparison to overall consumer legitimate spending.

The cutting-edge companies that are advertising to banks and credit card companies about fraud prevention services highlight their ability to recognize legitimate customer transactions better than their competitors. Banks and credit card companies know that if a legitimate user gets blocked from doing a legitimate transaction more than once or twice every few years, that person will use another credit card product that doesn't "false-positive block" them. It makes sense. The average credit card rate is 14 percent to 16 percent. If they block legitimate consumers too much, they stand to lose 14 percent to 16 percent of every future $100 of that person's unpaid balance and not just 0.05 percent to 1.1 percent from a cybercriminal. Once you see those comparative figures it's not as surprising to learn that credit card vendors care more about not blocking legitimate customers than decreasing fraud. Fraud is merely background noise. Making too many customers mad by rejecting their legitimate transactions could lead to catastrophic revenue problems, and ones they are still working on to lower.

NOTE On an almost unrelated note, banks and credit card companies are constantly fighting fake identities, known as *synthetic identities,* in the industry. These identities are created when fraudsters use and abuse credit cards and other financial transactions. They consist of purely fake identities, slightly modified real identities, identities of infants and deceased persons, and so on. They are not accurate in one or more ways and are used fraudulently (like a baby's identity artificially aged to 40 years old so that the fraudster can attempt to buy a house). They appear to have names, addresses, financial transactions, and even credit scores. Many applicable laws require our financial institutions to root out and remove these fake identities. One credit card vendor lamented to me in a private meeting, "Too bad we have to get rid of them. They often have great credit scores, even better than most of the real identities. We otherwise have zero incentive to remove them. Because they have great credit scores we can sell them as marketing leads and make a lot of money. Too bad they are fake and we have to remove them."

Unhackable Fallacy

Even if you could make the most secure MFA solution possible, it would still be hackable. Nothing is unhackable. Nothing. If someone tells you something is unhackable, they are either lying and trying to sell you something or mistaken. Either way, you shouldn't trust them. In 2019, there were 12,174 publicly announced vulnerabilities (according to CVE Details, `www.cvedetails.com/browse-by-date.php`); see Figure 4.1. These are only the ones publicly announced. Most are caught and fixed privately. Other bugs are lying inside of software, hardware, or firmware sitting undiscovered waiting for someone to find them.

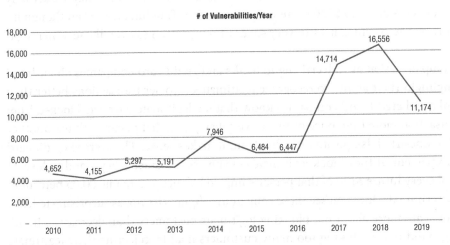

Figure 4.1: Number of known public vulnerabilities by year

About a fourth to a third of all reported vulnerabilities are given a critical rating of high or critical, meaning that if the vulnerability is successfully exploited it can be used to take over the system it is executed on. Figure 4.2 shows public reported vulnerabilities by numeric criticality score. Vulnerabilities with scores 7–8 are considered high criticality and vulnerabilities with scores 9 and higher are considered critical. You can run an updated list of vulnerability criticalities by visiting www.cvedetails.com/cvss-score-distribution.php.

Criticality Rating	0–1	1–2	2–3	3–4	4–5	5–6	6–7	7–8	8–9	9–10	Total
# of Vulns/Crit. Rating	959	860	4,392	3,882	24,278	21,761	15,158	25,393	502	15,176	112,361
Percentage	0.85%	0.77%	3.91%	3.45%	21.61%	19.37%	13.49%	22.60%	0.45%	13.51%	100.00%

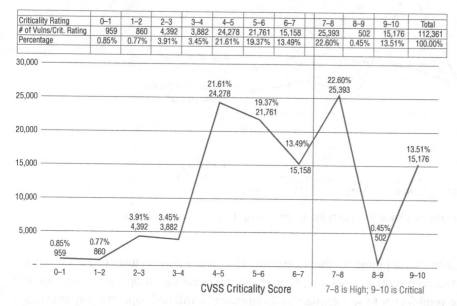

Figure 4.2: One-fourth to one-third of all vulnerabilities are ranked with a score of high or critical.

To make matters worse, the majority of vulnerabilities have low complexity, which means they are easy to execute, as Figure 4.3 shows. The data is a little aged in this figure, but the trend line has remained fairly static over time. So, we have many thousands of vulnerabilities a year, the majority are easy to exploit, and one-fourth to one-third of them have the highest criticality ratings. It's not a pretty picture if you're a computer security defender.

Every software program has bugs. Most have critical security bugs. Even hardware has bugs. Most hardware chips contain hardwired instructions, and some of those instructions have bugs. If you look into any computer processor chip from Intel or AMD, you'll see they all have multiple bugs, which get fixed in successive versions or firmware or software updates. There's no such thing as bug-free hardware.

Some of the bugs are bad security bugs. Perhaps the two biggest computer security bugs discovered in my lifetime, so far, are the 2019 Meltdown and Spectre (meltdownattack.com) chip vulnerabilities. They are hardware bugs that impacted the most popular CPUs manufactured since the late

1990s, and if you did not apply the related patches, the attacks that exploited them could not be stopped or even detected by anything in software or the operating system. We are just lucky that malicious hackers aren't exploiting hardware bugs more often.

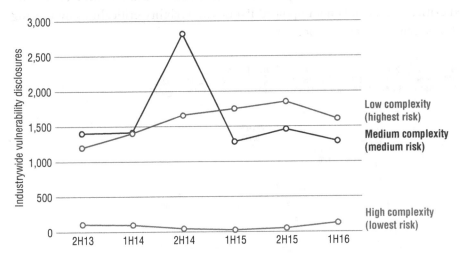

Figure 4.3: Most vulnerabilities have low complexity, meaning they are easy to exploit.

If you read about hardware "appliances," those certainly also have many security bugs. A *computer appliance* is a dedicated computer or special-purpose device running an operating system and application. Appliance vendors try to sell appliances as running "hardened" operating systems as if they are harder to attack. If the vendor really does their job right—minimizing services and aggressively keeping up on updating when impacted bugs are announced—that claim can be true. But many vendors do a pretty poor job, and the claims of "hardening" are nonsense. Either way, appliances are often harder to patch and are usually patched with far less frequency than software. If the hardening is done correctly, the appliance won't need nearly as much patching. If done as many vendors do it, they just become bug-ridden appliances ripe for the picking.

When I reviewed hardware appliances for a living for *InfoWorld* magazine's Testing Review Center, I probably reviewed over a hundred appliances. None arrived to me, the tester, without multiple security bugs. Most had publicly known bugs many years old. Most appliances could not be updated by the user, even if they knew it contained a bug that had a patch out for it. The best appliances were updated at most once a quarter. Some were only updated when big new sets of features for the primary software were updated by the vendor. Some appliances were never updated. There were even several vendors that I had to threaten to publicly disclose their unpatched vulnerabilities to their customers if they did not patch it. When you see the words "appliance" or "firmware" just think, "harder-to-patch software," because that's all they really are.

Unbreakable Oracle

In 2001, Oracle started a new "unbreakable" campaign. It claimed that its products were essentially unhackable. It didn't take long for the first security bugs to be found. Over the next few years, over a hundred bugs were found in Oracle's core products. It was an embarrassment. There was no one in the computer security world who thought Oracle's claim would be found to be true for very long. Everyone was wondering why Oracle's CEO, Larry Ellison, even decided to go with the "unbreakable" marketing campaign that was bound to fail. But even so, it was likely a good marketing campaign for Oracle. It put them in the news, and it showed that Oracle was at least trying to make a better product, albeit just asking for trouble from hackers who hadn't previously concentrated on Oracle products.

DJB

Daniel J. Bernstein (he is widely known as djb) is one of the leading cryptographers and secure coding teachers in the world (cr.yp.to/djb.html). According to what I remember at the time, he is so good at secure coding that student developers sign up to take his classes, even though in some of his classes nearly everyone fails. In one of his classes, he required that everyone find at least 10 previously undisclosed security bugs, and all the found bugs were immediately released to the public without giving the vendor any time to patch ahead of the public announcement. Students who didn't find 10 previously undisclosed vulnerabilities failed the class. Most students found only a few bugs and ended up failing his class. Still, the best programmers in the university fought to take (and likely fail) his class. He was that good of a teacher and that highly respected.

> **NOTE** It is possible that my recollection of everyone failing his classes because they did not find and disclose 10 new vulnerabilities may have been a false rumor. But I'm pretty sure this is the truth or near the whole truth. I had some of his students write and confirm what I'm sharing here, but djb, himself, never responded to confirm my understanding.

Dr. Bernstein is a respected programmer who has written many respected, very secure open source programs, including qmail and dbjdns (found here: cr.yp.to). His programs are known for not having very many security bugs. djb is a fierce critic of the huge number of security bugs found in most software programs. He chides developers and vendors for having too many bugs, using too many lines of code, and simply not caring enough to aggressively minimize security bugs. He used to offer $1,000 rewards for anyone finding a security bug in any product he wrote that could be exploited. Over a few years, at least two bugs were found. I wrote about one in 2009 (www.csoonline.com/article/2633162/djbdns-security-vulnerability-found.html). I don't believe he offers his $1,000 rewards anymore.

Dr. Bernstein cares about avoiding programming security errors almost more than anyone else alive on the planet. If his code had errors, anyone's code can have errors. I don't want to take away anything from what he's accomplished. He does write some of the most secure code on the planet, and he put his personal money where his mouth was. His code has held up over time. But his code is fairly simple with limited functionality (as compared to his competitors' products). It's great code with some decent functionality, but it truly can't compete in the marketplace of other similar programs. Why? Because most people don't care about security as much as he does. Most people are willing to accept just okay security to use a program with a ton of functionality. And if djb couldn't write bug-free code, what chance do the rest of us have? Not a lot.

The average number of exploitable security bugs per lines of code ranges from one bug per thousand to three hundred thousand lines of code (`security.stackexchange.com/questions/21137/average-number-of-exploitable-bugs-per-thousand-lines-of-code`). More to the point, I've never heard of a published piece of code, software or hardware, that did not eventually get one or more bug fixes to address found security vulnerabilities. A bug-free program doesn't exist, and I'm fairly confident there will never be one. All code is hackable.

Unhackable Quantum Cryptography

My previous book, *Cryptography Apocalypse* (Wiley, 2019), is on quantum computers and how quantum computers will one day break traditional public-key cryptography. It also covers how quantum computers and devices can be used to make hard-to-break quantum cryptography. According to quantum physicists, the very laws of physics prove that quantum cryptography can't be broken—that to break quantum cryptography you have to break the laws of physics, and you are not doing that. So, you'll hear all these theoretical physicists state how quantum cryptography is unbreakable. Of course, they are wrong.

Although quantum cryptography may be theoretically unhackable, practical application is far different. One, it really isn't unhackable in the first place. What they mean by "unhackable" is that quantum information cannot be eavesdropped on without the sender and intended receiver knowing. That's not the same thing as "can't be eavesdropped on." It just means that if it does get eavesdropped on, the legitimate parties will know it happened. If critical information was eavesdropped on, it was still stolen—it's just that the legitimate parties know it happened.

Second, and more important, referring to the previous section, "Unhackable Fallacy," humans have never made anything that is unhackable. We've tried. We've intended to. We've thought we did it. And in every case, we've been wrong. To be human is to be fallible. We make mistakes. And those mistakes lead to hacks.

Even if we were somehow able to make unhackable quantum cryptography, we would mess up implementing it in the real world. It's always what happens. We take something that is perfect in theory and ruin it in practice. It's the way of the world. And I don't see quantum properties and quantum physics, which are as inherently complex as anything humans have messed with, suddenly being the thing we got right. Nope, odds are quantum cryptography will be hacked to death just like everything else in the world we have created.

All MFA solutions are hackable. All contain security bugs. More examples and information in Chapter 15, "Buggy Software."

We Are Reactive Sheep

Part of the reason that we accept less security in trade for higher usability is that it's far harder to sell people on something that will bring more inconvenience to their lives now before the bad thing you are trying to warn them about happens. It's easy to sell batteries just before a hurricane hits. It's easy to convince people to do the right thing after the pain happens.

The best example is what happened in the United States on September 11, 2001 (aka "9/11"). On that day, terrorists overcame the flight crews of four airliners and flew them into famous buildings (and a Pennsylvania farm field). Nothing they did was surprising or new, other than the sheer audacity and scope of the plan and who did it. We had long known that terrorists could take over control of planes and use them as mass casualty weapons. The box cutters the terrorists used were already illegal to have on a plane and were supposed to be stopped by current airport security procedures. The U.S. intelligence agencies were on high alert about a pending huge terrorist attack. A flight school warned the FBI about one of the alleged terrorists and how he was mostly concerned with flying the plane, but not so much about landing. Subsequent (failed) terrorist attacks were attempted using bomb-laden water bottles, shoes, and underwear.

Airport security and counterterrorism officials have known for a long time that water bottles, toothpaste tubes, shoes, and underwear could be used to sneak in bombs. But if airport security told us before 9/11 that we would have to throw away all liquids over 3 ounces, take off our shoes, and undergo full-body scans, we Americans would have revolted in such numbers that the airlines would have forced the security people to relent. After 9/11, we are all standing in longer lines taking off our shoes, throwing away our bottles of water (and tiny screwdrivers, lighters, etc.) and going through the security scanner of the Transportation Security Administration (TSA) screener's choice. The pain had to happen first.

It's the same with computer security. Passwords have been working fairly well for decades. It's only now that all the computer security issues (covered in Chapter 1) have accumulated and caused enough damage that companies and people are being forced to do something better. Super-damaging ransomware attacks are forcing people to make sure their backup and restore operations truly work as advertised, because if they don't and they get hit by a ransomware attack, they'd better be prepared to pay the ransom.

In school and college, we are taught to be proactive, that being proactive is a good thing. And it is. But in the real world, trying to argue for additional and better security defenses before the pain has happened is a very tough sell. Do it enough times and with too much vigor, and you'll be seen as the "Boy Who Cried Wolf," and you may even be fired.

It's the same with authentication and MFA. It's taken a lot time and a lot of cybersecurity damage for people to start moving in significant numbers away from passwords to MFA. Phishers have stolen billions of passwords. You would have thought that when a million or a hundred million of them were stolen the whole world would have noticed and required MFA. But even with many billions of passwords stolen, society's move to MFA is still very slow—so slow that by the time most of society is using MFA by default, we will probably be on to the next best authentication solution (covered in Chapter 24, "The Future of Authentication").

Security Theater

There are also instances of security that are more theater and spectacle than true security (known as *security theater* by critics). The world is full of security theater. One of the best examples is signing checks or credit card/ATM receipts for purchases in the United States. It has nearly zero real security value in stopping fraud from being committed. With a check, you might possibly have a sales clerk compare the signature on your check with your ID, but probably not. And if that clerk notices a difference, they probably won't say anything to you and certainly won't stop your purchase. There is a chance that a fraudulent signature can help support your case of fraud in the event that fraud is noticed on the backend a long time later, but it rarely actually stops the fraud from being committed in the first place.

For decades, I have signed all my checks and credit cards with a known bad signature. I have signed thousands of my credit card receipts and checks with "Yogi Bear" and "ThisIsNot MyRealSignature" and I have never been stopped from purchasing something. I've had a few people laugh, but none have stopped me from my purchase. I think, originally, most of us thought it was important to make sure our signature was our legal, valid signature. We must have thought that there was a chance that someone was sitting in a backroom somewhere actually comparing signatures and that person would notice the discrepancy and stop the transaction. It has never happened. That person, that position, that security action does not exist. We are legally required to provide that signature by law, supposedly for some security purpose. But that review does not happen. Most of the time, we are just wasting our time. I'm not sure why we as a society even tolerate having to sign signatures that do almost nothing. Perhaps it's because it doesn't take us long. If signing a signature took 20 seconds on average, I bet the requirement to use signatures would be changed.

> **NOTE**   In some countries, the user's signature is electronically validated at time of purchase or soon thereafter and can actually decrease the incidences of fraud. But in the United States signatures on credit cards and checks have almost worthless security value.

Sometimes it's theater, but it appears to be working in at least some limited way. For example, at the airport: the TSA security checks aren't that hard to get around. Every day dozens of lethal weapons, including guns, get past the TSA security checks. I can easily think about how to get a bomb past TSA security. I don't want to share the idea in print, but my method would work at any airport and I could do it every day for a year and never be caught. Many people admonish TSA as security theater.

But it appears to be working. It's not perfect, but the TSA does stop many loaded guns from getting on planes each day (most are accidentally left in carryon luggage by mistake and the offender meant no ill harm). The TSA can't really stop all bombs and terrorists, but for whatever reason since the TSA was invented and put in place, the United States hasn't suffered any additional successful terrorist attacks using airliners so far. One day that record may change, but it's been over 15 years and not a single terrorist has again successfully used a plane to attack us. They have tried. We've stopped underwear bombers (barely), shoe bombers (barely), and bombs placed in laser printers to be shipped in cargo holders.

Despite the many ways to bypass the TSA, warts and all, they have quite the success record. At this point I have to ask, is it security theater? I mean, 15 years without a successful attack means something. It can't just be dumb luck. Perhaps it's enough security to scare terrorists into using some other form of attack? And remembering that security isn't binary, isn't it perhaps not perfect security but good enough security? They can't stop all imaginable attacks, but they have, at least so far, stopped all real-world attempted attacks. With that said, I'm not sure I'm ready to call it security theater. The TSA has a far better record than the signature used to sign credit card receipts.

Security by Obscurity

Most computer security practitioners are taught early on that "security by obscurity is no security." The idea is that attackers might be able to discover any fact surrounding your security system, so you can assume they have all the necessary facts and you should design your security system to be secure even if they have perfect knowledge of it (for everything but the ultimate authentication secrets). The "security by obscurity is no security" dogma is believed and repeated so much that it borders on religion. However, it isn't any truer than the old password policy beliefs.

The truth is that obscurity is a great defense and often one of the best ways to get the biggest bang for your security dollar. It just shouldn't be the only or the primary way your system is secured. You should still design a system as if the axiom is true. It can only help you. But there's a fundamental difference between not relying solely on security by obscurity and refusing to benefit from it at all. If you look at the security scenarios that use it, you should absolutely include some obscurity as part of your overall security defense. Any variable that a hacker has to guess or look for slows them down and makes their job harder. If obscurity is no security, then why don't the world's armies tell each other where their nuclear subs are traveling and where all the nuclear missile silos are located? I can tell you why. Obscurity has good security value.

MFA Will Cause Slowdowns

Most MFA solutions slow down implementation and operations as compared to non-MFA solutions—not all, but most. It takes more time planning and implementing an MFA project versus using simple logon names and passwords. It takes more time to convince management that they need to use MFA rather than logon passwords. It takes more time to educate coworkers on how to use MFA. It takes more time to train help desk and support staff on how to support and troubleshoot. It takes more time for people to input and use multiple factors as compared to single-factor solutions. It is the very rare MFA solution that actually speeds up everything. If you can do that, it's a win-win for everyone.

There are even claims (krebsonsecurity.com/2019/11/study-ransomware-data-breaches-at-hospitals-tied-to-uptick-in-fatal-heart-attacks/) that requiring MFA has caused an increase in deaths at a hospital due to slowdown issues. On first read, it seems a strong conclusion to reach on just one study, and perhaps it's just an anecdotal anomaly, or maybe MFA wasn't a causative reason for the increase in deaths—but it might be. We haven't studied a computer security problem with these types of potential severe consequences before. Until we conduct more studies with similar findings and more data that rules other possible causes in or out, we might not know for sure.

MFA Will Cause Downtime

Years ago, when I was a child my mother bought the first car we ever owned that had electric windows. Prior to that, in any car we owned you had to manually roll up or down the windows using a knob of some type. We loved our new car and its fancy, high-tech windows. Until we broke down on the side of a Florida highway during a torrential summer rainstorm and we could not roll up our windows. It rained so much that not only did we get wet, but it ruined the inside of the car. We had to buy a new car. It was a lot of rain. Ever since then, I haven't trusted things with too many fancy gadgets. I've learned that every additional feature or gadget is just one more additional thing that can break.

MFA is like electric car windows. The reason password authentication has survived so long in the face of growing hacking adversity is that it just works—from a usability perspective. MFA costs more to implement and to operate. It takes longer to enroll users in MFA authentication; it's far more likely to cause problems, far more likely to have false positives and false negatives, and far more likely to cause downtime. Here's an example: www.bleepingcomputer.com/news/microsoft/microsoft-365-authentication-outage-users-unable-to-login. It was barely any downtime, only two hours, but it has happened before, multiple times (including another 14 hours: www.securityweek.com/microsoft-details-cause-recent-multi-factor-authentication-outage). It's not much downtime, but it's downtime that would not have been incurred if MFA did not exist.

No MFA Solution Works Everywhere

Perhaps the biggest usability argument, at least right now, is that no MFA solution works everywhere. None. You can take the most popular and widespread supported MFA options, which are supported by millions of sites and services, and they don't account for 1 percent of sites and services people need to log on to. In every case, administrators have to pick incomplete solutions and users have to use the MFA solution for some things and a non-MFA (or other MFA solution) for others. The lack of global support for any MFA option is absolutely slowing down its proliferation.

The best an admin looking for a new MFA solution can do is to inventory which applications must be covered and which are optional. And then they need to find which MFA solutions cover their "must-haves" and which critical applications will not be covered. I've yet to see an organization where a single MFA solution covered everything they needed, unless it was a very specialized, high-security environment where MFA coverage was *the* primary requirement above all else. Or perhaps they had an MFA-enabled SSO solution that allowed a single MFA sign-on to then open other (really non-MFA-protected) applications.

If you are interested in seeing whether your favorite websites support MFA, you can visit `twofactorauth.org`, but I've yet to find a single information source that has a definitive list of what MFA solution is supported where inclusively. Most of the time, it takes an admin doing the grunt work of tracking down where a desired MFA solution will and won't work based on their mission-critical application needs. All the needed work makes MFA less likely to be used than if some (seemingly magical) solutions worked everywhere by default. Of course, there are more considerations than just whether the MFA solution works with your applications, and I'll cover those factors in Chapter 23.

Summary

Security has always been a struggle between usability and safety, and that struggle is definitely challenged by any MFA solution. This chapter explored many of the main points of usability versus security, including the fact that users actually don't care about security as much as we do and they don't want the best security possible. Instead, the solutions that will win in the long run provide us with the right balance of security and ease of use.

Chapter 5, "Hacking MFA in General" investigates the general methods for hacking any MFA solution.

Hacking MFA

5 Hacking MFA in General

hapter 5 will cover hacking MFA generally, without showing any specific techniques. Anything can be hacked. Anyone telling you that they have something that can't be hacked is lying or naïve. Either way, they shouldn't be trusted. Multifactor authentication (MFA) has many components and supporting infrastructures many of which the MFA solution vendor has no control over, and each can be hacked by various means. This book is dedicated to showing dozens of ways that all, or specific implementations, can be hacked, although this particular chapter just addresses the topic in a generalized way.

This book will not be able to show all the ways MFA can be hacked, although I'll fit as many as I can within these pages. There are ways that I don't know about; I haven't thought of them or encountered them, or I've simply forgotten them. Many MFA vulnerabilities are only known to the potential attacker who is keeping them secret until they are otherwise needed. Or they are used sparingly and rarely in a way that the exploited victim isn't even aware of. The biggest nation-states have thousands of nonpublic vulnerabilities cataloged away, awaiting a specific need. Others are known by their vendors and kept secret because the vendor doesn't know a good way to mitigate the risk.

Many MFA vulnerabilities haven't been discovered yet. The world is full of examples of hacked things that had vulnerabilities that went undetected for decades, until they were finally discovered by a single, curious soul. Vulnerabilities often sit in plain sight for years, until someone reviewing the code or trying a specific action saw a potential weakness and explored it. Many vulnerabilities are found by accident. Someone is trying to do something new, such as extend or automate functionality, and they end up accidentally causing an error that reveals a previously unfound vulnerability.

Many, if not most, vulnerabilities will go undiscovered, without anyone recognizing the vulnerability that could be exploited. Humans are imperfect. Just as we can't stop all programming mistakes, we don't find every mistake or vulnerability. We will always create more vulnerabilities than we will find. It's just the nature of programming. Even the software that we design to specifically find vulnerabilities doesn't find every one; it can only find the vulnerabilities we all already understand and know how to find.

Chapter 5 is not only a generalized look at how MFA vulnerabilities are found, but also summarizes all the different components. This chapter should be used by nonmalicious hackers looking to ensure that an MFA solution they are considering is as secure as possible as well as by MFA developers to ensure that the solution they are delivering is as secure as possible from the start when they offer it to consumers. Nothing is vulnerability free, but by learning and using the lessons of past exploits, the number of future bugs can be minimized. Many of the discussions in this chapter apply to most digital solutions and not necessarily just authentication or MFA. The rest of Part II will cover specific examples of MFA vulnerabilities that illustrate the generalized vulnerabilities covered here.

MFA Dependency Components

No MFA solution is an island. Every MFA solution is just one part of multiple components, relationships, and dependencies, as visually depicted in Figure 5.1, and each of these components is an additional area where an exploitable vulnerability can occur.

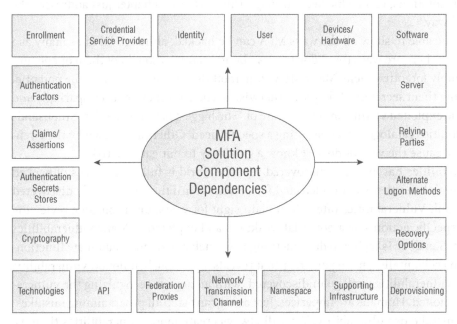

Figure 5.1: MFA dependent components

Essentially any component in the entirety of the MFA's life cycle, from provisioning to deprovisioning and everything in between, is subject to having exploitable vulnerabilities and hacking.

And like the proverbial chain, it's only strongest as its weakest link. Here is a list of the phases and components involved in MFA:

- Enrollment
- User
- Devices/hardware
- Software
- Authentication factors
- Authentication secrets store
- Cryptography
- Technology
- Network/transmission channel
- Namespace
- Supporting infrastructure
- Relying party
- Federation/proxies
- APIs
- Alternate authentication methods
- Recovery
- Migrations
- Deprovision

The rest of this section will explore these components in more detail. Some of this chapter will repeat terms learned in early chapters, but they are included here again for completeness and redundancy can't hurt when discussing authentication systems.

Enrollment

Enrollment (also known as *provisioning*) is the process of a subject being registered and verified to get an authenticated identity (label). An unverified and unregistered subject is known as an *applicant*. They are applying for an authenticated identity. The *credential service provider* (CSP) asks for and receives one or more (unique) subject attributes, which can be used to clearly identify the subject. This process is known as *identity proofing*. The subject can enroll themselves or have another *enrollment agent* trusted by both the applicant and the CSP do it on their behalf.

A critical part of the process is that the CSP verifies the applicant's submitted attributes. Without the CSP strongly verifying the applicant's submitted attributes and ensuring that the applicant is who they say they are and that the submitted applicant attributes truly belong to the applicant, authentication is nearly worthless. How strongly the CSP verifies the identity and attributes of the applicant determines the level of *assurance*.

Think of the enrollment process like a person applying for a driver's license. The person must pass a physical driving test to show that they have basic driving skills, answer a set of knowledge-based questions to prove they know the "rules of the road," and prove they are who they say they are. The latter involves providing sufficient proof to the driver license issuer (the CSP in this example in the United States is the Department of Motor Vehicles [DMV]) to get the official driver's license. The applicant does this by providing multiple forms of acceptable identity attributes, such as a birth certificate, Social Security card, and a bill sent to their home residence to verify the address. Years ago, the DMV didn't require as much assurance as they do now, but previous weak validation allowed serious identity crimes to occur, and so now the DMV requires stronger identity assurance.

But if you get a driver's license issued to you, almost anywhere (e.g., law enforcement, liquor store) that requests proof of your identity will accept the DMV-issued driver's license as proof of your identity. It's the same thing with CSPs. Any relying party that trusts the CSP will trust that a CSP-verified identity submitted by a subject to them is accurate. But if the CSP doesn't do their job and doesn't accurately verify the subject's identity and attributes before issuing a verified identity, then the whole process breaks down.

A good, everyday digital example of this is the use of Pretty Good Privacy (PGP) asymmetric encryption keys. Created in 1981 by Phil Zimmerman, PGP is a very popular encryption program that comes in both open source and commercial versions. Everyone who gets a PGP public key from someone else is supposed to validate it before using it. But almost no one does so in practice. In the past, fraudulent users have pretended to be someone else by using fake PGP keys and none of the involved recipients noticed that the supplied PGP public key was invalid (e.g., had an invalid digital fingerprint). So, everyone thinks they are participating in this higher level of privacy and authentication when it really is no better than regular, nonencrypted, unauthenticated email (or perhaps even worse, because people think they can rely on it).

A verified identity (and their verified attributes) is known as a verified *subscriber*. The CSP usually maintains overall ownership of the issued identity and can renew, cancel, or update it, solely at its discretion. The authentication factors associated with the identity and stored by the CSP are also known as *authenticators*. When the subscriber goes to authenticate to a relying party (e.g., device, system, site, service), they are known as the *claimant*. The claimant can also provide, along with their authenticators, one or more claims/attributes, which have also been verified by the CSP.

This is a good overall description of the enrollment process and the other involved components, but individual enrollment processes vary greatly. The generalized common enrollment process is summarized in Figure 5.2. It is a far simpler view of the authentication life cycle process presented in Figure 2.7 in Chapter 2, but summarizes the same process (without all the other complexity).

The biggest risk to the enrollment process is a malicious subject being fraudulently enrolled to become a verified subscriber backed by the CSP and trusted by the relying party. Malicious actors do this to obtain inside access to an authenticated population, where they can introduce maliciousness. An authenticated identity gets seen as more legitimate than if they posed as an anonymous user.

Of course, the trust given any identity depends on the steps the CSP takes to verify the subscriber's identity before issuing them a "verified" account. For some of the most popular CSPs the verification party is little to no verification before being issued an account. Every day the largest Internet properties using authenticated accounts (e.g., Facebook, Google, Microsoft, Twitter) suffer from millions

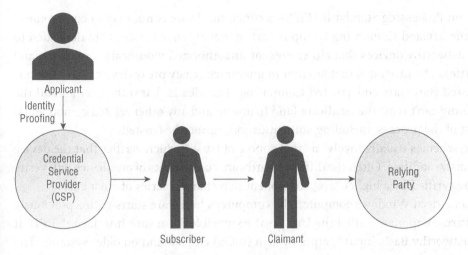

Figure 5.2: Generalized common enrollment process

to tens of millions of fraudulent accounts. Each of these entities spends many millions of dollars to fight fraudulent applicants and to detect and proactively remove fraudulent, now verified subscribers.

Most people probably can't visualize the breadth of this type of problem. In 2019, Facebook reported (www.huffpost.com/entry/facebook-fake-accounts-transparency_n_5dcce729e4b03a7e0294d419) that they removed over 3.2 billion fake accounts over six months and that, despite its monumental effort, over 5 percent of their remaining 2.45 billion accounts are thought to be fake as well. That's a third of a million fake accounts created every day, 365 days a year. And that's just what Facebook doesn't easily find and delete. Google, Microsoft, and Twitter face similar enormous enrollment problems. There is even a cottage industry of firms whose sole objective is to help CSPs better recognize fake accounts as well as another industry that is bent on helping semi-legitimate and malicious actors to continue bypassing the newer and changing defenses. It's truly a war of daily attribution, with both sides winning some early battles that are then successfully fought back by the other side using new techniques.

User

The number one way that malicious hacking successfully happens is by maliciously manipulating the user. This will be covered in more detail in the section "Human Element" later in this chapter.

Devices/Hardware

Any of the devices involved in authentication can be maliciously compromised. Devices include computers, phones, authentication devices, storage, memory, network interfaces, antennas, and any other physical device involved in the authentication process. They can be compromised to steal authentication secrets, steal the resulting access control token, eavesdrop, steal data, and redirect the user or authentication process to a fraudulent site or service. If a hardware device is compromised, it is difficult (although not impossible) for the authentication process to be trusted. This is not to say that some hardware isn't more hacking-resistant than others.

Federal Information Processing Standards (FIPS)-certified hardware is not easy to compromise. Other groups, like the Trusted Computing Group (trustedcomputinggroup.org) are dedicated to providing proven trustworthy devices that either prevent unauthorized modification or detect and alert the relying parties. The programs that attempt to guarantee trustworthy devices have various names, such as Trusted Hardware and Trusted Computing. The idea is that if the user and all the software that is running can't trust the hardware (and firmware and any other related components) to be secure, the rest of the process, including authentication, cannot be trusted.

Trusted hardware schemes usually involve a "root source of trust," which verifies that the device has not been maliciously modified. Often the different hardware components of one device will verify themselves and/or be verified by a higher-level component in a chained series of trust checks.

For example, on a modern Windows computer, the computer's hardware starts with a previously trusted basic hardware component called the Universal Extensible Firmware Interface (UEFI). It replaced the less trustworthy Basic Input/Output System (BIOS) chips found on older systems. The UEFI firmware boot chip contains coding that is digitally signed as authentic by the vendor. Each higher-layer relying hardware component relies on the previous level component to verify its digital signature. This system of chained trust checks continues until the entire Windows operating system software boot sequence is accomplished, using processes called Secure Boot, Trusted Boot, and Measured Boot. You can read more about how it works here: docs.microsoft.com/en-us/windows/security/information-protection/secure-the-windows-10-boot-process.

Every authentication device should have a similar trusted measurement performed and verified. Although it's rare in today's world, every device in the authentication process (i.e., every computer, router, server, service) should have similar hardware and software trust verification processes. The very best authentication devices promise to deliver a highly trustworthy process even if all the other components are compromised.

But essentially, if any of the hardware devices are compromised, it's "game over." You cannot trust the authentication processes if the devices involved have been maliciously manipulated. A vendor and designer can do their best to prevent it and to minimize the impact of a compromise in the chain of components, but a compromised process can never be completely trusted.

Software

Just as all the hardware must be trustworthy and uncompromised, so too must be all the software. Software includes firmware code, boot code, operating system, and applications. The most trustworthy software not only checks itself for unauthorized changes, but also has other higher-layer processes and/or trust-verified software check it. Like the risks to hardware, any malicious change to the software involved anywhere in the authentication process threatens the trustworthiness. The best authentication takes software threats into account and tries to remain as trustworthy as possible.

API

Many MFA solutions come with a private or open (i.e., shared) application programming interface (API). These APIs can contain vulnerabilities or be maliciously used by an attacker. Chapter 19, "API Abuses," will cover this category in more detail.

Authentication Factors

The authentication factors themselves can be compromised. For example, any biometric attribute (fingerprint, retina print, etc.) can be captured and reused maliciously. Malware programs can steal passwords and PINs, or users can be tricked into giving them out. Authentication secrets can be stolen off authentication devices.

It is also possible for an involved claim/assertion to be maliciously manipulated. For example, a user's authentication solution may have verified them as *not* belonging to an elevated security group but the attribute is modified to appear as if the user does belong to an elevated security group. Many hacks are against the authentication factor or claim.

> **NOTE** Another increasing concern is the privacy rights of a claimant. Every authentication system should strive to allow the subject to decide which claims are revealed in specific authentication events. Many attacks seek to gain access to more claims than the relying party is supposed to be privy to.

Authentication Secrets Store

Many times, the hack is made against the database/store where authentication secrets are stored. Unauthorized access to the authentication secrets store are among the most devastating attacks possible, because an attacker can get access to every secret the store has and reuse them.

For example, as covered previously, Windows network authentication secrets are stored on Active Directory domain controller databases with the filename `NTDS.DIT`. There are many hacker tools, such as Mimikatz (`github.com/gentilkiwi/mimikatz`), that attempt to "dump" all the authentication secrets stored there, if the hacker has enough elevated access. The NT hashes of user and computer passwords are stored in `NTDS.DIT`. As covered in Chapter 1, "Logon Problems," those hashes can be replayed to create new network, drive, and device connections. They can also be "cracked" back to their plaintext password equivalents and then used anywhere that accepts the plaintext password alone (email, logon portal, etc.). An attacker gaining access to an authentication secrets store is a "game over" attack. When an attack obtains access to the ultimate authentication secret, there is nothing the attacker cannot do. They have the keys to the kingdom. The entire authentication system was essentially set up to prevent that occurrence, and once it has happened, the authentication system can no longer be trusted as a way to verify who is or isn't associated with a particular identity (label).

Cryptography

Most authentication solutions (although not all) use cryptography to protect themselves and their secrets. Most authentication systems use "industry-accepted" cryptographic algorithms and key sizes. Many hacks try to compromise either the cryptography itself (by finding an inherent weakness) or by finding a flaw in the implementation. The latter is many, many times easier and more common. The world is full of hundreds of vulnerabilities found because MFA developers did not correctly and securely implement the otherwise secure cryptography. Attacks like this are often described as "leaving the keys of the kingdom under the doormat."

All industry-accepted cryptography standards become weaker over time. Cryptographic attacks only get better over time, either because of increasing computational resources or because the attacks find increasingly better ways to take advantage of an inherent cryptographic flaw in the cipher. The nature of cryptographic use is that vendors must always be aware that existing cryptography is constantly being weakened over time and that an MFA solution relying on that cryptography must be prepared to move to newer, stronger cryptography standards. If it is relatively easy for the MFA vendor to move their solution to other, newer cryptographic standards, if their solution is "crypto-agile." Unfortunately, many MFA solutions are "hard-coded" as to what cryptographic algorithms and key sizes they can use, and they often cannot be upgraded without a complete replacement of the hardware and/or software.

On a related note, as of 2020 quantum computers are soon becoming powerful enough that they may break most traditional public key cryptography (RSA, Diffie-Hellman, Elliptic Curve, etc.) and weaken in half most traditional symmetric algorithms (e.g., AES), hashes (e.g., SHA-2), and random number generators (RNG). See my previous book, *Cryptography Apocalypse* (Wiley, 2019), if you want to learn about the quantum crypto break in more detail and how you can start preparing now.

No matter what, an MFA solution should always be aware that any involved cryptography can become compromised at any time and make their solutions crypto-agile in anticipation.

Technology

Like cryptography, any of the technology being used by the MFA solution can be compromised. For example, many physical MFA device solutions rely on the Universal Serial Bus (USB) standard. USB is a software, API, and hardware specification, and each of those components can come under attack at any time.

Transmission/Network Channel

Most authentication solutions require and use a transmission or network channel, especially when network authentication or access is involved. The channel is composed of software and hardware and can be compromised like any other software and hardware.

Namespace

Most underlying MFA solutions rely on a digital namespace. A *namespace* is a way of naming, locating, storing, and categorizing objects. Common digital namespaces include Active Directory, Lightweight Directory Protocol (LDAP), Domain Name System (DNS), and Internet Protocol (IP) addresses, among others. The identities and other components are often referenced in the namespace and used by other involved components in locating and verifying other components. Examples of DNS addresses are rogerg@knowbe4.com, www.knowbe4.com, or www.knowbe4.com/resources. An example (Distinguished Name) Active Directory name could look like CN=Rogerg, OU=Users, OU=PRDept, DC=knowbe4, DC=com. Namespaces can hold not only objects, but also claims, assertions, and attributes of objects. Chapter 10, "Subject Hijack Attacks," and Chapter 18, "DNS Hijacking" will cover examples of MFA attacks against namespaces.

Supporting Infrastructure

Many, if not most, MFA solutions depend on a host of supporting infrastructures, like DHCP, TCP/IP, and IP addresses. The routers involved in helping the MFA solution work across a network running router protocols, such as Router Internet Protocol (RIP), Interior Gateway Routing Protocol (IGRP), Enhanced Interior Gateway Routing Protocol (EIGRP), Open Shortest Path First (OSPF), Intermediate System to Intermediate System (IS-IS), and Border Gateway Protocol (BGP). Network addresses are converted to physical Media Access Control (MAC) addresses by the Address Resolution Protocol (ARP). Most computers get their IP addresses from Dynamic Host Configuration Protocol (DHCP) services. Networked Windows computers use Active Directory services to connect. Linux computers often use LDAP. Apple computers often use Bonjour for zero-configuration network services. New USB devices are often automatically registered and recognized because of the Universal Plug-n-Play (UPNP) standard.

The idea is that almost all MFA solutions ultimately rely on multiple standards, protocols, and technologies, which they themselves did not invent or control. And each of these technologies and supporting infrastructures can be attacked and hacked to compromise an MFA solution. For example, it is possible for a malicious USB port to rewrite a USB device's firmware instructions or to eavesdrop and record the device's data. If you are not familiar with USB firmware hacks, type **usb charger hacks** in any search engine and prepare to be amazed. Most of the hacks are simply proof-of-concept projects, but it's not hard to see how devastating they would be against a USB-enabled MFA device. For example, the firmware of a USB security token could be secretly rewritten not to provide the security the device was capable of before being maliciously modified, or a protected secret key could be stolen and used by adversaries to read protected information.

Relying Party

The party that is requesting or relying on your authentication can be compromised. The attacker can hack around the relying party's authentication requirement or even hack their authenticating party. Every component participating in the authentication is a potential attack vector, and this includes the ultimate relying party.

Federation/Proxies

Many sites and services rely on another site's or service's authentication process when deciding to allow a subject to authenticate to them. The relying site or service is saying, "I trust your authentication service enough to trust that you authenticated the subject correctly and I'll rely on that authentication." This can be done through shared APIs, proxied authentication, shared single sign-on (SSO) services, and federation. Federation is becoming the most common of the solutions. *Federation* is a linking or use of verified identities across multiple identity management systems, sites, and services. Federated services can just be between internal departments of the same entity, between multiple entities, or globally between all participating parties. Latter examples include Microsoft Accounts, Facebook authentication, Open Authorization (OAuth), and Google Accounts.

The risk is that all of these technologies are involved in authentication and many, like federation, are SSO solutions. If you compromise the SSO authentication or token, you can more easily compromise everything that allows or relies on that solution.

Alternate Authentication Methods/Recovery

Most of the major MFA solutions, providers, and relying parties (Google, Microsoft, etc.) have alternate means for participants to authenticate. This is because MFA solutions are always more inherently complex than 1FA solutions and thus are subject to failures of all types. People forget their PINs, lose their smartcards, and accidentally break their devices. For the big vendors, these sorts of MFA failures happen millions of times every day. If they had to spend a lot of time helping users to recover or log on using another alternate method (most of which are far less secure than MFA), then their support costs would skyrocket. Instead, the vendors create simple, automated methods so that the user can log on if they can't use their MFA solution in the original way intended. Attackers often abuse these alternate methods. Several of the chapters in Part II of this book will focus on hacking the alternate/recovery methods.

Migrations

Migration is a less common hacking method and is included here only for completeness. Rarely does an organization use or get a single authentication method that they use the rest of their online life. Usually, the authentication system or its identity databases gets upgraded or moved to newer, better methods. Organizations, through mergers and acquisitions, often change. These changes often require that older and existing authentication systems and users be migrated to a newer or another system. There are specific hacks that can occur in these migrations.

For example, there is an older known escalation of privilege (EOP) hack known as a SID History attack (attack.mitre.org/techniques/T1178/) that can occur during Active Directory network migrations. All AD security principal accounts (user, computer, group, etc.) have an attribute field named SID History. This field was intended to allow administrators to prepopulate a security principal's current and/or future security group memberships when an existing security principal is migrated to a new AD forest or domain. AD migrations happen all the time due to network consolidations and mergers. The SID History field was not well known, protected, or monitored until Windows Server 2003 came along. Prior to that, a malicious admin could add highly elevated group memberships (e.g., Scheme Admin, Domain Admins, Administrators) to a security principal's account, and when it got migrated it would become a member of the elevated security group, sometimes without the destination forest's or domain's admins intending it to be so or even being aware that it happened. It was a little used but critical privilege escalation attack for many years. Starting with Windows Server 2003, AD "filtered" out SID History values by default to stop the possibly unintended security elevations. Even today, enabling or disabling SID History Filtering requires only changing a single binary value in AD. All a malicious admin has to do to is change a 1 to a 0 in one place to allow the SID History attack to work again. See docs.microsoft.com/en-us/previous-versions/windows/it-pro/windows-server-2008-R2-and-2008/cc794757(v=ws.10) for more details.

Here's another common example of an attack which takes advantage of migrations: When everyone is migrated to a new system, the administrator often assigns everyone a common, identical password, or the assigned password for each user is different but is based on an easily recognizable and predictable pattern (say, the user's first initial of their first name followed by the last name). Or when users are set up for the first time on a new MFA device, all MFA devices in the same system may have a common PIN of 1234 and everyone knows this fact. Any malicious user learning of the repeated password or password pattern could take advantage of it by using other user accounts.

Migrations are usually infrequent, irregular acts. Many processes don't check for potential mitigation exploits, and a lot of administrators don't check or worry about such attacks. Because of this, as uncommon as migrations are, they are still a valid risk for any organization.

Deprovision

To complete the authentication life cycle processes, *deprovisioning* is the process of deleting, removing, or inactivating identities. This is usually done by the enrolling CSP, but it can be done or requested by a relying party. Deprovisioning is often weakly managed and controlled. It is not uncommon for there to be many more inactive and unused accounts than there are active, used accounts in an authentication system. Every inactive, unused account that is not deprovisioned is a potential threat to everyone else in the system. This is especially true of the unused accounts which have admin access in the authentication system being used. All authentication systems should strive to have strict measurement and control over which accounts are active and being used and which ones become inactive and not used, and deprovision the latter.

MFA Component Conclusion

Many times a successful hack or bypass of an MFA solution was accomplished via a method that actually had little to do with the MFA solution. It often was done via a weakness or issue in a component the MFA solution must rely on but has no control over. The MFA vendor often doesn't have the ability to strengthen the component it must rely on. It is forced to trust the security of the relied-on component and be held hostage by that dependency's own security—in both good and bad times.

One of the lessons to take away from this chapter and book is that MFA solutions are rarely dependent only on themselves. More often, if not always, an MFA solution is one part of a multipart authentication system. An MFA vendor or user's job is to implement and secure the components they are in charge of and can control, and secure them with the right amount of security. As for the relied-on components you cannot control, you should threat model as well to see whether you can implement mitigations and controls to offset the potential risks from required reliance. An MFA vendor or consumer should not just throw their hands up in the air just because they don't have ultimate control over something. No, their job is to predict, access, and mitigate risk no matter how it is involved. And only when they've done the best reasonable job at mitigating the risk from others does the MFA vendor or consumer now recapitulate and accept the risk.

Main Hacking Methods

There are three main methods to hack anything digital, including MFA solutions: technical, human, and physical. Many attacks against MFA are combinations of more than one.

Technical Attacks

Technical attacks are assaults against the technical elements of the digital solution. They are attacks against the solution itself, how it is designed, and how it operates. They are a direct attack on the digital components of the solution. For instance, a technical attack can be a method to expose stored authentication secrets.

For example, as mentioned earlier Windows Active Directory network authentication logon secrets are often kept in a database called NTDS.DIT stored on every participating domain controller, and local logon secrets are stored locally in a registry or file known as the SAM (Security Accounts Manager) store. In both instances, Microsoft has gone to great technical lengths to protect the stored authentication secrets. Even the all-powerful local Administrator or members of the Domain Administrators security group cannot directly access the secrets stored in the Windows or Active Directory authentication databases. To view the stored authentication secrets, a subject or process must have the even higher elevated SYSTEM (i.e., local system) permissions or equivalent. Additionally, the operating system processes that protect those secrets try to prevent known attacks and attack tools from accessing those secrets, even if the attacker has the necessary permissions and privileges. But each year at least a few attacks are announced that thwart Microsoft's best attempts to stop them. It's a constant cat-and-mouse game.

Other examples of technical attacks are compromising the encryption that protects the secrets, finding predictable patterns in what should be truly random information, locating accidental plain-text copies of what is supposed to be encrypted information, compromising involved endpoints and other participants, hijacking namespaces, eavesdropping on communication channels, and other similar attacks. A technical attack is finding a flaw in the digital technology that underpins the solution's safety and security.

Human Element

There is a common saying in the computer security world: "The weakest part of any computer defense is the human." I'm not sure if that is always true, but social engineering of humans in some form accounts for 70 to 90 percent of all successful malicious breaches. No other root hacking cause comes close! The second biggest cause for malicious hacking is unpatched software, which is involved in 20 to 40 percent of all malicious data breaches (they are often paired with each other in an attack, as I explain in a moment). Every other hacking root cause you can think of—misconfigurations, eavesdropping, data malformation—combined only account for 1 to 10 percent of the risk in most environments. Social engineering has been the number one or two reason for successful malicious hacking for the entirety of networked digital computers.

NOTE The percentages were measured from a private study I did using the largest public data breach database in the world, the Privacy Rights Clearinghouse (privacyrights.org). It currently tracks over 11.6 billion breached records. I spent months researching to find the root cause behind every breach. I weeded out nonmalicious data breaches, such as people leaving records behind or accidentally sending records to the wrong patient in email. I concentrated on intentionally malicious breaches or those that could have likely exposed the records to a malicious person. Other studies back up my figures (for example, this study says phishing is responsible for 91 percent of all cyberat-tacks (digitalguardian.com/blog/91-percent-cyber-attacks-start-phishing-email-heres-how-protect-against-phishing), but I consider my study the most accurate within the constraints of my consideration. A coworker of mine, Javvad Malik, did a meta-study (info.knowbe4.com/threat-intelligence-to-build-your-data-driven-defense) of one hundred other root cause studies and found that, although they differed greatly on the actual percentage, all one hundred concluded that social engineering and phishing were the number one root cause of cybersecurity incidents.

Social engineering can be defined as the process of maliciously masquerading as a trusted entity to acquire unauthorized information or to create a desired action that is contrary to the victim's or their organization's self-interests. Simply put, social engineering is a "con," with criminal or unethical intent, that focuses on manipulating otherwise legitimate human behavior. It can be done a number of ways, including in-person or by using email or instant messaging, Short Message Service (SMS), social media, and voiceover phone. Depending on the social engineering form and intent, it can also be called phishing, spear phishing (i.e., targeted), spamming, or vishing (i.e., done via voiceover phone). Social engineering schemes can involve authoritative subjects claiming to be law enforcement, government officials, friends, coworkers, popular social websites, banks, auction sites, or IT administrators. Any relationship that might be able to motivate someone to follow suggested instructions is commonly used to lure the unsuspecting victim.

It can be argued that any authentication failure resulting from a human mistake or bad risk decision more rightly can be blamed on a technical failure. You might think that if the solution were better designed, the human would not be asked to make a risk decision that could possibly result in self-harm. And if it were possible to design a system that did not involve a human being, this would be true. But all user authentication systems inherently involve the user. At a bare minimum, a human is usually involved (although not always) in invoking the authentication system to gain access to a protected resource they are trying to access.

Most other systems of any type involving trust also require that the involved human beings make critical trust decisions, often because the technical systems cannot be trusted enough to make the correct decisions in all cases. For example, one day we will have self-driving cars, which never (or very rarely) make a mistake. We badly need self-driving cars to save millions of otherwise innocent lives. But right now, the technical sophistication of self-driving cars cannot be fully trusted. Cars are coming with numerous self-driving features, which monitor and warn of us about other vehicles driving in our blind spots, as well as sensors that will automatically stop the car if it is going to otherwise get involved in a front-end collision. And these systems are improving every day. They are even more accurate and safe than the humans in many scenarios. But still, overall, they aren't safe enough to completely trust. Today, we still have self-driving cars running over pedestrians, running into the sides of firetrucks, and causing accidents that a human could easily avoid. Recently, I even saw a relative of mine ignore an overtly loud warning that there was a car right beside her as she diverted into the other vehicle's lane and almost caused a severe accident. One day they will be more perfect and able to outdo humans in almost every case, but that day has still not arrived.

It's the same with authentication. Perhaps one day we will have authentication so perfected that a human being won't be asked to make a trust decision that could possibly result in self-harm, but that day is not here yet. And until someone can develop that perfect system and have a large percentage of humans trust it enough to rely on it as their sole method for authentication, human beings will be involved in making critical trust decisions and initiating actions involved with their authentication. But for now, without a doubt, the human element is behind many MFA hacks.

Physical

Many hacking attacks require physical access to the object being hacked. The simplest type of physical attack is the theft of the device the MFA solution was protecting (i.e., stolen laptop or phone) or theft of the MFA solution itself (e.g., someone steals the authentication token itself). Theft is a denial-of-service (DoS) attack.

But in this book, as it related to MFA, physical attacks refer more to ways the secrets of an MFA solution can be compromised or bypassed by an attacker having physical access to the MFA device. Physical possession is the key to the method required to pull off this type of attack. For this category, the attack cannot be done remotely or virtually, or at least nearly as easily. Some of the physical attacks require great expertise and/or expensive equipment. Others require very little expertise and little to no hardware. For example, in Chapter 17, "Physical Attacks," I'll detail an MFA attack that requires a million-dollar electron microscope and another that requires only a $5 can of compressed air. You can't get any cheaper than that.

Two or More Hacking Methods Used

Many of the MFA attacks shown in this book use two or all of these main hacking methods. Often social engineering is used to start the attack and to get the victim to click on a link or to activate a process, which then uses one of the other methods to actually accomplish the necessary technical hacking. For example, a user gets a phishing email that directs them to a fake website, which accomplishes a man-in-the-middle (MitM) attack, which then steals credential secrets. Or physical theft of a hardware token is performed and then the token is forensically examined to find the stored authentication secrets. MFA hacking most often requires that two or all of these main hacking methods be used.

"You Didn't Hack the MFA!"

On a related note, after learning that many of the attacks against MFA require or involve methods not directly related to the MFA method (say, hacking a DNS entry), many MFA vendors have accused me of being disingenuous in my claim that any MFA solution can be hacked. "You didn't hack my MFA solution! You hacked something else that I don't have control over!" My retort always is, "Did a user rely on your MFA solution to protect themselves from hacking? Did you tell the user that your MFA solution would protect them from hacking and that's why they should buy it? And if relying on your solution, was the user still hacked?" Too bad hackers can't just be artificially constrained to hacking only in specific ways in a lab under controlled conditions the way the vendor determines is the "correct way" to hack!

How MFA Vulnerabilities Are Found

Over the last few decades, hundreds of specific vulnerabilities have been found in various MFA solutions. You may wonder how so many have been found. First, as covered previously, everything is hackable. There is no perfect anything. Everything has flaws and vulnerabilities even if we can't readily see them. The key is in finding them. They are found using many different methods, including official threat modeling, code review, fuzz testing, penetration testing, vulnerability scanning, human testing, and by accident—either by well-meaning people or malicious actors.

Threat Modeling

The best way to prevent and find vulnerabilities is to do threat modeling. Threat modeling is when the developers or subsequent reviewers look at a component, or better, the totality of a system, and try to predict all the different ways it can be maliciously compromised or even accidentally broken. When done appropriately, threat modeling helps us design in better security by default. One of the best books on threat modeling is Adam Shostack's *Threat Modeling: Designing for Security* (Wiley, 2014).

The process of threat modeling begins by summarizing the proposed solution, breaking down the individual component steps, and brainstorming all the possible ways each can be errored and compromised. It involves thinking about the different security boundaries and trusts and figuring out how each can be abused. Threat modelers can create "attack trees" (aka cyber kill chains), which show how an attacker can go from one or more exploits to achieving the end objective (bypassing security protections, viewing protected information, etc.). There are models (such as Microsoft's STRIDE), tools, and structured measurements of risk to help with threat modeling. If successful, a threat modeling team can look at all the known threats and risks and minimize them by using built-in controls and mitigations. Any MFA solution using well-considered threat modeling is likely going to have fewer errors and vulnerabilities than one that did not.

Code Review

All MFA solutions involve programming code. The code can result in software, firmware instructions, or both. All code contains errors. A code review, accomplished by either humans or automated software scans, can find predefined vulnerabilities. The best code reviews include both, as each often finds what the other misses.

Fuzz Testing

Fuzz testing software finds potential exploits by varying inputs dozens to hundreds of different ways. Suppose, for example, a piece of software asks users to input their logon name, where the expected logon name would be composed of twenty or fewer characters. A fuzzer would run the program and possibly input logon names composed of hundreds of different combinations. It might put in overly long logon names, logon names composed of numbers only, printer control characters, or executable code, for example. The idea is that a fuzzer would proactively try all sorts of combinations, expected and unexpected, looking to see if the accepting program would throw an error—and if an error is thrown, whether it is an error that might be exploited. Many of today's most aggressive bug-finding hunters use fuzzers to ferret out programming bugs.

Penetration Testing

Penetration testing involves software-driven or skilled human adversaries looking to exploit a target. They might use fuzzing techniques, but usually go far beyond just varying responses to inputs. They will focus on all the involved components looking for new and old vulnerabilities. As with code reviews, the best penetration testing uses a combination of automated and human-based attackers.

Vulnerability Scanning

Vulnerability scanning is almost always performed by automated software that looks for known exploitable vulnerabilities. Vulnerability scanning is a subset of penetration testing, but it's focused only on finding application vulnerabilities caused by errors and weaknesses. Usually it's looking for known vulnerabilities that have been patched by the vendor but that remain unapplied on the investigated target. But it can also include looking for common coding bugs, misconfigurations, default passwords, and performance-reducing issues. The best vulnerability scanners have upward of over 50,000 tests. Vulnerability scanners are great tools, but if they are the only things used by a defender to find and prevent vulnerabilities, they can come up short. Other methods, such as those suggested earlier, should also be used.

Human Testing

Many vulnerabilities have been found simply by a person looking at a particular solution and trying to guess at different possible exploits. Any professional penetration tester uses a combination of their favorite automation tools and their own wits to find bugs and vulnerabilities. It takes a combination of experience, ingenuity, and persistence to be a good human bug finder. In my personal experience (with over 20 years of professional penetration testing), I found at least half of the most critical bugs by simply manually hunting for vulnerabilities and bugs. Sometimes I've simply guessed and tried something randomly. I've found bugs right away using my first hunches and found bugs just before the moment I gave up in exhaustion.

I think a good bug finder is like a good poker player. Everyone is playing by the same rules, but some people seem to have more talent at it because they tend to "win" a lot more than others. Most bug testers tend to specialize in the type of bugs they find. They focus on one operating system type (say, Windows versus Linux versus Apple iOS), one language (say, Python), one type of server functionality (web, database, file, etc.), and so on. The best have expertise at multiple disciplines.

Accidents

One of the modern medical miracles is the discovery of penicillin. Its founder, a Scottish scientist named Alexander Fleming, discovered it when an accidentally discarded Petri dish containing Staphylococcus bacteria was left uncovered near an open window. A blue-green mold, later identified by Fleming as a strain of penicillin, landed on the Petri dish and started to kill and inhibit the growth of the bacteria. Fleming noticed the impact the mold had on the bacteria, and after a lot of serious work, his finding has saved and improved billions of lives. Very happy substantial accident.

Many found digital vulnerabilities were happened upon accidentally. The person or tool that found them was not intentionally looking for them. Sometimes it's because an end user types in something wrong (like a fuzz tester might try) or does something in the wrong order. Other times it is from a third-party vendor looking to use and extend the functionality of an MFA vendor's solution.

MFA solutions that use threat modeling, code review, fuzzers, penetration testing, and vulnerability scanners tend to have fewer found bugs after the solution's public release. The smartest MFA vendors both employ internal resources who focus on finding bugs and encourage friendly external "bug hunters." Some even invite bug hunters and offer public rewards to encourage friendly bug hunters in a process known as *bug bounties*. Some vendors, including MFA vendors, have bug bounties offered at $100,000, although the overall payout depends on the severity of the found bug.

Even if an MFA vendor is not utilizing all, or even a single, of these vulnerability-hunting methods, you can always assume that malicious hackers and adversaries are. It's always best if the MFA vendor tries to find as many bugs as they can in their products first.

Summary

The security of an MFA solution depends on far more than only the inherent properties and technologies of the solution itself. Most also rely on potentially dozens of other, not-in-their-control, components and infrastructure issues. Each component can be hacked to compromise or get around the involved MFA component. In general, MFA hacks can be accomplished using technical methods, human elements, physical attacks, or two or more of these methods. MFA vulnerabilities are found in a variety of ways, including human review, automated scans, and even accidents. An MFA solution and designer must be aware of all the involved factors and potential attack vectors. The remaining chapters of Part II will give specific examples of MFA attacks. Chapter 6, "Access Control Token Tricks" will begin with one of the most common and hard-to-stop attack methods: hacking the access control token.

6

Access Control Token Tricks

hapter 6 begins a detailed look into dozens of examples of how to hack various multifactor authentication solutions. Specifically, we'll look into hacking the access control token, which is likely one of the oldest and most popular methods. Attacking the access control token usually means the attacker doesn't care about what type of authentication was used, be it a single-factor password or multifactor, biometric, super-MFA device. An access control token hacker only cares about re-creating or stealing the resulting access control token, which in most cases is given to a subject after a successful logon.

Access Token Basics

Access control, in general, is a system or set of defined processes, people, and policies implemented to prevent unauthorized subjects from accessing protected resources. In the real world, it's the keys to your house and car. It's every guarded gate. It's a barbed wire–topped fence. It's every building key card entry system. Digital access control systems attempt to do the same with digital systems needing separate security domains for trusted and secure operations.

As you learned in Chapter 2, "Authentication Basics," when a subject successfully authenticates, most authentication systems then generate and transmit an *access control token* (aka *access token*) to the subject, or more accurately to the processes running on behalf of the subject. The token can come in many forms. It is often in the form of a plaintext "cookie" after a user logs on to a website or service, and on Microsoft Windows systems it is often in the form of an NT token or a Kerberos ticket. It can even just be a temporary memory variable value set in a way to allow the operating system or application to know that the user has successfully authenticated.

The purpose of an access control token is to allow subsequent decisions requiring authenticated subjects to be more quickly made without requiring a subject to completely reauthenticate again, especially during the same session or overall action. Imagine, for example, that if every time you clicked on a different page in the same authenticated website you had to completely reauthenticate again, over and over, or if every time you opened a document in Microsoft Word from your own folders that you had to type in your logon name and password again.

Instead, with access control tokens, after successfully authenticating once (for whatever is considered a single session), an authenticated subject can pass along its session access token to any processes requiring proof of a successful authentication to access a protected resource. In reality, it is rarely the actual subject passing along its access token; it's one or more processes acting on behalf of the subject. For example, when accessing a website or service, your web browser often uses your access control token on your behalf. If you're using Word on Windows, it's Word and the Windows operating system executables using and evaluating the access token. What processes are involved depends on the operating system, applications, and tasks being performed.

The access control managing systems protecting resources (such as files, folders, sites, and services) can use a subject's access token in the access control process to determine whether a particular authenticated subject can access a particular object. The access token is sort of a "driver's license" providing proof of a subject's authenticated identity and possibly related permissions, memberships, and privileges.

Access Control Token General Hacks

Unfortunately, accessing or duplicating a subject's access control token often allows any acquirer, legitimate or not, to be seen as (or identical to) the legitimate, original acquirer. Access tokens can be likened to physical "bearer bonds" in the financial world, where the physical holder of the bearer bond is considered the legal owner.

If an unauthorized party is able to reproduce or steal an authenticated subject's access control token, they can often start interacting with the access control system as if they were the legitimate user, and there is little to no way for the access control system to know any different. This type of attack is generally known as *session hijacking*. Attackers can view and manipulate everything the legitimate subject could, including changing the subject's authentication factors so that they no longer work for the legitimate user. There are two general ways access control tokens are hacked: reproduction/guessing and theft.

Token Reproduction/Guessing

Every access control token contains information unique to the authenticated subject and/or session that essentially identifies the subject to the access control management system. That identifying information *should* always be long, random, unique, and unpredictable. A trustworthy, reviewed process must be used to create unique, unpredictable session IDs, which are then used within the access control token.

As an example of a possible simple, trustworthy process, let's suppose the user's unique identity account number is combined along with a randomly generated seed value (generated anew for each session) and that the result is then hashed by an industry-accepted hashing algorithm (SHA-256, bcrypt, etc.) to create a unique and random session ID (as the process is graphically represented in Figure 6.1). The session ID information should never be repeated after the one session has expired, not even for the same user, and should expire after a preset amount of time.

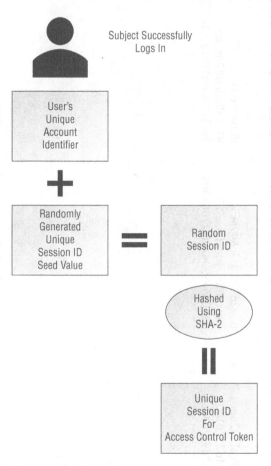

Figure 6.1: Example of a trustworthy session ID creation

Following the simple example shown in Figure 6.1, let's generate three unique user session IDs for users with sequential account numbers. Let's assume the users' account numbers are 1234, 1235, and 1236. Table 6.1 shows the randomly generated information and the resulting hashed outcome that would be used as the unique user session IDs.

NOTE In real life, both the account numbers and length of the random number would be far longer, likely generating even more secure session IDs.

Table 6.1: Example of randomly generated user session IDs

	User1	User2	User3
Account Number	1234	1235	1236
Random Number	17851561988734442051	79301558109136489	19744833112320865368
Account Number + Random Number	123417851561988734442051	123579301558109136489	123619744833112320865368
SHA-256 Hash Result	7be2b867b9c5b8f26dc457199 a5a25371351d25781007 b9fd90e0447b912042c	0432629d7bdc649ae5e 12bc76ff4a4be6fbee599 43b055e590479f1270020ff2	90043e041c3c0c510 91e699e8e0ff04ccb5 2fb522e67fa978c36e14772702b65

You can see that the resulting outcomes are unique, long, random, and unpredictable. Using a good cryptographic hash, like SHA-256, with an additional random portion ensures that any hacker viewing one session ID won't be easily able to guess another. The session ID should be time bound (i.e., expire after a specified time limit) to ensure that one stolen session ID can't be reused for the same user in another session after the first one expires. At the same time, as long as the site or service is storing the calculated values, it will be easy for it to track the user across multiple actions and transactions during the allowed session.

All the protections provided session ID are nullified if the session ID turns out to have an easy-to-see predictable pattern. If someone can easily view or guess the unique identifying information, they can easily craft an identical access control token. Access control token hackers often look for predictable patterns in what is supposed to be random and unpredictable. Hackers will authenticate to a website many times with many different identities and review the different resulting access control token information for predictable patterns. If they see a suspect predictable pattern in the cookie's supposedly unique identifying information, they will begin to construct additional cookies, slightly modifying them in different ways, and connect to the website to see if it (a) accepts the cookie, and (b) authenticates them as another valid user account. If (a) and (b) are true, the attacker has hacked their way in. There are many hacking tools (Firesheep, Burp Suite, Cookie Cadger, to name a few) that help with cookie theft, re-creation, and hacking. Then it's a matter of generating as many possible legitimate subject IDs and cookies as possible. This part can be easily scripted. If the attacker figures out the pattern, then there's nothing to stop them from harvesting the whole database. Many of the data breaches you read about in the news are really just hackers who figured out a session ID pattern and used it to dump an entire database.

Token Theft

If the attacker has the appropriate access, it's probably just easier to steal a user's legitimate access token. Most access tokens contain correctly generated randomly unique session IDs, as shown in Table 6.1, and so trying to guess them or find a repeatable pattern is *nontrivial* (i.e., very hard to impossible using known technologies and techniques in a reasonable amount of time). Access control token theft can happen locally or over the network. Locally, if an attacker has complete admin control of a user's computer or device, usually this is enough to let them access, view, steal, and/or manipulate and use the access control token.

Admin access doesn't always guarantee immediate access to an access control token. Many operating systems provide special protections to access control tokens and the processes around them, and even the highest admin access won't let a user directly access the token. But most of the time, ultimately, if an attacker has unencumbered access to a device or token, with enough time and resources, access to the access token will be gained, one way or another.

Other times, especially if the token is stored on a cryptographically protected token device, it can be difficult outside of exceptional attempts to access and steal or duplicate the access token. Instead, it would probably be easier for attackers to manipulate or reuse the token when it is being used by the legitimate user. You'll learn more about this latter type of scenario in later chapters.

Another method is to steal the access control token during its use or transmission over a network medium. In most of these instances, the attacker must inject themselves in the communication's stream between client and server, in what is known as a man-in-the-middle (MitM) attack. The MitM attacker can eavesdrop and view and/or manipulate the access control token. Network theft of access control tokens has been done for decades and is among the most common ways to hack any authentication solution, including multifactor authentication solutions.

Reproducing Token Hack Examples

As many website penetration testers can attest, at any minute on the Internet there are probably thousands, if not tens of thousands, of websites that use easily guessable session IDs. You can find them all over the place, but when I taught for Foundstone in the 2000s, most Foundstone hacking instructors used the same website to demonstrate access token attacks. It was even written into some of our instructional guides. It was a real website that a previous instructor had found that contained multiple token vulnerabilities. It was a perfect "demo" site because its control token session IDs were sequential. That fact made vulnerabilities easy to see and exploit. We never took malicious advantage of the exploit, and we told our students not to attack it. But showing them how easy it was to hack a real-world website gave our classes some increased cred.

We used the same website so much that I think most instructors must have come to believe that it was a fake site built to help us demonstrate the exploit. (I know I initially thought it was a fake site.) But one day one of my students told me they had successfully purchased several expensive pieces of equipment for free using the exploit we had taught them. He, too, thought it was a fake site and that he was "fake exploiting" it, but then the items arrived on his doorstep charged to someone else's credit card. Needless to say, we had to correct the "mistake" with the vendor and the instructors stopped using that website as a demo.

But know that everyday thousands of web penetration testers, including old, inactive pen testers (like me), are looking for signs of repeatable patterns whenever they are visiting any website. It's not anything you even think about—it becomes part of your DNA. You find yourself looking at URLs (where the session IDs are sometimes displayed) and in cookies to see if you can find guessable, repeatable patterns. Once you understand what the vulnerability is and how prevalent it is, it becomes a lifetime game of virtual bug hunting.

Upon finding a guessable session ID in a real-world website, a good and ethical hacker always reports the found bug to the owner of the website and never uses it illegally or unethically. Unfortunately, it can be difficult to impossible to inform the website owner of the problem. Many sites do not display who to contact if a problem is found. Others include information, but the sent warnings are never read by anyone. The email address they included in the website was created long ago and whoever it belonged to has long since left the company or stopped maintaining the website. Worse, I've had a few people email me back and what they say indicates that they do not understand the criticality of the bug. A few have accused me of being a criminal hacker. I'm pretty clear with them. I have never done anything illegal or unethical on a computer. I'm not going to publicly report my finding or tell anyone else. But really, if they don't fix it after a long period of time, an ethical hacker could be forgiven for publicly announcing the vulnerability so that the site's customers are aware of the problem and don't risk personal information by remaining with the site unprotected. In my 30-year-plus computer security career I have had to warn one website that I was going to go public (after over a year) if they did not fix the problem. It happens. More often, my emails to vulnerable websites end up helping the website get rid of the vulnerability, and that makes everyone safer.

Guessable session IDs are a popular exploitable bug because programmers are rarely taught how to avoid common security vulnerabilities in school or while using self-study resources. It is the rare programming instructional guide that covers security development life cycle (SDL) educational topics. So, it is very common for new programmers, when designing a system involving authentication and access control tokens, to flub the process that generates session ID numbers. Unless they have been trained about the importance of making authentication and access control tokens random and unpredictable, they usually don't realize how easy they are to exploit.

Creating random, unique, and unguessable session IDs has become a part of the Open Web Application Security Project (OWASP) Top 10 list (`www.owasp.org/images/7/72/OWASP_Top_10-2017_%28en%29.pdf.pdf`). OWASP is a not-for-profit group dedicated to helping web programmers program more securely. The OWASP Top 10 list is considered one of the top guides of its kind and has become a global de facto standard. OWASP explains poor session IDs and how to defend against them in its *A2:2017: Broken Authentication* tranche. In particular, OWASP recommends the following to prevent insecure session IDs: "Use a server-side, secure, built-in session manager that generates a new random session ID with high entropy after login. Session IDs should not be in the URL, be securely stored and invalidated after logout, idle, and absolute timeouts."

That's the long way of saying that you should make sure that your session IDs are unique and unguessable. When hackers can guess or predict session IDs, the IDs can usually be exploited to further compromise the website or its users. Sometimes the patterns are so easy to see that they just stick out like a sore thumb. This is usually the case when an attacker can see sequential patterns that increment just a single number or letter at a time (as shown in Figure 6.2). In this first example of insecure session IDs, the session IDs are located in the URL, where they are easier to examine and are identical except for the last digit. It doesn't get any easier to spot the vulnerability than that.

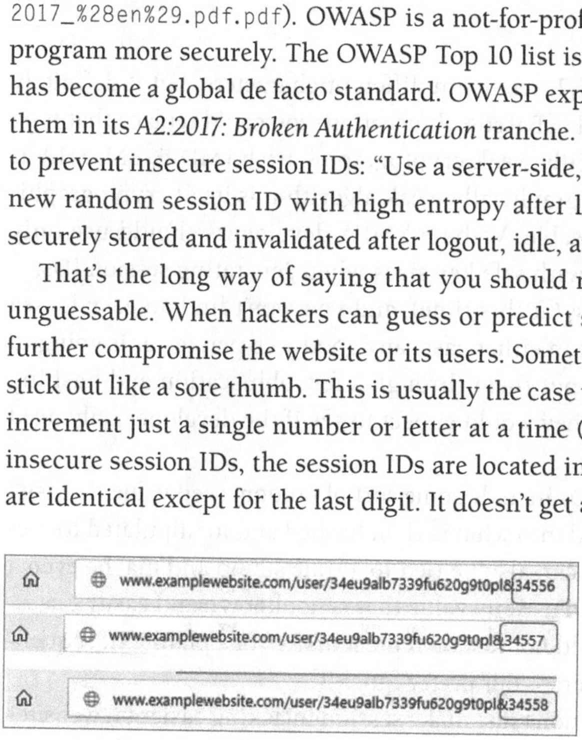

Figure 6.2: Example of sequentially incrementing session IDs located in a URL

Although many real-world examples of insecure session IDs are as simple as that, most of the predictable patterns are a bit harder to see but nevertheless not that difficult to see once you know what you're looking for. For example, many sites create session IDs based solely on the user's account number (without a randomly generated portion added), which is then weakly obfuscated or hashed. For example, let's suppose that three users have account numbers 1234, 1235, and 1236, respectively. Many sites will convert the user's account numbers into a Base64 (en.wikipedia.org/wiki/Base64) representation or simply hash the account number. Table 6.2 shows the user's plaintext account numbers converted into weakly secure Base64 and SHA-256 representations.

Table 6.2: Example of weakly generated user session IDs

	User1	User2	User3
Account Number	1234	1235	1236
Base64 representation	MTIzNA==	MTIzNQ==	MTIzNg==
SHA-256 representation	03ac674216f3e15c761 ee1a5e255f0679536 23c8b388b4459e13f97 8d7c846f4	310ced37200b1a0dae 25edb263fe52c491 f6e467268acab0ffec 06666e2ed959	7b0838c2af7e6b1f3fe 5a49c32dd459d997a 931cee349ca6869f3 c17cc838394

The Base64 conversion, you can see in Table 6.2, results in different characters, but it definitely has an easy-to-discern, repeatable pattern. Instead of Base64 obfuscation, you could replace that type of vulnerability to a lesser extent with any provenly weak cryptographic hash (MD-5, LM, SHA-1, etc.). Any modifier routine that includes a cryptographically weak algorithm is itself cryptographically weak, and potentially hackable, and guessable. Web and MFA developers should use only industry-accepted safe and secure cryptography with safe key sizes when generating session IDs.

The SHA-256 hash is cryptographically strong (at this time), and you won't find an easy-to-see pattern just by examining the hashed output. But in either case, any good web pen tester is going to take known account numbers or logon IDs and put them through a few obfuscation and hashing routines to see if what comes out matches what they would expect to see if the developer only used a conversion or hash routine as the session ID.

For good protection, it is critical that session IDs include some sort of random seed value that isn't easily predictable and have that component added into what is then hashed and manipulated to create the final outcome. Perhaps the final outcome can also be tied to a time stamp and maybe even a user's previously registered device. Developers can use any value that is not known and easily guessable by an attacker. But the hashed outcome should not just be representative of a plaintext, sequentially updated number. Hackers figure those schemes out pretty quickly.

It's important to note that insecure session IDs don't just make session hijacking easier on websites and services. Anywhere a session ID is used, including in an MFA solution, they need to be securely generated. A weakly generated session ID can bring down an otherwise solid MFA solution.

Network Session Hijacking Techniques and Examples

As I shared earlier, it's often easier to steal the legitimately issued access control token than it is to try to reproduce or guess it. Tokens can be stolen and reused locally or from over a network. Session hijacking over a network is a popular attack against MFA solutions and one that we will explore in more detail here.

Network session hijacking requires that the attacker intercept the access control token somewhere between the client and server. In the earlier days of networking, most networks used shared network media known as Ethernet. Ethernet networks can be wired or wireless. On a pure Ethernet network (no switching), any participating network node can listen to the traffic sent between any others on the same local network. Normally, an Ethernet node simply ignores or discards any packet on the same shared network that doesn't directly involve it (or that isn't a broadcast) because it doesn't involve them. But eavesdropping Ethernet devices, malicious or otherwise, don't discard that information. Instead, they read every packet that passes by their interface. So, in the early days, without any additional network security protections, on a pure Ethernet network it was easy for any participating network node to listen to and even maliciously manipulate other nodes' network traffic.

Firesheep

For at least two decades, the online world has been full of legitimate and malicious tools that will "listen" to other node's traffic. If that traffic contained an unprotected access control token from another node, as was often the case, the malicious listener could intercept and copy it. There were and are dozens of hacking tools that focused on stealing other people's access control tokens off shared media networks.

One of the most popular tools, focusing mostly on website cookies, was Firesheep (en.wikipedia .org/wiki/Firesheep). Released in late 2010, it was a browser extension program that could be installed on a popular Internet browser named Mozilla Firefox. It took the world by storm because it showed how easy access token theft was.

To use Firesheep, you enabled it within the Firefox program and it would immediately listen for and collect as many unprotected access control tokens as it could. Then all you had to do was double-click one of the collected tokens, as represented in the program, and it would immediately log you in as the person it was collected from. It was that simple.

It was stunning to see if you were not already aware of how easy access token theft was to accomplish. Many pen testers would enter coffeeshops, airports, and other areas where lots of people were using shared wireless public networks, and steal as many access control tokens as was possible. It was a great way to wow your friends and make them think you were some great uber hacker. The technique was frequently used by corporate security employees to show senior management how easy network session hijacking was to accomplish. It dropped jaws and opened budgets.

Two of the key requirements for Firesheep, and other tools like it, to be successful were (a) the tool had to be able to sniff on shared media Ethernet networks with other people connected to websites that used cookies, and (b) the access control tokens had to be transmitted over an unprotected, sniffable network connection (i.e., HTTP, not HTTPS). Eventually, largely due to the success of Firesheep and other similar hacking tools, shared media networks like Ethernet quickly evolved to nonshared, switched Ethernet networks, and most websites eventually switched to HTTPS (vs. HTTP) network connections, which prevented the easy access control eavesdropping. Within a few years of Firesheep's release, decades of easy network eavesdropping had almost disappeared. It was a victim of its own success. There are still lots of network session hijacking tools (Burp, Cookiesnatcher, Paros, WebScarab, etc.), but the attacker has to first find a way to "inject" themselves into the now default private communications between a client and a server. No longer do lots of shared network media networks rule the wires and airwaves.

MitM Attacks

Normally MitM is done by the attacker either injecting themselves into an already existing network connection between the client and server or tricking either the client or server into accidentally connecting to an attacker node first. This can be done in dozens of ways to get the same outcome. Then, unbeknownst to the client or the server, the attacker's node acts as a proxy, sitting between them (as shown in Figure 6.3). The proxy will forward all commands and content originating from the client and the server to the other. And anything it proxies, it can record and/or manipulate. Neither the client or the server is generally aware that there is an intermediate proxy intercepting or eavesdropping on the traffic. To the client, it appears as if it is communicating directly to the server, and vice versa. MitM attacks can be accomplished in a bunch of different ways, although they tend to vary based on whether the attacker is on the same local network as either the client or the server or operating on a different network, such as over the Internet.

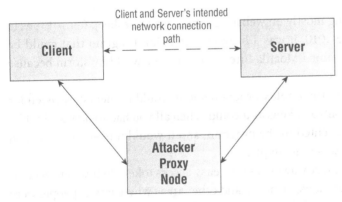

Figure 6.3: Basic attacker proxy setup

ARP Poisoning

MitM attacks can be accomplished on a local area network (LAN) in a variety of ways, including an Address Resolution Protocol (ARP) "poisoning attack." ARP is used to convert higher-layer Internet

Protocol (IP) addresses (e.g., 192.168.1.10) to their lower-layer Media Access Control (MAC) addresses (e.g., 9C-B6-D0-C7-F3-C8), which are ultimately used to transmit network information between nodes on a local area network. When a computer on the local network needs to know where another computer on the local network is, it will issue an ARP broadcast, something akin to asking, "Where is 192.168.1.10?" And the computer with the 192.168.1.10 IP address will get the broadcast (sent to all nodes) and respond, "I'm 192.168.1.10 and I'm at 9C-B6-D0-C7-F3-C8." This is the way two networked devices on a local network send and receive traffic to each other.

In an ARP poisoning attack, the attacker's device maliciously answers on behalf of the legitimate computer using its own MAC address instead. If the ARP poisoner's ARP response is received ahead of the legitimate ARP response, the victim will take the fraudulent ARP response as legitimate and start communicating with the attacker's node instead. The ARP poisoning machine will attempt to fake out both the client and server into connecting to it instead of to a legitimate node. Dozens of hacking tools are out there that make ARP poisoning as easy as clicking a button within a tool made for such a purpose.

> **NOTE** Many layer 2 switches contain anti-ARP poisoning capabilities, such as storing the more common legitimate MAC addresses for each IP address in a special table and noting if the MAC address suddenly changes for a particular IP address. Each anti-ARP poisoning feature works and can cause additional problems with varying levels of success and failure.

Proxy Attacks

In attacks from different networks or over the Internet, the MitM attacker fakes out a victim by using a range of other tricks, including fraudulent routing, DNS, email, or other naming tricks. If a client or server relies on a service or human action to get routed to the other side, which is usually the case, there is a chance that intermediate reliance can be abused to create an MitM proxy attack.

A common MitM method is to send a victim an email pretending to be from one of the user's legitimate, beloved services that they frequently interact with. The email is formatted to look like it is arriving from the legitimate service with a potentially legitimate-looking request that involves the user clicking on an embedded malicious link, which takes them to the attacker's malicious proxy service instead.

An MitM proxy attacker doesn't care how the victim is authenticating. Again, it can be any method. They just want to capture and reuse the resulting access control token after the victim's successful authentication. Here are the basic steps of this type of MitM proxy network session hijacking attack:

1. Attacker convinces victim to visit rogue (usually a name-alike) website, which proxies input to real website.
2. Real website, through proxy, prompts victim to put in logon credentials, which can include an MFA solution.

3. Victim puts in required credentials, which bad guy relays to real website.
4. Attacker intercepts victim's resulting access control token coming from real website.
5. Attacker logs into real website as the victim.
6. Attacker takes control over user's account.
7. Attacker changes anything user could use to take back control.

There are five primary ways to pull off an MitM proxy attack, each with increasing levels of attacker sophistication:

- Level 1—Look-alike URL and website (without TLS)
- Level 2—Same as the previous Level, but with a trusted digital TLS certificate tied to the look-alike DNS domain
- Level 3—Same as Level 1, but with DNS spoofing of a legitimate domain (without TLS)
- Level 4—Same as Level 3, but with trusted (but fraudulent) TLS digital certificate tied to a legitimate domain
- Level 5—Same as Level 4, but with a stolen/duplicated, legitimate, trusted TLS digital certificate and private key tied to a legitimate domain name

NOTE The "trusted" in trusted digital certificate means that the user's device, operating system, browser, or application automatically "trusts" the certification authority (CA) that issued it. A digital certificate from an untrusted CA will usually create a warning message indicating that the CA that issued the certificate is not trusted and will prompt the user to confirm or deny the trust of the CA and/or the digital certificate. Each warning a user has to read and decide on defeats a certain percentage of possible attacks, so hackers like to obtain and use trusted digital certificates so that the trust warning message is never displayed. Most operating systems and browsers have predefined lists of CAs they trust or don't trust, and the user can usually add their own as they need or come across them.

The first MitM proxy method, Level 1, is simply tricking a user into clicking on a look-alike URL that directs them to a look-alike domain and website. The fake website is not hosted and does not appear as hosted at the legitimate domain name. With Level 2, a MitM proxy attack, an attacker also gets a valid, trusted digital certificate for the rogue, look-alike domain. Currently, these are the most popular type of MitM proxy attacks—over 70 percent of rogue websites have valid, trusted digital certificates.

It can be difficult for even good CAs to police and determine which TLS certificates they issue are for legitimate domains with good intentions and which are not. Many CAs don't even try and even publicize that fact. If you want a TLS certificate for your server and domain name you can have it, even if it's fairly obvious to anyone who reads the name what is likely going on. Hackers appreciate the blind eye.

NOTE The most widely trusted CAs do at least some small amount of checking for malicious intent before issuing a digital certificate, although what they do to verify the legitimacy and intent of a particular domain varies greatly by CA. But the good ones try to stop the easy-to-spot rogue domain names that appear to be attempting to spoof well-known, legitimate domains.

Today, most scammers use the Level 2 method in their phishing scams. With either Level 1 or Level 2 attacks, unless the user realizes they are connecting to a fake website or their authentication solution doesn't mitigate them, it's easy to fool unsuspecting users. These types of MitM attacks can be defeated by the user being aware of what the legitimate URL is and ensuring that they never get tricked. But as we know, humans can be socially engineered into clicking on the wrong links. Far more superior is automatically enforcing the use of site-specific authentication credentials, as FIDO does, to prevent these types of MitM attacks.

With the Level 3 MitM proxy method, the attacker somehow redirects the victim to a look-alike website, which appears to the victim's device or software as hosted at the legitimate domain (or is actually hosted at the legitimate domain but without a valid, trusted TLS certificate involved). The attacker can poison DNS so that the victim's software is redirected to the fake website even when the user types in or clicks on the legitimate name. For example, the user types in or clicks www .bankofamerica.com and it redirects them to a fake Bank of America website that appears to the victim's software to be hosted at www.bankofamerica.com even when it is hosted elsewhere. DNS poisoning attacks used to be more popular over a decade ago, but they have significantly diminished in popularity as various anti-DNS poisoning techniques have been widely adopted. Still, there are various ways to accomplish DNS poisoning and these attacks do still occur.

Attackers sometimes steal the legitimate site's domain name from the legitimate DNS domain owner and use it to redirect victims to their fake website now hosted under the legitimate website's domain name. This does happen and is covered in more detail in Chapter 18, "DNS Hijacking."

The Level 4 MitM proxy attack method involves a fake website that appears hosted at the legitimate domain and has what appears to be a legitimate TLS digital certificate. The TLS digital certificate is not the same as the legitimate site's real TLS certificate, but nevertheless it is tied to the real website's legitimate domain. Usually this is accomplished by a trusted CA being compromised and then being used to issue fraudulent but trusted digital certificates. This sort of attack first became big news in 2011 with the compromise of DigiNotar (www.computerweekly.com/news/2240105500/ DigiNotar-digital-certificate-fraud-could-affect-millions-of-users-says-SecurEnvoy).

A newer defense called *certificate transparency* and another older defense known as *channel binding* both try to mitigate Level 4 attacks by comparing the previously stored and verified digital fingerprint (hash) of the legitimate site's known and trusted TLS digital certificate with the currently provided digital certificate that a user (or more realistically, the software on their behalf) is interacting with during a current connection.

Certificate transparency was created by Google in 2013, as RFC 6962 (tools.ietf.org/html/ rfc6962), and is becoming more widely adopted as time goes on. With certificate transparency, legitimate sites register the digital fingerprint of their legitimate TLS digital certificates in publicly accessible, trusted certificate transparency logs—for example, with logs maintained by Google or some other well-trusted CAs. The idea is that if someone submits an additional TLS digital certificate for an already registered domain—with an already existing, valid, trusted, not-expired digital certificate—the duplicate registration would be quickly noticed and evaluated.

Initially, I didn't like the idea of certificate transparency, and I even wrote a few articles against it. To me, and others, it was re-creating the protection we had with already existing certificate revocation lists (CRLs) that are already widely used and deployed by most CAs. But over time I've come to appreciate one of certificate transparency's main arguments: that the existing CRL protection was not working well or timely enough. Although certificate transparency has its own issues (such as requiring legitimate websites to register their valid TLS digital fingerprints in one or more public logs), it has proven itself by helping protect end users against rogue domains and certificates used in Level 4 attacks.

For more information on certificate transparency, see

- `www.certificate-transparency.org`
- `en.wikipedia.org/wiki/Certificate_Transparency`
- `searchsecurity.techtarget.com/news/4500253976/Certificate-Transparency-catches-bad-digital-certificates-from-Symantec`

Channel binding, RFCs 5056 (`tools.ietf.org/html/rfc5056`) and 5929 (`tools.ietf.org/html/rfc5929`), also uses digital fingerprint comparisons of digital certificates, like certificate transparency, but in a distinctly different way. Certificate transparency involves centralized databases, which everyone else can connect to and use. Channel binding, on the other hand, is done locally on a per device, OS, application, or authentication solution basis and uses distinctly different methods. Certificate transparency logs can contain millions of digital certificate fingerprints. Local channel binding databases often just store the sites a user or their authentication solution have intentionally decided to trust, store, and use specifically with channel binding.

NOTE There are three types of channel binding, but I'm only covering the most relevant type known as *tls-server-end-point*.

Authentication solutions that support channel binding can have it: 1) enabled by default, 2) turned off by default but recommended, or 3) simply offered as a possible option but not really recommended. For example, FIDO has channel binding enabled by default in their specification, although it is not enabled in most implementations (i.e., by popular browser vendors) because of some false-positive use case scenarios and current disagreement by the big browser venders on the ultimate solution.

NOTE There are other similar technologies such as Online Certificate Status Protocol (OCSP) stapling, trust anchors, and key pinning that attempted to do similar things to certificate transparency and channel binding. However, they never caught on as broadly, likely because they did not have the backing of Google, which controls much of the Internet and protocols these days.

Level 5 MitM proxy attacks are the most sophisticated and difficult to detect. Either the attacker has been able to access the legitimate site's real digital certificate and copied it in its entirety, including the private key, or they have otherwise somehow been able to duplicate it. These types of attacks are extremely rare. I've not heard of one being used to fake a website (although I do know of several stolen or fraudulently duplicated digital certificates used to sign trojan malware).

These types of attacks, if they occurred, would be hard to prevent. The user wouldn't likely notice anything is wrong since the website is a look-alike and is appearing to be at the correct domain with the legitimate digital certificate. Certificate transparency and channel binding would not prevent the attack because both the original and copied/duplicated digital certificates would have the same digital fingerprint.

All five levels of MitM attacks could be mitigated by a defense known as *token binding*, RFC 8471 (tools.ietf.org/html/rfc8471), introduced in late 2018. Token binding involves tying a client's long-lived authentication token to the authentication instance registered or located on both the client and the legitimate website or service. Here's how it works: A user's authentication solution generates a unique public/private key pair for each website, providing the public key to the website and proving possession of the corresponding private key, on every future TLS connection to the server. The pre-registration of the token to the site and of the site to the token is a very difficult hurdle for attackers to overcome—the preregistration of shared secrets allows only the legitimate site and token to successfully negotiate authentication. A few authentication standards, like FIDO, support token binding (fidoalliance.org/fido-technotes-channel-binding-and-fido), but like channel binding, it is not enabled by default in most use case scenarios for the same reasons.

Kevin Mitnick MFA Bypass Attack Demo

My friend and coworker Kevin Mitnick, the world's most infamous hacker and KnowBe4's Chief Hacking Officer, demoed this exact type of attack against MFA as used on a very popular website. You can see a video of Kevin demonstrating this attack method, which bypasses MFA authentication like it doesn't even care, at the following site: blog.knowbe4.com/heads-up-new-exploit-hacks-linkedin-2-factor-auth.-see-this-kevin-mitnick-video (a screenshot is shown in Figure 6.4). This demo is important to understanding this type of attack—so important that if you haven't already watched it, you should stop reading right now and do so.

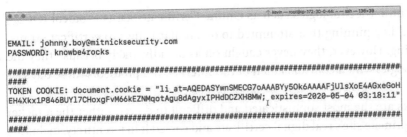

Figure 6.4: Kevin Mitnick demo getting around a common MFA solution involving a popular website and stealing the access control token cookie

In summary, here's what Kevin did in his demo:

1. Kevin set up fake lookalike/sound-alike website that was really an evil proxy.
2. Using an email containing a fraudulent URL, he tricked "the victim" into visiting the evil proxy website.
3. Victim typed in credentials, which were proxied, now pretending to be the legitimate customer, presented to legitimate website.
4. Legitimate website sent back legitimate session token, which Kevin then stole and replayed to take over victim's session.

NOTE   Kevin used Evilginx (`breakdev.org/evilginx-advanced-phishing-with-two-factor-authentication-bypass`). It's a great network session hijacking tool. But there are dozens of hacking tools you can use to accomplish the same thing.

This is just one example hack out of the dozens, if not hundreds, of ways to do network session hijacking, even if MFA is involved. When Kevin originally demoed this attack in May 2018, many reviewers thought his attack was due to a flaw in the website (i.e., LinkedIn) or to a flaw in the MFA solution. They wanted to know when Microsoft (LinkedIn's parent company) was going to fix its website or when Kevin was going to file the CVE (Common Vulnerabilities and Exposures) paperwork notifying the world of his brand-new hack.

Kevin and I laughed because we both knew that even though it was another great example of Kevin's demos, what he did has been done for decades, and it wasn't due to a flaw in the site or the MFA solution. The actual hack was just due to the inherent disconnect between the successful authentication and the resulting access control token and tricking an end-user. There were no bugs. This was one of those many unfortunate "as-designed" issues. And these aren't just theoretical attacks. They occur all the time in real life.

Accidental Token Leak

Sometimes people don't realize how important session token information is and inadvertently leak it to others. It happens all the time when friends send URL links to each other with "You've got to check this out!" invitations. For example, the original person copies and forwards a link to a video they are watching, not realizing the link contains their unique session ID. When the other people paste the link into their browser, they may not realize that they are actually authenticating or being seen by that host system, as the original user. But people like me look for it and do realize what has happened.

But sometimes even knowledgeable hackers can make mistakes. In 2019, a professional penetration tester sent a link (arstechnica.com/information-technology/2019/12/hackerone-breach-lets-outside-hacker-read-customers-private-bug-reports) to other testers on one of the world's most popular vulnerability testing and reporting sites, not realizing that he accidentally included his session token. The receivers could access a larger confidential database. Accidental session ID leaking can happen when shared services which display URLs accidentally forget to stripe out the identifying information, such as is discussed here: community.spiceworks.com/topic/2265465-alienvault-otx-gives-away-zoom-sharefile-and-other-urls. In the latter example, the URLs the author is discussing link to unauthenticated sessions, but those URLs he is referencing could contain legitimate authenticated token information as well, since this particular web service just stores and lists all involved URLs (and does not strip any information). This sort of issue can be mitigated by websites/services using server-side tokens as OWASP recommended earlier.

Access Control Token Attack Defenses

There are not many, if any, safeguards an end user can use to prevent the generation of insecure access control tokens. At the most, buyers should ensure that any MFA solutions they choose include the defenses we'll explore in this section. MFA developers can implement the following defenses to prevent attackers from guessing, reproducing, and stealing access control tokens.

Generate Random, Unguessable Session IDs

The best and simplest defense is to generate truly random and unguessable session IDs. Always include some other randomly generated information that an attacker could not otherwise obtain or guess. Use a random generator process that is truly random (don't build your own or rely on the "random" functions included with most programming or scripting languages that have not been tested and certified as truly random). If you are unsure how to create truly unique or random session IDs, connect with someone who has the appropriate knowledge and experience. Too many developers get this part wrong, and it can be embarrassing if you have to admit this sophomore mistake in a public advisory about the error.

Use Industry-Accepted Cryptography and Key Sizes

If cryptography is involved, use industry-accepted cryptography and key sizes. Don't try to make your own. Many developers who have taken a cryptography course or two think they can create a new cryptography solution that is uncrackable. Very few of them can. Strong cryptography is much more difficult than it seems, and only a few dozen people in the world at any given time are any good at it. Unfortunately, tens of thousands of people think they can design a very strong cipher. Even the very best cryptographers get it wrong.

As an example, the National Institute of Standards and Technology (NIST) received 82 newly proposed quantum-resistant cryptography candidates during round 1 of its recent post–quantum cipher contest (`csrc.nist.gov/CSRC/media/Projects/Post-Quantum-Cryptography/documents/call-for-proposals-final-dec-2016.pdf`). Most of these submissions came from highly respected, experienced cryptographers, many with PhDs in cryptography. Of those original 82 submissions, only 26 were selected to compete in the next round. Although there were other disqualifications and consolidations, most of the rejections occurred because of obvious cryptographic security flaws that others easily discovered. Of the 26 remaining ciphers, observers are still finding errors. Some very promising candidates have turned out to have huge cryptographic flaws that, had they been prematurely implemented, would have caused huge security issues.

And this is the result from experienced cryptography professors and practitioners. Good cryptography takes many years and a ton of testing to prove. If cryptography isn't your day job, don't even think about making your own cryptography. If cryptography *is* your day job, you're likely not going around trying to invent your own cryptography when many other great candidates already exist and are trusted as secure around the world. Don't try to prove how smart you are. Just use industry-accepted cryptography and key sizes.

For bonus points, code your application in such a way that the cryptography used is easily changed out (crypto-agile) as new cryptography ciphers and schemes become available as recommended replacements. Make it so easy that even your customers can easily upgrade and replace them without having to do a complete installation or replacement. Don't hard-code the cryptography in a way that is not easily replaceable or upgradeable.

NOTE Quantum computers are expected to soon break most traditional forms of public key cryptography and weaken by half the remaining symmetric ciphers, hashes, and random number generators. It is likely that, by 2022 or soon thereafter, we will be upgrading our asymmetric ciphers and digital signatures to newer, quantum-resistant cryptography. If you are a developer, help make the world's move to quantum-resistant ciphers and schemes easier for everyone. For more information, consider reading my book on the coming quantum crypto break, *Cryptography Apocalypse* (Wiley, 2019).

Developers Should Follow Secure Coding Practices

You would be surprised by how all security solutions contain bugs and the numbers of bugs in each. All developers, especially MFA solution creators, should learn and aim to use security development life cycle (SDL) tools and techniques. SDL is a process that builds in security from the very beginning of any programming process or project. Even before the first line of code is written, all the people involved in the project are using threat modeling to evaluate all the different ways the code can be attacked and abused, and then striving to mitigate the most likely and significant attacks.

One of the earliest and biggest SDL proponents were employees of Microsoft, and soon thereafter, Microsoft itself. No other company shares as much information about secure coding practices and tools than Microsoft. If you are a developer and you don't already master SDL practices, I beg you to learn as much as you can about SDL concepts, processes, and tools. You can't do any better in starting your journey than to visit Microsoft's SDL website: www.microsoft.com/en-us/securityengineering/sdl. Web developers, specifically, should also check out anything that the OWASP Foundation offers: www.owasp.org/index.php/Main_Page.

Use Secure Transmission Channels

Any time the access control token is transmitted, it should only be done over secure channels. Internally, on the local OS or device, this means the access control token should be protected by the OS or device against easy eavesdropping. More importantly, this applies to any time the token is transmitted over an otherwise unprotected transmission network channel. At the very least, the network channel should be protected by industry-accepted cryptography and key sizes. HTTPS using TLS is fine as long as it is an acceptable version and does not contain known vulnerabilities. The participating client and server nodes should be authenticated and trusted, as well as any infrastructure supporting the authentication or authorization actions.

Include Timeout Protections

All access control tokens should come with server-side-enforced expirations, after which the issued session token should no longer be valid. Token validity dates can range from minutes to days—the idea is that you want to prevent theft and replay of one token to be a threat forever.

Tie the Token to Specific Devices or Sites

The most effective defense against token theft is to tie all access control tokens to previously registered devices. That way, if an attacker steals it they cannot reuse it on another nonregistered device or new location. At the very least, if an access token is used on a new device or location, the user should be prompted for additional authentication to ensure that the legitimate user is using the access control token.

This is a good time to bring up the FIDO Alliance's (fidoalliance.org) method of tying tokens to sites, and vice versa. As explained here (fidoalliance.org/how-fido-works), the FIDO registration process starts with the user beginning registration on the intended FIDO-enabled website as they would any site requiring authentication. The site's registration web page is tied to a FIDO API, which hooks to a FIDO server. The website queries the user's connected FIDO-compliant browser or application to see if the user has registered a FIDO authenticator that complies with the site's required authentication policies (e.g., requiring user verification in order to provide strong 2FA in a single step). If one is found, the website prompts the user to select the FIDO authenticator they want to use for this website registration instance. When the user selects the FIDO authenticator they want to use, the website asks the FIDO server for a challenge (a large random number), and it sends it to the user's FIDO authenticator along with its unique FIDO AppID/RP ID and other information. The FIDO authenticator prompts the user to provide a gesture to the authenticator (pushing a button, using a biometric attribute, etc.) and the authenticator creates a unique private/public key pair registered for the website or application by its DNS domain name. The key pair is unique for the website's domain name or application developer, the user's account name, and FIDO authenticator binding.

> **NOTE** The private/public key pair is not a traditional x.509 digital certificate because a trusted third party (i.e., the CA) is not needed.

The public key is sent to the website along with the FIDO authenticator's response to the challenge. If the challenge is successfully verified by the website, the user's FIDO authenticator instance is registered along with the related public key. The private key and any other authentication information, such as a biometric attribute, never leaves the FIDO authenticator. Each website gets a unique public key for each registered user account and FIDO authenticator. Each user account and authenticator will use a different key pair with each website. The combination of the authenticator as a possession factor plus the biometric or a PIN leads to MFA in a single step.

When the user starts to log on to a FIDO-enabled website they have previously registered with, the site will request and send a FIDO challenge to the user's FIDO-enabled browser or application, which passes it along to the FIDO authenticator. The user must provide a gesture to unlock the related private key, which signs the challenge and sends it back to the FIDO website. The website verifies the signed response using the FIDO authenticator's public key instance and, if verified, allows the user's logon to proceed.

When the user connects to what they think is their intended website, the FIDO authenticator can only be involved if the DNS domain name of the site is the one that was previously registered with the FIDO authenticator. If the domain name is not previously registered—say, because the user is accidentally connecting to a malicious MitM proxy website—the FIDO authenticator will read the proxy site's domain name and ignore it because it was not previously registered. Additionally, the authenticator will always automatically use the authentication key (FIDO credential) related to the specific website—and the machine does a better job in distinguishing look-alike URLs than humans. This is effective protection against many types of MitM attacks. There is still a chance an MitM proxy site could get the user to register with their fake site, and if they successfully accomplish it, that's not good. But it still would not allow the MitM site to interact with the legitimate website.

Optionally, FIDO channel and/or token binding can be enabled and used to prevent the more advanced versions of the MitM proxy attacks discussed here, if they are supported by the website and FIDO browser or application (which unfortunately most of the time is not true). Authentication solutions, like FIDO, requiring site and/or authenticator preregistration make many MitM attacks significantly harder to accomplish. Other authentication solutions use similar preregistration requirements, but FIDO, as a public, open consortium and set of protocols, is steadily gaining in popularity.

Summary

In this chapter, we discussed access control token tricks to get around MFA solutions. A common theme to all these access control token attacks is that the attacker does not care what type of authentication you use. The user could have used simple logon names and passwords or some seven-factor MFA scheme that seems impossible to fool. The session hijack attacker doesn't care; they just re-create or steal the resulting access control token after the victim successfully logs on. MFA solution developers should ensure that their session IDs are hard to predict and steal. Chapter 7, "Endpoint Attacks" will cover endpoint attacks.

7

Endpoint Attacks

In this chapter, we'll explore endpoint attacks. If an attacker has control over your computing device, it is often "game over," but MFA developers and end users can take many proactive steps to minimize risk from these types of attacks.

Endpoint Attack Risks

There has always been this general guiding security dogma that if an attacker has complete control over your endpoint there is nothing you can do to stop them from doing something malicious. No doubt every computer security professional innately knows this early on, even without being officially taught it, just because it seems like the most universal, plausible, commonsense fact anyone can understand in this field of study. Still, it never hurts to communicate and educate.

If a person or a team with unauthorized intent and with unlimited resources has uncontrolled physical or logical access to a device and the data that it contains, it would be the rare device and/or protection control that would prevent it from being compromised. Even the best controls with the best intentions will fall. It's just a matter of time. This is not to say that protecting against these types of attacks is worthless and should not be done. No, to the contrary. Computer security isn't binary, and if an attacker (or most attackers) can be prevented from doing easy compromises for a reasonable period of time, even if they have complete control of a device, that is a goal we should work toward. Don't let perfection be the enemy of doing something. Still, it's a long-standing maxim that if an attacker has complete control of a system, physical or logical, it's pretty difficult to defend against, especially in the long run.

In early 2000, Microsoft published an informal codification of this security canon as part of its 10 Immutable Laws of Security (blogs.technet.microsoft.com/seanearp/2007/03/25/immutable-laws-of-security). The 10 Immutable Laws are as follows:

Law #1: If a bad guy can persuade you to run his program on your computer, it's not your computer anymore.

Law #2: If a bad guy can alter the operating system on your computer, it's not your computer anymore.

Law #3: If a bad guy has unrestricted physical access to your computer, it's not your computer anymore.

Law #4: If you allow a bad guy to upload programs to your website, it's not your website anymore.

Law #5: Weak passwords trump strong security.

Law #6: A computer is only as secure as the administrator is trustworthy.

Law #7: Encrypted data is only as secure as the decryption key.

Law #8: An out-of-date virus scanner is only marginally better than no virus scanner at all.

Law #9: Absolute anonymity isn't practical, in real life or on the web.

Law #10: Technology is not a panacea.

The first four "laws" are essentially (redundantly) stating that if a malicious person can control your software or device, then they can do really bad things. And this is true. Any trusted device that is in a malicious person's hands or that is running malicious code is no longer trusted. If an attacker can modify an operating system, it's no longer the creator's operating system; it's the attacker's version. They can do anything that the software and device is capable of. The risk of malicious compromise or physical access is any attack, possibly only limited by the ability of the device and software to operationally accomplish it.

NOTE   Conversely, many security defenders mistakenly oversimplify malware risks when they say or write that an attacker "can do anything!" when the attacker controls the endpoint. That's almost true, but the attacker's maliciousness is limited to the type of access they have and what the software and device is logically and physically capable of doing. For example, decades ago some early virus writers making spurious claims said they had written malware that could "slam" the read/write heads of hard drives against the hard drive's central spindle, over and over, until the heads flew apart, irreversibly physically damaging the drives. I laughed when I heard this and taunted them because I knew that all hard drive read/write heads were physically incapable of landing against their central spindles. The physical, mechanical, metal components of a hard drive prevent it. And no amount of "genius" malware coding was going to get around a physical limitation. Sometimes unskilled, immature attackers make impossible, overreaching, salacious claims to induce additional panic in unknowledgeable readers of their diatribes.

What many people forget is that although an attacker having physical access or code control over an endpoint is not a good thing, it doesn't have to be easy for the attacker. It's not always guaranteed that an attacker having that sort of control will absolutely bypass all security defenses. In fact, many computer security defenses, like storage encryption, firmware-level hypervisors, and special memory protections, are specifically built to inherently fight attackers who gain physical or code-level access to a device. Many controls are specifically built to stop attackers who have complete control of a device but who don't have authorized access. While it's still true that an attacker having control of an endpoint is a huge risk to the device, its data, and any of its transactions, that doesn't mean the device and the involved software can't be designed to prevent, slow down, and mitigate the success of such attacks. Every MFA solution should be designed and built to withstand easy endpoint compromise attacks.

General Endpoint Attacks

Endpoint attacks can be broken down into two main categories of compromises: programming attacks and physical access.

Programming Attacks

Programming attacks are code-level assaults where the attacker exploits a software or hardware vulnerability to gain unauthorized logical access to the device and/or involved software. They are very popular. Programming attacks usually happen because the end user is tricked into running some sort of trojan horse malware program or because a hacker remotely executes a programming attack, such as a buffer overflow, against the user's active and running device, programs, or services. In general, an attacker or malware program that exploits a programming bug gains the same level of security access that the program or user running it has. If the program is running as part of the operating system or has system-level access, exploiting the program gives the attacker or malware program system-level access to the operating system and device. And if the hacker or malware program exploits a program running in user mode, the attacker or malware program ends up with the same set of privileges and permissions as the currently logged-in user.

In most cases, attackers want to get elevated (i.e., admin) access to the exploited device/software to get more complete control. Getting elevated access allows an attacker to more easily accomplish current and further future actions, but it isn't always immediately gained or needed. Sometimes, lower-level, user-mode access control is enough for the hacker or malware program to accomplish all the required maliciousness. It is also very common for an attacker or their malware creation to initially gain only user-mode access but then use that level of access along with an additional exploit to gain higher elevated access (using what is called a *privilege escalation exploit*).

Physical Access Attacks

Physical access attacks are when an attacker has local, physical possession and control of a device (or network transmission media). It is not in the authorized user's physical possession and control, but in the hacker's. An attacker can use their physical possession of a device to deploy both physical and logical attacks against it. The most simple, unsophisticated form is an attacker or thief stealing or physical disabling or destroying an involved device. That is a denial-of-service event to the legitimate owner or users. On the other end of the spectrum are physical attacks that use sophisticated machinery to bypass physical controls, such as using an electron microscope to figure out secrets by viewing them at the molecular level. An intermediate-level physical attack example might be using a boot disk or removable media drive to boot an alternate operating system to directly access a protected disk, or using a local software hacker tool to disable or change a password that would be more difficult to do when the operating system was fully booted. Another physical attack could be a bit-level disk scan against a protected hard drive or memory scan against an encryption-protected removable USB key, looking for plaintext secret key copies accidentally made and left behind outside of the secure spaces. Physical attacks will be covered in Chapter 17, "Physical Attacks."

NOTE The phrase "physical attack" is often broadened to include wireless and other types of attacks that do not involve a human with physical possession of a device.

There are benefits to either hacking approach (i.e., programming or physical), although remote programming attacks are far more common than physical attacks. Physical attacks need a human being with physical possession of the attacked device to accomplish and are very high risk as compared to remote programming attacks. Programming attacks can be accomplished from different legal jurisdictions (i.e., other countries) and "weaponized" using malware into billions and billions of attempted attacks with very little risk for the attacker.

However, if I have physical possession of a device, I can often do both programming and physical attacks against it and get the best of both worlds. With physical control I can have unlimited access and time. For example, suppose I steal a fully patched server. If I want, I can hold onto the server for an undetermined amount of time, run it on a private network, and wait for a remote software exploit to be announced that I could use to remotely break into the server. There are usually over a hundred vulnerabilities announced against the most popular operating systems (Microsoft Windows, Linux, Apple) each year, and at least one of those is usually able to break into the targeted OS remotely. So, given enough time, I as an attacker can just wait and attack a device I have physical possession of when the right exploit is publicly announced. The biggest risk to an attacker from having physical possession of a device (if they get away with the crime) is that the legitimate owner/user will usually be aware that it is missing and may take appropriate countermeasures (such as remote data wiping or locating).

What Can an Endpoint Attacker Do?

Once an attacker has complete control of an endpoint, there is little they cannot achieve that is legitimately possible with the software or device. Here are some of the things a successful endpoint attacker can do to MFA solutions.

Attacker Can Do Anything the User Can Do

At the very least, any attacker gaining control to a program or device can "see" what the user is seeing and likely perform similar actions to what the user can legitimately do. For example, if a user uses an MFA solution to access a database to view and update records, an attacker controlling the user's device can access that same database to review, copy, and update records. The attacker can remotely accomplish the same steps and actions as the user, or use a macro, script, or API to accomplish what the user could have otherwise typed. If the user has an online bank account, the hacker can transfer money. If the hacker has control of the user's trading account, they can maliciously trade stocks and transfer money. The hacker can use the user's email to send targeted spear phishing emails to the user's contacts. Attackers can also install additional malware like backdoors, rootkits, and keyloggers. Whatever the user can do, the attacker can do, but with malicious intent.

Attacker Can Steal the Access Control Token

As we discussed in previous chapters, most of the time an attacker in control of another person's access control token is treated by systems as identical to the legitimate holder. An attacker with control of a system can view (and re-create) or steal access control tokens off the compromised system. Once a token is stolen, an attacker can, unless specific protections are already enabled, reuse the access control token from a different location and device. Access tokens are often valid for hours to years, depending on the type of access control token.

Attacker Can View MFA Secrets

Most MFA solutions involve and/or store secrets. For example, a USB security token device could securely store and protect the private keys of asymmetric key pairs. An attacker with complete access to a system using a USB security token device could surreptitiously view a private key and then use it to view systems and information protected by it. MFA and encryption secrets are often stored in memory, either in plaintext or obscured form. An attacker with elevated access can usually view those secrets in memory, even if that memory is supposed "protected." An attacker who's able to view the secrets used by an MFA solution can then view and manipulate any system or data protected by the compromised solution, often without the legitimate user being aware.

Attacker Can Modify MFA Solutions

An attacker can modify an MFA solution so that it is no longer protecting a system or user but the user doesn't know it. Instead of viewing the MFA secrets, they can modify them. For example, an attacker can change an MFA secret to be a secret that they also know and can read. Or they can modify the solution so that it is actually invalidated or operates at a weaker, easier-to-compromise state. For example, suppose your MFA solution can use a host of different cryptographic algorithms and by default uses a well-known, strong encryption cipher (for example, AES). The attacker could secretly change the MFA solution to use a far weaker encryption algorithm, say DES, and the MFA solution would begin using it (as long as it supports it), likely without the user noticing. Most MFA solutions involve software. An attacker could modify the software of an MFA solution so that it simply does not provide the protection the user thinks it is providing. For example, the user might think that they are using a secure VPN connection when in fact no secure connection is started or used.

Attacker Can Start a Second Hidden Session

A very common endpoint attack is when the attacker or their malware program starts a second hidden session that reuses the same access control token or approval as the first, legitimate session. Most authentication solutions allow multiple simultaneous user sessions and are unable to distinguish between the user's legitimate sessions and additional sessions initiated by an attacker or malware program. I'll cover this more in the "Specific Endpoint Attack Examples" section later.

Attacker Can Change Transaction Details

Attackers are also known for surreptitiously changing transaction details of a legitimate transaction the user is conducting to do something other than what the user intends. The user thinks they are accomplishing one thing, and yet another entirely different set of transactions is going on. This has been a fairly common type of MFA attack. It can be related to the previous topic and uses a second hidden browser session to conduct a second transaction event but refers more specifically to when an attacker modifies the details of the same session the legitimate user is involved in.

Attacker Can Maliciously Influence Infrastructure

Attackers are also good at manipulating the infrastructure services and components that MFA relies on so that a malicious instruction or value gets consumed by the MFA device, which diminishes its overall protective capability. Many MFA attacks begin by the attacker maliciously manipulating DNS, Active Directory, DHCP, Windows access control, ARP, and other infrastructure support services. Examples of these will be covered in future chapters of this book.

The most frustrating part for MFA vendors is that their solutions can often be compromised for something that is beyond their control. Some of the things they rely on can be verified before they're used, but for others the MFA solution has no way of determining whether or not it has been maliciously manipulated. Every MFA designer should threat-model all their necessary dependencies and determine whether they can build in verification checks to detect or prevent relying on a compromised supporting service. Designing a secure MFA solution always means considering more than just what is directly under the MFA vendor's control.

When an attacker or their malware creation has complete control over a device or MFA solution, they can do anything that the device or software is capable of doing. While I just covered seven different things an attacker with endpoint control can do, what they can do is limited only by human imagination and device and software limitations.

Specific Endpoint Attack Examples

Here are some specific endpoint attack examples.

Bancos Trojans

Bancos is the word "banks" in Spanish. *Bancos trojans* refers to a class of trojan horse programs that are specifically designed to steal money from people's bank accounts. They are known as bancos trojans because they first became popular in South America because South America and other Spanish-speaking countries had a lack of widely accessible physical banking locations and automated teller machines (ATMs). When ATMs are available, oftentimes they are expensive to use, unreliable, and untrustworthy. They have high fees, they are often out of service, and users often have their card information stolen and reused to make fraudulent transactions. Consequently, South American banks jumped on the "e-banking" movement quicker than other nations to serve their remote customers. So, too, did hackers and malicious mobile code.

Early on, banking hackers just broke into PCs and stole banking logon credentials. As antivirus programs got better, they started to conduct man-in-the-middle (MitM) attacks on the network connections between the customer and the bank. They would sniff the unprotected HTTP connection, steal user logon credentials, or modify the user's commands to cause an unseen malicious transaction to occur. The banks responded by enabling HTTPS, which made MitM attacks much more difficult, and by requiring users to use SMS-based MFA. South American banking customers were among the first customers to use MFA as part of a large-scale, public deployment. Using MFA seemed to thwart the hackers for a little while, but hackers responded by creating bancos trojans.

Bancos trojans work by exploiting end-user systems and waiting for the user to successfully log on to an intended targeted host system. After the user successfully logs on, no matter how they logged on, MFA or not, the bancos trojan can do many things, including the following actions:

- If not using MFA, steal the user's logon credentials and send them to the hacker
- Steal the access control token and send it to the hacker
- Inject code into the bank's web page (called web injection) that prompts the user for logon credentials or other additional private information (such as email address, SSNs, or their phone number) which is then sent to the hacker
- Open a remote backdoor session, dial home to the hacker, and let the hacker remotely do anything they want to the system
- Intercept the user's typed-in commands and mouse clicks and modify them on their way to the bank to conduct another malicious transaction
- Start an additional hidden browser session and conduct a clandestine malicious transaction that is not known to the user

With the latter action, the bank doesn't know that a malicious trojan is conducting the transaction. Every instruction appears to be coming from the legitimate computer and user who just successfully logged on. The user thinks they are securely logging on to check their bank balance or to transfer $40 to their kid, but in the background the trojan is transferring $10,000 to a bank in Russia. The latter type of bancos trojan is part of an attack type known as a *man-in-the-browser* (MitB) attack. The bancos trojan can be coded to recognize how much money they can transfer without setting off the financial institution's fraud checks. It may even change the user's email address, phone number, mailing address, and logon method. That way, if the bank decides to contact the user to confirm the transaction, the bank ends up calling a Skype number where the hacker answers in the name and personae of the targeted victim.

Alexandre Cagnoni of cybersecurity company WatchGuard (www.watchguard.com), and one of this book's tech editors, has years of experience in fighting bancos trojans in Brazil. He shared that a couple of years ago, some Brazilian hackers started selling a self-teaching toolkit, with code and everything needed, teaching how to create your own banking MitB trojan. It was around $200, as far as he remembers. One of his friends who worked on fraud prevention at a bank bought a kit. He said that it came in a nice, professional-looking box with a CD and was very well explained.

Cagnoni also shared that around April 2019, banks in Brazil started suffering an unknown banking-related attack. Criminals in the streets were stealing iPhones and Android phones from people in the streets of Sao Paulo. Forty minutes later, the victim's money was being transferred from the customer account to another bank, using the mobile banking application, even if the phone and banking app were both protected by PIN and biometrics (face or fingerprint). His team was baffled. At that time, the only thing they discovered was that all the phones were being taken to the same GPS location— a neighborhood in Sao Paulo (called Santa Ifigenia), where there were a lot of shady electronics stores. Their only guess was that the attackers were using some specific high-end hardware to bypass the biometrics check within the phone and mobile banking app.

Bancos trojans have now been around for nearly two decades and have stolen billions of dollars. Single bancos trojan families have been implicated in stealing a billion dollars (www.dsolutionsgroup.com/spyeye-caused-1-billion-losses). They are still very popular today. Bancos trojans target not only banks but also any organization the hackers can transfer money or value from. This includes stock trading, cryptocurrency, and money transfer sites.

NOTE   I first wrote about bancos trojans in March 2006: www.infoworld.com/article/2657551/ssl-trojans-getting-ever-nastier.html.

Bancos trojans are a major class of malware and can contain hundreds of different features, but in general most of them work the following way:

1. First, the trojan gains unauthorized access to the victim computer using any root cause exploit, usually social engineering or unpatched software.

2. It modifies the system so that it can remain in memory or be re-executed if the computer is rebooted. This is known as *persistence*.

3. It checks running processes to see if any of the most popular Internet browsers (Google Chrome, Microsoft Internet Explorer, Microsoft Edge, Apple Safari, etc.) are installed and running.

4. It monitors the URL address to see if it matches any one of the predefined URLs that indicate a bank or other targeted host system.

5. When the user connects to one of the predefined URLs, the bancos trojan monitors the session, waiting to confirm a successful logon. Usually this involves simply detecting the web page (usually via its URL) that is displayed after a successful logon.

6. Then the bancos trojan performs one of the malicious actions listed earlier.

Good examples of popular bank trojan can be found here: www.enigmasoftware.com/clientmaximus-removal and www.americanbanker.com/news/the-dridex-threat-how-to-block-the-latest-malware-aimed-at-banks.

Banking trojans often make their hacker gangs many millions of dollars. Figure 7.1 shows an example news report about a single banking trojan gang who stole over $100 million from more than 41,000 victims. That's just from one hacker gang. The king of all banking trojans was Zeus. It evolved from a generic botnet trojan, which through sharing and code leaks, was used by many newer bancos trojans over the years, many of which bypass MFA. It even has its own Wikipedia page: en.wikipedia.org/wiki/Zeus_(malware).

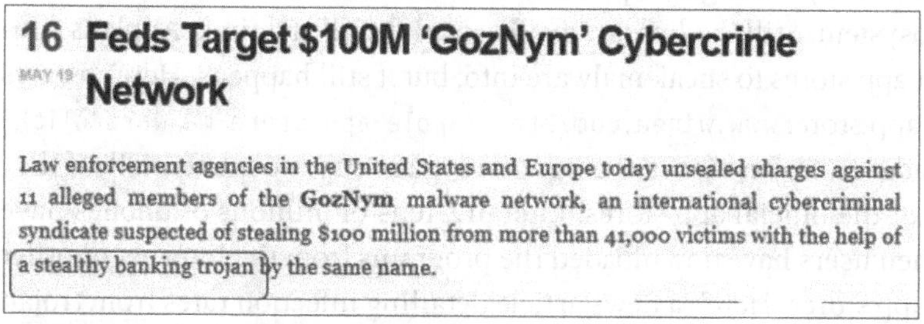

16 Feds Target $100M 'GozNym' Cybercrime Network

MAY 19

Law enforcement agencies in the United States and Europe today unsealed charges against 11 alleged members of the **GozNym** malware network, an international cybercriminal syndicate suspected of stealing $100 million from more than 41,000 victims with the help of a stealthy banking trojan by the same name.

Figure 7.1: Example news report about a single banking trojan gang arrest

Transaction Attacks

When bancos trojans first came out, they were simply stealing the customer's logon credentials or access control tokens and conducting other fraudulent transactions from another computer. The bank could not tell whether or not the transaction was from the legitimate user. So, the banks implemented SMS-based MFA, where the bank sent the user a one-time code via their phone that the user had to type in to confirm the transaction they wanted to complete.

The bancos trojans quickly moved to the MitB method, where the trojan intercepted and modified the user's typed responses to the bank or used a second hidden browser session to conduct a new fraudulent transaction. The bank's method of using a one-time code to confirm the user's transaction didn't work, because the trojan could just modify the user's typed commands (say, the user thinks they are transferring $40 to their kid) to be something else (say, transferring $4,000 to a Russian bank account), and the bank would have no way of knowing that the user didn't intend to commit the latter transaction. The bank would just send a code that was valid for the $4,000 transfer and the user would type it in their screen, thinking they were initiating a $40 transfer. The user had no way of knowing that the transaction the bank was seeing and the transaction they were trying to do were completely different.

Banks updated the SMS message to include the details of the transaction (i.e., date, time, transaction type, amount, and recipient) along with the one-time code that was cryptographically linked to the other transaction details. Now, the critical details of what the bank was seeing was sent to the user, who could then verify the transaction before they typed the one-time code into the bank's website. This frustrated banking trojans for a long time until SIM swapping attacks came around (covered in the next chapter).

Mobile Attacks

As our computer world has become a more mobile world, malware and programs that bypass MFA have migrated to mobile as well. Many trojans that bypass MFA come in the standard form of trojan horse programs: the user gets tricked into installing it and then it performs malicious behavior. Both Android and Apple have created heavily managed "app stores," which cut down on the malicious programs that sneak into the ecosystem. Still, bad programs do sneak by all the time. Apple is considered to have one of the hardest app stores to sneak malware into, but it still happens. Here's a news article about malware in Apple's app store: www.wired.com/story/apple-app-store-malware-click-fraud. Chances of a user downloading a trojan malware program increase super-exponentially if they download that program outside of the official app stores. Literally, tens of millions of phones have been compromised by trojans when users have downloaded the programs from the Internet or other supposedly "safe" but unofficial app stores. Here's a news article detailing infection rates from trojan Android apps downloaded outside the Google Play Store: www.wired.com/2016/12/never-ever-ever-download-android-apps-outside-google-play. Never download any app from an untrusted vendor, especially outside the phone ecosystem's official app store.

Bancos trojans, many of which bypass MFA, get installed on cell phones all the time. Kaspersky Labs reports 30,000 to 60,000 detected mobile banking trojans a month on just their monitored customers: www.kaspersky.com/about/press-releases/2018_phantom-menace. Here's an example of a mobile banking trojan that steals money via PayPal even if the user enables 2FA: www.welivesecurity.com/2018/12/11/android-Trojan-steals-money-paypal-accounts-2fa. The trojan poses as a battery optimization app. When executed, it waits for the user to successfully authenticate to PayPal and then it quickly mimics a user transferring $1,000 very quickly. You can see the trojan in action here: www.youtube.com/watch?v=yn04eLoivX8. Figure 7.2 shows a screenshot of the trojan in action as it types in 1,000 EUR and transfers the money. It's better to watch the YouTube video to see it in action and its full glory. This is a good trojan to study and learn the details about to understand exactly how devious mobile banking trojans can be. The only redeeming feature is that it doesn't seem to have a ransomware feature, as many of the mobile banking trojans often do. But it can be remotely updated at any time, so that feature can be added and activated at a later date by the managers. And this news story (www.scmagazineuk.com/2fa-stealing-android-malware-gives-enterprises-cause-concern/article/1681863) discusses mobile malware which looks for passwords to over 200 financial apps and can bypass SMS-based MFA.

Figure 7.2: Mobile trojan transferring 1,000 EUR by mimicking the user's keystrokes

Compromised MFA Keys

It is possible for an attacker to "zero out" (i.e., erase) the encryption keys of an MFA solution if they can get write access to the involved encryption keys. But erasing the encryption keys might make the encryption functionality error out or be noticed by the user. Instead, a smart attacker would just view and record the encryption keys or supply their own known keys that the target would unknowingly rely on.

I've only heard about this sort of MFA attack involving the intelligence agencies of nation-states. In one story that I read a long time ago, when the United States was first looking for Osama bin Laden, they learned that suspected terrorists were using cell phone subscriber identity module (SIM) cards, which allowed symmetric encryption keys to encrypt the messages and voice communications between all the involved co-conspirators. The terrorists would insert the secure SIMs when needing secure communications and frequently buy and update their secure SIMs so that they would be using new SIM information and new encryption keys. It was a pretty good plan. The U.S. intelligence agencies could not break into the encryption, but they contacted the vendor of the secure SIM manufacturer and convinced them to use symmetric keys known to the intelligence agency on all secure SIM encryption cards sent to the particular Middle East area. Everyone, terrorist or not, who bought the same brand of secure SIMs received encryption keys known by someone else. But indeed the terrorists did get the compromised keys and the U.S. intelligence agency was able to listen in on terrorist communications.

In a more public case, which came to be known as the Great SIM Heist, the U.S. and UK intelligence agencies broke into the world's most prolific supplier of SIM chips, Gemalto, and potentially compromised over 2 billion SIM encryption keys (theintercept.com/2015/02/19/great-sim-heist). An April 2010 intelligence agency document details the automated collection of SIM encryption keys in fairly good detail: theintercept.com/document/2015/02/19/pcs-harvesting-scale. There is no reason to believe that similar intelligence agency actions are not still occurring around the world.

Endpoint Attack Defenses

Endpoint attack defenses break down into two different categories: developer and end-user defenses.

MFA Developer Defenses

MFA developers can do many things to limit or slow down physical and logical endpoint attacks.

Threat Model and Protect All Dependencies

Few MFA solutions work solely alone. Most rely on a host of other services out of their control, including host computers and operating systems, networks, supporting infrastructure, namespaces, the humans involved, and all the other entities, as summarized in Figure 5.1. An MFA developer should consider all relied-on services as untrusted and potentially compromised. Then the developer should decide which ones are critical to the security of their solution and create code that can detect and determine whether the underlying infrastructure is compromised to the best of their ability to detect an anomaly. MFA solutions should be designed to detect unauthorized hardware and/or firmware changes. All critical functions should be securely stored and run in secure memory areas. There should be secure boot checks and the runtime operational code should check itself for integrity. Only secure, authorized updates should be allowed.

The MFA device should stop operations (i.e., "brick") on any critical error. Any detected anomaly should be displayed descriptively to the end user if possible and the MFA solution should error out or refuse to operate further. Most developers work with an attitude of trusting the other components to be uncompromised and reliable. A good MFA developer takes the opposite attitude, threat-models, plans, and codes accordingly.

Secure All Network Communications

Ensure that all communications between an MFA device and the system and networks are secure against attack. These days most network connections are protected using HTTPS/TLS, which is a great default as long as the code can be updated in the future if the current version used is found to have flaws. HTTPS/TLS is frequently updated over time to fix identified flaws.

Tie Access Control Tokens to Registered Devices

If possible, tie access control tokens to previously registered devices. That way, an attacker cannot compromise the token and move it to another device and reuse it.

Prevent or Notify the User of Second Instances

Stop or communicate with end users when a second, concurrent, authenticated instance using the same MFA or access control token is used by an additional process or additional instance of the same process. This can be very, very difficult to do in practice for at least two reasons. First, allowing multiple instances to share the same MFA or access control token at the same time often makes the user's life easier. It's single sign-on. Users do not want to have to completely reauthenticate every time they are starting a new instance to connect to or to do the same things. Having to reauthenticate for each additional instance, depending on how it's done and when it is needed, can be overly burdensome to the end user. And if you make it too hard on the end user to use, they will often choose not to use your product or work around it in such a way that it invalidates the overall protection.

Second, many operating systems do not easily allow programmers the ability to prevent one security identity instance from being used with a second process. In fact, the only general-purpose operating system I know of that does allow this by default is Qubes (www.qubes-os.org), which is used by very few people even though it is open source and free. Some other versions of Linux allow process separation but do not enable it by default. And enabling strict process separation can cause operational issues. Microsoft Windows is still, as of 2020, struggling to allow stricter security process separation and handling by default, but they are working toward that goal and toward something closer to what Qubes has already achieved.

If MFA or access control token reuse cannot be prevented, try to notify the end user or make sure they are easily aware of the second instance. Try to prevent "hidden" instances. Additionally, you might even want to log all uses by location and process and let the user know that information. Many software programs and services will proactively display to the user when a second instance seems suspicious, such as the user seemingly connecting from the United States and China within too short of a time. The second connection isn't always prevented, but it is logged and presented to the end user to view and confirm.

Notify the User of Encryption Key Changes

Notify the user of any encryption key changes since the last time the MFA token or process was used. You can do that by securely storing the hash of the previous encryption key and comparing it with the current encryption key upon startup. Notify the user if the key changes and allow the user to confirm the change was expected.

Host Should Use Dynamic Adaptive Authentication for Uncharacteristic or High-Risk End-User Actions

Host programs and services should ask for additional authentication for high-risk actions and events. For example, if I ask for a new Amazon purchase to be shipped to a mailing address I've never used before, Amazon will ask me to enter my stored credit card's three- or four-digit security code. The idea is if an attacker stole my credit card information and is now using it to buy and ship goods to their location, the hacker might be less able to put in the credit card security code. Or when I buy an expensive item on my credit card, my credit card company will send an SMS message to me asking whether or not the purchase should be allowed. Your MFA solution should ask for additional authentication, perhaps something as simple as asking for the user to reenter a PIN for high-risk transactions. If I'm doing business with my bank or PayPal and I suddenly request that a large sum of money be transferred to a Russian-located bank for the first time, verify that I'm making that request from my normal registered device and that none of my contact information has changed, and ask for some sort of additional verification before performing that action. I'm giving examples that are usually outside of the control of the MFA solution provider, but the idea is to program your solution in a way that asks for additional authentication factors for very high-risk or unusual events, if possible.

There are several vendor and industry efforts to better publicize and standardize "continuous authentication" schemes and recommendations. One, from the industry analysis giant Gartner, is called CARTA, or Continuous Adaptive Risk and Trust Assessment (blog.acceptto.com/gartner-carta). Gartner's analysis is heavily respected in the industry, and most of what it recommends has strong and long ramifications in the computer industry. CARTA has four pillars:

- Continuous discovery (identifying and including assets as they get inserted and removed from the managed device networks)
- Continuous monitoring
- Continuous threat assessment
- Continuous risk assessment and prioritization

Clearly, CARTA and other similar approaches are far better than the "single-approval-at-the-start-and-you're-in-forever" approaches that control 99 percent of the access control world today. The future of authentication will be a more adaptive approach, and anything you can do, if possible, to start moving your organization to it is a step in the right direction.

Transaction Verification Requests Must Include All Critical Details

When asking a user to verify a transaction, be sure to include all critical details. For example, if I'm buying a new, expensive television from Walmart, don't just send me a message saying, "Do you approve the transaction for $3,200?" Instead, use something like the following: "Do you approve a transaction for $3,200, location Walmart in Clearwater, FL 33755 on 1/22/20 at 8:07PM EST?" Give all the relevant critical details so that the user can make the appropriate judgment call. Any missing information gives an attacker the ability to create a fraudulent transaction.

End-User Defenses

End users also have defenses they can employ.

Use Endpoint Protection

It goes without saying that all devices used by an end user should have strong endpoint protection when allowed and when it makes sense from a risk perspective. Your computers and phones should have endpoint protection. But it's not always possible to get protection for your smart TV, smart wristwatch, and Internet of Things (IoT) devices. From a risk perspective, you do not need specialized endpoint software until a real-world "in-the-wild" attack happens to your device. If your wristwatch, TV, or smart toaster has never been attacked in the wild, then you likely don't need additional specialized endpoint defenses. But history isn't static. It used to be that TVs didn't get attacked by hackers. Now some smart TVs do get attacked. Unfortunately, there are no antivirus software programs to protect your TV—yet—but there will be. But for those devices for which you do need endpoint defenses, and doing so is possible, make sure you have at least the basics: firewall, antimalware detection, intrusion detection, and secure configurations.

> **NOTE**   It won't hurt to have a network security device protecting your own network if you have the ability to get one and/or have the skill. Some cable network vendors provide decent network protection in their cable modem/routers; you just need to explore and use the advanced capabilities. You can also purchase a network security device if one is not otherwise provided. Most come fairly securely configured out of the box, but you shouldn't install and use one without understanding what it does, how it is configured, and how to manage, configure, and troubleshoot on your own.

Download Apps from Official App Stores

Make sure all apps for your phone are downloaded from the phone's official ecosystem app store. If you download an app directly from a vendor, make sure you absolutely trust the vendor and understand what the software does. Encourage the vendor to submit their app to the official app store. Don't "jail break" your phone. Phones that are "jail broken" are much more likely to be compromised. Pay attention to the permissions any app is requesting that you approve. Most malicious programs ask for far more elevated permissions than is reasonable for what the app it is pretending to be needs. Any app asking for admin access should be denied and not installed.

Don't Get Socially Engineered

Social engineering and phishing is the number one way that most people end up with malicious installed trojan horse programs. Use every technical control at your disposal (antimalware detection, content filters, etc.) to prevent social engineering and phishing content from getting to your eyes. Then make sure you get good security awareness training to educate yourself, and others, about real-life examples of how malware was unknowingly installed by someone.

Keep Up with Critical Patches

After social engineering, attackers exploiting unpatched software (which usually has available patches) is the way they break into a computer or device. Unpatched software often allows an intruder to "silently" install their malware. Be sure to keep up with critical security patches and apply them in a timely manner (i.e., right away or at least within one week). If possible, enable auto-patching. Let the device and software check for new patches at least every day and patch itself whenever new updates are available. If you're prompted to apply a patch, do it as soon as possible. However, one caveat: Never apply a patch or update recommended while you are in a browser session. If prompted for patch by a browser while browsing the Internet, close the browser and see if the prompt to update still occurs. Better yet, go to the software vendor's official website and check for patches. Don't allow any website other than the official vendor's website direct you to install patches and updates.

Split Secrets if Possible

If possible, don't store all the authentication secrets on one device. This means requiring separate authentication factors whenever possible. Don't use 1FA devices, even if they appear to be "MFA" devices. 1FA devices are more susceptible to hacking than 2FA, and when using 2FA solutions, make sure they use different types of factors (e.g., something that you know, something that you are, something that you have). It is simply harder for an attacker to steal multiple types of factors at the same time.

Summary

In a very real sense, a physically or logically compromised endpoint is game over from a security standpoint. Once an attacker has gained admin-equivalent access, what they can do is limited only by the inherent constraints of the device and software that runs on it. They can do anything the system is capable of, only they have malicious intent. This chapter presented specific endpoint attack examples that are capable of bypassing MFA solutions, including common, ordinary bancos trojans, transaction attacks, mobile attacks, and compromised MFA keys. But as you learned in this chapter, there are defenses developers and users can use to prevent easy compromise.

Chapter 8, "SMS Attacks" covers attacks against SMS-based authentication.

8

SMS Attacks

hapter 8 will cover Short Message Service (SMS) attacks. Today's incredibly functional smartphones are where a lot of the world conducts most or even all of their computing. Many people have only a cell phone to connect remotely to another person, be it a phone call, messaging, or email. For many people, especially younger people, most of their Internet browsing is conducted from a cell phone. So, it makes perfect sense that criminals will go where their potential victims are.

The small form factor and inability to easily distinguish between real and fraudulent SMS messages has led to an entire new genre of crime. In many cases, the insecurity of SMS makes MFA solutions that rely on it even less safe than simple logon names and passwords.

This chapter describes what SMS is and why it is abused, presents examples of real-world attacks, and finishes with how SMS-based MFA developers and users should defend themselves.

Introduction to SMS

SMS is a popular text-based messaging service standard that nearly all cell phones support. Already in widespread use by the 1990s, it is rare that a cell phone doesn't support SMS. It was and is the original chat-based "killer app" that took over the world. Today, many people use other chat apps like WhatsApp, Skype, Facebook Messenger, Google Hangouts, and Instagram, but almost everyone uses SMS because everyone else has it and it's always active and loaded.

NOTE There is a competing service called Multimedia Messaging Service (MMS), but it isn't nearly as popular or is used as part of SMS to deliver multimedia content. Either way, it isn't covered in this book. If you want to learn more about MMS, visit `en.wikipedia.org/wiki/Multimedia_Messaging_Service`.

SMS originally allowed a maximum of only 140 to 160 characters to be sent in a single message to one or more other recipients using their cell phone numbers. Today, depending on the mobile network vendor and applications, SMS-based apps can send longer messages and more than simple text-based characters (such as emoticons, pictures, and videos). Figure 8.1 shows an example of an SMS message including messages, pictures, and emoticons from my wife one day.

Figure 8.1: An SMS message including messages, pictures, and emoticons

Every SMS message includes at least the following information, even if much of it is not displayed directly to the user:

- Originating address (originating mobile number or generated code)
- Header – Message Type, Service Center Time Stamp, Protocol Identifier, Data Coding Scheme, Length Of User Data
- User Data (the message)

The originating address is usually the sender's phone number, but it can be a variety of codes, usually all numeric. It can be a simulated phone number or any code that any part of the network system involved in sending and directing the SMS message wants to inject. It doesn't have to be a valid phone number or even originate from the phone number it says it is from. Phone numbers can be spoofed using several different methods and tools. Here's a story about spoofed phone numbers which were used to compromise user's credit card accounts: `krebsonsecurity.com/2020/04/would-you-have-fallen-for-this-phone-scam`.

One of the key facts to note is that if an SMS message comes from a phone number or code we already have stored in our contact lists, such as my wife's telephone number in this example, SMS-based applications typically will convert the attached phone number to the name as listed in the contact list. If the phone number is not found in the contact list, the user is just shown the phone number the SMS message was sent from or what is known as the *short message code*. This applies to both senders and receivers (as shown in Figure 8.2).

Figure 8.2: Example of SMS message displaying the short message code from where the message was sent

SMS is the most popular application used on a cell phone, surpassing using it as a telephone. For many users, SMS is the primary way they communicate with another person for many reasons, not the least of which is that people can easily communicate with other people without being outwardly noisy or distracting other people. All around the world you can see people with their heads down, typing and reading SMS messages. Many a parent has admonished their children to verbally communicate more, and people often send messages to each other even though they are in the same room or right next to each other.

SMS is a popular way for businesses and organizations to communicate with their customers and members. More importantly, and the reason for this chapter, SMS-based MFA solutions are very popular. Many companies and organizations use SMS-based MFA solutions because they are fairly easy to deploy and often use "out-of-band" channels for authentication (and that is a good thing regardless of the other issues), and because nearly everyone actively uses SMS. Figure 8.3 shows real-world examples of various vendors using SMS messages as part of their MFA solutions. Examples include SMS messages from Bank of America, Google, Microsoft, Marriott, and an anti-identity theft service.

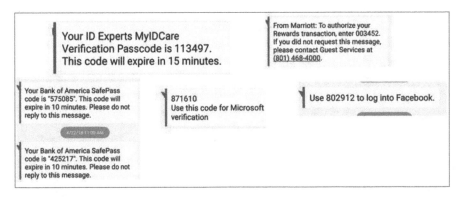

Figure 8.3: Real-world examples of SMS-based messages as part of their MFA solutions

I don't have any solid data on SMS-based MFA solutions, but I'm fairly confident in saying that SMS-based MFA solutions are the most popular type of MFA solution on the Internet and in the world. And this is unfortunate, because SMS can be so easily hacked.

SS7

The original small message size limitation of SMS was due to its reliance on an underlying phone protocol known as Signaling System No. 7 (SS7). SS7 is the international standard and protocol that made regular voice telephone calling, known as the *public switched telephone network*, possible. SS7 splits the "voice part" of the channel apart from the "control" or "signal" channel, which helps originate, manage, and disconnect calls. It takes both channels, the control and data, to make a telephone conversation happen. In the early days of telephones, human operators handled all the background setup work. Eventually, everything the human operator could do was replaced by control signals sent along with the voice portion of a phone call. It was not unusual for a caller or receiver to hear the control instructions (usually modulating tones).

SS7 gained popularity because it allowed the control portion to be "out-of-band" from the data or voice portion. They can even take different paths from the originating caller to the destination as long as they both end up in the same location. Earlier versions had both the control and voice components in the same channel together (called *in-band*), which made phone hacking (known as *phreaking*) easier. Phreakers even made whistles that mimic important tones to abuse the phone system. You can read about one of the early and most interesting phone phreakers, John Draper (aka Captain Crunch), here: en.wikipedia.org/wiki/John_Draper.

NOTE If you are wondering, yes, there were previous versions of SS7 known as Signaling System No. 6 (SS6), Signaling System No. 5 (SS5), and so on. SS7 partially came about because hackers were too good at hacking previous versions. First implemented in 1975, SS7 is regularly attacked and abused today. If you want to learn the details and ins and outs of SS7, protocols, and formats for today's digital phone networks, you can read this document: www.etsi.org/deliver/etsi_ts/151000_151099/15101001/12.05.00_60/ts_15101001v120500p.pdf. But be aware it is over 6,000 pages long.

Since SS7 was invented, hackers have concentrated on finding weaknesses in it and abusing it. Many hacks directly against cell phones and cell phone networks can happen only because of cell phones' and cell phone networks' reliance on SS7. For example, when you read about "stingray" devices that fraudulently act as a cell phone tower so that the user can eavesdrop on cell phone calls and locations, it's due to vulnerabilities in SS7. SS7 white-hat researchers and attackers have intercepted people's phone calls and read their SMS messages for decades. They have even performed nearly identical MFA-bypass attacks, as we discuss later, but using methods exploiting SS7 directly (thehackernews.com/2017/05/ss7-vulnerability-bank-hacking.html). SS7 vulnerabilities are so well known and easy to abuse that in 2016 a U.S. congressman called for an official investigation (www.theguardian.com/technology/2016/apr/19/ss7-hack-us-congressman-calls-texts-location-snooping), although nothing came out it.

Most nation-states and governments don't want to fix SS7 vulnerabilities because they use them when they want to spy on their own targets. They like that their populace isn't paying that much attention and doesn't seem to mind that their communications can be regularly intercepted and redirected at will. Regardless, the inherent issues in SS7 underlie many of the hacks of the upper-layer applications, like SMS, which rely on SS7 for the basic connection handling between phones. Of course, SMS has its own problems that go above and beyond what SS7 has, but together it's a problem that any MFA solution relying on them is weakened by. So knowing that, we can't fully trust it.

Biggest SMS Weaknesses

Ignoring the inherent SS7 issues, the biggest problem with SMS-based MFA solutions from a security perspective is that an SMS sender or receiver is often not authenticated beyond an attached phone number. And phone numbers are amazingly easy to steal. Anyone sending or receiving an SMS message can only, at best, be assured that the phone number the SMS message comes from or is sent to is accurate, and even that isn't guaranteed. Many rogue applications allow users to send SMS messages from spoofed or borrowed/shared telephone numbers. If the receiver doesn't have the phone number previously registered as a contact in their phone, the SMS message shows up on their phone as originating from a particular phone number and that's it.

SMS is unauthenticated, meaning anyone can send another person an SMS message by simply knowing the recipient's phone number. And as long as that person hasn't previously noted the number as a particular sender's ID and stored it in their contact list, it will show up looking like any other SMS message without an authenticated name attached. I, and anyone else, can pretend to be nearly anyone via SMS. A receiver might not believe the sender is the president of the United States (unless they already have a formal relationship with the president), but otherwise most people are susceptible to simply accepting that the SMS sender is who they claim to be.

Even if the SMS message appears to come from a phone number the receiver trusts or is in the contact list, it may not be from that number. It is possible for attackers, using a variety of methods, to specify whatever sending phone number (or code) they want. Many web-based interfaces and APIs allow the sender to specify any phone number or code they like. Figure 8.4 shows sample Active Server Pages (ASP) code that someone might use to send an SMS message from within an accepting web-based console.

```
<%
' create SMS message
set Sms = Server.CreateObject("SMSSenderName.Sender")
' parameters
Sms.Username = "logonname"
Sms.Password = "password"
Sms.MobileNo = "[mobile_number]"
Sms.SMSType = "LongSMS"
Sms.Message = "This is Google tech support. We have detected a problem with your gmail account and are going to send you a second text
message to your previously registered phone number to verify your account. Please retype that sent verification code to this reply within
the next 10 minutes or your Gmail will be permanently deleted."
' sending SMS message
%>
```

Figure 8.4: Example ASP code showing how to construct and send an SMS message via a web portal or gateway that would accept it

When web-based portals, APIs, or SMS-based apps are involved, it is often possible for a malicious user to construct a malicious SMS message that would normally not be valid. This involves including any phone number they would like the phone number to appear to be from. Most of the time the network service provider would have code or services that recognize fraudulent or malformed messages, but that isn't always possible. For example, if the SMS message originates on one network service provider's network but the destination belongs on another, it is difficult for the recipient network to verify all the details of the message originating from the sending network. Many receiving networks simply take the sent information as valid, trusting that the sending source performed all the critical verification steps first. This is an unfortunate and overly optimistic stance to take by default. It is ripe for abuse.

Additionally, many URL links sent via SMS are often harder to inspect for security issues without completely loading the web page and being exposed to whatever content it sends. SMS URL links are often "shortened" to some innocuous-looking link that makes it hard to figure out where it ultimately links to. So, a URL link might say something like `bit.ly/Y7acoe` and, when open, might redirect to something that looks like `thisisabadwebsite.com/virus.php`. Most *smishing* (i.e., phishing via SMS messages) includes shortened URLs that are intended to hide the eventual destination.

Security people aren't big fans of URL shortening services in general, but when paired with limited pre-inspection capabilities of SMS and lack of authentication, there are even more reasons to be skeptical. Users cannot "hover" over an SMS URL to find out where it ultimately goes to, and SMS applications don't contain nearly as many anti-malicious controls as the typical browser does (although many times, SMS URLs are opened up in the user's browser anyway). As our online world is increasingly becoming one conducted by cell phone, smishing is growing in popularity with attackers.

Example SMS Attacks

Let's look at some popular SMS attack methods that can bypass SMS-based MFA solutions.

SIM Swap Attacks

Before I can discuss SIM swap attacks, I need to make sure everyone understands what a SIM is.

Subscriber Identity Module (SIM)

Most mobile devices that accept cell phone calls and messages have several globally unique numbers associated with and stored on them. Each cellular device and network can have different requirements and often store many pieces of various information, but most have at least a few minimum types of unique numbers.

One is an *International Mobile Subscriber Identity* (IMSI) number. An IMSI contains three parts:

- Three-digit *Mobile Country Code* (MCC), which identifies the country the mobile device is registered in
- Three-digit *Mobile Network Code* (MNC), which identifies the device's registered network provider (visit the following for example codes: `www.roamingzone.com/mnc`)
- Nine-digit *Mobile Station Identification Number* (MSIN), which identifies a specific subscriber no matter which device they use

Most cell phones also have an *International Mobile Equipment Identity* (IMEI), another 15-digit number that identifies the specific mobile device and stays with the device. Another common number is a *Mobile Station Integrated Services Digital Network* (MSISDN) number, which is the full phone number of a mobile device subscriber, beginning with and including the national country code (e.g., 1 for the United States and Canada, 44 for the UK, 61 for Australia).

These numbers are used to identify you and your device on a cellular network and to route and manage voice and message conversations to you and your device. In essence, it is these numbers that allow your cell phone to be *your* cellphone. When some of these codes are moved from your current phone to your next, it's what makes the new phone now *your* phone.

Originally, most cell phone and cellular network providers stored this information, and anything else they liked, in a physical small memory card (shown in Figure 8.5) known as the *subscriber identity module* (SIM) card or chip. Each SIM chip or storage area has a 19-digit or larger globally unique *Integrated Circuit Card Identifier* (ICCID) number.

If you ever had to move from one cell phone to another back then, your cellular service provider would make you move the existing SIM card from the old phone to the new phone. Most cell phone users would spend time trying to find where exactly the SIM card was (often in a tiny slot on the end of the phone or underneath the removable battery, when batteries were removable), and get a paper clip to eject or pop the card out. It was an exercise in patience.

Figure 8.5: Much larger than scale representation of a physical SIM microSD card

If you lost or replaced your old phone, SIM chip and all, the cell phone provider would provide you a new SIM chip and tell you to place it into the new cell phone, and then you would dial a special short phone number (say #69#) and that service would push down your SIM information to the new card and phone. Increasingly, future cell phones will not come with SIM slots or cards anymore. Instead, the information that was normally stored on a SIM card will be stored on the cell phone's permanent memory storage in a protected location. This technology is known as *virtual SIM*. Even when the physical SIM card is no longer present, most people will still refer to the stored information as the SIM card or SIM information. For more information on virtual SIM, visit www.allinallspace.com/virtual-sim-card-esim-the-full-guide and www.kaspersky.com/blog/virtual-sim/11572.

The SIM storage area can also act as storage for the cell phone, holding application data such as the user's pictures and contact information, although using a SIM for customer data storage is being deprecated. As I said earlier, it is the SIM information that makes your current phone *your* phone.

The SIM information allows calls and messages to be routed to your current mobile device and phone number.

SIM Swap Methods

For well over a decade, hackers have been obtaining a legitimate subscriber's SIM information and transferring it to a phone in their possession. This can be done in many ways:

- Social engineering of the user
- Social engineering of the network provider
- Insider attack at the network provider
- SIM information–stealing malware
- SMS network infrastructure exploitation

It is very common for SIM information thieves to socially engineer a user, via email or phone, to get enough information so that the hacker can than socially engineer the user's cell phone network provider into switching the user's SIM information to the hacker's cell phone. Hackers have also paid cell phone network provider employees to perform SIM transfers.

No matter how it is accomplished, once the SIM information is installed and active on the new cell phone, the old (original, legitimate) cell phone stops receiving calls and messages. Other than an "out of network" icon indicator, most victims don't realize for hours that their SIM information has been transferred. Usually the victim finally notices much later on that they haven't received any calls or messages for a few hours. Then they realize they can't send any messages or make calls. Usually, it's only then that they realize they don't have cellular service. The victim may think they are involved in a normal, temporary disruption. By the time they realize it isn't a temporary service disruption, they have to find out a way to call their cell phone network provider's technical support. Usually at this point the victim is still unaware that they are a victim of a crime and that their SIM information has been transferred to an attacker's phone.

Normally they call their cell phone provider's technical support line and are told something like "You activated your new phone" or something like that by the technical support person. When the victim says they did not do that, both the victim and the tech support person begin to realize that a SIM swap attack has occurred and begin the process to get the SIM information back to the original phone. It can take as long as several days for the victim to get their cell phone service back. And during all those hours the attacker is usually using their ill-gotten SMS access to their advantage and to the victim's disadvantage.

When a hacker does a malicious SIM swap, those SMS-based MFA messages are sent to the hacker's cell phone instead of the victim's. The hacker can then compromise your online account using the misrouted SMS-based MFA message. Usually what the hacker does is go into the user's MFA-protected services (Gmail, Microsoft 365, etc.) and act like they cannot access the account without getting an SMS recovery message. The service sends the SMS recovery code to the user's previously registered phone number, and because that phone number is now under the control of the hacker and linked to the hacker's cell phone, the SMS message is sent to the hacker instead of the legitimate user. The hacker then uses the SMS recovery message to get access to the account. Once in the victim's account they change as much authentication information as they can to prevent the victim from reasserting immediate control.

I have read many stories of victims arguing over and over with technical support about how the recently changed information was not done by them and how the technical support person had a hard time validating that the person claiming to be the "victim" was really the victim. How is the technical support person supposed to know that the person claiming to be the victim really is the victim, especially if the hacker used supposedly secret information that only the legitimate owner was supposed to know in the first place?

> **NOTE** Here is a great 2020 research paper on how easy it is to do SIM swap attacks: `www .issms2fasecure.com/assets/sim_swaps-01-10-2020.pdf`.

Real-Life SIM Swap Attack Examples

Rogue SIM swaps have happened many tens of thousands of times, as shown in the news headline examples in Figure 8.6. Some of the world's largest and most notorious hacks have involved SIM swapping. One cryptocurrency millionaire had over $24 million stolen from his crypto-wallet (`www .bankinfosecurity.com/att-sued-over-24m-cryptocurrency-sim-hijack-attacks-a-11365`) because it relied on SMS-based MFA. He sued AT&T for $224 million because they transferred his SIM information without authorization.

Figure 8.6: Headlines from real-life SIM swap attacks

A SIM-based attack was also used in 2018 to compromise Reddit's company network (`www.wired .com/story/reddit-hacked-thanks-to-woefully-insecure-two-factor-setup`), an attack that led to

Reddit's source code and network login credentials being compromised. Here are other SIM swap attack examples:

- ■ krebsonsecurity.com/2018/08/florida-man-arrested-in-sim-swap-conspiracy
- ■ coolwallet.io/smartphone-crypto-hack
- ■ motherboard.vice.com/en_us/article/a3q7mz/hacker-allegedly-stole-millions-bitcoin-sim-swapping
- ■ krebsonsecurity.com/2018/08/reddit-breach-highlights-limits-of-sms-based-authentication
- ■ blog.knowbe4.com/sim-card-attack-may-affect-over-1-billion-mobile-phones-worldwide

SMS Impersonation

SIM swap attacks take at least a bit of advanced knowledge and preparation on behalf of the attacker. But some attacks against SMS-based MFA solutions are so easy even a child can do it. You can do it; I can make you an SMS hacker. Of course, never do so against anyone who hasn't given you written permission. The key to SMS impersonation attacks is that SMS is not authenticated to anything other than to a phone number or code and most people don't know if the phone or code is legitimate. Here are some common examples of SMS impersonation.

Fake Technical Support Messages

Here's how the attack goes:

1. The attacker sends the victim a fake text message, claiming to be from Google Gmail security support (see Figure 8.7), and tells the victim to expect a shortly forthcoming recovery code via SMS from another phone number, which needs to be sent back in reply to the message.

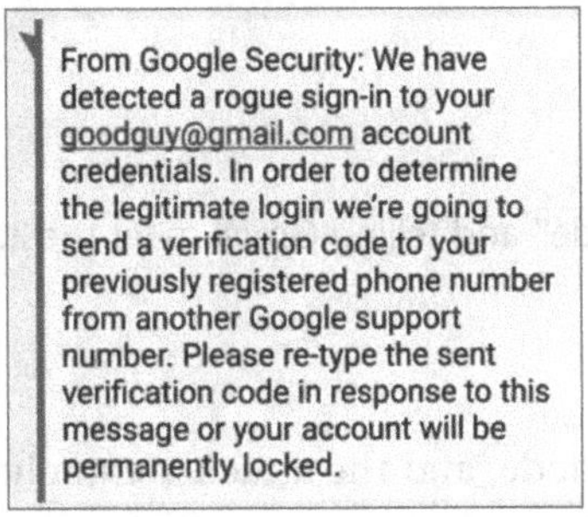

> From Google Security: We have detected a rogue sign-in to your goodguy@gmail.com account credentials. In order to determine the legitimate login we're going to send a verification code to your previously registered phone number from another Google support number. Please re-type the sent verification code in response to this message or your account will be permanently locked.

Figure 8.7: Fake tech support SMS message

2. The hacker then attempts to log in to your legitimate service, but then acts like they do not know the right password to put the Gmail login in "account recovery" mode (see Figure 8.8).

Figure 8.8: Example Gmail logon by attacker acting like they are the legitimate user and have forgotten their password

3. In this example, Gmail first offers to let the attacker/user to use their previous password if it is known. An attacker would just click "Try another way" to get a list of recovery choices, as shown in Figure 8.9.

Figure 8.9: Example of Gmail being put in "recovery mode" and telling Gmail to let the attacker/ user select their recovery method

4. Gmail then offers a selection of options for recovery mode, and the attacker can choose the SMS option, which brings up the screen in Figure 8.10.
5. The legitimate recovery code gets sent from the service to the victim's previously registered phone via SMS message (see Figure 8.11).
6. The tricked victim then sends that recovery code back to the originally requesting hacker's impersonated message (see Figure 8.12).

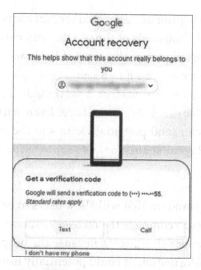

Figure 8.10: Attacker/user choosing to recover the account using the SMS method

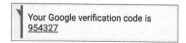

Figure 8.11: Example of Gmail sending a legitimate account recovery code via SMS to the victim

Figure 8.12: Example of victim sending back real Gmail account recovery code to the hacker's original impersonated message

7. The hacker then takes the code and types it into the user's legitimate service's recovery code prompt that they initiated, gets authenticated to the account, and then takes control of it.

This is a very common type of phishing scam, although the scammer may claim to be from your bank, investment company, PayPal, airline, hotel company, or any other entity with whom you have a membership and financial information. In all cases, they will claim to have detected some sort of rogue activity or attempt and claim to be saving you from the criminal activity. They will then claim to be sending you a code via SMS that you need to tell them to verify that "you are who you say you are," and when you tell them that code (sent by your service's legitimate automated recovery service), they take over your account. This type of scam is likely done thousands of times a day and can fool even the most skeptical among us. Here are two real-world examples of this type of hack: `www.msn.com/en-us/news/crime/a-scam-targeting-americans-over-the-phone-has-resulted-in-millions-of-dollars-lost-to-hackers-dont-be-the-next-victim/ar-AAJpE2J` and `nakedsecurity.sophos.com/2019/08/23/instagram-phishing-uses-2fa-as-a-lure`. Even without asking for recovery reset codes, SMS impersonation scams can send potential victims to the rogue websites. Here is a real-world news story about related PayPal scams: `nakedsecurity.sophos.com/2020/02/05/paypal-sms-scams-dont-fall-for-them`.

> **NOTE** Some Apple engineers have proposed a new SMS standard that will allow users to be sent legitimate recovery codes in SMS that they can simply select to complete the recovery process (`www.ehackingnews.com/2020/02/apple-engineers-unveils-proposal-to.html`). Because the proposed standard relies on the user's previously registered device information, it could potentially mitigate the types described in this section.

SMS Buffer Overflow

You can be sent SMS messages containing malicious URLs, which if opened can try to exploit your cell phone and its software. In most cases, the victim must have some vulnerable piece of software installed that can be taken advantage of by the exploit code. This attack method has occurred many times before, although usually it is accomplished by a nation-state. The most famous example to date is Saudi Arabia's exploitation of Amazon CEO Jeff Bezos's cell phone (`www.wired.com/story/bezos-phone-hack-mbs-saudi-arabia`). In this case, it involved WhatsApp and not SMS, but the modality is the same.

In this next case, the messaging app *was* SMS. A journalist was apparently targeted, but he was too suspicious of the message to trust it or to click the included link. Instead, he had his phone and the message analyzed. The message link pointed to software called Pegasus, made by Israeli company, NSO Group. If executed, it would have likely compromised the journalist's phone. This article includes good detail about what the journalist did to confirm that the message was bogus and how he avoided getting exploited: `www.nytimes.com/2020/01/28/reader-center/phone-hacking-saudi-arabia.html`.

This article details the hack, along with an excellent screenshot of the original message in its Arabic form: `citizenlab.ca/2020/01/stopping-the-press-new-york-times-journalist-targeted-by-saudi-linked-pegasus-spyware-operator`. So far Citizen Lab has identified 13 people targeted by the same software and group. The real number is likely in the many hundreds to thousands.

Once your cell phone has been taken over, the attacker can read any SMS secret MFA codes sent to your phone, read your passwords, and see any site or service you log on to using your cell phone as an MFA solution.

Cell Phone User Account Hijacking

Attackers will also compromise a user's cell phone provider's user account portal using any valid hacking method that works to gain access to the web-based console that allows any supported cell phone user to send SMS messages from the portal. Figure 8.13 shows an example web-based SMS-sending portal.

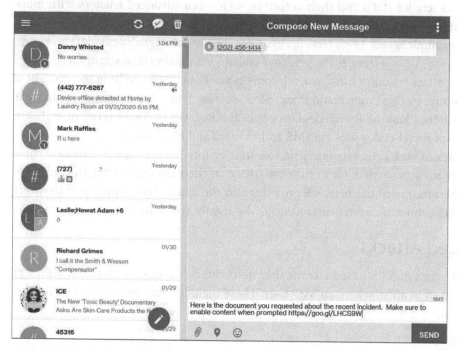

Figure 8.13: Example SMS-sending web portal

Once the attacker has achieved access, they can send SMS messages to other people and they will appear to have come from the victim's phone. A message will appear on the victim's cell phone in the SMS path and message history, but it will appear to be a regular sent message. It does not proactively notify the cell phone user that a message was sent, it doesn't cause a sound notification, and the message is not highlighted in any way. Unless the victim happened to be staring at their phone's SMS message history right at the moment the message was sent, it probably would not be discovered right away. And users seeing the rogue message would be confused about how it happened. During those minutes of ignorance or confusion, the attacker could be pushing an active deception scheme against the victim's trusted relationships. Here you can read about an example of a real-world attack using this method: nakedsecurity.sophos.com/2019/10/18/phishy-text-message-tries-to-steal-your-cellphone-account.

Attacks Against the Underlying Supporting Infrastructure

Sending and receiving SMS messages involves many components under the control and management of different parties. These include cell towers, base stations (transceivers and controllers), SS7, routers, switches, gateways, servers, databases, interfaces, websites, and anything else involved in SMS transmission. Any of these components can be an access point for maliciousness. And just as hackers can exploit telecom and retailer staffs and their accounts, so too can advanced hackers with more knowledge of how SMS works exploit the weakest link in the SMS messaging chain.

Here is a real-world example (`www.fireeye.com/blog/threat-research/2019/10/messagetap-who-is-reading-your-text-messages.html`) from 2019. A custom-coded Linux malware program was inserted by Chinese nation-state attackers into a European telecom's network on SMS-handling servers. There it could steal phone numbers, IMSI information, and SMS message texts. It included a feature that could do text-based searches looking for particular people and key words. These types of malware programs could intercept secret codes sent via SMS and redirect and block them.

It is likely that advanced attackers, especially nation-state or intelligence agency attackers, routinely perform such attacks as needed. Or even more likely, in their country of origin they have authority to request permission of the network provider and the appropriate equipment to insert themselves into the SMS communication center as needed—legally and frequently.

Other SMS-Based Attacks

There are many other types of SMS-based attacks that don't directly impact SMS-based MFA but that could still be involved in an attack on an SMS user. These include silent messaging and denial-of-service (DoS) attacks.

Silent SMS Messaging

For example, law enforcement agencies can send "silent" SMS messages to a user, which do not show up in the SMS-based application and which the user does not know about, but which allows the sender to track the user's whereabouts and learn other identifying information. These types of SMS messages are known as Type 0, which refers to the numeric code that the sender puts in the SMS message header's Type field. This approach was intended to be a way that a cell network provider could push or collect needed information to the phone without bothering the holder. Check out the following news story: `www.theregister.co.uk/2011/02/04/silent_sms`.

Regular users may be able to send silent SMS messages to other receivers, depending on what the receiving and sending network providers allow. There are even open source applications anyone can download to their phone, including this one: `github.com/domi007/silentSMS`. I don't recommend that you download and use this app since it requires that you allow an untrusted app to be installed on your phone and you never know if there is or isn't something more nefarious hiding in the code (unless you know what you're looking for and inspect each line of code). Still, it can be done.

A related "control-type" of SMS message is known as "Flash SMS" messages. Flash messages are sent by SMS, but they appear on your phone across the screen and aren't seen or stored in your regular SMS application or inbox. Flash messages are used to send Amber Alerts, weather warnings, and other types of official warnings. An attacker who is allowed to craft an SMS flash message that is not stopped by the network provider could likely pose as an otherwise trusted critical authority to cause maliciousness.

SMS Denial-of-Service Attack

An SMS-based attacker could also send a flood of SMS messages nearly anywhere into the system that supports and sends SMS messages and overwhelm the involved component. In the simplest form of the attack, a sender could send a flood of messages to a receiver, which then overwhelms the user's ability to handle the incoming messages and obfuscates important legitimate messages. An attacker could make it nearly impossible for an SMS user to be notified, view, or use an SMS message related to SMS-based MFA solutions.

And these attacks can be done silently. A more advanced attacker could flood the underlying network provider's system as well. Here's a great whitepaper detailing how SMS works and some possible DoS attacks: mo.co.za/open/silentdos.pdf.

Even without DoS attacks, SMS is very unreliable. It is known as "connection-less," meaning its delivery from source to destination isn't guaranteed. And some studies have shown that 1 percent to 5 percent of SMS messages are never delivered. That's a bad delivery rate when almost every other type of authentication method is as near to 100 percent as you can get without just saying it's 100 percent.

SIM/SMS Attack Method Summary

In summary, there are many ways that SIM information can be stolen and SMS fraudulently used, including the following:

- SS7 hacking
- SIM swapping
- SMS impersonation
- Cell phone network provider account hijacking
- Mobile phone malware that steals SIM information
- Social engineering cell phone network provider's employees
- DoS attacks

Many of these attacks start by the attacker sending a simple phishing email to or calling the legitimate user, posing as the cell phone network provider to obtain the user's legitimate information (account logon, password, etc.). Once learned, the user's fraudulently obtained information can be used to accomplish the SIM/SMS takeover. SMS has been so successfully abused that many authorities, including the U.S. government, frown upon or forbid SMS to be used as authentication.

NIST Digital Identity Guidelines Warning

In June 2017, the U.S. National Institute of Standards and Technology (NIST) released version 1.0 of their Digital Identity Guidelines, Special Publication 800-63 (`www.nist.gov/itl/tig/projects/special-publication-800-63`). These guides are the U.S. government's official recommendations and are often requirements for entities that must follow NIST guidelines. NIST guidelines usually carry great weight and are often adopted as the de facto standards and requirements used throughout much of the world. SP 800-63 was especially controversial compared to previous NIST authentication guides because it stated that the long-held, traditional password policy guidelines of requiring long, complex passwords and forced periodic changes were actually *increasing* a follower's risk compared to using simple, shorter, nonchanging passwords. Yes, you read that right. The U.S. government claimed that using the type of password you are probably forced to use at work increases your risk of being hacked. Despite the government declaring their new password policy recommendations, as of this writing not a single major public cybersecurity guideline (PCI-DSS, HIPAA, NERC, etc.) follows it. Instead, they still require organizations to use the older, higher-risk password policy recommendations.

The Digital Identity Guidelines made another fact clear: SMS-based MFA solutions are not desired. In SP 800-63B (`nvlpubs.nist.gov/nistpubs/SpecialPublications/NIST.SP.800-63b.pdf`), NIST said that authenticators using public-switched telephone networks, including phone and SMS-based one-time passwords (OTP) are *restricted*. Most SMS-based MFA solutions send OTP codes as part of their authentication solution.

NOTE One-time passwords will be covered in detail in the next chapter.

Restricted means the authenticator has elevated risks and should not be implemented without all the involved parties understanding the risks. Furthermore, NIST is signaling that restricted authenticators may not be acceptable in the near future. This is the U.S. government and one of the most respected computer security entities in the world telling you how insecure SMS is. They are basically saying do not use it. Officially, they are saying do not use SMS without everyone involved understanding the risks. Most people involved with SMS-based MFA solutions do not understand the risk. So, don't use SMS-based MFA solutions if you can avoid them. If you're planning on developing or using an SMS-based MFA solution, think about this: the U.S. government, over three years ago, said you really shouldn't use them. Should you or your business be depending on an SMS-based MFA solution that the government says isn't that good? If you somehow said yes, there are lot of SMS victims that would like to share their experiences with you.

Defenses to SMS-Based MFA Attacks

The best protection against SMS-based MFA attacks is to not use or rely on SMS-based MFA solutions. However, as I said earlier, SMS-based MFA attacks are the most popular type of MFA on the Internet. Often you cannot get access to a site or service that requires MFA without using SMS-based MFA. Sometimes a vendor may even have a phone app for their services, but they will often resort to sending SMS codes because everyone has SMS active but not everyone has their app running. So good luck trying to avoid using SMS-based MFA. Many times you have no choice. If you have to use SMS-based MFA, here are some developer and user defenses.

Developer Defenses

First, let's look at some developer defenses.

Security Awareness Training

Any SMS-based MFA vendor should share examples of the risks of using their solution, educating users about the types of rogue attacks that could be accomplished even while the users rely on their solution. Educate the users about common risks and scams.

Way to Verify SMS Message Legitimacy

As long as SMS doesn't have an easy way for a user to verify a vendor's SMS message legitimacy, the vendor's solution should include a method that the user can quickly verify that an SMS message claiming to be from the legitimate vendor really is from that vendor. It can be something as easy as creating a user portal where the user can verify the legitimacy of all sent SMS messages. The user should be able to easily pull up that portal and verify that it is on the real website for that purpose.

Expire SMS Codes in Ten Minutes or Less

All sent SMS codes should have a useful life of 10 minutes or less. You don't want to let an authentication code sent via SMS to be used indefinitely. Having an unexpired SMS code increases the risk of unauthorized viewing and reuse. Make sure all SMS secrets are only sent to previously registered phone numbers, and if the user generates the SMS recovery code, they should have to provide not only at least a portion of the preregistered phone number that the SMS code is being sent to but also another piece of authentication information that only the user should know.

Tell Users to Put Your Contact Info in Their Contact List

Tell users to put the phone number or code related to your SMS-sending service in their phone so that when you send an SMS message it automatically comes up as a validated contact name. Educate users not to accept SMS messages from phone numbers outside of the communicated contact information.

Prevent Suspicious SMS Messages from Being Sent

If the user can initiate SMS messages, look at the actions of the user and see whether or not they are suspicious. Is the request coming from the user's usual devices, locations, and other normal behavior characteristics? If not, require additional authentication before sending the user the requested SMS code.

Use Push Authentication

MFA solutions involving "push" authentication have become increasingly more popular over the last few years. Push authentication is when an authentication service transmits, or "pushes," a message or code to a preregistered device or application involved in an active logon sequence, which the user then acknowledges (or declines). A common scenario is a user logging into a website and after the user provides their logon name, the website's authentication solution automatically pushes a message to the user's MFA phone app. The user gets the authentication message, reviews, and approves. The approval process generates a response back to the website, which then automatically logs the user on. There are even popular push notification cloud services, like Google Cloud Messaging and Apple Push Notification service, that developers and MFA providers can use as part of their solution to push their messages.

Because the server is pushing it to the user via a preregistered, usually out-of-band app installed on the mobile device, it makes many forms of hacking harder to achieve. For example, if the user's session was compromised by a MitM attack, the eavesdropping would not capture any of the out-of-band messages, as it might if the user typed in an in-band OTP code. In most instances, the pushing is done to the user's phone, to an authentication app directly tied to the logon experience. Because of the inherent issues with SMS as covered in this chapter, push authentication to a phone app or hardware token is preferred over SMS.

There are even "pull" messages. Because push messages often rely on potentially unreliable phone and cellular phone service, the push notification services cannot guarantee delivery. Some MFA vendors, such as WatchGuard, will use their client-side app to send "pull" messages to the server side. When you open the MFA phone app, the WatchGuard app will proactively check for waiting, outstanding push messages to make sure one wasn't lost or delayed (for example, as it would be if it was sent while you were on a long flight) and is still waiting for a retry somewhere.

Most push messages are sent to an "app ID" that ties the push message to a particular user application. If the push message is sent using a general push service servicing multiple sites and services, the push message should include all the necessary authentication "transaction" details so that the user can acknowledge the push is tied to the correct, desired authentication experience. Without the necessary details, an attacker could possibly create a logon credential to a second website or service the user is also registered with, but doesn't know they are logging onto, and inadvertently be tricked into responding to an alternate Push message tied to a second website or service they are unaware is involved. The attacker could trick the user into logging into an incorrect site or use the push acknowledgement to log on to the second site themselves using the victim's identity. Another potential security issue is that if the device or app being used to receive the push is compromised and/or in the hacker's possession, then the push will be sent to the attacker, who can then acknowledge the push message. Phone apps should always require authentication as well, such as a PIN or biometrics, to prevent a lost phone from being used to further compromise the victim's online experiences as well. But in general, push messages are a good thing and usually improve MFA security.

User Defenses

The number one defense is to use any MFA solution other than one that relies on SMS. Outside of that, if you must use and rely on SMS-based MFA devices, here are some other defenses you can implement.

Security Awareness Training

The best piece of defense advice I can give you is to let users know they can still be hacked even though they are using an MFA solution. Make sure users are educated about the risks and scams specifically associated with SMS-based MFA solutions. You definitely want to cover SIM swap attacks, SMS impersonation, and rogue SMS URL links that can lead to device takeovers. Educate users so that they understand they don't have all the normal protections they may have on a full-sized computer, such as the ability to hover over a link. Make sure all SMS-based MFA users get this training at least once a year if not once a month.

Be Aware of Rogue Recovery Messages

Users should be aware of rogue SMS recovery schemes and what they look like. Examples include unexpected SMS messages or voice calls warning them of a possible compromise.

Be Wary of SMS Recovery PIN Scams

Users should be told that, if they are sent an SMS recovery PIN, it would be suspicious if they were instructed to type it back into another separate SMS message or have to tell someone over a phone the sent PIN number.

Try to Place a Lock on Your SIM Info

Some cell phone network providers allow high-risk users to place a "lock" or "block" on their SIM information. That way, if someone calls requesting that their SIM information be moved to another phone, that individual must know the additional piece(s) of information to get the lock removed. Be aware that this could frustrate users if they cannot remember the information needed to remove the block.

Protect Your Cell Phone Network Account Logon with MFA

This may sound like circular logic, but it can't hurt to protect your cell phone network provider user account with MFA if that is an available option. Yes, MFA can be hacked, but protecting logon accounts with MFA usually provides you with more security. So use it.

Be Wary of Short URL Links

All users should be wary of short URL links—you don't know where they go. When I get them, I usually just ignore those messages. If I see one that might be legit, I usually open it on a computer virtual machine where potential malware can do no permanent harm.

Minimize Posting Your Phone Number

I used to be a guy that posted my personal cell phone number in every email I sent. No more! Many SMS scams begin with an attacker having your valid phone number. Sure, there are lots of services that they or anyone can use to look up your phone number, but why make it too easy? If they don't know your phone number, they can't scam you via SMS.

Is RCS Here to Save Mobile Messaging?

Rich Communication Services (RCS) is the heir apparent to SMS. Conceptually, it is intended to be the less hackable and more feature-rich replacement of SMS. I'm sure SS6 proponents had the same hope when SS7 was announced. As with all new technologies that claim they will be more secure, the devil is in the details. Companies and hackers are already hacking it plenty (see `www.wired.com/story/rcs-texting-security`). They can even hack RCS users while sitting on the same Wi-Fi network. That's something that couldn't be done with SMS, so it seems that RCS may yield even more hacking opportunities.

Part of the problem is that even though RCS is supposed to be a new international standard, it is being implemented in different ways by different vendors. In addition, there is the need to be backward compatible with previous technologies such as SMS, which means some of the new and improved security features can't be used. Some RCS security researchers think that it is far easier to hack and results in worse consequences than SMS. So I wouldn't hold my breath thinking RCS was going to make our phone chatting conversations more secure.

> **NOTE** Interestingly, Bruce Schneier makes the same arguments when comparing the new 5G networks to 4G, security-wise: `www.schneier.com/blog/archives/2020/01/china_isnt_the_.html`. He says the need to continue supporting 4G at the same time as 5G on the same networks leads to many insecurities. Unfortunately, this is a common security story.

Is SMS-Based MFA Still Better than Passwords?

In the earlier chapters I stressed that using MFA isn't a bad thing. In most cases, using MFA for protecting confidential information is preferred and more secure than using a regular logon name and password and other 1FA solutions. But let's not breeze over the word "most" so quickly. SMS-based MFA solutions have been hacked so many times and so many people relying on them have lost great sums of money (especially well-to-do crypto-currency holders and traders) that many previous

SMS-based MFA solution users have gone back to traditional simple logon names and passwords. They literally don't trust SMS-based MFA solutions to protect them nearly as well as simply using a dedicated logon name and password. Security experts can argue all they like as to whether the switcher reacted wrongly or too strongly, but it cannot be denied that the user who depended on an SMS-based MFA solution was successfully attacked, suffered harm, and no longer trusts an SMS-based MFA solution to protect them. And trust is what authentication is all about.

Many would argue that SMS is better than a simple name and password and that people should use it as an MFA solution instead of 1FA. I understand this argument. Still, I think the biggest problem is that most people do not understand how utterly easy it is to hack SMS, and until that education becomes widespread or the SMS services update themselves to be less hackable, I'm not a big fan.

Summary

This chapter covered the ways SMS-based MFA solutions can be abused. The attacks boil down to the fact that SMS is based on insecure protocols and does not have adequate authentication for our digital world. SMS impersonation and hijacking makes SMS-based MFA solutions among the riskiest authentication solutions available. We discussed the promise and risks of RCS, the evolving standard that is supposed to replace SMS, and the steps that developers and users of SMS-based MFA solutions can take to minimize risk.

Chapter 9, "One-Time Password Attacks" will cover time-based OTP-based MFA solutions and attacks.

9

One-Time Password Attacks

This chapter will cover attacks against one-time password MFA solutions. These solutions have long been among the most popular types of MFA and are continuing to grow in popularity. This chapter will explain how these types of MFA solutions work, give some example attacks, and then cover various defenses to reduce the risk of successful attacks.

Introduction to OTP

One-time password (OTP) authentication solutions have been popular for decades and are based on a concept that many people believe to be the cryptographic Holy Grail solution for authentication.

The idea is that when a subject is asked to authenticate, they provide a seemingly random set of characters that is valid only for that one request and known or predictable only between the subject and the authentication system. Once used, it will never be generated or used again (i.e., the "one-time" part). So, even if an attacker learns a particular OTP, it will never work again on any other authentication session. Any successful future authentication challenges would use a different, unpredictable, code.

The never, nonrepeating claim of an OTP solution is only true of a conceptualized, perfect OTP solution. In a perfect world, the OTP would never be repeated. But the reality is that it's impossible to avoid repeating OTP characters given a long period of time, especially when the number of characters used is limited. For example, an OTP may use a core algorithm capable of generating trillions of different possibilities, but if the OTP solution only uses and displays 6 numerals, 0–9 (as most of them do), then only 10^6 (i.e., 1 million) possible combinations can be generated and used. And if a new OTP code is shown every 30 seconds, as is common, that means all million codes could be shown in 347 days, if the codes never repeated (which isn't even a guarantee). So, in the real world, the codes do repeat, but often not close together and not predictably so. This still allows OTP codes to be used securely, even in our imperfect world.

The seemingly random requirement is essential. If an attacker were able to predict any future OTP code and the time it would be valid, they could use it as if they were the legitimate user. A perfectly and truly random number that only the legitimate user and the authentication system can generate and know at a given time period or event is key to the security of an OTP-based authentication system. The biggest problem is how to create a truly random and unpredictable OTP.

In the early days of cryptography and authentication codes, the legitimate parties could just generate and share a big list of random numbers as codes and agree to use them in the future. But that type of scheme has at least two big problems. First, how do you make the codes truly random? How do you truly create the codes randomly and verify that they are truly random? Humans could simply "guess" at code characters—say, have each of the legitimate parties "randomly" guess a number between 0 and 9 over and over until all the codes are created and shared. For instance, suppose they need a four-digit OTP. The first person might say 3, the second person might say 5, the first person then says 9, and the second person says 2. This would give a shared four-digit code of 3592. And they could repeat the guessing and sharing until they have shared all the codes they need to share for all the possible future authentication transactions.

To the average person, this seems fairly random and fair. But it is not. Humans simply cannot do anything truly random. Humans tend to be fairly "un-random" and have a hard time doing anything truly random, especially in picking numbers and codes. If humans were asked to participate in a task like that above, they would invariably pick some numbers considerably more than others without realizing it. For example, humans are far more likely to pick lower numbers than higher numbers and to avoid repeating numbers. In a truly randomly selected set of numbers, over time, each number (0–9) would have a 10 percent chance of being selected. But if you had humans pick the numbers you would surely see numbers selected below 10 percent of the time and numbers picked over 10 percent of the time. In studies of this human behavior, some of the numbers were picked nearly 20 percent of the time and others less than 5 percent. No matter what your loved one says to the contrary, humans just aren't random.

> **NOTE**   One of my favorite things to suggest is to read the reviewer comments for the Rand Corporation's book *A Million Random Digits with a 100,000 Normal Deviates* (American Book Publishers, 2001) on Amazon: www.amazon.com/Million-Random-Digits-Normal-Deviates/dp/0833030477. This book was supposed to be used by humans "randomly" opening to any page and just "blindly" picking a set of numbers. Providing what looks like very random numbers was supposed to help fix the human error part, but it really doesn't work that way. Humans just end up picking non-random areas of the book to pick a "random" number, skipping over early and ending pages altogether, which a computer selecting the same pages would never do. But please look at a sample of the book's pages and then read the reviewer comments. Anyone who has ever followed my advice ends up laughing until they cry—or at least computer geek types with a similar sense of humor.

Computers and their ability to pick seemingly random numbers are often used in place of more flawed human code selection. Unfortunately, prior to quantum computers, even computers could not be truly random. The best any traditional computer could do was to generate a seemingly random set of numbers. But they were not truly random. Some developer somewhere had to create an algorithm that tried its best to simulate randomness, but by its very definition any algorithm is a set of steps that follows a common process every time. And that's the opposite of random. Over the years, computers have gotten better at appearing truly random, even if they were not truly, perfectly random. Computer scientists acknowledge this fact by calling all traditional computer *random number generators* (RNGs) *pseudo-random number generators* (or PRNGs).

NOTE Noted cryptographer and industry luminary Bruce Schneier has pointed out to me that our PRNGs are nevertheless pretty good. He claims that, essentially, trying to compare the accuracy of a good PRNG to a truly perfect random number generator is like building a mile-high wall and arguing over whether it can be made one or two feet higher.

Quantum-based computing devices, using the inherent natural properties of quantum particles, can actually generate truly random numbers, and certifiably so (www.nist.gov/news-events/ news/2018/04/nists-new-quantum-method-generates-really-random-numbers). Unfortunately, quantum devices capable of generating truly random and certifiable random numbers are not yet widespread. Developers creating OTP codes should make sure any random-generating algorithm has been analyzed to provide as near true randomness as is possible (see more details in the "Developer Defenses" section, later in this chapter).

NOTE If you are interested in learning more about quantum computers and quantum random number generators, check out my 2019 book, *Cryptography Apocalypse: Preparing for the Day When Quantum Computers Break Today's Crypto* (Wiley).

Second, another similar big problem with manually created physical OTP codes, is where to hide the one-time codes until they are needed. When the two authorized parties generate and share one or more preshared codes, they need to protect them from unauthorized viewing until they are needed and can be used in a secure way (i.e., from unauthorized eavesdropping). Even today, there are MFA solutions that use preprinted OTP codes as one of their authentication factors. How are the codes securely generated and shared? How does a user securely store them? Where? In our increasingly digital world, where do we store a piece of paper? Or, if the OTPs are digitally represented, where do we securely store them on a computer? How can we readily call them up whenever we need them? How do we use them without others seeing them as well? Do the codes ever expire? Can any code be used at any time or must they be used one at a time, in order?

Solving this problem was a multi-century issue for the cryptography world. In the middle of the 1970s, asymmetric cryptography was created (with several different independent groups and people initially claiming credit without knowing about the other), and it solved the problem for digital operations (although not on the printed, non-digital side). Asymmetric cryptography with two cryptographically related keys, a private and a public one, allows two people to securely share any information (in our case, an OTP) over digital transportation channels without having to divulge any previous secret information. This solved the problem in the digital world, at least for transmission security, but not in the real world for printed OTPs.

A partial solution for preshared printed OTPs was for any printed OTP only to be part of the required OTP needed to successfully authenticate. Every OTP transaction would be formed by the preshared printed portion along with another code that was not physically printed. For example, the user could be instructed ahead of time to always add the code 1234 to the beginning of every typed-in OTP. The preshared printed portion of the OTP may be something like 9913, but when the user typed it in as part of an authentication try, they would type in **12349913**. That way, if the preprinted OTP portion was viewed by an unauthorized party, the entire OTP code would not be fully compromised. Of course, an attacker capturing a few of the user's subsequent logons might notice a pattern of all the user's OTPs beginning with 1234 and figure out what was going on. Solving that problem ends up returning to the primary issue: the one of generating truly random numbers and codes that the adversaries cannot guess or predict.

One way to stop an adversary from seeing or predicting the constant portion of a preshared key is to make it hard to predict in the first place instead of having some portion fixed and some portion randomly generated. But how do you generate a seemingly random OTP between two authorized parties without it being intercepted or easily predictable?

Seed Value-Based OTPs

The answer was OTPs that used a random, but unchanging, number preshared among all the legitimate parties that leads to a shared, seemingly random, and frequently changing OTP that can be computed by either party independent of the other. Each side does its own calculation, and the side trying to log on submits their calculated answer to the authenticator. The authenticator does its own calculation and then compares. If they match, the subject is successfully authenticated. All the protection is due to the true randomness and secrecy of the preshared randomly generated number (known as the *seed value* or *nonce*).

For example, let's supposed that all the authorized parties shared a randomly generated number of 508. All involved parties would have knowledge of the seed value and use it as part of every authentication transaction, but no one else would know its value. All the involved parties would also share a common OTP algorithm, which even adversaries might know.

As an example, for simplicity's sake, let's say the involved legitimate parties are using a made-up Roger's algorithm, which is $X \times Y \times 13$, where X is the constant random seed value and Y is a newly generated value that anyone, including an adversary, could know or view. Y is known as the *counter value*. It is known as the counter value because early on it was simply a changing value that incremented each time it was used, say from 1 to 2 to 3 and so on (although cryptographically it was likely more complex than that). The seed value never changes, and the counter value changes every transaction.

Continuing our example, for the first authentication transaction let's suppose the countervalue is 1. Using Roger's algorithm to generate the OTP, the answer would be 6604 (i.e., 508 × 1 × 13). Then let's suppose the counter value was 2 and then 3, respectively. The next valid OTP results would be 13,208 (i.e., 508 × 2 × 13) and 19,812 (i.e., 508 × 3 × 13), respectively. Perhaps to make it slightly less obvious to any observers as to what is going on, we decide as part of our algorithm to use only the first four digits (known as *truncation*) and always remove the second digit so that the respective results become three-digit codes of 604, 120, and 181. It might appear to a simple observer that the resulting codes are fairly random and unpredictable (although they are not even close to being random and unpredictable). The only truly unknown value was the seed value of 508.

Now, take this sort of OTP calculation and involve really long numbers (128-bits or 16-digits long) as a bare minimum. A 128-bit code can store 2^{128} different codes or 340,282,366,920,938,463,463, 374,607,431,768,211,455 different codes. Now add true randomness (or as close as you can get) and a more realistic OTP algorithm that involves more advanced math and strong cryptographic functions—things like trigonometry, moduli, and hashes. Essentially what you get is a very, very, very hard-to-guess and -predict OTP number without having knowledge of the shared seed value.

Early on, lots of OTP creators used homemade algorithms and their own math to create their seemingly random-looking OTP codes. Unfortunately, creating truly secure OTP codes is really, really hard to do. Many early OTP codes that looked very hard to guess and predict ended up being figured out and 100 percent predictable. In response, over time the OTP industry came up with a tested and proven standard OTP algorithm and told OTP solution creators to use what was tried and true instead of making up their own.

HMAC-Based OTP

Enter *hash-based message authentication codes* (HMAC-based OTP, or HOTP). Cryptographic *hash algorithms* (also known as *hash functions* or simply *hashes*) are used to create unique output results for every unique content input. In our discussion, the unique input would be whatever values the OTP solution supplies as part of the OTP initial code calculations (i.e., seed and counter values), although in crypto circles it would simply be known as the *message* to be hashed. The hash output after the "hashing" is known as the *message digest*, *hash result*, or simply *hash*.

A secure, trusted hash has four important traits:

- For every unique input, a unique output result must be generated.
- Every time the same input is hashed, it should result in the same hash output.
- No two different inputs should ever result in the same hash output (i.e., a *collision*).
- If given the hash output, it should be impossible or near impossible (known as *nontrivial* in the crypto world) for anyone to derive the original content input.

A good hash has all these attributes. Hash algorithms usually result in fixed-length hash results regardless of the length of the input. Common hash output lengths range from 128 to 256 bits.

Because in the real world the hash outputs are often shorter than the messages they hash, it absolutely means that you can end up with the same hash for two different messages (i.e., a hash collision). You can't represent all the possible set of larger messages with a smaller set of unique messages. You just can't. But like the never-repeating and truly random assumptions we accepted earlier as not being truly perfect either, if the outputted hashes are usually unique (even if not truly guaranteed to be unique), it's acceptable for most uses.

NOTE   Some of the material on hashing has been previously discussed in Chapter 3 but is repeated here for completeness. It also doesn't hurt to read it again.

There have been many different generally accepted, widely used hash standards over the years, including Message Digest 5 (MD5), Windows LANManager (LM), Windows NT (NT), and Secure Hash Algorithm-1 (SHA-1). All of these previous standards, except for NT, are considered weak and broken.

Today, the most popular hashing algorithm is Secure Hash Algorithm-2 (SHA-2 or SHA2), although in 2015 NIST recommended that SHA-2's successor, Secure Hash Algorithm-3 (SHA-3 or SHA3), be used instead because SHA-2 has known weaknesses that will only get weaker over time. So far, almost everyone is still using SHA-2. SHA-2 has many different output sizes, including 224, 384, 256, and 512 bits. Table 9.1, which is a repeat of Table 3.1, shows the hash result output for the word "frog" using various popular hashes.

Table 9.1: Example hash outputs for the word "frog"

Hash algorithm	Hash result for "frog"
MD5	938C2CC0DCC05F2B68C4287040CFCF71
SHA-1	B3E0F62FA1046AC6A8559C68D231B6BD11345F36
SHA-2	74FA5327CC0F4E947789DD5E989A61A8242986A596F170 640AC90337B1DA1EE4
SHA-3 (512)	6EB693784D6128476291A3BBBF799d287F77E1816b05C 611CE114AF239BE2DEE734B5Df71B21AC74A36BE12CD 629890CE63EE87E0F53BE987D938D39E8D52B62

An HMAC algorithm uses a strong hash and a trusted calculation algorithm along with a preshared key (seed value) in a way to generate unique outputs for unique supplied content.

HMACs have been around for decades, including as defined for everyday use in the 1997 Internet Engineering Task Force (IETF) Request for Comment (RFC) 2104 (tools.ietf.org/html/rfc2104). In 2008, RFC 2014 was codified by NIST in Federal Information Processing Standard (FIPS) Publication 198 (csrc.nist.gov/publications/detail/fips/198/1/final). Although back in 1997 the original developers were talking about MD5 and SHA-1 hashes, which were later deprecated, it speaks to the resiliency of the idea and algorithm that decades later all we had to do was update to stronger hashes and the concept and math didn't substantially change. HMACs and HMAC-based OTPs have proven to be a very good idea. See en.wikipedia.org/wiki/HMAC for more information on HMACs in general.

Most OTP vendors immediately understood the value of using a tried-and-true HMAC-based OTP algorithm and stopped trying to "roll their own" OTP algorithms. You can read more detail about HMAC-based OTP solutions based on the agreed-on standard here: en.wikipedia.org/wiki/ HMAC-based_One-time_Password_algorithm. A popular specification and implementation of HMAC-based OTPs is the Initiative for Open Authentication (OATH) and is known as the OATH HOTP-standard. You can learn more about it here: openauthentication.org. Several venders provide OATH HOTP devices, including Yubico (www.yubico.com/wp-content/uploads/2016/02/ YubicoBestPracticesOATH-HOTP.pdf), one of the leading OTP vendors in the world.

Most HMAC-based OTPs deliver 6- to 8-digit OTP codes, usually numeric only, for use during authentication. There are still custom OTP algorithms, but most are still fairly close to the standard one and (hopefully) include security improvements. In order for HMAC-based OTP solutions to be secure, the following components must be trusted, secure, and strong:

- HMAC algorithm
- Hash algorithm
- Seed value needs to be randomly generated.
- Seed value must forever remain a secret between the involved authenticating parties.
- Counter value should change and not repeat.

Of these components, only the seed value needs to be secret. Everything else, including the counter and algorithm, could be known and the overall OTP result should remain secure. The overall protective power is in the ability of the hash to output a nonpredictable and seemingly random string based on the inputs. If you have a good hash and a good algorithm used against something that involves a secret, you're good to go.

When you're using an OTP with a counter value, the question is what should increment the counter and cause the solution to use a new counter value. There are several different possibilities.

Event-Based OTP

One answer is what is known as an event-based OTP, which is really a subset of HOTP. The event can be and often is simply the passage of time. For example, every 10 minutes the OTP device updates its code. This requires that both the OTP device and the authenticator keep in time sync (which is often more difficult than it sounds). Even identically created time sources using identical materials can vary in what time they report over time.

The "event" can also be a user pressing a button on the OTP device or setting a physical set of characters, as sort of an initialization code, to kick off the new OTP code calculation. In those cases, the authentication system may start by communicating with the authenticating user, and communicate some set of numbers, letters, colors, sounds, and so forth. The user has been instructed to look or listen for the codes and then input them into their OTP device. Another example could be that the user needs to biometrically authenticate to the OTP device first or hold the device up to a computer screen so that an optical code can be communicated to the OTP device (the latter example will be discussed in more detail in Chapter 21, "Test - Can You Spot the Vulnerabilities?").

With any OTP MFA solution, the device or software the subject is using to authenticate must be synchronized with the authenticating resource. Both the subject and the authenticator must share, use, and store the same seed value to compute future resulting OTP codes. They must also share the same method for generating current and future counter codes and algorithms. And they often get time-synchronized.

In practice, there is an authentication database (store) on both sides, and they share the seed value and also track a globally unique identification value that ties the subject's authentication device and/or software instance to the right authentication record within the authentication database. Usually the identification number is some sort of unique serial number or GUID. It may be globally unique or just unique for the vendor's implementation. The database can be stored in a number of places, but it must always be stored (or readily accessible) in a location where the authenticator can access it during authentication of the subject.

During authentication, the subject's authentication solution and the authenticator's service must be able to separately, consistently, and accurately calculate the resulting OTP result for any participant for any particular instant (when all involved requirements are satisfied). They must be able to calculate the result separately, and then the authenticator compares what it calculated by itself to what the subject's authentication solution submitted. If they match, the subject is considered successfully authenticated.

There is always a chance that someone learning all the involved components except for the secret value could, with enough time and processing power, compute the secret value, which, if learned, would make everything come tumbling down. If given enough sequential OTP outputs, there's always a chance that an attacker can figure out what the static seed value is. The counter value helps offset the risk so that part of the computation is always changing, and an attacker will have a harder time determining which part of the changing output is due to the static seed portion and which part is due to the changing counter value.

OTP designers help further counteract this threat by routinely changing the counter value. That way, if an attacker was ever able to successfully compute a single OTP result code (never mind figuring out the seed value, which is much harder), by the time they likely did so, the resulting OTP code would be expired and no longer work. OTP designers make the codes expire, and when they do, both sides must use the new counter value to generate a new OTP output code. Since the counter codes are often routinely changed, and the more frequent the better, many times it just makes sense for the counter to synchronize and key off the current time value.

TOTP

Time-based one-time password (TOTP) authentication solutions involve a current date and/or time value in the counter calculation. As the time changes, so too does the counter value, usually at fixed predetermined intervals, like every 30 seconds to 10 minutes. I think anyone who has used a TOTP device has learned the minor stress that is caused when you are rushing against an expiring time clock to type in the current TOTP code before it expires and you need to begin typing in a new one.

NOTE Some MFA texts don't call the nonstatic value that a TOTP solution uses a *counter*. They reserve the term *counter value* for non-TOTP OTP solutions.

Like HMAC-based OTP, TOTP-based OTP solutions have gained a common standard (en .wikipedia.org/wiki/Time-based_One-time_Password_algorithm) codified in IETF RFC 6238 (tools.ietf.org/html/rfc6238). Considered a special subclass of HBAC-OTP, TOTP solutions are considered trusted and secure when following the same rules (i.e., shared but secret static random seed value, trusted hash involved, trusted TOTP-based algorithm involved, etc.). The only added requirement for a TOTP is a trustworthy time source for all involved authenticators that can stay in time sync (i.e., "sync'd") with each other.

Any trusted time source can be used and the time can be "grabbed" using any language or device, but in general the time value tends to be the date (YYYY-MM-DD) followed immediately by the time (HH:MM:SS), although I have also seen the hundredths of the seconds involved as well. The date and time is usually measured in Coordinated Universal Time (UTC), which is also known as Greenwich Mean Time (GMT) and Zulu Time. UTC is usually used because it does not have to be converted and modified by location and time zone in order to be used (unless displayed or wanted). The current time read is often converted into other numeric values such as the number of seconds since January 1, 1980 or the number of 30-second periods since January 1, 1970 (known as *Epoch* or *Unix time*: en .wikipedia.org/wiki/Unix_time). Most of today's TOTP solutions use "epoch time" as the time value of their OTP calculation.

Many times, the only difference between an HOTP solution and a TOTP solution is that the TOTP solution uses the current timestamp as the counter value and HOTP uses something else. Plus, when an HOTP gives a result, it remains valid until used or another HOTP counter action occurs. A TOTP is always updating based on time all the time, and older TOTP values automatically invalidate more frequently based on time. The distinction is that an HOTP value may be potentially valid much longer, and thus attackable much longer, than a TOTP, which is always moving on.

TOTP Popular Examples

The two most popular TOTP-based MFA examples are RSA's SecurID and Alphabet's Google Authenticator. RSA offers hard token and software versions (also known as "soft tokens"), whereas Google offers software-only versions that run on phones and other computing devices.

RSA SecurID   I don't know if RSA SecurIDs (see an example in Figure 9.1) were the first hard-token TOTP-based MFA device, but they have been around for decades. For many of us long-term, experienced, computer security types, a SecurID was the first hard-token MFA device we had ever seen and, most of the time, the only TOTP device we had ever used. If it wasn't the first, it was one of the most popular. The little parallel bars on the left-hand side of the token display were countdown timer bars. One by one, they went away as the time for the current TOTP code expired. When they all went away, a new code with a full set of bars would be displayed and the timer and countdown bars would begin all over again.

Figure 9.1: Example RSA SecurID token
Source: Photo by Alexander Klink is licensed under CC BY 3.0 (`creativecommons.org/licenses/by/3.0`).

The RSA SecurID Wikipedia page (`en.wikipedia.org/wiki/RSA_SecurID`)—yes, it has its own Wikipedia page—says that in 2003 they commanded over 70 percent of the MFA market. RSA themselves claim that 93 percent of Fortune 500 companies use one of their products, although that figure likely includes both hard-token and software solutions.

Early on, most implementations required that a user type in a static set of characters that only the user and the authentication system knew, in combination along with the newly generated TOTP code portion. Eventually this requirement was relaxed or made optional so that RSA could provide a more seamless experience, as some of their competitors only required the TOTP code and not the combination of both the static password and TOTP code. Requiring both the static code <u>and</u> the TOTP is a more secure method, but as frequently happens in the computer security world, higher security requirements are often relaxed to make a better user experience. RSA SecurID and other RSA products remain among the top, most popular, MFA solutions today, although there is a lot more competition now.

Google Authenticator   Giving RSA a strong run for its money, or perhaps even surpassing it in popularity now, is the Google Authenticator, created in 2010. Google Authenticator is a software-based TOTP used with any website or service that supports it. See Figure 9.2 for an example Google Authenticator output result.

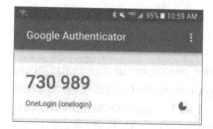

Figure 9.2: Example Google Authenticator logon code

The website or service using Google Authenticator for authentication must include code that requests Google Authenticator during logon. Before a user can use Google Authenticator with a website or service they must be sent a pre-shared 80-bit code using Base32 text or a graphical Quick Response (QR) code; see Figure 9.3 for an example QR code. The QR code contains an 80-bit key which is used as the pre-shared see value.

Figure 9.3: Example QR code

Base32 is an encoding system, using all capitalized English letters (A–Z) and numeric digits 2–7. That's 32 characters (26 letters plus 6 numbers). Each Base32 character can represent 5 bits of information. So, an 80-bit seed value takes 16 characters to send. People typing in sixteen Base32 characters can be a bit challenging, so Google Authenticator administrators often choose to send QR codes instead. QR codes can hold thousands of characters of information, so it has no problem representing the 80-bit seed value needed for Google Authenticator as well as other information, such as what site or service the code is tied to.

The user takes the received QR code and holds it up to the waiting Google Authenticator app installed on their phone or computing device, and the code then transfers to the Google Authenticator app for that particular instance. When Google first created Google Authenticator, it was an open source application and Google shared the algorithm used. Google turned Google Authenticator and its algorithm into a proprietary app, and the open source version (github.com/google/google-authenticator) became the FreeOTP project (en.wikipedia.org/wiki/FreeOTP), which is now used by Linux distros, such as RedHat.

The initial open source nature of Google Authenticator allowed anyone to see the (original) Google Authenticator algorithm. The Google Authenticator algorithm is posted on the Google Authenticator Wikipedia page (en.wikipedia.org/wiki/Google_Authenticator) and is implemented in an open source project called Pharo (smalltalkhub.com/#!/~SvenVanCaekenberghe/GoogleAuthenticator/). Figure 9.4 shows the Wikipedia description/pseudo-code of Google Authenticator's TOTP generation.

```
function GoogleAuthenticatorCode(string secret) is
    message := floor(current Unix time / 30)
    hash := HMAC-SHA1(secret, message)
    offset := last nibble of hash
    truncatedHash := hash[offset..offset+3]  // 4 bytes starting at the offset
    Set the first bit of truncatedHash to zero  // remove the most significant bit
    code := truncatedHash mod 1000000
    pad code with 0 from the left until length of code is 6
    return code
```

Figure 9.4: Wikipedia description/pseudo-code of Google Authenticator

Pharo allows anyone to code up a virtual instance of Google Authenticator. So far, it does not seem as if the underlying algorithm has changed since Pharo was created. Pharo's author created a document that steps through the Google Authenticator algorithm (medium.com/concerning-pharo/the-code-behind-google-authenticator-9c59c606a572). It should not be surprising that the Google Authenticator algorithm process, although fairly simple, goes through a lot of conversion steps, and so it can appear complex to someone unaccustomed to doing programming, computer cryptography, and byte conversions.

Here's an example conversion routine based on the Google Authenticator algorithm according to Pharo's author:

1. The 32-character Base32 secret key (seed value) is used and converted to a byte array.
2. The current time is taken and converted to Unix/Zulu time, which is the number of 30-second time periods since January 1, 1970.
3. The seed value and the time value are used in an HMAC-SHA-1 hashing event, with the seed value as the secret key and the time value as the message acted on by the hashing algorithm and secret key.
4. This outputs the 160-bit results from the hash calculation (i.e., the hash).
5. The 160-bit SHA-1 result is converted to a 20-byte array (8 bits per byte).
6. The 20-byte array is converted into a 32-bit integer, which has 9 numeric characters.

7. The first one or three numbers are truncated, depending on whether the Google Authenticator instance is supposed to return 6- or 8-character codes.

8. What remains is the Google Authenticator TOTP code.

The TOTP code return will be the same code every time if measured during the same 30-second Unix epoch cycle. Every 30 seconds a new code is generated and is only good for 30 seconds, although it appears that a second or two is allowed after the expiration period to account for a user quickly typing in a just-expired code. The TOTP code can be typed in as sequential digits, although it is often displayed and will be taken as two different sets of numbers separated by a space.

There are dozens of other vendors creating OTP, HOTP, and TOTP MFA solutions, using both hard-token and soft token versions. In the world of MFA, TOTP-based solutions are hot. Microsoft also uses a TOTP soft token solution known as Microsoft Authenticator (docs.microsoft.com/en-sg/azure/active-directory/user-help/user-help-auth-app-download-install). It, too, can use a QR code, as one of a few different methods, to communicate the initial seed value.

As great and popular as they are, OTP and TOTP solutions are not unhackable.

Example OTP Attacks

Like everything in the world, OTP-based MFA solutions can be attacked and hacked. This section examines some methods and examples.

Phishing OTP Codes

Without a doubt, one of the most common ways to hack OTP-based MFA solutions is for the hackers to phish and/or intercept the resulting codes, especially if all that is needed to log on is the account logon identifier and the OTP code. The OTP code is essentially just replacing a password as the secret needed to get in.

The most popular hacking method to get the OTP code is similar to what was shown in Chapter 6, "Access Control Token Tricks," with the Kevin Mitnick hacking LinkedIn video. The attacker somehow convinces an OTP-based MFA user to visit a rogue, lookalike website that is functioning as a man-in-the-middle proxy site between the victim and their intended ultimate destination. Everything the victim types is proxied to the ultimate server/service, and everything from the real server/service is proxied to the user. When the user is prompted to enter in their OTP code, the hacker grabs it and uses it to log on to the real website.

With HOTP tokens, a hacker could somehow trick a user into inputting multiple valid, sequential HTOP codes. Maybe they create a simulated logon page that asks the user to log on. The user types in their current HOTP code, and the fake website returns an error and asks the user to type in their next HOTP code, which the fake logon website then records. The first (and valid) code is now forwarded on to the real logon portal, and the user is moved to the real website. But the attacker has a second valid code that they can also use. In this type of attack, the hacker could induce the victim to type in a bunch of HOTP codes, storing up multiple valid future codes. Either way, by sending the first code to the valid website and then redirecting the user there, the user thinks their second (or subsequent) codes are the ones that worked (instead of the first). When the legitimate user goes to log on again, because their HOTP token is now unsynchronized with the logon portal, their future logons will not work, but the attacker's list of stolen HOTP codes will.

Here are some additional examples of successful attacks involving OTP codes that were phished or intercepted:

- www.wired.com/story/hack-binance-cryptocurrency-exchange
- www.bleepingcomputer.com/news/security/this-citibank-phishing-scam-could-trick-many-people
- nakedsecurity.sophos.com/2019/01/11/2fa-codes-can-be-phished-by-new-pentest-tool

Figure 9.5 shows an example screenshot of a Binance victim discussing how his stolen Google Authenticator TOTP code was stolen and used against him.

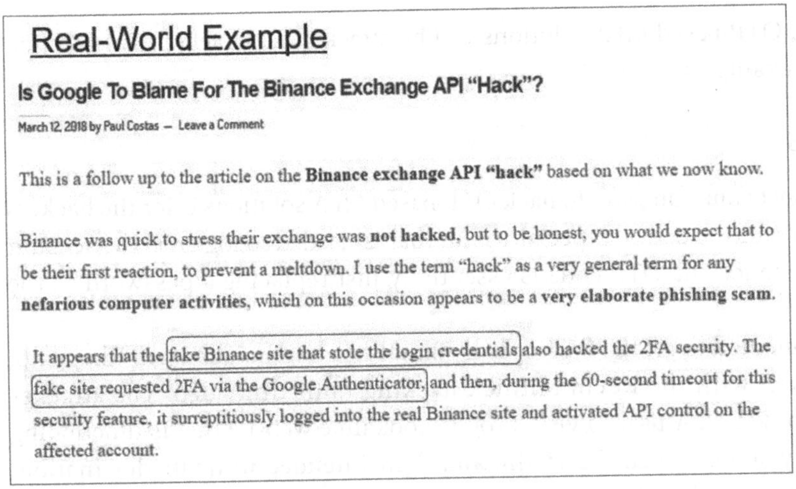

Real-World Example

Is Google To Blame For The Binance Exchange API "Hack"?

March 12, 2018 by Paul Costas — Leave a Comment

This is a follow up to the article on the **Binance exchange API "hack"** based on what we now know.

Binance was quick to stress their exchange was **not hacked**, but to be honest, you would expect that to be their first reaction, to prevent a meltdown. I use the term "hack" as a very general term for any **nefarious computer activities**, which on this occasion appears to be a **very elaborate phishing scam**.

It appears that the fake Binance site that stole the login credentials also hacked the 2FA security. The fake site requested 2FA via the Google Authenticator, and then, during the 60-second timeout for this security feature, it surreptitiously logged into the real Binance site and activated API control on the affected account.

Figure 9.5: Victim detailing how his stolen TOTP code was used to compromise his account

I have many more real-world examples to share, but I'll present them in Chapter 12, "Social Engineering Attacks." For now, just be aware that socially engineering people out of their OTP codes is very, very common.

Poor OTP Creation

It goes without saying that OTP solutions not using tried-and-tested standards such as those documented in IETF RFC 2104 (OTP) and/or RFC 6238 (TOTP) are often full of calculation vulnerabilities that don't make them nearly as difficult to figure out as the vendors thought. The risk goes up significantly if the OTP vendor creates their own cryptographic routines. Strong and secure cryptographic algorithms are very hard to create, even for the most advanced and studied cryptographers with decades of advanced degrees. If your vendor starts talking about proprietary or secret cipher algorithms, run, don't walk, away from them. I get a few "new" cryptographic cipher claims a month from vendors who can't wait to tell me about their new super-duper proprietary encryption scheme that has solved all the problems of the previous ones. Never has this been true. If you get told about distributed-split keys, quantum-distribution, or million-bit keys, you can be assured that the person doesn't know what they are talking about and anything they can create will be worthless to wasteful. Only rely on and use tried-and-true cipher routines long trusted by everyone in the public domain.

On a related note, Google Authenticator uses an 80-bit seed value. An 80-bit key gives a lot of potential combinations of secret keys (i.e., 2^{80}) but the official RFCs on the matter, 4226 (`tools.ietf.org/html/rfc4226`) and 6238 (`tools.ietf.org/html/rfc6238`), recommend minimum OTP secret seed sizes of 128 bits, and really 160 bits (double what Google Authenticator uses). OTPs should use random seed values equal to or greater than the key size of the involved hash. When Google Authenticator was created, SHA-1 was the most common hash and SHA-1 has a 160-bit hash. Today, the most common hash is SHA-256, meaning it is SHA-2 with a 256-bit key. Any OTP solution should use a minimum of 256-bit seed values and 256-bit hash keys.

With that said, much of the digital security protection provided as part of the hash's longer key length is significantly diminished by eventual multiple truncations of the message digest from a 20-byte array into a 32-bit integer, which has 9 numeric characters, which is eventually truncated to 6- to 8-characters. In the end, the answer can have a max of only 64 bits of different information. The truncated, short OTP codes are probably far too hard to crack, especially when they are only good for 30 seconds. Still, if an RFC recommends a 160-bit key, it doesn't seem encouraging that we have a very popular solution that intentionally only uses half of that.

NOTE   Soon quantum computers, using Grover's algorithm, will lessen the protective capabilities of hashes and symmetric keys to half their stated key size. So, the 80-bit seed value will essentially have the security of 40 bits, and that is considerably more in the range of a realistic break.

OTP Theft, Re-Creation, and Reuse

If an attacker can physically steal or re-create an OTP device, they can see the code that it generates and reuse that code as if the legitimate user was using it. I think everyone can readily understand that having physical access of an OTP device gives the holder the same powers as the legitimate owner (unless other offsetting mitigations are implemented), but it's just easier for an attacker to re-create it. If an attacker steals an OTP device, the legitimate owner will notice and report it missing, and it will be decommissioned. But if it is re-created, the legitimate owner likely will not know, and it can be used by the attacker multiple times at will before the unauthorized access is noticed.

Google Authenticator has this risk in spades. The 80-bit seed value communicated in the original setup (via text or QR graphic) is all that is needed to create one or more instances of the same Google Authenticator OTP code. Worse yet, it never expires! If anyone obtains the setup information at any time before the Google Authenticator instance is decommissioned, they can create additional, potentially maliciously intended instances of the same Google Authenticator instance.

There have been many instances where someone's "old" Google Authenticator initial setup email or picture was later on compromised by a hacker. The hacker either found the original setup email or found a picture of the QR code that some users take as backup safety. Once they have the 80-bit code or QR picture, it's game over. An example real-life story can be found here: www.reddit.com/r/ CoinBase/comments/6sesol/2factor_can_be_hacked_apparently/. Figure 9.6 shows an example screenshot of that story on Reddit.

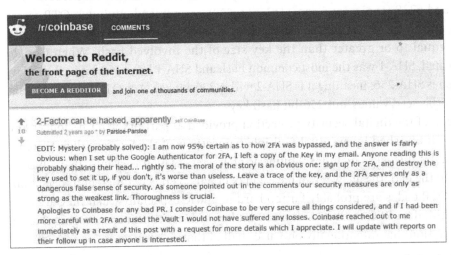

Figure 9.6: Reddit posting about a stolen Google Authenticator setup email that led to a real-life compromise

Stolen Seed Database

The shared, secret, random seed values can be compromised wherever they are stored. Seed values are typically stored on the participating OTP device/instance and authenticating database, wherever that database is stored. They are often stored at the OTP solution vendor and may be additionally stored on a database near the logon server/service. These databases have been compromised in the past, although these compromises are not super common. But when they have happened they are often accomplished by advanced persistent threat (APT) adversaries on behalf of nation-states.

The most famous example was a compromise of several RSA customers in 2011 (www.wired .com/2011/06/rsa-replaces-securid-tokens/). An APT actor phished multiple RSA employees with emails containing malicious attachments (i.e., Microsoft Excel spreadsheets). Some of the multiple RSA employees who fell for the ruse had long unpatched versions of Microsoft Office, and when they opened the malicious files the included malware program compromised their workstations and then eventually much of RSA's network. Even with the unpatched software, the employees had to ignore or bypass multiple warning prompts from Microsoft Office products. They did. Among other things, it was rumored that several RSA customer databases, including Lockheed Martin's, containing their RSA SecurID seed values and device GUIDs were compromised.

Over the years I've heard conflicting stories from the press and RSA employees as to whether the APT attackers did truly obtain RSA SecurID secret information and use it to compromise customer accounts. I've heard RSA strongly denounce that the popularly believed set of events never happened. This is made more difficult to believe because of a few factors. One, RSA themselves confirmed the breach and volunteered, after months of pressure, to replace all customer's RSA SecurID devices. This of course could have been out of an abundance of caution and to head off continuing negative goodwill headwinds. Second, at least a few RSA customers said they were compromised directly because of the RSA compromise, including Lockheed Martin (www.theregister.co.uk/2011/05/27/ lockheed_securid_hack_flap/) and L-3 (www.wired.com/2011/05/1-3/).

Lastly, I have re-created SecurID tokens myself. I'm not alone. Likely hundreds of interested computer security people did. For over a decade a common hacker tool called Cain & Abel provided an easy way to mimic any RSA SecurID if you knew the serial number and seed value. Cain & Abel contained dozens of features. It was a cornucopia of hacking tools all wrapped up in one package. It excelled at sniffing passwords off the wire and doing easy man-in-the-middle network attacks, ARP poisoning, and password cracking. It also included a feature that would allow anyone to create virtual instances of RSA SecurID tokens and even included a way to import any supplied SecurID key files. Figure 9.7 shows an example test of that Cain & Abel functionality.

For well over a decade I used to gladly direct people to download and use Cain & Abel as a versatile hacking tool. But it hasn't been upgraded much since the days of Microsoft Windows XP Pro (2004) and is no longer hosted on its creators' original website (oxid.it). I'm not sure if you can trust a Cain & Abel download today not to have some malicious modification to abuse people who use it. So, it's best if you avoid it unless you can be assured you can get and use a clean version. These days I assume since the big RSA hack that RSA has updated the SecurID token algorithm so that even if you had a clean copy of Cain & Abel it would not work against today's SecurID tokens. RSA is likely using updated hashing algorithms and other more secure changes.

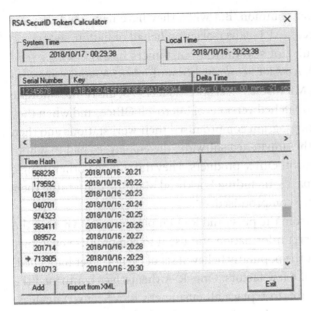

Figure 9.7: Example of using Cain & Abel to simulate an RSA SecurID token OTP code generation

But any time someone can learn what components and algorithms an OTP device uses, they can create virtual device instances of it. Pharo and FreeOTP show that as well. Here's another example of a single private company getting badly compromised because of an OTP database breach: www .securityweek.com/how-attackers-likely-bypassed-linodes-two-factor-authentication-hack-pagerduty.

To summarize this section, the most popular way attackers hack people using OTP-based MFA solutions is by phishing and social engineering, but there are other ways such as OTP re-creation and compromised seed databases. The attacks aren't theoretical. They happen in the real world.

Defenses to OTP Attacks

There are methods developers and users can take to decrease the risk of attacks against OTP-based MFA. Unfortunately, most of the heavy lifting is on developer shoulders, although the single best defense against OTP attacks is solely accomplishable by users.

Developer Defenses

The following sections explain some developer defenses against attacks against OTP-based MFA solutions.

Use Reliable and Trusted and Tested OTP Algorithms

Unless you are or have access to some of the world's best cryptography experts who the cryptography industry trusts, don't attempt to make your own OTP algorithms or cryptography. Today's tried-and-trusted algorithms and cryptography are more than sufficient for whatever purpose you need.

If you are lucky and your OTP solution survives for a long time (say over half a decade. . .most do not last this long), you will likely need to update the cryptography associated with your OTP solution. Assume whatever cryptographic algorithms you use will eventually need to be updated or replaced and make your solution "crypto agile." This means that you and your customers can easily update the involved cryptography without major actions or issues. All cryptography weakens over time and does eventually get replaced. It's routine. Survive long enough and it will happen. Don't hard-code the algorithms and cryptography in a way that makes it difficult to replace or upgrade. But at the same time ensure that no unauthorized changes can be made to your solution.

OTP Setup Code Must Expire

Any initial seed value/code used to set up a unique OTP instance should expire within a reasonable period of time. You don't want an "old" code sitting around waiting for an unauthorized user to discover. This also applies to master, backup, and travel codes. All codes which allow a new instance or to bypass an existing MFA instance should expire in a reasonable period of time.

One interesting related solution is Dynamic Symmetric Key Provisioning Protocol (DSKPP). Officially described in RFC 6063 (`tools.ietf.org/html/rfc6063`), DSKPP is a standard for implementing shared symmetric secrets between two authenticating participants—between the client and server of an OTP solution, for example. DSKPP allows a shared secret, like a seed value, to be generated between the OTP participants securely. And—this is important—it could be used over and over to establish new secret values anytime they are needed. So that if the original seed value database or any old values were compromised, the information learned could not be used as easily to duplicate future OTP codes. An OTP token, for example, could generate a new shared secret every day or at any predefined time interval. Although DSKPP is new, I'm already thinking that any OTP solution using it has a leg up on the competition.

OTP Result Code Must Expire

Any resulting OTP code should expire whether or not the code was created by an TOTP. If OTP codes did not expire or took a long time to expire, then an unauthorized user might be able to use an "old" found code for a future authentication event. This is a big problem, particularly around HOTP solutions. There is a very popular HOTP vendor solution that never expires old or used HOTP codes. Some knowledgeable people and competitors go around showing how 20 HOTP codes generated over a year ago still work just fine during current logons. This is unacceptably dangerous.

Prevent OTP Replay

Some OTP solutions allow previously generated or used OTP codes to continue to be valid into the future. This is crazy! All OTP codes surpassed by newer OTP codes should no longer be valid. Some OTP solutions include timestamps that are recorded and stored with the involved OTP code when it is generated and used. This can help to prevent easy replay. An OTP system should not allow multiple OTP codes to be generated, used, or remain valid all at once. This prevents an attacker from obtaining older OTP codes and re-using them as easily.

> **NOTE**   This recommendation causes an issue for MFA solutions with master codes, which are often generated in multiples at the same time and either never expire, are given long expiration periods, or don' expire until the user generates new ones or cancels the old ones.

Make Sure Your RNG Is NIST-Certified or Quantum

OTP security protection strength relies on the true randomness of the static seed value and the involved hash. Mess that up and the rest does not matter. Most traditional popular operating systems contain fairly trusted random number generators (RNGs) and you can rely on them. Don't "roll your own." Today's better RNGs are known as pseudo-RNGs (PRNGs) and inspire a bit of confidence because they are acknowledging that they aren't perfect. Funny, but by acknowledging that they aren't perfect makes them seem more trustworthy. I avoid RNGs that don't understand that they aren't as perfect as they pretend. Quantum random number generators are truly and provably random. All other factors considered equal, I would trust any true quantum random number generator (QRNG) over an RNG/PRNG.

NIST created a series of tests that any—quantum or otherwise—RNG vendor or customer can run to see how good or bad their RNG/PRNG is compared to a theoretically perfect random number generator. NIST documented the tests and requirements in NIST Special Publication 800-22 (nvlpubs .nist.gov/nistpubs/Legacy/SP/nistspecialpublication800-22r1a.pdf).

Increase Security by Requiring Additional Entry Beyond OTP Code

One thing that RSA got right early on was requiring that logons involving their TOTP devices also use an additional static code that the user provided during the time of the logon. While the additional static code could be compromised as easily as a seed value or typed-in OTP value, it does make that sort of attack slightly harder to accomplish. Additionally, if the seed database gets compromised and the other static values are not located in the same place, the seed value alone will not give the hackers immediate access.

Stop Brute-Forcing Attacks

When OTP codes are typed in, the authentication system should have an "account lockout" feature that prevents attackers from guessing over and over again unsuccessfully until they guess successfully.

Most of our organizations do it for logon name/password combinations, but for some reason many new OTP vendors forget to put similar logout features on their new solutions. Here are three examples:

- `threatpost.com/researcher-bypasses-instagram-2fa/146466`
- `hackerone.com/reports/121696`
- `www.cloudfoundry.org/blog/cve-2018-11082`

Figure 9.8 shows some two headlines from MFA solutions that did not include account lockout features.

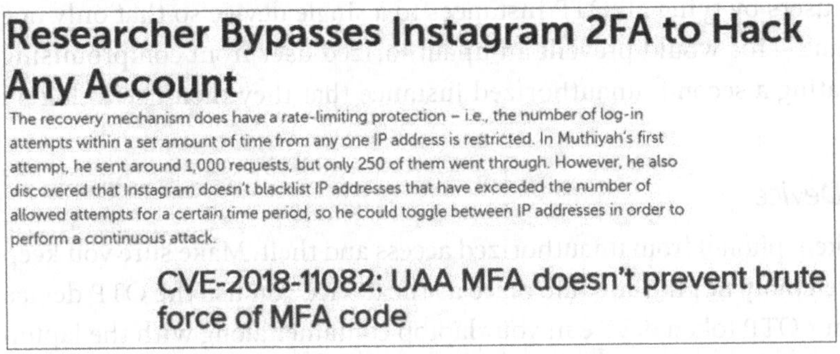

Researcher Bypasses Instagram 2FA to Hack Any Account

The recovery mechanism does have a rate-limiting protection – i.e., the number of log-in attempts within a set amount of time from any one IP address is restricted. In Muthiyah's first attempt, he sent around 1,000 requests, but only 250 of them went through. However, he also discovered that Instagram doesn't blacklist IP addresses that have exceeded the number of allowed attempts for a certain time period, so he could toggle between IP addresses in order to perform a continuous attack.

CVE-2018-11082: UAA MFA doesn't prevent brute force of MFA code

Figure 9.8: Example headlines from MFA solutions that did not include account lockout features

Secure Seed Value Database

Seed value databases are the targets of hackers. All seed value databases should be particularly secured as the high-risk assets that they are. Wherever they are stored, they need to be protected by field-level encryption, data-leak protection, containerization, heightened security monitoring, and quick incident response methods. Ensure that any additional static secrets used in OTP result code calculation are not stored in the same databases as the seed values.

User Defenses

Let's look at some defenses users can take to protect themselves against OTP attacks above and beyond what developers can do.

Don't Get Socially Engineered Out of Your OTP Code

The single best thing any OTP user can do is not to allow themselves to get socially engineered out of their request OTP code. Users need to be aware of phishing scenarios, how to spot rogue URL links, and about rogue proxy servers. Many end users think that if they have an MFA solution they don't have to be as worried as if they had a simple logon name/password solution. A false sense of security can be as dangerous as a weak security solution.

Delete Setup Codes

Delete and erase MFA setup codes. Don't simply delete and forget. Delete and empty the trash. Make sure there is no way your setup code can be recovered by another unauthorized person and used to create an additional identical OTP instance. Developers, of course, could make this a non-worry by expiring setup codes after a reasonable period of time or by implementing DSKPP as described earlier.

Tie to Single Device/Instance

Developers can decrease risk to users by tying all OTP instances to a single device so that only one person can use it at the same time. This would prevent an unauthorized user from compromising the original instance and generating a second, unauthorized instance that they then use to log on as the legitimate user.

Physically Protect Your OTP Device

Protect your OTP device (e.g., token, phone) from unauthorized access and theft. Make sure you keep your device in a secure place, preferably not in the same place as the device you use the OTP device with. For example, don't keep your OTP token device in your laptop container along with the laptop that you use the OTP device with. With one theft, a thief could have both your OTP device and your laptop where it is to log on to. If your OTP device goes missing or gets compromised, report the issue to IT security immediately. They should disable your ability to OTP log on until they decommission the old device.

NOTE   Remember to securely protect any "backup" or "travel" master codes so that they cannot be easily discovered by a hacker.

Summary

This chapter covered the different types of one-time password MFA solutions, including HMAC, event-based, and TOTP. Most successful attacks against OTP occur due to users handing over their OTP code because of social engineering and phishing. Other real-world attacks have occurred because of stolen setup codes, non-expiring codes, and compromised seed databases. This chapter ended by discussing the various defenses developers and users can implement to prevent attacks.

Chapter 10, "Subject Hijack Attacks" will cover subject hijack attacks.

10

Subject Hijack Attacks

Most of the topics and hacks in this book have been well covered previously by lots of different sources, and the attacks they explore have been performed in the public domain for many years. This chapter is different. It examines a topic that is not well discussed and includes demo attacks that, as far as I know, have never been performed publicly. It does not make what this chapter covers, component abuse and subject hijacking, any the less concerning for people interested in authentication security.

Introduction

In Chapter 5, "Hacking MFA in General," we looked at more than 20 different authentication components, all of which can be attacked and exploited to compromise or get around multifactor authentication. It's a large, complex system of reliance that is rarely all controlled by a single entity. But even when a single entity controls all the factors, making sure they don't get abused to allow a hacker to get around authentication is a challenge.

In this chapter, we'll cover a specific type of authentication component abuse in order to illustrate the power of the namespace dependencies. I'll show that simply changing one field of unprotected information can drastically change and invalidate authentication in unexpected ways. This chapter will just focus on one scenario in one particular type of environment, but the larger lesson can be applied to all forms of MFA in all sorts of environments.

The key takeaway of this chapter is to understand that not only can dependencies be abused to get around authentication checks, but that all dependencies must be protected as if they are critical authentication secrets. Our computer security industry is very good about instructing administrators to protect passwords, password hashes, and other authentication secrets, but it gives scant coverage to every other critical reliance even though they are just as important. This chapter is society's wake-up call to how important all the dependent components can be.

Example Attacks

There are a myriad of ways to show dependent component attacks, but in this chapter I'm going to show a simulated subject identity hijack involving Microsoft's Active Directory and smartcards. By simply changing a name value, an attacker can make an entirely different authentication outcome happen and make it very difficult for anyone to learn that it happened. Before I show the hack demo, I need to quickly explain what Active Directory is and how it works with smartcards.

Active Directory and Smartcards

Microsoft Active Directory (AD) is easily the most popular enterprise network directory and authentication service in the world. Based on open standards, Lightweight Directory Services and its Lightweight Directory Access Protocol (LDAP), AD was introduced by Microsoft in 1999 along with Windows 2000. It is, at its most basic level, a database and service for sorting and storing logical objects, such as user accounts, files, printer, and their attributes (i.e., fields and data). It can also be used for authenticating users, groups, computers, and other participating subjects against protected objects (e.g., servers, files, folders, sites, services). Today, AD is also supported in the Microsoft Azure cloud, although the cloud version is currently not as feature-rich as the "on-premises" version. That is changing quickly. Microsoft likely plans to make their cloud-version an irresistible "must-buy" for enterprise users.

Active Directory supports smartcards and has since the beginning of AD, although newer versions of Microsoft Windows and AD support more functionality and flexibility than earlier versions. As previously covered in Chapter 3, "Types of Authentication," traditional smartcards are physical devices about the shape of a thick credit card, which contain a digital certificate with an Object Identifier (OID) field containing the following value: Smart Card Logon (1.3.6.1.4.1.311.20.2.2). Applications accepting smartcards look for this particular OID value.

NOTE   Some smartcard-enabled applications will accept other non-smartcard OIDs, client (1.3.6.1.5.5.7.3.2), and server (1.3.6.1.5.5.7.3.1) authentication, as example alternatives. But officially, any smartcard-using application should explicitly look for and only accept the one and only Smart Card Logon OID (1.3.6.1.4.1.311.20.2.2). The smartcard OID supposedly means the digital certificates containing them have been very securely generated and the associated private keys have only been generated and stored on the smartcard's chip.

The smartcard usually contains both the public and private keys of each digital certificate. The smartcard's integrated circuit chip cryptographically protects the private key of stored certificates from ever being accessed by external programs or intruders. The private key is stored on the card and remains there, even when used. Most smartcards require a user PIN to be entered as a second factor whenever the digital certificates on the card are to be used. Smartcards are tamper-resistant and may be disabled if someone tries to hack them or physically access them (although Chapter 17, "Physical Attacks," will cover how to successfully attack them).

Every MFA solution is tied to one or more particular subject identities. In AD, smartcards are tied to different user accounts using the user's User Principal Name (UPN) value. The UPN value is defaulted to as the user's logon name followed by an @ sign and the user's Active Directory forest domain name (e.g., `rogerg@knowbe.ad`), but can be many other custom values. A popular alternate UPN format is the user's email address (e.g., `rogerg@knowbe4.com`), which may or not be the same as the user's default UPN name or the user's Active Directory domain name. A user can have only one UPN value at a time, and it must be unique in the Active Directory forest. If an AD administrator fills out a user's UPN, they do so in the user's user account field labeled as Logon Name (see Figure 10.1). In the Figure 10.1 example, the user's logon name is Super Admin, the AD forest name is `victim.com`, and so their complete UPN is `SuperAdmin@victim.com` (letter case does not matter).

Figure 10.1: Example user UPN

When a user smartcard certificate is created for use with Active Directory, the user's UPN is written as a value in a x.509 certificate field called Principal Name under the certificate's Subject Alternative Name field (see Figure 10.2 for an example). A cert's Subject Alternative Name can have a lot of values (e.g., LDAP, DNS, IP address, Common Name, NetBIOS). A UPN is just one type of name, but it must present for a smartcard used by Active Directory, and the UPN must match the user's UPN value in their user account. When a user logs in using a smartcard, Windows and Active Directory links the smartcard to the appropriate user account using the UPN field.

When the user logs in using a smartcard, they don't type in their username. Instead, they simply insert their smartcard into the computer's smartcard reader (or it is wirelessly read for contactless smartcards), and Windows (if smartcard enabled) receives the logon event and automatically takes the logon identity from the smartcard's UPN value. If a smartcard has multiple smartcard certificates, the user will be prompted to choose which smartcard certificate to log on with. The user will then be prompted for their smartcard PIN (see Figure 10.3). The user's inputted PIN will be passed along to the smartcard and the evaluation of whether it was the correct PIN will be completely up to the smartcard and its own operations. Windows and Active Directory are not involved in the actual authentication event that determines success or failure other than passing along the information to and from the smartcard. All of the actual authentication information and processing is performed within the secure confines of the smartcard's integrated circuit chip.

After the user successfully authenticates, the user's public portion of the smartcard certificate is transferred to the user's Windows local certificate store, and Active Directory looks up the UPN of the certificate to confirm that it exists in the AD forest. Once found, the logon is then mapped to the user's account which contains it, and the user is assigned a Windows/Active Directory access control token.

Figure 10.2: Example user UPN written into a smartcard certificate

Figure 10.3: Example smartcard logon prompting for the user's PIN

NOTE   The smartcard must have been issued by a certification authority (CA) that Active Directory trusts. In Active Directory there is a security group called Trusted Certification Authorities, and the server name of the CA must be a member of that group in order for AD to accept the smartcard certificate.

Simulated Demo Environment

To demonstrate this simulated hack, we are going to consider two users in the same Active Directory forest named `victim.com` for this example. One user, called Super Admin, is a super administrator with every possible right and permission in Active Directory. Super Admin belongs to every highly privileged group, including Schema Admins, Enterprise Admins, and Domain Admins. For all intents and purposes, Super Admin is an all-powerful "god account" of the network.

The second user, called Help Desk, is a regular user account with no special network permissions or privileges beyond that of a regular user except that they have the ability to change user account UPNs. They do not have any elevated network group memberships. Both users have valid smartcards and must use those smartcards to log on to their computers and Active Directory. For the simulated attack, let's assume that the Help Desk user decides he wants to steal the Super Admin's security credentials and do something malicious he is not capable of doing with his regular permissions and privileges.

NOTE Microsoft goes to great length to protect who has permission to modify the UPN value, but this demo attack assumes that the Help Desk user has the ability to write this value (as do other admins). In my demo I give the Help Desk user only that one extra permission to demonstrate the power of one small change on one field.

The rest of the demo will be a series of narrated steps and pictures starting with the Super Admin logging on to their computer as they normally do to demonstrate what a regular logon looks like. When the Super Admin successfully logs on using his smartcard and PIN (shown in Figure 10.3 earlier), afterward his user account can be validated using the Windows `whoami.exe` command (see Figure 10.4); his memberships in the highest elevated groups can be seen in Figure 10.5.

Figure 10.6 shows the Super Admin's smartcard digital certificate details, including the digital certificate's thumbprint (i.e., 55FAD65667C33E23D122) and UPN. The certificate's digital thumbprint, which is unique for all certificates, will become important later on when we are trying to figure out what happened.

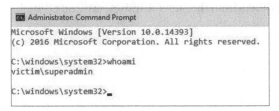

```
Administrator: Command Prompt
Microsoft Windows [Version 10.0.14393]
(c) 2016 Microsoft Corporation. All rights reserved.

C:\windows\system32>whoami
victim\superadmin

C:\windows\system32>
```

Figure 10.4: `Whoami` command showing Super Admin user

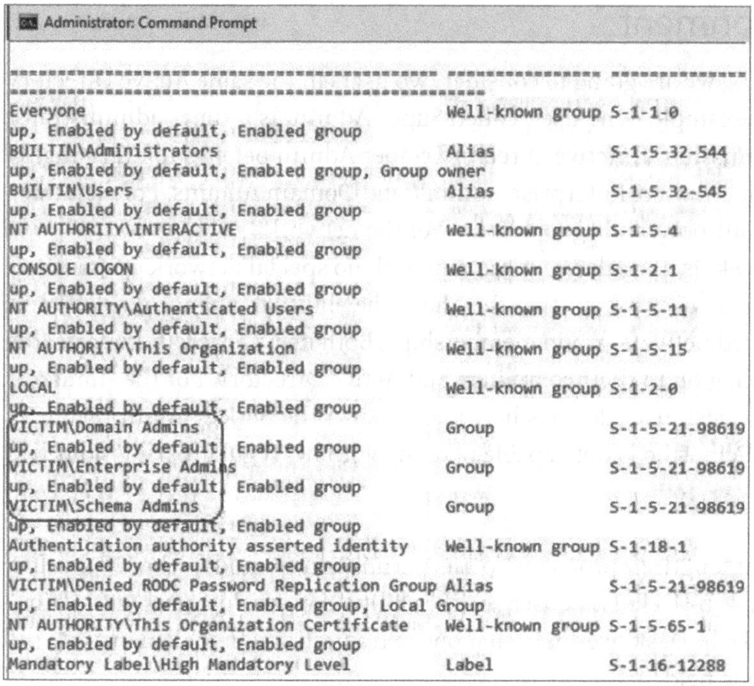

```
[■] Administrator: Command Prompt

===================================================== ================ ==============
============================================================
Everyone                                         Well-known group S-1-1-0
up, Enabled by default, Enabled group
BUILTIN\Administrators                           Alias           S-1-5-32-544
up, Enabled by default, Enabled group, Group owner
BUILTIN\Users                                    Alias           S-1-5-32-545
up, Enabled by default, Enabled group
NT AUTHORITY\INTERACTIVE                         Well-known group S-1-5-4
up, Enabled by default, Enabled group
CONSOLE LOGON                                    Well-known group S-1-2-1
up, Enabled by default, Enabled group
NT AUTHORITY\Authenticated Users                 Well-known group S-1-5-11
up, Enabled by default, Enabled group
NT AUTHORITY\This Organization                   Well-known group S-1-5-15
up, Enabled by default, Enabled group
LOCAL                                            Well-known group S-1-2-0
up, Enabled by default, Enabled group
VICTIM\Domain Admins                             Group           S-1-5-21-98619
up, Enabled by default, Enabled group
VICTIM\Enterprise Admins                         Group           S-1-5-21-98619
up, Enabled by default, Enabled group
VICTIM\Schema Admins                             Group           S-1-5-21-98619
up, Enabled by default, Enabled group
Authentication authority asserted identity       Well-known group S-1-18-1
up, Enabled by default, Enabled group
VICTIM\Denied RODC Password Replication Group Alias             S-1-5-21-98619
up, Enabled by default, Enabled group, Local Group
NT AUTHORITY\This Organization Certificate       Well-known group S-1-5-65-1
up, Enabled by default, Enabled group
Mandatory Label\High Mandatory Level             Label           S-1-16-12288
```

Figure 10.5: Whoami/groups command showing Super Admin's elevated group memberships

Now the demo will show what happens when the Help Desk user logs on. Figure 10.7 shows the Help Desk user logging on with their own smartcard and PIN.

After the Help Desk user is successfully logged in using his own user account, it can be validated using the Windows whoami.exe command (see Figure 10.8). The only elevated group membership the Help Desk user has is membership in the Local Administrators group, as seen in Figure 10.9. Being a member of the Local Administrators group does not confer any special permissions or privileges for something done on the network, as this demo shows.

Figure 10.10 shows the Help Desk user's smartcard digital certificate. Take note of this certificate's thumbprint (i.e., E9AE2A94225E6A740DA8) and how it differs from the Super Admin's certificate thumbprint (i.e., 55FAD65667C33E23D122).

Figure 10.6: Super Admin's digital certificate

Figure 10.7: Example of the Help Desk user logging on with their own smartcard and PIN

```
Administrator: Command Prompt
Microsoft Windows [Version 10.0.14393]
(c) 2016 Microsoft Corporation. All rights reserved.

C:\windows\system32>whoami
victim\helpdesk

C:\windows\system32>_
```

Figure 10.8: Help Desk user confirmed using the `whoami.exe` command

```
Administrator: Command Prompt
C:\windows\system32>whoami /groups

GROUP INFORMATION
-----------------

Group Name                                          Type              SID

==================================================  ================  ===============
=================
Everyone                                            Well-known group  S-1-1-0
oup
BUILTIN\Administrators                              Alias             S-1-5-32-544
oup, Group owner
BUILTIN\Users                                       Alias             S-1-5-32-545
oup
NT AUTHORITY\INTERACTIVE                            Well-known group  S-1-5-4
oup
CONSOLE LOGON                                       Well-known group  S-1-2-1
oup
NT AUTHORITY\Authenticated Users                    Well-known group  S-1-5-11
oup
NT AUTHORITY\This Organization                      Well-known group  S-1-5-15
oup
LOCAL                                               Well-known group  S-1-2-0
oup
Authentication authority asserted identity          Well-known group  S-1-18-1
oup
NT AUTHORITY\This Organization Certificate          Well-known group  S-1-5-65-1
oup
Mandatory Label\High Mandatory Level                Label             S-1-16-12288
```

Figure 10.9: `Whoami /groups` command confirming that the Help Desk user does not have any elevated network group memberships

Subject Hijack Demo Attack

Right now, everything is as it should be. But in our hacker fantasy scenario, we're going to assume the Super Admin user logs out and goes home and the Help Desk user hangs around to do mischief.

NOTE I must thank my longtime friend and former Microsoft coworker Adam Arndt for showing me this hacking trick nearly 20 years ago. Adam discovered this hack by accident while successfully trying to understand how Active Directory and smartcards interacted while we were both on-site at the same customer. He was installing a smartcard pilot project and I was part of a response team fighting foreign hacking adversaries that had successfully attacked this company several times over the years.

Figure 10.10: Help Desk user's smartcard certificate

The "hack" is the Help Desk user changing the Super Admin's UPN to helpdesk@victim.com so that when the Help Desk user logs on using their smartcard with a UPN of helpdesk@victim.com, AD maps the Super Admin's account to the Help Desk user's logon. To do this, he must first rename Help Desk's UPN to almost anything else (frogtemp@victim.com in this demo) because there cannot be two UPNs with the same values (i.e., helpdesk@victim.coms) at the same time in the same AD forest. So, by first renaming the Help Desk's legitimate UPN to something else, the Help Desk user can then rename Super Admin's UPN to helpdesk@victim.com. This sequence of steps is simulated in Figure 10.11.

After the UPN change, the Help Desk user must log out and wait for the user account change to replicate across Active Directory so that all user account databases get the new change. This can take up to 10 minutes (or longer) in some environments, but often takes only 1–2 minutes. At the very least, the UPN must be replicated to the Active Directory domain controller the Help Desk user is logging on to.

Then all the Help Desk user does is log into Windows and Active Directory using their own smartcard card and PIN (as shown in Figure 10.12). During the logon, anyone watching in real time would see the Help Desk username suddenly change to Super Admin a split second before the logon screen goes away to reveal the successful logon.

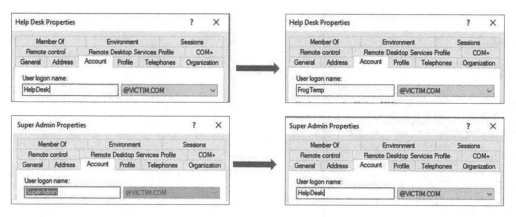

Figure 10.11: The Help Desk user renaming his existing UPN to `frogtemp@victim.com` first before renaming Super Admin's UPN to `helpdesk@victim.com`

Figure 10.12: Demo logon showing the Help Desk user logon using their smartcard, PIN, and UPN

When the Help Desk user runs `whoami.exe` (Figure 10.13) and `whoami /groups` (Figure 10.14), it now reveals the Help Desk user is logged in as Super Admin and has the elevated group memberships of Super Admin, even though they logged in using their own smartcard and PIN.

Now at this point you may be thinking that I could have just copied Figure 10.13 and Figure 10.14 from the previous Super Admin screenshots from Figures 10.8 and 10.9. And I could have, but I didn't. For one, you can see it happen real time. You can see a video of this simulated attack demo'd in action by the author here: `youtu.be/OLQ31AMuokI`. Second, when the currently logged-on user's (e.g., Help Desk) smartcard digital certificate is revealed (in Figure 10.15), it displays the thumbprint (i.e., E9AE2A94225E6A740DA8) from Figure 10.10 (i.e., the Help Desk user's cert) and not 55FAD65667C33E23D122 (i.e., the Super Admin user's cert thumbprint).

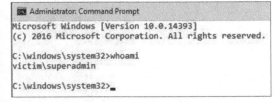

Figure 10.13: Help Desk user running `whoami.exe` and getting an answer back that he is Super Admin

```
Administrator: Command Prompt
C:\windows\system32>whoami /groups

GROUP INFORMATION
----------------

Group Name                              Type
==============================================  ========
==============================================
Everyone                                Well-kno
up, Enabled by default, Enabled group
BUILTIN\Administrators                  Alias
up, Enabled by default, Enabled group, Group owner
BUILTIN\Users                           Alias
up, Enabled by default, Enabled group
NT AUTHORITY\INTERACTIVE                Well-kno
up, Enabled by default, Enabled group
CONSOLE LOGON                           Well-kno
up, Enabled by default, Enabled group
NT AUTHORITY\Authenticated Users        Well-kno
up, Enabled by default, Enabled group
NT AUTHORITY\This Organization          Well-kno
up, Enabled by default, Enabled group
LOCAL                                   Well-kno
up, Enabled by default, Enabled group
VICTIM\Domain Admins                    Group
up, Enabled by default, Enabled group
VICTIM\Enterprise Admins                Group
up, Enabled by default, Enabled group
VICTIM\Schema Admins                    Group
```

Figure 10.14: Help Desk user with elevated groups of Super Admin as shown by `whoami /groups`

The Help Desk user IS the Super Admin user. This occurred because Active Directory had no way of knowing that the Super Admin user account should not have had a UPN of `helpdesk@victim.com`. Active Directory gets told by Windows that a successful smartcard logon has occurred and that the UPN of `helpdesk@victim.com` is part of that transaction. AD looks it up and finds the user with the associated UPN, and then gives that user the access control token of the Super Admin user, including groups and privileges.

Figure 10.15: Showing that the currently logged-on user, Help Desk, is using his own smartcard digital certificate

At this point, the Help Desk user can do anything the Super Admin can do. They can add their regular Help Desk user account to privileged groups; view, modify, and copy files they would not normally have access to; and install eavesdropping trojans and other malware. They can even modify operating systems and Active Directory itself.

And to make matters worse, Microsoft Windows and Active Directory would track all Windows Event Log events being committed by the Help Desk user as if they were committed by Super Admin. After committing any unauthorized actions, the Help Desk user could swap back the UPNs and log out. Unless UPN updates are being logged and the importance of those particular actions were noticed, it would be difficult to easily see what actually happened even if you suspected it had happened. In most environments, this sort of skullduggery would occur without anyone being the wiser.

Back when I was first saw this hack, Microsoft and Active Directory did not protect the UPN attribute as well as they do today. Back in the day, if you gave a help desk admin Full Control over user accounts, as is still a common assignment for help desk admins today, they could also change the UPN value of any user, including higher privileged users. Today, Microsoft protects the UPN field more strictly, and although a regular user account can still be assigned the ability to change UPN fields explicitly, if it's not done correctly AD just undoes the permission change.

Today, a more likely scenario is one admin changing their UPN field to another admin's UPN value so that everything they do is tracked to the other admin's account. So, it would be less about privilege escalation and more about hiding malicious tracks. For instance, using this trick would allow one admin to use the elevated custom group memberships of another admin without creating an alert of an unauthorized group membership occurring (as it could if the rogue admin just added themselves to a new elevated group). Or suppose the second admin had permissions on a second trusting forest. This trick would allow the malicious admin to acquire access to the second forest without having to ask for permission to the second forest. They could do all their needed deviousness in the second forest and their activity would not easily be traced back to them. And it would work for any escalation of privilege where one admin had the ability to do something another admin did not (for example, be an Exchange Administrator).

This is not to say that this type of maliciousness cannot be noticed and stopped. The changing of the UPN usually creates an event in the Windows log file that shows that the UPN is changed and what it was changed to. But unless someone was looking for that event and alerted on it, it would probably go unnoticed. And there are some logon events, such as Event ID 4768, registered at the involved domain controllers that would include each supplied smartcard's thumbprint, which could be reviewed as evidence to reveal that the Help Desk user's smartcard was now somehow associated with the Super Admin account. But forensics investigators would have to be aware of and seeking to validate this particular hack scenario. They would have to know that a particular certificate thumbprint belonged to the Help Desk user and not Super Admin. It would not be something most people looked for unless they knew it was even a possibility and what to look for. Even then, it's such a rare edge case (i.e., it's never been done in the wild that I know of), that it's probably not going to be the first thing most incident responders check for. It's not going to be what most incident responders ever check for, first or last. Beyond the people reading this chapter, perhaps a few dozen people in the world know about this strange link between smartcards and AD, and how it can be abused. Welcome to a very small group.

There are other related hacks. For example, anyone who is able to generate a trusted smartcard cert that contains anyone else's UPN can then log on as that user. In the first example, we modified the Super Admin's UPN to `helpdesk@victim.com`. But we could also simply generate a brand-new smartcard that contains the UPN of `superadmin@victim.com` and be able to log on as Super Admin. I've done this attack technique using a "foreign" CA (i.e., a CA belonging to another organization) that was simply installed as a trusted CA in the victim organization. The foreign CA can generate smartcards with the victim's organization's UPN. Again, the only evidence a forensic examiner might find is a certificate thumbprint in the logs that doesn't match the Super Admin's current certificate thumbprint.

To be clear, this is not really a hack or bug. Microsoft is not going to fix this. This is an "as-designed" outcome in which the way Active Directory–integrated smartcards work. Smartcards are tied to a user's UPN and the Help Desk user changed UPNs. So, in Active Directory's defense, it did map the "right" user account to the authenticated smartcard as it was defined in Active Directory. Active Directory has no way of knowing that one UPN is the correct UPN over another.

The defense to the smartcard hijack attack is not to allow people to make unauthorized UPN changes and to prevent smartcard administrators from simply creating any smartcard with any UPN they like. Or more realistically, log UPN changes (there are legitimate reasons why they occur such as due to name changes from marriage and divorce) and make sure the change was authorized. And make sure you trust your admins. Administrators are very powerful accounts that can do a lot of malicious things, well beyond just subject hijack attacks. You need to make sure your admins are trustworthy as rule #1.

The Broader Issue

As covered in Chapter 2, "Authentication Basics," the act of validating an authentication credential can, and often is, separate from the resulting authorization and access control processes. In this particular hacking scenario, the smartcard authentication process (i.e., that the user is presenting a valid, trusted smartcard with a valid UPN and knows the associated PIN) and the access control and authorization process (where the "validated" user is handed their group memberships and privileges in an access control token) are, to Active Directory, almost completely separate events. Once a valid, trusted smartcard and the correct PIN is typed in, there is no way (in the most common smartcard scenarios) for Active Directory to know the validated UPN being supplied shouldn't be mapped to the user account that contains it. It's the way Active Directory and smartcards were made to work with each other.

The general protection against these sorts of MFA abuses is to realize that any time you use an attribute, such as subject UPN, as part of an authentication solution, the involved attribute needs to be protected and monitored as if it were an authentication secret. Most administrators are taught to secure other authentication secrets, such as password hashes, as if they were the keys to the kingdom—and they are. But most admins are not taught to protect and monitor the other involved authentication attributes, even though their malicious modification can have similar security impacts.

Dynamic Access Control Example

Let me give another example attack to clarify further. Since Windows Server 2012/2016, Microsoft Windows and Active Directory allow Dynamic Access Control (DAC) and Central Access Policy (CAP) to control a subject's authentication (see `docs.microsoft.com/en-us/windows/security/identity-protection/access-control/dynamic-access-control` for more details) in a much more feature-rich, more granular way.

With traditional Windows security, what a subject (e.g., user, group, computer, service) can access is determined solely by their membership in groups and what individual permissions and privileges they were given on various protected objects. With DAC/CAP, dozens of other elements, such as attributes and location, can be used to determine whether or not a subject can access a particular object. For example, is the user in a U.S. location and in the Accounting department? As Figure 10.16 shows, that question can now be asked to determine whether or not someone in a group is given access to a file. With traditional Windows security, the question would have been much simpler: is the user a member of the Authenticated Users group? But with DAC/CAP, the question can be more granular: is the user a member of the Authenticated Users group, belongs in the Accounting department, and located in the United States? With DAC/CAP, nearly any object attribute can be used to create more complex expressions with ANDs, ORs, and NOTs. DAC/CAP gives you a lot more access control flexibility.

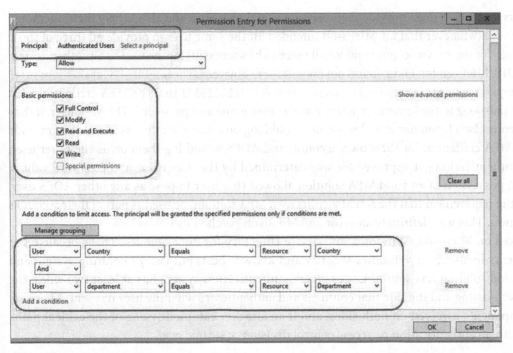

Figure 10.16: Example of using Microsoft DAC/CAP to determine if a user group can access a particular protected resource

The problem is that any attribute used to evaluate authentication or access control now becomes a critical evaluation point. Before DAC/CAP, the values of text fields on a user's account such as Department and Country didn't mean much. They couldn't impact security, access control, and authentication. They were informational at best, and superfluous most of the time. Most people who fill them in might not even care if they spell the text values correctly. But now with DAC/CAP, perhaps unknown to the original people who put in the values, they are being used to evaluate authentication and access control. When someone decided to use Department and Country as access control attributes, did they increase the security over who could or couldn't modify and change those attributes? Did anyone increase monitoring over those attributes to look for and report unauthorized changes? Likely not. Most computer security people see those fields and still think of them as text-based attributes that are part of a user's account description. But by including them as evaluation decisions in DAC/CAP, they are critically important and should be protected as you would protect logon names, passwords, and password hashes.

ADFS MFA Bypass

Another similar attack could have been performed with Microsoft's Active Directory Federated Services (ADFS). ADFS is Microsoft's service for federating authentication and identities between two unrelated organizations who do not share the same authentication system. When MFA is used with

ADFS, users logging on must provide their user name and password and also supply their integrated MFA credential (whatever that is). Microsoft intended for the same user to provide all three of those needed values for their own account and for all three to be successful for the user to be authenticated.

But in 2018, MFA vendor, Okta, found out (`www.darkreading.com/threat-intelligence/microsoft-adfs-vulnerability-lets-attackers-bypass-mfa/d/d-id/1332553`) that the MFA credential used didn't have to belong to the same user account as the user name and password. The MFA user, if they knew someone else's logon name and password, could log on on as the other user and then provide their own MFA credential for their own account, and ADFS would log them on as the other user. Who the authentication got approved for was determined by the user name and password values. Essentially, possession of an valid MFA solution allowed that user to pose as any other ADFS user, bypassing the requirement that the actual victim's own MFA solution be used as part of their account's authentication. This was definitely an error and Microsoft patched it.

I've picked on Microsoft, Windows, and Active Directory for my examples. That's because I've spent 30 years focusing on Windows security and know it best. But every operating system and authentication solution has similar issues. Every authentication system has at least two sides: the side the user is using and the side that confirms and authenticates what the user has sent. There are lots of components involved on both sides, and if an attacker can modify one of the critical paths involved with an authentication or access control decision, it's game over.

Defenses to Component Attacks

The following sections highlight some defenses to component attacks.

Threat Model Dependency Abuse Scenarios

All authentication solutions should be threat modeled and include all the various dependencies that the solution relies on to be accurate. Use Figure 5.1 in Chapter 5 as a starting point to begin discussions. I cannot recommend any higher Adam Shostack's *Threat Modeling: Designing for Security* (Wiley, 2014) for those of you who want to improve your threat modeling skills. All threat modelers should idesntify all the critical dependencies and see whether identified dependency risks can be mitigated or minimized. All inputs should be considered untrusted by default.

Secure Critical Dependencies

All critical component dependencies for MFA solutions should be as secure as possible. This means that user and group hygiene has been performed to minimize which users and groups can access and modify various components, and those remaining who are allowed should be given least privilege permissions. Better yet, make all modifications require a checkout of a time-bounded elevated credential whose access and use is tracked. Critical dependencies need to be treated like passwords and password hashes, and protected accordingly.

Educate About Dependency Abuses

Educate everyone, developer and customer, about possible dependency abuses. For example, in the dynamic access control example earlier, would everyone involved suddenly realize that the Department and Country attributes were now used for making access control decisions? Did anyone put stronger security and monitoring around those fields? Users should be educated about any threat models that the developers have defined, how they were minimized, and what risks still remain.

I can think of no better example than the FIDO Alliance's Security Specification document (fidoalliance.org/specs/fido-v2.0-id-20180227/fido-security-ref-v2.0-id-20180227.html). Every MFA solution should be so forthcoming and detailed. It includes a summary of the outstanding threat models (as shown in Figure 10.17) and then covers each in detail. I think all readers and security reviewers will have more faith in a solution that does good threat modeling and isn't afraid to show known risks and the mitigations and steps they have taken to minimize them. This document gives increased faith in the family of FIDO solutions.

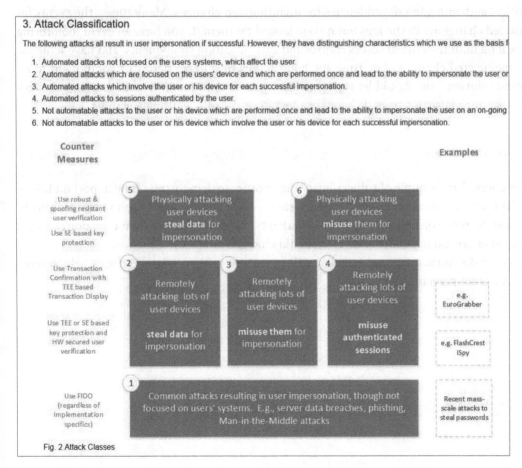

Figure 10.17: FIDO Alliance Security Specification document section example

Prevent One to Many Mappings

The ADFS example showed how two people's authentication processes were inadvertently allowed to co-mingle. In that example, the hacker opened two browser sessions. In one browser session they logged in as themselves using their own logon name and password. In the second browser's session they logged on using the intended victim's name and password. ADFS was then requiring a successful MFA authentication. But because ADFS didn't ensure that the successful event be tied to a particular logon account, the attacker was able to use their MFA logon for the victim's MFA logon. There was a mapping error or break. Sometimes they are known as channel errors. All authentication systems want to "bind" the logon credentials for all parts of the authentication event to prevent the one to many mappings that might otherwise be possible. Authentication solutions should use channel or token binding techniques or similar ideas to prevent inadvertent user mix ups.

Monitor Critical Dependencies

Monitor critical authentication dependencies for unauthorized changes. Many times, the events for an unauthorized change are in the logs but no one looked for them. If you have an event monitoring system, have it monitor the critical access control and authentication components, and have someone verify any unexpected changes. Any time someone adds a new dependency or component to an authentication solution, you should be trying to figure out how to monitor unauthorized changes and how to minimize false positives if there are a lot of events from legitimate activity.

Summary

This chapter covered an example of subject hijacking in order to demonstrate how important it is to protect all dependencies used in authentication systems. Most environments go to great lengths to protect passwords, password hashes, and other authentication secrets, but then they don't protect and monitor other critical dependencies. This should change.

Chapter 11, "Fake Authentication Attacks" will cover fake authentication attacks, which most forms of MFA cannot prevent.

11

Fake Authentication Attacks

T his chapter covers a type of attack that's possible against nearly all forms of authentication, including MFA. It's difficult to stop and not all that hard to pull off for the attacker. In a nutshell, malicious hackers can provide an experience to an end user that appears as if the user's authentication was successful and legitimate when it was not. The attacker can then trick the victim into revealing more confidential details or into performing actions that they otherwise would not.

Learning About Fake Authentication Through UAC

I often hear from MFA vendors and users who ask me if their favorite MFA solution can be hacked. My immediate response is always, "Yes!" Anything can be hacked. But more specifically, I know that "fake authentication" hacks can be accomplished against nearly any MFA solution. I learned this lesson firsthand over 15 years ago when my employer was trying to figure out a way to mitigate it.

I worked for Microsoft Corporation for almost 12 years as a principal security consultant, and another three years before as a consultant working on Microsoft Windows Server 2003 and Microsoft SharePoint security courses for internal staff and customers. I loved my time working for Microsoft. It taught me a great deal, including that there are many very smart people who know a lot about computer security. Many times, I would come up with what I thought was an excellent security defense only to find that my idea was already thought up by someone else—sometimes multiple someone elses!—and discussed and appropriately shot down years to decades ago. It's more difficult than you think to come up with a new, viable computer defense that works at the scale that Microsoft works at. They have hundreds of millions of customers, and the Windows ecosystem supports many tens of millions of software programs. I would come up with a defense to an existing problem that I thought was brilliant and find that if implemented it would cause problems with "only" one percent of existing software programs. When I heard this the first time, I thought it was great news and that certainly my "great" idea would be implemented. But one percent at Microsoft's scale translates into millions and millions of problems, with as many angry users and vendors. A 99 percent solution isn't good enough. It causes too many operational issues. A 0.01 percent solution causes too many problems.

Microsoft has to come up with security solutions that cause no problems or at least the least numbers of problems possible for the risk being mitigated. Causing too many problems could lead existing customers to use other platforms that don't have as many issues. It's something that Microsoft worries about with each security decision. Many times, otherwise great security solutions had to be shelved because they caused too many end-user operational issues. Other times the security risk was so big that Microsoft decided to implement the solution even if it caused problems. And a few rare times they implemented a security decision intentionally knowing it was going to cause a lot of issues and anger. In fact, it was the unavoidable intent, but the risk they were trying to mitigate was that important.

During the creation of Windows Vista, one of the big problems was that despite Microsoft's best efforts to the contrary, too many users (nearly all) were constantly logged on all the time as the fully permissioned and highly privileged Administrator—so much so, that most programs (nearly all) expected to run in that context. Nearly all the time, most users and programs were running with the highest level of permissions. This was a fact that hackers and malware loved to abuse. When a malware program or hacker "takes over" a program, they get whatever security context the user and/or their programs are running in. So, if the user and their programs are running as full administrator, that's what permissions and privileges the hacker or malware gets when they break in. And at that level of elevation, they can do anything that's possible using the software and hardware. It's a hacker's dream scenario.

In the Linux world, most Linux versions (called *distributions*, or *distros* for short) started to run all users and programs in a less privileged mode by default and require that all users and most programs intentionally elevate themselves if they needed elevated permissions. This is often done in Linux using the sudo (super user do) command. Figure 11.1 shows sudo in use. With the first command, without using sudo, I tried to open and view the Linux password file called shadow. Without sudo, I was denied. With the second command attempt, I added sudo to the beginning of the command and I was prompted for a root account (like Administrator in Windows) password and the file opened. This is a fairly common example, where a user attempts to run something, it fails, and the user remembers they have to add sudo to the command to make it work.

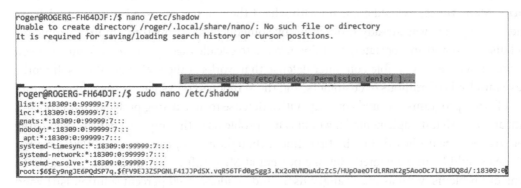

```
roger@ROGERG-FH64DJF:/$ nano /etc/shadow
Unable to create directory /roger/.local/share/nano/: No such file or directory
It is required for saving/loading search history or cursor positions.




                        [ Error reading /etc/shadow: Permission denied ]...
roger@ROGERG-FH64DJF:/$ sudo nano /etc/shadow
list:*:18309:0:99999:7:::
irc:*:18309:0:99999:7:::
gnats:*:18309:0:99999:7:::
nobody:*:18309:0:99999:7:::
_apt:*:18309:0:99999:7:::
systemd-timesync:*:18309:0:99999:7:::
systemd-network:*:18309:0:99999:7:::
systemd-resolve:*:18309:0:99999:7:::
root:$6$Ey9ngJE6PQdSP7q.$fFV9EJ3ZSPGNLF41JJPdSX.vqR56TFd0gSgg3.Kx2oRVNDuAdzZc5/HUpOaeOTdLRRnK2g5AooDc7LDUdDQ8d/:18309:0
```

Figure 11.1: sudo in action

Not allowing regular users and programs to run with the highest privileges and permissions (known as root) by default enabled Linux to have a stronger default user security profile than Microsoft Windows. The new default security posture broke a lot of programs, and Linux users had to be retrained in a new way of doing things, but for the most part it worked. Users complained early on, but within a few years the complaining had stopped and Linux people now know to use `sudo` when they need to run something elevated. After you've used Linux for a few months, you don't even think about it anymore. It's "muscle memory"—you do it without thinking about it.

Because Windows didn't have a similar `sudo` command, Windows users were far more likely to run in elevated contexts all the time. Until Windows Vista, Microsoft could easily take a large part of the blame. They didn't really care about the issue or highlight it beyond as part of a list of some general recommendations that no one really followed. Making matters worse, Microsoft didn't make it easy to run as a non-administrator. In the waning days of Windows Microsoft XP, some security professional colleagues and I decided to follow Microsoft's advice (and our own advice that we had been giving for years) and run as non-administrators as much as we could. Turned out it was very hard to do. Many applications simple broke or had critical errors, and we had to log out and back in as administrators all the time to do very simple, normal, frequently needed actions. Logging in and out, and saving all our open applications, could take minutes each time. In most cases, our "tests" lasted only a few days to a few weeks before we cried uncle and just went back to being logged in as Administrator all the time. Microsoft heard our collective cries.

While moving from Windows XP to Vista, Microsoft agreed they needed something similar to `sudo`, although sadly what they developed was many, many times more complex and confusing. Microsoft created a new default feature called *User Account Control (UAC)*. By default, if a user logged in as Administrator (or as a member of any elevated group or with elevated privileges), UAC would automatically "de-elevate" the logged-on user's permissions, privileges, and group memberships to that of a normal user. If the user or a program needed to run with higher privileges, they would need to approve a logon prompt (by clicking OK or entering elevated logon credentials) to get to the higher level of access. Figure 11.2 gives an example of the UAC prompt screen.

Overall, even though it looks fairly friendly and easy to use in the picture, I (and millions of others) were not big fans. Behind the scenes, the way it worked was complex, complicated, and clunky. It took me months to figure out what it did and how it worked. I did a presentation during this time, and it took me over 100 slides to discuss, in detail, how it really worked. Most people didn't understand it very much at all. But even without a thorough understanding most users and vendors *hated* it!

NOTE   I had to understand UAC in detail because I was writing a book on Windows Vista security (*Windows Vista Security: Securing Vista Against Malicious Attacks*, Wiley, 2007) and because I was going to teach Vista security to thousands of internal Microsoft employees and tens of thousands of interested customers.

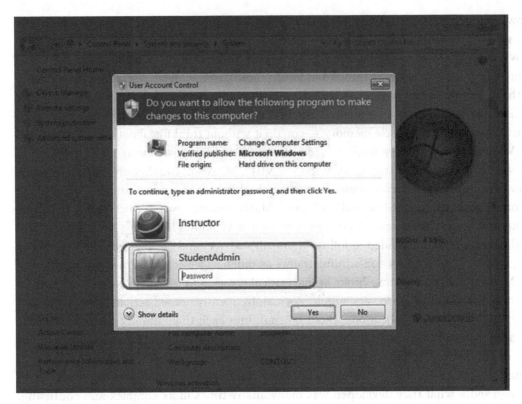

Figure 11.2: Example of UAC prompt screen

But as much as UAC was hated, in a year or two it had the same desired effect as `sudo` did in the Linux world: most users and programs were no longer running all the time as full administrators. Over time Microsoft tweaked UAC to be more user friendly and less bothersome (although the behind-the-scenes complexity stayed). Today, users barely notice UAC other than to have to click OK to install a program or enter their password again to change a system setting. UAC (and `sudo`) are success stories if you ignore the early warts and frustrations of the first few years.

I related this long narrative for two reasons. First, sometimes usability issues can't be avoided and the vendors just have to take a risk that users will understand the new, constant interruptions over the long term.

NOTE Keep in mind that far too many security vendors think this is always the case for everything they do and, in reality, forced instances of major changes should be used very rarely. As covered in Chapter 4, "Usability vs. Security," users will more often work around security blockers, turn them off, or use something else when faced with too high of a security obstacle—even when it is in the user's own best self-interest.

Second, and more important to this particular chapter, I wanted you to understand the background of how important UAC was to the success of Windows's enhanced security since 2007. Many people remember Vista with mixed emotions, but it contained a ton of upgraded security that improved the default security posture of Microsoft and its customers as well as computer security in general. Many of the security improvements Microsoft added was the first time they had been added to a major, general-purpose OS, with other operating systems following Microsoft's lead. Even then, though, UAC suffered from security issues that Microsoft could not overcome that are still potential issues today. One of those was the threat from fake authentication.

When a user or program requested elevated access, Windows and UAC tried its best to prevent potentially malicious programs from getting around the UAC user prompt. Microsoft didn't want malicious programs to be able to either click on or answer the UAC prompt themselves, bypassing it, tricking users into accidentally clicking on the wrong things (known as *clickjacking*), or interacting at all with the end user during the UAC elevation prompting interaction. If malicious programs can interact with UAC or the user during a UAC elevation prompt event, then the chances that a malicious program or user can do something bad are significantly higher. Every hacker wants to be able to interact with any security feature in a way that fools the end user or bypasses the protection. And every security-conscious developer tries to regulate what is known as *focus of control* so that only the legitimate programs are able to interact in authorized ways at the appropriate times.

UAC's developers decided they needed a way to prevent any unauthorized program from interacting with the UAC prompt during an elevation event and prevent the user from accidentally interacting with anything else but the UAC prompt until after the elevation event was finished. During a UAC prompt event, UAC's developers needed total isolation except for the one elevation decision for the one program the user needed to make. What the developers did (which was sort of genius) was that during a UAC prompt event, UAC takes a snapshot of the user's desktop and places it over the real desktop. Or Windows just creates a single-color graphic picture that becomes the temporary background, covering your real desktop during the elevation prompt action.

After that happens, only the true UAC prompt could display over the fake desktop picture. So, even if the user was accidentally tricked into clicking on anything beside the UAC prompt, nothing would happen. They would only be clicking on a picture and not the actual desktop behind the scenes. It was a pretty cool secret switch. Probably fewer than 0.001 percent of Windows users even knew this was happening. If you know how UAC works in detail and know what was happening and looked for it, you might see the millisecond switch-out. Most people just saw that their desktop was suddenly darker (Microsoft dimmed the photo to remove any user focus on anything other than the foreground prompt). The only major side effect was that some early video drivers couldn't handle the switch-out action and would not work with UAC. Those video drivers had to be updated to handle UAC or, until the driver was updated, the impacted users had to run commands to disable the protected UAC prompt screen.

It was a great example of a great security solution from the minds of top computer security experts. What Microsoft didn't share with people outside the company was that they could not solve the opposite problem: a malicious program faking the whole UAC experience. In fact, no one can easily solve it or other similar authentication problems like it. I have seen ways to solve it, but most are clunky and unlikely to become pervasive. More on that later in this chapter.

Let me go into more detail about the fake authentication experience involving UAC so that you'll better understand what I'm talking about. What Windows developers could not easily stop was malicious programs simulating the entire UAC experience when it did not really happen. With the real UAC experience, the UAC prompt comes up only when the user, program, or Windows requests it. But there is nothing to stop a malicious program that is actively running from faking that the UAC experience is happening when it isn't. All a malicious program has to do is take a desktop picture or offer up a single-colored, dimmed background; make a fake UAC prompt appear; ask the user to click OK or type in their logon credentials; and have it seem to have succeeded no matter what the user did. The user can even be tricked into providing their credentials to the fake UAC prompt, which is made to appear as if it failed, and then a real UAC prompt is called. The user will likely just think they must've typed in their credentials incorrectly the first time and then think the "second time" that they typed them in correctly. There is no way for Windows or UAC to accurately detect that a fake UAC experience just occurred or be able to block it with a high level of accuracy. Even if Windows actively tried to look for and detect known instances of fake UAC prompts, the fake UAC prompt could be changed just enough so that Windows never detects it no matter how much it tries.

If the user types in their credentials, the malicious program can record the user's elevated credentials and then use them behind the scenes to do anything the elevated user can do. The hacker or malware program will "own" the system. They can install more malware, record the user's keystrokes with a keystroke logger, dump all the system credentials, manipulate data, and spread around the network. What the malware or attacker can do would be limited only by their malware developer's or hacker's imagination and what is possible given the software and hardware constraints.

The user can also be tricked into providing other confidential information or into believing they had performed some necessary administrative action, such as fooling the user into thinking they had run a (fake) antimalware scan or install a new, legitimate (but really fake) Microsoft patch. A real UAC prompt will often show the legitimate vendor of the program if that program is signed by a trusted digital certificate. So, all the malware program has to do is fake the whole experience, including showing a fake trusted digital certificate that Windows itself appears to be saying is real and trusted. Fake authentication can be used to do many things, including:

- Steal logon credentials.
- Perform a man-the-middle attack, which is then used by the attacker to access the real site/service as the victim.
- Steal other confidential information.
- Take over the logon account.
- Make the victim think some legitimate action occurred that did not in actuality.

It is interesting to note that faking authentication is able to accomplish many of the same (although not all) goals such as bypassing MFA or actually hacking it. The key issue with faked authentication is that the end user is still relying on and trusting their experience as legitimate even though it is completely rogue.

Fake authentication is a very hard thing to stop. I know that all the best minds at Microsoft could not figure out a trustworthy, accurate, way to prevent it. And this is not just a Microsoft challenge. Fake authentication hacks pretty much pollute all the big vendors today. It is one of the most popular ways to hack someone and to hack MFA. It is the bane of the computer security authentication world. And it is not easy to mitigate.

Solve this problem the right way and you'll probably become rich. Many have tried. I have even seen a few solutions that actually did solve it, but the solutions are so heavy-handed and cumbersome that most organizations and users are unlikely to use them, at least widely. But without an easy-to-implement solution, authentication can never be truly trusted. Hackers are taking advantage of this attack vector with vigor. And unfortunately, fake authentication can be used in both the digital and nondigital arenas to bypass MFA.

Example Fake Authentication Attacks

I covered some of the most popular fake authentication attacks in Chapter 8, "SMS Attacks." Short Message Service (SMS) continues to be a top vector for fake authentication attacks. Let's look at other real-world examples of fake authentication attacks.

Look-Alike Websites

Fake, look-alike websites are even more popular than fake SMS messages. Fake websites are perhaps the most popular attack vector used by phishing attackers for decades when attempting to steal credentials. When people think of phishing, they think of emails pretending to be from some otherwise trusted, legitimate vendor and their related look-alike websites. When the victim is tricked into visiting the fake website, they can be tricked into using their real credentials, and this trick works even when using MFA (as was illustrated in Chapter 6, "Access Control Token Tricks" with the Kevin Mitnick hacking video: blog.knowbe4.com/heads-up-new-exploit-hacks-linkedin-2-factor-auth.-see-this-kevin-mitnick-video).

Once a user is tricked into thinking they have logged into a fake website, they can be easily prompted for more confidential personal information. This often occurs with fake banking websites. After the victim "logs in," the fake banking website sends a pop-up message asking the victim to verify and update more information. Figure 11.3 shows such a prompt.

Worse yet, many of the rogue websites have valid, trusted digital certificates (www.infosecurity-magazine.com/news/boom-in-look-alike-retail-domains). This is often due to the existence of free, online digital certificate authorities (CAs), like Let's Encrypt (letsencrypt.org), which have been a boon for rogue websites. Free CAs, which allow any website to request a valid, trusted certificate without significant verification of legitimacy of function and ownership, have been a security concern since they were envisioned and implemented. The results have shown that the concern was valid. Oftentimes there are far more malicious, "trusted," look-alike websites for every real website they are pretending to be.

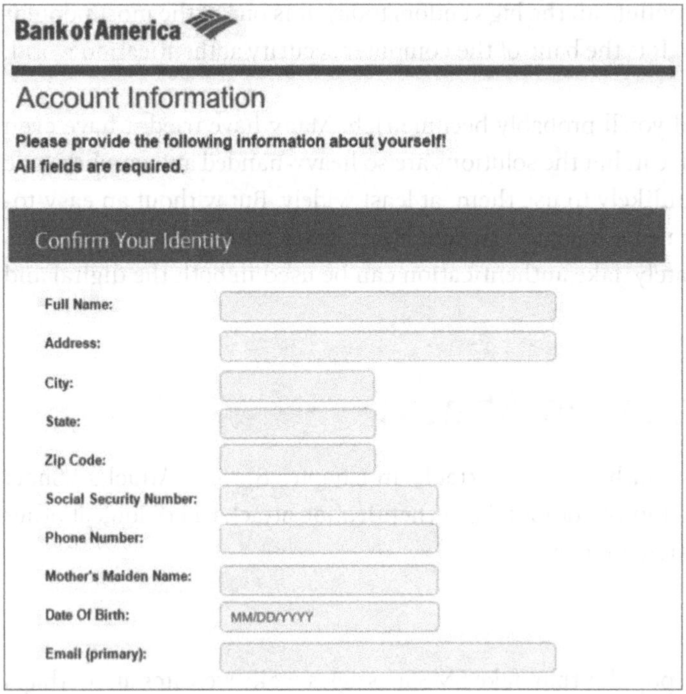

Figure 11.3: Fake bank website prompting for more confidential information

Fake Office 365 Logons

Another very popular fake authentication request that can bypass MFA is the fake Microsoft Office 365 request. Microsoft Office 365 is Microsoft's premier and most popular application and cloud service. Depending on the edition and version, Office 365 can include Word, Excel, PowerPoint, SharePoint, OneNote, Teams, Outlook, and OneDrive. It's the latter two applications/services that hackers love to take advantage of the most lately, although malicious Word and Excel documents are running a close third and fourth, respectively.

Usually it starts with a realistic-looking phishing email claiming to be from almost anyone. Office 365 is so popular that it is very normal for you to receive an email that then prompts you for your Office 365 logon credentials to access a stored or protected document. The following site gives a great picture-by-picture example of a sophisticated Office 365 scam involving fake voicemails:

thenextweb.com/security/2019/10/31/scammers-are-now-faking-voicemail-notifications-to-steal-office-365-login-credentials/. Sadly, it's all part of a malicious kit that anyone so motivated can purchase and use.

To stop malicious hackers from stealing Office 365 credentials, Microsoft recommends that users be required to log on using MFA solutions that work with Office 365. Microsoft provides a few MFA solutions (that work with Office 365 and Azure AD), which they sell, and they also work with selected compatible MFA solutions, such as Duo, RSA, and Trusona. Microsoft and security experts recommend using MFA instead of passwords for all the reasons we've already covered.

If the user uses MFA to protect their Office 365 logon, it can be bypassed using fake authentication. Like the Kevin Mitnick MitM attack demonstration, here is a video of a good guy hacker demonstrating that he can bypass Office 365 MFA using the same hacker tool Kevin used, Evilginx: www.youtube.com/watch?v=k4bq5A-icBw. Here's another video example of the same technique: www.youtube.com/watch?v=mNOBOWZw8D4. And this blog posting covers using Evilginx against Office 365 and how to mitigate the risk: www.thecloudtechnologist.com/defending-against-evilginx2-in-office-365/. It is easy to say that bypassing MFA using this method is not a secret. They all begin with a fake email that drives the user to a fake authentication page.

NOTE   Bypassing MFA using fake authentication attacks is not just a Microsoft problem. Hackers frequently attack Google's G Suite applications and Dropbox just as readily.

Using an MFA-Incompatible Service or Protocol

Another common, but unrelated, method to bypass MFA requirements is by implementing an attack that uses a protocol that the MFA solution does not work with. When vendors like Microsoft try to move to MFA-required solutions, many times legacy requirements prevent all the vendor's services, methods, and protocols from requiring MFA. Attackers will try logging into different services to see if there are any that will bypass the MFA requirement.

For example, it was reported (securityaffairs.co/wordpress/82480/hacking/imap-protocol-attacks.html) that password spray attacks utilizing the legacy email protocol Internet Message Access Protocol (IMAP) allowed attackers to bypass MFA requirements on both Office 365 and G Suite. Not only could attackers bypass MFA requirements, but the multiple logon attempts did not cause account lockout to become enabled. One in four tenant customers were successfully compromised. That's incredible if true.

A cybersecurity analyst friend of mine, Rob Tompkins, discovered that he could bypass Microsoft Intune's and Office 365's MFA requirement if he used a Chromebook, an application called Bluemail, and Microsoft's ActiveSync service/API. He could log on to any email account that would normally require MFA using only a logon name and password. It was an obscure find at the time, but it points to the difficulty any longstanding vendor in implementing MFA in all scenarios. Another older legacy service that allowed logons without using MFA (at the time at least) was Exchange Web Services, according to this article: www.theregister.co.uk/2018/07/13/2fa_o365_bypass_attacks/. Microsoft responded to these legacy-style type of attacks by stating that legacy protocols can either be disabled or protected (in some instances), and that legacy devices can be prevented from logging on (blogs .msdn.microsoft.com/oncloud/2018/06/06/blocking-legacy-clients-with-azure-ad-conditional-access). This is true, but admins have to be aware that this sort of proactive defense is available and needed. Many admins are just happy to get a new cloud service running and don't realize that MFA protections can be bypassed in some scenarios that they may have in their environment.

> **NOTE** Microsoft is desperately trying to eradicate users who must use the older legacy protocols which do not support MFA. Microsoft understands the weaknesses of using older legacy protocols, but when you have hundreds of millions of customers, shutting off older, weaker protocols takes much longer than you would think.

It is very common for trusted services to access other services using application programming interfaces (APIs). When doing so, services cannot easily (or at all) log on to the other service using MFA. So, instead the services are not required to log on at all, they are allowed to use hard-coded credentials, or they can use something else to mitigate the risk. An attacker knowing that MFA is not required and knowing what mitigations are used may be able to log on to an otherwise MFA-requiring service. For example, in this blog article (www.agilepointnxblog.com/bypass-multi-factor-authentication-in-office-365), the researchers revealed that many Office 365 APIs are locked down using only IP addresses. The involved parties often will lock down the APIs so that they can accept logons only from predefined, trusted IP addresses while every other connection coming from anywhere else will require MFA. An attacker learning this information could try to modify the IP address range to include an IP address they are originating from or make sure they originate their logons from within the previously approved IP addresses. Other types of API attacks will be discussed in Chapter 19, "API Abuses".

Fake authentication attacks can be very difficult to detect and stop. It's even difficult to blame the MFA solution developers. The MFA developers might have done everything possible within their control to ensure that their MFA solution, when used correctly, prevents bypasses and hacks. But in fake authentication instances, the hackers are simply simulating the MFA solution experience or bypassing MFA being needed. Using fake authentication, the hackers can trick the user into revealing other confidential information or performing other actions that are contrary to the victim's own self-interest.

Defenses to Fake Authentication Attacks

Here are some developer and user defenses against fake authentication attacks.

Developer Defenses

Although there isn't much developers can do against fake authentication attacks, let's look at some defenses they can consider.

Educate Developers

Many MFA developers have not heard of the threat from fake authentication attacks. All developers should be educated about the threats and likely scenarios against their involved solution in order to ensure that they are considering it when threat modeling and developing solutions. If you don't even know that it can easily occur, you're probably not going to make defenses against it when opportunities for defenses present themselves.

Educate Customers

Developers should include warnings to all their users about the threat of fake authentication attempts. You don' t want your customers to be unaware of this particular type of attack. So, include warnings about it in your customer literature along with any possible recommendations that might prevent it.

Implement Channel and Token Binding

As covered in Chapter 6, authentication solutions which use channel or token binding are resilient to MitM attacks. So, implementing binding protection can prevent many common types of fake authentication.

Lock Authentication to a Single Digitally Authenticated Site

Require that all authentication be done to a single, digital certificate-authenticated website for which the user can easily verify the URL address. The user should be instructed to always look for a particular URL and verify that it is the legitimate website address before authenticating. This, of course, is easier said than done. If users could easily do this, fake authentication on fake websites would not be the problem that it is today.

Registered Logon Devices

Perhaps the easiest defense against MitM attack methods is to require that all MFA devices be previously registered and verified to the service that uses them. That way, if an attacker tries to send captured codes from the victim to the logon server, the MitM device being used would not be the same as the previously registered device and the logon would be denied (or more authentication information could be requested).

Disable Legacy Protocols and Services That Bypass MFA

Developers and administrators can disable legacy protocols, services, and devices, that cannot be MFA-enabled. APIs and other services that cannot use MFA should be sufficiently restricted by other security controls, such as IP address and approved VPN tunnels. For example, with Microsoft Office 365, you could disable Basic Authentication (which can bypass MFA), or just enable it for a smaller select group of users or machines. All or most users and computers should be forced to use Microsoft's Modern Authentication, which supports and enforces MFA.

NOTE Around the time this chapter was being written, Microsoft had announced plans to disable Basic Authentication to prevent MFA bypass and other types of legacy attacks, but their previously announced deployment date was delayed because of customers with backward compatibility issues.

Forced Logon Apps

One of the more common defenses against fake authentication is to require that the user always begin all authentication attempts from within a safe, trusted application. Most MFA solutions allow the user to use any compatible browser. MFA solutions wishing to prevent fake authentication attacks will sometimes require that all authentications be originated from a single trusted application. I recently saw an example of this type of solution from a new MFA solution developer. He created a phone app (and planned to make apps for Windows and Apple computers) that asked the user to type in all URLs to which they needed to authenticate with his solution. Each participating website had to include code that accepted logons from only that application and the user had to use that application to connect to those predefined websites. It's a very heavy-handed approach and most customers will not accept that sort of solution, but it does work fairly effectively.

User Defenses

Fake authentication attacks are hard to stop, but the user can defend against them by simply being more aware. Defenses include the following.

Security Awareness Training

Nothing beats a user being aware of the different types of fake authentication attacks and being on the lookout for them. Most users are unaware of these types of attacks, and because of that, they never look for them. Be honest with yourself; before I told you about fake UAC attacks, had they ever occurred to you? Had you ever looked out for them? Now, after reading a few pages about them and how hard they are to stop, you are probably at least going to be slightly more aware and look out for any unusual signs whenever a UAC prompt pops up.

Trusted URL Verification

After education, nothing beats the user looking to confirm what the URL address is of the location they are logging into to confirm they are logging into the legitimate location. It never hurts to make sure that the URL is HTTPS-protected, but as was previously discussed, many rogue websites contain "trusted" TLS-enabled digital certificates. Users should verify that the URL visually points to the desired, legitimate, location first and foremost.

Some readers may wonder why I didn't recommend or mention URL reviewing, antimalware, reputation-scanning tools, which look out for rogue URLs. That's because most of us already have one built into our browsers and email applications by the vendors that make them, but more importantly, because they are largely inaccurate. One recent large study (blog.knowbe4.com/heads-up-a-whopping-21-percent-of-phishing-attack-urls-are-not-detected-as-malicious-for-days-after-they-go-live) said that as many as 21 percent of all rogue URLs go undetected as malicious for multiple days. With accuracy that bad, I'd rather users relied on their own senses. Additionally, I've also seen executing malware that faked he URL review as being successful when it really wasn't. Just like faking the whole UAC approval process, an active malicious application can fake a URL approval process.

Summary

This chapter covered fake authentication attacks where the attackers simulate the MFA solution experience to collect victim confidential information or trick them into performing otherwise rogue actions. Fake authentication can be simulated by any malicious program that fakes the whole experience, by fake websites, or by forcing the use of a legacy protocol or service that bypasses MFA requirements. This chapter also covered some developer and user defenses against fake authentication attacks.

Chapter 12, "Social Engineering Attacks" will explore many of the ways social engineering can bypass MFA defenses.

12 Social Engineering Attacks

A significant portion of all crime involves social engineering—always has, and likely always will. Accordingly, social engineering is one of the most popular ways hackers can bypass MFA solutions. This chapter explores social engineering attacks on MFA and other hardware authentication solutions.

Introduction

Social engineering is the process of someone or something (e.g., email, malware, program) fraudulently and maliciously masquerading as someone or something else to acquire unauthorized information or to create a desired action that is contrary to the victim's or their organization's self-interests. Simply put, it's a "con" with malicious intent. It is often done in person, using mailed advertisements, using email, in messaging apps, or over the phone.

There are various forms and applications of social engineering, each having their own descriptive names, such as phishing (digital social engineering), spear phishing (targeted phishing), smishing (phishing using SMS), vishing (phishing using voice over phone), and whaling (targeting senior executives). Social engineering includes emails, messages, SMS, and voice calls claiming to be from work, vendors, bosses, friends, coworkers, popular social websites, banks, auction sites, or IT staff. Any weakly authenticated or unauthenticated communication channel that can be used to successfully lure any unsuspecting victim will be used.

Social engineering and phishing are the number one cause of successful digital attacks. As covered in Chapter 5, "Hacking MFA in General," social engineering is responsible for 70–90 percent of all malicious digital breaches (blog.knowbe4.com/70-to-90-of-all-malicious-breaches-are-due-to-social-engineering-and-phishing-attacks). It wasn't always that way, although social engineering and unpatched software have been either the number one or number two reason for successful hacking attacks for over three decades. For a long time, unpatched software was the number one reason why people got hacked. For almost two decades, unpatched Internet browser "add-ins," like Sun/Oracle Java, Adobe Acrobat Reader, and Adobe Flash, were responsible for most successful attacks.

In many years, a single unpatched program was accountable for most hacks. For example, according to the Cisco 2014 Annual Security Report (`www.cisco.com/assets/global/UK/pdfs/executive_security/sc-01_casr2014_cte_liq_en.pdf`), unpatched Java was responsible for 91 percent of successful web attacks. Imagine that; patch one program successfully and 91 percent of your cyber-security risk goes away!

Eventually, over time, browser and operating system vendors made unpatched Java less of a threat. They made it less likely that an unauthorized Java program would be able to run without approval by an end user or administrator. Around 2015, social engineering became the predominant way computers were compromised, and that hasn't changed. Attackers are so successful at using social engineering to get what they want, and it works cross-platform—attackers don't need separate exploits for different operating systems and programs—that it's likely to stay the number one exploit vector until social engineering can be defeated overall, which is not any time soon.

And it comes as no surprise that social engineering is used to defeat and get around MFA solutions. Many of the chapters of this book are full of different types of MFA attacks that involve social engineering. Social engineering greases the skids of attacks and makes them easier. Want to get someone to run a trojan horse program that gets around MFA? Socially engineer them into running it. Want to get a user to click on a malicious URL link? Then socially engineer them. There is little maliciousness that social engineering can't make easier to accomplish.

Part of the problem is that most humans just inherently trust other humans. We do it as a part of our daily lives. When someone says something, most of us believe it. Most of us don't see other human beings as inherently evil or untrustworthy. We all make incredible risky risk decisions as a part of our daily lives. Heck, any woman who goes on a date with a guy, who is usually bigger and stronger, is making a big risk decision in her life. We all order pizza or other delivery food that gets delivered by someone who we really don't know. Many of us get into Uber and Lyft cars even though we've read the many stories of other drivers doing harm to previous customers, and those drivers continue to welcome new customers into their personal cars even though there are tens of thousands of reports of other customers harming drivers. We are a world of people who inherently trust each other. Phishing and social engineering takes advantage of that inherent human trust.

Even when humans explicitly know the risks, we don't always avoid them or fear them in relation to their actual incidence of harm. For example, I live in Key Largo, Florida. My friends and visitors love to go with me and my wife on our boat out on the ocean to go swimming, snorkeling, and sometimes scuba diving. I've never had a guest who didn't ask me, ahead of the planned ocean trip, if there were sharks in the water. I always laugh and reply that all saltwater on the earth has sharks, and yes, that although the water around Key Largo has sharks, too, there has never been an unprovoked shark attack in Key Largo's recorded history (since the 1880s). They always ask, what does unprovoked mean? I tell them it means they aren't petting or pestering a shark or aren't holding a bloody fish or lobster. My guests never care. They are nervous about sharks because they saw the famous movie *Jaws* or watched Discovery Channel's *Shark Week*.

I often respond with the facts: that your chances of being bit by a shark anywhere are about 1:3,700,000 and that your odds of dying in your car during your lifetime are about 1:100 to 1:50. Your odds of dying of cancer (1:7), heart issues (1:6), or falling in your home (1:111), are much higher than even that. This is a great site to see your odds of dying from a particular event: `injuryfacts .nsc.org/all-injuries/preventable-death-overview/odds-of-dying/`. Various sites give you widely different statistics, but the relative comparisons are roughly the same (i.e., you should be worried far more about your car ride to the ocean than a shark attack in the ocean). One of my favorite related statistics is from a 2018 report from the Bill and Melinda Gates Foundation (`www.gatesnotes.com/ Health/Mosquito-Week-2018`). It revealed that more people die every day from the impact of mosquito bites than from the last hundred years of shark attacks altogether, yet far more people are afraid of shark bites than mosquito bites. There is no Mosquito Week on Discovery channel. We are often worried about the wrong things and can't help ourselves. There is something far more visceral and emotional about getting eaten alive by a shark than sickened slowly by a blood disease transmitted by a mosquito. And attackers understand emotions and fear as big motivators. As I discuss in a moment, phishers often use "stressor events" as an emotional motivator to help compromise their victims.

Social Engineering Commonalities

Anyone can lie to another person. But professional social engineering is a special kind of thoughtful lying. Here are some of the common traits of social engineering scams.

Unauthenticated Communication

Criminals don't like to get caught. So, the first rule of business for a scammer is to use a communication's channel that is largely unauthenticated, weakly authenticated, or if authenticated, easy to break into so that the scammer can easily pretend to be someone else. As examples, anyone can send a physical document via the postal service claiming to be anyone else. You could claim to be the president of a country or the Pope and as long as you got the logos right on the document, there's no one to say that it isn't you. The post office doesn't take the time to authenticate that who is sending the mail is the same as the person it is claiming to be from (with rare exceptions).

Email is only authenticated to the receiver by the sending email address (maybe). Any email can claim to be from anyone, and many times even include fake sending email addresses. Unless the receiver's receiving email services check for fake sender email addresses, it will not be discovered. There are common email standards that check to see whether or not the sending email address is accurate (e.g., Sender Policy Framework (SPF), Domain Keys Identified Messaging (DKIM), and Domain -based Message Authentication, Reporting and Conformance (DMARC), for three), but nearly all of these can be gotten around in multiple ways.

NOTE If you are interested in learning more about SPF, DKIM, and DMARC, see my webinar on these topics: info.knowbe4.com/dmarc-spf-dkim-webinar.

More often, phishers use valid email addresses from valid domains that look like some other valid email address. For example, phishes often send emails with sender addresses formatted like bill-gates-microsoft.com@biz-microsoftemail.com, where an unsuspecting user might not understand that the email is not really from Microsoft.com. Or as covered in Chapters 6, "Access Control Token Tricks" and this chapter, a fake LinkedIn email may really point to llinkedin.com and not linkedin.com, and many victims would not notice the difference.

Chapter 8, "SMS Attacks," covered how phone calls and SMS text messages are not authenticated beyond the attached phone number, which may or may not be accurate. I can call from any phone claiming to be the president of the United States, perhaps using a second person acting as my "call setup" press assistant, and with enough accurate mimicry it might be tough for any receiver to prove that I'm not the president. Comedic radio DJs appear to do it all the time. When someone calls us claiming to be from our cable company, bank, or telephone company, rarely do we actually tell the caller to prove it in some trusted, irrefutable, way.

NOTE For years as a demo at small presentations, I would initiate a call to everyone in the audience who gave me their phone number before the start of my talk, a call that appeared to come from the White House (phone number 202-456-1111) with a mimicked message purportedly from the president saying it was impossible to spoof phone numbers. It was always a big hit.

Most phishing scammers avoid real-life phone calls for a number of reasons, including that many times the scammer is of a different nationality and may not even speak the victim's native tongue well enough to pull off the scam or answer basic questions quickly. Most phone call receivers expect any vendor's call, even if coming from someone sounding foreign, to be able to fairly easily communicate in the customer's expected language and know basic details about the customer's referenced matter. Using a real phone number (versus the Internet) slightly increases the risk of being caught, but only very slightly.

Nonphysical

Direct person-to-person social engineering happens all the time, but criminals like it the least of all the possible methods. First, and foremost, the scammer can be more easily detained and arrested. Second, it involves appearing in person and having to answer another skeptical person's questions. Third, it's a very inefficient way of scamming a large group of people. Most people don't fall for social engineering scams. This means that scammers must try their phishing scam on a bunch of people for each unlucky victim who takes the bait. When a scammer is doing the scam in person, that's 1:1 scamming. They have to take the time to try and fool each and every person, one at a time. They can't begin the second scam until they have physically ended the first scam, whereas a single online scammer can send out millions to hundreds of millions of phishing emails in a day, with a far less chance of getting caught. Or a scammer using a phone, even though it involves 1:1 scamming (unless they include a robocall portion), can more quickly end one unproductive scam and begin the next far quicker as soon as they realize the current target isn't falling for the scam. A physical scammer has to physically walk from one victim to the next.

Usually Involves Well-Known Brands

Most social engineering and phishing scams involve the names of well-known companies with which the victim is familiar. This is because well-known companies are often known to have many proactive marketing campaigns and, as such, would have a valid reason for reaching out to a person "out of the blue." Well-known brands are also often well thought of by the potential victim so that the scammer gets the goodwill the victim has for the company being used. Scammers pretending to be from beloved, well-known companies are more likely to be successful than if using company names no one has heard of.

NOTE   Well-known companies are not always beloved. For example, many scammers pretend to be the Internal Revenue Service (IRS) or law enforcement. The widespread fear of such organizations can also play a major role into getting the victim to drop their normal skepticism quicker.

Scammers will often use look-alike or sound-alike email addresses and websites of well-known brands and include content taken from or linked to the defrauded organization. Many times, the only truly malicious content beyond some of the fraudulent text is the one URL link the scammer is hoping the victim will click on. Figure 12.1 shows some example fake URL links that create the impression they are legitimate domains approved by well-known brands. They aren't.

Figure 12.1: Examples of fake URL domains created to look like they are affiliated with well-known brands

A scammer website will often include a trusted digital certificate, and the majority of the world thinks that means the website is valid and trustworthy. Most websites (over 80 percent of the web as of 2020) use a TLS/HTTPS digital certificate to help authenticate a site and encrypt data transmissions between the visitor and the website. These digital certificates are handed out by trusted

CAs (covered in more detail in Chapter 3, "Types of Authentication") to each website. One of the most important things CAs can do is confirm that it's a valid website and that the certificate is being requested by a legitimate person on behalf of the website. Most users also think that every CA goes further and actually makes sure the website is not malicious. In many cases, especially in free, public CAs, like Let's Encrypt (letsencrypt.org), it is absolutely not true. Most of the major CAs try their best not to distribute trusted digital certificates to malicious customers, but at any CA some percentage of their customers is likely doing bad stuff. At CAs like Let's Encrypt, they do such little checking, and knowingly say (letsencrypt.org/2015/10/29/phishing-and-malware.html) they will not check, that hackers and malware pushers use them as their go-to trusted digital certificate issuer (www .infoworld.com/article/3019926/cyber-criminals-abusing-free-lets-encrypt-certificates .html). To be fair to Let's Encrypt, they clearly state what they do and don't do. But it's sad that many browsers and users automatically "trust" whatever digital certificate is sent to them without understanding the ramifications.

Yes, your browser and your antimalware scanner are supposed to warn you when you access a malicious URL, but as previously covered over 21 percent of malicious URLs are not detected as such for days after they've been launched (blog.knowbe4.com/heads-up-a-whopping-21-percent-of-phish-ing-attack-urls-are-not-detected-as-malicious-for-days-after-they-go-live). The end result is that no one can trust a digital certificate to mean that a website is or isn't malicious, but malicious websites take advantage of the fact that most people inherently trust HTTPS-enabled websites more than they should.

Often Based on Notable Current Events and Interests

Phishing always increases and focuses during popular notable events, such as natural disasters, celebrity deaths, and big global events. Phishers know that people are interested in notable events. and they will prey on their interest in the topic. As I write this, the global coronavirus COVID-19 pandemic is accelerating—and predictably, the amount of phishing using COVID-19 as a hook is increasing. Here are a couple of blog news stories: blog.knowbe4.com/hackers-use-interactive-malicious-covid-19-map-to-spread-malware and blog.knowbe4.com/extreme-measures-the-epidemic-of-covid-19-phishing-emails-rages-on. Phishers will often post contrarian, counter-factual news stories in forums dedicated to specific topics, knowing that a certain percentage of the readers will be emotionally incentivized to click on the embedded phishing link.

Uses Stressors

Phishers like to use *stressors* in their initial contacts. Stressors are descriptive stories that are intended to push the receiver's thoughts into a base "fight or flight" mode. Stressors include things such as someone pretending to be the victim's boss saying that such and such thing needs to be done ASAP or some big business deal will fail, or someone's grandchild has been arrested and bail needs to be paid to the police, or the IRS has found a tax discrepancy and will be arresting the victim unless they pay some penalty fee immediately. The phishers say something that is supposedly believable to the victim but that is an emergency request. Or they prey on people's personal shame and embarrassment, such as when phishers claim they've recorded the victim privately masturbating to pornography using the victim's web cam and will release the video to their friends if they don't get paid. Stressor events demand immediate action. They don't want to give the victim time to research the request more to determine the validity.

Advanced: Pretexting

Pretexting is used in advanced phishing attacks. *Pretexting* is when the phisher initiates multiple contacts with the victim, with the first communication being something that is not asking the victim for anything super suspicious. The phisher is "laying the groundwork" and establishing an ongoing relationship so that when they do have a requested action in the future, the victim already feels comfortable with the phisher.

An example pretexting phone call might be a hacker calling a company's human resources number and talking to the accounts payable clerk and acting as if they are now the new primary contact for an existing company that regularly sends invoices for payment. In the first call, the phisher just says hello and communicates that they are the new contact, gives them new contact information, and tells the accounts payable clerk that all questions and requests related to the company should now go to them. They may even indicate that the change is happening as part of a "big update" and that they will even be changing banks to a new bank that gives them more favorable terms, or something like that. Then the phisher waits a few days or weeks and then asks the accounts payable clerk to update the payment information supposedly due to a new banking change. When the regular invoice from the real company comes into the accounts receivable clerk, the clerk not knowing anything different, sends the regularly scheduled payment to the new bank and phisher. Scams like this are often not discovered for months.

I often have friends and people tell me that they could never fall for a phishing scam. I always laugh, because anyone can be tricked. One of my favorite methods is to have someone, my accomplice, call that skeptical person at home posing as a road construction survey crew member and say, "I'm calling to get permission to be able to access your front yard to take a survey for the upcoming road widening and regional sewer project involving your street and the future new highway exit ramp at [some location between the closest interstate and their house]." The victim is never happy to hear this. No one wants more traffic in their neighborhood or their yard ripped up for huge sewer lines. When the victim complains, the caller will then tell them they will be glad to send information about the pending road widening project and information on how they can vote against the road project in an email. The victim then gives their email address and the phisher (i.e., me) sends an encrypted PDF document containing potential malicious links (as examples) to the victim from a Gmail or Hotmail address that is a look-alike for the pretend construction survey company my accomplice introduced on the phone. I've never had the intended victim not open the PDF document and click on the links. Never. Pretexting works. You don't want to bet me.

Third-Party Reliances

One of the fastest growing segments of phishing is rogue emails from taken-over, compromised, computers of trusted people and partners you have an ongoing relationship with. Most of the normal antiphishing advice, such as "Don't open emails from people you don't know," don't apply. Spotting a phishing email sent from someone you have an ongoing relationship with is very hard. Defenses mainly come down to "Call the person at a previously communicated phone number any time they request you to do something out of the ordinary to confirm."

Here's a good example of this type of phishing. In the United States, most people buying a house get a home mortgage loan. As part of that process, the buyer usually has to make a down payment (ranging from 1 percent to 20 percent of the loan or property's value). The down payment must be held in "escrow" by a third party that everyone trusts before the mortgage can be approved and the buyers take possession of the property.

Phishers will break into loan officer or escrow agent computers and inventory the pending property closings and note which ones have large pending down payments. Then they will send the buyers an email, which the buyers have been told to expect on the day they are expecting, telling them to make an escrow payment that they have been told to expect, for the amount they have been told to expect, for the property they want to buy. The email arrives from a person the buyer already trusts and every detail in the email is legit except for the wiring instruction information. The phisher switches out the legit banking wiring instructions for instructions to their bank. They then usually create an email rule on the compromised system that deletes any future outgoing emails from the legitimate agent to the victim and re-routes in any incoming emails from the victim to the scammer's email account. Usually by the time everyone finds out what has happened, the money is long gone. The victim is out their down payment and everyone else in the financial pathway that was going to get a piece of the mortgage finance fees (usually more than a handful of people) are out of their money because the mortgage does not close. The buyer loses their wanted property and everyone involved other than the phisher is out their money. Phishing using previously compromised trusted third parties is really dastardly stuff.

All of these characteristics are common traits of phishing content. It goes without saying that social engineering and phishing is often used to bypass and to access user accounts protected by MFA solutions.

NOTE Anyone can be tricked by social engineering and phishing. Anyone! How susceptible you are or aren't has nothing to do with measured intelligence or "street smarts." Anyone, appropriately motivated, can be tricked into doing something that is against their own self-interest.

Example Social Engineering Attacks on MFA

Many attacks on MFA solutions involve social engineering. Chapters 6, 7, "End-Point Attacks," 8, and and 11, "Fake Authentication Attacks," all had examples of attacks that involved social engineering, and many of the next chapters will as well. As stated previously, social engineering is involved in the vast majority of attacks and has been since the beginning of computers. Here are some more examples.

Fake Bank Alert

A very common scam these days is for someone to message or call a victim, claiming to be from that victim's bank, PayPal, hotel company, stock investing site, and so forth, and claim to have detected a potentially malicious fraud. When they call, they will say something like, "Hello, Mr. Grimes, we are from your bank [or insert real bank name here] and we have detected some potentially fraudulent transactions on your account. Did you buy two tickets from Dallas Fort Worth airport to Nigeria?" The victim will say, "No!" Then the scammer continues, "We didn't think you did. Don't worry, we have blocked those two transactions and we are going to take care of you. We think we have detected other fraudulent transactions on your account and we want to block them so you won't be responsible for the charges. We just need to confirm that you are really Mr. Grimes and your relevant account information. What is your account number?" The victim gives the account number. The scammer continues, "What is your logon name?" The victim gives the account logon name. The scammer then asks, "What is your PIN or password?" The victim gives them that information.

The scammer then tries to log to the victim's account using that information. If the victim has MFA enabled, the scammer will put the account in "recovery mode" and get the bank to send a login code to the victim's cell phone using SMS. The scammer will say something similar to "We are going to send you a code to your previously registered cell phone to verify that you are who you say you are, Mr. Grimes. I need you to read me back that code once you receive it." The victim receives the account recovery PIN code sent by the real bank and reads it back to the scammer, who then uses it to take over the account. The scammer then changes the user's logon method, often disabling MFA and the current password. If the user is currently logged on to their account, they ask the user to log out and back in again. Of course, the victim can no longer log in to their account. The fake bank support team tells the victim that they are taking care of everything and will call the victim back in a few minutes. Of course, within those few minutes, the attackers steal as much money as they can. The victim usually ends up waiting hours, gets frustrated, and tries to call the "bank" back. The "bank" never answers the victim's call. The victim then has to look up his bank's real tech support number, which he then calls, and after a hour or many hours determines he's been scammed. I've heard of many victims who could not easily convince their bank that they were the real account holder. It sometimes took days to get everything figured out and locked back down.

Here's a link to a real-world example of a similar crime: www.msn.com/en-us/news/crime/a-scam-targeting-americans-over-the-phone-has-resulted-in-millions-of-dollars-lost-to-hackers-dont-be-the-next-victim/ar-AAJpE2J.

Crying Babies

Earlier I wrote about how humans just want to help other humans. This applies even when there are rules designed to stop malicious instances of social engineering to get around those helpful humans.

Almost every major customer service vendor is well aware of phishers and social engineers and how they abuse their customers and customer support engineers to steal money or services. Most vendors have been exposed to this type of criminality for years and have implemented rules that if their staff strictly follows, will prevent most social engineering attacks. They train their staff to let them know about the risk of social engineering and create "scripts" that the support staff is supposed to follow that will prevent most social engineering. Still, it's tough to remove the humanity out of the human, and trained customer support representatives can still be tricked. Here's a great example: www.youtube.com/watch?v=lc7scxvKQOo.

In this video a young man asks a hacker if they can hack his phone account at the 2016 DEF CON convention, which is attended by white- and black-hat hackers alike. In the video he asks white-hat hacker female, Jessica Clark, to see if she can compromise his cell phone account using only his cell phone number, name, and the identity of his cell phone provider. He did not give her any other information.

She starts with two things. First, she downloads and uses a recording of a baby crying from a YouTube video (you can find any on YouTube) and she fakes her call as originating from his cell phone number. When someone calls into their cell phone provider using a subscriber's cell phone number, a lot of information prepopulates the cell phone provider tech support's call screen, and this gives them a false sense that the caller is who they say they are. The tech support person also hears the baby crying in the background and pictures an overtasked mother and is being told the mother is behind in a chore assigned by her taskmaster husband. The social engineering hacker begins to get confidential information within 30 seconds and, within a few minutes, is able to get his password changed and herself added to the account.

This is a perfect example of humans helping humans.

Hacking Building Access Cards

I'm lucky. I work with one of the world's best social engineering hackers, Kevin Mitnick (en.wikipedia .org/wiki/Kevin_Mitnick). Kevin was arrested many years ago in 1995 for hacking cell phone networks and businesses. There is even a best-selling book, *Takedown: The Pursuit and Capture of Kevin Mitnick, America's Most Wanted Computer Outlaw – By The Man Who Did It* (Voice, 1996) by Tsutomu Shimomura with John Ma Markoff, which talks about Kevin's exploits and capture. I eventually wrote about Kevin and his turn into a white-hat hacker in my 2017 book, *Hacking the Hacker* (Wiley, 2017). It's still delightfully surprising to me that I now work for him and call him a true friend.

Kevin was such a creative hacker that he has become one of the few infamous legends in our field. I don't want to downplay any harm that his hacking caused, but his hacking was never particularly malevolent or primarily financially motivated. Much of it involved pranks and just seeing what he could do. Since his release from prison (over 20 years ago), he has spent his life helping people and businesses to be more secure. Two decades ago, when I barely knew Kevin, I realized that he had learned his lesson and become a good guy hacker. Not all black-hat hackers successfully make the turn to permanent white-hat hacker, but Kevin did. He was one of the first famous hackers who I trusted had made the turn.

Kevin is now co-owner and chief hacking officer of my current employer, KnowBe4, Inc., and he runs his own very successfully penetration testing company. I've come to know and love Kevin Mitnick. He's a solid, upstanding, moral person. And he loves to teach others how to hack, legally, especially using social engineering. If you ever get a chance to see one of Kevin's hacking seminars or presentations in person, you'll see what I mean. Kevin's hacking demos are a combination of uber hacker and nearly untouchable showmanship, which points back to his original love of magic and magicians.

One of my favorite demos and stories is from Kevin about how he often clones building entry cards as part of his professional penetration testing engagements. Building entry card often work on principles similar to MFA solutions. This particular long video from one of my company's national conferences shows Kevin explain these hacks: `www.youtube.com/watch?v=iFGve5MUUnE`.

When Kevin is hired to penetration test a company, the purpose is often to see whether he can penetrate the company's physical security. Most of the places he is hired to hack have building entry cards that are required to enter the building and open doors. Kevin loves to tell two stories about how he secretly clones building entry cards.

If the customer is located inside a big building that offers rental space to other companies, he will often call the rental office posing as a prospective future rental customer of that same building. Usually he meets with a rental person on-site to "see the space." The building rental officer usually has a master building entry key that lets them into the building and on all the floors of the building. Unbeknownst to the rental officer, Kevin has card cloning hardware that will make an exact copy of the building entry card when it gets within a few centimeters of Kevin's wireless scanner. Kevin places the hardware inside a thin, leather-bound notebook, the type of which you often see used by business professionals around the world. He will ask to see the card used by the rental agent and "innocently" swipe it over his handheld notebook. Little does the rental agent know that their card has just been completely duplicated.

The second story he loves to tell is how he went into the public bathroom of a company and put himself at the urinal right next to the building's head maintenance person. Any male knows that no other male should come up to a row of large vacant urinals and place themselves right next to the only other person going to the bathroom. In the male world it's considered poor etiquette for a bunch of reasons. But that's what Kevin did. He went right up to the urinal next to the maintenance man, faked urinating, and in doing so placed his notebook close enough to the maintenance man's master key card that he successfully cloned it—despite the nervous eye rolling of the maintenance man who felt Kevin had invaded his personal space. Kevin regales the audience with these stories as he calls for anyone from the audience to volunteer bringing up their own building entry card to use in a current hack demonstration of the same. Kevin has never not been able to clone the volunteer's building entry card in any of the many demos I've seen him do, although I'm sure there are some models that would not be so easy to clone.

The lesson here is that if you have a wireless MFA product that is not protected from cloning (smartcards have anticloning protections), then it might be possible for a physical social engineer to clone your MFA device.

Defenses to Social Engineering Attacks on MFA

This section discusses developer and user defenses against social engineering.

Developer Defenses to MFA

Let's look at some MFA developer defenses to social engineering.

Education and Threat Modeling

It is difficult to call out specific anti–social engineering defenses for developers to use without see-ing the specific MFA solution and its design. Each type of MFA class would have different social engineering mitigations. The default answer is that every MFA solution must be threat modeled, and any potential for social engineering must be considered as part of that modeling and then the appropriate mitigations implemented.

On top of that, and something that isn't done nearly enough, MFA solution vendors should share all threat modeling, including social engineering threat scenarios, with their customers. Most MFA vendors hide social engineering threats from their customers. They certainly don't proactively speak and educate about them. Their customers are not as aware of the different social engineering threats that are posed against their particularly chosen MFA solution and, as such, don't look out for them and can't as easily mitigate the risk from them. So, my best advice to developers to prevent social engineering attacks against their MFA solution is to threat-model all the possible social engineering scenarios and share those scenarios and possible defenses with customers. Be transparent and forth-right. Your customers will thank you for it. I can think of no better example than the FIDO Alliance's Security Specification document (`fidoalliance.org/specs/fido-v2.0-id-20180227/fido-security-ref-v2.0-id-20180227.html`) that I previously shared in Chapter 10, "Fake Authentication Attacks". It's such a good example of what every MFA vendor should do that it deserves to be promoted twice.

Provide Better/Best Authentication

Many communication channels have weak to no authentication. This includes voice calls, SMS messages, and email. Anything the industry can do to improve default authentication is welcomed. Phone com-panies are attempting to improve voice call authentication, at least by making it harder for scammers to spoof phone numbers using the new STIR/SHAKEN protocols. Voice-over-IP (VoIP) products, such as Microsoft Skype, need to take great care to prevent malicious VoIP calls. Email has SPF/DKIM/DMARC, but it isn't enabled by default everywhere. Neither STIR/SHAKEN nor SPF/DKIM/DMARC are perfect or enough. We need more and better authentication, especially with phone calls and SMS messaging. Anything any industry can create or adopt to decrease social engineering success rates is welcomed.

Provide Contextual Information

If possible, push/deliver contextual information about any authentication or transaction details to the user to help them make better decisions. Phone calls should provide antispoofing hints, such as the true phone number and location origination. SMS should be tied to verified corporate identities and phone numbers. VoIP calls should at least indicate origination location. Online MFA transactions should be tied to preregistered devices and authenticated websites and, if possible, show those details on the MFA solution. Any transactions should include enough detail so that the user can be assured that they are safely conducting the purported transaction and decision. Figure 12.2 shows an example of a good, proactive push notification providing contextual details for MFA logon approval.

> Logon attempted to https://web.vzw.com, a verified Verizon Wireless web site, was recorded on 5/7/2020 at 9:39AM EST from a new device with the IP address 206.78.7.12 with the hostname Roger's Laptop from physical location Dade County. Respond with Y to approve or N to disapprove. Choose D to discontinue notices.

Figure 12.2: Example of proactive push notification providing contextual details for MFA logon approval

User Defenses to Social Engineering Attacks

To defeat social engineering, it takes three main classes of mitigations: policy, technical controls, and security awareness training.

Review Any Vendor Threat Modeling

First, users should check with the vendor to see if the vendor has done threat modeling and, if so, what the threats and mitigations were to the various threat models. Download and study any threat modeling and mitigation documents that the vendor shares and figure out if you need to design additional mitigations. If they do not have any threat modeling to share with you, which is likely, do your own threat modeling on any MFA solution before you buy it.

Policy

You should produce written documentation to minimize the chances that your coworkers will be socially engineered, including from attacks against their MFA solutions. Look at the various threat models that involve social engineering and the examples given in this book, and think about any policies that might mitigate those risks.

Technical Controls

Any technical hardware or software solution that can prevent social engineering should be deployed, including firewalls, antimalware, intrusion detection, antispam, antiphishing, and content filtering products. Unfortunately, even the very best technical controls will allow some amount of social engineering to get by your defenses. What will save you then is good security awareness training. I have a fairly comprehensive webinar that covers every possible defense: policy, technical, and training, that I can think of to defeat social engineering and phishing. You can watch it by registering at this link: info.knowbe4.com/webinar-stay-out-of-the-net.

Pulling Off Top-Notch Security Awareness Training

Security awareness training is supposed to give your coworkers a healthy level of skepticism to recognize, stop, and report social engineering attacks. For years, we wondered how to pull off great security awareness training. I'm fortunate enough to be working at the world's number one security awareness training vendor. They have looked at the way their customers have deployed security awareness training and have determined what methods work the best. I will share them with you.

Publicize the Security Awareness Training Program   Let all your coworkers know that you are doing a formal security awareness training program. Explain how you will be doing it and how you expect them to participate. Don't surprise anyone. No one ever got promoted for surprising someone, least of all senior management. Instead, let everyone know that you do regular security awareness training and how you will do it. This phase of the system is part of the training.

Establish a Baseline   Send a simulated phishing email test to all your coworkers. Create a phishing email that accurately represents a common phishing email that you've seen before. It should not be crafted to be sneaky and hard to recognize. You want to send a phishing test that you believe most people would readily recognize as a phishing test and not click on. You'll likely be surprised at how many people will click on this easy-to-spot phish. It is not uncommon for up to 30 percent of employees of an organization to fall victim to a simulated phishing test.

Train at Least Once a Month   Send your coworkers to some sort of training at least once a month in addition to performing the simulated phishing tests. The training should vary, should be interesting enough that people won't hate it, and should be short. Monthly trainings shouldn't be longer than a few minutes each. Ideally, the training would be around current popular social engineering trends or focus on preventing social engineering for your implemented MFA solution.

Do Simulated Phishing Tests at Least Once a Month   Send your coworkers a simulated phishing test email (or SMS message or voice call) at least once a month. Like the training, the simulated phishing should be focused on current social engineering trends. If someone fails a simulated phishing test, they should be provided with immediate feedback on what they should have noticed to have successfully seen that it was a phishing (test) and not a legitimate email. As your user base gets better at spotting phishing emails, you can increase the level of sneakiness. You want to ramp up the training as your end-user base knowledge of phishing increases.

Stay Current on Your Training   Make it a priority to keep the social engineering training current on up-to-date real social engineering trends. When a world event happens that real phishers are using, model your simulated phishing tests and training after what the phishers are doing.

If you follow these recommendations, you will likely see a significant reduction in the amount of successful social engineering. KnowBe4's average customer who follows these recommendations cuts the percentage of employees who can be easily socially engineered from around 30 percent to 2–5 percent within a year. That's not the best customers or some customers. That's all customers who follow these recommendations.

NOTE   I cannot recommend a better book on how to craft and deliver the best security awareness training program than the recommendations in my friend and coworker Perry Carpenter's book, *Transformational Security Awareness Training: What Neuroscientists, Storytellers, and Marketers Can Teach Us About Driving Secure Behaviors* (Wiley, 2019). I also recommend you check out articles published on my current employer's blog website, www.knowbe4.com/resources, which features many useful free tools, whitepapers, and dozens of webinars, including many of mine.

Summary

This chapter covered social engineering and provided examples of how it can be used to bypass MFA solutions. You learned about common social engineering attributes and how to educate your MFA users against social engineering attacks. Chapter 13, "Downgrade/Recovery Attacks" will explore downgrade and recovery attacks.

13 Downgrade/ Recovery Attacks

This chapter will cover additional sneaky ways hackers take advantage to get around MFA solutions focusing on alternative authentication methods vendors provide to recover MFA-protected accounts.

Introduction

No matter what your MFA solution is, implementing it is more expensive, both initially and ongoing, than traditional logon name and password solutions. If you use MFA, your organization is nearly guaranteed to have increased support calls and costs. It's the nature of using a more involved, complex solution. It takes longer to train people in how to appropriately use MFA solutions. MFA solutions involving additional hardware devices naturally mean those hardware devices will break and be lost or stolen. Even if all your MFA solution uses is SMS or an app on a cell phone, that means more support calls and more operational disruption as compared to password-based solutions.

Large-scale MFA solutions with hundreds of thousands to millions of users are challenged with how to provide technical support to all those customers and at the same time keep support costs to an acceptable minimum. Because of this, I've yet to see the large-scale MFA solution that didn't offer a recovery method that ultimately didn't involve something less secure than the MFA solution it was backing up. I've even seen many MFA solutions that had an admin or user option that enabled the user to "REQUIRE MFA", that in the end didn't allow a logon method that didn't require MFA. Required apparently doesn't always mean required. Ironically, this often means that although the legitimate user is using and requiring multifactor authentication, attackers can use something less. I will cover three example downgrade/recovery attacks, one of which is so weak that it should be outlawed.

Example Downgrade/Recovery Attacks

I already covered some of these types of attacks in previous chapters, where they were slightly more representative of the particular chapter topic. In Chapter 8, "SMS Attacks," we explored recovery attacks involving SMS. These included the run-of-the-mill fake technical support SMS messages and fraudulent phone calls, both of which are hard to authenticate. Chapter 11, "Fake Authentication Attacks," covered fake authentication attacks, where the victim is led through a completely fraudulent experience. As previously discussed, these types of experiences are very hard for authentication vendors to stop. And the previous chapter, Chapter 12, "Social Engineering Attacks," covered multiple social engineering attacks, which allow hackers to bypass MFA protections. All of the previous attack types could be classified as downgrade/recovery attacks, but here are three more common attack types specifically related to recovery issues: alternate email address recovery, master code abuse, and guessing personal-knowledge questions.

Alternate Email Address Recovery

Most major MFA solution providers allow an account recovery code to be sent to an alternate email address. Most of the time, the alternate email address must be previously registered during the initial registration, but not always. Figure 13.1 shows two examples of alternate email addresses used as account recovery options.

Account recovery options

If you forget your password or cannot access your account, we will use this information to help you get back in.

Recovery email   roger@▮▮▮▮▮▮   >

Recovery phone   (▮▮)▮▮▮▮   >

Microsoft account

Security code

Please use the following security code for the Microsoft account ro*****@hotmail.com.

Security code: **0152772**

If you don't recognize the Microsoft account ro*****@hotmail.com, you can click here to remove your email address from that account.

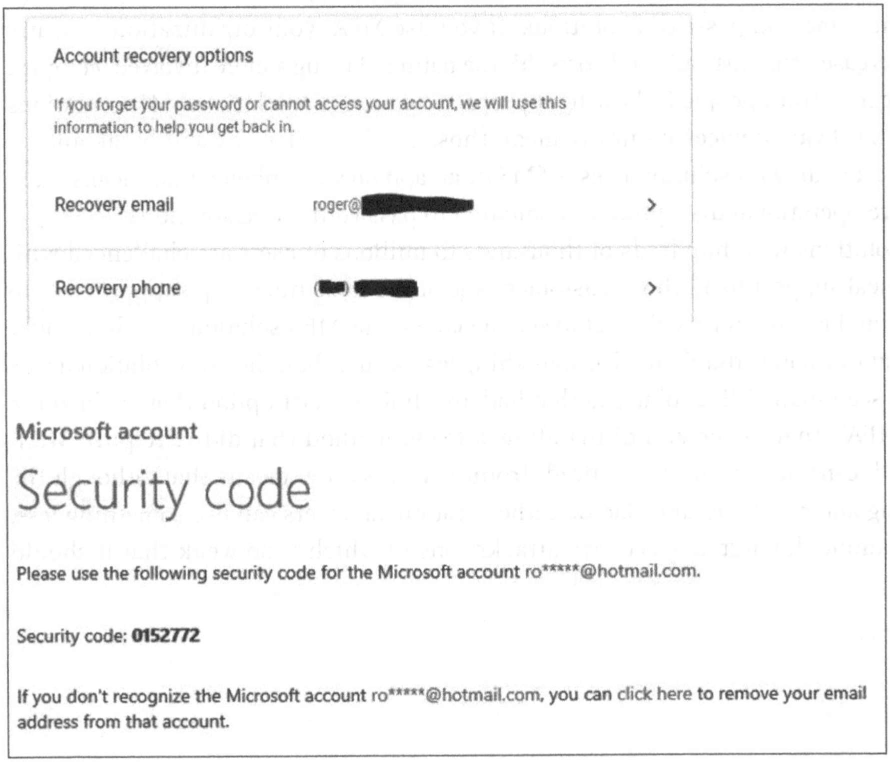

Figure 13.1: Two examples of alternate email addresses used as account recovery options

Attackers abuse alternate email address recovery in at least two ways: takeover of alternate email addresses and rerouting recovery.

Takeover of Alternate Email Addresses

In this method, attackers will confirm what alternate email address a particular victim is using and then compromise that alternate email address (usually using social engineering or phishing, or by learning the password from a previous password dump), and then send the MFA-protected account into recovery mode. I've also heard of password guessing being used to compromise the alternate email account, although it doesn't seem to be as popular these days since most major email accounts have password lockout settings enabled.

Compromised email accounts happen every day. Many users have free Gmail, Microsoft, or Yahoo email addresses as their personal email accounts, which often are used for MFA solution alternate email address account recovery. A small percentage of these free email accounts are compromised every day. But because these services have tens to hundreds of millions of email accounts, a "small percentage" of accounts translates to millions of compromised accounts every day.

The large free email providers cannot afford to provide human tech support technicians. It's too expensive. They'd go bankrupt trying to staff up for email account recovery. Instead, they automate the account recovery process. The hardest part can be finding the "account recovery" link to start the process. But once done, the automated process goes through a series of questions and steps to help the involved party self-recover the account. Figure 13.2 shows an example of the beginning of the Microsoft email account recovery process.

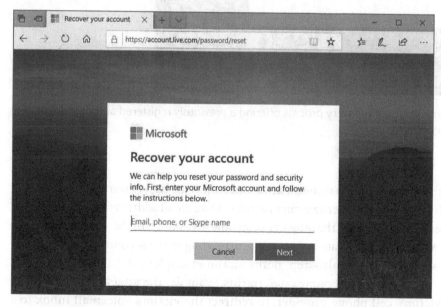

Figure 13.2: Beginning of the Microsoft email account recovery process

Unfortunately, the first recovery option offered by Microsoft is a previously registered alternate email recovery account (see Figure 13.3). Oftentimes the recovery process will provide a partial email address of a previously registered email account, which could give the attacker a clue as to what the alternative recovery account they need to compromise should be. Some email account recovery processes will even offer to let the recovery person use new email accounts that have not been previously registered, but most services will require additional previously known details before using any newly registered account. (More on this in the "Developer Defenses to Downgrade/Recovery Attacks" section).

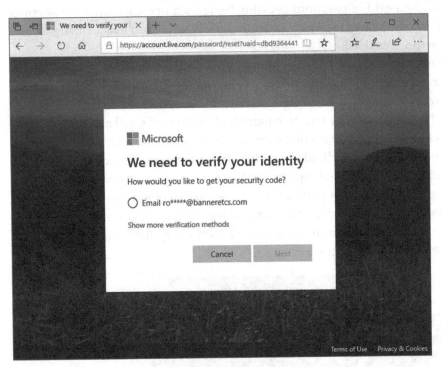

Figure 13.3: Microsoft email account recovery process offering a previously registered alternate email address as the first recovery option

Rerouting Recovery

The second popular alternate email address recovery attack method is the hacker somehow convincing the MFA solution provider to switch the alternate email address to an email address the hacker already controls. This attack usually requires that the attacker somehow get enough of the victim's details to successfully answer the MFA account update features or utilize a bug in the account update process.

Here's a real-world, sophisticated, multi-step, multi-victim example: `blog.cloudflare.com/post-mortem-todays-attack-apparent-google-app`. In this example, the attackers successfully convinced AT&T, the victim's cell phone provider, to redirect the victim's voicemail inbox to a new, temporary phone number. When doing this, the attackers did not know any of the normal recovery questions that the AT&T technical support person asked but knew the last four digits of the victim's social security number, which the tech support person accepted as valid authentication.

NOTE The victim was at a loss as to how AT&T had his Social Security number.

The attackers then put the victim's Google Gmail account into account recovery mode and chose, out of the multiple options offered by the automated recovery process, to have Google send the recovery account PIN to the victim's previously registered phone number. The victim did not recognize the incoming phone call from Google and let it go to voicemail. The AT&T hack had rerouted the victim's voicemail to a number under the hackers' control, and the hackers listened to the voicemail from Google tech support and heard the Gmail recovery code.

The hackers used the Gmail recovery code to take over the victim's Gmail account. They then put the victim's CloudFlare account (their ultimate victim target) into recovery mode and had CloudFlare send the recovery code to the victim's Gmail account. The attackers then used the CloudFlare recovery code to take over the victim's CloudFlare account.

The attackers then used the victim's CloudFlare account to make changes to victim's DNS records, which allowed the attacker to take control of the victim's domain and services. They then used those admin abilities to change the DNS address of the hacker's ultimate attack target. Whew!

The intermediate victim, the chief executive of CloudFlare, was actively involved during the incident and fighting unsuccessfully against the hacker while his authentication was being stolen. The attackers turned out to be hacktivists that wanted to punish their ultimate target, 4Chan, for not self-policing well enough.

You can read more about it at krebsonsecurity.com/2012/06/attackers-target-weak-spots-in-2-factor-authentication/, www.darkreading.com/vulnerabilities-and-threats/google-apps-security-beat-by-cloudflare-hackers/d/d-id/1104666 and www.csoonline.com/article/2222511/hacktivists-ugnazi-attack-4chan--cloudflare-and-wounded-warrior-project.html. The CloudFlare executive said the attackers were eventually arrested by the FBI, but the link to that statement is no longer any good and I cannot confirm the arrests.

There is a third and fourth way to take over or change the alternate email account, but they are not as common. The third way is if the recovery process contains a vulnerability that allows a knowledgeable programmer to bypass the MFA requirement and update the recovery code option. This has happened a few times to major MFA services in the past, although I could not find URLs to relevant articles to include in this chapter in time for publishing.

The fourth way is when an attacker compromises a victim's related device, which then allows MFA bypass on the targeted device. This can be done in some rare scenarios (and are more of "man-in-the-endpoint" attacks), and luckily, I don't know of any real-world malicious attacks. An example of this type of attack is commercial password hacking company Elcomsoft's announcement (blog.elcomsoft.com/2017/11/breaking-apple-icloud-reset-password-and-bypass-two-factor-authentication) of its ability to bypass Apple's iCloud MFA solution using their software if it is installed on the victim's PC. Altogether, though, bypassing a victim's MFA solution by using an alternate email address recovery is a very popular type of attack.

Abusing Master Codes

MFA services understand that users don't always have access to the primary, default MFA solution, but they still want their users to be able to access the protected service. Many of these services offer permanent, non-expiring, "master," "backup," or "travel codes." These codes can be set up when the MFA solution is first established and can often be generated any time thereafter, such as when the user knows they will be going on vacation.

Google calls them backup codes (see Figure 13.4). When you enable them, Google displays ten 8-digit backup codes, which you can screenshot, download, or print. Microsoft calls them "recovery codes" and generates one at a time (see Figure 13.5).

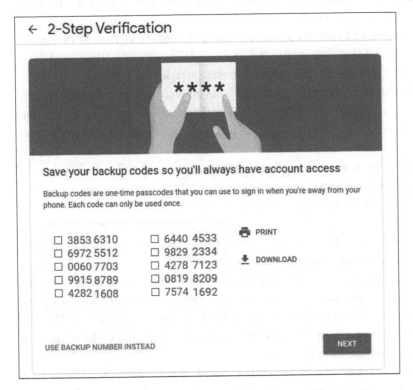

Figure 13.4: Google backup codes

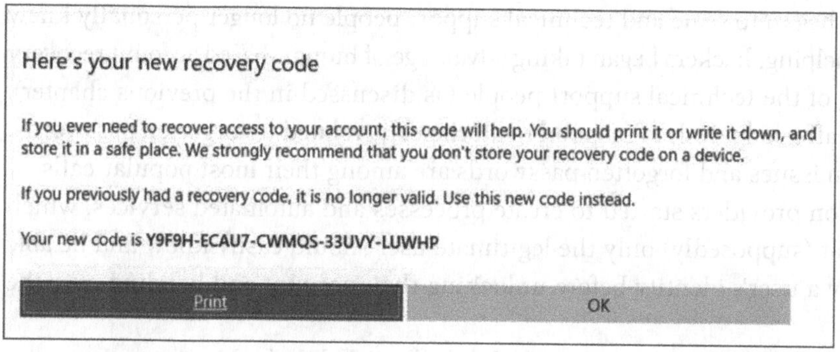

Here's your new recovery code

If you ever need to recover access to your account, this code will help. You should print it or write it down, and store it in a safe place. We strongly recommend that you don't store your recovery code on a device.

If you previously had a recovery code, it is no longer valid. Use this new code instead.

Your new code is Y9F9H-ECAU7-CWMQS-33UVY-LUWHP

Print	OK

Figure 13.5: Microsoft recovery code

The problem with master codes is that they often never expire and securely storing them is difficult to do. Many people are told to back up their backup codes. That makes them exist in two or more places. Google used to tell users on the default backup code screen to store the backup codes in their wallet. That sounds like a reasonable idea until you realize that backup codes in both downloaded and printed form contain the Gmail address as well. If an attacker comes across the backup codes, they can use them at will from anywhere in the world. The codes do not expire, although you can get new codes and cancel the old codes at any time.

> **NOTE**   It is not super easy with either Google or Microsoft to find the right place to generate and manage the backup codes. On a good note, it makes it harder for users to learn about and enable them in the first place, but it also makes it harder to reset or disable them.

Guessing Personal-Knowledge Questions

Of all the ways someone can recover their MFA-protected account, perhaps answering, fairly simple, preregistered personal-knowledge questions is the least secure and easiest of all to hack—so easy, in fact, that many people, including this author, believe the traditional way of using them as implemented by most websites should be forbidden by law. Several large authentication providers, including Google and Microsoft, have forbidden their simplistic use on their sites and services.

Sadly, simple personal-knowledge questions have been one of the most popular account recovery methods and have been for decades. They came out of a need for authentication providers to allow users to recover their forgotten passwords without needing human intervention. Before automated self-service account recovery, a user locked out of their account or forgetting their password had to call a human technical support person, explain the problem, and have the tech support person unlock their account and give them a new temporary password.

This method worked fairly well when the number of people, including users and technical support people, was small enough that they would likely be familiar with one another (voice recognition authentication). As systems began to scale and technical support people no longer personally knew most of the users they were helping, hackers began taking advantage of human-based account recovery by using social engineering of the technical support people (as discussed in the previous chapter). It's also very expensive to staff a help desk to respond to all the calls related to forgotten passwords. In most organizations, logon issues and forgotten passwords are among their most popular calls.

In response, authentication providers started to create processes and automated services, which often involved questions that (supposedly) only the legitimate user should easily know and be able to answer, as a way to verify a user's identity before unlocking their account and handing over the new temporary password.

Someone—I don't know who was first—came up with the "brilliant" idea of asking users to answer a series of pre-canned questions, and those questions and answers could be used with the automated systems to verify the person's identity when they needed their password reset. Thus, "What is your mother's maiden name?" became the first widely used personal-knowledge question. How anyone ever thought that question's answer could not be easily looked up by nearly anyone is a mystery to me. A woman's maiden name has been widely available in public records for decades, well before the Internet made it child's play to look up.

At first, personal-knowledge questions were few and hard-coded. A user didn't have a choice as to which ones would be involved. In many systems the number of hard-coded questions increased, but you still could not make up your own questions. In a minority of systems, users were/are allowed to create their own custom questions. Some personal-knowledge question systems ask only one question and anyone successfully answering that one question is good enough for authentication. On other systems, the user must successfully answer two or more questions. In some instances, if the user wrongly answers a question, they will get other opportunities with other questions. In more secure systems, a single wrong answer means the user must unlock the account another way.

The *huge* problem from the beginning is that many of the questions and answers are public knowledge or can be learned by socially engineering the user. Even the ones that aren't common knowledge or that are a bit harder to socially engineer someone out of (such as "Model of your first car?" or "Your favorite elementary school teacher?" or "Your first pet's name?") are far easier to guess than guessing at a password. A typical password (e.g., 6–8 characters long and using multiple character types) can have billions of combinations. A password guesser has to come across an extremely poor password choice (such as password or qwerty) to actually outright guess someone's password.

But the number of models of cars that someone can possibly have to guess through is maybe a few thousand. I counted the current number of car models sold in the United States today (en.wikipedia .org/wiki/List_of_automobiles_manufactured_in_the_United_States). It was just over 100. If an attacker was faced with the model of car that someone used or liked as their first car, they only have to guess through 100 or less models that were available around the year that person was of legal driving age. The attacker would have to think up or otherwise find out all the readily available common car models that could be in existence during the time the victim was first of legal driving age, but most models repeat many years in a row. The victim's first car was likely not a Bentley. Most people's first car is usually a lower-end vehicle. Some personal-knowledge questions ask a person's favorite car. It's probably not an AMC Pacer or Ford Pinto. It could be, but odds are less likely. It's more likely to be a "sexy" car like Mustang, Charger, Corvette, Lamborghini, or Lexus. In any case, if the personal-knowledge question involves cars, the number of potential guesses an attacker has to make are far less than what a person's password might be (unless the attacker already knew the person's previous passwords or interests).

Lest you think I'm making up how easy personal-knowledge questions can be, here's a list of questions I was given to choose from during a February 2020 flight when I was purchasing inflight Internet services (see Figure 13.6).

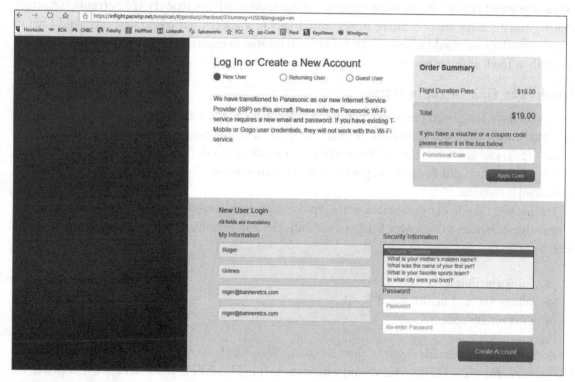

Figure 13.6: Personal-knowledge questions

There have been several studies about the efficacy and use of personal-knowledge questions over the years, but perhaps the defining paper on the subject was a Google whitepaper, "Secrets, Lies, and Account Recovery: Lessons from the Use of Personal Knowledge Questions at Google" (www.a51.nl/sites/default/files/pdf/43783.pdf). This paper was one of the big reasons Google got away from using simple personal-knowledge questions for account recovery. Here are some facts taken from the paper:

- Some recovery questions can be guessed on the first try 20 percent of the time.
- Forty percent of people were unable to successfully recall their own recovery answers.
- Sixteen percent of answers could be found in the person's social media profile.

Those facts should be astounding to you. I think we've all been there, having trouble correctly answering our own questions months or years later. "Was my favorite teacher Mrs. McKree or Mr. Mutach?" You try both and both fail. Turns out, the failure rate of the legitimate user to successfully answer starts to go way up quickly for questions that are any harder than mother's maiden name or father's middle name.

In fact, if I look at the rate at which people successfully answered all their questions (60 percent) versus the attacker's rate at guessing some of the questions with the first try (20 percent), it appears that legitimate users are only three times more likely to answer their own questions. And I bet in more cases than we would admit to, hackers would be able to research or guess the correct answers faster than the legitimate users.

Sarah Palin Email Account Hack

Attackers have long been putting accounts into recovery mode and then successfully answering personal-knowledge questions for decades. One of the most popular and well-known attacks (en.wikipedia.org/wiki/Sarah_Palin_email_hack) involved Sarah Palin, who was running as a U.S. vice presidential candidate on the Republican ticket against Barack Obama and Joe Biden in the 2008 presidential election.

The hacker, the son of a democratic state representative, answered three of Sarah Palin's personal-knowledge questions to take over her personal Yahoo! email account. The three personal-knowledge questions were:

- Palin's birthdate
- Where she met her husband
- Current zip code

According to this article (nypost.com/2008/09/19/dem-pols-son-was-hacker/), the 20-year-old hacker was able to find her birthdate and where she met her husband, Todd Palin, on Wikipedia. He knew from a little research that Sarah had married her high school sweetheart and figured out the most likely place they had met was in high school. There's only one high school in Wasilla, Alaska, but it is also located in Sarah Palin's Wikipedia entry (as shown in Figure 13.7). The hacker found out that Wasilla had only two possible zip codes, which he looked up on the U.S. Postal Service's website. It's a misnomer to call him a hacker; he's really a guy who knows how to use Google. The attacker was eventually identified by the FBI, arrested, tried, and sentenced to a year plus one day in jail, plus three years of probation.

Early life and family

Palin was born in Sandpoint, Idaho, the third of four children (three daughters and one son) of Sarah "Sally" Heath (née Sheeran), a school secretary, and Charles R. "Chuck" Heath, a science teacher and track-and-field coach. Palin's siblings are Chuck Jr., Heather, and Molly.[6][7][8][9][10] Palin is of English, Irish, and German ancestry.[11]

When Palin was a few months old, the family moved to Skagway, Alaska,[12] where her father had been hired to teach.[13] They relocated to Eagle River in 1969, and settled in Wasilla in 1972.[14][15]

Palin played flute in the junior high band. She attended Wasilla High School, where she was head of the Fellowship of Christian Athletes[16] and a member of the girls' basketball and cross-country running teams.[17] During her senior year, she was co-captain and point guard of the basketball team that won the 1982 Alaska state championship, earning the nickname "Sarah Barracuda" for her competitive streak.[18][19][20]

Figure 13.7: Partial Sarah Palin's Wikipedia entry showing where she went to high school, which was used by the hacker to answer her Yahoo! email account personal-knowledge questions

Celebrity Nudes

Hacking by answering personal-knowledge questions has always been a popular way for attackers to take over user accounts. And sometimes those users are famous. For quite a few years, Hollywood celebrities were apparently too trusting of Apple's iCloud to keep their personal photos, often containing nudes of themselves, safe from unauthorized users. They apparently didn't get the link between taking personal photos with their iPhone and the phone's default behavior of backing up all data to the celebrity's iCloud account as the big risk it really was.

A few hackers were eventually arrested and found guilty. Initially, there were so many stolen celebrity photos that it was speculated that the attackers had discovered an unknown vulnerability in Apple's iCloud service. After doing an internal investigation, Apple publicly posted (www.businesswire.com/news/home/20140902006384/en/Apple-Media-Advisory) that all the compromised iCloud accounts were accomplished using social engineering and "by a very targeted attack on user names, passwords, and *security questions* [emphasis mine], a practice that has become all too common on the Internet."

Today, although some of the big vendors like Google and Microsoft don't allow account recovery based on simple personal-knowledge questions, it is still a very, very popular recovery method. Many popular sites will not allow a user to register an account without setting up multiple personal-knowledge questions. Figure 13.8 shows all the personal-knowledge questions a popular bank allows users to choose between.

The list of questions are more creative and a bit harder to look up than your mother's maiden name, but not that much harder. Many are far easier to look up than the creators probably think and certainly easier to guess with a little research than a user's password.

One of the big unknowns is how many times you can guess against a personal-knowledge question before being denied access. It varies widely between sites. Some allow only a few wrong guesses before the account is locked, whereas many others will allow continued guessing as long as you don't guess too many times in a row without a break. For many sites that use personal-knowledge questions, all the attacker has to do is to close the website down after one or a few guesses and then start the whole account recovery process all over again to get a few more guesses. As long as they restart/reload the website after a few guesses, they will never be locked out. And there is a small percentage of sites that will simply let a person guess as many times as they like without ever locking out the account. And regardless of the number of times a person is allowed to guess at a personal-knowledge question before being denied access to their account, once is too many. As used by most sites, personal-knowledge questions are a high security risk and should be avoided when possible.

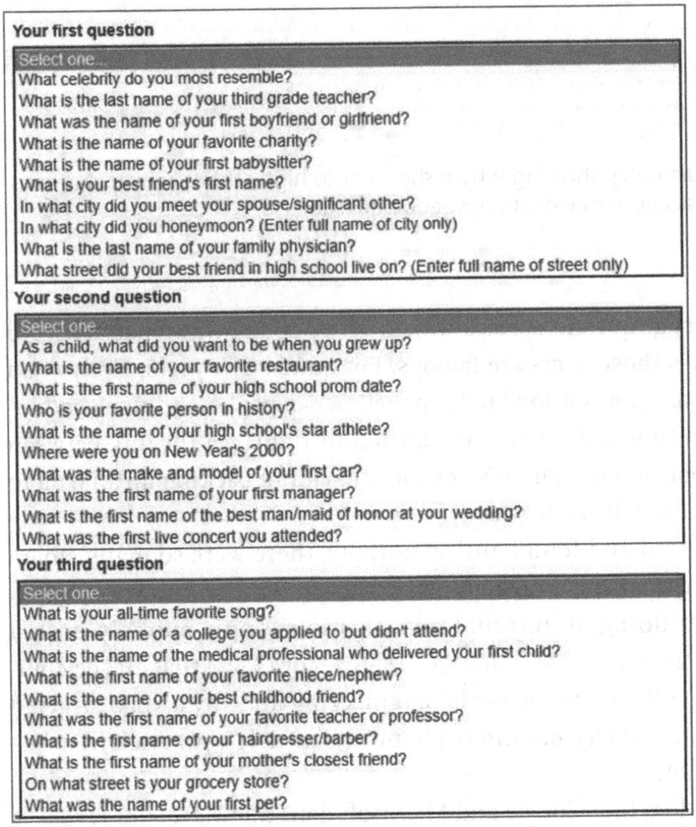

```
Your first question
┌──────────────────────────────────────────────────────────────────┐
│ Select one...                                                      │
│ What celebrity do you most resemble?                               │
│ What is the last name of your third grade teacher?                 │
│ What was the name of your first boyfriend or girlfriend?           │
│ What is the name of your favorite charity?                         │
│ What is the name of your first babysitter?                         │
│ What is your best friend's first name?                             │
│ In what city did you meet your spouse/significant other?           │
│ In what city did you honeymoon? (Enter full name of city only)     │
│ What is the last name of your family physician?                    │
│ What street did your best friend in high school live on? (Enter full name of street only) │
└──────────────────────────────────────────────────────────────────┘
Your second question
┌──────────────────────────────────────────────────────────────────┐
│ Select one...                                                      │
│ As a child, what did you want to be when you grew up?              │
│ What is the name of your favorite restaurant?                      │
│ What is the first name of your high school prom date?              │
│ Who is your favorite person in history?                            │
│ What is the name of your high school's star athlete?               │
│ Where were you on New Year's 2000?                                 │
│ What was the make and model of your first car?                     │
│ What was the first name of your first manager?                     │
│ What is the first name of the best man/maid of honor at your wedding? │
│ What was the first live concert you attended?                      │
└──────────────────────────────────────────────────────────────────┘
Your third question
┌──────────────────────────────────────────────────────────────────┐
│ Select one...                                                      │
│ What is your all-time favorite song?                               │
│ What is the name of a college you applied to but didn't attend?    │
│ What is the name of the medical professional who delivered your first child? │
│ What is the first name of your favorite niece/nephew?              │
│ What is the name of your best childhood friend?                    │
│ What was the first name of your favorite teacher or professor?     │
│ What is the first name of your hairdresser/barber?                 │
│ What is the first name of your mother's closest friend?            │
│ On what street is your grocery store?                              │
│ What was the name of your first pet?                               │
└──────────────────────────────────────────────────────────────────┘
```

Figure 13.8: List of personal-knowledge questions allowed by a popular banking website

You may be wondering, "What should sites do for automated password recovery then?" Although relying on the standard types of simple personal-knowledge questions is a poor security practice, advanced recovery systems (covered in a moment) are still based on personal-knowledge questions but implemented in a way that does not allow easy social engineering or guessing.

No matter how it was stolen, once an attacker has successfully taken over the victim's account, they usually disable the MFA solution, "downgrading" the victim's account to use something less secure. They always change the password, often change the phone number (to stymie phone-based account recovery processes), and may change other information as well. They then utilize the stolen account to steal money or to use it to fraudulently pose as the victim to other potential victims. It can take the real victim many hours or even days to recover the account. I've read of people who never regained use of their stolen account and some who permanently lost content they had been saving in the account for decades.

NOTE Always back up your important content in two or more places. Don't trust that you'll always have access. Many of the taken-over accounts are owned by a third party and they are under no legal obligation to make sure you re-obtain control and use of it.

Defenses to Downgrade/Recovery Attacks

Here are some developer and user defenses to downgrade/recovery attacks.

Developer Defenses to Downgrade/Recovery Attacks

First we'll look at developer defenses to downgrade/recovery attacks.

Educate Users

Users need to know that master codes must be stored securely and not stored along with the identity of the accounts they are related to. Users need to understand that personal-knowledge questions and their answers can be socially engineered and guessed, so they should not choose questions with answers that are super easy to research or guess.

Threat Model Recovery Processes and Tools

Threat model recovery processes and tools for legitimate and illegitimate recovery attempts. Design your processes and tools and educate technical support people to mitigate cybersecurity risk. Educate tech support staff in how to detect and handle possible social engineering.

These processes, tools, and education should model ahead of time how to distinguish between legitimate and unauthorized users if they are in a real-life struggle to obtain and maintain control over the account. You want to be able to return control of the account to the legitimate owner and not make them struggle too hard in regaining control after a malicious takeover. You need to decide ahead of time what information a person posing as a legitimate user can provide that proves legitimate ownership of the account. Make it too easy, and an unauthorized user can more easily fake being the legitimate owner. Make it too hard, and the legitimate owner has trouble regaining control of their account.

Expire and Anonymize Master Codes

Any master codes should have reasonable expiration dates, and the associated linked account identity should never be fully printed and attached to the list of codes. Instead, the full identity label (i.e., rogeragrimes3@gmail.com), if printed out or saved next to the codes, should be instead partially represented (e.g., ro*s3@gmail.com). You don't want a compromise of the master codes to be immediately available to use for logon by an attacker.

Require an Acquaintance to Approve Recovery

Personal approval by a preregistered acquaintance, boss, coworker, or friend is one way to significantly cut down on rogue recoveries (although even acquaintances can be socially engineered). Early on, support technicians manually approved account recovery by personally recognizing a person's voice (or in-person request). On large systems not every tech support person can recognize every possible legitimate user. Instead, an authentication recovery system can ask any new user to designate two or more acquaintances who can be used to help verify the requestor's account recovery request. Any approval must first go to at least one of the designed verifiers, who are instructed to confirm, by voice or in person, that the legitimate party needs the account recovery. This type of control was used in Microsoft when I was there and worked well, although there were times when the designated acquaintances were unreachable and so the recovery operation was delayed until they responded. Implementing a defense like this isn't easy to do in an online, automated way, but it has been done, such as in the case of Facebook's Trusted Contacts feature www.facebook.com/help/119897751441086.

Use Advanced, Adaptive Personal-Knowledge Questions

This chapter singles out personal-knowledge questions with specific criticism. The detailed recommendation is that simple personal-knowledge questions should not be used, but there are many, far more secure implementations of advanced, adaptive, personal-knowledge questions that many of the major sites now use, such as the recovery process and questions used by Google and Microsoft. Anyone wanting a master's class in how to do advanced personal-knowledge questions should study what either of those two vendors do.

First and foremost, they do not ask for or store the kinds of simple personal-knowledge questions listed earlier. They know how easy they are to hack and guess, and how hard they are for users to remember. Second, they store the unique identity of the devices used by the user (e.g., computer, cell phone) and consider to be high risk any account recovery coming from a new device. They also consider to be high risk any account recovery coming from a new location where the user has never before successfully authenticated from. When elevated risk is detected, the questions and processes require more proof to be successful.

They start by asking a more advanced series of questions that the site already knows the answer to without the user having to provide. And these questions get progressively harder and detailed as the risk increases (due to incorrect answers or other measured authentication traits). Figure 13.9 shows how Microsoft asked me a progressively more detailed set of questions as I tried to simulate an account recovery. Microsoft initially offered to send a recovery code to my previously registered alternate email account, but I acted as if I had to use a new account. This set off Microsoft's adaptive and progress set of advanced personal recovery questions. In each case I answered one or more questions wrong and then clicked the Next button. Each time, instead of approving my account recovery, Microsoft didn't say which of the previous answers I had put in wrong. They simply asked me one or more questions, such as my previous buying experience, which led to more related, more detailed questions. This is the way to do detailed, adaptive, personal-knowledge questions.

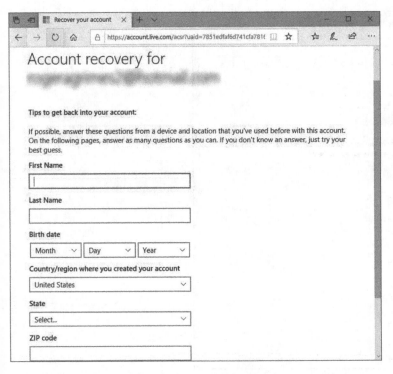

Figure 13.9: Microsoft uses advanced, adaptive, account recovery questions.

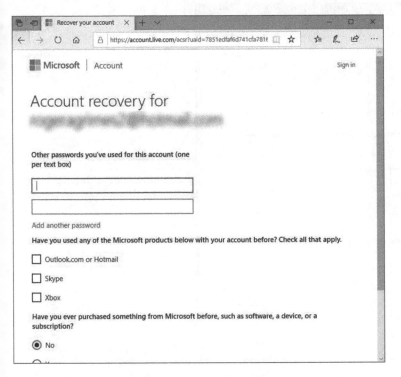

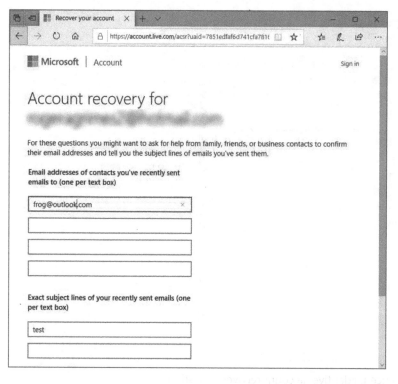

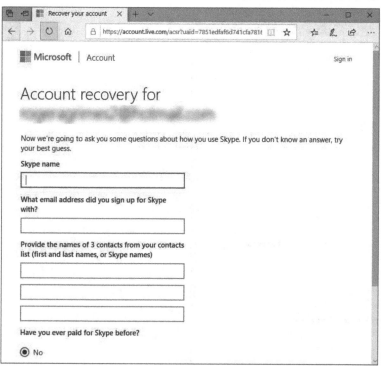

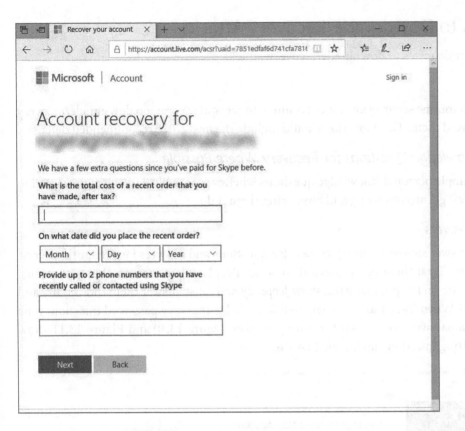

Ultimately, Microsoft is asking the same questions that a human-based technical support person could, just in an automated way. Eventually, the user must answer enough questions successfully to automatically recover the account. The questions are so thorough that I'm not sure if a user could successfully recover their account by calling and talking to a human Microsoft technical support person. The support person would likely ask the same questions and be guided by the same policies to determine the user's legitimacy—although any time a human is involved, a good social engineer can possibly win out over policy.

Google Gmail's advanced recovery process eventually asked me to verify my identity using the preregistered phone device and the Google Authenticator app. As I purposely tried to fail various authentication attempts, Google eventually displayed a code on my computer screen, the number 23, and then sent to the Google Authenticator app on my phone three different one- and two-digit values and asked me to pick the value that was displayed on my computer screen. When I choose the correct value on my phone screen, I was successfully authenticated on my computer. This sort of authentication was possible because I was using two previously used devices from locations Google had previously detected. The future of authentication will use both of these factors (device and location) as primary determinations of adaptive risk.

User Defenses to Downgrade/Recovery Attacks

Now we'll look at user defenses to downgrade/recovery attacks.

Education

Users should be given routine security awareness training to recognize common downgrade/recovery attacks and how to avoid them. The education should include the next three recommended defenses.

Avoid Personal-Knowledge Questions for Recovery Where Possible

Users should avoid simple personal-knowledge questions whenever possible. I often get prompted to input them, but if I can get around using and answering them, I do.

Give the Wrong Answers

If forced to use and answer simple personal-knowledge questions and answers for account recovery, give incorrect answers. Treat them like passwords instead. People, when they get these questions, seem to feel that they are on the popular gameshow *Jeopardy* and must answer them thoroughly and correctly. Instead, lie! When forced to use a personal-knowledge recovery password question, type something closer to a password or at least the wrong answer. Figure 13.10 and Figure 13.11 show some examples of setting questions up for the first time.

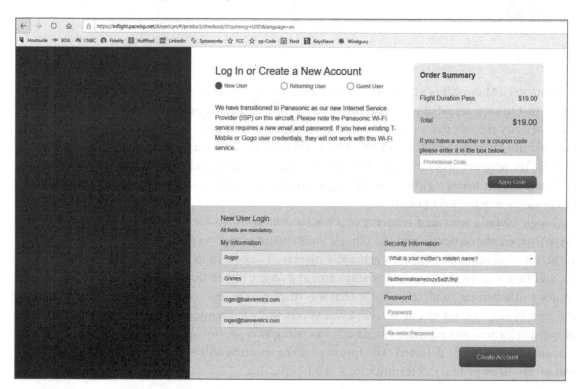

Figure 13.10: Answering personal-knowledge question wrong

Solution: Never answer the questions with the real answers!

Question:	What was your high school mascot? ▼
Answer:	pizzapizza$vgad2@M1
Repeat Answer:	**********

Question:	What is your mother's middle name? ▼
Answer:	**********
Repeat Answer:	**********

Question:	What is your father's birthdate? (mmdd) ▼
Answer:	***

Question:	What is the name of your best friend from high school? ▼
Answer:	**********
Repeat Answer:	**********

Figure 13.11: Example of answering personal-knowledge questions wrong

The answers you use should be unique for each site; again, treat them as you would passwords. In some cases, I am able to use the same answer for each question on the same site, and when possible I do. But most of the time every answer for each question must be different—they check.

The biggest complication, and it's not great, is that answering your personal-knowledge account recovery questions wrong and uniquely means you'll definitely have to write them down. You will likely not remember them weeks, months, or years later, when you might have reason to use them. I write both the questions and the answers down in my password manager in the section devoted to each logon and site. You can write them down in a separate password-protected document if you like. In either case, never write down the entire answer in full text so that if the manager or document gets compromised, the full-text answer is not visible. For example, for the fake answer in Figure 13.11, pizzapizza$vad2@M1, I might write down pp$vad2@M1 and have to memorize that the pp stands for pizzapizza. Of course, if a bad person compromises your password manager or password document, it's pretty much game over anyway. They already have the keys to the kingdom. But it can't hurt to use abbreviations as long as you don't forget what the abbreviations are. In any case, stop feeling an obligation to answer the questions correctly if you're allowed to supply the answers. Make up the answers, store or write them down somewhere securely, and get rid of the risk.

Protect Master Codes

If you like to have master codes as backup authentication, securely store them. I store them in my password manager, where I can readily access them on my phone if I need to. If printed out or downloaded, do not store the account identifier (e.g., email address) they are linked to in full text along with the codes. That makes it too easy for unauthorized discoverers. At least make the attackers work for it.

Summary

In this chapter, we covered downgrade and recovery attacks. We discussed how attackers use fraudulent account recovery methods, master code abuse, and personal-knowledge questions as attack methods. Finally, we explored developer and user defenses to mitigate most risks.

Chapter 14, "Brute-Force Attacks" will cover brute-force attacks against MFA solutions.

14 Brute-Force Attacks

This chapter will cover brute-force attacks against the underlying technology of MFA solutions. Some of this material was covered in earlier chapters, but it's worth repeating and expanding on.

Introduction

Brute-force attacks are considered the most primitive type of cyberattack. They don't require a lot of intelligence. You just attack a target over and over again, slightly changing or incrementing one value each time, until you get success. If you don't have any defensive controls blocking all the tries, it's the one cyberattack method guaranteed to eventually win.

As covered in Chapter 1, "Logon Problems," brute-force guessing at passwords is one way to guess at passwords. A brute-force password guesser, with zero knowledge of the allowed minimum length of a targeted password, would start with the letter a, let's say, and when that didn't work, try the letter b, and so on, until they had tried all the letters, numbers, and symbols in the possible character space and come up empty. Then the password brute-force guesser would try aa, then ab, and then ac, and so on, again moving through all the possible characters in the second position. Sequentially they add more characters in each position, trying every possible combination, one at a time, until they eventually found the correct combination of characters that make up the targeted password. Not surprising, brute-forcing passwords or anything cyber-related is relatively slow. Computer automated guessing can seem very fast, but as compared to more advanced methods, brute force guessing is still comparatively slow.

Most attackers, even guessing at passwords, like to add a little intelligence to their guessing, hoping to be successful faster. As discussed in Chapter 1, password guessers likely know that most people form passwords based on their native language and the natural formatting of that language. Certain characters, like the vowels a, e, i, and o, will be used far more frequently on average than consonants. Usually, most passwords will start with a consonant, followed by a vowel. If users are forced to use uppercase characters, usually it will be an uppercase consonant in the first character position. If they are forced to use numbers, they will usually choose 1 or 2, and it will be at or near the end of the password. Using a little intelligence, attackers find that most passwords (and PINs) can be broken faster with fewer tries than by using brute-force methods.

But if a defender starts their password with a less popularly used character, say q or z or }, an intelligent password guesser is likely to be slower than an attacker using a brute-force method for that particular password. Brute-force guessing and hacking are good for an attacker to use when they have all the time in the world and can guess a bunch of times very quickly. When those factors are available, the brute-force guesser will be more successful, more often, than an intelligent guesser, across a wider population of passwords (or PINs).

NOTE Although the brute-forcing attack is one of the slowest ways to approach a hack, computers make brute-force methods far easier and faster than doing it manually. For instance, some brute-force guessing password attack tools and computer rigs allow hundreds of billions of guesses to be made a second. See `arstechnica.com/information-technology/2012/12/25-gpu-cluster-cracks-every-standard-windows-password-in-6-hours/` for an example.

Birthday Attack Method

Attackers using the brute-force method can have great increases in speed by randomly guessing among the total population of possible guesses. Traditional brute-forcing just starts at the beginning and sequentially increments one value at one position after another until it solves the target problem. But by simply randomly guessing among all the possible values, while still cycling through all the possible values, brute-force guessers can often be successful faster. This phenomenon is known as the *birthday attack* method (among various other names).

It's widely known as the birthday attack method because of a simple experiment to demonstrate the logic anyone in a middle-sized group can perform. In the experiment, which is best performed with at least 20 people, each person is asked, one at a time, to announce their birthday date (July 19th, September 2nd, etc.), without the year. And any time someone says a birthdate that matches someone else's, the person with the matching birthdate announces the match and the experiment ends.

You would think that the odds of someone else having the same birthdate as anyone else would be 1 in 365.25 (the number of days in a year, including leap years), because anyone can be born on any day. Ignoring the realities of naturally occurring birth clusters and cultural aggregations (like after a war), people can generally be born on any day during the year. But the odds of any two people sharing the same birthday (known as a *collision* in statistically analysis or cryptography) in a group of people exponentially increases as additional people are brought into the group. A single person may have odds of 1:365.25 of being born on a particular day, but as another person is added, it increases the odds of a collision by half for each person added. . .so that the next person has 1:182.625 odds (i.e., 2:365.25) and the third person has 1:91 odds, and so on, until the odds of two people sharing the same birthday actually become quite high. It takes just 23 people for the odds of two people having the same birthday to be above 50 percent. By the time that you get to, say 30 people, the odds are 70 percent that two people in that group share the same birthdate.

I've performed this test many times in classrooms of 20 to 30 people over 30 years, and I've only once not gotten a match. Many times, the match is announced within the first 10 people. It's a fun exercise if you want to teach statistical odds to a group of people. It rarely fails to generate excitement, interest, and understanding. If you want more details on the birthday attack method, visit en .wikipedia.org/wiki/Birthday_attack.

So, most brute-force methods guess randomly at whatever their target happens to be—password, PINs, or whatever—across the entire population of possible answers. And of course, some guessers implement even more logic, trying out what is statistically the most logical answers before trying the less likely answers. It makes sense to do things the fastest way even when performing brute-forcing. But the latter approach decreases the speed of the solution if the solution isn't one of the most likely, earliest, answers. It is always an accuracy versus speed trade-off. If the number of possible guesses is relatively small and the attacker can make an unlimited number of guesses, then it makes sense to use the brute-force attack, because eventually you will find the solution. And sometimes brute-force attacks are the only attack type a hacker has for the situation, as shown in the next section.

Brute-Force Attack Methods

There are two main ways to conduct brute-force attacks: manual and automated.

Manual

Manual brute-force guessing is a human being taking guesses one at a time. For example, perhaps you have to guess a four-digit PIN. You can sit there and try four-digit combination after four-digit combination. Manual, human-based guessing has a benefit that any known information about the victim, such as their birthdate, their children's birthdates, favorite numbers, or any known previously used PINs can be used to try to figure out the correct PIN faster than brute-force guessing alone.

The biggest problem with human-based, manual guessing is that in a short amount of time after a limited number of guesses most humans can't remember what combinations they already tried and what combinations they didn't try. After a few dozen guesses, the average manual human attacker is likely to start making duplicate guesses using previous values without realizing it. Computer-based, automated tools are great at guessing really fast and in keeping track of what was previously tried that already did not work so that they won't waste time trying them again.

Automated

The hacking world is full of hundreds, if not thousands, of automated brute-force guessing programs. All an attacker has to do is find the right tool that is allowed to interface with a particular target, set operational parameters (such has how many guesses to try in a particular time period), and launch the tool. Hacking tools, free and commercial, such as John the Ripper (www.openwall.com/john/), Cain and Able, L0phtcrack (www.10phtcrack.com), 0phtcrack (ophcrack.sourceforge.io/), Burp

Suite (portswigger.net/burp), and Hydra (www.hackingtools.in/free-download-hydra-v-7-4-fast-network-cracker/), are infamously used by millions of white- and black-hat hackers to brute-force their way past various logons. This is not to say that brute-force guessing can't be mitigated, and I'll discuss how in the "Developer Defenses Against Brute-Force Attacks" section later in this chapter.

Example of Brute-Force Attacks

Let's look at some real-world brute-force attack examples.

OTP Bypass Brute-Force Test

The first example comes from a white-hat hacker who successfully brute-forced a site using a one-time password (OTP) MFA solution (medium.com/bugbountywriteup/how-i-bypassed-the-otp-verification-process-part-1-e5b333274ae9). He connected to the website and performed the normal logon/account registration process until the website requested the OTP code to validate his logon/registration. His previous knowledge and testing confirmed that the site used six-digit OTP codes.

He then used Burp Suite to capture the website's packet request around the OTP submission packet. He located the OTP code submission field (see Figure 14.1) after the label *validatedcodetextbox*. The developer could have tried to hide the field's purpose and its value in different ways to at least somewhat obscure the purpose of the field and its value, but they did not. They didn't enable account lockout either, so this is not a surprise.

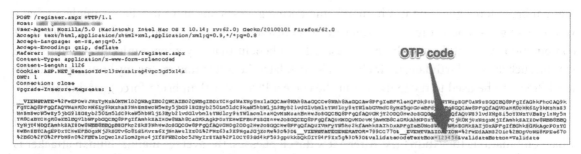

Figure 14.1: OTP code submission value being located in a packet submission request opened in the Burp Suite hacking tool before being used in a brute-force attack
Source: Image courtesy Aditya Anand

The white-hat hacker then used the "Intruder" mode/tab of Burp Suite to try different OTP combinations for another logon/registration attempt. A six-digit OTP, composed solely of numbers, digits 0–9 (i.e., 10 numbers) has a million possible combinations, ranging from 000000 to 999999. That's a lot of possible combinations to try. The white-hat hacker then claims he put in the correct code at try 150 and instructed Burp Suite to attempt a bunch of different combinations to see if it would allow him to be successful. It did. So, the website allowed at least 150 different tries and the 150th try was successful. Lest you think these types of attacks work only on anonymous or lesser known sites, let me tell you about the next two examples.

Instagram MFA Brute-Force

Instagram was acquired by Facebook in 2012 and is arguably one of the most popular Internet services in the world. It has over one billion users. In July 2019, a white-hat hacker announced that he had successfully brute-forced Instagram's MFA six-digit OTP solution (`threatpost.com/researcher-bypasses-instagram-2fa/146466/`).

The hacker started off by trying to guess at Instagram's OTP solutions from a single location. Through his testing, he quickly learned that Instagram allowed a maximum of only 250 guesses per originating IP address. With potentially a million guesses to try, that would mean the hacker would need 4,000 IP addresses (although it says 5,000 in the article). He found out he could send double the guesses per IP address if he used different IP addresses for each sequential guess and limited how many guesses he did at once and within a certain time period. He found out that Instagram was not permanently blacklisting IP addresses that guessed wrongly too many times, blocking them only temporarily for a given set time period. After the time period passed, they were welcome to try again. He then calculated that using 4,000 different IP addresses using a commercial cloud service would run about $150. The hacker eventually sent over 200,000 guess attempts without being blocked. For his trouble and publicly reporting it to the vendor so that it could be fixed, the hacker was awarded $30,000 from Facebook's bug bounty program.

So, to be clear, as recently as 2019, one of the largest and most sophisticated and well-funded websites in the world has a brute-force MFA vulnerability. Brute-force bugs don't just happen to naive websites and services to clueless people.

> **NOTE** You may wonder why Instagram allowed so many guesses, 250, at a time before blocking a particular IP address. Is that too many to allow? Possibly. But it's also possible that Instagram has seen many legitimate logons or processes that guessed wrong a lot, and then determined from their own experience that allowing 249 bad guesses was a good decision for them. More on this decision in the "Defenses Against Brute-Force Attacks" section later in this chapter.

Slack MFA Brute-Force Bypass

In this example (`hackerone.com/reports/121696`), a white-hat hacker discovered that brute-force attacks could be used to get around Slack's MFA solution. Slack (`slack.com`) is a very popular messaging app. It's used by tens of millions of people around the world.

The hacker discovered that, even if MFA is enabled on Slack, anyone could go into a user's password-reset feature, which would then send an OTP code for verification. He tested and found out that he could submit random OTP codes without any limits until he guessed the right code. For his efforts and for reporting it to the vendor so it could be fixed, he was awarded $500.

UAA MFA Brute-Force Bug

In this 2018 responsibly reported and fixed bug announcement (www.cloudfoundry.org/blog/cve-2018-11082), the vendor revealed that someone who had the victim's logon name and password could brute-force attack the victim's MFA credentials. It was reported by another corporate security team and fixed.

Grab Android MFA Brute-Force

This MFA brute-forcing attack applied to Android cell phones. A white-hat hacker let the vendor, Grab, know about a successful brute-force attack against their app (see hackerone.com/reports/202425 and hackerone.com/reports/205000). Grab is a very popular app, similar to Uber, in Southeast Asia. Users can hail cars, get food delivered, and so forth.

The hacker discovered that Grab's four-digit SMS codes could be guessed at a rate not to exceed six attempts a minute, equating to 8,640 attempts a day. A four-digit numeric code only has 10,000 total possibilities, and the birthday attack means it will likely take far fewer attacks. In the hacker's own tests, he was successfully able to guess multiple codes after several hours each.

All of these examples were found and ethically reported to the vendor by good-guy, white-hat hackers. But it makes you wonder how many other MFA solutions are susceptible to brute-force attacks and how many malicious groups are exploiting them without publicly reporting them to get them fixed. Luckily, to stop these types of attacks just takes awareness about them by the developers and some commonly implemented controls.

Unlimited Biometric Brute-Forcing

Attacks against biometric MFA solutions will be covered in Chapter 16, "Attacks Against Biometrics," but need to be mentioned here. Many, if not most, biometric solutions allow unlimited brute-forcing attempts, and the ones that don't are usually very liberal.

For example, when I walk up to my building's fingerprint entry system I can try over and over again using my fingerprint. It will beep and tell me I've failed, but it doesn't lock me out. The same thing with a retina scanner I used at a previous company. I could put my eye up to the retina scanner and try over and over for hours, and it would keep letting me try. Why? Because most shared biometric scanners can't tell the difference between a single person trying over and over and the next (different) person trying for the first time. They just accept all tries as new ones. For many biometric implementations there is no such thing as "account lockout."

Additionally, most biometric scanners experience tons of false-negative scans, where your fingerprint (or retina or whatever) is read too early as you are just placing your finger down on the scanner or moving your finger around to get it "situated" or placed for scanning. The scanner doesn't know the difference between your finger almost being placed solidly on the scanner and your finger being solidly placed on the scanner. Instead, it's scanning over and over many times a second just waiting for the right fingerprint image to be placed in the right way.

All biometric scanners are intentionally "de-tuned" to be less be less accurate. If they were fine-tuned to be as accurate as possible, it would result in too many false negatives due to variations in legitimate fingerprints from normal wear and tear. This de-tuning, along with a lack of rate limiting, opens up the opportunity for an attacker to try many, many biometric attributes until it hits one that "sort of" matches a legitimate one. Your fingerprint or retina may be unique in the world, but the way it is stored and analyzed is usually a lot more susceptible to rogue brute-force guessing.

Defenses Against Brute-Force Attacks

The risk of brute-force attacks is exacerbated by the fact that most MFA solutions that require input use only numbers 0–9 and have a maximum number of 4-to-6-digit positions. In the regular password authentication world, common rate-limiting and bad-attempt lockout controls against brute-force attacks have been the norm for decades—not in every logon portal, but for most. For some reason these controls, which have proven their value in the password world, just aren't seen as important in the MFA solution world. In fact, brute-force controls are often ignored as unneeded until some hacker tries a brute-force attack and tells the vendor. It seems almost uncommon for a new MFA vendor to implement anti-brute-forcing controls from the very beginning. I don't know why. But perhaps it is because the MFA vendors and their users think that MFA has some mysterious property that makes them far less likely to be hacked using the normal, everyday methods. Even when the flaws are reported, the vendors, big or little, often take months to close the holes.

Here are some developer and user defenses against brute-force attacks. Most of the controls are developer-focused and the end user's risk is mostly controllable only by the MFA solution vendor.

Developer Defenses Against Brute-Force Attacks

First, let's explore some developer defenses.

Enforce a Maximum Number of Guesses in a Particular Time Period

Developers should allow a maximum number of bad attempts in a particular time period before either making the attempter wait for a set period of time to try again, require an unlock from a more trustworthy service or person, or permanently lock the device. How many attempts and in what time period is up to the developer. I will say I was surprised to read that Instagram allowed 250 attempts. That seems insanely high to me, but they must have their reasons. A value of six attempts within five minutes as the maximum without causing a lockup seems reasonable to me.

Why would Instagram, or any other vendor, allow hundreds of bad attempts before locking out an account? It may be because of their past experience or simply their personal belief about what the right settings are. For example, for decades Microsoft's default bad password lockout policy was that five bad guesses within 30 minutes caused a 30-minute lockout. After 30 minutes without any further bad password guessing, the counter would be restarted and bad guess attempts would be set to 0. The recommended defaults (which often varied with the default settings set in their products) changed, starting with Windows Vista/Server 2008, to allow more bad attempts before a lockout occurred. Today's Microsoft is not recommending a one-size-fits-all default policy for any organization (`docs.microsoft.com/en-us/archive/blogs/secguide/configuring-account-lockout`). Why?

I can give you a couple of reasons. First, Microsoft felt that if an organization's password policy was sufficiently strong—requiring at least eight characters and multiple character sets of complexity with a 90-day or shorter expiration period—then an attacker was unlikely to successfully guess at anyone's password before it expired. With a sufficiently strong password policy, it would take a hacker billions of guesses before they would be successful, and even with automated guessing, the password would be changed before the automated tool had guessed any password.

Account lockouts are used to stop guessing against passwords using online methods. Using online portals means that the logon name and password have to be entered and the Enter key pressed or OK button clicked to send the logon to the authentication system for verification. The roundtrip process of entering in a particular logon name/password combination and waiting for the authentication system to validate, either successfully or with a failure message, normally takes 2–3 seconds in most online scenarios. So, automated (online) guessers can guess at a single logon combination only every 2–3 seconds per logon portal instance (usually). At 2 seconds per guess, at best it would allow a guesser 3,888,000 attempts in a 90-day period with no account lockout or throttling enabled. That's a lot of guessing but far less than what it would take to randomly guess an average eight-character, "complex" password (without any usable knowledge or birthday attack hits). If you limit passwords to just eight characters and rule out any bigger passwords, you get 95^8 possible passwords. That's billion of billions, over six quadrillion possible passwords (i.e., 6,634,204,312,890,625). If all that was allowed was 26 lowercase characters (26^8), it would still be 208,827,064,576 possible different passwords. This is of course ignoring the human entropy issues discussed in Chapter 1 and premature birthday attack collisions. But suffice it to say, guessing at "complex" passwords one at a time using an online portal is nontrivial if the passwords are sufficiently "complex." So, the thinking is that if you've got sufficiently complex passwords required by the password policy, you don't need account lockout enabled because a malicious password guesser or their tool will never be successful.

Second, Microsoft tech support had seen tens of thousands of instances where legitimate scripts or tools caused big account lockout problems and operational issues because someone updated a user account password the script or tool was using (as recommended by every password guide and regulation) but didn't update it in the script or tool. So, the automated tool was trying to do some legitimate, routine task and in the process unintentionally causing account lockout issues across the network. Microsoft tech support also saw a lot of password-guessing malware programs (like Conficker), which often tried up to 100 different common passwords, cause widespread account lockout issues on networks. It turned out that stricter account lockout policies were causing a lot of unintentional, unneeded widespread lockouts in networks where the password policy by itself without any lockout rules was sufficiently strong that the malware programs would never have been success-ful anyway. And, on a more limited basis, sometimes attackers will knowingly cause an organization to have a denial-of-service (DoS) event by guessing with every known valid logon name and a bunch of passwords against a public-facing logon portal. For example, maybe the company has an Outlook for Access (OWA) email logon web portal employees use. An attacker knowing a bunch of company email addresses could guess against the portal (using passwords they know won't work, like frog, dog, or toad) just to intentionally cause DoS problems with users. In the end, Microsoft decided against recommending a one-size-fits-all account lockout policy (although there are still built-in defaults in some products, features, and versions).

Still, deciding on the "right" password account lockout policy is not an exact science and is debated even within Microsoft, which has thought about it more than most. For example, their Azure Active Directory default settings are 10 bad guesses in a row leads to a one-minute lockout (docs.microsoft .com/en-us/azure/active-directory/authentication/howto-password-smart-lockout). Each subsequent bad guess after 10 leads to a 1-minute or longer lockout period for each additional bad attempt. Microsoft Active Directory Federated Services (ADFS) has different account lockout policy recommendations depending on the feature being used and version (docs.microsoft.com/en-us/ windows-server/identity/ad-fs/operations/configure-ad-fs-extranet-smart-lockout-protection and docs.microsoft.com/en-us/windows-server/identity/ad-fs/operations/ configure-ad-fs-extranet-smart-lockout-protection). There are differences between on-premises Active Directory user accounts and products and those same entities and features in the Azure cloud. It just goes to show you that account lockout policy setting is not an exact science. There is no "right" policy.

With that said, I think having any password account lockout policy with any reasonable setting is better than having no policy. That's because when you enable account lockout policy, when someone or something makes wrong guesses too many times, most systems will generate an account lockout security event, and that event can be sent to an alerting mechanism and can be investigated. It's just another tool in a defense-in-depth strategy to help organizations defeat malicious hackers and mal-ware. Without account lockout, most environments would probably be unaware that a bunch of bad password attempts were happening (either unintentionally from misconfigured scripts and tools or from malicious hacking). Account lockout gives you early warning of potential issues.

So, why did Instagram decided to allow a default of 250 bad attempts against their MFA solution? I don't know. Perhaps they had a history and experience of many "bad" logons inadvertently caused by legitimate issues, just below that threshold they now recommend. Maybe they read one of my previous books where I was recommending the settings be set above 100 bad attempts because of my belief that a strong password policy offset needs a strict account lockout policy. In any case, when you are using MFA it's because you've decided you want stronger security than what is normally provided with passwords. MFA solutions should use stricter account lockout policies by default, especially when the number of characters a malicious hacker may have to guess is only 4–6 digits long and contains only numbers. What that number should be I'm not sure, but should be at a level that reasonably protects users and prevents hacking attacks from being successful. Without relevant, contradictory facts, allowing 250 bad attempts per IP address at the same logon doesn't seem like a reasonable policy.

Rate-Limit Number of Concurrent Attempts

Many MFA solutions allow multiple code attempts at one time against the same MFA instance. I'm not sure why more than one within a reasonable time period (say 2 seconds) should ever be allowed. Anything faster than that is indicative of automated brute-forcing and should be prevented.

Blacklist Rogue IP Addresses

Multiple bad attempts from the same IP address should force the IP address to be blacklisted so that no further attempts are allowed for a long period of time (say months), or a manual process must be accomplished to get the IP address "un-blacklisted" for future attempts. Security logs should log bad attempts and alert on obvious brute-forcing attempts.

> **NOTE**   When you're locking out future attempts from IP addresses, take care to confirm that the originating IP address is the true originating IP address. You don't want to block IP addresses that are just being forged in the IP packet header by an attacker hoping not to be detected or hoping the IP address being fraudulently used gets locked out, causing a DoS event to the legitimate owner. Typically, all that is needed to confirm that the claimed originating IP address is the "true" IP address is a completed TCP handshake. The connection-oriented, three-way TCP network packet handshake (i.e., ACK, SYN-ACK, ACK) is intended exactly for that purpose. Of course, an attacker could be temporarily controlling an otherwise innocent host or doing some sort of "reflection" attack, but at least make an attempt to verify the originating IP address is the originating IP address of an attack before blocking it.

Increase Wait Time Between Each Allowed Guess

Each bad attempt should be penalized with longer and longer waiting periods before another attempt, successful or not, can be attempted. For example, 10 seconds must go by before a second attempt can be made, 30 seconds before a third attempt, and 60 seconds before a fourth. Microsoft implemented this sort of rate-limiting control in Windows for regular logons with their latest versions, and it has been effective at slowing down automated guessing attacks. Trusted Platform Module (TPM) chips have the same mechanism enabled for people entering the wrong TPM PIN to unlock their secrets. If I remember correctly, TPM version 1.2 chips had a set waiting period between guesses and after too many guesses locked out the user until some extraordinary reset event was accomplished. TPM version 2.0 chips implemented an increasing and random minimum time limit between incorrect guesses but don't lock out the chip permanently or require a hard reset no matter how many bad guesses.

Increase the Number of Possible Answers

Increase the number of possible answers so that it is harder for a brute-force guesser to be successful. Requiring six-digit PINs (1,000,000 possible answers) is far better than four-digit PINs (10,000 possible answers). Having more possible answers just makes the brute-force guessers job take longer. This is where non-OTP MFA solutions gain an advantage.

Enforced Answer Complexity

If possible, require that a larger number of possible characters be allowed or required. With most PINs that use only numbers 0–9, that is hard to do. But if a MFA solution allows letters and symbols to be used along with numbers, it's so much the better. If it requires them, so much the better. Allowing or requiring greater character set complexity increases the number of possible answers and makes the brute-force attacker's job harder.

Offsetting this recommendation is the fact that users don't want to use an OTP solution that uses something besides numbers only. There have been a handful of OTP solutions in the past that used more character types than numbers, and all have eventually failed in the marketplace. A better solution for any MFA vendor is to allow customers' admins or users to choose among required character sets. Some admins and users, desiring stronger security, can require complexity. Others can disable complexity or leave it at the default or using numbers only. That way, you get the best of both worlds that satisfy the security-minded and less friction mindsets at the same time.

Send Emails to Warn End Users

All MFA users should be warned if their devices or instances were involved in multiple bad input attempts. The user should be made aware of the issue and they can determine whether it came from something they did, a broken faulty, or a legitimate process, or was the result of some hacker attack. Either way, the user should be made aware of the multiple bad attempts, along with the relevant details, so that they can make the appropriate response to the risk.

User Defenses Against Brute-Force Attacks

Sadly, there isn't a lot an end user can do to prevent brute-force attacks, especially when using OTP-based solutions. Most of the possible controls can only be determined and implemented by the developer. The only "control" a user has is when buying or renewing a particular solution. Or if you or someone else discovers a new brute-force against your MFA solution, you hope the vendor takes action and closes the hole quickly.

Education and Using Only Solutions That Fight Brute-Force Attacks

MFA solution buyers should be aware of brute-force attacks and ask the right questions when investigating a new MFA solution. Don't always assume your solution or a solution you are looking to buy has defenses against brute-force attacks. All the users of the previous examples thought, "Sure, account lockout is enabled"—and it wasn't. Ask your vendor. And if they don't have account lockout, insist that it be enabled at a reasonable value.

Summary

In this chapter, we covered brute-force attacks against MFA solutions. You learned about common brute-force methods and saw multiple examples of real-world brute-forcing examples found by white-hat hackers. We concluded with a look at seven developer controls and one user control designed to help mitigate brute-force attacks.

Chapter 15, "Buggy Software" will cover MFA solution vulnerabilities.

15 Buggy Software

This chapter will cover vulnerabilities in MFA solutions, discussing common types of software vulnerabilities, potential exploitation outcomes, real-world examples, and defenses.

Introduction

There is no such thing as perfect, flawless computer programming, at least not yet—in the real world—even by the very programmers who tried their hardest to prove it was possible. Today, it's quite the opposite situation. Software, firmware, and chip vulnerabilities are everywhere. As Figure 4.1 showed in Chapter 4, "Usability vs. Security," we had 12,174 publicly announced vulnerabilities in 2019. We had 16,556 the year before and 14,714 the year before that. So far humans have been pretty poor at making flawless code. Some argue that artificial intelligence (AI) will one day make flawless code, but I find it a specious argument at best. The AI that humans would need to code would be flawed like everything else we have ever done, and somehow I'm supposed to believe that the flawed AI code would magically be capable of making flawless code? I don't buy it.

As Figure 5.1 from Chapter 5, "Hacking MFA in General" showed, every MFA solution has a lot of components. We have to assume that every component and dependency in an authentication solution has one or more vulnerabilities and can be a potential attack vector. And there have been many hundreds to thousands of security vulnerabilities found on all sorts of authentication software. If you want to see if your favorite authentication solution has had any publicly known vulnerabilities, you can do a CVE (Common Vulnerability and Exposures) search here: www.cvedetails.com/google-search-results.php. An example search on the vendor RSA, who has been around and doing cryptography and MFA longer than anyone, turns up at least 79 different published vulnerabilities (see Figure 15.1).

Publicly announced vulnerability sites only list the publicly announced vulnerabilities. Most vendors don't announce vulnerabilities found internally or those found in software preproduction. These days, some of the world's biggest vendors keep their publicly released software in "beta" for years and feel that doing so somehow reduces their responsibility to have to report security bugs to public databases.

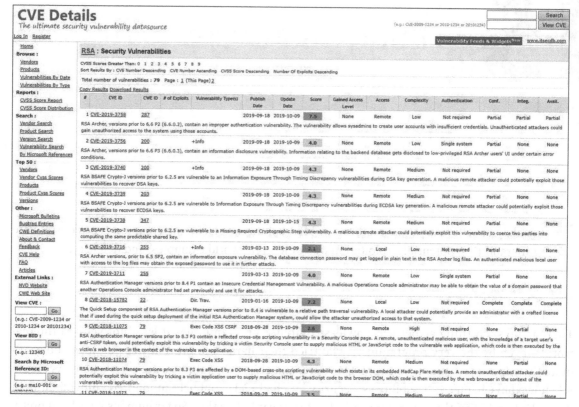

Figure 15.1: CVE search showing RSA vulnerabilities

Of course, the key worry is whether a malicious hacker finds and exploits an unpatched vulnerability. Not all vulnerabilities result in critical security issues. Most programming vulnerabilities result in program interruptions and unintended consequences, but those mistakes cannot always be leveraged to commit a security violation. Only a subset of vulnerabilities can be used in some sort of security exploit. If the vulnerability is not publicly known and/or doesn't have a patch from the vendor to close the hole, we call it a *zero day*.

Common Types of Vulnerabilities

Programming vulnerabilities can occur with any programming, not just with software. Vulnerabilities are frequently found in firmware and hardware devices, including CPU chips. Programming is the way all computers and electronic devices work, although much of the time that programming is hard-coded into the hardware and much harder to fix. One of my favorite sayings is, hardware and firmware are just harder-to-patch software.

So, what are these programming mistakes developers make that lead to potential security vulnerabilities? There are many hundreds of types of mistakes that any programmer can make, although only a few dozen account for more overall vulnerabilities than all the rest added together. Over the decades, there have been many different lists enumerating the most common types of vulnerability mistakes made by programmers; one of the most common is called the Top 25 Most Dangerous Software Errors: `cwe.mitre.org/top25/archive/2019/2019_cwe_top25.html`.

NOTE The Common Weakness Enumeration (CWE) site lists 1,190 different possible programming vulnerabilities. Their Top 25 list is made up of many dozens of other supporting "child" vulnerabilities that make up the larger "parent" vulnerability listing.

If you're not a programmer, some of those errors may not be super recognizable, but for my money here are the programming mistakes that seem most common and worrisome to me over my 30-plus years of experience.

Buffer Overflow

A *buffer overflow* happens when a program expecting a certain type or range of data as an input gets something else that overwhelms the storage area the program set aside for the input. For example, the program may have a field asking a user for their first name. The programmer expected someone to type in Roger, Richard, or Angela, or something like that. But instead, a hacker pasted in a bunch of binary executable code, which overwrites not only the storage area set aside for the first name and other inputted data, but also the current executable code that is part of the programming. The entered data is essentially overwriting and rewriting the current program's coding instructions (as simply conceptually diagrammed in Figure 15.2). If the overflow can be done "neatly" without causing the program to lock up or quit, there is a chance that the hacker's executable code will start being executed instead of the original program. The overflow usually results in the attacker's program running in the same security context as the program that was overflowed.

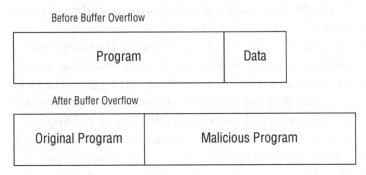

Figure 15.2: Simple conceptual representation of a buffer overflow

NOTE There are lots of different types of buffer overflows. The previous description is just one popular type.

Buffer overflows are one of the most common types of exploitable vulnerabilities. The most dangerous ones are those that reside in "listening" services or daemons. Listening means they accept incoming connections (locally on the same computer or device or over the network from other computers and devices). A listening vulnerable network service reachable over the network can be remotely abused.

The fastest spreading malware program to date, the 2003 SQL Slammer worm (en.wikipedia.org/wiki/SQL_Slammer), buffer-overflowed nearly every unpatched listening Microsoft SQL instance reachable from the Internet or from an infected computer on the local network in just a few hours using a 376-character payload against UDP (User Datagram Protocol) port 1434. It did not appear to do anything other than spread, but it spread so fast and wide that it came the closest to shutting down the Internet than any other malware program in the modern era (so far). Because of SQL Slammer and other malicious worms using remote buffer overflows, most operating system and application vendors go to great lengths to harden their services and daemons against remote buffer overflows, although buffer overflows requiring the end user to be involved (by using social engineering) are still quite popular.

These days, most of the time an end user must be tricked into clicking on a malicious link or running a trojan horse program in order for the buffer overflowing program to be executed. Either way, attacks against programs that can be buffer overflowed are among the most feared vulnerabilities. They are many different types of buffer overflows (e.g., memory corruptions, underflows, stack-based, heap-based), but most can be prevented by the targeted program preventing invalid input when requesting information. On top of that, most modern-day operating systems and some hardware have several anti–buffer overflow mechanisms built into them by default these days.

Cross-Site Scripting

Cross-site scripting (XSS) is when a hacker can inadvertently trick someone's local program into running their malicious code or instructions instead of simply displaying it as data. Let me give you my favorite personal example from the time when I was an instructor and penetration tester for Foundstone (now a division of McAfee: www.mcafee.com/enterprise/en-us/services/foundstone-services.html). My team was testing a new cable device for one of the world's largest cable providers. The device was fairly sophisticated and even included a fully functional firewall that any of us would be glad to have on our home networks. The firewall not only logged any attacks against the cable device but logged all the detailed data and payload from within any network packet it blocked. We realized, almost by accident, that any HTML coding or scripting displayed in the firewall log would be executed on whoever's browser was looking at the firewall data. We sent a small "Hello World!" scripting test to the firewall on a blocked port, and sure enough, when we looked at the firewall log using a browser, a "Hello World!" message popped up—confirmation of the cross-site scripting vulnerability.

Someone on the team—I forget who, now, but it wasn't me—created a malicious script and "attacked" the firewall. We then called the cable company's technical support team and pretended to be regular cable customers who believed we were being attacked by hackers. We asked the technical support person to look at our firewall to see if we were indeed being "attacked" to confirm our suspicions. They agreed to look at the firewall logs, and when they did, their Linux-based system sent us their passwd and shadow files (the password files on a Linux system). The stolen root credentials worked across every computer in their corporation. So, from a single XSS vulnerability in a single product, we were able to take over the entire corporation. You can see why this is my favorite XSS story.

Another common XSS example is an example of what is called a *reflected XSS attack*. An attacker sends you a link that looks like any link you would normally click on and use to visit a website. But unknown to the user, it has additional commands added to the end of the link that wind up executing extra, malicious content. For example, you click a link to connect to a website that looks familiar to you, but the link not only goes to that website, but also abuses a feature of that website that allows users to be automatically redirected somewhere else. Here's an example: `www.reddit.com/r/sysadmin/comments/d9ndnf/heres_a_phishing_url_to_give_you_nightmares/`. In this instance, any user connecting on what they are shown as the legitimate `adobe.com` website would have been redirected to a website of the attacker's choosing (before the bug was corrected). An attacker would usually redirect the user to a look-alike website and then probably get them to download fake trojan Adobe software.

Defending against XSS attacks relies on any program that can accept and display scripting or coding to ensure that the scripting or coding is always displayed like regular data or writing and not executed locally. For example, web application developers need to write or use mechanisms that sanitize all inputs by looking for and removing "escaping" special characters that often get used to indicate to a browser that a script or piece of code is involved or being injected. In general, developers should always sanitize all user inputs to programmatically ensure that clients can only enter the specific type of data required for that particular input. Nowadays, many programming tools have these sorts of input sanitation controls built in, but they aren't always enabled by default and it's up to developers to take advantage of them.

Directory Traversal Attacks

Directory traversal attacks are a vulnerability where an attacker tries to navigate to otherwise security-protected directories, files, and folders without supposedly being allowed to those locations or the parent locations. A good, super-simple, example is to suppose that I can get to the folder `C:\parent\child` when I'm not allowed to get to folder `C:\` or `C:\parent`. Simply having and using the full pathname (i.e., `C:\parent\child`) allows me to bypass the parent directories where I had less permissive access.

A real-life example of a common hacker directory traversal attack test string is `../../../` or something like that. The forward slashes represent folder subdirectories and the dot-dot (`..`) represents a parent folder in many operating systems. You can test this by going to a DOS prompt on a Microsoft Windows computer, which will usually drop you off at a subfolder (i.e., `C:\Users\<userlogonname>\`) and if you type `cd..` and press Enter, you will be in the parent folder (e.g., `C:\Users`). A single dot represents the current folder. Hackers learned decades ago that using combinations of dots and double dots as names along with forward slashes (and sometimes backward slashes) would sometimes, if you were lucky, let you get to folders that you had been told that you did not have access to.

Back to my previous example where my Foundstone penetration testing team was attacking a cable box device. In order to access the device, you went to its IP address with a browser (e.g., 192.168.1.1). That gave you a web-based logon prompt. We tried password guessing against it and nothing was working. I ran a web server identification hacking tool called Nikto (`cirt.net/nikto2`) against the cable box, because any device you can connect to using a browser is running a mini-web server of some sort. Nikto will try to identify the web server/service by vendor and version and run a bunch of common attacks against it. Nikto wasn't successful in finding a vulnerability, but it did identify the web server edition. It was something called Notebook. I had never heard of it, and it was difficult to research, but I found a single Google reference to a Digital Research web server called Notebook discontinued over two decades ago. I knew nothing about Notebook, but I knew that web servers from that era were full of directory traversal vulnerabilities. So, I tried the standard test string I listed earlier, and voilà!, just like that, I was into the device with full administrative control. We did not need a logon or password to be authorized as the root account with the highest level of access possible on the box. We were able to completely control the device, sniff credit card information, steal paid cable shows for free, and completely manipulate the code of the device. The next day, we did the XSS attack listed earlier and took over the whole global corporate office. So, in two days we had not only completely owned the device we were paid to hack, but had also taken over the entire corporation. That is one of my best hacking memories to this day, and I'm still smiling as I type this.

Directory traversal attacks aren't as common these days, but they can still be used to get around permission controls on operating systems and other (non–web server) programs. People who build web servers know all about directory traversal attacks and code against them, but it seems that other developers are not as familiar. Preventing directory traversal attacks is usually solved by correct permissioning—and that leads us to our next topic.

Overly Permissive Permissions

A very, very common vulnerability these days is overly permissive permissions, meaning that whoever created a system did not correctly define the correct permissions for all users—be they admins, regular users, guests, or the infamous "everyone" groups. Whoever defined them inadvertently allows users and visitors who should not be able to read or write protected files the ability to do so. So, a regular user or visitor who normally should only be able to read files or execute code the developer intended ends up with the ability to maliciously modify or add critical files or read and download confidential files.

These days the most popular attacked targets due to overly permissive permissions is that of Amazon Web Services (AWS) cloud storage "buckets." An organization buys and uses AWS storage and that storage often has overly permissive permissions.

Here are some examples of real-world attacks:

- www.upguard.com/breaches/cloud-leak-accenture
- www.forbes.com/sites/thomasbrewster/2017/12/19/120m-american-households-exposed-in-massive-consumerview-database-leak/#1667d9e97961
- www.wired.com/story/exactis-database-leak-340-million-records/
- www.zdnet.com/article/accenture-left-a-huge-trove-of-client-passwords-on-exposed-servers/
- www.hackread.com/personal-data-of-over-50000-honda-connect-app-leaked/

Even before cloud storage became so popular, when hired as a penetration tester one of my favorite hacks was to look for overly permissive permissions on shared network logon files and local computer files for programs that ran with the ultra-privileged System permissions. Many networks run a number of shared common executables and scripts on each connecting device after people log on to the network. I liked to look for those shared files and scripts, and if it allowed regular users to modify those objects, I would modify it to include some potentially malicious program or script. If I was hired to pen-test a regular computer, I would look for local programs I could find with elevated privileges. I found quite a few antivirus programs with overly permissive permissions. I would replace or modify one of the files to sneak in my potentially malicious backdoor programs, reboot the computer, and then take it over. I always found it ironic that the programs designed to defend an asset were the ones I most abused to successfully attack something.

Defenses against overly permissive permissions is for the developers to ensure that the correct permissions have been set in the beginning and for administrators and developers to run periodic file audits to look for overly permissive permissions on potentially dangerously misused files and folders.

Hard-Coded/Default Credentials

Another common vulnerability is for programs to contain hard-coded, can't-change logon credentials or to have very common, well-known logon credentials that the users frequently don't change. Many developers either don't know the risk of hard-coded credentials or use them during early development and forget to remove them. The only way to fix hard-coded credentials is to update the software or programming with updated code that removes the hard-coded credentials. The Common Weakness Enumeration site has a great description and examples of this type of vulnerability: cwe.mitre.org/data/definitions/798.html. Hard-coded credentials can be mitigated by developer education and tools that look for and alert on such instances in programming code.

One of my favorite real-world examples comes from the cyberwar malware program Stuxnet (en.wikipedia.org/wiki/Stuxnet). Stuxnet was a malware program, created by U.S. and Israeli intelligence forces, that successfully attacked and destroyed Iranian nuclear fuel centrifuges in 2010. It contained several attack methods, including zero days. One of the methods was abusing credentials hard-coded into involved Siemens controllers. The involved Siemens interface software, known as WinCC, connected to Siemens controllers using a permanent logon name of wincconnect along with a password of 2WSSXcder. The hard-coded password was revealed to the world in a public forum in April 2008. And over two years later, not only was this publicly known hard-coded password to Siemens SCADA systems not fixed, Siemens did not proactively tell their customers about the issue. When this hard-coded password was revealed to the world by those taking part in Stuxnet, not only did Siemens not fix the huge security issue right away, but they also sent out an official field notice telling its customers not to change the hard-coded password because it would cause too many operational issues. Hackers love to read that sort of stuff.

Anyone interested in reading more details about Stuxnet should see www2.cs.arizona .edu/~collberg/Teaching/466-566/2012/Resources/presentations/2012/topic9-final/report .pdf and read Kim Zetter's excellent book, *Countdown to Zero Day* (Broadway Books, 2015).

But really, anyone who works with penetration testing SCADA systems knows that many industrial control systems have hard-coded passwords, not just Siemens (although many different types of Siemens control systems have hard-coded passwords as well). It's rife in the industry and isn't uncommon anywhere. You would think that developers would understand how risky using hard-coded passwords are and never do it. I first had this exact thought in 1990. I had assumed this particular security issue was so well known that no developer would ever be so stupid as to make this mistake. I was wrong. Security defending is not about intelligence; it's about education and awareness. And if the developers and managers involved with a particular programming project aren't aware of the problems with hard-coded passwords, then they can't minimize their use.

During my 30-year-plus penetration testing career, I've found hundreds of hard-coded passwords in programs and systems I've been hired to test. Once, not that long ago, I was advising a Fortune 10 company who developed software and services on how to better remove security bugs from their systems. When they ran Qualys vulnerability scanners, the resulting reports would often list 50 or more "critical" bugs that were found on each scanned system. The task to fix them all at once over thousands of systems was overwhelming, so they asked me for my advice. I pride myself on figuring out what should be fixed first. I even wrote a book about it (*A Data-Driven Computer Defense*, independently published, 2019).

I told them to ignore the voluminous reports and asked, "What is the vulnerability type that has been most successfully used by attackers to exploit your systems in the real world?" I figured there was no better answer than to fix the way the systems had actually been exploited the most as the first, best step they could take. They had to research the data. And it turned out that of thousands of publicly exposed systems, only eight had been successfully compromised that they knew about. But of those, when I asked how most were exploited, they answered, "Hard-coded logon credentials!"

I think it surprised everyone in the room, including me. I think we all thought that unpatched software, buffer overflow, or some other more sophisticated type of attack was going to be involved. But the real answer was simple, hard-coded password problems. So, the problem persisted in one of the largest and successful companies in the world just a few years ago, and it exists on a multitude of systems we all use all over the world.

Many computers and devices come with built-in default credentials. There are dozens of sites around the Internet that list common default passwords—such as datarecovery.com/rd/default-passwords—that any hacker can look up and attempt to use when faced with a device logon.

Default passwords that are never changed are so common that popular malware, like Mirai bot (en.wikipedia.org/wiki/Mirai_(malware)), tries default passwords to take over vulnerable devices. Mirai bot alone has taken over tens, if not hundreds, of millions of devices (like IP cameras and cable modem routers). Those devices are often then organized into huge *botnets* (malware networks), which then attack other devices and networks.

Defenses include developers implementing customized default passwords for each unique device. For example, many home cable modems now come with the unique password printed on a sticker stuck to the side of the modem or the password is autogenerated off some unique attribute of the device, such as its MAC address. The best solutions use unique logon credentials stored in "security enclaves" like TPM chips or other facilities built into CPUs and other chips.

Insecure Authentication

Good authentication is hard to do, and there are a lot of involved dependencies. It is easy—probably easier—for a developer to do authentication incorrectly and insecurely than to do it right and securely. There are so many ways a developer can mess up authentication that entire books could be devoted to just single types of mistakes. The Common Weakness Enumeration website lists 18 ways a developer can incorrectly code authentication (cwe.mitre.org/data/definitions/1211.html), and most of them have several different sub-methods listed under them. Suffice it to say, doing good authentication is difficult work. Defenses include everything that I will list in the "Developer Defenses Against Vulnerability Attacks" section, later in this chapter.

Cleartext Storage or Transmission of Confidential Information

Another common vulnerability is the insecure storage or transmission of confidential information, either data that is supposed to be protected or some type of authentication secret. Many times, all an attacker has to do to see a supposedly protected secret is look. For example, many early encrypted USB storage devices stored the private encryption key that "locked" the devices on the device in plaintext. All an attacker needed was the right equipment and software to inspect the storage device at the "bit level." There have been cases where private encryption keys generated on the fly were left in what was supposed to be temporary storage areas. Or data that was touted and designed to be sent over HTTPS was sent using HTTP instead. Defenses against inadvertently revealing confidential information include a good understanding, enforced use, and review of cryptographic systems and processes.

There are, of course, many more types of vulnerabilities than just the ones I've covered here. Keep in mind that social engineering and phishing are responsible for the vast majority of successful malicious hacking (70–90 percent), whereas unpatched vulnerabilities are "just" responsible for 20–40 percent. That's still a huge portion of successful attacks.

Vulnerability Outcomes

The exploitation of any vulnerability can result in a myriad of outcomes, although most of them can be grouped into three major categories: security bypasses, information disclosure, and denial of service.

Security Bypass

As the name implies, vulnerabilities often allow an attacker to bypass whatever security the system has in place. This is the most common type of outcome when the attack is against an MFA solution. Security bypasses can range from an attacker gaining regular user privileges on a device they are not authorized to be on all the way up to completely compromise where the attacker can do anything the device and programming is capable of without further limitations.

Some security bypass attacks are known as *escalation of privilege* (EoP) attacks, where the attacker is elevating their current security access to one with more permissions and privileges. For example, many times a hacker's initial exploit of a device results in the attacker only getting the security context of the logged-in user or program they are using. An EoP attack allows them to gain more privileged security contexts, which permits them to do more sensitive operations and potentially more damaging actions.

Information Disclosure

This is essentially a security bypass, but one where the security bypass only allows the attacker to see information they otherwise could not. In this case, the attacker is not normally "in control" of the system they have compromised. They are simply seeing something their default level of access should not have allowed them to see. They can't modify or delete the information—they can only see, read, download, and share it. Unfortunately, most security systems exist to protect information; it's the reason for the security in the first place. Like security bypasses, information disclosures range from low risk to high risk, from the ability to see just one bit of confidential information to being able to see all information on the involved system.

Denial of Service

Denial-of-service (DoS) events allow an attacker to prevent legitimate and authorized users and systems from using allowed systems and information in a timely manner. For example, an attacker may target a web server with tens of billions of useless network packets, overwhelming the processing capabilities of the server, which results in "404 errors" being displayed to users trying to access it. Other types of DoS attacks can result from a vulnerability that doesn't allow security bypass or information disclosure. Instead, it just corrupts the program to a point that it can no longer run.

I've even implemented attacks (e.g., Smurf attack) where a single malformed network packet locked up an entire server or device. I have twice locked up smart televisions by sending them single malformed packets.

Many security vulnerabilities result in a device or service becoming "locked" up. Sometimes all that needs to happen is for the impacted device or software to be restarted or rebooted, and sometimes the lockup is more permanent. Attacks against firmware can result in "hard lockups," which make the impacted device unusable until the firmware gets rewritten back to a good state.

Examples of Vulnerability Attacks

When I first started in computer security over three decades ago, I thought that anyone in computer security just magically knew how to stop all potential security issues. I felt like I did, at least in my areas of expertise. But I soon found out that most programmers, even programmers of security software and hardware, had very little, innate, understanding of computer security issues, including how to avoid common software vulnerabilities. This isn't that surprising, since very few programming schools and universities devote much time to teaching secure programming. Currently, I only know of two universities that offer a complete course in how to program securely. So, it should be no surprise that most of our programmers, even security software programmers, aren't so strong in avoiding vulnerabilities in their own code.

I remember being shocked when I worked for Foundstone when they were purchased by McAfee in 2004. One of the first tasks McAfee asked us to do was a vulnerability analysis of all their security software. McAfee was one of the largest sellers of computer security software in the world. We found hundreds of vulnerabilities, often in a single program. At the time, I couldn't believe how many errors we found. I was worried the news would leak out. Over the years since, I've learned that McAfee's buggy software is not an outlier. It's very normal. The reality is it's unusual to find computer security software without a lot of bugs. Still, to this day, most computer security programmers do not get training in how to avoid common vulnerabilities. And this includes the programmers of MFA solution software and hardware.

Let's look at examples of vulnerabilities found in MFA solutions.

Uber MFA Vulnerability

The popular ridesharing vendor, Uber, has offered MFA since 2015. A white-hat hacker noted a two-factor bypass in 2018 and reported it in the legitimately trusted Hackerone (www.hackerone.com) bug bounty program. Uber responded by saying that his finding was not that substantial and that at best all that was needed was a documentation update. Frustrated, the hacker contacted the media and after being contacted by a popular tech media site (ZDNet), Uber finally fixed the bug and paid the hacker for the report. But for over two months after it was reported, Uber did not fix the bug. For more details, see www.zdnet.com/article/uber-security-flaw-two-factor-login-bypass.

Google Authenticator Vulnerability

The Google Authenticator time-based one-time password (TOTP) app was extensively covered in Chapter 9, "One-Time Password Attacks." In that chapter, it was stated that the secret seed values of any OTP need to be heavily protected. If an adversary can get access to these values, they can generate additional unauthorized instances and use them to respond as if they were the legitimate users.

In order to implement and use Google Authenticator with your website, an admin has to install and configure the Google Authenticator software on a server that is configured as the authentication provider to the sites the admin wants to protect. Google Authenticator is implemented by installing the pluggable authentication module (PAM) `pam_google_authenticator.so` on a Linux host computer. The installation process creates a secret file containing seed origination codes that must be kept secret from unauthorized users.

In 2012, it was discovered that the secret file had overly permissive permissions, in this case, readable by all users, instead of more secure settings. The Google Authenticator PAM's operations were changed so that it worked with stricter permissions and required elevate user access (i.e., `sudo`) to access. To see more details, see `www.openwall.com/lists/oss-security/2013/04/18/10` and `www.cvedetails.com/cve/CVE-2012-6140`.

A second Google MFA bypass (`www.cvedetails.com/cve/CVE-2013-0258`) was discovered in 2013. If a user's account was enabled for Google Authenticator but their token was not associated with the account, anyone could log on to the user's account using the logon name alone (no password required). Details are here: `www.drupal.org/node/1903282`.

YubiKey Vulnerability

Yubico makes some of the most beloved MFA devices and tokens on the Internet. They are used by millions of users and might be the second-most popular MFA solution (after RSA) of all time. In 2018, a researcher discovered multiple vulnerabilities in various versions of Yubico supporting software that would allow someone with knowledge of those vulnerabilities to craft a custom MFA device that would successfully bypass YubiKey authentication checks on devices where the software was installed. The attacker could insert their custom device and they would immediately be logged on as if they successfully presented a legitimate YubiKey device. It was due to buffer overflow vulnerability. Details are here: `www.yubico.com/support/security-advisories/ysa-2018-03/`. A more widespread exploit, known as ROCA, that worked against Yubico devices was found in 2017 and will be discussed in a moment.

Multiple RSA Vulnerabilities

Founded in 1982, RSA Security, Inc. has been around longer than most other security vendors. They were the earliest implementers of public key cryptography and MFA authentication. RSA was so popular that for decades if you saw an MFA solution, it was most often an RSA token (RSA SecurIDs) or RSA piece of software. So, it should be no surprise that RSA has a higher number of vulnerabilities than most of its current competitors.

CVE shows 79 different RSA vulnerabilities (`www.cvedetails.com/vendor/334/RSA.html`) since 1999. There are at least nine security bypasses (`www.cvedetails.com/vulnerability-list/vendor_id-334/opbyp-1/RSA.html`). Many involved MFA solutions, including this one: `www.cvedetails.com/cve/CVE-2010-3321/`. With this particular vulnerability, someone with authorized access to an impacted SecurID token could export the device's private key off the device. Private keys on smartcards and SecurID tokens are supposed to be protected from being able to be exported off the devices. If someone can export it, they can essentially duplicate the device and how it authenticates. RSA Security was also purportedly involved in one of the largest seed value thefts, as discussed in Chapter 9.

SafeNet Vulnerability

I've been a big PKI guy for decades. In that world, the three most trusted companies for securely storing PKI secret keys for certificate authorities (CA) and other critical PKI equipment were Thales, SafeNet and Gemalto (which was a target of a massive SIM card hack in 2010, covered in Chapter 8, "SMS Attacks"). Now all three brands are owned by the single company, Thales (`www.thalesgroup.com`).

NOTE   Thales is pronounced "Talice," similar to malice or Alice but with a t.

In 2016, SafeNet announced (`labs.nettitude.com/wp-content/uploads/2016/03/160125-1-Gemalto-IDSS-Security-Bulletin-SAS-Agents-Privilege-Escalation.pdf`) 10 separate CVEs dealing with overly permission permissions. In particular, the Microsoft Windows Authenticated Users group had Full Control permissions to SafeNet critical files. This would allow any authenticated user on those impacted systems to see confidential authentication information and be able to maliciously modify SafeNet files.

Login.gov

Login.gov (`login.gov`) is a website that allows anyone "secure and private online access to participating government programs." It's the way tens of millions of Americans access their public government resources. In 2017, a hacker reported an MFA bypass bug (`hackerone.com/reports/264090`). He was able to start the registration process, which then sent him a confirmation email. The website expected the user to click the link to continue their registration process and told him he had only 24 hours to do so. Then he noticed that it did not require him to confirm that the registration code was tied to a specific email address, that it could be used multiple times, and that it did not expire in 24 hours. Using the initially provided authentication, he was able to log on to involved websites without any authentication beyond the authentication code. It took `Login.gov` two months to close the bug after it was reported. See `mustafakemalcan.com/bypass-two-factor-authentication-on-login-gov/` for more details.

ROCA Vulnerability

There are vulnerabilities and then there are *vulnerabilities*! The 2017 ROCA vulnerability is one of the most severe authentication vulnerabilities of the modern area. It involves public key asymmetric cryptography. As you learned in Chapter 3, "Types of Authentication," asymmetric cryptography involves cryptographically related private and public keys. Whatever one key in the pair can encrypt, the other key can decrypt. Public keys are meant to be shared with anyone, and private keys are intended to be known only by one (or a few users or devices if it is purposefully shared). If an unauthorized person is able to access the private key, that encryption pair is considered broken and useless. Private keys must be protected.

A company called Infineon Technologies (www.infineon.com) created a cryptographic subroutine program known as a cryptographic library. It was named RSALib. It was implemented in the software and hardware routines of hundreds of millions of devices. It could be called on by software and hardware to generate public–private key pairs. In 2017, it was discovered that any RSA-generated keys (sizes from 512 to 2048 bits) had a severe vulnerability—if you could access the public key (which theoretically anyone in the world could do), you could immediately determine the related private key. This was such a big deal that even though it was discovered by researchers in February 2017, it was not publicly disclosed until October 2017. The intervening time was used to involve vendors and make patches. I had heard inklings of something related to a widespread security vulnerability a few weeks before it was publicly announced, but no one I personally knew had any idea of the severity of the discovery. It was a well-kept, but somewhat selectively known, secret among the involved vendor's chosen employees. In an instance, as soon as the flaw was made public, hundreds of millions of devices (e.g., Windows computers with TPM chips running Microsoft BitLocker, smartcards, YubiKeys) were essentially announced as being easily exploitable. We had emergency meetings at Microsoft, where I worked at the time, about what we needed to do. It was determined that all impacted Microsoft administrator smartcards needed to be replaced immediately. It was followed by device and software updates across hundreds of thousands of devices, just at Microsoft.

Tens of millions of devices had to be upgraded. Impacted smartcards had to be replaced. What scares me to this day is that I frequently run into vendors who sold impacted smartcards and MFA administrators who more than likely had impacted devices, who have never heard of ROCA. Early on we estimated that millions if not tens of millions of vulnerable devices and asymmetric keys were never fixed. Two plus years out, most of the vulnerable keys have now likely expired (the average impacted asymmetric key is only good for 1 to 2 years). But there is no doubt that some vulnerable keys with longer lives are still being used around the world. For more information, check out the following sites:

- en.wikipedia.org/wiki/ROCA_vulnerability
- crocs.fi.muni.cz/_media/public/papers/nemec_roca_ccs17_preprint.pdf
- thehackernews.com/2017/10/rsa-encryption-keys.html
- arstechnica.com/information-technology/2017/10/crippling-crypto-weakness-opens-millions-of-smartcards-to-cloning/

If you are interested in learning if your favorite MFA solution has any software vulnerabilities, you can search, by name, on any CVE site, including this one: www.cvedetails.com.

Defenses to Vulnerability Attacks

This section looks at developer and user defenses against vulnerability attacks.

Developer Defenses Against Vulnerability Attacks

Here are some developer defenses against vulnerability attacks.

Education—SDL

All developers must be thoroughly trained in security development lifecycle (SDL) education, tools, and processes. SDL is an encompassing way to significantly reduce programming vulnerabilities lower than the numbers without SDL involved. It begins by teaching all programmers how to program securely. With it, they learn about the common vulnerabilities, how they were allowed to occur, and how to defend against having them appear in your code by using secure development tools and secure development defaults. Good, secure programming does not come naturally. If it did, we would not have global vulnerability counts over 10,000 each year, year after year. It takes education and teachers. We need to do SDL "train-the-trainer" programs, and have those educators train all the other programmers. Universities and other programming schools should make programming securely a definitive part of their required curriculum. Companies who hire programmers need to make SDL skills a requirement for a job. Together the SDL training and the job requirements would make more competent, security-conscious programmers. You want a culture with a healthy respect for secure coding to be the norm.

Microsoft has the most comprehensive, free, SDL resources on the Internet: www.microsoft.com/sdl. They share most of what they have learned and practiced in one of the largest programming shops with the rest of the world. They not only don't mind if competitors and everyone else programs more securely, they hope they do. Microsoft has worked with many other competitors, such as Adobe and Apple, to help them establish SDL programs of their own as well. There are also many books on secure programming and many other websites and methods dedicated to secure programming.

Use Secure Tools with Secure Defaults

Not all programming tools are equal. Some programming tools have more secure defaults and more easily help programmers deliver more secure code by default. All organizations should ensure that their developers are using the best, most secure tools, and implementing them with the most secure options possible. Risky languages and functions should be banned and discontinued from use.

Code Checks

All submitted programming code should be checked for vulnerabilities—using a combination of static code analysis, fuzz testing, and manual code review—both by the original developer and by their peers. The best organizations should have development tools that refuse to compile well-known vulnerabilities so that the code check finds fewer and fewer issues over time.

Pen Testing

All code should be penetration-tested by internal and external teams to see if vulnerabilities can be located that the previous methods missed. External teams should be changed or cycled through every year or two so that fresh eyes and approaches get tried. Further, every vendor writing code for external use should participate in a bug bounty program, where penetration testers are encouraged to look for and responsibly disclose bugs and be rewarded for doing so.

Automate Patching

All externally used code should have an automated, daily-checking, self-updating patching routine enabled by default. It should not require any user input. It should just regularly check for and update the code automatically when critical vulnerabilities are known.

User Defenses Against Vulnerability Attacks

Finally, let's explore user defenses against vulnerability attacks.

Education

All users should be educated that MFA solutions and computer security software in general have vulnerabilities, most of which may not be known. Users need to generally understand and expect that they will need to routinely update the software, and to a lesser extent, firmware and hardware, of their MFA solution on a regular basis. If your MFA solution doesn't have regular, at least semiannual, patch updates, you can assume they aren't doing a good, proactive job of bug hunting and all the security issues that invites.

Require Vendors to Use SDL

Customers have the most ability to impact MFA solution vendors before they purchase a solution. Customers should ask all potential MFA solution vendors if they use SDL training, tools, and processes. If the vendor doesn't know what SDL is, that should be concerning to you. If they answer in the affirmative, ask for details. Don't just take a "yes" response without confirming the extent of their SDL participation.

Timely Patching

Even when using SDL, vendors' programming will have vulnerabilities (although hopefully fewer of them). Remember, there is no such thing as perfect software. After vendors release a security notice and related patch, customers should patch their impacted software, firmware, and hardware in a timely manner. What's a timely manner? Some people think it means immediately or within a few days, and others say it means within one month. Most security practitioners probably think that one week to one month sounds like a reasonable amount of time.

NOTE If your MFA solution vendors are not issuing security notices and updates at least once every year or two, you should wonder if the vendor is looking for and taking security vulnerabilities seriously. Most of the risk happens between the time a vendor first announces a security vulnerability and releases a patch until the time the customer applies it. A vendor with an active, aggressive patching program is usually a good sign, not a weakness (although we all would prefer fewer security bugs in the first place).

Vulnerability Scanning

MFA solution users should routinely scan their environment (at least once a month) for security vulnerabilities. Be sure to include all the components of your MFA solution. Good patching doesn't just mean checking for software vulnerabilities; firmware and hardware must be scanned and checked as well. When critical vulnerabilities are found, they should be patched in a timely manner.

If vendors and customers follow these recommendations, malicious attackers will have fewer opportunities to exploit vulnerabilities, and that is good for all of us.

Summary

This chapter covered vulnerabilities, and vulnerabilities in MFA solutions in particular. We discussed common types of vulnerabilities, damage impacts from successful exploitation, and examples of MFA vulnerabilities. You also learned how to defend against them.

Chapter 16, "Attacks Against Biometrics" will cover attacks against biometric-based MFA.

16 Attacks Against Biometrics

This chapter covers attacks against MFA solutions that use biometrics as part of their authentication factors and explores the various ways to hack them. This subject includes a lot of information, so it will be one of the longer chapters.

Introduction

Many years ago, I was on a team that was tasked with seeing if we could hack fingerprint readers. The organization we were working for was considering requiring biometrics for network logon and wanted to know whether or not the fingerprint readers could be fooled. If you watch spy TV shows or movies, it seems like any fingerprint reader can be easily fooled by any spy, but we wanted to see if that is reality. Fingerprint system vendors would have you believe that it is mostly hype and is far more difficult in real life.

We purchased 22 different fingerprint readers—some as part of laptops in which they were built in and others as stand-alone devices. We had finger swipe–style, bar readers, where you swipe the first joint section of your finger front to back across a thin fingerprint reading sensor, as well as pad-style, where you simply pressed or rolled your first finger joint across a flat glass or plastic pad.

Long story short, we hacked *all* of them with fake fingerprints using multiple methods. Nearly every single method we tried worked across a majority of them. Fake gelatin fingers, check! Silly Putty fingers, check! Rubber glue fingerprints, check! My favorite hack was simply cupping my hands around a fingerprint pad reader and blowing a few chest-fulls of hot air on the sensor. The warm, hot, moist breath swelled the existing fingerprint oils from the last person who'd logged in and the sensor took the reinvigorated fingerprint oil as a new, successful logon. We tried fingerprinting powder and that worked as well.

Because of the success of the last two types of hacks, we recommended to fingerprint pad vendors that they never accept someone's fingerprint that is in the exact same place as the previous fingerprint logon after a logon attempt. We reasoned that fingerprints would rarely ever be in the exact same places two times in a row during additional real logons. A year later, I retested some of the devices that had failed using the latest updated software and drivers. Most of the original devices that had been hacked using the "breath trick" or fingerprinting dust still could be tricked. Only one seemed to consistently fail now, as if the vendor had heeded our report and done something different.

Since then, I've been involved with several teams that have investigated hacking and tricking various types of biometrics. We have always been successful in hacking them. I have never once been on a team that didn't successfully trick or hack all the devices being investigated. Most of the time, everyone but me were surprised by how easy the biometric equipment was to fake out. Many times, the team would anticipate weeks of testing to find a sophisticated hack that would get by the devices only to discover that their first, mostly unsophisticated, attack worked fine across many of the devices. This is not to say that extremely accurate biometric devices don't exist or aren't being used. It's just that most of us are not using those types of more sophisticated biometrics. Most of us would not tolerate using them. Though, to be fair, biometrics are improving over time—more on this below.

Biometrics

In computer security, biometrics are personal authenticators linked to physical human body composition (i.e., physiological) or behaviors that can uniquely identify a person. To be used in biometric authentication, a biometric trait should meet the following requirements:

- It is universally unique to a specific person.
- It is permanent; it does not change except perhaps very slowly over many years, if at all.
- It is measurable in most people.
- It is fairly easy to measure.
- It can be measured quickly (no longer than a few seconds).
- It's fast and easy to make comparisons against stored biometric traits to confirm or deny an authentication attempt.

The most common biometric traits used for authentication are fingerprint, face, or voice, but only slightly less popular is hand geometry, palm veins, iris, and retina. There is increasing interest in typing patterns and rhythms known as *keystroke dynamics*, which essentially links biometric attributes to distinct, unique behavioral outcomes. There are even obscure biometric projects based on traits like eye veins, walking gait, handwriting, brain activity, heart activity, and even scent/odor. One day I suppose if we can get an immediate, very detailed DNA analysis, that may become the ultimate biometric trait to use for authentication (although it turns out fingerprints are far easier to use and are likely more unique).

NOTE Biometrics are even being used to recognize individual animals (e.g., zebras, manta rays, dolphins) based on their physical characteristics to better track them.

Biometrics are based on the core idea that many different physical traits (and sometimes behaviors) are unique within the known world. Most were established during embryonic development and with us since birth. No one else has our fingerprints. No one else has our same irises, retina, face, or voice. Or that's the theory, and so far, no one has ever conclusively demonstrated anything different for those particular traits. But it's not like we have actually taken everyone's biometric traits and done a thorough search to conclusively prove that our biometric traits are truly unique in the world. We haven't taken every one of the world's over 7 billion living people's fingerprints and compared them to one another, much less compared them to the over 100 billion people who ever lived. We'd have to do that to get a definitive answer. Until then, we will have to agree that we haven't found any definitive matches in the people we have tested (beyond identical twins for some traits), and the likelihood of two (identical twins excepted) individuals sharing the same biometric traits is at least exceedingly rare.

NOTE There have been a few cases where someone's fingerprint was (likely mistakenly) identified as someone else's, as in this murder case from the 1990s: en.wikipedia.org/wiki/Shirley_McKie.

Note that even identical twins, originating from the same single egg and sperm, and sharing the same DNA, have different fingerprints and often varying genetic material. Twins usually have genetic differences and environmental differences that can and do shape some of their biometric traits differently. That's why even most identical twins can be differentiated by humans (and computers), even though they can be very similar looking, especially the older they get. Small genetic differences (which exist 80 percent of the time) can be detected using special tests. Read more on detecting the genetic variations in twins here: www.nytimes.com/2019/03/01/science/twins-dna-crime-paternity.html.

Common Biometric Authentication Factors

Biometric authentication has become popular because our biometric traits are likely unique in the world; change slowly, if at all; and are carried on us all the time without any additional effort. We can't easily lose them like we can a smartcard or USB token. This section explores the most popular biometric traits used in digital authentication systems.

Fingerprints

Fingerprints are created by the naturally existing, uniquely shaped peaks and valleys (officially known as *friction ridges*) on a person's fingers (and hands, feet, and toes, albeit named differently). A person touching nearly every surface that isn't thoroughly aqueous or a gas is leaving behind a fingerprint imprint (at least partial) due to the natural oils (a mixture of water and fatty acids) or dirt located on the fingers or on the surface touched. Flat, solid surfaces are best, although fingerprints are routinely lifted from clothing, rubber, and even powders.

Fingerprints have been used by law enforcement for over a century to identify criminal suspects and for decades to register and document applicants for high-security jobs, security clearances, licenses (e.g., concealed carry gun permits), and today, for passports and visas. Fingerprints were among the first used computer security biometric authentication factors and are the most popular biometric used today. One or more fingers may be measured for potential authentication candidates.

Many vendors have included fingerprint readers and applications with various models of computers and laptops for at least two decades. Some models of mobile phones started offering fingerprint authentication over a decade ago, but it really took off in popularity with Apple's front-located, Touch ID implementation on the iPhone 5s in 2013. Today, many if not most smartphones come with a fingerprint sensor that can be used to unlock them. Many USB-style MFA devices include a fingerprint sensor (as shown in Figure 16.1).

Figure 16.1: Fingerprint reader sensor incorporated on a relatively inexpensive FIDO (Fast ID Online) USB device

Fingerprint reader sensors come in four basic technologies: optical, capacitance, ultrasonic, and thermal. An optical scanner records an image of the fingerprint. Capacitance, ultrasonic, and thermal readers all use their underlying technology (i.e., weak electrical current, high-frequency sound waves, or temperature differences) to identify and map ridges.

NOTE Most fingerprint readers require a person to touch or swipe their fingerprint across a physical surface above a sensor. There is a developing class of touchless fingerprint readers. These readers usually work using lasers, light, ultrasonically, but touchless fingerprint reading can also be done using a digital camera on a cell phone. Touchless fingerprint readers have benefits over the traditional, touch-based sensors. First, because the user is not required to press their finger on a flat surface, the finger isn't unnaturally deformed (called *elastic deformation*) and flattened. Instead, held in the air, the finger retains its more natural 3D shape, which when measured should help cut down on spoofing attacks. Second, because there is no touching of a surface, disease transmission will be near zero as compared to touch-based sensors. For more information on touchless fingerprint readers, see `www.bayometric.com/touch-less-fingerprint-standard-fingerprint-recognition/` and `www.researchgate.net/publication/320077009_Full_3D_Touchless_Fingerprint_Recognition_Sensor_Database_and_Baseline_Performance`.

The peaks and valleys of a fingerprint bounce back minute differences depending on whether the involved signal wave has hit a peak or a valley. Optical readers are considered the older, legacy technology. The newer reader types were created explicitly to defeat spoofed fraudulent fingerprints just printed out as images or placed on flat surfaces, like glass or pictures. The newer *liveness-* or *realness-detection* technologies supposedly work because they require a 3D surface (i.e., the shape of a real fingerprint) and/or something that conducts current back as a real finger would. The idea is that using these newer three technologies should make it harder for hackers to spoof fingerprints. But as you will see, these particular three anti-spoof technologies are not undefeatable.

Fingerprint readers will ultimately record the entire visible fingerprint as a single image, map/trace the ridges and artifacts, or record the main points where the ridges change pattern and other minutiae. In fingerprinting science, there are nine generally recognized patterns known under the general classifications of whorl, loop, and arch. See this article for more details on the different patterns: `legalbeagle.com/7287158-nine-different-types-fingerprints.html`. *Minutiae* is a technical term in fingerprinting referring to artifacts smaller than a ridge with names like ridge ending, bifurcation, island, and bridge.

NOTE Many U.S. and international standards cover fingerprint data formats and interchanging, including the ANSI/INCITS 381-2004 Finger Image-Based Data Interchange Format and the ISO/IEC 19794-4 Finger Image- Based Interchange Format.

Fingers have veins and arteries underneath the skin that can be mapped like fingerprints. Like fingerprints, finger vascular vessel shapes, positions, and patterns are thought to be universally unique per person. Finger vascular vessel biometrics isn't nearly as popular as fingerprints but has some potential advantages. Finger vein scanners use near-infrared light (700–900 nanometers of the electromagnetic spectrum), which the hemoglobin of blood absorbs far more than the other components of the finger, allowing the scanner to get a very accurate picture of the finger's vascular vessels. It is harder for a forger to secretly capture a potential victim's finger vascular vessels because vessel patterns aren't left latently lying around after a person has touched something. To capture them, a forger would have to have the victim inadvertently put their finger in a finger vein reader or steal the data from another system where it was already stored. There's more information on finger vein biometric authentication here: `en.wikipedia.org/wiki/Finger_vein_recognition`.

Hand Geometry

Hand geometry readers measure the outlining shapes and lengths of a candidate's hand, including:

- Hand length and width
- Individual finger length and width
- Individual joint length and width
- Angles and geometric shapes between different fingers, joints, and features

Hand geometry researchers have identified 30 distinct measurements that can be taken and compared to identify a specific hand, and each hand is believed to be unique. Hand geometry is not considered as provable globally unique as compared to fingerprints and other biometric attributes, but I haven't read of a documented exact match yet.

Hand readers usually have small posts that separate the fingers and help place the hand in the right position and orientation. See Figure 16.2 for an example of a popular hand geometry scanner.

Figure 16.2: Popular hand geometry reader example
Source: Z22, used under the Attribution-Share Alike 3.0 Unported license, creativecommons.org/licenses/by-sa/3.0/deed.en

I used a hand geometry reader as part of my employer's computerized time clock system well over two decades ago. My current health-care system uses hand geometry scanners to register and identify ER patients. Hand geometry scanners are often used in conjunction with fingerprint readers (using more than one biometric attribute for authentication at the same time is known as *multimodal*) in order to improve their overall accuracy, and this does indeed seem to be the case in the systems I've been involved with. My current employer, KnowBe4, uses this combination for building entry. We had more false-positives before using multimodal scanners.

For more information on hand geometry scanning, see `cdn.intechopen.com/pdfs/40073/InTech-Basic_principles_and_trends_in_hand_geometry_and_hand_shape_biometrics.pdf`.

Palm vein scanning, using the same technology as finger vascular vessel scanning, is a semi-common biometric solution as well. Palm vein readers have been used in corporate and high-security offices. I've even heard of banking ATM systems using palm veins of their customers as a way to authenticate cash flow card users and even portable user tokens based on palm vein reading. But many of these early, more public, projects eventually went away because of complexity, cost, and disease transmission concerns.

NOTE Microsoft Windows Hello allows palm vein scanning as well: `newatlas.com/windows-10-palm-vein-scan/53344`.

Iris

The iris is the colored part of the eye (see example in Figure 16.3), which is attached to sphincter muscles that control the size of the pupil to regulate how much light enters the internal structures of the eye. The iris's scannable image is composed of the pigment, muscles, fibrous tissue, texture, and blood vessels. This combination is considered highly unique within humans.

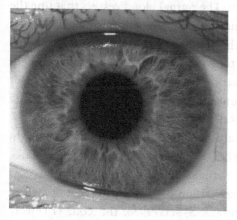

Figure 16.3: Example of an eye iris
Source: `FreeImages.com/Sofi gamache`

Biometric eye readers will read one or both eyes. Iris scanners work using visible light or near-infrared light, with the near-infrared light revealing more detail, especially in (very common) brown-eyed people who typically have less visible distinctions. Iris recognition works even if the candidate is wearing glasses or contacts. Irises usually change very slowly, often over decades. There can be acute iris changes, and a good overview of what they may be due to can be found here: www.aao.org/eye-health/tips-prevention/why-are-my-eyes-changing-color. But in the general population, iris changes are usually almost rare and occur slowly over many years. Most people's irises do not change over their lifetime after the first year of age.

Iris recognition has been used for decades, initially mostly in high-security corporate environments, but it is increasingly used in different nations as part of their border control measures. A good list of major iris recognition projects can be found here: en.wikipedia.org/wiki/Iris_recognition. One major disadvantage to shared iris readers, like most tactile fingerprint readers, is potential disease transmission. No one wants to get "pink eye" from an ill coworker.

Potential iris recognition forgeries are prevented using a variety of methods, including confirming the submitted image is not completely flat, measuring lighting changes to confirm pupil constriction changes, confirming natural eye movement, and other spectral checks.

NOTE   An interesting related story involves one of the most famous faces ever portrayed on the cover of *National Geographic* magazine, that of a 12-year-old Afghan girl. She was photographed 18 years later and iris recognition technologies were used to confirm it was the same individual: www.cl.cam.ac.uk/~jgd1000/afghan.html.

Retina

The retina is the internal rear structure of the eye that converts light into electrochemical neural signals, which then get sent along the optic nerve to the brain. The retinal blood vessels that line the retina create a pattern that is unique and unchanging in humans from birth to death, except in cases of disease and injury. Retinal patterns are considered among the most unique biometric traits possible.

With retinal scans, usually performed across both eyes at the same time, low-energy infrared light is sent through the pupil and bounces off the retina and back to the scanner. The candidate user must stare closely into the retina reader's eyepiece and wait until the scan is confirmed. This usually occurs in a few seconds, but it can take up to 10–15 seconds depending on various factors.

The first commercial retinal scanner was created in 1981 and was quickly adopted by many high-security organizations. The Federal Bureau of Investigation (FBI), Central Intelligence Agency (CIA), National Aeronautics Space Administration (NASA), and the National Security Administration (NSA) were early adopters. I saw my first retinal scanner when visiting Verisign's high-security location, where the Internet's top-level domain (TLD) Dynamic Name System (DNS) servers for the .com TLD were located. The Verisign employee giving me the tour, which included several other high-security protections I had never seen before, had to get his retinas scanned as the last check before we could enter the server room. It was all very impressive at the time. However, in my experience, I haven't seen a company buy a new retinal scanner system in a lot of years—they seem to have plummeted in popularity.

NOTE Other parts of the eyes are also used in biometrics, such as the veins of the sclera, the "whites" of the eyes. You can read more about this type of eye vein scan technology here: en.wikipedia.org/wiki/Eye_vein_verification.

Face

It is often said that, today, in any industrialized country, a person's image is recorded without them being aware at least several times, if not several dozen times, a day by video cameras. Using facial biometric recognition and authentication is becoming very popular, perhaps surpassed only by fingerprint biometrics by sheer number of users and corporate interest.

NOTE There are serious, global, concerns about appropriate use of facial recognition identification. So many law enforcement agencies are starting to use biometrics for identifying wanted people in crowds that much of the world is asking for national or global privacy controls to determine what should or shouldn't be allowed by default.

Facial recognition is built into many modern-day smartphones and operating systems. Apple introduced Face ID (en.wikipedia.org/wiki/Face_ID) facial biometrics in their iPhone X and iPad Pro devices to allow users to unlock their own devices, and many other smartphone providers followed suit.

Microsoft followed by introducing fingerprint and facial recognition biometric authentication for Microsoft Windows with Windows Hello (www.microsoft.com/en-us/windows/windows-hello), and later added palm vein recognition support. Users with the appropriate minimum hardware requirements and Windows 10 can enable it. It has fairly strict requirements for accuracy and security (and anti-spoofing) and is one of the harder systems to hack among the more popular technologies as far as general operating systems and biometrics go. Here's a real-world picture of Microsoft Windows Hello (see Figure 16.4) using facial recognition to log me into my laptop.

NOTE If Microsoft Windows Hello facial recognition doesn't recognize your face, it allows you to log in using another previously registered method, like a PIN. This could be another potential example that could be listed in Chapter 13, "Downgrade/Recovery Attacks." Face biometric recognition consists of image acquisition, algorithmic analysis, storage, and comparison.

The acquisition of the face and its characteristics can be done using regular light, infrared light, skin texture analysis, or thermal imaging. Face ID apparently uses over 30,000 separate points of infrared light to map a face. The image is then analyzed and normalized to identify key features (e.g., mouth, eyes, chin, skin color, teeth, lips) photometrically and geometrically; then these features are stored as data points.

Figure 16.4: Real-world example Microsoft Windows Hello facial recognition screen actively scanning my face during an automated logon at my laptop. You can see the infrared camera at the top of the laptop shining light on my face.

NOTE Infrared light is often used for facial recognition because it works in low lighting conditions and is harder to spoof. Infrared light will not map a 2D picture of a face as a 3D image.

Comparing and identifying faces requires identifying data points on a newly acquired image and comparing it to existing stored images and determining the likelihood that stored data points most accurately match a candidate image. It usually isn't a 100 percent match; it's more like a "preponderance of evidence" wins the day. Although the basic underlying physical features and bone structure of someone's face doesn't change that often, more minor, transient traits in people's faces vary on a day-to-day basis, and certainly more over time. People get new skin blemishes, tans, different hair growths (e.g., hair, eyebrows, mustaches, beards), and weight changes. We have different facial expressions for the situation, and facial traits for a frown are distinctly different than for a big smile. Hairstyles, hats, scarves, and glasses can cover up a lot of our face. And few of us look like our high school yearbook photos. Facial recognition algorithms make a weighted guess about the probability of any two images matching and propose a potential match for the one(s) with the highest probability.

The comparison part can take longer than most other biometric comparison analyses. It's a very complicated analysis, with lots of math involved. If you are interested in learning more about how facial recognition works and its algorithms, check out the broad class of facial recognition algorithms known as *eigenfaces* (en.wikipedia.org/wiki/Eigenface), but there are dozens of different facial recognition algorithms used by various systems. Each algorithm is trying to 1) identify the unique characteristics of every face they capture, 2) store those data points efficiently, and 3) allow comparisons to be made as fast as possible. It's far from an exact science, but they are getting better all the time.

Facial recognition systems tend to work better when looking to authenticate one or a few people to a small selected group of stored images, like might be the case with an individual's cell phone. Broadly used facial recognition/identification, where a single person is being looked for out of a crowd of people or sifting through many stored images, reveals some of the inherent weaknesses of facial identification systems. The average broadly used facial recognition system I've been involved with has a lot of false positives (it wrongly proposes a stored image that is not a correct match with the newly acquired candidate image). Many times, the person the system is proposing as a likely match doesn't look anything like the newly captured image to most people, although usually obvious similar traits exist.

At the same time, a human will likely take far longer if asked to find a single match among thousands or millions of people. Computers can do that sort of rote searching quite quickly (albeit with a lot of false positives). Our human senses seem especially adept at determining true matches between a few candidates if given lots of time, but we cannot make a match of a completely unknown subject in seconds out of millions or billions of possible images the way a computer system might be capable of doing. I've also seen a facial recognition system successfully tell 200 pairs of identical twins apart without a mistake when the human control group had a 5 percent failure rate looking at the same twins. Somehow the computer was able to tell twins apart who looked absolutely identical to people.

The only reason facial recognition hasn't been able to take over the world more completely is it can be fooled many different ways and has a high false positive rate when used with large datasets. Most broadly used facial recognition systems rely on a human to review and approve their final recommendation(s) to confirm a match. No facial recognition system I've seen, so far, is accurate enough to confirm matches on their own across a broad population.

Long used for biometric applications, facial recognition for purely identifying people has become a popular use worldwide for nation-states and law enforcement. They have cameras scanning public places and events looking for wanted people. One U.S. company, Clearview AI (`clearview.ai`), claims to have over 3 billion face images alone (much of it purportedly taken without explicit permission from Facebook and other social media sites). More than 22,000 organizations in over 27 countries have accounts with Clearview (`en.wikipedia.org/wiki/Clearview_AI`). That's one company and its customers—and there are hundreds of facial recognition companies.

Voice

A growing biometric field is voice analysis. Voice biometric systems analyze a person's speech to identify everything that makes up verbal language, including frequency, pitch, cadence, words used, dialects, and so forth. Identifying a particular, expected person (I'm Roger and this is Roger speaking), also known as *speaker recognition*, has a higher success rate than when randomly trying to identify unknown people out of a huge possible population of potential candidates (just like facial recognition).

Confirming that a candidate is a particular, expected person is being used by many companies to confirm whether a person who is calling in for support help really is the person calling. There is a huge industry offering voice identification solutions to save time by not requiring technical support folks to have to additionally verify a person's identity before offering help. Normally, the first factor in the voice identity is the phone number the person is calling in from, followed by a second verification done using the person's voice. If both match what is already stored on the system, the person calling in may be considered automatically validated before they reach a tech support person. I have not personally seen voice recognition used inside companies for network logons or building entry, although Hollywood seems to think it's often used at super-secret organizations.

In my personal experience, I've seen many voice identification systems correctly validate me and not accept other people pretending to be me in vendor tests at conferences and presentations. I've even witnessed tests where a person's voice was recorded and then played back in an attempt to fool voice-recognition systems without success. Hacker tools are available that will take a recorded person's speech and turn it into future, custom selected sentences or words that the person never said. Demonstrations using these tools and methods are pretty fun to watch being done. Still, in the tests where I've been physically present, even these hacker tools failed to fool the involved voice-recognition systems. But these tests were limited, in time, resources, and quality. The vendors of voice-recognition systems often indicate that if an attacker has enough time and effort, they can probably fool their systems. That's why voice-recognition systems are usually paired with another factor.

NOTE Here's an example of an open source tool anyone can use to try to fool voice recognition: github.com/CorentinJ/Real-Time-Voice-Cloning. Lyrebird AI is a commercial tool: www.descript.com/lyrebird-ai. A sample video of Lyrebird AI being used to create a fake President Barack Obama's voice is here: www.youtube.com/watch?v=YfU_sWHT8mo. To me, the fake audio of the president still sounds strange. Faking voices is not yet perfected, but that will likely change over time. Many experts expect fake audio in the future to be so good that neither humans nor computers will be able to readily tell the difference.

There are many other biometric factors that various vendors and researchers have implemented or tried to implement. Most do not become widespread because they are not as guaranteed to be universally unique, are too hard to measure, vary too widely in between measurements, or are too costly. As you'll recall from Chapter 4, "Usability vs. Security," the world is not waiting for a better new biometric solution. We have plenty already. We just need more accurate solutions with the least amount of user friction. In any case, from a purely security view, any biometric when paired with another factor (biometric or not) is widely seen as more secure than using a 1FA biometric factor as a sole authentication factor.

NOTE One of the broadest biometric projects is the idea of a biometric passport (en.wikipedia.org/wiki/Biometric_passport). The concept is that a person's biometric attributes be securely stored on a chip that is embedded in their passport and that biometric information can be pulled up by passport officers and compared to currently measured biometric traits to confirm a person's identity. Various nations have implemented it at different levels of participation.

How Biometrics Work

Each biometric system has its own strengths and weaknesses, but most work across a general, common set of phases (as graphically represented in Figure 16.5). I'll cover each step in more detail in the following sections.

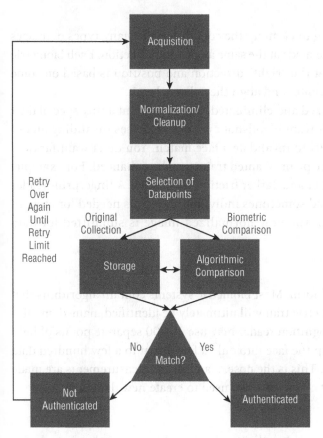

Figure 16.5: Graphical representation of the biometric authentication process

Acquisition

Collection of the biometric trait starts the process. If it is the first time someone is being registered to a system for future use, it is part of the enrollment process. Or it can be collected to compare the current subject against previously stored images as a part of identification or authentication. The collection can be *unimodal* (one biometric trait collected or using only one sensor) or multimodal (multiple sensors and/or multiple types of biometric traits collected together at once). The user involved may or may not know that the biometric trait is being collected or be asked to give permission, such as when a crowd of people walk past a facial identification camera set up in a public area.

> **NOTE** The National Institute for Standards and Technology (NIST) has a document dedicated to the collection of biometric traits: NIST Special Publication 800-76-2 (`csrc.nist.gov/publications/detail/sp/800-76/2/final`).

Normalization/Cleanup

Every collection event includes preprocessing to clean up the collected trait. Many types of images are "right-aligned" so that comparisons can be made at the same angles and direction. Each biometric system has its own way of determining what the "right" direction and position is based on some biometric trait characteristic that is used to center and align the collected trait.

Unwanted noise and artifacts are recognized and eliminated. You don't want a tiny spec of dust invalidating an entire fingerprint. You don't want bloodshot eyes or eyeglasses invaliding an eye print. You don't want a fallen-down hair curl to invalidate a face match. You don't want faraway background noise or cold invalidating a voice print. Wanted traits may be enhanced. For example, a submitted fingerprint image often has lighter and darker friction ridge lines. A fingerprint reader will lighten and darken the overall image and sometimes individual ridges as needed for more of the fingerprint detail to be distinct. Then, the now normalized image is submitted for data collection.

Selection of Data Points

All biometric traits are converted into digital form. Most biometric systems contain algorithms that determine which parts of the submitted biometric trait will ultimately be identified, named, manipulated, and stored. For example, a facial recognition reader may use 30,000 separate points of light to capture a face, but the algorithm breaks up the face into only a few dozen to a few hundred data points. These are the eyes. These are the lips. This is the nose. . .and so on. Measurements are made on the individual parts and between the parts. Math is often used to create new data points.

Storage

The biometric images and data points are stored locally in a database located on the same device on which the biometric measurement is made and/or in a remote location. To increase comparison speed, commonly accessed data points may be uploaded to each remote device or local memory for faster local processing. Wherever the storage is, it needs to be securely stored on disk, in memory, and during transmission.

Comparison

When requested, comparisons are made between the newly acquired traits and the stored biometric traits. Comparisons are done during initial enrollment, to make sure the new acquisition doesn't match an existing stored, different subject, and during subsequent authentications.

It is almost always done using data analysis and is not a direct comparison of acquired optical images or sound. For example, when two faces are compared it isn't done image to image as a human would analyze it. Instead, it's done using stored data points and measurements of the new candidate image of the same data points. The system will look to find images that agree on more data points than not.

Another good example is fingerprints. The actual fingerprints, even if stored and available for later retrieval, are not used in the comparison. Collected fingerprints are stored as specific points where the friction ridges begin and end, along with identified shapes and artifacts. Stored fingerprints look more like a star constellation (e.g., Orion's belt or the Big Dipper) than a picture of a fingerprint. The more points that are compared and found to be the same, the more accurate the fingerprint match will likely be. Unfortunately, it's not always possible to collect all the points that a fingerprint recognition system would like to collect during each acquisition, because people are always placing differing areas of varying points during each fingerprint submission. That's why many initial fingerprint collections will ask the submitter to press their finger several different times in different ways—to collect as many different data points as they can to better represent the overall fingerprint. A fingerprint collection system is essentially comparing "star constellations" looking for partial overlapping matches where different data points match.

Authentication

If authentication is requested, the system will usually make a determination of whether someone is authenticated based on the preponderance of evidence over the various data points. If successfully authenticated, a person will be allowed to access the protected system or resource. If accessing a digital access control system, as used in an operating system or website, the authenticated user will be assigned an access control token, as you learned in Chapter 6, "Access Control Token Tricks."

Problems with Biometric Authentication

Most of the world has come to believe that biometric authentication is the most accurate authentication method there is. Biometric vendors say their biometric identification systems are accurate to 1:100,000,000 and can't be faked. They sound like that antivirus industry trying to convince us that their products can successfully detect 100 percent of all malware when the thriving malware industry over 30 years old obviously proves otherwise.

And it isn't just security newbies who think biometrics are some dare-to-dream, magic, Holy Grail authentication solution. Many computer security people think that too. I've been in the room of supposed world-renown computer security experts determining the future of online and in-person commerce tell the room making the next international standards how they could not wait for the near-term magic of biometrics to make fraudulent authentication and transactions finally be a thing of the past. They sound like they've been waiting their whole professional careers for biometrics to mature to the point that online and computer crime won't be a problem anymore.

They could not be more wrong! Biometrics are not great authenticators for a variety of reasons, including high false error rates and theft of biometric traits causing irreversible damage. There are other bothersome issues as well. Personally, I'm less impressed with biometrics than most other MFA solution methods. Here's why.

High False Error Rates

Every authentication solution has a certain number of false positives and false negatives. A false positive is an authentication transaction determined to be successful when it should not have been. This is known as a *Type II error* or *false-acceptance rates* (FARs) in the biometric world. A false negative is a legitimate authentication denied that should have been successful. These are known as *Type I errors* or *false rejection rates* (FRRs) in the biometric world.

If you've ever been in a company that uses shared biometric scanners, you can probably relate to the experience of having to wait behind someone (or yourself) as the biometric scanner incorrectly doesn't accept the validly submitted biometric trait over and over. . .until it finally does work as it should have done the first time. If you are in that type of work situation, it happens so often that many of us don't even cognitively notice it anymore. It's just a way of life around shared biometric authentication devices. We are standing around waiting for legitimate people to finally get recognized. It happens to us personally if our cell phone has a fingerprint scanner as we wait and try over and over placing our finger on a phone fingerprint scanner. . .wipe the sensor, wipe your fingertip, and try again, until it finally recognizes us and unlocks.

As sensitivity of a biometric system is tuned up or down, these errors start to increase or decrease, often inversely to each other. There is also the *crossover error rate* (CER), where Type I errors (percentage of) equal Type II errors. Figure 16.6 shows this basic biometric error comparison.

False acceptance rates are clearly dangerous because the system is admitting someone who should not be admitted. That's a safety and security issue. In the password world, it would be like someone submitted the wrong password of froger instead of the correct password of frogger and still the authentication system accepted the incorrect password and authenticated the user. A false rejection in the password world would be like the legitimate user typing in the correct password of frogger and it still did not work.

In the biometric world, it's also not uncommon for a biometric trait being seen as close enough to the legitimate trait that it is accepted (false acceptance). Perhaps a different fingerprint is smeared in a comparison region and the fingerprint reader incorrectly marks it as a friction ridge change or whorl. Or conversely, a legitimate person puts their correct fingerprint on the scanner over and over,

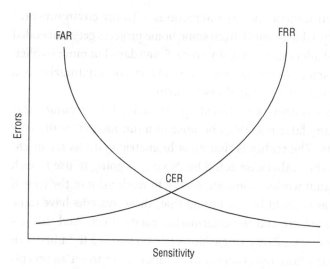

Figure 16.6: Biometric error rate comparison summary

but never completely places the entire needed fingerprint section on the scanner or has some small skin abrasions that the scanner picks up as a new bridge or bifurcation.

Either way, many biometric systems have a higher percentage of both false negatives and false positives as compared to every other sort of non-biometric authentication. This is because of a number of variables, including some we'll look at next.

Natural and Artificial Biometric Variances

The biggest impediment to more accurate biometrics is simply that biometrics are measuring living tissue in a changing world. There isn't a second when our bodies are exactly the same as before. We are constantly replacing and sloughing off old cells for new cells. Our environment is changing us every second. The light, air, and dust we interact with every second is changing us. Quantum mechanics says that billions of particles are entangling with our bodies every second of every day.

NOTE Not to get too astrophysics on you, but there are 65 billion particles called neutrinos passing at the speed of light through every square centimeter of your body every second. Look it up.

Every day our biometric traits are changing in some way. Most of those changes don't show up with enough volume or intermediacy to change our biometrics in a noticeable way that would be detected by most biometric authentication systems. But eventually they do accumulate in enough quantity to make a noticeable change. Our skin ages. We get wrinkles. Our irises and blood vessels change. Our eyes change color. One day I didn't have noticeable varicose veins and then one day I did. Our voices change. I distinctly remember my voice noticeably changing in just a few days as I entered puberty. My face is notably plumper than it was in high school. I've become far more gray-haired over time.

Day-to-day changes occur due to my environment and my interactions with my environment. I get abrasions on my face and hands. I get dirty. Glue or caulk from some home projects gets embedded on my fingers. I get cuts and scars. Colds and allergies change my voice. Some days I'm more swollen than others. On cold days my skin is contracted. Every day the friction ridges on my fingers are a slightly different size and have slightly different dirt and artifacts in them.

If face, hand, or fingerprint authentication systems were tuned up too high where accuracy was everything, it would end up causing too many false rejections because of minutiae that really isn't due to different faces, hands, or fingerprints. The reality is that most biometric systems are intentionally "de-tuned" to be less accurate than they otherwise could be. No one is going to use iTouch to unlock their cell phone if it fails more than it works. Nope, we want it to work most of the time if not every time, even if it is not as accurate as it could be. And to do that, these systems have to be far less accurate than the sensors and software are and the information they collect. And this de-tuning increases the risk of false acceptance errors. Every single biometric system is a fight between too many false acceptance errors and too many false rejection errors. Vendors have to set an acceptable level of both that most of their customers will accept. Too many errors in either direction and potential customers are using someone else's product that gets the ratio right (for the customer).

Missing Biometric Traits

Not everyone has the biometric traits being measured. Our world is full of people missing digits, hands, and eyes. Eight in every 10,000 people are born mute. Many people have glass eyes and more are blind. Millions of people have eye injuries and diseases that change their eyeball physiology significantly in short periods of time. People with adermatoglyphia have no fingerprints. I have musician friends who have played guitars long enough that they have no fingerprints on the main pads of their fingers. I had a friend who worked in a factory making sandpaper for a living. His hands were permanently stained and looked dirty; he had to dip his hands into acid before his vacation days to make them look clean, and this process removed his fingerprints. Some criminals intentionally modify their fingerprints (see an example: en.wikipedia.org/wiki/Fingerprint#/media/File:Altered_Fingerprints_of_Alvin_Karpis.jpg) or get face-altering plastic surgery.

Many times for reasons that cannot be easily explained, some people simply cannot not be validated day-to-day using the same biometric trait as everyone else in the organization. Anyone who has administered a large biometric network for a living will tell you there are some people who cannot use the selected biometric system day-to-day for one reason or another, often unknown. I knew a woman whose fingerprints would not authenticate a second time no matter when the fingerprints were taken, be it a day or just minutes later. Everyone involved looked at her fingerprints and they seemed to us to be as normal as any we had ever seen. She didn't shake or move her fingers strangely when placing them on the fingerprint reader. There were no obvious defects or dirt. She just could not successfully use our fingerprint authentication system, and she was as frustrated as we were. I've heard of similar measurement issues from other biometric system administrators. That doesn't happen with passwords, USB tokens, or most of the other MFA solution methods.

Easy to Bypass Using Fake Traits

There isn't a biometric system that can't be faked. Some are harder to fake than others, but they all can be bypassed using faked, simulated biometric traits. If someone is telling you that a biometric system can't be faked, then they are trying to sell you it. There's often some 16-year-old kid on YouTube showing he can fake it using $2 worth of materials. More on this in the example attacks later.

Theft Causes Irreversible Damage

The majority of our most commonly used biometrics are easily spread everywhere we've traveled and/or aren't particularly difficult for someone to get if they really want them. Our fingerprints and DNA are everywhere, even on our trash. Anyone can call us and record our voice. Our hand geometry isn't a state secret. Getting our eye biometric data might be a bit more difficult, but a determined social engineer with the right equipment could offer a free glaucoma or premature retina detachment test, or simply break into your eye doctor's office to steal any recorded eye scans. With enough physical access, an adversary could secret a "skimming" device at any legitimate biometric reader to record submitted biometric traits just like gasoline pump/ATM skimmer criminals capture credit card details. Capturing internal blood vessels with enough accuracy to be useful might be the exception, although it probably wouldn't be that hard to trick anyone into submitting to a rogue biometric reading to get the needed biometric trait either.

Far more common are the wholesale thefts of entire biometric databases (several examples covered in a moment) used by vendors and customers. And once your biometric trait is stolen, how can any system that relies on that trait ever be assured that it really is you trying to log in? For example, if someone steals your fingerprints (it happens), how can any system that uses fingerprints for authentication truly be assured that a submitted fingerprint is really you? Theft of biometric traits is irreversible damage and is likely to become far more common as the use of biometrics increases. There is a chance one day that a few big biometric database breaches could reveal everyone's biometric traits, and what do we do then?

Compare that to non-biometric authentication factors like passwords or tokens, where all we need to do to replace a stolen one is disable the old one and enable a new one. Very easy to do. We do it all the time. The damage due to theft is not permanent, unless that theft led to your biometric traits being stolen.

How to Compare Biometric Error Rates

Biometric error rates are essentially a fight between sensitivity to differences. As sensitivity is increased, false rejection errors go up. As sensitivity is decreased, false acceptance errors go up. Each biometric solution has its own error rates. What works in one environment may not work in another. For example, a high-security military system would tolerate far more false rejections than the average corporation or cell phone user. False acceptance errors at a top-secret military installation incur too much risk. But most corporations and general consumer devices (e.g., phones and laptops) would rather have low rates of false rejections.

The crossover error rate, where false acceptance errors and false rejection errors equal each other, gives you a bit of insight into how any particular biometric solution is configured as far as errors versus sensitivity is concerned. When comparing biometric systems, look at all the error rates, but for super quick comparisons you can use the CER alone. It allows apples-to-oranges comparisons about where the sensitivity settings begin to equal out error-wise. Be aware that many biometric vendors, like car manufacturers trying to promote overly optimistic average gas mileage ratings, tend to post error rates that aren't nearly as small when tested in the average, real, environment. I've yet to meet the biometric solution that was truly as accurate as it claimed. Try before you buy, so to speak.

There are, for sure, biometric systems with a low number of errors. Most are more expensive, slower, and only able to be used in a limited number of high-security scenarios where the cost is worth the decrease in errors. The vast majority of biometric systems are cheap and high in errors, and knowingly so. It's not known to the customers and users, but it's known to the vendors and to people who evaluate biometric systems for a living. For example, the vendors that make fingerprint and facial recognition scanners for cell phones know they have very high rates of false acceptance. Their customers would not have it any other way.

NOTE Microsoft Windows Hello is known for its relatively low error rates, especially for the price range and general use of it. You can read about its required error rates at these sites: `docs.microsoft.com/en-us/windows-hardware/design/device-experiences/windows-hello-face-authentication` and `docs.microsoft.com/en-us/windows-hardware/design/device-experiences/windows-hello-biometric-requirements`. But even it has errors. I have several friends who get routinely false-negatively rejected and we don't know why.

Most customers would not even put up with very accurate, low-error, biometric solutions because of the cost and slower processing time. I've been around more accurate biometric systems used at high-security organizations. When using fingerprint or eyeball readers, users have to stop, slow down, and let the reader spend 3 to 15 seconds to complete its scan and make a decision. This may not sound like a lot of time, but it is too much time for most scenarios. Imagine if you had to wait still and calmly for 10 seconds to pass to enter your building or unlock your phone, while a line of other people around you are waiting as well. Most users, as described in Chapter 4, are fine with faster approval and just okay security.

Privacy Issues

Privacy issues surrounding biometrics is a big deal. People are worried about the increasing number of companies and databases that have their biometric traits and for what reason they are being stored and used. A large percentage of people would probably not agree to having their pictures scraped from their social media accounts and used by a biometric vendor for identification purposes (at least without their explicit permission). A large majority of the population does not want mass government/nation-state surveillance. They worry about their biometrics being used against them in some harmful way. Many people are worried that their DNA may be used by health insurance companies to charge them higher rates due to preexisting conditions or genetic anomalies that may make them at higher risk of critical conditions.

The overall problem is that our biometric data is being used by many companies for many reasons for which we did not give our explicit permission. And that data can be stolen from any of those companies and used in further unauthorized ways or even to fraudulently authenticate as us to a system we belong to.

NOTE As an example, there is strong blowback on law enforcement, which has been using large DNA databases to solve hundreds of old, previously unsolved, murders. Some DNA services have begun to deny the ability of law enforcement to use their services because of privacy invasion concerns of their customers.

Disease Transmission

Lastly, shared biometric readers that require physical touching using a common device (e.g., fingerprint readers, handprints, hand geometry, finger vessel scanners, eyeball readers) can easily spread disease. Even if a company offers disinfectant solutions or wipes for users to avail themselves of, there is absolutely no assurance those quick remedies actually work. Any discussion from health-care officials on preventing the transmission of diseases between people recommend copious amounts of disinfectants and handwashing over a minute or longer period of time—certainly more than just a quick, simple application of a gel or wipes. Not to mention airborne diseases that will collect in common waiting areas where shared biometric devices are forced to be used.

Taken as a whole, biometrics aren't the perfect or perfectly accurate authentication solutions that many people make them out to be. This is not to say that they can't be used or aren't a good solution in many application scenarios. People just shouldn't think they are highly accurate and without flaws. If you use biometrics, you should do so with a clear idea of their strengths and weaknesses.

Example Biometric Attacks

Let's look at some example attacks against biometric authentication.

Fingerprint Attacks

There are probably more successful attacks against fingerprint biometrics than any other biometric attack. That should not be surprising, since fingerprint biometrics are the most popular type of biometric authentication and have been around longer than any other method. Here's a good sampling of real-world attacks.

Stolen Biometrics

If an attacker can steal a whole bunch of biometrics at once, what can a victim impacted by the incident do? Their biometric traits are now out and controlled by an unauthorized party and available for reuse and duplication at any time.

OPM Fingerprint Theft The biggest known biometric trait theft was the 2014–2015 theft of 5.6 million people's fingerprints (`en.wikipedia.org/wiki/Office_of_Personnel_Management_data_ breach`). Everyone who had ever applied for a U.S. government security clearance and had submitted fingerprints (all 10 digits in most cases) were victims of a nation-state attack against the Office of Personnel Management (OPM). Even the fingerprints of our secret spies, now living under different assumed names, were taken. My fingerprints from an application for U.S. government work security clearance 15 years ago were involved. My wife's fingerprints from her work at a local shipyard in the 1980s as a teenager were taken. The fingerprints were among a total of nearly 22 million records stolen, including detailed personal background data of every government applicant (e.g., previous employers, family member information, relatives, addresses, travel, drug use, psychological issues)— all the information any good social engineer would love to have.

The theft was traced to China. Eventually, some arrests were made and some of the key perpetrators were identified. Years later, all the records were returned at the request of President Obama by agreement of Chinese President Xi Jinping, but there are no assurances that no copies were made. If I was a nation-state, I'd make a copy before "handing" back.

Suprema BioStar 2 Theft BioStar 2 is a fingerprint and facial recognition biometric security platform made by a company called Suprema. It allows admins to control secure access to facility areas and user permissions. In August 2019, security researchers announced (`www.vpnmentor.com/blog/ report-biostar2-leak`) that BioStar's biometric database could be breached, potentially exposing over 1 million users' fingerprints, facial recognition information, and passwords. The security researchers said Suprema was generally unresponsive and unhelpful to their report, although the reported breach hole was closed a week later. The question is, did anyone else discover the breach hole before it was discovered by the researchers and closed?

Fake Fingers

Making fake fingers and fingerprint images may seem like the stuff of spy movies, but you really can create fake fingers and fingerprints that fool fingerprint readers. I've done it. You can do it. Here are some examples.

Play-Doh Fingers This is a great example (`www2.washjeff.edu/users/ahollandminkley/ biometric/index.html`) of how easy it is to use common household materials to make successful fake fingerprints. Several teams tried various materials against two popular fingerprint readers. One team had good success against one of the scanners using soft wax that was then stiffened by putting in a refrigerator. The wax failed on the second scanner. But Play-Doh molding clay worked on the second scanner (you can see a video of one of the successes here: `www2.washjeff.edu/users/`

aholländminkley/biometric/MVI_4421.avi), but wouldn't work on the first scanner. I like this example because it is similar to what I have experienced in my biometric testing. Not all techniques work on all scanners, but all scanners can be faked out one way or another. And sometimes it only takes $12.82 worth of glue, gummy bears, wax, and Play-Doh.

Defeating Apple iTouch with Gelatin Fingers In this example (www.iphoneincanada.ca/news/touch-id-bypassed-fingerprint-gelatin-finger), white-hat hackers successfully hacked Apple's iTouch fingerprint scanner using a fingerprint image imprinted on plastic backed by smeared glue to give it texture. A second hacker did it using common food gelatin. A video of the former method is shown here: www.youtube.com/watch?v=HM8b8d8kSNQ. Here's a second video successfully hacking Apple's iTouch using another method: www.youtube.com/watch?v=2u4ZLGswlzo.

Tencent Fingerprint Hack At Tencent, a large Chinese security company, researchers used fingerprints printed on glass (www.tomsguide.com/news/hackers-unlock-any-phone-using-photographed-fingerprints-in-just-20-minutes) to fool supposedly every phone fingerprint reader they tried, using materials that cost $140. They demo'd their technique at a Chinese computer security conference. They asked a member of the audience to bring up his phone, they took a picture of his fingerprint, and in under 20 minutes they had hacked into his phone.

> **NOTE** Of course, sometimes all it takes to defeat fingerprint sensors is the wrong type of screen protector: www.theverge.com/2019/10/23/20929178/samsung-galaxy-s10-note-1o-fingerprint-recognition-issue-patch-ultrasonic-sensor.

Using 3D Printers to Create Fake Fingerprints This is probably the best overall example (blog.talosintelligence.com/2020/04/fingerprint-research.html) of the bunch. It's a great resource on fingerprint readers, fingerprint collection, and how to create great fake fingerprints. In this case, they used a sculptor's clay known as Plasticine, silicone, glue, conductive powders, and 3D printers, depending on the sensor type they wanted to fool. The conductive powders (aluminum and graphite) were needed to provide more lifelike feedback to the fingerprint readers that could not be fooled by simple, nonconductive, fake fingerprints. They established that all three types of fingerprint readers (capacitive, optical, and ultrasonic) could be fooled, although it often took different methods to do so. Ultimately the researchers concluded that ". . .there is a lack of a clear advantage between the different types of sensors."

They tried to fool lots of different devices and systems, with mixed success. They were able to fool phones fairly regularly but not a Samsung A70 device (which had a high false rejection rate with real fingerprints as well). They had no success against Microsoft's Windows Hello on multiple devices either, but they did against a MacBook Pro. They successfully broke into a biometric-protected padlock but were not successful against two-tested biometrically protected USB encrypted drives.

NOTE Make authentication too hard and criminals may just cut off your finger: `news.bbc` `.co.uk/2/hi/asia-pacific/4396831.stm`. Bet that guy wishes he never bought a car with fingerprint biometric protection.

Hand Vein Attack

In December 2018, some members of the infamous European-based Chaos Computer Club (CCC) faked out hand vein recognition (`motherboard.vice.com/en_us/article/59v8dk/hackers-fake-hand-` `vein-authentication-biometrics-chaos-communication-congress`). It wasn't easy. It took over 30 days of effort, but by the end they were routinely fooling the vein scanners by using vein-shaped lines printed on a hand-shaped flat surface covered in wax.

NOTE CCC members also made news in 2014 when they claimed they had successfully cloned a German politician's fingerprint from a conference using a regular camera: `www.bbc.com/news/` `technology-30623611`.

Eye Biometric Spoof Attacks

Eyes can be spoofed to biometric readers like any other biometric trait. In particular, iris spoofing is a common area of research for scientists and researchers around the world. Iris spoofing attacks (known as *presentation attacks* in the biometric world) usually involve reprinted images of irises, replayed video of irises, or textured contact lenses. The latter method has the best spoofing ability.

Unfortunately, there aren't a lot of YouTube videos showing spoofing attacks against eyeballs, irises, or retinas, because these attack demonstrations are more expensive and difficult to pull off than the average computer security geek can do. That doesn't mean eye biometric spoofing can't be done. In fact, it's proven that it can be done. It's a huge worry for the vendors that make eye biometric devices and the high-security customers who rely on them. So, the research and demos of eye biometric spoofing attacks tends to be done behind closed doors by university PhDs. But researchers around the world are trying their best to both hack and defend eye biometric solutions.

There are even international competitions to both defeat and defend against iris spoofing attacks. The LivDet – Liveness Detection Competition Series (`livdet.org`) is held every two years around the world. In 2017, the "winner" of LivDet was able to successfully get 15 percent of his spoofed irises, using specially created contact lenses, past the involved iris recognition scanners. This is against the best anti-spoofing, state-of-the-art technology in the world.

One researcher who is part of the competition, Daksha Yadav, has written extensively on the accuracy to detect and ability to spoof eye biometric systems. Here is a presentation from a group of researchers that includes Yadav: `www.youtube.com/watch?v=HSHg-IXIxpg`. You can read more of his multiple individual papers on the subject here: (www.researchgate.net/scientific-contributions/2059653303_ Daksha_Yadav) or download one of his relevant papers here: www.researchgate.net/publication/ 326915028_Fusion_of_Handcrafted_and_Deep_Learning_Features_for_Large-Scale_Multiple_Iris_ Presentation_Attack_Detection/download. If you spend just a little time researching eye and iris presentation attacks, you'll see that there are plenty of them and that lots of researchers are having great success performing them and stymieing the others (and themselves) who try to prevent them.

Facial Recognition Attacks

Next we'll look at some example facial recognition spoof attacks.

Spoofing Windows Hello

As stated earlier, Microsoft Windows Hello is one of the more difficult general public fingerprint and facial recognition technologies to fool, and this is still true. That doesn't mean it can't be hacked. At the end of 2017, some German hackers (www.syss.de/pentest-blog/2017/syss-2017-027- biometricks-bypassing-an-enterprise-grade-biometric-face-authentication-system/; although the article starts out in German, there is an English version that follows) found out they could take a picture of someone using a near-infrared camera and then place that 1D image in front of Windows Hello, and it would accept it. You can see a video of how they did it here: www.youtube.com/ watch?v=Qq8WqLxSkGs&feature=youtu.be. More details can be found here as well: seclists.org/ fulldisclosure/2017/Dec/77.

Part of the reason it worked is because Microsoft did not enable the enhanced anti-spoofing feature by default in Windows Hello. So, what is "enhanced anti-spoofing" and why doesn't Microsoft enable it by default? I could not find exact details of the Microsoft requirements for a biometric device to be branded as supporting Windows Hello enhanced anti-spoofing, but there are differences between the facial recognition cameras that claim they support enhanced anti-spoofing and those that do not. The best I can tell is that cameras supporting enhanced anti-spoofing support more pixels of infrared resolution and try their best to determine the difference between a fake spoofed face (2D images— pictures and videos and 3D masks and objects) and real faces—liveness detection. Hardware and software with enhanced anti-spoofing capabilities likely do this by a combination of one or more of the following:

- Checks to ensure submitted image is 3D and real by checking for depth, lighting, and texture differences. Paper and masks are likely to be far more uniform across all these checks.
- Checks to see if eyes are moving
- Checks to see if head is moving
- Checks to see if the area around the face is distinctly different (i.e., not just a picture of a face held up on a piece of paper)

For more information on facial anti-spoofing checks, see `ynd-consult.com/blog/anti-spoofing-mechanisms-in-face-recognition-based-on-dnn` and `towardsdatascience.com/anti-spoofing-techniques-for-face-recognition-solutions-4257c5b1dfc9`.

Window Hello with enhanced anti-spoofing can be enabled if you have a version of Windows 10 or newer that supports the feature as well as a facial recognition camera that supports enhanced anti-spoofing, and you have enabled the enhanced anti-spoofing feature (it is not enabled by default). To enable it in Windows 10 (assuming you have supporting software and hardware), open the local Group Policy Editor (`gpedit.msc`) and navigate to:

```
Computer Configuration\Administrative Templates\Windows Components\Biometrics\
Facial Features
```

Then enable the Configure Enhanced Anti-Spoofing setting. Figure 16.7 shows the Enhanced Anti-Spoofing Group Policy key.

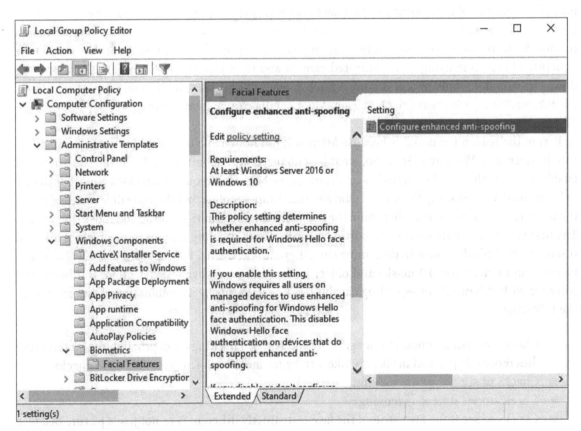

Figure 16.7: Microsoft's Enhanced Anti-Spoofing Group Policy key

Why doesn't Microsoft enable enhanced anti-spoofing by default? The answer is probably twofold. One, they don't know for sure that your hardware supports it, although they likely could require vendors to include a way to verify it using an API if they really wanted to. Second, and probably more importantly, enabling enhanced anti-spoofing probably causes high false rejection rates and slower acceptance. That's the double-edged sword with all biometrics. As you decrease false acceptance rates, you unavoidably cause higher false rejection rates and slower processing. I've yet to meet a biometric vendor that did not struggle with this issue. Companies using Windows Hello with facial recognition should probably enable enhanced anti-spoofing. Those of us at home are probably fine without it.

Faking Out Apple's Face ID

In 2017, a Vietnamese security company printed out and pasted 2D face images on 3D masks and fooled Apple's Face ID on iPhone X: nakedsecurity.sophos.com/2017/11/16/apples-face-id-security-fooled-by-simple-face-mask/. There is a long, nearly 52-minute video of the spoofing if you want to watch it: www.youtube.com/watch?v=B8FL1Ovqt8I&feature=youtu.be. Start at the 8:30 minute mark if you just want to see it in action. Some other hackers did it using pictures of eyes taped over eyeglasses here: www.forbes.com/sites/daveywinder/2019/08/10/apples-iphone-faceid-hacked-in-less-than-120-seconds.

Here's a video of a 3D-printed head fooling lots of different cell phones, but not Apple's iPhone: www.youtube.com/watch?v=ZwCNG9KFdXs.

Twins Fooling Apple's Face ID

If you want to see a set of identical twins fool Face ID, see (NSFW because of crude language): www.youtube.com/watch?v=GFtOaupYxq4. They aren't even the most perfect-looking set of identical twins I can imagine. They have different artifacts on their faces and don't look, to me, 100 percent perfect clones of each other. So, why did it work? Likely Apple allowed the false-acceptance error rate of Face ID to be higher than Windows Hello so that more legitimate users were able to quickly log on using Face ID than if they set it less high.

Conversely, I've seen Microsoft's Windows Hello not be faked out by dozens of very near perfect sets of identical twins. Here's a video of a twin test against Windows Hello: www.youtube.com/watch?v=J1NL246P9Vg. Windows Hello didn't fail.

Spoofing 42 Smartphones

In January 2019, Dutch researchers tried spoofing 110 different smartphones by holding up a simple 2D face picture. It worked on 42 of the phones, although not the Apple iTouch: www.zdnet.com/article/facial-recognition-doesnt-work-as-intended-on-42-of-110-tested-smartphones.

Tech editor Corey Nachreiner did a test spoofing Android's 2D Trusted Face biometrics: www.youtube.com/watch?v=_L_UFY3Bg74. He placed his wife's low-resolution picture on a high-quality laptop screen image, and it was good enough to fool the Android facial recognition check. By the end of 2019, Google stopped including Trusted Face as a default feature, according to this article (www.androidpolice.com/2019/09/04/trusted-face-smart-unlock-method-has-been-removed-from-android-devices) and intends to build a more reliable facial recognition feature closer to Apple's Face ID.

To summarize all these different types of biometric attacks: there are lot of them and they are hard to stop. Biometric vendors are improving their ability to prevent spoofing attacks, but it is a constant war between the good and the bad trying to get around their biometric solutions. So far, no one has ever invented a biometric device that could not be fooled, and there probably will never be such a device.

Defenses Against Biometric Attacks

This section explores developer and user defenses to mitigate attacks against biometrics.

Developer Defenses Against Biometric Attacks

First, we'll look at some developer defenses against biometric attacks.

Education

Developers must be educated to understand all the threats to each type of biometric solution they are developing and how to mitigate those threats. Developers must threat-model their solution and use security development lifecycle (SDL) programming techniques to lower potential vulnerabilities and errors.

Strive for Lower Error Rates

It goes without saying that developers should strive for lower error rates. Microsoft Windows Hello proved that relatively low error rates could be required and implemented without upsetting the customer too much. Apple's Face ID used to be very hackable, and now it is less so. The conventional wisdom that high error rates must be acceptable on general use devices to make customers happy is being disproven every day. All developers should strive to lower error rates whenever possible.

Implement Anti-Spoofing Measures

Implement the strongest anti-spoofing, liveness-detection technology you can. What that means depends on the biometric technology used, but in general it means recognizing and discounting the very simple presentation attack methods and ensuring that the submitted sample comes from a live person.

Bayometric has a great article on liveness detection regarding fingerprint scans here (www.bayometric.com/spoofing-fingerprint-scanner-and-spoof-detection/) and here (www.bayometric.com/liveness-detection-anti-spoofing-challenges). They are using a variety of methods to try to prevent spoofed fingerprints. One way is using a light embedded in the fingerprint sensor to sense whether various common, inorganic spoofing materials are being used. Another is to take very fast sensor readings of the submitted fingertip and compare them to see how much "ridge distortion" there is. Supposedly real fingers have more distortion. They look for perspiration. Apparently spoofed fingerprints show more uniformity than non-spoofed fingerprints. They do other things, such as looking for signs of artificial artifacts (such as air bubbles in glue) and confirming the presence of a pulse. A lot of research is going on in anti-spoofing technologies, and these technologies are getting better all the time.

But no matter what anti-spoofing, liveness-detection techniques are used, they can *always* be hacked around. There is no unhackable technology. But by keeping up with the latest technology with the best anti-spoofing methods, you can cut down on easy spoofing. Security is not binary. Don't let the goal of perfect be the enemy against doing anything.

Limit Number of Attempts

Most of the hackers in the attack demos talk about how many times the biometric device spoof attempt failed over and over between successful attempts. Limiting the number of failed attempts before a successful authentication is a good way to reduce spoofing success. Treat biometric attempts like a password and enable account lockout. On a related note, extend wait times between failed attempts so that each failed attempt begins to exert more of a cost on the hacker. Don't just let them try over and over really fast until they are eventually successful.

Require MFA with Biometrics

Biometric authentication should always be paired with a second, non-biometric factor. The whole reason most of the world is going to MFA is because it requires two or more factors and makes it harder for a hacker to be successful against a potential victim. Biometrics should not change that. 1FA solutions are usually weak solutions. Biometrics don't change that and, in some cases, are weaker than simple passwords.

Securely Protect Biometric Trait Databases

All developers need to ensure that their biometric trait databases, wherever they are, are strongly secure. They need to be secured with least privilege permissions and encrypted. For example, Windows Hello uses secure symmetric and asymmetric ciphers and protects the most critical keys with an additional private key stored on a Trusted Platform Module (TPM) chip on the motherboard and an OS protected by Unified Extensible Firmware Secure Boot. It's a pretty great combination.

Fairly secure storage can be done even without encryption and special encryption chips if the stored biometric factors are obscured enough to be unrecognizable and unusable outside the system from which it was stolen. For example, I've heard of biometric systems where the data—say, fingerprints, iris patterns, or hand vein data—is converted into a digital matrix that is unusable and unrecognizable outside of the system. As stated earlier, most pattern-recognition systems convert the images they see to inflection points, sort of like star constellations, and it is those "star constellations" that are stored and not the actual images. Going one step further, those star constellations can be mapped to a matrix grid, which is then converted to numbers or coordinates. As a simple example, let's say my right pointer finger maps to 32,AB, 56,7F,01,45,43,20,02,66,67,AF. Any subsequent fingerprint submitted for matching would also be converted to the star constellation and then converted to the matching numbers. Perhaps, as a further security step, those numbers were then hashed. Just to continue our example, the hash outcome might be, say, A52BBB17F189943F34066A. And the only value that would need to be stored for future comparison is the hash.

An attacker compromising the biometric attribute database and stealing the only information available, the hash, would have no clue as to the original fingerprint that created the star constellation that in turn created the matrix coordinates and produced a single hash. As long as the biometric developer is using a good hash with enough inputted data points, an attacker would have a difficult time figuring out the original fingerprint. The data (i.e., the hash result) they could steal would be essentially useless to them, even within the system they stole it from unless they were able to insert themselves where the final step, hash comparison, was made. I love this sort of protection and wished more biometric vendors implemented protections like it.

User/Admin Defenses Against Biometric Attacks

There are not many defenses that end users can employ against biometric attacks other than to possibly be extremely paranoid and not to leave your DNA and fingerprints hanging all around all over the place where someone can steal it. I'm not a person who likes to live in fear, and so I'm not going to recommend that people go around wiping their fingerprints off everything they touch. Here are some other recommendations.

Education

Instead, users and admins just need to be aware that biometrics can be hacked and stolen. Biometrics can be good, but they aren't perfect. Simply understanding the strengths and weaknesses of biometric authentication is a big part of the battle. So many people are running around this world thinking that biometrics can't be hacked, and that's dangerous thinking. If you believe biometrics can't be hacked, you're more likely to let your guard down and be open to risks that you would otherwise avoid. So, start and finish with good security awareness training that teaches the strengths and weaknesses of any biometric authentication solution you have or plan to deploy.

Require MFA with Biometrics

If you use biometrics for authentication, they need to be in an MFA solution that is paired with a non-biometric factor for best security. Don't buy or use 1FA biometric solutions to protect your valuable data. Out of all of the recommendations I make in this book, this is the one most likely to be ignored, because millions of people use 1FA biometric solutions. I use a 1FA biometric solution every day to enter my current office building. It's a fact of life. But this is often only the case because of the next related recommendation.

Don't Allow Use in Isolated Scenarios

One of the big reasons we allow so many 1FA biometric solutions in our lives (on our cell phones, computers, and buildings) is that the solution is really a low-risk, convenience solution (I don't really think spies are trying to break into my cell phone) or the risk is offset because the biometric submission is being done in a private place watched by other people. When I submit my fingerprint to enter into my building, I'm usually being watched by many other coworkers, who would likely notice if I was a stranger or if I didn't have my company badge displayed. If I was a hacker who broke in using biometric authentication, then I'd be surrounded by tons of employees, who would be following me and asking who I was. In high-security locations, a guard is often watching the biometric scanner as people authenticate directly in front of them. Biometric 1FA solutions aren't as risky in these public/ private in-person scenarios because there are other people around, and the chance of the hacker getting caught and detained is high. The hacker isn't going to be trying their fake fingerprint or iris over and over as people line up in a queue behind them.

This all changes if biometric authentication is allowed to be used remotely, in a completely isolated environment (say, from home). Allowing 1FA biometric solutions from home is a huge risk. An attacker with a stolen or spoofed biometric trait can attempt remote authentication over and over from the safety of their remote location until they eventually break in. Part of the reason biometric authentication works is because there is usually a public record of people using and watching other people use it. The risk is high for an attacker doing a biometric attack in front of other people. But put them in a remote location, and they can try as much as they like with little risk of getting caught.

Summary

This chapter covered attacks against biometric solutions. You learned what biometrics are, which traits are commonly used in biometric authentication, and the problems with biometrics. We looked at example attacks and explored defenses against such attacks. The takeaway is that biometrics are easily faked and should never be used alone as 1FA or remote solutions. And anyone relying on biometrics should be aware of the problems and challenges.

Chapter 17, "Physical Attacks" will cover physical attacks against MFA solutions.

17 Physical Attacks

This chapter covers possible attacks when the attacker has complete, physical control over an MFA solution. Many of the previous chapters included physical attacks related to the particular subject of the chapter, but this chapter examines physical attacks that could be successful against any, or most, physical MFA solutions.

Introduction

If an attacker has unrestrained physical possession of your MFA device with unlimited time and resources, they are very likely going to compromise it. That's just a fact of life. In Chapter 7, "Endpoint Attacks," I mentioned the infamous Microsoft 10 Immutable Laws of Security (blogs.technet .microsoft.com/seanearp/2007/03/25/immutable-laws-of-security). Three of those laws directly apply here:

Law #3: If a bad guy has unrestricted physical access to your computer, it's not your computer anymore.

Law #7: Encrypted data is only as secure as the decryption key.

Law#10: Technology is not a panacea.

These laws have so far never been proven wrong. Several types of physical attacks are covered in the next section.

Types of Physical Attacks

Let's explore three types of physical attack categories that impact MFA solutions.

Physical Viewing of Secrets

Viewing or obtaining the authentication secrets held by an MFA device is one of the most common physical attacks. The most commonplace method is *shoulder surfing*, whereby an attacker is able to view an authentication secret as it is viewed and/or used by the legitimate user. It's called shoulder surfing because it is often done by an attacker viewing the secret behind the victim, over their shoulder from the rear, without the victim being aware of the unauthorized viewing. Criminals have been shoulder surfing to steal PINs for a long time, and it's not that hard to see what lines and shapes someone has selected if logging on while using a graphically based swipe screen (as covered in Chapter 3, "Types of Authentication" and shown in Figure 3.2).

NOTE   Because of shoulder surfing, many banks and ATMs contain small mirrors to let a person typing in a PIN quickly check to see if anyone is looking over their shoulder without having to turn around.

A more technical physical attack is to look for and identify digital authentication secrets on a device by directly accessing the MFA device and its electronics. All digital authentication secrets are stored as bits on memory or storage areas. An attacker can use specialized electronics to look for authentication secrets in these areas. Sometimes the secrets are heavily protected and encrypted, but they can still be accessed and decoded if you know what you're looking for and have the right equipment. Other times the digital secrets are accidentally left in insecure memory or storage areas during temporary processing, or the storage area that was supposed to delete the secret did not even when told to do so. For example, flash memory and solid-state drives (SSDs) do not normally erase data even when told to unless specific commands are used—and even then it is not guaranteed.

An attacker can also physically disassemble and modify the normal processing of an MFA device to obtain the stored digital secrets. Thousands of people have the ability to look at almost any device, see chip numbers and layouts, and figure out which components are either storing the digital secrets or are critical in protecting the digital secrets. And they can modify the hardware—add or remove components, create physical jumpers/bridges between components, or do whatever it takes to interrupt the normal processing to access protected data. Here is an article that discusses using memory chip cloning to access a terrorist's locked cell phone: www.npr.org/2016/03/28/472105583/listeners-questions-about-unlocking-phone-battle-answered.

Unfortunately, I can't show you videos or links to the people who physically hack MFA devices for a living, as they often work for nation-states and law enforcement and are prevented from publicly revealing their techniques. But I can show you a video of a woman who recovers pictures off a "dead," PIN-protected iPad that belonged to a 79-year-old man who passed away while hiking. The iPad lost its power 10 months ago and was exposed to rain and snow. His daughter-in-law wanted to get the pictures back that he took with the iPad to possibly understand what happened and why, and to have the photos for keepsake memories. The video is over an hour long, but worth watching: www.youtube.com/watch?v=zMuap2fgGuY. It will restore your faith in humanity and give you a sample of the types of skills I'm talking about. In this video the repair person has the PIN, so she doesn't have to electronically bypass it, but she likely could. If not, there are many people and companies who can. Law enforcement authorities are routinely gaining access to cell phones and devices protected by MFA. It's not even unusual to hear about it anymore.

For example, years ago you would hear about law enforcement asking Apple for help in bypassing iPhone PINs and biometric features to access the locked cell phones of terrorists and other high-value targets. Apple declined to assist the authorities with bypassing their own protection features. But you don't hear about law enforcement asking Apple about it anymore because a small cottage industry now exists to break into iPhones and other cell phones protected by biometrics, PINs, and MFA. For a while, it looked like U.S. law enforcement's requests were going to head to the Supreme Court to get a ruling to compel Apple to comply. The legal cases have been withdrawn because they are no longer needed. Law enforcement has the access they need now. Here is an article revealing one of the companies that specializes in breaking into iPhones by name: `www.forbes.com/sites/ thomasbrewster/2018/02/26/government-can-access-any-apple-iphone-cellebrite`.

NOTE   Also included in this type of attack is the method where a hacker has physical possession of an MFA device and waits for a new vulnerability involving the device to be announced and then attempts that particular exploit at that time. For example, in October 2017 when the ROCA vulnerability was announced (`www.securityfocus.com/bid/101484`), potentially hundreds of millions of MFA devices were suddenly identified as vulnerable to anyone who could access them or the solutions they used.

Side-Channel Leaks

Most living and electrical things emit unintentional waves, signals, or currents that are different based on the type of information or activity they are involved with. It's not completely out of the range of possibility that one day someone will be able to point a scanner at your head and determine what you are thinking. And if we break things down to the smallest quantum levels, all things are composed of quantum particles and states that ultimately can be translated into 1s and 0s (i.e., information and data). All MFA devices are certainly generating unintended information leaks; it's just a matter of looking for them and interpreting them.

A side-channel attack is accomplished by eavesdropping on an unexpected signal that is directly tied to operations or stored secrets. It can be due to a number of unintended leaks, including those from power consumption, electromagnetic waves, timing, light, temperature changes, and sound. Most electronic devices have one or more of these unintentional leaks.

My first exposure to a side-channel attack was when I was fairly new to computers in the mid-1980s and an acquaintance of mine worked in the U.S. Navy to protect our military ships against side-channel eavesdropping. He showed me how he could plug a voltage monitor into his home's wiring that could display what letters a nearby dot-matrix printer was printing. He explained that every strike of the "dots" of the printer that created each individual character produced a minute current resistance change in the electrical circuit voltage the printer was connected to. I tested it by sending some random characters that he could not see to the printer from a word processor. Sure enough, his voltage scanner reproduced the sentence I had sent. He made me a believer. He told me that he could detect sound vibrations from the printer head impacts as well to do the same thing, and he could even detect those changes by sending an ultrasonic signal against a nearby window pane. It blew me away. I also remember him saying that the biggest threat to what he was trying to do was laser printers, because laser printers didn't create individual impacts when creating an image on paper and all his listening devices didn't work against them. Still, the real-world image of him "spying" on a printer changed the way I thought about computer signals the rest of my life.

Today, detecting side-channel leaks is another common way that nation-states and law enforcement get ahold of authentication secrets. Hundreds of research papers and presentations are available that detail the successful ways people bypassed the security protection on electronic devices. And the people who can prevent side-channel eavesdropping attacks is a subspecialty of computer security defense. Figure 17.1 shows a power differential analysis that derives RSA key bits from a side-channel attack (en.wikipedia.org/wiki/Side-channel_attack#/media/File:Power_attack.png). The peaks are 1s and the valleys are 0s.

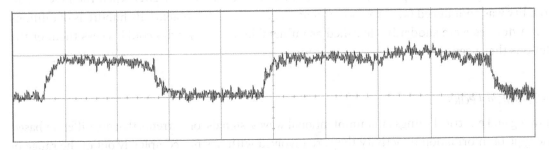

Figure 17.1: Peaks (1s) and valleys (0s) that reveal the bit information of an RSA operating from electric power differential analysis
Source: Audriusa/Creative Commons License Deed Attribution-ShareAlike 3.0 Unported

NOTE   There are many test cases of unintentional secret leaking from the sound or electrical signals from someone typing on a keyboard (see www.berkeley.edu/news/media/releases/2005/09/14_key.shtml). Monitors supposedly leak information from unintentional ultrasonic emanations (www.wired.com/story/monitor-ultrasonic-sounds-reveal-content-side-channel). Apparently 3D printers are the new dot-matrix printers of the past as far as side-channel attacks are concerned (escholarship.org/uc/item/6c52g94w). It has even been shown that talking and singing can be remotely recorded from changes in lighting due to sound vibration impacts (www.zdnet.com/article/lamphone-attack-lets-threat-actors-recover-conversations-from-your-light-bulb). The broad category name for sound side-channels attacks is *acoustic cryptanalysis*.

Sometimes the inherent construction or implementation of a protective device or method makes it more or less susceptible to potential side-channel eavesdropping attacks, physical or wireless. For example, today, many encryption algorithms and devices under serious consideration for security protection are evaluated, from their very beginning, for their potential susceptibility to eavesdropping side-channel attacks.

One of the side-channel attack possibilities arises when a particular encryption algorithm takes a different amount of CPU time when working with 1s versus 0s. An attacker with the right sensitive equipment could possibly determine an encryption private key by looking at the minute jumps in CPU processing time as it reads and processes the different bits of a particular key. Today, for an encryption algorithm to be successfully selected as a "standard" it must undergo side-channel analysis and be shown to be resistant to easy, known, side-channel attacks. Otherwise like encryption algorithms are dismissed because they are overly susceptible to side-channel attacks. Other times, modifications are made to the algorithm to fix the potential side-channel issues.

NOTE A story I have heard many times from people I trust concerns the ability for the U.S. government to use remote listening devices to detect secret keys stored on hardware security modules (HSMs) located within a building from outside that building. I have talked to two people who supposedly witnessed a test like this working at a company I was involved in. In their recounting, a vendor told a senior executive at a large Fortune 10 company that they could read that company's private keys stored on an HSM in the middle of a building inside a locked computer room from a car in the parking lot. The purported bet was if the vendor could successfully perform the eavesdropping test, then the company would buy the vendor's protection product. The vendor proved they could remotely eavesdrop from outside the building and sold their product. I'm not sure if the bet and test were real, but I do know that the rest of us were told to open up our existing HSMs and insert new shielding products from that vendor, and from then on every new HSM had to come with the vendor's shielding product already installed.

Side-channel attacks have been fairly well understood and defended against for decades. Many governments name the technologies that both attack and defend against side-channel attacks TEMPEST (Telecommunications Electronics Materials Protected from Emanating Spurious Transmissions). You'll find a good summary of TEMPEST attacks and defenses here: en.wikipedia.org/wiki/Tempest_(codename). Defenses against side-channel attacks include design, shielding, jamming, filtering, distance, and isolation.

Physical Theft/Destruction

Of course, an attacker can always just physically destroy or take your MFA solution—which is an availability issue. You've got a time-based-one-time password (TOTP) device? A thief can just steal it. Many people keep their MFA device stored in their carrying satchel or backpack along with the device that it is used with. Or they may place their TOTP device on their keyring or put their smartcard in their wallet or purse, and once that is stolen, so too, is their MFA solution. Or as covered in the last chapter, most biometric traits are easy to steal.

We aren't just worried about physical mechanical attacks. Wireless attacks can be a problem, too, in the physical category. In the nation-state arena, *electromagnetic pulse* (EMP) attacks have worried the world's governments for over half a century. Most major nations are believed to have EMP weapons, nuclear and otherwise, which everyone assumes will be deployed in any major war to disrupt an adversary's electronic devices. Large electromagnetic pulses have been proven to permanently disable electronic devices. That means our computers, phones, radios, generators, lights, air conditioning, networks, power grids, cars—anything with an electronic component is thought to be susceptible. Which is pretty much nearly everything in our world. The fear is we would be back to bicycles, spears, bows & arrows, and guns, if an EMP attack comes. Because of that fear, most major governments require anti-EMP defenses on their electronics and have national plans to mitigate the threat. Here's a recent 2019 story on America's latest EMP defense planning (www.forbes.com/sites/arielcohen/2019/04/05/whitehouse-prepares-to-face-emp-threat). Of course, it seems Hollywood never tires of making films that involve EMP attacks. My favorite recent film using an EMP bomb as part of its main plot was 2001's *Ocean's Eleven* (www.aps.org/publications/apsnews/200203/oceans-eleven.cfm), and there is a Wikipedia page devoted to the genre (en.wikipedia.org/wiki/Electromagnetic_pulse_in_popular_culture).

We can make it very difficult for an attacker with physical possession of an MFA device (or server or client) to compromise an MFA solution, but we can't make it impossible. This is not to say that we should not make it as hard as possible to stop physical attacks. You'll learn about some common methods in the section "Developer Defenses Against Physical Attacks" later in this chapter.

Example Physical Attacks

This section shows examples of real-world physical attacks against MFA solutions that haven't already been covered in earlier chapters.

Smartcard Side-Channel Attack

As discussed in previous chapters, a smartcard contains a specialized integrated circuit chip—the small, squarish metallic chip (as shown in Figure 17.2). It contains a microprocessor, memory storage areas, an operating system, and eight distinct areas known as "pins." Some of the pins are involved in powering up the chip, and others are data input/output (I/O) areas. The chip is the "smart" of the smartcard and is designed to securely protect storage secrets (which often include an asymmetric key pair, including a private key). It was specifically designed to protect authentication secrets, and in most normal circumstances, it does a pretty good job at it.

However, at least since 1998, researchers and smartcard hackers have known that smartcard chips and the secrets they protect are vulnerable to side-channel attacks, specifically differential power attacks. Here is a great 2002 paper on these attacks: www.cs.uic.edu/~sloan//my-papers/ieee-messerges-proof.pdf. Smartcard attackers can essentially monitor the power differences between the ground pin and the true ground, and using a resister and a digital oscilloscope, note voltage differences that equate to 0s and 1s. You can read the *IEEE Transactions on Computers* article listed

Figure 17.2: Smartcard integrated circuit chip shown from smartcard-enabled credit card

above for the details. It is very enlightening and only moderately difficult to understand. The article concludes with the following sentence: "Ways an attacker might maximize side-channel signals have been investigated and were found to be very effective." That pretty much says it all right there. So, in theory, an attacker could monitor a smartcard as it was used and determine its stored secret key and other information.

This white paper covers over a dozen different types of attacks against smartcards (www .infosecwriters.com/text_resources/pdf/Known_Attacks_Against_Smartcards.pdf) and tells anyone how they, too, can do it. It's a great smartcard hacker resource. Essentially, you physically cut the smartcard chip away from the card, use an acid to remove any remaining attachment resin, and then use an optical microscope to map out the chip's different component boundaries and connections. Then a series of metallic probes are used to send and record voltages and information (different I/O scenarios), and at least one of those probes is attached to a digital signaling processor card and/or oscilloscope (or other measuring device). It also includes many different known types of attacks. And there are many.

A 2014 paper (portal.sinteza.singidunum.ac.rs/Media/files/2014/43-46.pdf) says that "The results of this study show that leakage current can be easily exploited as a side-channel by an attacker to extract information about the secret key in cryptographic hardware in CMOS crypto-design, while TDPL [three-phase dual-rail pre-charge logic] can be a reliable countermeasure to use in future design of smart cards." So, it confirms that smartcard side-channel attacks can be performed but suggests a possible countermeasure. Smartcards using TDPL gates result in more evenly distributed power consumption while working on 1s and 0s, which makes it harder for differential power attacks to succeed. Unfortunately, almost all smartcards still use the traditional, more hackable design. And even if you solve this one attack type (different power analysis), there are dozens of other methods that will be successful.

NOTE If you are interested in learning more, here is a great two-hour tutorial video on how to hack smartcards and other MFA tokens using side-channel attacks: vimeo.com/26765734.

The key lesson is that even very specialized hardware designed to protect authentication secrets can be hacked, often dozens of different ways, and there are thousands of people who know how to do it. It takes awareness of these specialized side-channel attacks and how they are accomplished to defeat them. And sometimes if an attacker looks hard enough at the microscopic level, they can even defeat those defenses.

Electron Microscope Attack

A typical microscope works using light, which is made up of photon particles. When you want to measure very tiny things, microscopic, down at the nanometer scale and smaller, light doesn't work because the photons are bigger than the objects being measured. It would be like trying to use a yardstick to measure a pea.

For very small things, scientists and researchers use an electron microscope. Electron microscopes, not surprisingly, use electrons. Electrons are up to 100,000 times smaller than photons and can be used to measure microscopic, subatomic objects of all types.

A new electron microscope (there are several types) can easily set back a research facility $3 million to $5 million, but you can buy used ones in multiples of tens of thousands of dollars. Here's an online marketplace for electron microscopes: www.labx.com/electron-microscope. Of course, the purchase cost is only part of the cost equation. Electron microscopes consume tremendous power to create their electron beams and are usually housed in environmentally controlled labs, with teams of professional people using and maintaining them. Still, in the United States, many small community colleges and even high schools (www.hssemgroup.com/high-school-sems/school-url-s) have them or have access to them. They aren't the super rare commodities that they once were. Certainly, nation-states have and use them.

An electron microscope can be used to search for and identify authentication secrets at the molecular level. The first time this was largely publicly discussed was in 2010 (gcn.com/Articles/2010/02/02/Black-Hat-chip-crack-020210.aspx) by Christopher Tarnovsky. Over nine months, using a focused ion beam electron microscope, Tarnovsky was able to find and retrieve the authentication secrets stored on an Infineon SLE 66PE, a microcontroller chip, which carried the security label of Trusted Platform Module (TPM).

TPM chips are specialized chips designed to prevent the unauthorized retrieval of authentication secrets. Microsoft has been requiring a TPM chip to protect critical boot secrets for years on all enterprise levels of Microsoft Windows hardware. Tarnovsky revealed that anyone with access to an electron microscope could get at those secrets. Tarnovsky also found that the TPM chip had several anti-tampering technologies built-in and that triggering any one of them would destroy the chip. He ended up destroying more than four dozen chips in the process, but eventually he learned how to get at the secrets without destroying the chip in the process. Tarnovsky estimates he has reverse-engineered over a thousand chips in his career, and he continues to attack chip protections to this day. He often shares how he does what he does, including this 2019 talk: media.hardwear.io/exposing-the-deep-secure-elements-of-smartcards-christopher-tarnovsky.

> **NOTE** If you want to learn a little more about electron microscopes and how they can be used against computer chips, here's a great video: www.youtube.com/watch?v=Mam2ktODcvg.

> **NOTE** There are lots of hacker websites devoted to reverse-engineering chips and their designs, including siliconpr0n.org, zeptobars.com, and visual6502.org.

Cold-Boot Attacks

But suppose you don't have the money or time to own and run your own electron microscope. If you have $5, you might be able to reveal protected secrets with a can of compressed air. Let me explain.

On most devices, in order for encryption and decryption to work, the encryption/decryption key(s) must be in plaintext in memory (or at least eventually derivable to plaintext from what is located in memory). It has to be that way. You can't encrypt the encryption/decryption key while it is actually being used to encrypt or decrypt data. If you can use a memory inspection tool, you can look for and locate the encryption key. And sometimes that key is left in memory even when it shouldn't be. Turns out many types of memory chips, especially nonvolatile memory, will keep the encryption key in memory even when power is not currently supplied. For decades, it was popularly believed that if you powered off a computer device, the information located in its memory chips would be gone. Turns out that wasn't and isn't always true.

If you lower the temperature or freeze the memory chips, it's even more likely that memory contents will last longer after the power goes away. This new understanding led to what is now known as *cold-boot attacks*. Essentially, you lower the temperature of the memory chips as much as possible while they are still energized, and then power off the device the memory is currently located in and move the memory to another device, which can dump and analyze the contents of the memory as it is powered back on in a static state. For a few years after the first public revelations, cold-boot memory attacks became all the rage. Stopping them wasn't so easy because the problem was with how electronic memory inherently worked; it wasn't a bug that could be fixed with a patch. See www.thewindowsclub .com/cold-boot-attack and en.wikipedia.org/wiki/Cold_boot_attack for more details.

The first time I saw a cold-boot attack in person, I had just learned about these types of attacks in 2008. A Princeton University team, including well-known Java and voting machine hacker Edward Felten (en.wikipedia.org/wiki/Edward_Felten), announced (citp.princeton.edu/our-work/memory/) to the world that they could hack a variety of well-known disk encryption programs using a simple and inexpensive cold-boot attack method using canned air, like the type anyone can buy to dust off their computer and keyboard. The programs they could break included Microsoft's BitLocker Drive Encryption.

NOTE Even though BitLocker is named "Drive Encryption," it really doesn't encrypt a whole disk as the name might imply. BitLocker, like many other disk encryption programs, just encrypts smaller, logical disk volumes and not the entire disk. It's a small but important distinction. True disk encryption usually requires equipment or software in the disk microcontroller or some other external hardware encryption component sitting higher/prior in the execution stack than on the disk itself.

This was startling and newsworthy because Microsoft had just released Microsoft Windows Vista with BitLocker the year before and was trying to capture the trust of more enterprise customers with the promise of stronger, built-in, reliable disk encryption. And here were college kids saying they could break the encryption technology from the work of a multibillion dollar company with a $5 can of compressed air. And it truly worked! Felten's team supplied (`citp.princeton.edu/our-work/memory/`) a white paper, FAQ, and even source code so that anyone could replicate what they had done. Their technique had worked not only against Microsoft's BitLocker, but also against Apple's FileVault as well as open source dm-crypt and TrueCrypt. The Princeton team were equal opportunity hackers.

> **NOTE** TrueCrypt was a very popular open source encryption program for over a decade. It was eventually discontinued after subsequent analysis showed it was overly vulnerable to other forms of hacking (or that is the well-known rumor). Either way, it is not used anymore.

At a security conference held by Microsoft (where I worked at the time), a hacker demonstration of the cold-boot technique was going on. The hacker asked for volunteers. I raised my hand and gave him my BitLocker-protected laptop. He flipped it over, removed the panel that was covering the laptop's memory modules, and sprayed a can of air on the memory modules until an icy frost appeared on the chips. He then held down the power switch, killing power to the laptop, and continued to spray the chips, putting more icy frost on them until the whole can was drained. He then popped out the memory chips, put them into his external memory tray attached to his computer, ran a program that copied all the memory to his computer storage, ran a search program, and found my BitLocker encryption keys.

With Microsoft BitLocker, the master keys that protect the BitLocker encryption keys are located on the TPM hardware chip on the computer's motherboard. You can't simply take someone else's BitLocker-encrypted hard drive to another computer and boot it up because the master keys to unlock the BitLocker encryption keys are located *only* on the original computer. A BitLocker-protected disk will not boot without its encryption keys, which are protected and unlocked by the TPM chip. The hacker moved my hard drive to his computer and hooked it up as an external drive. Since the TPM chip was not on the hacker's computer, my disk should not have booted on his computer. But the hacker booted my hard drive and supplied the spied-on BitLocker encryption/decryption key, and my hard drive booted like it normally would to my regular Windows logon prompt. He then began doing keyword searches on my BitLocker-protected hard drive.

I was astounded. Everyone in the audience was. It was big world news at the time, not only in the computer security world, but even in the mainstream news markets. Today, you can do an Internet search for *cold boot attacks* and find dozen of videos showing you how it is done. The key is that the decryption keys (or whatever protected information you are seeking) has to be stored in plaintext in a memory area where it stays at least semi-permanently when power to the original device's memory is no longer continuously supplied. Most of the time, the memory copying is done on the original device, if possible, with the least amount of power interruption to maximize the chances the secrets will remain in memory. But I've seen the memory moved to other devices plenty of times and seen the attack work. Example basic cold boot memory steps often are as follows:

1. Confirm the targeted device will allow booting to an external device such as a USB key, and modify it to boot to this external device (i.e., hacker computer or device). This may require modifying the CMOS BIOS or UEFI settings.

2. Ensure the targeted device has protected information in memory.
3. Lower the temperature of the memory chips to near freezing, if possible.
4. Connect the hacker device to the target device using the connection method indicated as the primary boot sequence connection.
5. Power down the targeted device (do not do a normal shutdown, which might clear memory).
6. Boot up on the externally connected hacker device.
7. Run a program to copy the memory of the targeted device. There are dozens of forensic tools that can copy memory contents to an external storage device.
8. Search for and identify the protected information from the copied memory.

Many cold-boot hacking guides are available that will help you identify the areas in memory where encryption keys are likely to be stored and that show you how to identify and copy the correct encryption keys. For example, here is the Princeton group's source code for finding RSA and AES keys: `citp.princeton.edu/our-work/memory/code`.

Snooping On RFID-Enabled Credit Cards

Radio-frequency ID (RFID) is a near-field communication (NFC) wireless technology that many products use to communicate wirelessly. It uses radio waves (part of the electromagnetic spectrum) from 120 KHz to 10 GHz. Most wireless credit cards (and smartcards and other contactless products we use for wireless payments) operate at the 13.56 MHz frequency (known as the *ISM band*).

The RFID components in credit cards are known as "passive" (versus "active") and get energized by external devices that wirelessly supply a DC power current (a process known as *induction*). When an RFID device comes within range of the RFID power source and signal, it turns on and does what it was preprogrammed to do—just as if it had been inserted into a physical reader device. Passive RFID credit cards must be within a few centimeters for a standard passive card reader to supply the power and energize the passive device, although active RFID devices (with their own power supplies and operating at different frequencies) can communicate with each other up to several thousand feet away.

As an end-user convenience, an RFID interface is now commonly installed on credit cards (and other devices) so that the cards can transmit wirelessly to the payment card reader during a transaction. The user usually hovers their card within a few centimeters over the wireless reader and the transaction is confirmed in one to three seconds. Wireless credit cards usually fall under the ISO/IEC 14443 standard and are also known as *proximity cards*. RFID-based credit cards are the most common type of contactless card used for electronic payment. To see if your current credit card is RFID enabled, look for a symbol similar to the one shown in Figure 17.3. There are a handful of different RFID-symbols placed on RFID-enabled credit cards, but this is the most common one.

Anyone can install an RFID reader app on their cell phone, hover it over an RFID-enabled credit card, and read a limited amount of unprotected information, including the credit card account number and expiration date (an example is shown in Figure 17.4).

Figure 17.3: RFID symbol indicating that the credit card it is printed on is RFID-enabled

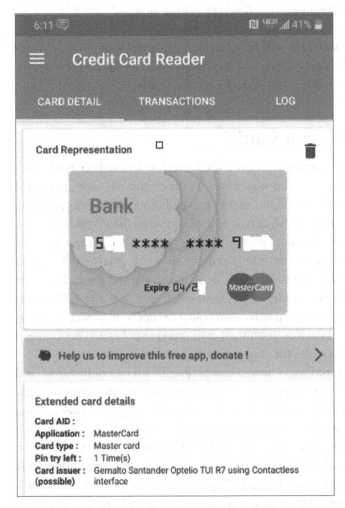

Figure 17.4: RFID-enabled credit card information being read by a RFID cell phone app

The risk is that hackers will walk past you or you past them and the hacker will record your RFID credit card information and use it to make future fraudulent purchases and transactions. If you search on YouTube for *RFID hack*, you can find dozens of videos of hackers and reporters breathlessly showing you how easy it is to do. I've done it myself to demonstrate RFID transmission hacking to friends and coworkers. You, too, can easily do it.

The ability for RFID-enabled credit cards to be remotely sniffed, along with the fear of wireless hacking of credit cards, has resulted in a thriving billion-dollar protection industry known as *RFID shielding*. You can buy cheap credit card shields (see Figure 17.5), and they are frequent giveaways at computer security conferences. You can also buy wallets, purses, and even clothing, like stylish jeans with shielding material covering the pockets.

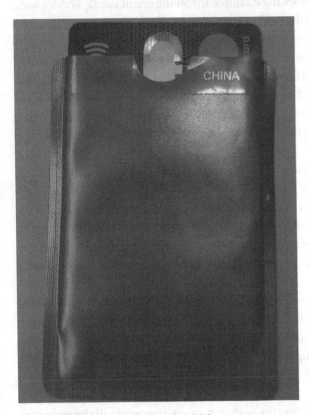

Figure 17.5: RFID credit card shield

There is a huge caveat to this potential wireless threat: there has never been a publicly documented, real-world, crime by a real criminal where an RFID-shielding product would have prevented the credit card theft. The theft could happen and the card information be used, but there is no public evidence that such a real-world incident has occurred. And that is pretty important. There are a lot of risks we need to defend against, but one that has never occurred before and isn't likely to happen isn't one of them. Still, RFID-enabled chips are being placed on more and more things all the time, such as passports, building entry cards, and MFA security tokens. Depending on the information that can be accessed remotely, what can be stolen could be a big deal in the future.

> **NOTE** Much of the content for this RFID section originally appeared as part of a 20-page white paper I wrote in December 2019: `www.linkedin.com/pulse/all-i-want-christmas-certainly-isnt-rfid-credit-card-sleeve-grimes`. It covers credit cards, RFID, and RFID hacking in detail.

EMV Credit Card Tricks

Let me end this section by describing a low-tech hacking example involving credit cards. For decades, credit card thieves have stolen credit cards or credit card information to create new fraudulent transactions. In order to fight that, credit card merchants have been steadily adding more advanced security options to the cards. At first it was adding a three- or four-digit security code that was not stored on the magnetic stripe on the back of the card. Today, most credit cards are chip-and-PIN-enabled. Chip-and-PIN credit cards are often part of the EMV (Europay, Mastercard, VISA) standard. EMV chips on credit cards are essentially smartcard chips, which more securely store and protect critical credit card information from easy eavesdropping (especially when compared to how easy it is to steal from the magnetic stripes of credit cards).

When we make local, in-person purchases, most (but not all) vendors require that the chip be used as part of the transaction. Brand-new EMV cards must be activated before they can be used. They can be easily activated by someone calling from the previously registered phone number already associated with the user of the card. Since the chip cannot be easily copied or cloned by regular criminals (they don't usually have electron microscopes or oscilloscopes handy or the skillset), attackers have come up with another interesting, physical, hack to steal and use EMV-enabled credit cards.

Credit card hackers will (somehow) intercept someone's legitimate EMV credit card and send the victim another completely fake card with the same information (e.g., merchant name, user's name, card number, three-digit security code, phone number to call, etc.) printed on it. It may or may not have an (empty and fake) EMV chip on it. Creating fake credit cards can be done with a few hundred dollars of supplies and equipment, all of which is readily available for purchase by anyone over the Internet.

When the victim gets the fake card and assumes it is the legitimate card, they will call the activation phone number, which activates the real card in the criminal's possession. The criminal tries making very small transactions each day until the first one finally goes through, and when it does, they use the now activated card to make big purchases. It's a low-tech attack against a high-tech defense.

Defenses Against Physical Attacks

Let's next explore developer and user defenses against physical attacks.

Developer Defenses Against Physical Attacks

First, we'll look at developer defenses against physical attacks.

Threat Model

Physical attacks are easy to overlook. MFA developers need to ensure that physical attacks are included in their threat modeling and mitigated. Encryption keys and other critical secrets should be as securely protected as possible. Developers need to make sure the secrets don't accidentally "bleed" out into less protected areas.

Educate

Programming team managers need to be sure that all involved developers are educated about the possible physical attacks discovered during threat modeling so that they can be mitigated. Vendors should share potential physical attack scenarios with customers so that they can do their part in preventing physical attacks.

Allow/Require Split Secrets

Many physical attacks can view stored, supposedly protected, authentication secrets. If possible, store the secret across two locations so that a compromise of one location does not reveal the entire secret. For example, with BitLocker, Microsoft recommends users use at least two different locations for the secrets needed to unlock a BitLocker volume. As an example, BitLocker can store part of the key in a local TPM chip and also require a PIN entered by an end user. An electron microscope may be able to discover the master key located on a TPM chip, but it won't be able to see the PIN stored in someone's human memory. It's the whole reason MFA can be more secure than 1FA.

Implement Anti-Tampering

Any time MFA-related software or firmware starts up, it should check itself for unauthorized modification. At the very least, it should be an integrity self-check. But it's better to allow an external component, which has already been checked and verified for legitimacy, to do the check. For example, in Microsoft Windows, the TPM chip has self-checks and "roots of trust" to verify itself. The TPM chip has secret keys that unlock other keys, including the roots of trust of UEFI Secure Boot, which then unlocks BitLocker, which in turn unlocks the disk volume and loads Windows. Critical Windows drivers go through another integrity check before they load. It's one big integrity-checking trust chain, from beginning to end, before the end user can even log on. Each verified component then checks the next component's integrity in the chain. Only authorized updates should be allowed to update any of the involved components.

Any MFA physical device should be designed to prevent physical tampering. You can do Internet searches on anti-tampering and TEMPEST to get plenty of recommendations and guidance. Design and engineering should make it hard for an attacker to logically or physically tamper. MFA physical device cases should be resistant to easy opening. If a case is opened by an unknowledgeable technician (or opened at all), the device should trigger a "dead switch," which then permanently disables the device.

Mitigate Side-Channel Attacks

You can find hundreds of papers online with recommendations for how to mitigate side-channel attacks. Defenses against side-channel attacks include design, encryption, shielding, jamming, filtering, distance, and isolation. Authentication secrets can be encrypted to prevent easy eavesdropping or stored in areas that are not as easy to attack (like CPU registers). All MFA devices should contain anti-electromagnetic shielding to prevent wireless side-channel attacks. Devices can contain voltage regulators, electrical containment, random signal noise, and jamming to prevent easy wireless eavesdropping. Encryption algorithms should be used that are not susceptible to easy side-channel attacks.

Enable Viewing Disruptors

If authentication secrets are displayed to end users so that they can view or type them, the viewing method should stop easy shoulder surfing. Viewing display screens can be made with angled or shaded optics, which prevent easy offset view (much like a privacy screen makes it harder for someone else not directly in front of the screen from seeing the data).

Allow Easy Remote Decommissioning

MFA devices get lost, stolen, and broken. It will happen. In the event that an MFA device is not in the possession or under the control of the legitimate user, allow for easy disabling and/or remote decommissioning. In all cases, allow reuse of a lost, stolen, or disabled MFA device to be prevented from being used in future authentication.

> **NOTE**   There is some disagreement about whether one of a developer's defenses should be "security by obscurity." Some developers think that the less an attacker knows (e.g., chip designs, encryption algorithms used), the better. And this is true. But the best security designs assume that an attacker has perfect knowledge of what they are attacking and the solution is designed so that it still stays as secure and hard to compromise as possible even with near perfect knowledge of the MFA device.

User Defenses Against Physical Attacks

Now we'll explore user defenses to physical attacks.

Education

Users of any MFA solution should be made aware of the physical attacks that can be possible against their solution and use them in a way to minimize future potential physical attacks. A simple educational component is to tell users of physical MFA devices to take care of the devices and to report as soon as possible if they're missing or broken.

Use a Split Key Solution if Possible

If a split key solution is available, use it. For example, with Microsoft BitLocker, users have over half a dozen ways to unlock a BitLocker-protected volume, including TPM chips, PINs, USB keys, and network-unlock. Methods include 1FA, 2FA, and 3FA. When worried about physical attacks, use a 2FA method that splits the secrets among two or more physical locations, such as TPM + PIN or TPM + USB key. Splitting the secret in half prevents the compromise of a single location from revealing the whole secret.

Protect MFA Solutions Against Physical Attacks

High-security devices, such as HSMs, should be stored and isolated from public areas and should be protected by shielding that prevents electromagnetic emanations. Users should not carry their MFA devices in places or ways (e.g., key rings, wallets, purses) that can be accessed by criminals. Users should not place MFA devices in the same transportation bag as the device the MFA solution is being used with (e.g., not in the laptop bag or purse). Users should carry their MFA device in such a way that a single theft or loss event does not compromise both the computer it is used with and the MFA device used to authenticate.

Replace Devices with Wear Signs

MFA devices with keypads that show signs of obvious wear patterns, like the device shown in Figure 3.1 of Chapter 3, should be replaced. You don't want obvious wear patterns giving hints to an attacker which numbers or characters are likely involved.

Report Lost, Stolen, or Missing MFA Devices

Users should be instructed to report lost, stolen, or missing MFA devices as soon as is safely possible. If a phone number is involved that the user should call, the number should be given or stored in an area that the user will still likely have access to if the MFA device is stolen. I've seen many MFA devices with the number to call to report the lost device printed on the device. That's a great idea until the device is no longer in your possession.

Improve Your Physical Safety and Awareness

Everyone should strive to live a generally commonsense safe life. This means avoiding areas and times that may be at increased risk for physical crime. Don't advertise electronics in public places or leave them out where they are easily visible to strangers. Part of being safe is simply being more aware of your surroundings and what others are doing.

Some computer security experts also recommend disabling Bluetooth on a device when you aren't using it, even when you think the device is in "sleeping" mode. There are stories of thieves walking up to cars with Bluetooth readers, searching in "pairing mode." Any active Bluetooth devices secreted away may still be wirelessly advertising themselves, by product name, to savvy criminals looking for easy score.

Taking self-defense courses can help, but if someone attempts to rob you of your MFA device or computer, let them have it. Rarely is it worth getting physically injured over a device that the thief will often reset/erase or resell without ever looking at the previously stored data.

Is Your Physical Safety Worth It?

You may want to ask yourself whether your physical safety is worth the defense you are using, There's a famous computer security XKCD cartoon (xkcd.com/538/) where the answer to any fancy, expensive, super-duper computer security system is to physically hurt the legitimate user until they just give up and let the bad guy in. This is a real consideration to any computer security system protecting valuable assets wanted by others.

As covered in the previous chapter, a Malaysian man lost his finger because his car's antitheft system could only be deactivated using his fingerprint. The criminals chopped off his finger and solved the problem. This sort of situation, portended in multiple Hollywood films for years, has come to life in the real world. The thieves could have learned how to take his fingerprint and cloned it, resulting in no bad harm to the end user—but they didn't. They likely didn't have the intelligence or the time, or want the additional risk from what it would take to make a 100 percent, accepted-all-the-time, cloned fingerprint. So, they took the easy way out and cut off his finger. Easier for them, not so much for the victim. I don't think there is any scenario where the victim would have traded his finger for keeping his car, which was likely insured.

A more common example is thieves who hack technology to steal wirelessly protected cars. Today, many cars are protected by keys that contain a wireless activation device, often built into the physical keys, that control whether the car can be started and driven away. The thinking is that even if the thieves are able to break into the car, it can't be started without the legitimate keys, which contain a wireless chip synced to the car. Today, many cars can be started remotely using cell phones and remote key systems.

In the many older stories and videos on the Internet, such as www.youtube.com/watch?v=bR8RrmEizVg, the thieves use an electronic device to extend the key's electronic signal from inside the house where the car is parked and the owners sleeping, to the car, which they then start and drive away. I'm assuming they then drive to a safe spot, disable the wireless ignition component and any theft-tracking devices, and quickly disassemble the individual parts.

There is a school of thought that says that if we are able to make cars impervious to stealing without the thief getting access to the actual electronic device, doesn't that just incentivize potentially dangerous criminals into coming into your house, where you and your family members are, to get to the device they need to steal the car? When I now interview car vendors that offer wireless starting security options, they often tell me that the wireless relay tricks of the past will no longer work on today's newer car models. Today, they say, a thief would need to have the actual authentication token (usually stored in the owner's house) to start the car. Is that a good thing? Is that really a security improvement?

Do you want potentially dangerous criminals in your house? The car is likely covered by insurance. Wouldn't you rather the thieves stay out of your house and not need to come into it to steal your car? For most of us, we'd rather criminals stay out of our houses and not lop off our fingers.

Summary

This chapter covered physical attacks against MFA solutions. We started by discussing the three major categories of physical attacks: physical viewing of secrets, side-channel attacks, and physical theft or destruction. We then covered five example physical attacks and ended by discussing several developer and user defenses.

Chapter 18, "DNS Hijacking" will cover DNS hijacking attacks.

18

DNS Hijacking

T his chapter covers DNS and other similar namespace hijacking attacks. DNS attacks are the most popular type of namespace attack, but this chapter covers multiple types of namespaces used by the Internet, some of which not all readers may be aware of. But each may be involved as a dependency in an MFA solution and can be hacked and abused.

Introduction

As discussed in Chapter 5, "Hacking MFA in General," most underlying MFA solutions rely on a digitally represented namespace of some sort, most often Domain Name System (DNS). There isn't a conclusive definition of namespace, but it can be most commonly thought of as a way of naming, locating, storing, and categorizing objects within a shared system. The governing domain of a namespace can be something used only locally on a single device where it is located; used between multiple, remote participating entities who agree to use it (like Extensible Markup Language [XML]); or used globally throughout the world. Namespaces govern the very small, such as the natural taxonomy (kingdom, phylum, class, order, etc.) to classify microorganisms, like bacteria, to almost unfathomably large celestial objects, like galaxies and star nebulas (named and classified by various space-related organizations such as the International Astronomical Union). Namespaces give participants an easier and agreed upon way to name, classify, store, and locate objects.

Our home mailing addresses are a sort of namespace. You can point to any property in the world and it's likely to have a country, state/province, city/county, and zip code associated with it, even though each country can use its own labels and boundary definitions. The mailing namespace is thorough enough that each of us can mail a package from our house or business to another house or business in almost any part of the world. We can do the same thing with emails and email addresses, which are based on DNS.

It's easy to get millions or even billions of objects in a digital domain, so it only made sense that namespaces would extend to our computer domains. There were earlier precursor implementations, but for the Internet, DNS became the official standard in the early 1980s. Many other digital namespaces are still in use today, including Abstract Syntax Notation One (ASN.1), Active Directory (AD), and Lightweight Directory Access Protocol (LDAP). Any filesystem used by an operating system can also be thought of as a namespace. Other naming conventions, services, and protocols that could be construed as a namespace of sorts are NetBIOS, Internet Protocol (IP) addresses, and AppleTalk, among others. The commonality is that the identities and other components named and identified in the namespace are used by other participants in the same namespace to locate each other. DNS is the most popular namespace and the one most familiar to people. Many toddlers can rattle off their favorite DNS addresses before they are three years old. Examples of DNS addresses are `rogerg@knowbe4.com`, `www.knowbe4.com`, and `www.knowbe4.com/resources`.

In the enterprise world, Microsoft's Active Director namespace is very popular. An example (Distinguished Name) AD name looks like CN=Rogerg, OU=Users, OU=PRDept, DC=knowbe4, DC=com. Namespaces can hold not only objects, but also claims, assertions, and attributes of objects.

Namespaces can be attacked to circumvent MFA solutions. I covered a related attack in Chapter 10, "Subject Hijack Attacks." That one involved Microsoft's AD and smartcards, and it revealed one of the few attacks covered in this book that has, as far as I know, not been used in a single real-world attack.

Attacks against or using DNS are the polar opposite. Attacks against DNS occur thousands of times a day and are routinely used to bypass authentication defenses. And there have been some involving other types of namespaces. I'll cover a handful of them in this chapter.

Someone using MFA would likely not be able to prevent the vast majority of namespace attacks. This should not be surprising. If I can hack a dependency, I can often hack or bypass the thing that relies on the dependency. It's fairly difficult to stop an attack against a namespace dependency, but I'll cover some possible defenses later in this chapter.

DNS

We'll cover a few types of namespaces and attacks in this chapter, but certainly attacks against DNS are the most important and popular. DNS (along IP addresses) is the backbone of our Internet, and the majority of organizational networks also use it to work.

DNS converts the "common names" we type in or click on, such as `www.knowbe4.com`, to their officially registered IP (version 4 or 6) host addresses (e.g., 104.17.113.180, 16A7:F1E0:10B2:51::8, etc.) used by Internet routers behind the scenes to transmit our intended communications. Each computer or device accessible directly from or to the Internet must have a unique (fully qualified) DNS name and associated (public) IP address. No other directly addressable device on the Internet can have the same DNS name or IP address.

NOTE Directly contactable Internet devices must have unique "public" IP addresses, but one public IP address can front many thousands of "private," non-unique, addressable IP devices using a protocol known as Network Address Translation (NAT). Only public IP addresses can be routed to and from directly on the Internet. But there are millions of private IP addresses that anyone can use on their private networks as long as they don't try to connect them directly to the Internet.

DNS was officially put to use on the Internet in 1983. Prior to DNS, each communicating computer or device that wanted to connect to another computer or device across the Internet (at the time called ARPANET) had to use the destination computer's IP address, even though most computers also had more easily typed-in English-language hostnames. The humans using and configuring those computers were not as good at remembering a whole bunch of long numbers (i.e., IP addresses) as they were hostnames. Everyone agreed that using hostnames for connections would be far easier; they just needed a method for converting hostnames to IP addresses.

Initially, computers' operating systems (and/or applications) were updated to include and use a file named HOSTS (or hosts, `HOSTS.TXT`, or `hosts.txt`), which listed the names of the desired computers followed by their IP address. Users could then use a computer's hostname and the OS or application would look to the HOSTS file to convert the hostname to an IP address, which it then used to connect to the destination computer(s).

NOTE You can still find a HOSTS file on most computer systems. On a Microsoft Windows computer, the HOSTS file is located under `\Windows\System32\drivers\etc`.

This method still required a human or local automated process to update the HOSTS file on each participating computer with the necessary computer hostnames and IP addresses any time someone wanted to just use the hostname with a computer not already documented there. It was a manual pain even before it began to scale to much larger networks. According to industry lore I've heard, by the time the HOSTS file included just eight computer names, many people started to see that a more robust, automated, centralized service was needed to handle the hostname-to–IP address conversion. A computer scientist named Paul Mockapetris, along with Jon Postel, created DNS. Within a few years, a computer service/component known as Berkeley Internet Name Domain (BIND) was created in Unix so that any Unix-like computer could participate. Today, BIND (`www.isc.org/bind`) and Microsoft's DNS service (server and client) handle the vast majority of DNS queries.

NOTE Some malware still manipulates the HOSTS file in order to maliciously redirect victim computers to rogue computers. The HOSTS file, if present, is often checked by OSs and applications before they will use DNS. But it's an older, legacy file that is rarely used, so humans don't often look there when investigating suspicious computer redirection behavior. So, if malware modifies the HOSTS file, the malicious modification can go undetected for a long period of time.

The DNS namespace is a hierarchical, tree-like structure, where the upper layers control and link to lower layers. On the Internet, the upper top-level DNS zones are known as *top-level domains* (TLDs). Many of the Internet TLDs are well known, such as COM, EDU, MIL, ORG, with newer ones such as BIZ and INFO. Each country has its own two-letter TLD domain if someone wants to use them, such as RU for Russia and AU for Australia. DNS addresses are written in reverse order, with the TLD portion always at the right end of a fully qualified DNS domain name.

Subdomains (such as knowbe4.com) and their devices are hosted by lower-layer DNS servers. Each DNS server either hosts its own domain(s) or points to other DNS servers in other domains that host their resolution information. DNS servers that are the "owners" of a DNS registration record (i.e., hostname to IP address) are considered "authoritative." Every device that can directly access to or from the Internet is usually registered on one or more DNS servers within its domain by its hostname and IP address. For example, the www in www.knowbe4.com refers to a DNS hostname of www within the knowbe4 domain that falls under the COM TLD.

DNS servers provide DNS services to DNS clients. DNS clients point to DNS servers to ask hostname-to–IP address resolution queries. A server can be both a DNS server and use a DNS client. But the vast majority of devices and computers connecting to the Internet are DNS clients only, asking DNS servers (which are naturally fewer) DNS resolution queries. For example, when someone on the Internet types www.knowbe4.com on their computer to look for the KnowBe4, Inc. website, their computer and DNS client will typically do a DNS query that looks something like this:

1. It checks to see if the IP address of www.knowbe4.com is already cached in memory from a previous resolved query.
2. If not, the application/OS checks the local HOSTS file.
3. If it is not located there, the DNS client sends out a single DNS client query to its locally defined DNS server essentially asking, "What is the IP address of www.knowbe4.com?"
4. The local DNS server returns the IP address if it is already cached in its local memory from a previous successful query, and if not, may or may not check its own HOSTS file.
5. The DNS service may check its own DNS database if it is authoritative for the domain (i.e., knowbe4.com) being requested.
6. If the DNS query answer is not in either location, or if DNS service does not check, the server attempts to ask another DNS server to resolve the query or directly connect to the "root" DNS servers.
   Most DNS servers are configured with a list of 13 root DNS servers (www.iana.org/domains/root/servers), which then point to the TLD DNS servers that are authoritative for the TLD domains. Most of the time, because of previous queries, at least a few of these are already cached in memory.
7. The querying DNS server essentially asks a root DNS server, "Where is the TLD DNS server that is authoritative for the TLD domain I am requesting?" (COM in this example).
8. The root DNS server returns one or more IP addresses of TLD DNS servers for the TLD.
9. The querying DNS server directly connects to the TLD DNS server that is returned and asks the TLD DNS server, "Where is the authoritative DNS server for the subdomain I am requesting?" (knowbe4.com in our example).
10. The TLD COM DNS server returns the DNS answer.
11. The querying DNS server connects to the DNS server that is authoritative for the subdomain (knowbe4.com in our example) and asks, "What is the IP address for the www.knowbe4.com DNS name?"

12. The authoritative DNS server returns the requested IP address, which the original querying DNS server then returns to the original requesting client (and to any intermediate DNS servers still involved in answering the query).

NOTE This is a simple explanation of a common type of DNS query, and in real life the query may be far more complex.

All of this happens in a few seconds or less. The user types a hostname, and fairly quickly their application is redirected to the right computer or site anywhere around the world. It is quite amazing when you think about.

All the DNS servers below the TLD DNS servers will cache the DNS entry they were involved in for a set period of time limited to the shortest of the maximum DNS cache period allowed by the service or attached to the DNS query answer (which usually has a preconfigured cache timeout value as well). Cached answers are always faster than if the DNS service has to execute additional DNS queries and answers. Figure 18.1 gives a graphical example of our theoretical DNS query.

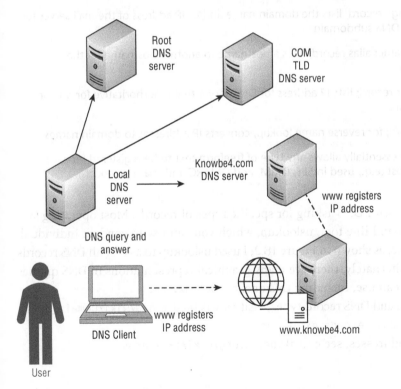

Figure 18.1: A graphical example of a theoretical DNS query for `www.knowbe4.com`

The DNS client sends out one request and gets back one answer, which then allows it to connect to its intended destination. The original querying DNS server can be involved with connecting to many other DNS servers while trying to service the original, single DNS client query.

DNS Record Types

DNS servers can contain dozens of different DNS records, most of which convert a DNS domain name to its associated IP address, although they can also point to other DNS records and hostnames (and other information). Table 18.1 shows common DNS record types.

Table 18.1: Common DNS record types

DNS record type	Description
A	Host record; most common DNS record type; lists a DNS hostname and its associated IP address (IPv4)
AAAA	IPv6 host record
MX	Mail Exchange record; lists the domain name and/or IP address of the mail server for a particular DNS subdomain
CNAME	Canonical name; alias record; links a hostname to another hostname for the same device
NS	Name server record; lists IP address for DNS server that is authoritative for one or more domains
PTR	Pointer record; for reverse name lookup; converts IP addresses to domain names
TXT	Text record; essentially allows any type of freeform text to be registered for a particular host (e.g., used in SPF, DKIM, and DMARC anti-spam protocols)

You may hear people familiar with DNS asking for specific types of records. Most operating systems come with a built-in command-line tool, nslookup, which you can use to conduct individual, manual DNS queries. For example, as shown in Figure 18.2, I used nslookup to ask for all DNS records associated with knowbe4.com. Alternately, there are many graphical representations of DNS queries out on the Internet that anyone can use, including this one: mxtoolbox.com.

For more information on DNS and DNS record types, visit en.wikipedia.org/wiki/Domain_Name_System and ns1.com/resources/dns-records-explained.

For more information on IP addresses, see en.wikipedia.org/wiki/IP_address.

Common DNS Hacks

One of the most common dependencies for an MFA solution is DNS, and subsequently, DNS has long been used to commit malicious hacking attacks. Let's explore some common types of DNS hacking.

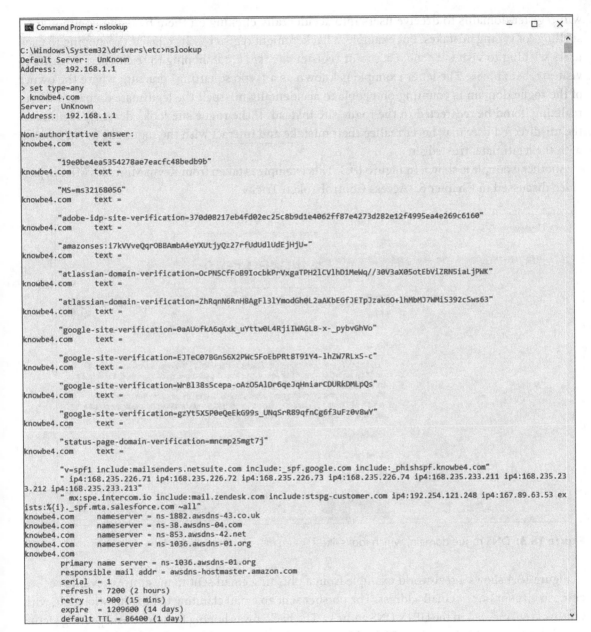

```
Command Prompt - nslookup                                                    —    □    ×

C:\Windows\System32\drivers\etc>nslookup
Default Server: UnKnown
Address: 192.168.1.1

> set type=any
> knowbe4.com
Server: UnKnown
Address: 192.168.1.1

Non-authoritative answer:
knowbe4.com     text =

        "19e0be4ea5354278ae7eacfc48bedb9b"
knowbe4.com     text =

        "MS=ms32168056"
knowbe4.com     text =

        "adobe-idp-site-verification=370d08217eb4fd02ec25c8b9d1e4062ff87e4273d282e12f4995ea4e269c6160"
knowbe4.com     text =

        "amazonses:i7kVVveQqrOBBAmbA4eYXUtjyQz27rfUdUdlUdEjHjU="
knowbe4.com     text =

        "atlassian-domain-verification=OcPNSCfFoB9IocbkPrVxgaTPH2lCVlhD1MeWq//30V3aX05otEbViZRN5iaLjPWK"
knowbe4.com     text =

        "atlassian-domain-verification=ZhRqnN6RnH8AgFl3lYmodGh0L2aAKbEGfJETpJzak6O+lhMbMJ7WMiS392cSws63"
knowbe4.com     text =

        "google-site-verification=0aAUofkA6qAxk_uYttw0L4RjiIWAGL8-x-_pybvGhVo"
knowbe4.com     text =

        "google-site-verification=EJTeC07BGnS6X2PWc5FoEbPRt8T91Y4-lhZW7RLxS-c"
knowbe4.com     text =

        "google-site-verification=Wr8l38sScepa-oAzO5AlDr6qeJqHniarCDURkDMLpQs"
knowbe4.com     text =

        "google-site-verification=gzYt5X5P0eQeEkG99s_UNqSrR89qfnCg6f3uFz0v8wY"
knowbe4.com     text =

        "status-page-domain-verification=mncmp25mgt7j"
knowbe4.com     text =

        "v=spf1 include:mailsenders.netsuite.com include:_spf.google.com include:_phishspf.knowbe4.com"
        " ip4:168.235.226.71 ip4:168.235.226.72 ip4:168.235.226.73 ip4:168.235.226.74 ip4:168.235.233.211 ip4:168.235.23
3.212 ip4:168.235.233.213"
        " mx:spe.intercom.io include:mail.zendesk.com include:stspg-customer.com ip4:192.254.121.248 ip4:167.89.63.53 ex
ists:%{i}._spf.mta.salesforce.com ~all"
knowbe4.com     nameserver = ns-1882.awsdns-43.co.uk
knowbe4.com     nameserver = ns-38.awsdns-04.com
knowbe4.com     nameserver = ns-853.awsdns-42.net
knowbe4.com     nameserver = ns-1036.awsdns-01.org
knowbe4.com
        primary name server = ns-1036.awsdns-01.org
        responsible mail addr = awsdns-hostmaster.amazon.com
        serial  = 1
        refresh = 7200 (2 hours)
        retry   = 900 (15 mins)
        expire  = 1209600 (14 days)
        default TTL = 86400 (1 day)
```

Figure 18.2: Using nslookup to query the DNS records for a domain

Look-Alike Domains

The most common type of DNS hack is tricking the user into clicking on a rogue domain that looks similar to a legitimate domain they are familiar with; this is one type of social engineering. Hackers will register domains to deceive users into accidentally clicking on them by using common misspellings or typing mistakes. For example, a hacker might register `vvatchguard.com` hoping to trick users wishing to visit `watchguard.com` or register `micosoft.com` hoping to trick users wishing to visit `microsoft.com`. The latter example is known as a "typo squatting" domain, where the owner of the rogue domain is counting on people to accidentally misspell the legitimate domain without realizing it and be redirected to the rogue site instead. If the rogue site looks decently legitimate, the misdirected user may never realize their mistake and interact with the rogue site as they would with the legitimate, trusted site.

Another example is shown in Figure 18.3. This example is taken from Kevin Mitnick's MFA bypass video discussed in Chapter 6, "Access Control Token Tricks."

Figure 18.3: DNS rogue domain, which looks like `linkedin.com` but really is `llinkedin.com`

Figure 18.4 shows a real-world example from a phishing email sent to me at my previous `roger_grimes@infoworld.com` email address. The phisher sent an email claiming to be from Microsoft, with `microsoftonline.com` in the URL's DNS address. The hacker was hoping I was an unsuspecting victim who didn't thoroughly know how DNS addresses work. They hoped I would see the `microsoftonline.com` and assume it was the origination domain. The real origination domain is `devopsnw.com`, which is not affiliated with Microsoft. `Devopsnw.com` was likely an innocent domain that was successfully hacked and used for this phishing campaign, or a real domain registered by the phisher. (In the latter case, such domains are usually removed when enough complaints come into the DNS registrar, or they are listed on blacklisting services.)

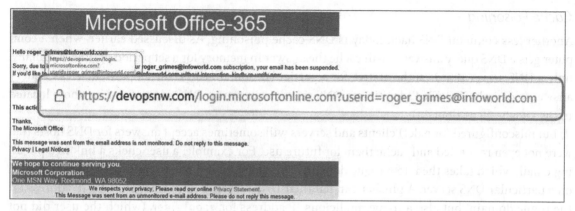

Figure 18.4: Real-world example of DNS domain naming tricks being used to try to fool unsuspecting victims

Everyone using a computer on the Internet should understand DNS at least at a basic level and learn how to recognize true domain names versus the various tricks that hackers and phishers use to fool unsuspecting victims.

NOTE If you are interested in learning more about how to determine legitimate versus rogue DNS addresses, see my "Combatting Rogue URL Tricks" webinar at event.on24.com/wcc/r/23925 82/4771996D68E43BFFA396FED7B0224967.

Hacked DNS Record(s)

Known as *domain hijacks*, the second most common type of DNS hacking is when an intruder takes control of a DNS administrator's account or the authoritative DNS server and changes the IP address of a DNS record to point to another rogue location. The hacker either takes over the user account of the legitimate DNS record owner at the DNS service and makes the change, or they hack and take over the entire DNS server. There have been decades of these types of attacks, and they still continue to be very popular.

DNS-Changing Malware

Hundreds of malware programs are around that, if run on a computer, will attempt to change the computer's DNS client settings. They will either maliciously modify the hosts file to point particular queries to their wanted locations or change the user's default DNS server to point to their rogue DNS server, which then serves up malicious IP addresses to DNS queries. Here is an example of a service warning about DNS-changing malware: www.enigmasoftware.com/dnschanger-removal. And here is a Wikipedia entry on that topic: en.wikipedia.org/wiki/Trojan.Win32.DNSChanger. Some DNS-changing malware specifically targets people's home Internet cable modems, routers, or gateways to intercept DNS queries.

Cache Poisoning

Another less common DNS hack today is DNS cache poisoning. As discussed earlier, when a computer gets a DNS query answer, it will cache the answer in memory for a set period of time. Normally, only a DNS server that is authoritative for a particular domain can return a particular DNS query answer (e.g., only KnowBe4's legitimate DNS servers can return DNS answers for any host located in the `knowbe4.com` domain).

But misconfigured (or older) clients and servers will sometimes accept answers for DNS hosts that were not even requested and cache them for future use. For example, a user clicks a link in a phishing email, which takes them to a rogue domain. That domain, if it exists and works, will be hosted on a particular DNS server. A phisher can tell their DNS server to return not only the IP address for the rogue domain, but also a rogue, malicious IP address for `google.com` (which the user did not request). The DNS client might be tricked into caching both responses in memory. The user, unaware of the DNS cache poisoning, might be directed to a fake Google site on their next Google query.

DNS cache poisonings were never super popular, but they did occur. Over a decade ago, Microsoft DNS servers and clients prevented DNS poisoning (by default), and BIND soon followed (not allowing DNS servers to answer for domains not in their authority). Because the two biggest DNS server and client vendors in the world prevented DNS caching by default, cache poisoning died in popularity a long time ago. Still, you will occasionally come across a DNS server or service that is still susceptible to cache poisoning, such as in home Internet cable modems or routers, so you will still hear about these types of attacks occurring in some rare instances and scenarios.

Name Collisions

Most namespaces have "reserved" names, which refer to specific services or objects. For example, on Windows systems at the command-line prompt, you cannot create files or folders with the names of AUX, CON, or LPT1, or CON2, because they are reserved words that refer to specific objects or handles used by the operating system.

There are also words and locations that mean something in one namespace that can conflict or be used with objects or words in another namespace. These are known as *name collisions* or *namespace collisions*. Let's look at two common, real-world examples.

WPAD A dangerous, easily hackable name collision that isn't super well known by the general public is the WPAD (Web Proxy Auto-Discovery) protocol. WPAD allows Windows and Microsoft applications to automatically discover proxy services that applications (like Internet Explorer and Edge) can use to connect to the Internet. Microsoft intended WPAD to be used as a way to help Windows computers connect to the Internet more easily without having to manually hunt down the proxy settings and enter them. Every Windows computer and related WPAD-enabled applications will generate DNS queries that ask for the location for WPAD. Most networks don't use WPAD, so the query gets ignored and receives no response.

But knowledgeable hackers can register WPAD on their local DNS servers. For example, they can name their Windows computer WPAD and reboot. When they do this on a Windows network, most Windows DNS servers will automatically register their WPAD hostname and related IP address in the local DNS servers authoritative for the domain. Thus, any other computer on the same network or using the same DNS server asking for WPAD will then be given the IP address of the hacker's computer. All the hacker has to do is set up a rogue proxy server (many free proxy servers or services are available for download on the Internet), and they can then start directing all the victim's network traffic to their computer or to other rogue locations. It really is a dastardly hack.

For more information on WPAD hacking, see `resources.infosecinstitute.com/hacking-clients-wpad-web-proxy-auto-discovery-protocol` and `auth0.com/blog/heads-up-https-is-not-enough-when-using-wpad`.

Corp.com Microsoft is involved in this namespace collision example as well. Microsoft released Active Directory, their primary network namespace, in 1999. AD uses DNS as its primary name resolution service (along with NetBIOS and LDAP), and anyone using Active Directory has to set up their network using DNS naming conventions. Not every AD administrator understood DNS super well, and for over a decade, tens of thousands of legitimate instruction guides used the `corp.com` domain as their example when telling an admin how to build or configure something, including Active Directory. As a result, tens of thousands of private AD domains have `corp.com` in their Active Directory domain name (e.g., `roger.corp.com`). Before all corporate networks were connected to the Internet full time, this wasn't a problem. But as every network started to be connected to the Internet, the `corp.com` part of the address started to cause a name collision issue. For example, if I (or more likely, a computer or program on my behalf) looked for `www` on my `roger.corp.com` network, the way DNS resolution works, the hostname of `www` would be looked for on not only `roger.corp.com` but `corp.com` as well. Someone owning `corp.com` could end up causing a lot of havoc if they wanted to.

For over a decade, a single American private citizen actually owned the `corp.com` domain on the Internet. Some early testing showed that over 375,000 computers were trying to send his domain information it did not request. One day, as a nonmalicious test, the owner set up an email server "answering" in the `corp.com` domain to see what would happen. Within an hour, he had over 12 million emails sent to the server. Many of these emails contained confidential information. The owner understood the problem well, and he eventually sold the `corp.com` domain to Microsoft for $1.7 million. Kudos to the owner and to Microsoft. The man didn't have to sell the valuable domain to Microsoft and Microsoft didn't have to spend $1.7 million because people didn't understand how DNS worked on Active Directory networks. But both parties were able to come to an agreeable resolution that benefited many Windows users. To learn more, check out `krebsonsecurity.com/2020/02/dangerous-domain-corp-com-goes-up-for-sale/` and `krebsonsecurity.com/2020/04/microsoft-buys-corp-com-so-bad-guys-cant`.

> **NOTE** Here is a great 2014 paper on risky DNS namespace collisions: `www.icann.org/en/system/files/files/name-collision-mitigation-study-06jun14-en.pdf`.

Needlessly to say, there are many different ways to do DNS and namespace hijacking. When DNS or another namespace is hijacked, it can lead to many different crimes, including:

- Bypassing MFA authentication
- Collecting email destined for the domain
- Collecting web traffic destined for the domain
- Collecting logon credentials used on the domain

And this has been done in the real world, many times. Let's get to some more examples.

Example Namespace Hijacking Attacks

Let's look at example namespace hijacking attacks.

DNS Hijacking Attacks

As covered earlier, one of the most popular types of DNS hacking is for a hacker to take control of a DNS record administrator's account or an entire DNS server to change the IP address of a well-known hostname to a malicious IP address. This is done thousands of times a year. Sometimes it's done by individual hackers and sometimes by nation-states. In 2019, popular and respected security vendor CrowdStrike reported (www.crowdstrike.com/blog/widespread-dns-hijacking-activity-targets-multiple-sectors) that 28 organizations in 12 countries had their DNS hijacked. Once hijacked, the hackers started receiving any traffic destined for those domains. The domains were hijacked anywhere from less than a day to over a month. The hackers were fairly sophisticated and even created trusted digital certificates for any connections requiring TLS. Security firm FireEye concluded (www.fireeye.com/blog/threat-research/2019/01/global-dns-hijacking-campaign-dns-record-manipulation-at-scale.html) that at least some of the attacks were accomplished by Iran. You can read more details here: krebsonsecurity.com/2019/02/a-deep-dive-on-the-recent-widespread-dns-hijacking-attacks.

MX Record Hijacks

As noted in Table 18.1 earlier, MX records are DNS host records that point to the IP addresses of email servers. If an attacker can move a victim's MX record to point to another IP address, they can often capture email headed to the victim. It works even if the victim's email users have MFA protecting their accounts.

In one example, fabricegrinda.com/hacked-cryptocurrencies-stolen, a cryptocurrency trader who protected his account with MFA was the victim of a SIM swap attack (covered in Chapter 8, "SMS Attacks") and had his MX record stolen. The hackers called his cell phone company pretending to be him, said he had lost his cell phone, and asked the company to activate another SIM with the same number. After the hackers redirected his MX records to their new rogue Microsoft Exchange server, they reset the passwords on his Bitstamp, Coinbase, Dropbox, Gmail, Twitter, Uphold, Venmo, and Xapo accounts. All the password reset messages and links were sent to his registered email address, which was now under the hackers' control. The hackers then tried to transfer all his bitcoin to their bitcoin wallet using Venmo. He was saved only because he had already nearly hit his maximum sending amount on Venmo.

In this example (arstechnica.com/information-technology/2014/01/how-i-lost-my-50000-twitter-username/), a man with a single-character Twitter handle (@N), which he valued at $50,000, had his MX record stolen while it was registered with GoDaddy. The hacker socially engineered tech support agents at PayPal and GoDaddy to do so. They then tried to steal his valuable Twitter handle and got access to his Facebook account and other websites. The victim contacted GoDaddy to regain control of his DNS MX record, and he was asked by GoDaddy tech support to verify his account information, all of which had been recently changed by the hacker. Because the legitimate account owner could not convince GoDaddy that he was the real owner, he could not regain control. He even contacted a GoDaddy executive through a friend, and that did not fix the problem. The victim eventually relented and let the attacker have his @N Twitter handle to minimize the damage. The hacker then shared how he did everything (social engineering) and suggested what he should do to protect himself next time. Nice hacker!

Dangling CDN Hijack

Content delivery networks (CDNs) are hosted by companies with servers all over the Internet and lots of fast and widespread Internet bandwidth. If you are a company that wants the fastest response to all your potential customers on the Internet, you can buy the services of a CDN. The CDN will host your server, services, or objects on their servers, and when one of your customers goes to access your domain services, they get that content delivered by the closest or fastest CDN server. For example, when Microsoft pushes out a new patch, they will often use a CDN to make that patch available to everyone very quickly. To use a CDN, the vendor must have DNS records that point to the CDN instead of their own DNS domains for the content. Read here for more details on CDNs: www.cloudvps.com/helpcenter/content-delivery-network-cdn/how-does-cdn-work.

In 2016, a white-hat hacker noticed (hackerone.com/reports/168476) that Snapchat had "dangling" MX records. Dangling DNS records occur because of a few reasons (e.g., abandonment, unintentional orphaning, etc.), but the end result is that the domain can be claimed by an unintended party and maliciously redirected elsewhere. It's the digital equivalent of moving out of your house and not putting in any mail forwarding request or an unauthorized intruder in your home to open up your mail. You can read more on dangling DNS records here: nominetcyber.com/dangling-dns-is-no-laughing-matter.

In this case, the hacker noticed that Snapchat had left some of their MX records pointed to a CDN domain that was no longer registered with their DNS registrar, GoDaddy, which controlled those records. He then opened an account with GoDaddy, registered those domains, and moved the dangling DNS record names to his account. He was a good guy hacker, so he contacted Snapchat on the HackerOne bug bounty program and got a $250 reward for reporting the dangling DNS.

Registrar Takeover

Why just take over a few DNS records when you can take over the whole DNS registrar? If you don't already know it, the companies that allow you to buy and/or register your DNS hostnames and IP addresses are known as *DNS registrars*. In the early days of the Internet, they used to be a very controlled and limited group. But today, there are tens of thousands of them, with varying levels of security and ethics.

Brian Krebs revealed (`krebsonsecurity.com/2015/02/webnic-registrar-blamed-for-hijack-of-lenovo-google-domains`) that Google's entire Vietnam subdomain (`google.com.vn`) was hijacked by a group called Lizard Squad. The hackers had taken over the Malaysian DNS registrar called `Webnic.cc`, along with over 600,000 domains it controlled, using a web server injection exploit. The hackers also took over `Lenovo.com`, which is a top laptop vendor and maker of all other sorts of computer equipment. For Lenovo, the hackers also switched their MX record and began directly responding to emails the media had sent to Lenovo to confirm the attack (you can see a screenshot of the email here: `www.tripwire.com/state-of-security/security-data-protection/how-hackers-can-hijack-your-website-and-read-your-email-without-hacking-your-company/`).

It's notable that in this attack, the hackers also gained control of "transfer codes," which are secret codes registrars use to authenticate themselves to one another for quick domain transfers behind the scenes. This particular hack was done by a hacking group more interested in pranks than in real espionage, but the damage to Webnic's customers and the broader Internet could have been way worse if a serious group had gained control.

DNS Character Set Tricks

Most of us type in our DNS URLs using English or our local language, whatever that may be. But many apps, including browsers, will accept different character sets, and those character sets can be used to hack users and bypass defenses.

Computers display characters on a screen or printer by choosing a particular number of an agreed-on character set that displays a particular character. For example, if I wanted to display a lowercase "f" using ASCII, I would use ASCII decimal number 102. To display an uppercase "F" using ASCII, I would use decimal number 70. And on any computer supporting ASCII, my program could use an ASCII table to look up and translate the numbers to letters. Here's a full ASCII table: `en.wikipedia.org/wiki/File:ASCII-Table.svg`.

A character set is also a way for one language to be converted into another. For example, suppose I wanted to allow users of my U.S.-centric application to type in the word *frog* and wanted my users in Russia to type it in Cyrillic (i.e., лягушка) and have my program understand it either way. I could code my application to have two or more languages or use a character set that can automatically translate and display between different languages. Character sets are usually defined at a device, OS, or application level.

The first computers used the ASCII character set. It could only support 128 English characters. The first 32 ASCII characters are "control characters" like line feed and end-of-text delineators. The rest cover uppercase and lowercase English letters, the 10 numerals, and common symbols you find on your keyboard (like !@#$%^&*). But a limit of 128 characters is a bit restrictive for non-English speakers.

Early on, Windows used what is known as the American National Standards Institute (ANSI) character set. It supported only 218 characters, which was better than 128-character ASCII, but it wasn't built to handle more complex languages like Cyrillic and Chinese. With Windows 2000, Microsoft began to use Unicode. Unicode supports every known language, active and ancient, and it can represent over millions of different characters.

Since 2009, the World Wide Web (essentially the Internet) uses a character set known as UTF-8 (Unicode Transformation Format 8-bit). It's a subset of over 1 million Unicode characters. Consequently, most of the world, including DNS (which officially only supports ASCII), actually uses UTF-8. When you type a character into your browser, behind the scenes the computer is dealing with the typed in character as its Unicode number. It's the way the web and web applications work behind the scenes.

Many websites and applications support a subset of UTF-8 with what is known as Punycode (en.wikipedia.org/wiki/Punycode) translations. Punycode is just a Unicode version for hostnames. You may also see IDN (internationalized domain names; en.wikipedia.org/wiki/Internationalized_domain_name), which is a method for converting and displaying domain names between languages using Unicode and Punycode.

Hackers can use Punycode and IDN characters that look like other language characters to create look-alike domain names. These types of attacks are known as *homograph attacks* (en.wikipedia.org/wiki/IDN_homograph_attack). They not only fool users but often get by expensive defenses. For example, the Unicode Latin "a" (U+0061 hex) and Cyrillic "a" (U+0430 hex) may look the same in a browser URL but are different characters represented in different languages. Any DNS address containing one versus the other will be different DNS addresses and can point to different IP addresses, even though they may look the same when sent in an email or displayed in a browser. A great example of this is to click the apple.com link at the beginning of this article: www.theguardian.com/technology/2017/apr/19/phishing-url-trick-hackers. You can read more about these types of attacks at these sites:

- thehackernews.com/2017/04/unicode-Punycode-phishing-attack.html
- www.wordfence.com/blog/2017/04/chrome-firefox-unicode-phishing
- en.wikipedia.org/wiki/IDN_homograph_attack
- blog.knowbe4.com/homographic-domains-make-phishing-scams-easier

NOTE It's even possible to use Punycode hacking tricks with SMS: www.zscaler.com/blogs/ research/smishing-punycode.

ASN.1 Tricks

ASN.1 is a standard interface description language for defining hierarchical, tree-like data structures. It is widely used in computers, telecommunications, and cryptography. It is used by X.509 digital certificates; Simple Network Management Protocol (SNMP); Kerberos; LDAP; wireless radio tags; and 3G, 4G, and 5G wireless networks. You can learn more about ASN.1 here: en.wikipedia.org/wiki/ Abstract_Syntax_Notation_One.

In 2004, hackers used an ASN.1 vulnerability to carry out a denial-of-service attack against Microsoft's core network authentication protocol NTLMv2 (www.itworldcanada.com/article/hackers- take-advantage-of-microsoft-asn-flaw/15081). In 2016, an ASN.1-based attack allowed hackers to execute code across a broad range of telecommunications equipment: commsrisk.com/asn-1-bug- lets-hackers-attack-mobile-carriers. These types of ASN.1 attacks could easily be used to allow SMS SIM hijacking. Here's an example of a videoconferencing system being hacked using its ASN.1 elements: media.blackhat.com/eu-13/briefings/Jodeit/bh-eu-13-hacking-video-jodeit-wp.pdf.

I bring up ASN.1 attacks to show that our OS and devices rely on shared standards that can be avenues into many different, often unexpected avenues of attack. Oftentimes the protocols are full of unknown vulnerabilities because of their rather obscure technical use. They aren't in everyone's face every day the way DNS is. But when hackers look at Punycode, ASN.1, and other supporting protocols and standards, they often find exploitable vulnerabilities.

BGP Hijacks

I want to finish this chapter's example attacks with another protocol standard that is essential to the running of the Internet but yet only known and worried about by a small percentage of hard-code networking professionals: Border Gateway Protocol (BGP).

When you are on the Internet, whether it's reading content from a website, watching a video, or sending an email, your keystrokes and received content go through a lot of devices, usually routers, between your computer and the other side and back. The average Internet network packet goes through 15 to 22 different routers between source and destination. That's a lot of routers and routing. Anyone sniffing on those routes or routers could potentially eavesdrop on your nonencrypted data (or metadata). But in order to focus on someone or an organization in particular, an attacker would need to know exactly which routers or routes your traffic will take. The Internet has millions of routers, and it's hard to predict where one network packet will go versus another (although there are well-known router aggregation points in every country). That's the beauty of the Internet.

A remote hacker trying to eavesdrop on a specific person or organization would essentially have to force the victim's traffic to go over a particular route in order to capture it. Turns out they can.

Since 1994, most of the major routers on the Internet have used BGP. It's the way the Internet's routers work. Each participating Internet BGP router is assigned a unique autonomous system number (ASN). BGP routers send and receive traffic from other BGP routers, and most of the traffic on the Internet depends on BGP routers and their BGP routing tables. You can learn more about BGP here: `en.wikipedia.org/wiki/Border_Gateway_Protocol`.

Unfortunately, when BGP was created and released, it didn't have a lot of security or integrity checks built into it. Essentially, any BGP router automatically trusts what any other BGP router tells it. One mistake by an errant BGP router administrator who updates their BGP routing table in the wrong way can cause huge routing issues with the Internet. Sometimes those mistakes seem indistinguishable from intentional hacking.

Starting in 2013, huge BGP "mistakes" have sent large percentages of domestic Internet traffic through other countries, often countries engaged in a digital cold war with the other country. Here's the first article I remember reading about it: `arstechnica.com/information-technology/2013/11/ repeated-attacks-hijack-huge-chunks-of-internet-traffic-researchers-warn/`. Since then I've read dozens of articles on BGP "mistakes," which just happened to send some country's Internet traffic through another country's routers, including these:

- `asiatimes.com/2018/10/beware-china-may-be-reading-your-email`
- `arstechnica.com/information-technology/2018/11/strange-snafu-misroutes-domestic- us-internet-traffic-through-china-telecom`
- `asiatimes.com/2018/10/beware-china-may-be-reading-your-email`
- `www.zdnet.com/article/russian-telco-hijacks-internet-traffic-for-google-aws- cloudflare-and-others`

Here's a military white paper on a Chinese series of BGP misdirections: `scholarcommons.usf.edu/ cgi/viewcontent.cgi?article=1050&context=mca`.

When a BGP hijacking happens, any unencrypted traffic rerouted through the hijacked network points can be captured and read. Even if the data is encrypted, an attacker can at the very least read source and destination IP addresses and determine relationships. If the attackers get fake, trusted digital certificates, as is often the norm with regular phishers, they might be able to read email and other web traffic. And like DNS hijacking, BGP hijacking has the distinct likelihood of bypassing MFA authentication.

I hope this chapter has convinced you of the importance of namespaces in our computer security and how their malicious manipulation can easily bypass MFA.

Defenses Against Namespace Hijacking Attacks

This section examines developer and user defenses against namespace hijacking attacks.

Developer Defenses

First we'll look at some developer defenses against namespace hijacking attacks.

Education

Education is always the primary key to fighting cybersecurity threats. Developers should understand the importance of namespaces to their MFA solution and understand the dependencies well enough to threat-model possible attacks.

Threat Model

We rarely think of namespaces when doing cybersecurity threat modeling, but if your authentication solution depends on them—and it probably does—any dependencies have to be threat-modeled, analyzed for threats, and mitigated.

Default Packet Encryption

Encrypt all traffic headed to and from your MFA solution so that if someone tries to eavesdrop on network traffic or manipulate a namespace with redirection, what little they can read will be of limited value. The encryption should always use industry-accepted ciphers and key sizes.

DNS Registrar Record Lockdowns

If your MFA solution uses DNS as part of its solution and that DNS points back to your records, make sure that no unauthorized person can hijack your DNS records. Discuss with your DNS registrar how they and you can prevent DNS hijacks and what the recovery actions are, if needed, and document them. Require that the registrar "lock" your DNS records. Even though this is a book on hacking MFA, have your DNS registrar require MFA to log on to your DNS admin account. Any changes to your DNS records should result in an email to a nonchanging, frequently checked email address.

Enable SPF, DKIM, DMARC

Enable Sender Policy Framework (SPF), DomainKeys Identified Mail (DKIM), and Domain-Based Message Authentication Reporting and Conformance (DMARC) in DNS and on your email servers. Enabling these three anti-phishing protocols enables your customers to verify that any email sent to them claiming to be from one of your protected domains is really from an email server authorized to send email on your behalf. It prevents unauthorized domains from sending email claiming to be from your domains. Require TLS between email servers (if possible).

NOTE If you are interested in learning more about SPF, DKIM, and DMARC, see my webinar called *How To Prevent 81% of Phishing Attacks From Sailing Right Into Your Inbox With DMARC* located at www.knowbe4.com/webinar-library.

Hard-Code Values Where It Makes Sense

If the names and IP addresses in your MFA solutions are permanent and unchanging, think about hard-coding them into your software or firmware to decrease your reliance on the namespace resolution if possible. As an example, if your MFA solution uses DNS, think about using permanent IP addresses instead. Both Microsoft and Google hard-code critical DNS addresses in their software so that even if someone malicious manipulates the DNS namespace, their software will always be able to "dial home" and find the parent company.

This is very tricky since it's incredibly difficult to predict whether or not hostnames and IP addresses will change over time. For example, today most IP addresses use IPv4 but are likely to move to IPv6 (version 6) if they haven't already. There is a chance that hard-coding any name or IP address could create a critical interruption issue in the future if your names, IP addresses, or namespaces change. So, only hard-code values you know for sure will not change for the lifetime of your product or those that you can fairly easily update when needed.

Decrease Chance of Namespace Manipulation

Instead of hard-coding values, a better solution is usually to program your solution in such a way that it would be difficult to manipulate expected namespace values without detection. For example, if your MFA solution connects back to a common website, have the website and MFA solution do a known challenge-response handshake as part of the initial authentication. For example, the website might already know a hard-coded value ahead of time that the MFA device uses to start the process, sort of like a TOTP device. Anyone eavesdropping on the initial connection might see data being passed but not know how the data is being composed or constructed. They would be unable to predict the value needed for the initial handshake connection. Any site without the correct handshake information would not be sent information from participating clients, and vice versa.

Site and Device Preregistration

Requiring that all sites and MFA devices get identified by a GUID and preregistered with the sites and services they will be involved with helps prevent man-in-the-middle attacks.

Don't Support IDN or Punycode

I understand the appeal of IDN and Punycode for international language support. However, I read more about malicious bypasses and social engineering of end users using these standards than anything else. The best of both worlds would be to create filtering that prevents the malicious misuse of these character set translation mechanisms while still allowing them to be used. Today, the most popular browsers attempt to recognize common IDN/Punycode redirections. But in the absence of those sorts of defenses, just ban both code sets instead. They are just not worth the risk.

User Defenses

Next, we'll look at user defenses against namespace hijacking attacks.

Education

All users should be educated about malicious namespace attacks, especially common DNS tricks, including IDN and Punycode mischievousness. Users need to understand how to determine between legitimate and malicious domains and be made aware of how a namespace compromise can impact their MFA solution of choice. Admins should choose MFA solutions that take namespace attacks into account and mitigate against them. Users should be made aware of DNS-changing attacks and malware.

Implement DNSSEC

DNS Security Extensions (DNSSEC) is a long-standing protocol that attempts to make DNS hijacking and other malicious manipulations harder to pull off for attackers. When DNSSEC is enabled, the DNS servers involved contain digital certificates that allow them to sign their zone files and answer the DNS clients. DNS clients, when also enabled, can verify that the DNS answers they receive come from the verified authoritative DNS servers that sent them. DNSSEC doesn't prevent all types of DNS attacks, but it does prevent some, and for that alone it should be enabled. It can even prevent routing tricks like BGP from working. For more information on DNSSEC, see en.wikipedia.org/wiki/Domain_Name_System_Security_Extensions.

Sadly, even after over a decade of attempts to get the world to embrace DNSSEC, it hasn't been widely adopted. At first, many DNS vendors, such as Microsoft, did not fully support DNSSEC for many years after it came out, and when they did, it was difficult to configure and/or did not conform to open standards. Today, most DNS vendors have made enabling DNSSEC far easier than it used to be.

In order to get the full protection, all the DNS servers involved in answering a query need to be DNSSEC-enabled. The root DNS servers were DNSSEC-enabled in 2010. Since then, the most popular and important DNS TLD servers (COM, EDU, ORG, MIL, and NET, among others) have been enabled for DNSSEC as well. The only thing left is for each participating subdomain DNS server to be DNSSEC-enabled. Unfortunately, that is where strong compliance ends. As of 2020, less than 1 percent (0.8 percent or 1.7 million domains) of COM subdomains participate with DNSSEC. You can get up-to-date statistics here: scoreboard.verisignlabs.com.

It cannot hurt to enable DNSSEC on the DNS servers you control. You likely cannot enjoy its best protection by telling all DNS clients to reject any answers from DNS servers that do not have DNSSEC enabled, because that would mean DNS clients would probably be rejecting 99 percent of the DNS answers they get to their queries. But for the DNS domains that do support DNSSEC, it means hackers will have a harder time with malicious DNS misdirection.

Detect and Alert on Unauthorized DNS Changes

User systems should detect and alert on unauthorized changes to DNS settings (and the HOSTS file), however that is accomplished. No one can guarantee that they can prevent 100 percent of malicious DNS attacks. But if a significant DNS change is made, if the event always generates an alert message that will be read and investigated if unauthorized, you can limit the damage. DNS clients should always report changes to their local HOSTS files or changes to their relied-on DNS server addresses. Both types of changes are fairly rare in most environments. DNS domain owners should get alerts of DNS server address changes and DNS record ownership changes. If you can't prevent an attack from happening, quick warning is the next best defense.

Summary

This chapter covered DNS and other namespace hijackings like BGP and ASN.1 exploits. We discussed common DNS hacking methods and seven example real-world attacks. We concluded by describing developer and user defenses against namespace hijackings.

Chapter 19, "API Abuses" will cover API abuses.

19 API Abuses

This chapter will cover hacking multifactor authentication solutions through or using the application programming interface. I'll review some previous terms and technology and introduce new ones so that you can understand what these terms mean in context when you read about MFA APIs.

Introduction

As covered earlier in Chapter 3, "Types of Authentication," application programming interfaces (APIs) are created by developers of their underlying technologies or services to allow other developers and users to programmatically interface with their product. APIs allow other people and services to quickly interact with a product or service and to easily extend its functionality. APIs are a staple of the computer world, especially if you want your product to be widely adopted and used. If an API is created and the general public can access and use it, it's known as an *open* or *public API*.

As an example, the HaveIBeenPwned website (`haveibeenpwned.com`), which can tell you if a particular logon name and password has been part of a known breach, has an API (`haveibeenpwned .com/API/v3`) anyone can use. In fact, it's on its third version. HaveIBeenPwned's API allows a different account lookup every 1.5 seconds. If you tried to look up different accounts or passwords manually using the website, you'd probably be lucky to request a new one every 10–15 seconds. So, using the API is at least a 10× speed increase when doing multiple lookups. On top of that, what the website can look for and return is limited to what the website has been preprogrammed to do. With its API, you can look for dozens of different types of information and perform actions that simply aren't possible using the default website interface.

Many other sites and services link to HaveIBeenPwned using the API, and its availability and low-cost use ($3.50 per month as of this writing) is likely responsible for much of the overall site's success. Instead of having to look up compromised accounts one at a time, an external programmer or service can look up a bunch of accounts and passwords (HaveIBeenPwned stores over 500 million stolen passwords) much more quickly. Any potential passwords it may share are delivered as SHA-1 hashes of the underlying plaintext passwords, so someone requesting them cannot easily determine what the underlying plaintext passwords are, but the password hashes can be used to compare against other existing, known (hashed) passwords to see if they are identical to other existing, known passwords for that account. That way, a hacker can't as easily learn someone else's password by querying HaveIBeenPwned, but an existing, known password for a particular logon account can be compared to a known, breached password.

Many existing, legitimate services use HaveIBeenPwned's APIs to perform bulk compromised account lookups. For example, my employer, KnowBe4, has a free tool called Breached Password Test (www.knowbe4.com/breached-password-test) that utilizes HaveIBeenPwned's API to look for logons related to the person's company who runs the tool. That way, if someone has hundreds to thousands of user accounts and passwords they need to test, the API allows them all to be tested far more quickly. KnowBe4's password testing tool tests for more things than just breached passwords (such as weak passwords), but the breach checking component is one of the main features. Figure 19.1 shows an example report snippet from the KnowBe4 Breached Password Test tool.

Many existing open source hacking/research tools work with HaveIBeenPwned's API as well to look up compromised user accounts and passwords. For example, the hacker reconnaissance tool called recon-ng (tools.kali.org/information-gathering/recon-ng), contains modules (the names contain the abbreviation *hibp* for HaveIBeenPwned) that allow users to confirm whether or not particular accounts and their passwords have been involved in a known breach, and it does this by using HaveIBeenPwned's API. Figure 19.2 shows recog-ng and the related breach password lookup modules.

Nearly every API has rules, usage agreements, connection points, commands, and syntax to learn in order for users to be able to successfully and efficiently use it. To use HaveIBeenPwned's API, users must first obtain a HaveIBeenPwned API license key. An HIBP API key is a unique 32-digit hexadecimal string for every different user, such as:

```
b163ce018a4147e5ad83c11d8187aaaf
```

Then to use the API to look up account logons that may have possibly been breached, the user connects to HaveIBeenPwned's API URL and issues a command that looks similar to this:

```
GET haveibeenpwned.com/api/v3/breachedaccount/rogerg@banneretcs.com hibp-api-key:
b163ce018a4147e5ad83c11d8187aaaf
```

The API query essentially says, "Look to see if any breached logons have the logon identity, rogerg@banneretcs.com, and here is my unique API key to prove I registered to use the API." Then the HaveIBeenPwned service will return all the possible documented breach cases involving that logon identity along with the name of the breaches they're associated with.

Then, whatever script or program interfaces with the HaveIBeenPwned API simply uses that command string over and over, varying the account name being looked up until all the sought identity accounts have been queried. There are many other commands and types of lookups anyone can perform using the API's commands and syntax.

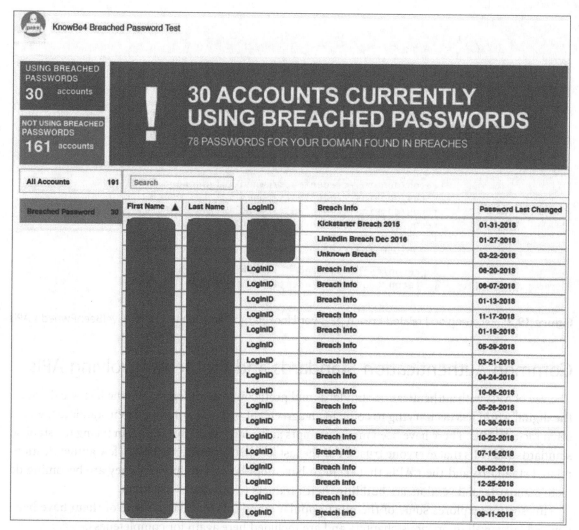

Figure 19.1: Partial example report from KnowBe4's Breached Password Test tool

Behind the scenes of the Internet, billions, if not hundreds of billions, of API calls are being made every day between various services. Without hyperbole, it is the way the Internet works at a programming level. A common programmer saying is "If you have to do it more than once, automate it." APIs allow interfacing and automation.

NOTE Many of today's protocols and APIs use Extended Markup Language (XML) to communicate messages, formats, and data between two communicating parties. XML was designed to work with and be familiar to programmers who used HTML, because each line of data is encompassed between "opening" `<section>` and "closing" `</section>` brackets. This makes anything that uses XML both human- and machine-readable if the programmer chooses not to encode the enclosed information further. You can read more about XML here: en.wikipedia.org/wiki/XML.

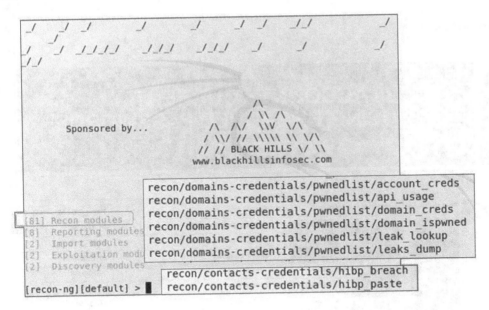

Figure 19.2: Recon-ng and related breach password lookup modules that leverage HaveIBeenPwned's APIs

Common Authentication Standards and Protocols Involving APIs

The use of APIs with authentication standards and protocols is no different. For the last two decades, the digital world has been trying to come to an agreement on some common open standards, which often include APIs. There have been many attempts and nearly as many failures in trying to establish standards and APIs that everyone trusts. For the last few years, there have been a few authentication-related standards and their APIs that seem to have popular staying power. They are becoming de facto standards, and vendors are building their products to interface with them.

This section explores some of the most popular standards and APIs. Some of them have been covered fairly well in previous chapters and are included here again for completeness.

OAuth

As covered in Chapter 3, Open Authorization (OAuth) is one of the most popular open federated authentication standards used on the web today. Because of its widespread adoption and use, I'll spend more space on it than some of the other standards.

Most of the major, huge websites and services (e.g., Facebook, Twitter) support it. OAuth is a framework that describes how unrelated servers and services can safely allow authenticated access to their assets without actually sharing the initial single logon credential. An identity provider, which may or may not be a website or service the user has authenticated to, attests to the already existing successful subject authentication and helps the subject to log on/access additional sites or services.

It's important to mention that OAuth is about authorization, not authentication, even though it involves authentication as well. With OAuth, the user has to authenticate, at least once, to the identity provider or first site/service, but after that, the first sites and software the user is using exchange authenticated access control tokens. The user doesn't have to reauthenticate to additional sites or services, although they usually have to approve (click Logon or Allow) the new logon/access to the new site and service (see examples of approval prompts in Figures 19.3 to 19.5). The subjects involved in the additional accesses aren't reauthenticating. They don't provide additional authentication proofs. They are past that part of the authentication process and are now in the authorization part of the identity life cycle. A user's authentication proofs are not being shared between sites. The original site/service is attesting to the subject having successfully authenticated and helps to establish the subject accessing future sites and services.

The future sites and services may involve another logon, but the user will not be asked to reauthenticate if they have already authenticated the selected identity recently somewhere else. In Figure 19.3, the user is accessing a new site, Grupz Vacation Rentals, and the Grupz site is detecting that the user has already successfully authenticated to two previous OAuth providers (in this case, Facebook and Google). Many of the times when you see "log on with Facebook," "log on with Google," or "log on with Apple," what you are seeing is OAuth involved and working. Any site working with OAuth needs to register with one or more OAuth identity providers. In this example, Grupz has previously registered with at least both Facebook and Google. Many participating websites have only one or the other, because they figure most people are going to have either, and why waste the effort of offering additional OAuth providers.

The user need only click on one of the shown buttons and Grupz and Google/Facebook will exchange the necessary authorization information to allow the user to log on without providing additional authentication information (although the user can log on using non-OAuth credentials as well).

If you haven't logged into your OAuth identity provider (shown as Facebook or Google in Figure 19.3) in a while, you may be asked to authenticate to them again before they authorize you to log on to the additional site/service. But the logon credentials you would be submitting are to the site/service you already trust (i.e., Facebook/Google) and not to the new site (Grupz, in this case). The new site/service never gets your authentication proofs. If the additional sites or services are compromised, attackers would get only a single access control token that is only good for the single, site/service and not your authentication proofs.

Figure 19.4 shows OAuth recognizing that the subject has more than one identity account registered with the same OAuth identity provider (Google in this example) and is asking the user to choose which identity they want the future authorization to occur under.

Figure 19.3: An example OAuth approval/logon prompt as a user goes to access an additional site or service

A site/service can also request access to your personal information, files, and data. Figure 19.5 shows Dropbox requesting access to see and download a subject's Gmail contact list. You should only allow the access if you trust what the requesting site/service plans to do with that access. Not allowing the requested access cancels the requesting site/service's ability to use OAuth with that provider, so if you don't allow the permission request, you can't use OAuth with that additional site/service.

NOTE Be aware if that site/service gets compromised, any attackers would have the same access to your personal information, so give out any personal access to your data and information skeptically and sparingly.

OAuth identity providers allow you to see a list of every previously allowed site/service (see Figure 19.6 for an example), and you can remove that site/service from your list of OAuth site/services you allow to interact with that particular provider on your behalf (see Figure 19.7 for an example).

Figure 19.4: Example of an OAuth prompt where the user is being asked which OAuth identity they want to authorize the next site/service

NOTE   It isn't always immediately obvious which participating OAuth sites/services you have given access to by just looking at the list. For example, the Grupz website in Figures 19.3 and 19.4 is listed as project-939659317702. This is because of how it was registered by whoever did the registration for Grupz. You can open up the link to get more detail, including the site/service URL it is associated with to help make your decision on whether to keep it or not.

All users should periodically review their allowed OAuth providers and registered sites/services and permissions and remove those that are unused or not needed. It only takes a few clicks to reestablish them again if needed in the future. For more information on OAuth, visit oauth.net, 256stuff .com/gray/docs/oauth2.0, and aaronparecki.com/oauth-2-simplified/#user-experience-and-alternative-authorization-flows.

Much of what I have described about how OAuth works involves OpenID Connect, discussed next.

Figure 19.5: OAuth-participating website asking for access to a user's personal data while using OAuth to log on for the first time to Dropbox

Figure 19.6: OAuth provider listing all sites/services previously approved by the user

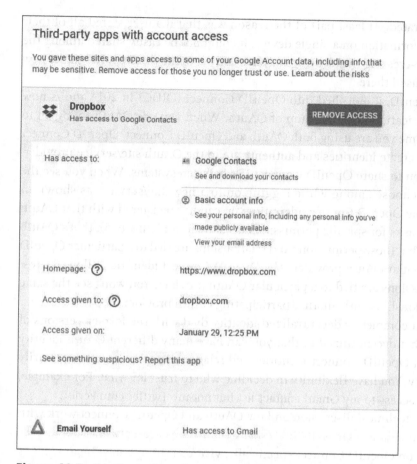

Figure 19.7: OAuth provider allowing a user to remove OAuth access to previously allowed site/service

OpenID and OpenID Connect

OpenID Connect (openid.net) is an authentication layer that goes on top of and is frequently used with OAuth. There was a preceding similar open and decentralized version known as OpenID (en.wikipedia.org/wiki/OpenID). It was an interesting authentication standard and was supported by many big members, including Microsoft, which deployed it as Windows CardSpace. The part that excited most identity experts was the ability to have a shareable identity and authentication that was completely decentralized. The identity and authentication information was stored by the user on their own system. There was no one entity or set of entities that controlled it or stored the authentication information (such as Microsoft Passport in the past). No one entity controlled the standard, which was good, and there was no one location that could be compromised, other than the user's device, that would lead to access to all the user's identities.

A slew of security concerns have been announced over the years against OpenID (see en.wikipedia .org/wiki/OpenID#Security), and in general, the idea of a completely decentralized standard, no matter how promising, evaporated. At least part of the reason was that if a user stored all of their identity and authentication information on a single device, it could not be easily shared among the user's other devices without re-creating the identities or physically copying the OpenIDs to the new devices so that they could be used there.

In the third version of OpenID, it morphed into OpenID Connect (OIDC) in 2014 and is now aligned as the official authentication layer over top of OAuth. When you use OAuth to log on to another website, most of the time you are using both OAuth and OpenID Connect. OpenID Connect is the protocol that helps you create identities and authenticate to the OAuth site/service provider. The OAuth provider allows you to share OpenID Connect IDs between systems. When you see the list of different IDs you can choose among while logging on to a new site/service (as shown in Figure 19.4), that's the available OpenID Connect identities you can use registered with that OAuth provider. When a site/service asks for specific permissions (as shown in Figure 19.5), that's OAuth and its authorization features, but those permissions and relationships are tied to a particular OpenID Connect identity with a particular OAuth provider. The OpenID Connect identities, allowed sites/ services, and approved permissions are tied to a particular OAuth provider. You won't see the same IDs, entities, and access relationships with another participating OAuth provider.

So, the original dream of a completely decentralized identity died with the former versions of OpenID, but it is still somewhat decentralized in that you can have many different OAuth identity providers, each with different OpenID Connect identities and relationships. You're not necessarily tied to one provider or identity. You have flexibility in deciding who to trust for what. For example, I may allow Dropbox to have access to my Gmail contact list but not my Twitter connections.

You can see a slightly more technical discussion on how OAuth and OpenID Connect work with each other here: stackoverflow.com/questions/1087031/whats-the-difference-between-openid-and-oauth. For more information on OpenID Connect specifically, visit openid.net/developers/specs and en.wikipedia.org/wiki/OpenID_Connect.

SAML

Security Assertion Markup Language (SAML) is an identity federation standard that allows the secure exchange of authentication and authorization information of subjects, identity providers, and service providers in or between security domains. It is frequently used to transmit security credentials of a user to log into something and is a favorite standard of corporate single sign-on solutions. SAML competes against OAuth + OpenID Connect in many areas. SAML gets used more in the enterprise space and OAuth + OpenID Connect in the consumer Internet space. One big benefit as compared to OAuth is that SAML can be used for both authentication and authorization, whereas OAuth, by itself, is used for authorization. For more information on SAML, see developers.onelogin.com/saml and www.csoonline.com/article/3232355/what-is-saml-how-it-works-and-how-it-enables-single-sign-on.html.

OATH

The Initiative for Open Authentication (OATH; openauthentication.org) is an industry consortium group focusing on strong authentication (i.e., token devices) and creating and using open standards. They focus on three major types of MFA solutions:

- Subscriber identity module (SIM)
- Public key infrastructure (PKI)
- One-time password (OTP)-based solutions

OATH has a large list of members and has created several widely adopted open token standards (most covered in previous chapters), including the following:

- HOTP: HMAC-Based OTP Algorithm (RFC 4226)
- TOTP: Time-Based One-time Password Algorithm (RFC 6238)
- OCRA: OATH Challenge/Response Algorithms Specification (RFC 6287)
- PSKC: Portable Symmetric Key Container (RFC 6030)
- DSKPP: Dynamic Symmetric Key Provisioning Protocol (RFC 6063)

Even though OATH seems to have a lot of promise and there are some fairly recent partner announcements, such as from Microsoft in 2018 (techcommunity.microsoft.com/t5/azure-active-directory-identity/hardware-oath-tokens-in-azure-mfa-in-the-cloud-are-now-available/ba-p/276466), it appears to have dissolved recently. The FIDO standard seems to be capturing the lion's share of news and forward progress, even from the same members. OATH seems to have come into existence, released a bunch of important RFCs, and then disappeared. Sadly, some of the methods that became more popular—such as generating keys in cleartext, like Google Authenticator does, instead of using Dynamic Symmetric Key Provisioning Protocol (DSKPP)—seem to have won out even though OATH is clearly technically superior. Unfortunately, that type of outcome, popularity over security, is not unusual in the field.

NOTE One other very interesting OATH initiative is Sharing Transaction Fraud Data, RFC 5941 (www.ietf.org/rfc/rfc5941.txt). It is an RFC that recognizes that the world would be better served if we could share information about security incidents in a faster, previously agreed-on format and structure. Information about fraud and cybersecurity incidents could be uploaded and shared by participants to help respond to existing and future threats faster. Unfortunately, it doesn't appear much traction has occurred since its submission in 2010. Something like this needs to happen and is likely to be part of whatever solutions end up making the Internet a safe place to be.

You can learn more about OATH here: openauthentication.org and openauthentication.org/wp-content/uploads/2015/09/AnIndustryRoadmapforOpenStrongAuthentication.pdf.

FIDO

As we covered in previous chapters, the Fast Identity Online (FIDO) Alliance specifications are a set of popular "passwordless" open authentication standards that rely on public–private key cryptography. FIDO supports a wide range of 1FA and MFA devices (computers, USB tokens, mobile phones, wired and wireless, etc.) and biometrics. FIDO2 (its second and current version) has two main authentication parts and four specifications. Any FIDO2-participating software (OS, browsers, websites, services, etc.) must use the World Wide Web Consortium's (W3C's) Web Authentication standard (WebAuthn) and APIs.

The Client to Authenticator Protocol (CTAP) specification covers wireless devices. The Universal Authentication Framework (UAF) specification is a passwordless method, which can be 1FA or MFA but does not necessarily have to involve a separate physical device. The Universal 2nd Factor (U2F) specification covers MFA and requires a second factor and device of some type. The U2F standard is the one being most adopted by MFA solution providers.

With U2F, the user registers their device with the participating site or service and chooses to implement an authentication factor, such as a PIN or biometric ID. When connecting to the site or service, or conducting a transaction that requires strong authentication, the device performs local authentication (verifying the PIN or biometric identity) and passes along the success or failure to the remote site or service. With U2F, an additional security device (such as a cell phone or USB dongle) is used as the second factor after the password or PIN has been provided.

Traditional TLS guarantees server authentication only to the client. FIDO2 authentication goes much further by linking "registered" devices to their users and those devices to the eventual websites or services. One authentication device can be linked to many (or all) websites and services. The pre-registration prevents many, but not all, types of authentication attacks.

U2F prevents most man-in-the-middle (MitM) attacks, such as those discussed in Chapter 6, "Access Control Token Tricks," and summarized in Figure 6.3. For example, the Kevin Mitnick MitM demo proxy attack against LinkedIn would not have worked. This is because U2F requires registration of the device and involved/allowed websites. Inserting an MitM proxy would have the link to the server and client coming from locations not previously registered, and the U2F authentication solution would not even respond (or would respond with an error). You can read about FIDO MitM protections in section 6 of this FIDO specification document: `fidoalliance.org/specs/fido-u2f-v1.2-ps-20170411/fido-u2f-overview-v1.2-ps-20170411.html`.

> **NOTE** Part of what I and others love about FIDO is that even in their specification section on how they prevent most MitM attacks, they tell you what would be needed to bypass even those defenses (it's a pretty specific set of circumstances that are unlikely to be present in the real world) and tell you how to prevent even those. They aren't afraid to say they can't prevent every possible attack and don't pretend to. This is distinctly different from most authentication solutions and standards. I wish more MFA solutions were as honest and direct. Transparency builds trust.

For more information on the FIDO2 standard and specifications, visit `fidoalliance.org/specifications/download`.

Other Common API Standards and Components

This section covers other common API standards and technologies and terms you may come across when you are looking at MFA APIs.

RESTful APIs

You may read about RESTful APIs. REST stands for representational state transfer web service standard. A RESTful API supports and uses the REST standard, rules, and syntax to allow interfacing with it. REST is language independent and uses very common HTTP commands and syntax to connect and communicate. If you are an HTTP programmer, you can use HTTP to connect to a RESTful API. Consequently, RESTful APIs are very popular and supported inherently by all sorts of servers and client frameworks (such as Node.js and Apache CXF).

Here is an example REST POST message trying to pass logon credentials to a server with an API:

```
POST /oapi/auth/logon HTTP/1.1
HOST: example.org
Content-Type:text/xml
<credRequest>
  <login name="administrator" password="password">
    <site contentUrl=""/>
  </credentials>
</credRequest>
```

REST isn't a very complex standard, which is both its strength and its weakness. Sophisticated interactions are more difficult to do and may be impossible without lots of additional programming outside the REST standard. Every REST request, like the underlying HTTP it relies on, is stateless, meaning the state of a client to a particular server is not inherently tracked between REST transactions. REST transactions must use methods like cookies and GUID numbers to track clients and servers between separate transactions. You can learn more about RESTful APIs here: restfulapi.net.

SOAP

REST's most direct (early) competitor is Simple Object Access Protocol (SOAP). SOAP is a messaging protocol and API that uses XML to communicate data between a client request and server. SOAP was created by multiple people at Microsoft in the late 1990s and never formally became a standard. But for nearly a decade it was a popular messaging format and API to develop to, especially for enterprise apps. Here is an example of a SOAP request message:

```
POST /Transaction HTTP/1.1
Host: www.example.org
Content-Type: application/soap+xml; charset=utf-8
<xml version="1.0"?>
<soap:Envelope xmlns:s="http://schemas.xmlsoap.org/soap/envelope/">
  <soap:Header>
    <Action soap:mustUnderstand="1"
```

```
          xmlns="http://example.org/transaction">
          http://example.org/IService/Operation
       </Action>
     </soap:Header>
   <soap:Body>
     <GetCount xmlns="http://example.org/TransAPI">
        <Item>345699</Item>
     </GetCount>
   </soap:Body>
 </soap:Envelope>
```

One of SOAP's benefits was that it used XML. Once you got used to reading XML, you could fairly quickly understand what the SOAP request or reply was attempting to do. But all the required header information and using XML also made the SOAP messages "bulky" compared to alternatives, especially as compared to REST requests and replies. Many programmers were distrustful of a standard made by and promoted by Microsoft, and Microsoft was late in submitting it as an open standard, allowing other competitors to overtake it.

> **NOTE** Another API standard you may come across is Common Object Request Broker Architecture (CORBA; en.wikipedia.org/wiki/Common_Object_Request_Broker_Architecture). Years ago, it was gaining a lot of traction inside enterprises, but it's now taking a backseat to REST.

REST's simplicity gained overwhelming popularity as SOAP and other earlier API standards started to dwindle. Today, SOAP and CORBA are basically "legacy" corporate standards.

SOA APIs and Web Services

Most of today's Internet-accessible APIs, including REST, are considered part of the *service-oriented architecture* (SOA) style of software design. In SOA, the client requests an action or service of a server using an API over a network using one or more network protocols. If this is done over the World Wide Web of the Internet, using HTTP/HTTPS, the service being accessed may be defined as a *web service*. Web service protocols, and there are many, are often defined by including *WS-* at the beginning of their name. Web services often offer and work with RESTful APIs.

JSON

JavaScript Object Notation (JSON) is a common way of communicating data between services. JSON is based on the JavaScripting language but is programming language independent. Most JSON messages are human-readable. Here is a simple example of JSON data within a message:

```
{
    "LogonName": "Administrator",
    "password": "TheyWillNeverGuess",
    "PrimaryGroup": Administrators,
```

```
  "address": {
   "streetAddress": "33 N Garden Ave",
   "city": "Clearwater",
   "state": "FL",
   "postalCode": "33755-6610"
  },
 }
```

JSON was recently involved in a Twitter data leak situation because Twitter's improperly con-structed JSON headers incorrectly allowed browsers to keep and leak confidential information if an intruder could get into a victim's browser cache. See `twitter.com/AlexMartin/status/1275439664808095744`. This is about as low risk as you can get. The bigger problem would be how an attacker got access to your browser's cache, but it goes to show that JSON is now yet another dependency component we have to worry about.

Physical Wireless Standards and APIs

Of course, most MFA solutions rely on multiple other standards, each often with their own API (if present), such as Universal Serial Bus (USB), smartcard, and Bluetooth. As covered in previous chapters, each of these is a potential area of exploitation and attack.

In closing this section, I want to add two points. First, none of these standards and APIs are inher-ently weak. There are standards and APIs that are fairly insecure as designed and lead to more than average exploitation. But the standards and protocols I've discussed here aren't considered poorly designed or overly weak. They are just another component dependency that can be a potential exploi-tation vector in a particular implementation.

Second, I don't want anyone to come away with the feeling that the examples of APIs and stan-dards I've shown are here to stay. No, APIs and standards change all the time—not all of them, but most of them. No doubt, some of these latest, greatest, agreed-on standards will become tomorrow's legacy standards. It could benefit the world greatly if a few single authentication and authorization standards were allowed to be the "winners" and stay for a significant period of time. Application developers would need to worry about creating only one way of sharing authentication data and improving automation. But standards, protocols, and APIs change over time along with technology. And maybe having varying and changing standards isn't always a bad thing.

Common, long-lasting standards also mean increasing chances for single point of failures. It also gives the malicious hackers of this world a common way of doing bad things. You'll see this discussed in computer security media as the weaknesses of a computer or security "monoculture." Monocultures allow malicious hackers to port malice across more things at once. In the same vein, when each system has its own way of operating and interfacing, it makes it harder for hackers to do widespread damage using the same tools. So, common standards and APIs are a dual-edged sword, giving us the ability to work and interface across platforms but at the same time open up potential vulnerabilities that might be exploited more widely.

Examples of API Abuse

APIs allow malicious hackers to do bad things involving the underlying technology faster and more destructively across a wider group of people. APIs have been used to rob people of hundreds of thousands of dollars in seconds and to compromise millions of accounts of very popular websites and services. The two main motives for API abuse are:

- To speed up automated compromise of a single victim
- To automate an attack of multiple victims

Turns out APIs are used by malicious hackers for the same reasons as legitimate programs: speed and automation. In either case, APIs can be used to bypass MFA. This section looks at examples of APIs being used to compromise MFA solutions.

Compromised API Keys

In 2019, popular cryptocurrency website Binance was compromised and exploited. As Binance's CEO explained (binance.zendesk.com/hc/en-us/articles/360028031711-Binance-Security-Breach-Update), hackers were able to steal 7,074 bitcoins (see Figure 19.8), equivalent to over $40 million in that day's conversion rate, by stealing users' API keys and ultimately their Binance "hot wallet," which used a TOTP token.

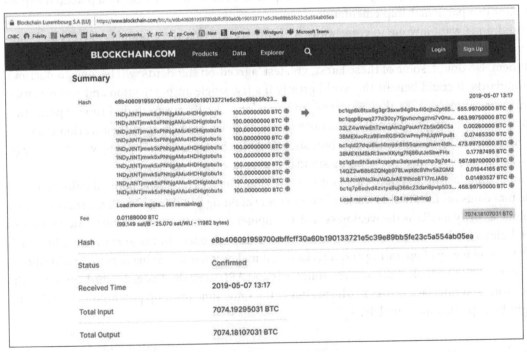

Figure 19.8: Binance transfer screenshot from theft confirming the transfer of $40 million of users' bitcoin to attacker's wallets

Binance has an API (see `binance-docs.github.io/apidocs/testnet/en/#general-api-information`), which it encourages users to get and use (`cryptopro.app/help/binance-api-key`) so that they can buy, sell, and trade cryptocurrencies very quickly. The API uses open standards, like REST and JSON, and is published and open. Binance's API allowed it to become very popular, and it quickly became one of the most used cryptocurrency portals in the world. It is even used for "trading bots," which do automated (high-frequency) trading based on predetermined entry and exit points. See an example of a trading bot that uses the Binance API here: `thebitcoinnews.com/setting-up-api-keys-for-trading-bot-on-binance`.

And when hackers took over multiple Binance user accounts using a socially engineered, fake proxy site, they used their knowledge of the API and the user's stolen API keys (and Google Authenticator TOTP codes) to steal their cryptocurrency very quickly. As Binance CEO Changpeng Zhao wrote in his blog: "The hackers had the patience to wait, and execute well-orchestrated actions through multiple seemingly independent accounts at the most opportune time. The transaction is structured in a way that passed our existing security checks." That's what having an API can assist with.

Bypassing PayPal 2FA Using an API

Reported in 2014, this incident is a little aged but provides another example of how APIs can be used in bypassing MFA and of the slowness of some vendors to respond to MFA security bugs. The bug was discovered by a single researcher and then reported to Duo Security (`duo.com/blog/duo-security-researchers-uncover-bypass-of-paypal-s-two-factor-authentication`), who got involved and more thoroughly investigated.

PayPal has a RESTful API that uses OAuth and JSON. PayPal also allows MFA to be required to use their service, but at the time MFA did not work with Paypal's mobile app. It was found that PayPal included in their OAuth message to their API an indicator of whether or not 2FA was enabled. The field was even named 2FA Enabled and possible values were True or False. Anyone sniffing the connection between a participating client and PayPal's service would have easily seen this.

NOTE Discovery of this bug would have probably been delayed a bit if PayPal had not labeled the field 2FA Enabled.

So, all any attacker knowing a victim's logon name and password would have to do is craft or intercept the authentication message headed to PayPal and change the 2FA Enabled value from a True to a False, and PayPal would take the user's logon name and password as valid credentials even if the victim had required 2FA. They also found an additional PayPal SOAP-enabled API that allowed money to be transferred.

To make matters worse, the original finder of this issue, Dan Saltman, reported this issue to PayPal via their official bug bounty program. For reasons not reported, PayPal did not reply to Saltman for over three weeks. In frustration, Saltman contacted Duo Security for their help, and they got involved through the bug bounty program and were assigned a case number. It still took PayPal another two weeks to request additional information about the vulnerability before they fixed it. This slow response is unacceptable in the computer security world, although these types of delays are likely more common than not, especially with the larger firms.

It is not unusual for large firms with millions of customers taking months to fix an issue to minimize operational issues. But what is not understood is why PayPal did not respond to the initial bug finder for three weeks and why it took almost two weeks to ask a second bug finder for more information. Perhaps one-off issues were involved in these instances. Unfortunately, too many firms seem to respond slowly to bug reporters, something that frustrates both the bug reporter and other security experts alike. While firms take their time responding, all customers of the exploitable product are at a higher risk. The bug is known by at least one or more people, and it could be known and used by others who have not responsibly reported it. Slow responses to bug reporters are likely responsible for more irresponsibly reported bugs than anything else (in my opinion). Frustrated bug finders often get disillusioned by the official bug reporting channels and just publicly release their finding in frustration.

AuthO MFA Bypass

Auth0 (`auth0.com`) is a popular authentication vendor offering MFA solutions. Their API (`auth0.com/docs/api/authentication`) uses OAuth, OpenID Connect, REST, JSON, and SAML. Auth0 MFA users use this API whenever they authenticate using an Auth0 MFA solution. The API uses a JSON web token standard named JSON Web Token (JWT), and tokens can assert claims (such as "I'm MFA and I'm using this algorithm for my digital signatures").

The issue is that the JWT standard allows a digital signature algorithm value (`alg`) of `None`, which was intended to be used by developers for solutions that previously assured API authentication messages using other previous means. In order for this to work securely, an MFA solution must verify any JWT token containing `alg: None` was previously authenticated before accepting anything it contains or asserts. Auth0's API did not. And someone discovered this bug in 2015 (`auth0.com/blog/critical-vulnerabilities-in-json-web-token-libraries`) and wrote an excellent article on the details and re-creation steps. That one mistake allows a ton of mischief, including the ability to bypass MFA.

It's also a good study in dependencies. The initial problem really wasn't Auth0's. Allowing an `alg` value of `None`, as the JWT standard does, is a strange decision. You would think that a standard dealing with authentication would require a valid digital signature to be used. Auth0 responded to the initial report by looking for and appropriately treating any JWT message with an `alg` value of `None`. Problem solved, right?

No. In April 2020, another person discovered (`insomniasec.com/blog/auth0-jwt-validation-bypass`) that Auth0 treated an `alg` value of `None` correctly, but any other case-sensitive value (i.e., `none`, `NonE`, `nONe`) would be treated as a valid JWT value of `None` but not subject to the offsetting, protective mitigations. And it wasn't noticed and publicly reported for another five years. The second bug finder even realized that he could enable and use a completely different MFA solution with the user's name, password, and Auth0 ID. So, they could bypass the Auth0 MFA requirement and create another rogue MFA instance tied to Auth0's API that could be successfully used once Auth0 fixed the first problem.

Authy API Format Injection

Authy is a popular MFA vendor. In 2015, a security researcher found out Authy's MFA initial token response to a new connection request did not encode user parameters of the token (sakurity.com/blog/2015/03/15/authy_bypass.html). This allowed an attacker to supply any other valid token user's ID, after the original user started their process, to log on without MFA. They traced the vulnerability back to a dependency on something called Sinatra "rack protection." Turned out other MFA vendors also had the same dependency and were susceptible to the same bug. The researcher also found a directory traversal attack (covered in Chapter 15, "Buggy Software") to throw in for boot. To quote the researcher, "Yes, the attacker was able to bypass 2 factor authentication on any website using Authy with something as simple as ../sms in the token field!"

Duo API As-Designed MFA Bypass

This is an interesting attack that speaks more to weak configuration defaults than anything else. As mentioned earlier, Duo Security (duosecurity.com) is a popular MFA vendor. When configuring a system to use a Duo Security MFA solution, one of the default install choices is a "fail open" option (see Figure 19.9).

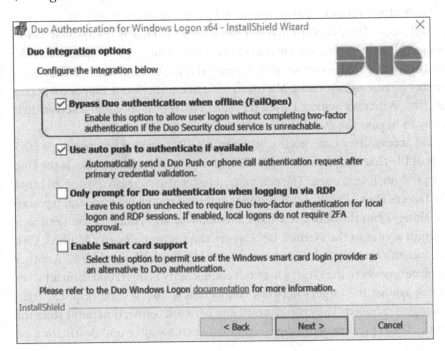

Figure 19.9: Duo Security install showing the fail open default configuration option

In the computer security world, fail open means that when something doesn't work, ignore it or just proceed as if the action worked. In this particular scenario, it says "If the Duo API URL location involved in this authentication transaction cannot be contacted, don't require MFA to log on."

Fail open configuration choices are not thought of highly in the computer security world. And if that fail open option is the default option, it's liked even less. Many people who install software take all the default options. The average person installing something just clicks Next, Next, Next. They assume the vendor made safe default choices for them. Users even get warnings from some software programs if they change a default install option to something safer. They worry that perhaps their change could cause operational interruption. I understand why Duo Security choose a default fail open, because they don't want an administrator unable to log on to one of their (own) Duo-protected servers just because there is a network problem or the API link involved (it's different per instance) is down for some reason. Instead, they want the logon to proceed. The user (or hacker) still needs to provide a logon name and password in most cases. And the risk is very minimal. On top of that, if a particular user is concerned with the risk they can just change the default option. It's a win-win.

But if an attacker (or insider) knows about this feature, they can bypass the MFA requirement by creating a connection problem between the computer being logged into and the API connection point. Before Duo had their "offline logon" feature added in late 2018, bypassing Duo's MFA requirement could be as easy as unplugging a network cable. But unplugging cables is a physical attack and requires physical access to the device or network being attacked. But network interruption can also be accomplished logically.

This was first brought to my attention by this article: `www.n00py.io/2018/08/bypassing-duo-two-factor-authentication-fail-open`. The penetration tester came up with a few ways to cause a connection problem that involved already having local access to the server. That begs the question: Why does a local attacker already on a targeted server need to bypass MFA in the first place? Well, there's a chance they have some sort of access (say, using Microsoft's PSExec utility), but they want access using a GUI logon console (say, Windows Remote Desktop Protocol [RDP]). They could leverage their non-console access as a way to bypass the Duo MFA requirement.

If they already have local access, they can "poison" the target's DNS service by creating a DNS entry in the target's DNS host file that redirects the Duo API URL link to somewhere else. If the Duo API connection fails for any reason, it fails open. The penetration tester also suggested using an MitM network attack, where the target's Duo API URL connection is captured on the network and replaced on the fly, to do the same thing. I can think of a few more methods for an insider on the same network. An attacker with admin access to the victim's DNS server can register a bogus API link URL address so that when the victim's target tried to connect, it would get a fake IP address. Another attack method could take place anywhere the target's network connectivity is interrupted; an attacker could attempt a DDoS attack against the target's network connection so that a valid response from the Duo API URL link never gets received. They could attack any network connection point from the target's host to the API link. The typical network connection between a source and destination on the Internet is often over a dozen nodes. Many of them are predictable and constant. Compromise any of those connection points or block the return traffic from the Duo API from getting back to the target, and it fails open.

I don't want to pick on Duo Security. The computer security world is full of default "fail open" configuration choices, although these types of settings are not nearly as routine today as they were in decades past. Today, most computer security choices more appropriately choose "fail closed."

> **NOTE** The author of the Authy bug also found another bug in Duo: `sakurity.com/blog/2015/03/duo_format_injection.html`.

Microsoft OAuth Attack

A security researcher discovered an OAuth attack (`www.scmagazineuk.com/new-phishing-campaign-bypasses-multi-factor-authentication/article/1683911`), which allowed attackers to send phishing emails that tricked users into granting permissions to their otherwise protected document using OAuth and OpenID Connect. The victims were sent an email that linked to a SharePoint document. Clicking the document redirected the user to a legitimate Microsoft Office 365 logon, but the document URL included an OAuth redirect to a bogus, look-alike website that then requested various permissions during the logon process (as is common during OAuth/OIDC logons, as shown earlier). The user could be tricked into granting permissions to the user's documents to the bogus website. If approved, the attacker would get the ability to read and write all of the user's files and documents of others they had access to (through the `File.ReadWrite.All` permission). And the newly granted permissions were indefinite. If the user was required to use MFA, the attacker would not be required to.

This attack can only be defeated if the user is aware of the permissions and access they grant to any website or service, and they take the time to make sure they grant permissions only to legitimate, expected sites and services. Sadly, many users don't understand OAuth and OpenID Connect well enough and simply click OK when prompted.

Sign In with Apple MFA Bypass

Sign In With Apple was a new SSO method announced (`www.apple.com/newsroom/2019/06/apple-previews-ios-13`) by Apple in June 2019. It uses OAuth and JWT to allow users who had previously authenticated to their Apple product using Touch ID or Face ID MFA to access other participating sites without having to reveal their email address or to reauthenticate. In May 2020, a researcher found that any previously validated user with a token could submit any other Apple email address (`bhavukjain.com/blog/2020/05/30/zeroday-signin-with-apple`) and get an approved, valid JWT token, which would then allow the attacker to authenticate as that user on the website. The bug was so critical that Apple paid this researcher $100,000 (`www.forbes.com/sites/daveywinder/2020/05/31/apple-pays-hacker-100000-for-sign-in-with-apple-security-shocker`).

NOTE It's stories like this one that I use to remind people that huge MFA security bugs still happen all the time even involving huge, well-known companies.

Token TOTP BLOB Future Attack

This is an interesting type of API attack suggested by Alexandre Cagnoni of WatchGuard (he's one of the tech editors for this book). Many companies store TOTP secrets as what is known as a BLOB, a binary large object. When a user uses their TOTP token to log on to, say, a bank, where this type of scenario is very common, the inputted TOTP code is compared to the stored TOTP secret (and other information) stored as a BLOB in the backend database. Attackers, using a well-known API and logon authentication, can reach the backend database and BLOB. These APIs are often known by the names of the vendors that created or popularized their use (e.g., OneSpan or Datablink).

The attacker must know how the API works and get a copy of the targeted TOTP BLOB or BLOB database or access to it (not an impossible hurdle to climb). Because the API is fairly well-known within the banking industry, this part is not difficult to learn at all. Then, the attacker changes the time on their computer to a future time—say, tomorrow at 6:00 a.m.—and then uses the API and their computer against the BLOB. With a six-digit TOTP code, there are only one million possible combinations of numbers. Using the API on their computer, the attacker can automate the process and guess very fast. At some point they are going to get an OK response from the API and learn what TOTP code works at what future time. The attacker can then use the TOTP code to implement a future fraudulent transaction. Alexandre performed this sort of test attack in his downtime to prove it could work, and it did. Luckily, neither he nor I are aware of this type of attack being used successfully in a real-world attack. And it just goes to show that if an attacker has access to the ultimate authentication secret, it's always game over.

NOTE While not specifically dealing with bypassing MFA, Akamai's 2020 State of the Internet report (www.akamai.com/us/en/multimedia/documents/state-of-the-internet/soti-security-financial-services-hostile-takeover-attempts-report-2020.pdf) stated that 75 percent of credential stuffing password attacks against the financial industry happened through APIs and not logon portals. Clearly, publicly accessible APIs are often attacked.

Defenses Against API Abuses

Now we'll look at developer and user defenses against MFA API hacking.

Developer Defenses Against API Abuses

First, let's explore some developer defenses to MFA API hacking.

Educate Developers

Developers should be educated about the past history of MFA solution API abuses. The inexperienced developer likely doesn't understand how APIs can be abused. Share with them the potential threats and show them real-world examples, like those discussed in this chapter, so that they can see it isn't just a theoretical concern.

Threat-Model APIs

Any developed APIs should be threat modeled for potential risks and attacks and the appropriate mitigations implemented. If you are not sure where to start, use the examples listed earlier as starting places.

Limit API Attack Surface

Minimize source code and attack surface area to limit what angles an attacker can attempt to abuse. With APIs, less is better for security.

Use Industry-Proven APIs, Standards, and Protocols

As stated earlier, the industry standards and protocols such as OAuth, OpenID Connect, SAML, REST, SOAP, and JSON are industry-proven methods. Nothing they do is inherently weak. Some MFA vendors try to "roll their own" methods, and in doing so many will inadvertently insert security weaknesses where security weaknesses didn't need to be. Don't fix what isn't broke. Use standards. Just make sure you implement them in safe ways.

Validate Authentication Workflow

Many API abuses were caused by authentication workflow issues, where if something later on was correctly done earlier, the attack would not have happened. Order matters in authentication. For example, with the Auth0 example earlier, the authentication system was treating the `alg` value as valid and relying on it, which then led them to rely on the "digital signature" in the API message. The message's header and digital signature should have been checked first, before relying on the information in the header.

Lock API Keys to Locations Instead of Email Addresses

Many API abuses only work because the API or API key is allowed to be used from anywhere. Today, most APIs either don't care a lick about origination location or tie it only to a provided email address. Preregistering users/devices of the API's IP address or other uniquely identifying location information would at least prevent hackers from using the API from other places.

Use Client-Side Security Enforcements Cautiously

Any time a client provides critical information that can impact authentication, that information should be validated, if possible, before accepting. Any security decision that essentially asks a client something similar to "Are you secure, valid, and safe?" is taking a risk that the client or an attacker targeting the client isn't maliciously changing the critical value before it gets returned. In the PayPal example earlier, PayPal was accepting a client's attestation of whether 2FA was or wasn't enabled. An attacker needed to change only a single value in a single API message to bypass MFA. That's not good.

Default Fail Closed

Whenever there is a decision between "fail open" and "fail closed," a security vendor should choose fail close. I know that's easy for me to write without any developer or customer responsibilities, and in practice, you need to be responsive to customer needs. But defaults matter. You can offer the fail open option—just don't offer it as a default, because nearly everyone takes the defaults. You're a computer security company in the 21st century. Act like it.

Obscure MFA-Related Values

Lastly, when vendors are passing values to and from their API, it can't hurt to use obscure naming conventions and values to make it less easy for people investigating your API and messages to see what values may or may not be impacting authentication decisions. Yes, this is a "security by obscurity" recommendation, but security by obscurity works. It's low cost and easy to use. A hacker seeing a field name of Field32 will have a harder time figuring out that Field32 equates to a particular critical authentication decision.

User Defenses Against API Abuses

User defenses against API abuses are limited, but I thought of a few good ones.

Education

Users need to be aware that APIs can be abused, and if their MFA solution has an open API, it, like any dependency, represents a potential area for exploitation. If your MFA solution has an API, ask the vendor if they have threat-modeled the API and implemented mitigations for weaknesses. If the vendor hasn't performed a threat model against their API, suggest that they do or explore what that means for your organization's risk profile.

Implement Secure Configuration Options

Look out for insecure default install configuration options and choose "fail secure" options whenever faced with a "fail open" versus "fail closed" decision. Realize that not all vendors always choose default secure choices. Vendors are under lots of pressure to avoid impacting user operations, even when those options could invalidate the whole reason you are using the product. Respect vendors who have secure defaults even when that sometimes causes operational disruption due to an "as-designed" default configuration option. We need to reward vendors who default to more security and not less.

Protect API Keys

If you have an API key, realize that it could be stolen by hackers to access your account and information. API keys are "keys." Treat them as such. Don't leave them in email or lying around on your hard drive. Instead, encrypt them or place them inside your password manager (if you use one).

Summary

This chapter covered API abuses. We began by exploring common API technologies and standards to help you better understand MFA APIs. We also discussed a handful of sample MFA API hacks. This chapter concluded by listing developer and user defenses against API abuses.

The next chapter will cover miscellaneous MFA attacks that didn't fit nicely into previous chapters.

20 Miscellaneous MFA Hacks

This chapter will cover some MFA solution hacks that didn't fit in previous categories and that were not discussed in earlier chapters.

Amazon Mystery Device MFA Bypass

This strange MFA bypass was reported by a U.S.-based Amazon user (`www.reddit.com/r/sysadmin/comments/dpbt3t/the_perils_of_security_and_how_i_finally_resolved`) in November 2019. This Amazon user woke up to discover several Amazon gift cards fraudulently charged to his Amazon account. This surprised him because not only did he *not* make the gift card purchases, but he, as an IT security professional, had protected his Amazon account with an OTP token. Amazon allows three different OTP options (see Figure 20.1): SMS Message, Voice Phone Call, and Phone App.

When enabled, the OTP code is required during the logon process to the Amazon user account, including any device the user connects to the account. The victim in this case thought that his account was thoroughly protected until the fraudulent charges happened. He tried to contact Amazon fraud support and sadly discovered that there was no option other than to send an email that has a promised 48-hour turnaround response time. So, he enabled another OTP option, deleted his credit card information from his Amazon account, disabled all current active sessions, removed all approved allowed devices, and even changed his banking and credit card website passwords.

After much research and talking to an offshore tech support person, he learned that someone (likely located in Asia) made the purchase from a Huawei smart television. He didn't own a Huawei television. To this day he does not know how his Amazon credentials were stolen. But he was perplexed by two things: 1) how the foreign television connected to his Amazon account when he has OTP protecting it, and 2) why he didn't see the foreign television on his list of allowed and connected devices attached to his account when he listed allowed devices under his account options. He learned that not only are non-Amazon devices (such as smart televisions, game consoles, and Roku boxes) *not* shown in Amazon's account device list, but they aren't displayed to most Amazon tech support as well. Only specialized Amazon senior tech support people have a tool that can see the foreign

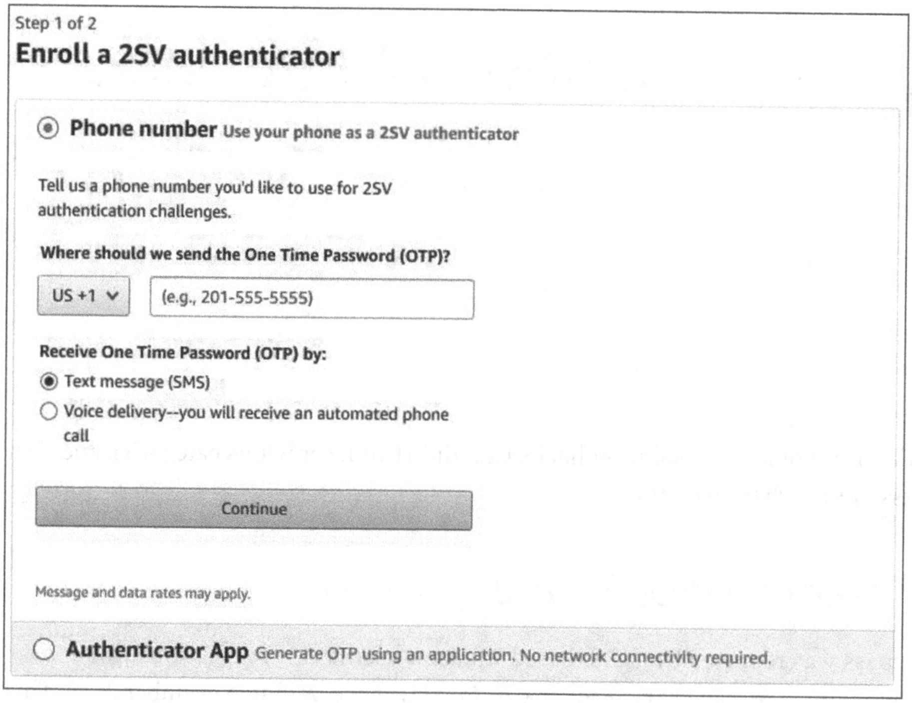

Figure 20.1: Amazon OTP options

devices. He also discovered that even when you specify OTP as required on your Amazon account, any existing connection will not be forced to use OTP until it is disconnected or deleted and reconnected. In the end, his whole experience was written up here: www.theregister.co.uk/2019/10/31/ amazon_account_hacking. This is a reminder that even when you think you've *required* OTP protection, that may not be the case—you may still be compromised using that account by an attacker that wasn't required to use MFA.

Obtaining Old Phone Numbers

In Chapter 8, "SMS Attacks," you learned about SIM swapping attacks, where an attacker obtains a legitimate subscriber's SIM information and transfers it to a phone in their possession. In this similar but different scenario, an attacker legally obtains a victim's old phone number, and simply having the ability to use the old number is enough to take control of the victim's current MFA solution.

In one example instance, the MFA vendor, Authy (authy.com), allowed Authy MFA users to register and use multiple devices (and phone numbers) with their MFA solution. This permitted any attacker knowing an Authy user's old phone number (previously used with their Authy solution) to get that number and then access the user's account using SMS (if the user did not disable Authy's Multi-Device feature, which was enabled by default). This oversight came to a head when Coinbase, the world's largest and most popular cryptocurrency trading site, stopped recognizing Authy as a valid MFA solution (www.reddit.com/r/Bitcoin/comments/6f0hhb/coinbase_recommendation_migrate_from_authy_to) and told all its Authy-using customers to change to Google Authenticator instead. Further, an outside security research firm found a vulnerability (bitcoinist.com/authy-vulnerability-exposed-users-affected) where attackers could learn Authy's users' personal information used to prove their identity to Authy. This information could have been used by an attacker to register a new fraudulent phone or phone number if the Multi-Device feature was enabled.

Auto-Logon MFA Bypass

Duo Security discovered (duo.com/blog/bypassing-googles-two-factor-authentication) that Android phones and Chrome OS devices could bypass Google's 2FA requirements by enabling the Auto-Logon flag in the Google Chrome browser. An attacker would have to have obtained access (local or remote control) of a phone or device that is linked to the user's Google account (a pretty big hurdle to begin an attack). But then the user (or attacker on the user's machine) could force the device to access Google's Account Recovery Options web page with the Auto-Logon flag enabled, and Google would allow the user (or attacker) to successfully authenticate (even with MFA required). The attacker could then send password reset codes to new phone numbers and email addresses. Google resolved the bug soon after it was reported.

Password Reset MFA Bypass

With this particular attack (www.reddit.com/r/msp/comments/ezr2bq/connectwise_controls_cloud_password_reset_mfa), anyone with control of an MFA user's email recovery account could initiate the password recovery process of an MFA-protected admin web portal. The recovery process would send an email to the attacker, and when the attacker clicked on the provided password recovery link, it would log them into the admin console automatically, without needing the password or MFA solution. The bug was fixed by the vendor to require the use of MFA even during email-based password recovery. Its logon would no longer be automatic just because someone clicked on a link sent in an email.

Hidden Cameras

Many MFA solutions can be compromised by an attacker using a hidden camera that records an MFA user's keystrokes or movements. For example, a user's PIN or password can be captured easily by camera. Swipe-style authentication screens can have the movements of the user captured and then duplicated by an attacker. MFA devices requiring end-user input should, if possible and reasonable, use some sort of shielding cover or antitheft screen to prevent camera recording. Users of MFA devices should realize their keystrokes and movements can be captured by a hidden camera and should try to minimize the risk by looking at their body position and potential angles of camera recordings.

Keyboard Acoustic Eavesdropping

For decades I've read of studies conducted in a laboratory in which an "attacker" could record the sounds of keystrokes on a keyboard and later determine which keys were struck. Here are two early studies on the hacking attacks: www.davidsalomon.name/CompSec/auxiliary/KybdEmanation.pdf and www.cs.cornell.edu/~shmat/courses/cs6431/zhuang.pdf. In one of the papers, the authors describe being able to successfully recover 96 percent of keystrokes typed in over a 10-minute period. In another study, what someone typed could be eavesdropped on if they were using Skype (spritz .math.unipd.it/projects/dst). Keyboard acoustic eavesdropping even works with smartphone keyboards (koddos.net/blog/hackers-can-detect-passwords-from-the-sound-of-your-keystrokes).

Wireless keyboards and mice can be eavesdropped on wirelessly, even if the communication is supposedly encrypted. You can read about it here:

- thehackernews.com/2016/02/mousejack-hack-computer.html
- www.computerworld.com/article/3101006/keysniffer-hackers-can-snag-wireless-keyboard-keystrokes-from-250-feet-away.html
- blog.emsisoft.com/en/12317/keysweeper-proof-that-its-relatively-simple-to-hack-a-wireless-keyboard

So, if your MFA solution involves typing something into a keyboard there is a chance someone could record your typing and recover and replay your keystrokes. I haven't heard of a single real-world attack that used these methods, but a nation-state attack force might have such capabilities.

NOTE White-hat hackers were able to recover typed-in keystrokes by aiming a laser pointer at a laptop from 100 feet way: www.zdnet.com/article/sniffing-keystrokes-via-laser-and-keyboard-power. The attack required $80 in equipment and worked through windows. In another demonstration, researchers proved that acoustic sounds could be accurately eavesdropped on by capturing the vibrations of light bulbs (www.popularmechanics.com/technology/security/a32851261/eavesdrop-light-bulb-vibration-attack-lamphone).

Password Hints

Many software- and phone-based MFA solutions are ultimately protected by a logon name and password. Once the user logs on once, the user can continue to use the MFA solution in perpetuity or for some set interval of time. But logically it means the solution's strength is tied to a logon name and password. That by itself is an issue. That's 1FA being used to protect 2FA. But to make matters worse, some of these MFA solutions allowing logon name and password to be used also allow a user to store, and anyone else to view, a password hint (see an example in Figure 20.2).

Create an account   or Log In

Email

Master Password   👁

Strength

Confirm Master Password   👁

Reminder (Optional)

Sign Up - It's Free

By completing this form, I agree to the Terms and Privacy Policy. I want
to receive promotional emails, unless I opt out.

Figure 20.2: Password hint protecting an MFA solution

HP MFA DoS

A 2019 bug (www.cvedetails.com/cve/CVE-2019-11989) was found that allowed an authenticated
attacker to remotely send a single network packet that would lock up Hewlett-Packard's IceWall
SSO Agent. If installed on an Apache web server and MFA was required, it would deny logon capabilities to those MFA users. A previous information disclosure vulnerability (www.cvedetails.com/
vulnerability-list/vendor_id-10/product_id-43910/version_id-238440/HP-Icewall-Mfa-4.0.html)
in the same software was found in 2014.

Trojan TOTP

Some cons are simple. In this case (blog.malwarebytes.com/threat-analysis/2020/05/new-mac-
variant-of-lazarus-dacls-rat-distributed-via-trojanized-2fa-app), malicious developers created
a rogue time-based-one-time-password (TOTP) application that was really a remote access trojan in

disguise. It masqueraded as a Chinese TOTP app known as MinaOTP. It appears to have been loose in the wild for three weeks before being discovered and revealed. You can't trust every MFA vendor to be scrupulous.

Hackers Turn MFA to Defeat You

In June 2020, Brian Krebs reported (`krebsonsecurity.com/2020/06/turn-on-mfa-before-crooks-do-it-for-you`) the story of a victim whose son had his Microsoft Xbox account taken over. As the father, a career IT security professional, tried to regain control of his son's account, he contacted Microsoft tech support, which, like a lot of tech support, is reachable only through email or online. The man started through the automated tech support forms to report the malicious account takeover and to initiate the steps necessary to regain control of the account. While doing this, he learned that any account changes would be sent to a rogue Gmail account, set up by the attackers, for approval. Not only that, but the attackers had set up MFA protection so that the legitimate users could not regain control without having access to the newly selected, rogue MFA protection instance.

Microsoft sent him a list of 20 increasingly sophisticated personal known questions, similar to what I revealed in Chapter 13, "Downgrade/Recovery Attacks," such as the serial number of his Xbox console. Even though he answered all 20 questions successfully, Microsoft refused to reset the account to his control because they did not have the (rogue) MFA option as the last confirmation. Microsoft had apparently never considered the scenario of an attacker enabling MFA after account takeover. After much wrangling, the victim had to create a new Xbox account (again, Microsoft had no way of recovering the original without the victim knowing the attacker's MFA code), and they were able to transfer his son's account and information to the new account. I guess the moral of the story is to enable MFA before the attacker does.

Summary

This chapter discussed eight miscellaneous MFA attacks. Chapter 21, "Test: Can You Spot the Vulnerabilities?" will explore a real life MFA solution to complete all the examples of real-world and theoretical MFA attacks explored in Part II, "Hacking MFA". Also, chapter 21 will cover a secure and sophisticated MFA hardware device and ask if you can spot the potential vulnerabilities.

21

Test: Can You Spot the Vulnerabilities?

This chapter is broken down into two main sections. It starts with showing how to quickly threat model any MFA solution and then it walks through example threat modeling a very solid, secure, real-world, MFA solution. It is intended for use by MFA developers or by buyers considering a MFA solution.

Threat Modeling MFA Solutions

Every MFA solution can be hacked. But how? Although you can take a haphazard approach to figuring out the potential vulnerabilities and weaknesses of a particular MFA solution, going in with a proven plan and process usually ends up being more efficient and inclusive.

Here are my basic threat-modeling summary stages:

1. Document and diagram the components.
2. Brainstorm potential attacks.
3. Estimate risk and potential losses.
4. Create and test mitigations.
5. Do security reviews.

Each threat-modeling stage has many steps, processes, and tools, associated with it. I'll cover some of them in more detail in this chapter—although, to be clear, I'm going to do it very fast. Really, it would take a multiday class or a book devoted to the topic to best understand how to perform a thorough threat-modeling risk management analysis.

> **NOTE** As indicated in earlier chapters, I'm a big fan of Adam Shostack's 2014 *Threat Model: Design for Security* (Wiley, 2014). You can get the Kindle version (www.amazon.com/Threat-Modeling-Designing-Adam-Shostack-ebook/dp/B00IG71FAS).

Document and Diagram the Components

You can't threat-model what you don't know about. Begin by first listing every possible operational component, device, service, relationship, trust, and security boundary you can think of that is related to the MFA solution. If you want, you can start with the list of common MFA components shown in Figure 5.1 in Chapter 5, "Hacking MFA in General," but diagram them in the logical order in which they're involved. Start with all the inputs to the solution, including the human component and how all information is input into the system. End with all the outputs of the MFA system. What does it provide? Does it provide an OTP code? Does it provide a public key? Does it provide a result code that simply communicates "Yes, the authentication was successful"? How does an identity get added to the MFA system? How does an identity get updated or removed? What happens when a device or token is lost or replaced?

Think of all the components involved in the authentication life cycle, from getting the inputs to the outputs and everything in between. What are the dependencies? What are the trust boundaries? If you plan to use a service, code library, or API, list it here. Then map and diagram all the steps in a flowchart that connects all the components, from beginning to end, so that anyone involved with the threat-modeling work (now or reviewing it later) gets a complete understanding of how the MFA solution works in all operational scenarios.

Brainstorm Potential Attacks

Start with threat-modeling the various attacker types and motivations, and the risks of one group versus another. For example, you could have nation-state attackers focusing on both a fingerprint-protected phone owned by a teenager or a smartcard-protected government laptop, but one is more likely than the other. A solution intended to protect cryptocurrency wallets is going to be attacked by a different class of attackers than one that protects Facebook or Instagram accounts. Is there a way automated malware could exploit the solution?

To be honest, I'm not as interested in hacker groups and motivations as I am in potential threat scenarios. To me, brainstorming attacker types and motivations is just a great way to get creative juices flowing for when you move over to brainstorming threat attack trees.

An *attack tree* (also known as a *kill chain*) threads together input points where a threat enters the event with a root cause exploit and then the series of steps along the way, including other exploits, until it achieves its ultimate objective and exits the tree with its goal accomplished. Look at every component and begin thinking of all the attacks someone could accomplish using it. These include the following:

- Social engineering
- Unpatched software
- Denial-of-service
- Eavesdropping

- Credential theft
- Spoofing
- Tampering
- Escalation of privilege
- Human error
- Misconfiguration
- Insider attack
- Physical attacks

Attack/threat trees are the series of steps from initial root exploit to the end that an attacker or malware program can do against an asset or component. They often get represented as nodes and subnodes, linked together in the order that they would occur in different attack scenarios.

These days, one of the most popular frameworks from which to pull individual nodes from to build attack trees is the MITRE ATT&CK matrix (`attack.mitre.org`). Figure 21.1 shows a snippet of the larger matrix. It contains 12 adversarial stages of attacks with over 185 individual elements, known as components and subcomponents. Many other standards-setting organizations tried to accomplish a global, agreed-on set of attack components in the past, but for some reason, none of the previous attempts stuck the way the ATT&CK matrix has. For all intents and purposes, the MITRE ATT&CK matrix seems to finally be the one attack model that people can agree on. With that said, it's a work in progress. MITRE is still asking for contributions and recommendations. I wrote an article about my recommendations here: www.linkedin.com/pulse/ you-can-help-improve-mitres-attck-matrix-roger-grimes.

Execution	Persistence	Privilege Escalation	Defense Evasion	Credential Access	Discovery
AppleScript	.bash_profile and .bashrc	Access Token Manipulation	Access Token Manipulation	Account Manipulation	Account Discovery
CMSTP	Accessibility Features	Accessibility Features	Binary Padding	Bash History	Application Window Discovery
Command-Line Interface	Account Manipulation	AppCert DLLs	BITS Jobs	Brute Force	Browser Bookmark Discovery
Compiled HTML File	AppCert DLLs	AppInit DLLs	Bypass User Account Control	Credential Dumping	Domain Trust Discovery
Component Object Model and Distributed COM	AppInit DLLs	Application Shimming	Clear Command History	Credentials from Web Browsers	File and Directory Discovery
Control Panel Items	Application Shimming	Bypass User Account Control	CMSTP	Credentials in Files	Network Service Scanning
Dynamic Data Exchange	Authentication Package	DLL Search Order Hijacking	Code Signing	Credentials in Registry	Network Share Discovery
Execution through API	BITS Jobs	Dylib Hijacking	Compile After Delivery	Exploitation for Credential Access	Network Sniffing
Execution through Module Load	Bootkit	Elevated Execution with Prompt	Compiled HTML File	Forced Authentication	Password Policy Discovery
Exploitation for Client Execution	Browser Extensions	Emond	Component Firmware	Hooking	Peripheral Device Discovery
Graphical User Interface	Change Default File Association	Exploitation for Privilege Escalation	Component Object Model Hijacking	Input Capture	Permission Groups Discovery

Figure 21.1: Partial snippet of a large MITRE ATT&CK matrix

No matter which attack tree or components you choose, pick the specific components or nodes you need to include in your threat-modeling analysis to describe the attacks and pathways attackers or malware might take against your MFA solution. Not all MFA solutions will be subject to the same risks. For example, a smartcard is subject to EMI (electromagnetic interference) side-channel attack analysis and (at least so far) a phone-based TOTP is not. TOTP-based MFA solutions are subject to having their seed databases stolen, whereas the private key of a smartcard is likely only present on the smartcard chip with no seed database that can be compromised. And so on.

Estimate Risk and Potential Losses

Collect all the possible attack methods and chain them together from start to end, assigning risk likelihoods of each step occurring against the MFA solution you are threat-modeling. What you'll end up with is something that will look similar to Figure 21.2.

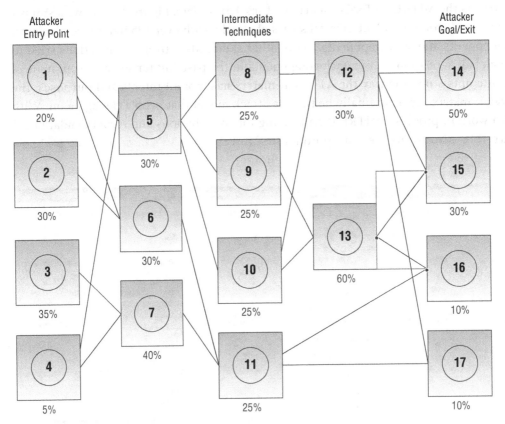

Figure 21.2: Example partial threat/risk tree

When assigning potential likelihoods of risks and different attack components, sometimes you'll be taking what we technical folks call a "guess." That's okay. You just need to take your best guess, whatever it is, and put it on the attack tree so that risk calculations can be made. But even when you guess, think about the methods and ways that have been most successfully used against your solution or organization or similar solutions in the recent past and that are most likely to occur in the near future. Real attacks by real malicious hackers mean the most. Theoretical attacks that have never been accomplished against your solution or a solution like yours have a far lower likelihood of occurring.

For example, in today's world, social engineering and attacks against unpatched software are common, making up the vast majority of the risk. We've also seen, as covered in this book, attacks against namespaces, but those types of attacks are a minority in the MFA world. Most are theoretical, but not all. More popular are credential theft attacks and exploits due to incorrect permissions—these are moderate, middle, risks for most solutions. Take your best guess at the likelihood of a particular type of attack component happening and put your best percentage guess to it occurring in a particular time period.

Then add or multiply the different likelihood values on each individual possible attack chain trees (e.g., 1, 5, 8, 12, 14 versus 3, 7, 11, 16 as examples from Figure 21.2) to calculate the highest risk, most likely attack trees. If I did my math right, the first tree (1, 5, 8, 12, 14) adds up to 155 percent. The second tree (3, 7, 11, 16) adds up to 110 percent. You need to perform this type of analysis across all the attack trees to find out which pathways have the highest risk of occurring. Then concentrate your analysis and mitigations on the most likely (and potentially most damaging) trees and individual risks first and best. In my hypothetical scenario involving Figure 21.2, we would concentrate on mitigating the first attack tree.

Some threat modelers assign damage values to the different hacker objectives and then use those damage (i.e., cost) values as the starting point value that is then multiplied across the various attack trees. For example, still using Figure 21.2, let's assume hacker objective 14 might cost the MFA solution vendor $2 million in damages but hacker objective 16 might cause $3 million in damages. If I took the first risk tree (1, 5, 8, 12, 14) that equates to $2,000,000 × 20% × 30% × 25% × 30% × 50% =$4,500 of estimated risk loss. In the second considered risk tree (3, 7,11, 16) that equates to $3,000,000 × 35% × 40% × 25% × 10% =$10,500. Just based on that analysis, mitigating the second risk tree first and best makes more sense.

After over 30 years of doing this, I've come to both hate and love the process of threat modeling and risk mitigation. But if done right, what I think it does is to force you to consider how your solution and scenarios can be attacked and make you think about what you need to mitigate first and best. I'm not so concerned with the exact numbers or percentages. I'm far more concerned with making sure I mitigate as much of the risk as I can, starting with the most likely stuff first. What I don't want to do is get my mitigation staff spending most of their time on a threat scenario that has never happened and likely never will. If nothing else, putting aside the numbers, make sure your threat modelers are thoughtful in what they think needs to be mitigated first and best.

Create and Test Mitigations

The next step is figuring out how to mitigate the biggest risks. Parts I, Introduction and II, Hacking MFA of this book list some of the most common attacks against MFA solutions and the mitigations a developer and a user can use to minimize abuse. Use this book as a starting point for your analysis and ideas for mitigations.

What mitigations can be deployed to reduce the risk? What do the mitigations cost? Do they outweigh the potential damage? Are they difficult or easy to implement? How long will they take to implement? What residual risks are you left with after all the mitigations have been applied? Remember, everything is hackable. Don't forget to use Security Development Lifecycle (SDL) tools and practices while creating and updating your product. Ensure that you include a way to automatically update your solution without end-user approval, and make it easy for people to report issues. Respond to vulnerability reports quickly and with care.

Do Security Reviews

After everything is applied, allow your MFA solution to be penetration tested. Use an internal team and use an external, more independent, team. Do external pen testing at least once a year, and change external teams every few years to get a different team's perspective on it. I recommend opening your solution up officially to one of the popular bug bounty programs like BugCrowd (www.bugcrowd .com) and HackerOne (hackerone.com). It's always better to be proactively notified of an externally found bug than to read about it in the computer security news press. Get a source code review done in-house by trained SDL professionals and use an automated tool that looks for security vulnerabilities in code. Always use a combination of automated tools and human reviewers as part of securing your product. One will catch what the other doesn't. Threat modeling and reviewing your MFA solution will likely decrease the number of found critical bugs after the MFA solution is released.

Introducing the Bloomberg MFA Device

In my 32-year plus computer security career, I've come across hundreds of MFA solutions. Most I've liked; a few I've hated. And some are so well built and designed they deserve a higher echelon of admiration. I would put the Bloomberg MFA device in that latter category.

Bloomberg, L.P. and the Bloomberg Terminal

Michael Bloomberg is the billionaire mayor of New York City who ran for the 2020 presidential democratic nomination. He got his billions of dollars from his Bloomberg, L.P. company and its much touted Bloomberg Terminal (`en.wikipedia.org/wiki/Bloomberg_Terminal`) device, which is used by nearly every stock trader who can afford it. It first appeared in 1982 as a "dumb terminal" device. It quickly moved to the PC platform when PCs became dominant and, today, is essentially a movable software program that remotely interfaces with the backend components. Most financial people and traders love Bloomberg Terminals. They are fast, relatively easy to use, and they have access to tremendous amounts of information. For example, you can ask "Show me the end-of-the-day stock price for IBM for every Friday since it was listed on the stock market" and get an answer in one to two seconds. You want financial statements for the last 20 years? They can get them in one to two seconds. You want to see the last 10 years of 10-Ks or the latest news? They have a ton of data and news about any public company, all in one place, all very quickly retrievable. It's amazing to see. The speed and ability to retrieve almost any financial information within reason is considered essential to high-end traders. Bloomberg Terminals are coveted. Many financial traders, before accepting a new job offer, will make sure that a Bloomberg Terminal is part of their new setup. If not, they won't take the job. If you thought Apple fanbois were cultish, you haven't talked to Bloomberg Terminal users. I've used one; I understand.

The quality and speed of what they deliver isn't accidental. Bloomberg has committed strongly to offering more information more quickly than any other company or product. It's their driving competitive advantage. If you're a computer consultant trying to help Bloomberg accomplish something, if your solution slows down a Bloomberg information response by even a few milliseconds, you won't have the job long. Information and speed drive all decisions. But Bloomberg is also pretty great in the computer security arena.

Early on, you had to own a physical Bloomberg Terminal to get access. Later on, you could download Bloomberg Terminal software and register your device and a subscriber key and run the software on your computer. Today, a Bloomberg Terminal session is remotely accessible from other computers in what is called Bloomberg Anywhere (`bba.bloomberg.net`).

The Bloomberg Terminal experience doesn't come cheap. Bloomberg Terminal licenses average $22,500 a year per person. Because of that, there has always been a great incentive for crooks and cheats to get or share free access to a terminal or the software that allows them to connect to one remotely. Bloomberg, from the beginning, has always had cutting-edge physical security controls, dongles, and MFA, to control who could run one of their terminals.

Many years ago, Bloomberg came up with their own custom physical MFA device. Since then it has gone through many iterations and improvements. Today, Bloomberg's MFA device is known as a *Bloomberg Personal Authentication Device* (or *B-Unit*). The main versions are known as B-Unit 1,

B-Unit 2, and B-Unit 3. Figure 21.3 shows the front of one version of the device with functionality callouts. You can read more about the B-Unit here: www.bloomberg.com/professional/support/b-unit.

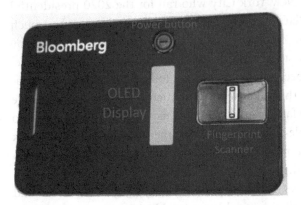

Figure 21.3: Example of a Bloomberg MFA device

As Figure 21.3 shows, the B-Unit has a fingerprint reader, an OLED screen (for displaying information and statuses), and a power button. The back of the card, not shown in Figure 21.3, has an eight-digit serial number and a photodiode light sensor. The bottom of the card has a micro-USB port for charging the internal lithium battery and updating. You can already see this is no ordinary MFA device. Using a B-Unit MFA device with Bloomberg software requires each user to register their device to link the user and device to each other and to their Bloomberg software instance. Thereafter, the user follows a similar but different set of steps to log on.

New User B-Unit Registration and Use

New Bloomberg Terminal users get a B-Unit device, start their Bloomberg Terminal software, and log on to the software instance with their username and password to begin the registration process. The software will prompt them to enter their eight-digit B-Unit serial number (tying their identity to a particular B-Unit device and software instance). Then, they power on their B-Unit device.

> **NOTE** If the B-Unit has been used before and contains information from a previous instance, the user is instructed to reset the unit the first time they use it to wipe out any potential remaining information and make sure they are starting with a blank slate.

The Bloomberg Terminal software will start to emit a series of light flashes from the center of the screen (similar to what an optical faux Morse code might look like). The user holds up their B-Unit within inches of the screen, and the MFA's light sensor reads the code from the Bloomberg Terminal screen that is flashing the light codes. This further syncs the user's B-Unit with their instance of the Bloomberg software. The user's B-Unit will then collect their fingerprint using the fingerprint scanner to be used for future authentication and, when successful, displays a four-digit alphanumeric code on the OLED screen that is then input back into the Bloomberg Terminal software.

> **NOTE** Other MFA solutions have used flashes of light. BRToken/Datablink (now owned by WatchGuard) had a similar light flash communication technology back in 2008. It sent a blinking light bit, flash for 1, no flash (i.e., dark) for a 0, every 60 ms. You can watch a (Brazilian Portuguese-language) demonstration of their device here: www.youtube.com/watch?v=nFRSD_74X0Y.

Once the user successfully registers and syncs the device, each time they want to log on to their Bloomberg Terminal software instance they go through the process just described, except their fingerprint will be used for authentication comparison instead of just registration and they won't be prompted for their eight-digit B-Unit serial number. You can read about the B-Unit 3 MFA device and how to register and log on with it in more detail here: data.bloomberglp.com/professional/sites/10/251767_BBGT_OVW_B-Unit_USRG_DIG_FINAL.pdf. Watch a video of the registration process here: bba.bloomberg.net/Video/BunitTutorial.

The first time I saw the four-factor Bloomberg B-Unit and its use, it. . .blew. . .me. . .away! I still think it is one of the top MFA solutions used widely by the general public. I'm a big fan. Let me summarize the pertinent MFA authentication steps:

1. User logs on to software using logon name and password.
2. User holds MFA device up to software screen so that software communicates optically to MFA device.
3. User swipes fingerprint to authenticate themselves to the MFA device.
4. MFA device displays a four-digit code, which user inputs into the software.

All of this must occur successfully, in order, for the user to be authenticated to the software. If any step fails, the user will not be able to use the Bloomberg Terminal software. Users can have only one B-Unit at a time.

I'll end this section by asking you to threat-model the Bloomberg MFA device. What potential vulnerabilities are even possible? Are there offsetting mitigations that can be deployed to minimize those vulnerabilities? Conduct a quick threat-modeling review, based on your limited knowledge of the Bloomberg MFA device, and then read further to learn how I did it.

Threat-Modeling the Bloomberg MFA Device

In this section I'm going to discuss some ways to possibly exploit users using Bloomberg Anywhere and relying on the Bloomberg B-Unit device. I'm not showing you this because I think the B-Unit device is weak or overly hackable. In fact, I think the exact opposite. I think the B-Unit is one of the best MFA devices and less hackable than most others that I've ever seen. The whole reason I'm using this device as an example is to demonstrate that all MFA solutions are hackable in one or more ways. There is a difference between saying an MFA device is making authentication significantly more secure in many scenarios and it not being hackable at all. This book, chapter, and section is a testament to this statement. Security professionals should be accurate in what they believe and communicate to others. Make sure you communicate the right education.

> **NOTE** A huge caveat to this section is that I have not hacked Bloomberg or any device or service they offer. They have not given me permission to do so and I have not asked. As an ethical hacker, I do not pen-test sites or resources of others without their authorized permission. This is purely a mental exercise, and my ideas of potential weaknesses and vulnerabilities are greatly limited by that fact. What I suggest as a potential attack may not work at all against the real device. It's important for you to understand the process of threat modeling more than whether a particular attack type I suggest would work against the actual device.

Every hack I list here is just a possible potential attack, used as an example, from public information available to anyone. I have no way of knowing if a particular suggested attack would or would not work. I may have made a mistake or bad assumption in my attack scenarios. I'm only human. I can only say that in my 20 years of professional pen-testing experience, when I saw similar signs I was often able to accomplish the various suggested hacks I recount here. Every potential attack I list may have been already successfully mitigated by Bloomberg (and I hope so). It's more important that you see the process and the ideas than whether they would or would not be successful in this specific example of the Bloomberg B-Unit device. The journey is more important right now than the destination.

Threat-Modeling the B-Unit in a General Example

Start out threat-modeling the B-Unit in general as I have suggested earlier as well as in previous chapters. First, consider all the potential components and dependencies of the B-Unit device. Here are the possible MFA components as listed in Chapter 5:

- Enrollment
- User
- Devices/hardware
- Software
- Authentication factors
- Authentication secret stores
- Cryptography
- Technology
- Network/transmission channel
- Namespace

- Supporting infrastructure
- Relying party
- Federation/proxies
- APIs
- Alternate authentication methods
- Recovery
- Migrations
- Deprovision

Let's start with what I don't know and can't or won't attack. A lot of these components I simply have no insight into. I don't know what cryptography the B-Unit uses, although I suspect it is secure enough. I don't know the hardware components involved or the expertise to attack the B-Unit at a physical level. I'm guessing there might be EMI emanations that could be used in a side-channel attack, or perhaps an electron microscope could see an involved secret at a molecular level. But I have no way of knowing. I didn't have permission to check their software, sites, or services looking for coding vulnerabilities. I'm not sure of what namespace they use other than DNS for Internet connectivity and locations (for logons, information, and APIs). I'm not aware of any federated authentication. I have no idea of any of their supporting infrastructure, programs, or patch status. I don't know where any authentication secrets are stored or how they are accessible. I'm not sure of their deprovisioning policies or procedures, but I suspect if a customer contacts Bloomberg tech support and says a specific user is no longer with their company and doesn't need the assigned Bloomberg license, the user's logon name and password are disabled and something likely happens with their B-Unit (it is reassigned or sent back to Bloomberg). There is a lot I don't know.

Specific Possible Attacks

Now, let's start with what I *do* know and some possible attacks. First, and most important, even though the B-Unit is a four-factor MFA device, the four factors are authenticating different things—not four factors authenticating the user to an application but *one* factor authenticating the user to the app, one of the app to the card, one of the user to the card, and one of the card back to the app. It's awesome to think about in one respect, but it's also only 1FA in two portions of the MFA. Those instances and disconnected instances become potential areas to explore when penetration testing. Let's explore my attack ideas.

Getting Logon Name and Password

The first step in Bloomberg Anywhere authentication is the user supplying their logon name and password at the public logon portal (`bba.bloomberg.net`). Without that information, a legitimate logon process cannot be started. As covered thoroughly in Chapter 1, "Logon Problems," there are lots of ways (theft, social engineering, guessing, etc.) that a user's logon name and password could end up being known by an attacker. But since 70–90 percent of all data breaches start with social engineering or phishing, if an attacker didn't already have a Bloomberg Anywhere user's password, I, as the attacker, would start trying any of the thousands of successful phishing attacks. A simple fake "Your Bloomberg Anywhere logon account password has expired" phishing email would likely work across more users than you would think.

The user's logon name is either their Bloomberg Terminal Username or corporate email address (as shown in Figure 21.4). So, any hacking knowing a Bloomberg Terminal user's business email address can use that to login as the victim. There are a lot of well-known trader names, and the companies they work for are known as well. A good password hacker can either find out a victim's email address or take a few guesses at it. It's not hard to find out what type of email naming format a particular company uses and then apply it to the victim's Bloomberg Anywhere logon.

Log In

Terminal Username or Corporate Email

Password   Forgot your password?

B-Unit may be required to log in.
Need help? Contact us

NEXT

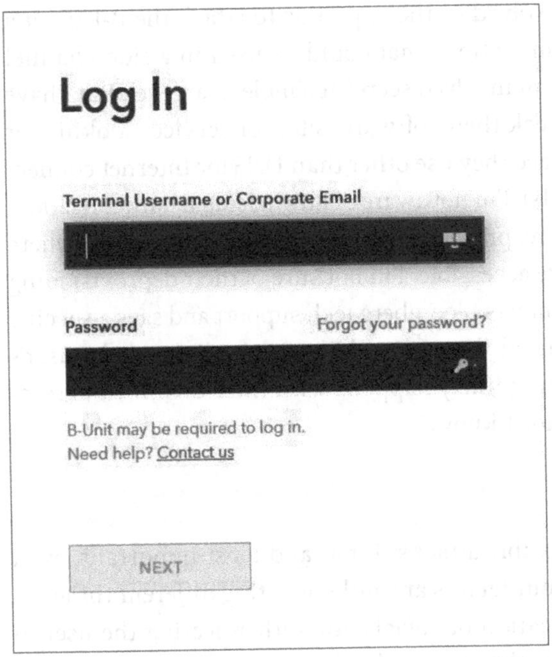

Figure 21.4: Bloomberg Terminal logon prompt

The password may be able to be attacked using a password guessing attack. The password entered here during an example Bloomberg Terminal logon seems to be five characters in the video `bba .bloomberg.net/Video/BunitTutorial`, but other public Bloomberg technical support pages indicate that passwords:

- Must be a minimum of eight characters long.
- Can't be the same password as used in the last three password changes.
- Cannot contain commonly used passwords or phrases.

But there is no character complexity required, so my commonly used "frogfrog" password would meet the requirements. I can't find evidence of a password expiration policy, although one may exist. I would tend to think that maybe one doesn't exist because it's not mentioned anywhere on any password resource I can find and B-Unit devices are good for two-plus years. Oftentimes, services with MFA solutions don't automatically expire passwords because they don't want them expiring out of sync with the associated MFA devices. It causes too much user friction and frustration. Remember, the world thinks one of the big benefits of having an MFA solution is that you don't have to be as strict with the password or PIN requirements associated with it. It's why you have the MFA solution involved in the first place.

I cannot find whether Bloomberg Anywhere has an account lockout policy either, but they most likely do. An attacker could just take a bunch of guesses against their public logon portal using a valid logon name (as covered earlier, it's not that hard to either guess or figure out) until they locked out the account (and in the process get the number of times they can guess incorrectly before the account gets locked out). Once they find out the account is locked out, they can time how long it takes for the account to become unlocked or determine how many times they can guess in a particular time period before the bad password counter gets reset to zero. It may take a day or two to identify this value, but by the end of one to two days, any decent hacker can determine Bloomberg Anywhere's account lockout policy. Requiring a call to technical support to unlock a targeted account would be the most frustrating to the hacker, so they would just learn to guess slow enough not to lock out the account in the first place. Hackers will often guess with a handful of "throw-away" logon names that they don't care about locking out, saving the true, intended victim's logon account for when they fully understand the password and account lockout policies.

Although I'm not 100 percent sure, it appears as if Bloomberg Anywhere's password reset portal asks only for the user to put in their previously registered email address (same as their logon name) to reset their password, as shown in Figure 21.5. In all the other instances where Bloomberg asks for the same information to reset a password (Bloomberg.com, Bloomberg Law, etc.), entering the email address causes a password reset link to be sent to the end user. The user clicks on the link and is asked to submit their new password, twice. No other authentication information is required. The link is all that is required. An attacker could take over a user's email account and request a password reset.

NOTE   On the Bloomberg.com site, a user can also log on with their Facebook or Twitter OAuth logon, but it doesn't appear to be possible on the Bloomberg Anywhere site. The hacker in me would love trying to see if I could comingle my Bloomberg.com OAuth credentials with my Bloomberg Anywhere logon. It's probably not possible, but I'd spend some time there.

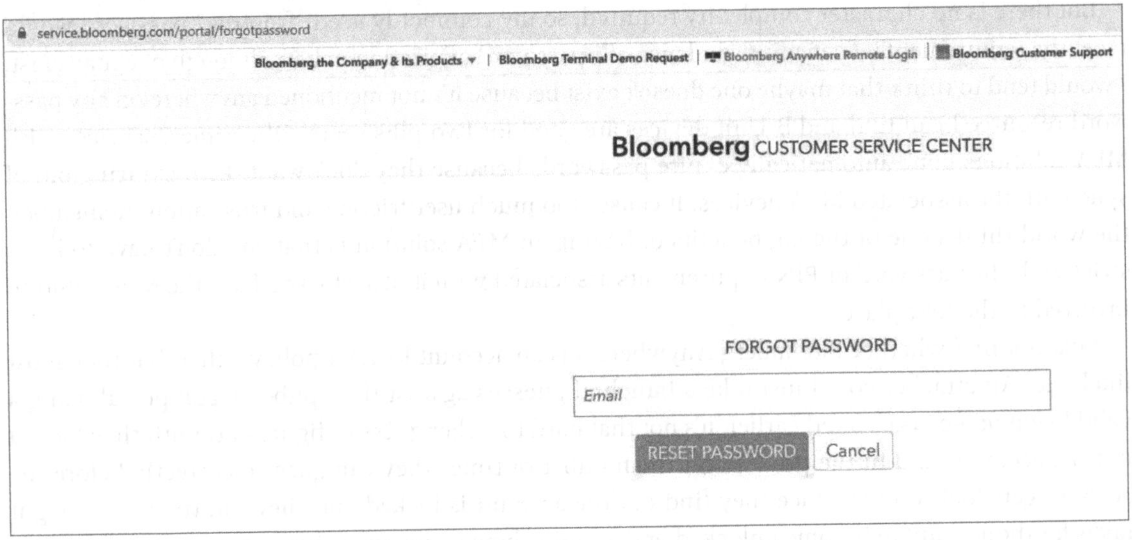

Figure 21.5: Bloomberg's password reset portal

MitM Is Possible

A MitM attack resembling what Kevin Mitnick did in Chapter 6, "Access Control Token Tricks," is very likely possible. Bloomberg Anywhere is touted as the solution for accessing Bloomberg Terminal from nearly any PC anywhere, as long as you have your B-Unit handy. No location pre-registraton information is required for the device. This means that everything passed from the legitimate Bloomberg Anywhere site to the user can be proxied, and vice versa.

Just like in the Chapter 6 LinkedIn MFA bypass example, the hacker could send the victim a fake email or somehow otherwise convince them to interface with a fake, look-alike website (which is really just an evil MitM proxy). Then, when the user typed in their logon name and password, the proxy could just record those values and pass them along to the real Bloomberg Anywhere site. The optic flashing from the real website could be passed along to the user on the proxy site like any other bit of information. The B-Unit would have no way of knowing that the light was coming from a fake proxy website. The user would use their fingerprint to authenticate to the B-Unit. The B-Unit would generate a four-digit code, which the user would type back into the proxy website, which in turn would send it to the real website. Now the hacker would be in control of the victim's Bloomberg Anywhere session.

Fake Authentication?

It may be possible for a hacker to fake the entire authentication experience, although I'm less sure of this. A hacker could create an entire fake, look-alike Bloomberg website. The victim would enter their logon name and password, which would, of course, be captured. Then the fake website would begin to send optical flashes on the screen. The user would be successfully authenticating to their B-Unit using their fingerprint. The question is what the B-Unit would do if the flashes being sent to it were nonsense? I don't know. Or could a hacker just do fake flashing that seems to be an accurate representation of the real flash sequences or record and replay another previous legitimate optical communication session and end up with the B-Unit generating a four-digit code? Would the B-Unit just error out and not generate the four-digit code, alerting the user? If the fake or replayed optical communications worked well enough to generate a four-digit code from the B-Unit, the user would likely enter it into the fake website and not know anything was amiss.

There is, however, a strong chance that the B-Unit message sent using flashing light has a particular sequence and checksum of that sequence to prevent fake flashing attacks. If so, an attacker would need to know what the lighting sequence and checksum is composed of in order to trick the B-Unit into sending back a code. If an attacker was interested, they could record as many flashing sessions as possible, convert them into their bit representations, and then look for patterns. If I was a betting man, and I am, I'd bet the sequence and checksum are much shorter than a typical, trusted cryptographic hash and closer to a four- to six-digit OTP code. If the latter is true, figuring out the sequence so you could fake future codes would not be that daunting. It wouldn't be easy, but it would not be impossible. Recording a previous legitimate session of flashing lights might work as a replay attack. I doubt the B-Unit keeps track of previous light sequences (i.e. codes), stores them, and would refuse to take them again in the future. But if tied to an OTP sequence, HOTP or TOTP, then the specific code sequence for the exact time period would need to be known to get the B-Unit to respond correctly.

Of course, faking an actual, valid, Bloomberg Terminal session after a fake logon would be insanely hard unless the attacker had access to a real terminal to proxy request and responses back and forth. But even then, a regular Bloomberg Terminal user would probably notice the speed delay. The second or two it would take a proxy to send and receive information from a real terminal would easily double to quadruple the user's waiting time, and that would be noticed for sure.

If I were an attacker, instead of worrying about faking the real Bloomberg Terminal experience, I would just immediately go into some message notification (e.g., "We are experiencing technical difficulties. Please wait") while some fake Bloomberg Terminal screen replayed in the background underneath the message. Or a message could say that something is wrong with the user's account and ask them to verify critical information (billing, credit card, banking information, etc.). This is one of those unusual instances where faking the whole authentication experience is actually harder to pull off than just doing the MitM attack mentioned previously.

Endpoint Compromise

As with any MFA solution, if the user's endpoint is "pwned," it's game over. If the user's computer is controlled by a hacker or malware program, they can do whatever the user can do. It doesn't even take admin or root access. The malware or hacker can wait until they have detected a period of slight inactivity but make sure they send "keep-alive" movements to the Bloomberg Anywhere terminal, because it locks out after 60 minutes. So, the attacker could keep the terminal always active and unlocked, and have unlimited access when the victim was away and/or asleep.

Downgrade Attack

Most popular public services using MFA realize that there are times when legitimate users don't have access to the MFA device. It happens a lot in the real world, and Bloomberg users are no different.

So, of course Bloomberg has many alternative logon methods that bypass the B-Unit. They even advertise this on multiple public help files (see Figure 21.6 for two examples): www.bloomberg.com/faq/question/i-forgot-my-b-unit-can-i-still-access-the-bloomberg-professional-services-software-via-bloomberg-com-bloomberg-anywhere-2.

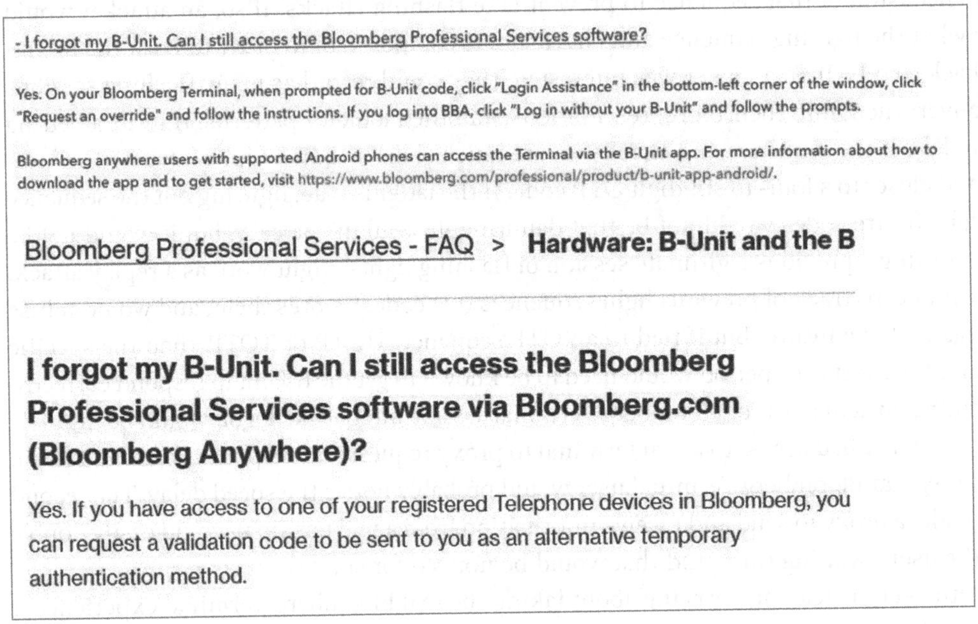

- I forgot my B-Unit. Can I still access the Bloomberg Professional Services software?

Yes. On your Bloomberg Terminal, when prompted for B-Unit code, click "Login Assistance" in the bottom-left corner of the window, click "Request an override" and follow the instructions. If you log into BBA, click "Log in without your B-Unit" and follow the prompts.

Bloomberg anywhere users with supported Android phones can access the Terminal via the B-Unit app. For more information about how to download the app and to get started, visit https://www.bloomberg.com/professional/product/b-unit-app-android/.

Bloomberg Professional Services - FAQ > Hardware: B-Unit and the B

I forgot my B-Unit. Can I still access the Bloomberg Professional Services software via Bloomberg.com (Bloomberg Anywhere)?

Yes. If you have access to one of your registered Telephone devices in Bloomberg, you can request a validation code to be sent to you as an alternative temporary authentication method.

Figure 21.6: Bloomberg help instructions for how to log on without a B-Unit

My guess is that a SIM swap attack, as shown in Chapter 8, "SMS Attacks," would work just fine. You might need the user's logon name and password, but the code being sent to the victim's phone (now swapped to the hacker's phone) gets around the four-factor B-Unit requirement.

Do Mobile Versions Have Less Security?

I don't know for sure, but this public link (mb.blpprofessional.com/m/android) seems to suggest that users can use a different "token" mode (see Figure 21.7). From what I could learn, this appears to be a secondary B-Unit OTP mode. Other information I found online indicated I could enter a password or token code.

This begs the question: if the token code is an OTP code (which is likely), how likely is it that it could be cloned, reused, or used in another of the attack methods shown in Chapter 9, "One-Time Password Attacks"? Help documentation also said that the token code would be needed only the first time when using a mobile solution, seeming to suggest that after it is entered the first time, the user's mobile device is being treated as the MFA device (instead of the B-Unit). Well, compared to B-Units mobile phones are distinctly easier to attack and "pwned." A hacker getting one token code could perhaps create a second Bloomberg Anywhere instance that the victim does not know about (although I did read that when an individual is using their mobile device, the Bloomberg Terminal service can lock out or log out the other instance, depending on the devices involved). I wonder why mobile devices aren't forced to use B-Unit authentication. If there is a reason, it might reveal an additional exploitation vector to pursue.

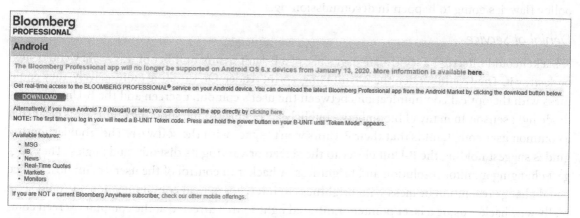

Figure 21.7: Bloomberg Anywhere Android showing "token code" requirement

Possible to Get a Second Unit?

Bloomberg Anywhere explicitly states (as shown in Figure 21.8) that a user cannot have two B-Unit devices. This is a secure, good policy. I applaud Bloomberg and their excellent security staff for it.

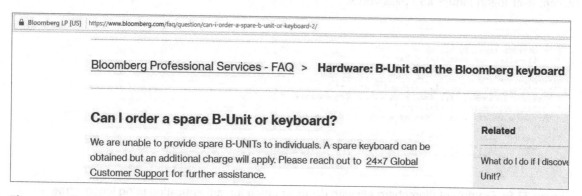

Figure 21.8: Bloomberg policy statement that a user cannot have two B-Unit devices

But in other help information, Bloomberg offers scenarios where a legitimate user can get a second unit, such as when a user's first unit is displaying a low-battery message (www.bloomberg.com/faq/

question/my-b-unit-is-displaying-a-low-battery-message-what-do-i-do-2). When that happens, a user can order a second unit. The question is if Bloomberg is super strict about still allowing only one device to be enabled on an account at one time. Likely this is the case. But as a professional hacker for 30 years, I've also seen these types of scenarios where technical enforcement is weaker than the policy. Or perhaps the decommissioning of the old device, when the new device is activated, happens slowly or takes a day. In general, if you're going to have a technical enforcement versus policy flaw, it's going to happen in decommissioning.

Denial of Service

A hacker could interrupt a legitimate user's use of a B-Unit in any number of ways. They could steal or destroy it. They could scratch the B-Unit's fingerprint reader. Or, thinking more suavely, they could mess with the optical communications between the user's computer screen and the B-Unit's photo-diode light sensor. In many of Bloomberg's publicly accessible troubleshooting guides, it is clear that a common user complaint is that their B-Units won't "sync" with the software. The troubleshooting guides suggest holding the B-Unit closer to the screen or varying its distance and angles. They suggest changing monitor resolution and brightness. A hacker in control of the user's main host device could change resolution or mess with brightness to interrupt optical communications. I could see a really wily hacker using a laser pointer or infrared light source directed at the computer screen communication area or the path in between the screen and the sensor to surreptitiously cause problems.

API Bypass

It's very common for APIs not to require MFA. Bloomberg Terminal has a ton of APIs (www.bloomberg.com/professional/support/api-library). You can download documentation and examples. In what little I can see (as shown in the example code snippet in Figure 21.9), it appears that their APIs will accept user logon names and passwords.

```
"\n"
"TLS OPTIONS (specify all or none):\n"
"\t[-tls-client-credentials <file>]\n"
"\t\tname a PKCS#12 file to use as a source of client
credentials\n"
"\t[-tls-client-credentials-password <pwd>]\n"
"\t\tspecify password for accessing client credentials\n"
"\t[-tls-trust-material <file>]\n"
"\t\tname a PKCS#7 file to use as a source of trusted
certificates\n"
"\t[-read-certificate-files]\n"
"\t\t(optional) read the TLS files and pass the blobs\n"
        << std::flush;
    }
```

Figure 21.9: Example of Bloomberg API with documentation for authenticating using logon name and password

There is a strong chance that an attacker attaining a user's logon name and password could use Bloomberg's API to access data and other objects without needing a B-Unit. Having never implemented Bloomberg's API, I don't know if they have any offsetting mitigations such as requiring an API key and registration or locking down API use by domains or IP addresses.

NOTE Bloomberg APIs also accept other forms of authentication, such as digital certificates, and which authentication method is used and sent is defined by the client using the API.

Social Engineering Tech Support

Suppose I am an attacker and I get the Bloomberg Anywhere user's logon name, password, and B-Unit. What am I missing? The user's fingerprint. I could try to capture and re-create it, as we discussed in Chapter 16, "Attacks Against Biometrics," to complete the theft of all four authentication factors, or I could try social engineering tech support. Bloomberg's help files say, "If you should need to re-enroll on the B-Unit with another finger, please contact Bloomberg technical support." If I've got all the other information, I should be able to get a new fingerprint added to the existing B-Unit device.

Bloomberg B-Unit four-factor MFA devices are among the most secure, coolest devices out there. Bloomberg is full of very smart security people. I've met some. They are very good. But even they would tell you that nothing is unhackable. Heck, they probably know of other ways to hack Bloomberg Anywhere access or B-Unit devices that I did not think of.

Most companies know of many weaknesses and bugs that they need to fix in some future version that haven't been resolved yet. That's just a fact of life. My attack examples emerged from just a few hours of brainstorming. With more time and authorized permission, I'm sure I could confirm the validity of these attacks and/or find more. If my past hacking experience is any prediction of my success with these scenarios, half would not be possible because of some fact I got wrong or some mitigation I did not know about, and I would discover just as many new ones that I didn't find here using a mental exercise alone. I've never not been able to hack an MFA solution in multiple ways. And it's not just me. I'm a mediocre hacker. Everyone I've ever worked with on an MFA solution hacking project has been able to find ways to hack and bypass them. Nothing is unhackable, not even awesome Bloomberg B-Unit devices (even if these hacks don't work).

The B-Unit is a fantastic device for what it does. The number of security precautions is likely overkill for what it protects, but it works, and its users don't mind using it. In fact, for many users, having a B-Unit is a status symbol. The B-Unit is a great MFA device and has worked to minimize stolen Bloomberg Terminal licenses. Could it be made more secure? Yes, but it really doesn't have to be modified at all. The B-Unit is a great example of the right blend of security and end-user usability for the use case scenario.

NOTE Any Bloomberg people reading this chapter probably aren't all that thrilled that I used their pinnacle MFA device as an example of how to attack an MFA solution. I apologize in advance. You and your company are great. Yes, I'm an idiot. Yes, I don't know what I'm talking about. Yes, of course, none of these attacks would have worked because I made multiple mistakes and assumptions and you already have existing mitigations for all of them. Now, let's meet and go have a beer!

Multi-Factor Authentication Security Assessment Tool

As I've mentioned a few times in this book, I work for KnowBe4, Inc. (knowbe4.com). Last year, after the huge success of my "12 Ways to Hack MFA" presentations, KnowBe4 asked me to write an e-book (info.knowbe4.com/12-way-to-hack-two-factor-authentication), which eventually led to the writing of this book. The 40-page e-book covers only 18 ways to hack MFA, whereas this book covers over 50, and in far more detail with far more examples in its over 500 pages. KnowBe4 even created a part of their website dedicated to hacking MFA (www.knowbe4.com/how-to-hack-multi-factor-authentication). You can check it for updates.

But my favorite thing that KnowBe4 did related to the topic was to create the Multi-Factor Authentication Security Assessment (MASA) tool: www.knowbe4.com/multi-factor-authentication-security-assessment. Created a year before this book, it doesn't contain every way I know of to hack an MFA solution, but it does contain over two dozen hacking methods. Using this checklist review tool/service, anyone can figure out how an MFA solution they are using or considering can be hacked. It was basically my brain on the subject a year ago. When you run the tool, it asks a series of a dozen or so questions, enough so that it can figure out exactly what type of MFA solution you are inquiring about. Then it spits out a report describing how your specifically submitted MFA solution can be hacked. It starts with a summary coverage page (see Figure 21.10 for an example). The cover page is followed by a decent discussion of each possible hack, much like the ones presented in this chapter in the last section, including a ton of other related information from the e-book. It's not perfect. It doesn't include every attack listed in this book. But it was a labor of love and I think useful to anyone who runs it to get a quick analysis of how their submitted MFA solution might be attacked.

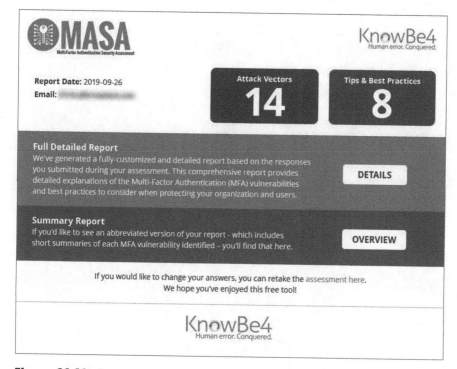

Figure 21.10: Example of the MASA summary cover page

Summary

This chapter highlighted a clever and sophisticated MFA physical token, the Bloomberg four-factor B-Unit MFA solution. We discussed how to threat-model any MFA device, and then explored the potential vulnerabilities with the Bloomberg device. We concluded by covering KnowBe4's Multi-Factor Authentication Security Assessment (MASA) tool.

This chapter ends Part II, Hacking MFA, of the book, which explored how to hack multifactor solutions with dozens of examples. Part III, Looking Forward will cover how to pick and design good MFA solutions, and I'll discuss what I expect the future of digital authentication to look like. Chapter 22, "Designing a Secure Solution" begins by discussing how to design a fairly secure MFA solution.

Looking Forward

22

Designing
a Secure Solution

Chapter 21, "Test: Can You Spot the Vulnerabilities?" discussed how to potentially hack one of the strongest real-world MFA solutions available. This chapter will challenge us to try to secure one of the hardest scenarios possible: remote electronic voting.

Introduction

It is very likely as time goes on that more and more people will be voting remotely in local, state, and national elections. In the United States, voting by mail-in or drop-off paper ballot has been allowed for decades. In five states, all voting (i.e., local, state, federal) is 100 percent done by mail-in ballot: www.ncsl.org/research/elections-and-campaigns/all-mail-elections.aspx. Paper-based voting, in-person or using a mail-in ballot, has worked fairly well and has a low number of incidents of voter fraud, but it's slow and requires a lot of time devoted to creation, storage, and transportation of paper. It is expensive even with much of the workforce around election day volunteering their time.

For "official" elections, voting machines at official in-person vote polling locations have become increasingly more electronic. Years ago, nearly all voting machines were mechanical contraptions—a voter inserted a paper voting ballot and selected their choices with a writing instrument (pencil or paper) or small hand tool. This process darkened selections or created holes in the paper aligned to particular selections and vote choices. Voters then manually placed their paper ballot into a mechanical vote-counting machine, which tallied the votes for the polling place. The equipment or a polling place manager would verify the integrity of the tallied votes and send or call in the results to central voting headquarters, which would then tally up all the votes and declare a winner. This is still how it works in many voting precincts in the US and all over the world.

Over time, the mechanical voting machines at polling places have been increasingly replaced by electronic voting machines, most of which are just customized computers running somewhat normal computer software. There are currently 19 registered and approved (by the U.S. Election

Assistance Commission) voting machine vendors in the United States: www.eac.gov/voting-equipment/registered-manufacturers. All of these manufacturers are working to create the most secure electronic voting machine that they can.

Dozens of organizations and overseers are dedicated to improving the security of electronic voting. Many hundreds, if not thousands, of white-hat hackers have been involved in penetration testing of electronic voting machines or conducting security reviews based on known information. The news so far is that many of our electronic voting machines are hackable—some easily so. Here is a story of a 11-year-old who hacked into a voting website replica in 10 minutes at a popular computer security conference: time.com/5366171/11-year-old-hacked-into-us-voting-system-10-minutes. Several hackers have publicly shown how they have, or could have, broken into real electronic voting machines. When confronted with irrefutable evidence, many electronic voting machine vendors have admitted their machines were or are vulnerable to hacking. Here's an example: www.theblaze.com/news/2018/07/17/largest-us-voting-machine-vendor-admits-using-software-vulnerable-to-hacking. In the rare times when professional security and code reviews have been done on voting machines, the results have not been good. Here's an example of a voting machine vendor's security code review report: votingsystems.cdn.sos.ca.gov/vendors/hart-intercivic/verity/verity-sc.pdf.

NOTE Security reviews are good for security, so I applaud this vendor for releasing the report. It was probably required by law for a state to consider using the voting machine, but I applaud that the security review was done and posted publicly (why and however it was done).

As covered in Chapter 1, "Logon Problems," hacking is so pervasive in our society that the prospect of any electorate using completely electronic voting, either at official polling places or remotely at homes, greatly concerns many people. If you understand what is at risk and how easy it is to hack most of today's electronic voting machines, you'd have to be crazy not to be concerned. Almost all computer security people familiar with the issues feel that there is way too much risk to go to pure electronic voting any time soon, but you don't even have to be a computer security professional to be wary of online remote voting scenarios. The general population, when asked about weighing the pros and cons of electronic voting, are nearly as worried as the professionals. It's not a hidden secret that our electronic voting machines are fairly hackable with a lot at risk.

Many organizations that have thought about electronic voting machine security for years or even decades have shared their opinions and potential solutions, including these examples:

- democracylive.com
- blogs.microsoft.com/on-the-issues/2019/05/06/protecting-democratic-elections-through-secure-verifiable-voting
- www.verifiedvoting.org/resources/internet-voting
- www.researchgate.net/publication/224673217_Secure_Remote_Electronic_Voting
- dl.acm.org/doi/pdf/10.1145/585597.585599

Here are some other related articles about electronic voting security and risks; you can find hundreds of them on the Internet:

- www.schneier.com/blog/archives/2004/11/the_problem_wit.html
- www.wsj.com/articles/agencies-warn-states-that-internet-voting-poses-widespread-security-risks-11588975848
- www.washingtonpost.com/news/powerpost/paloma/the-cybersecurity-202/2020/05/11/the-cybersecurity-202-internet-based-voting-is-the-new-front-in-the-election-security-wars/5eb85e4e602ff11bb1179347
- www.wired.com/story/online-voting-worked-so-far-doesnt-mean-safe
- www.scientificamerican.com/article/the-vulnerabilities-of-our-voting-machines
- www.csoonline.com/article/3114784/voting-machines-are-still-too-easy-to-hack.html

None of them are pro-"Let's getting voting remotely now!" articles.

How can we build very secure electronic voting machines or software that prevent every hacker attack? This worry is especially concerning for the concept of remote electronic voting, where every registered voter would vote for the candidates and ballot issues of their choosing from home or wherever they are. As I've stated repeatedly in this book, and in my career, everything can be hacked. So, how can we have very secure remote electronic voting?

Exercise: Secure Remote Online Electronic Voting

Our task for this chapter is to design a very secure voting MFA-protected solution for remote online voting.

Use Case Scenario

Remote voting involves two main possible implementations. One is to provide voters with either a dedicated voting device that they own full-time or a shared device that they access when needed on voting day (perhaps one per family or at a neighborhood voting station). The other idea is to allow anyone to vote anywhere as long as they have a working computer. We are interested in the latter, more challenging scenario, even though both would be difficult to securely protect. We'll go with the much harder scenario where we have to protect people and their vote no matter what computing device they choose. The solution has to be fairly easy to use and verifiably secure, and both the device and the inputted vote must be auditable by the user and vote overseers.

It must be recognized that this particular scenario is in some ways easier to design for. It requires high security and that the user base readily understands the need for high security, meaning that people are likely to tolerate higher user friction without too many complaints. Many MFA providers must design their solutions to work with an almost unforgiving general public who barely tolerates reasonable security friction. The voting public, once a year or once every four years, may tolerate some five-factor MFA device, but they would not be as forgiving toward an MFA solution that protected them when logging on to their computer every day or any time they wanted to buy something on Amazon. So, in this way our job is easier. Our users will tolerate a slower experience with more things to do. . .up to a point. No one wants to deal with a very difficult-to-use experience no matter what the objective is. There are boundaries to user understanding and patience.

Threat Modeling

Our voting scenario also gives us some risk advantages. For one, the fact that money isn't directly obtainable from hacking the solution cuts out 99 percent (or whatever the true percentage is) of cybercriminals who would want to hack it. Most hackers are trying to directly fill their pockets with money either directly (e.g., bank account fraud, ransomware) or indirectly (e.g., credit card fraud, seller fraud). Money could be made by hacking electronic voting machines, but only as payment by those parties (politicians, nation-states, hacktivists, corporate interests, etc.) that would pay for the private bug disclosure or for a hack fraudulently moving votes to a designed outcome. And that is a far smaller pool of potentially malicious actors than every petty criminal looking to line their own pockets.

I see two to four main threats, depending on how you count them, against remote online electronic voting. First, and the most obvious, is maliciously changing the vote. Hacking an electronic voting method could end up changing a lot of votes all at once or attack a collection point where individual votes are tallied and reported. Those are two different types of attacks. The first would need to target a substantial number of voters in a similar way nearly all at once. The second would need to target only the collection points, which would be a single location or at least fewer locations than the original number of votes/voters that would be impacted.

Another main threat would be a real denial-of-service (DoS) attack to interrupt or prevent legitimate votes. I think of this attack as two possible attacks. The first would be to truly interrupt a real vote. It could be against all voters or against voters who are seen as inclined to vote the opposite way of the desired vote outcome. The other, and fourth objective, would interrupt the vote just enough or make the electorate think the vote was interrupted or changed, no matter how little, to cause a scintilla of doubt in the integrity of the overall voting process. The side that loses a vote is always looking for signs of illegal or impacted voting as a reason to declare the already taken place election null and void. An attacker would not even have to actually do anything, except make it seem as if something malicious happened. It doesn't take much mischief to move our civil society to anger and violence.

There are 10 ways to accomplish any hack:

- Programming bug (patch available or not available)
- Social engineering
- Authentication attack

- Human error/misconfiguration
- Eavesdropping/man-in-the-middle (MitM)
- Data/network traffic malformation
- Insider attack
- Third-party reliance issue (vendor/dependency/watering hole)
- Physical attack
- Brand-new, unknown attack vector (without current/default mitigation)

NOTE A watering hole attack is where an attacker maliciously modifies a site and its contents that other developers or users frequently visit. For example, an attacker can surreptitious, maliciously, modify a piece of popular shared code that other developers often re-use in their own legitimate products.

Our design would have to assume that any other computing devices and networks involved are actively compromised and still operate securely. It will need to incorporate mitigations that prevent these types of attacks working against the components listed in Chapter 5, "Hacking MFA in General":

- Enrollment
- User
- Devices/hardware
- Software
- Authentication factors
- Authentication secret stores
- Cryptography
- Technology
- Network/transmission channel
- Namespace
- Supporting infrastructure
- Relying party
- Federation/proxies
- APIs
- Alternate authentication methods
- Recovery
- Migrations
- Deprovision

This is the process that every MFA security designer needs to go through when designing their solutions. The rest of this chapter discusses the suggested mitigations for our secure remote electronic voting MFA solution.

SDL Design

All design starts with the Security Development Lifecycle (SDL). All programmers and designers must be trained in SDL ideas, processes, and tools before being allowed to be a contributing member of the project. All programming tools used should have secure default settings. High-risk programming methods must be banned. Programmers should be given the basic threat models currently under consideration and be asked if they know of additional ones. They should be shown the components and the 10 general ways each of them can be hacked.

All code should be checked for common vulnerabilities before being allowed to be submitted as "checked-in" to the source code repository. Each programmer should review their own code for security bugs and submit their code to other team members for review. Rewards can be offered for the code with the least number of bugs per lines of code and for the most number of bugs found by someone else. Source code review should be done with automated tools by internal parties *and* by humans—that is, external code reviewers and pen testers. It is important to change external reviewers on at least a biannual basis. Source code should be released for public review, and an official bug bounty offering thousands of dollars in rewards should be established at one of the reputable bug bounty sites. Any reported bugs should be investigated immediately and aggressively. Bug reporters, even if incorrect, should be treated with dignity and respect. Vendors should monitor commercial bug payment sites and the dark web for any irresponsible bug disclosures or unauthorized commercial sales. When reasonable, any verified bugs should be purchased to prevent them from leaking outside the commercial bug sale service. Any known critical security bugs should be responsibly disclosed in a timely manner (no more than a few months) after patches (if reasonable and possible) are available.

> **NOTE** Many security electronic voting guides and organizations insist the code should also be "open," meaning not owned by any entity, containing patents, or copyrighted. Although I think this is a laudable goal, I don't find it a requirement for secure remote electronic voting. Over the last few decades, open code has not been proven to be less hackable or to have fewer bugs per lines of code than private, commercial code.

The MFA solution should have automatic updating enabled and should check automatically for updates any time it is powered up and at least daily thereafter. There should be no end-user involvement or approval needed. Only code digitally signed by an authorized agent should be allowed to update the MFA solution. All updates must undergo SDL processes. A failure to successfully update when a critical vulnerability is involved should result in automatic additional attempts to update the device or a "hard" locking of the device to prevent it from being used with a known vulnerability. Applied updates should not be able to be reversed except by emergency orders with an authorized digital signature, if at all.

All code-signing keys of the vendor must be stored on isolated, but duplicated, high-security hardware security modules (HSMs) stored in two or more separate locations that cannot both be compromised by same hacker or disaster event. HSMs and any attached computers should be "air-gapped" from any network, stored in physically secure areas, and protected from EMI, optical, and other types of eavesdropping and manipulation. It should take two or more people to initiate access and code signing, and any entrance to the code-signing area must be monitored, video-recorded, and documented. These latter processes are fairly common at high-value public key infrastructure installations and are part of what is called the *key-signing ceremony*. These processes are not new; everything I've described is fairly routine and normal. You can look up the steps and procedures for key-signing ceremonies on the web.

> **NOTE** I cover one of the pitfalls of highly secure key-signing ceremonies here: www.linkedin .com/pulse/my-key-signing-ceremony-gone-wrong-roger-grimes.

Overall, the electronic remote voting MFA vendor should invite review and scrutiny and actively promote and reward *responsible disclosure*. The HackerOne bug bounty program covers what responsible disclosure means fairly well in their definition: www.hackerone.com/disclosure-guidelines.

Physical Design and Defenses

Since I don't fully trust phones for high-security applications, our MFA solution will be a separate physical device. Because of the required feature set, it will look something like a Bloomberg B-Unit (i.e., a thick credit card). Like B-Units and smartcards, it should be built to withstand normal use and abuse, and should operate in reasonable temperature ranges. It should contain its own rechargeable power source (for now, that likely means a lithium-ion battery), have a useful life of at least 10 years, and be resistant to physical tampering. Any attempts to open the physical package should render the device permanently, logically broken. It should be designed to prevent EMI, electron microscope, and wireless side-channel eavesdropping.

Our MFA solution should have the most popular physical connections, such as micro-USB, and provide several popular physical connection types. It can include one or more wireless connection methods, such as Wi-Fi, Bluetooth, and cellular. Any wired or wireless connection points should be hardened against attack and operate at the securest implementation of their standards. Using any wireless method should require the user to physical press or move a switch that is clearly indicated for such a purpose; otherwise, the wireless connection methods remain off.

All connection points need to be protected by physical attacks, such as "Bad BIOS" or "evil USB cable" attacks, like the one discussed here: blog.knowbe4.com/new-evil-usb-cable-shows-how-attacks-can-leverage-physical-hardware. All communications, physical or wireless, must be encrypted and protected to prevent interception, modification, or eavesdropping. Any memory, chip, or storage areas should not be susceptible to cold-boot attacks.

The device should have an organic light-emitting diode (OLED) display area large enough to display codes and voter answers (e.g., candidates' names and Yes and No votes to particular ballot questions) along with enough detail that the voter is assured their vote was registered correctly.

NOTE The actual voting and display of the ballot is not done on the MFA device. The MFA device displays only authentication codes, validity-checking codes, and answers from the voter for verification. Most voting ballots contain far too much legally required text for a small MFA device to show all the required text in a reasonably readable way on a small form factor.

All hardware should have a "trusted boot" process, similar to what Universal Extensible Firmware Interface (UEFI) uses. All chips, firmware, software, processes, and components should check themselves for integrity upon boot up and continuously while in operation. Updates should be accepted only from preapproved sources using trusted digital signatures.

Cryptography

Any cryptography used should employ generally accepted open standard algorithms and key sizes. All cryptographic components should be easily updatable (by trusted sources using verifiable digital signatures) and be considered crypto-agile. The cryptographic algorithms and implementations used should not be overly susceptible to side-channel or timing attacks.

It is notable that Microsoft's proposed safe voting standard (`blogs.microsoft.com/on-the-issues/2019/05/06/protecting-democratic-elections-through-secure-verifiable-voting`) mentions using homomorphic encryption (`en.wikipedia.org/wiki/Homomorphic_encryption`), which we haven't covered previously.

Fully homomorphic encryption (FHE) systems promise perfect privacy, and Microsoft intends to use it to protect voter privacy and anonymity while still recording each person's vote to their identity. FHE is the idea that an organization can send encrypted content to a third party (in our case, it would be the centralized vote-processing center) and allow the third-party systems to purposefully manipulate the encrypted content in some authorized and intended manner, without the encrypted text (i.e., voter identity or vote choices) being decrypted by the third party.

Most homomorphic cryptosystems involve an additional evaluation algorithm that is cryptographically linked to the original cipher, which can be used by the third-party processor to do their work. Homomorphic cryptosystems would allow the necessary transactions (i.e., votes) to occur and be recorded without revealing individual votes or voter identity. This would better protect the entire voting ecosystem and the involved votes and voters from unauthorized data leaks.

Homomorphic cryptosystems have been postulated and created since the invention of public key crypto back in the 1970s, with varying results. Most of the attempts have resulted in halfway solutions, which could not be used in all situations and are known as *partially homomorphic*. A dozen or so FHE systems have been proposed in the pre-quantum world, but they have been more about the theory than implementation. Quantum computing, and especially the quantum property of *entanglement*, promises to allow more, better, and practically implemented solutions. Quantum entanglement is the key component that FHE has been waiting for. There is a subset of quantum cryptographers around the world who focus exclusively on this problem, using what they call *quantum homomorphic encryption* (QHE).

I'd call using homomorphic encryption in today's pre-quantum world a "big stretch" goal: fantastic if you can get it, but just sticking to existing generally accepted open standards (algorithms and key sizes) meets the requirements of this section. I do applaud Microsoft for making homomorphic encryption part of its desired future solution.

Provisioning/Registration

Voters should be given a free MFA device if they are an existing valid voter or when they register to vote for the first time once the new system is in place. All voter registration must be done in person. For people unable to go to the voter registration locations (e.g., disabled, elderly), an authorized, trained registrar should go to their location. The voter's identification should be determined beyond a reasonable doubt, however that is required by state or county voting regulations. Each voter should be given a global unique identification number tied to their specific voting identity no matter what they may be named throughout their life.

Each validly registered voter should be given a free MFA device and instructions on how to use it. Devices, each with its own GUID, should be tied one to one with the voter's ID, and only one MFA solution can be active per voter at one time and used only once per voting opportunity.

I considered biometrically identifying the voter to their MFA solution, like Bloomberg's B-Unit does. This can possibly be part of the solution, but I prefer nonbiometric methods or, if a biometric method is used, tie it to an additional authentication factor. In any case, I prefer a two-factor authentication method of the user to the device, if possible. One method might be that the user of that particular voter ID always must include a four-digit (personal knowledge) static code that they input to their MFA device whenever they use it. This code is locked to the device by the user when they first use it and thereafter permanently stored in the centralized voting database only, similar to how credit card CVV (card verification value) codes are done today, except the code is not printed on the device or anywhere else. If the voter forgets their static code, they must get a new MFA device assigned and registered to them. Registration to a new device should require physical identity verification just like the first one did.

NOTE Some readers may be wondering that since mail-in ballots, and the like, don't require in-person registration, why should our high-security electronic voting MFA device? First, I'll counter that even voters who can now use mail-in voting methods *at some point* had to register and be validated in person. Second, remote online voting is so high risk and subject to impacting every involved voter potentially at once that we should offset that risk with an in-person registration requirement until it is demonstrated that it need not be part of the requirement.

Any time a voter enters the static code, there should be an account lockout and throttling mechanism involved so that an attacker can't guess at the static code until they are successful. All bad guesses should result in a waiting timeout period longer before the next guess can be made and get progressively longer as each additional bad attempt is made. After too many bad attempts, the device should permanently lock itself and require a new device to be registered in order for the person to vote.

Authentication and Operations

Because it is nearly impossible to display a full-sized election ballot nicely on a small-form device, our MFA solution requires that the MFA device be plugged into another computer that meets the communicated minimum requirements, whatever they may be. The voting ballot will be displayed on the voter's other device and screen, and the voter interacts with that additional device to record their choices.

When the MFA device is plugged into a computer—say, by USB cable—the MFA device should power up and do its hardware and software self-checks. Then the user should execute the MFA device's main program (however that is done, depending on the operating system). This will launch a secure, very limited operating system and application, which is completely stored, contained, and loaded from the MFA device.

The user sees a voting application initialization message appear on their computer screen. The voter waits while the MFA device uses their existing Internet connection from the host device or a valid, supplied cell phone connection to check on updates and download any allowed, waiting online voting ballots. If updates are available, the device applies the updates and reboots. Upon rebooting, it checks again for both additional updates and waiting voter ballots.

Updates and ballot downloads are encrypted with an asymmetric key that is specific to the MFA device being used so that only a particular ballot package, tied to device and voter, is allowed to be decrypted and installed on any particular MFA device. No other device or voter ID can use that particular ballot package, and it can be run to completion only once. Incomplete voting requires that the whole process begin again with no previous choices shown or recorded.

Once updating and ballot downloading are finished, the device should confirm that it is securely communicating with the legitimate, expected voting website. If it is, the device should perform a challenge-response push to the device. Only the legitimate device and website can generate the agreed-on challenge-response sequence. If verified, the MFA device should display a big, green OK sign on the MFA device's OLED. The software should ask the user to confirm that the big, green OK sign appears on the MFA device. If not, something is wrong with communications, or it's possible that the user's authentication experience on the host computer's screen is being simulated by a fake website. The user should be educated not to proceed with typing in their credentials or participating with voting or updating until the big, green OK appears on the MFA device. This, along with the preregistration of the device and site, should prevent fake authentication attacks from being successful.

NOTE Of course, never underestimate the ability of users to ignore all signs of compromise and training no matter how well you've attempted to do.

Once the user confirms the green OK, they are shown a logon screen and asked to authenticate. The voter is asked to type in their voter ID and OTP code (plus the voter's four-digit static personal knowledge portion at the beginning). The entire authentication process and application is loaded from and originates from the MFA solution's secure enclave chip, much like a smartcard chip. The session shown to the user is a virtual session, protected by a hardware hypervisor to prevent tampering. All voter inputs are selected using touch-screen or mouse inputs. No keyboards are used to prevent easy keystroke logging. If higher security is desired, all inputs could be made on the MFA device by the voter using a button or wheel interface, as is often used on portable media players and voice recorders. Either way, great care should be taken to make sure the selections are recorded onto the voter's ballot within the secure confines of the MFA-provided application and hypervisor. It should be nontrivial for a host system to eavesdrop on the MFA-protected session.

The hardware hypervisor should protect the electronic ballot program from nontrivial eavesdropping or tampering. There are occasionally ways to hack hardware-based hypervisors to do "host-to-client" or DoS attacks, but doing so is not easy. And most hypervisor vulnerabilities can be remedied with a firmware or software update.

The OS and application should have minimal lines of code and footprint to cut down on possible attack vectors. All communications outside the secure enclave should be accomplished using a Transport Layer Security (TLS)-based VPN to predefined IP addresses or domain names.

Perhaps if the device is started up and finds no active ballot packages to download, it tells the user and either it powers off after a few minutes or it allows the user to perform a simulated ballot demo or provides user education to help with process training. Technical support websites and phone numbers should be physically located on the MFA device and displayed whenever the device boots.

The OTP code can be event based and key off each new election ballot package or, like a regular TOTP device, generate codes all the time. If it is event based (i.e., HOTP), the device should use the Initiative for Open Authentication (OATH) Challenge-Response Algorithm (`tools.ietf.org/html/rfc6287`) and incorporate critical parts of the ballot information and user's response as part of the challenge-response.

But the entry of the OTP code (either HOTP or TOTP) by the user into the voting software or process must require the four-digit static code portion in addition to the OTP code. The OTP code display on the device should have a physical printed area or sticker reminding the voter of the need for both portions, such as something similar to "Don't forget to enter in all codes using your 4-digit PIN plus the code displayed here: XXXX-XXXXXXX" or something like that. The screen can require the two needed codes separately as well.

Any OTP codes should use open standards and processes, such as those discussed in Chapter 9, "One-Time Password Attacks." OTP codes should expire in a reasonable amount of time. OTP codes should use Dynamic Symmetric Key Provisioning Protocol (DSKPP) to securely generate new shared seed values on a regular basis.

The MFA device should, similar to what FIDO Alliance devices do, require you to register the main voting site/service to the device (and vice versa), and the main voting site should always check for origination identification when a ballot download is requested. Channel binding should be enabled by default. If voter selections are not detected as originating from the specific MFA unit, then an MitM attack should be assumed and the vote not counted.

I love the Bloomberg B-Unit and Datablink examples' idea of having the application authenticate with the host device by using flashing light codes and an MFA device light sensor. However, this sort of authentication isn't needed because the application is originating from the device itself. It would be, in effect, authenticating to itself. In the Bloomberg B-Unit example, the application originates as already installed on the primary computing device being used or using a web service. The software is installed and executed prior to the MFA device being involved, and the software instance is being called from locations outside the MFA device's control. In our example, the code execution is under complete control of the MFA device and travels with the MFA device. But if additional application to MFA authentication is desired, I like the B-Unit's and Datablink's idea of flashing lights to communicate a code to the MFA device and having the user input a code back to the application.

Verifiable/Auditable Vote

After successfully authenticating, the current ballot is displayed on the screen and the voter reads it and makes their choices, with the ballot moving along as directed by the voter. The voter can see every vote on the computer screen and at the same time on the MFA device's OLED screen. On the full-sized computer screen, the entire ballot and text can be viewed. On the MFA device, only the question numbers and answers are shown. But a user could look at the computer screen where they are making their selections and compare it to the answers and choices being reported back by the MFA device.

When finished, the voter is asked if they would like to print a copy of their ballot and selections. Regardless of that answer, a custom link is sent to them via their registered email address (which is shown in partial form so they can verify it). They can click that link to see their choices immediately after the vote is finished. Alternately, the voter can always go to the main voting website, authenticate using the MFA device, and see their past voting history. The voter should have the ability to report incorrect votes at any point.

A verifiable voting paper trail is needed for any electronic voting solution, remote or in-person. It is essential that the voter be able to compare what they thought they voted for with what is printed. Solutions not allowing real-time printing of selections cannot be trusted. Solutions that send the verification through untrusted channels, like the Internet or only to the host device, cannot be completely trusted. That's why the verifiable voting option must also be displayed on the MFA device (i.e., transaction verification) so that the voter can verify it on the most trustworthy device and location. Any time they use the Internet (or other method) to verify their vote, the verification process must be as trustworthy as possible.

Communications

All connections to and from the MFA device and host computer must be encrypted end to end, preferably using a VPN from source (i.e., MFA device and application) to destination (voting registrar). The MFA device and application should be hard-coded to use a single DNS host address, which is heavily secured against malicious manipulation (on both the local side and server). It's even better if a hard-coded IP address can be used since it removes DNS from the equation altogether for the VPN, which is better from a security perspective. If an IP address is used, make sure to include both IPv4 and IPv6 addresses.

Note: If hard-coded addresses need to be changed they can be changed out slowly as old or existing devices expire and users get new replacement devices.

The central voting location should be hardened against DoS attacks, using load balancers and anti–distributed DoS protections. Connections from the MFA device to the voting location are the only connections allowed for voting and updates. Only one client-initiated connection can be active at any one time.

Backend Blockchain Ledger

All vote selections and other information should be recorded to a backend blockchain ledger. A *blockchain* is a distributed, decentralized ledger (i.e., records database) for tracking and verifying individual transactions. Each individual tracked transaction may be stored in a separate transaction "block," or multiple transactions may be stored together within a single block. The number of transactions stored per block depends on the implementation. An individual block contains the transaction information (it can be any information as defined by the application, including just a hash of the required transaction information) and at least one cryptographic hash, along with any other required information. A common blockchain block format is represented by Figure 22.1.

The "chain" of the blockchain refers to the fact that the hash of the previous block is stored in the next block, which is then hashed and stored in the next block, and so on. This makes each subsequent block "hooked" by hashing to the previous block in such a way that all blocks in the blockchain are cryptographically linked to each other. An attacker cannot easily tamper with any block without also modifying every subsequent block (because the hash of the tampered block would change). It's a pretty strong protection—as long as the integrity of the hashes are protected.

In order to maliciously manipulate any single block in the blockchain, any attacker would need to modify the information and hashes of all subsequent blocks and do so in a way that would not be detected and recovered by all (or at least half) the underlying participants. That's a very strong, underlying inherent protection. That's why blockchains are becoming so popular for transactions needing long-term integrity protection.

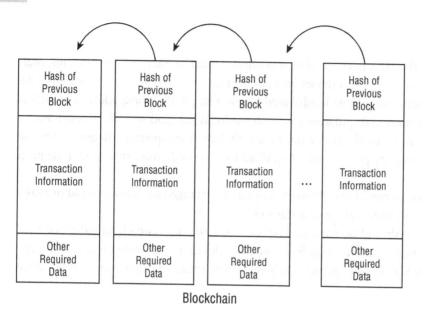

Figure 22.1: Representation of a simple blockchain

NOTE So-called "51 percent attacks" have been accomplished in the real world against less popular cryptocurrencies using blockchains. See www.ccn.com/ethereum-classic-51-attack-blockchain-security-researchers-reveal-full-implications for an example.

With that said, I've been a huge critic against using blockchains for every computer security problem. Here are some of my articles dismissing blockchain as the answer to every security problem:

- www.csoonline.com/article/3408317/what-blockchain-can-and-cant-do-for-security.html
- www.scmagazineuk.com/why-blockchain-isnt-holy-grail-cyber-security-strategies/article/1498777
- www.csoonline.com/article/3269236/why-blockchain-isn-t-always-the-answer.html
- www.csoonline.com/article/3241121/hacking-bitcoin-and-blockchain.html

Let's just say that I feel like I'm a fair and neutral party when it comes to talking about the "greatness" of blockchain.

Given that, I think it's the perfect solution for securely storing voting records. You can either store a person's voter ID and actual voting record in the blockchain, or for purposes of anonymization, store the hash output of a voter's choices for a particular ballot. For every ballot, different sets of answers could lead to different numeric summary answers. For example, if I voted yes for everything and for the first candidate for every position, my summary number might be 0196327, and if I voted another way, it might end up being summarized as 4530881. And that summary value could be hashed along with the ballot ID, my voter's ID, and my four-digit static code to end up with a hash that is unique for me and my particular vote. Or my votes could be stored in another database linked to my voter ID by another number. Either way, a value representing my choices could be hashed and then stored. An authorized voting registrar or system could look to the blockchain, find the hashed value, and then link to my voting record. I could also use the hash value to find my own voting record whenever I wanted to verify my recorded vote, and voting officials or law enforcement could do the same. Blockchains are difficult to hack and great at storing permanent records of important transactions.

Not everyone agrees with me. Here are two articles where someone disagrees that blockchain is right for electronic voting: www.verifiedvoting.org/wp-content/uploads/2018/10/The-Myth-of-_Secure_-Blockchain-Voting-1002.pdf and www.verifiedvoting.org/wp-content/uploads/2018/12/The-Myth-of-22Secure22-Blockchain-Voting-Onepager.pdf.

To summarize our secure MFA solution for online remote voting to the bare physical components, see Figure 22.2.

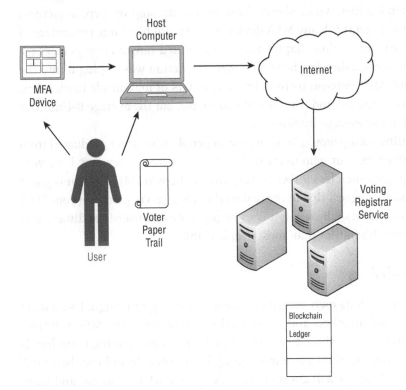

Figure 22.2: Summary of MFA solution for online remote voting

Migration and Deprovisioning

As with any physical MFA solution, inventories, policies, and processes need to be developed for lost, stolen, or replacement MFA devices. Any username changes due to marriage, divorce, or legal name changes can be handled outside the MFA device and application. The MFA device should stay linked to the person's voter ID. If a new device is provisioned, the old one is always deprovisioned first and disabled from being used (at least by that user). Users and anyone else should be able to easily initiate a device "hard reset" to wipe the device.

API

Any APIs used by the voting system should be locked by IP address and require special trusted digital certificates for initial authentication. The API should not be "open" and available to use by anyone. All API connections should happen over private phone lines or data connections and not over the Internet.

Operational Training

All users, tech support, and trainers need to be trained on device use and troubleshooting. Users should be provided with a written booklet, which shows them what to do, step-by-step, in pictures and text. No matter how easy to use you think any MFA device is, there will be a large percentage of people messing up. Remember earlier in this chapter when I discussed how a large percentage of people could not be trusted to work a device whose only real instruction was to plug it into the USB port and push a button. Our MFA vote-protecting device is orders of magnitude harder. Yes, Bloomberg's B-Unit is used by the "masses" and is more difficult to use, but the average B-Unit user is college-educated or at least of above average intelligence.

An MFA device for remote online voting would be going out to people who never graduated from high school, who have never driven cars, or who never had a driver's license. They may have very little to no experience on a computer, much less MFA devices. Any public-wide MFA rollout is going to take a lot of training and support. I suggest that in the real world, when you're planning your MFA device training, you consult with experts whose job it is to help you design user-friendliness and easy-to-understand documentation. It's harder than most people think.

Security Awareness Training

Every MFA solution needs to come with its own security awareness training campaign. Users must be taught about potential threats and attackers and the ways they might abuse the MFA solution. Online remote voting is no different. Users should be warned about attackers sending them fraudulent emails trying to infect their host machines or encouraging them to enable and use their MFA device against their bogus website. Hackers will always find ways to hack MFA solutions, and users need to be taught what those methods are, what to look out for, and how to defend against them.

Miscellaneous

There are lots of other considerations necessary with a real-world MFA online voting implementation, not the least of which is funding. A world of secure online remote voting isn't cheap. Someone (e.g., voter registration office, City Council, federal, state, or local government, etc.) has to buy the devices and give them away for free. Someone has to fund the infrastructure, ongoing operations, and tech support.

Not all people will have computers or the ability to use computers. How can special needs and disabled individuals vote? There will need to be alternative voting methods for them, or the MFA device and experience will have to be designed to handle all different types of disabilities. Will there be multilanguage support? How long will each version of a device be handled? How can we handle power outages, Internet outages, cell phone outages, and so forth? Will alternative methods of voting lead to other types of hacking?

So, what do you think? This was a quick security design review for a high-security MFA device for remote online voting. A real-world security design would take months and require the input of dozens of security experts. But you get the picture of what we are trying to do. Perhaps the only sad realization is that it is likely to be quite a while until we get MFA-protected remote online voting, if ever. We don't know yet if the wider voting electorate will tolerate the increase in user friction just to vote. To paraphrase my friend Dr. Cormac Herley, "You can design a system of how you think five billion people are going to react, but five billion people are going to react like five billion are going to react." And it may not match your model.

Send me your comments and recommendations for my secure online remote voting MFA device to roger@banneretcs.com.

Even with our best attempts to prevent hacking, this theoretical, ultra-secure MFA device could be hacked, potentially in several ways. But security isn't binary, and anything we do to decrease malicious manipulation is good. The primary security objective of a remote online remote voting implementation would be to create a highly secure solution that allowed more authorized voters to participate in the process with less hassle and with fewer errors and hacks compared to the existing systems. From a security perspective, if remote electronic voting actually resulted in fewer fraudulent votes overall (or rates per voters), it would be successful. It doesn't have to be perfect.

Summary

This chapter covered how to build a secure MFA device that would allow secure online remote voting. We discussed the use cases and did some quick threat modeling. From those scenarios, we developed a descriptive model for what we think is a highly secure MFA device for secure online remote voting.

Chapter 23, "Selecting the Right MFA Solution" will discuss how you can pick the right MFA solution for your organization.

23 Selecting the Right MFA Solution

This chapter will cover how to pick the right MFA solution for your organization and needs. We'll proceed as if you are tasked with choosing your organization's future MFA solution. You'll find dozens of questions and requirements, in checklist form, that you can use during any MFA evaluation project; a list of MFA vendors you can research; a summary project plan outline; and a link to a spreadsheet that lists over 115 MFA vendors, along with a summary of their particular features and options.This chapter will give you a leg up in evaluating MFA solutions for you.

Introduction

One of the most common questions I get from people who have seen my hacking MFA presentations or read my related articles is, "What MFA solution should I get?" Let's start off by setting expectations for this chapter. There is no perfect MFA solution that works for everyone. Without knowing a lot more about your organization, its risk tolerances, applications, budget, and security culture, I can't even begin to hazard a guess about what would be best for you and your organization.

I know what the questioner is asking and why. They are super busy and tasked with a hundred other things, and picking the right MFA solution for their company is just one of them. They want someone else, more knowledgeable about MFA, to pick *the* solution they need out of the hundreds available. Or they are looking for the one I would personally deem "least hackable." They want to start their research with solutions the MFA expert likes the most to cut down the learning curve. It's a plausible strategy. They may even think that I have a solution that I love above all others that I can recommend if only someone asks.

Unfortunately, there really isn't a single solution that works best for everyone. What is good for one organization may not work for another. And they are all hackable—in multiple ways. Asking anyone to pick the "right" MFA solution without knowing any of the relevant details is like someone you do not know at all asking, "What car or house should I get?" A lot of factors go into those sorts of big decisions to make someone happiest, especially if that "someone" is an organization full of people who often value drastically different things.

I have some crucial points to make to anyone considering buying a new MFA solution, not the least of which is that all MFA solutions are hackable and no single MFA solution works with everything. We've covered the first point well within this book. It's the second point that makes selecting the right MFA solution so difficult to start with. If you take the most popular and widely used MFA solutions, they likely work with less than one percent of the digital world. The most popular MFA solutions are software and hardware TOTP implementations and SMS-based options. You may already use one or more of them.

Think about the MFA solution you currently use and how many websites, services, and applications you authenticate with on a monthly basis. I don't mean just the sites where you purposefully turned on MFA, but all the websites and services you volunteer or are forced to authenticate to each month. These sites include social media, email, instant messaging, banking, health care, insurance, investment, Internet search engines, research, databases, payroll services, software downloads, file sharing, VoIP, remote meeting services, government services, blogs, auction/buying, news, educational, financial, wikis, television, video, taxes/tax preparation, package delivery services, pharmacy, magazines, gaming, security services, research, ancestry, hobby, hotel, airline, car rental, rating, charities, identity protection, music, conferences, utility, cable company, credit cards, loans, food, takeout, personal car services, and shopping. The average number of sites and services that an average business user authenticates with is about 190 (www.securitymagazine.com/articles/88475-average-business-user-has-191-passwords). I've got 176 different logons, so I'm about average.

Now, think about how many of those websites and services allow MFA. I'm guessing a significant percentage do, although whether that is a minority or majority percentage will depend on the person and the sites. But now you need to ask yourself what MFA solution you use or know about will work with the most sites that you use in a given month.

At my last company, we were lucky. We had a single sign-on (SSO) portal that was MFA-protected. Once we logged on using MFA to that portal, we could access 24 different applications. That's a pretty good number for a small business. But it's because of the SSO portal and not because of the MFA solution that we used. If I think about which of the 24 applications could be directly accessed by the MFA solution we used, that count would have been reduced to two. And there were nearly as many sites and services related to doing business for that company (travel, hotel, airline, car rental, 401K, investments, blogs, etc.) that were not located on the SSO menu that require me to provide entirely different logons. I also had different 1FA/MFA methods for entering the parking lot, building entry, elevators, and office space doors. I think this authentication amalgam experience is fairly normal in most business environments, even in businesses trying to truly get a single sign-on experience.

Regarding my personal accounts outside of business, the best example of the broadest deployed multiservice MFA logon I can think of is Facebook/Twitter/Google OAuth logons, where I require MFA to log on and then use OAuth to log on to other participating OAuth sites. Out of my 176 personal logons, I can use OAuth with five of them. I have a few dozen sites and services that use SMS-enabled MFA, but that is not by my choice, and I would not use SMS-enabled MFA if it wasn't required. I have three vendor phone apps that are MFA options for different services. They all work in drastically different ways. I think that my experience is fairly average for most people.

This explains why MFA has so far not replaced passwords as the most popular authentication method. No single MFA method works with as many sites as passwords. And passwords work so well that anyone could even use the same password across all their non-MFA sites. In fact, the computer authentication world spends most of its time telling people not to re-use the same password even though they could. Whenever I read articles claiming that passwords are soon to be gone, I want to ask the writer, "And replaced with what?" Because even if you wanted to do it, you couldn't do it. Passwords are going to be with us for a long time.

All MFA solutions have trade-offs. Some are easier to use than others. Some are cheaper to purchase, install, and operate. Some integrate with more things. Some require that separate devices be purchased. Some have authentication factors that simply seem to integrate and be accepted into your organization better than others. Some companies prefer external OTP tokens, some like software-only solutions, and some really like biometric protection.

You may want to consider that not using MFA at all may be the right solution for you at this time, either for everything or for particular sites and services. MFA doesn't work with everything, so that means you have to make trade-offs. Is that split of what MFA does and doesn't work with acceptable?

MFA is not always needed. I don't want to have to authenticate when performing Internet search queries or researching things on public, commonly available websites (like Google). I don't even like to have to authenticate to the various, one-off, websites I use to buy things during the year. I don't necessarily trust them to protect my personally identifiable information (PII). I'd rather do my buying as anonymously as is reasonably possible for the average person, although I don't go to the extremes of using one-use credit cards or using pseudo-anonymous identities. I like to use MFA where it makes sense for the things I value that I'm trying to protect to prevent easy malicious access by an unauthorized person.

We make similar risk decisions all the time in the real world. My house door is locked at night but my mailbox and external garage isn't. My garage has yard equipment I don't want stolen, but in the absence of any criminal theft issues over the last 10 years anywhere in my neighborhood, I accept the risk that goes along with leaving it unlocked. But I do have offsetting security cameras that will alert me to activity in my yard.

I do lock my cars all the time, but it's apparent that many people in my county don't from what I read in the local crime reports. I'm always amazed by how many people with loaded guns in their car don't lock their cars at night. They obviously have different acceptable risk profiles compared to me. So, in general, in real and digital life, we choose what we do and don't want to strongly secure depending on the scenario. That's life.

There are even potentially some scenarios that are far less at risk using regular logon names and passwords than using MFA. Just ask wealthy cryptocurrency traders. So many of them have had their digital fortunes stolen and never reimbursed (in many cases), because they overly relied on MFA to protect them. Since I've been doing my "Many Ways to Hack MFA" presentations and webinars, I've had dozens of people contact me to say they went back to using logon names and passwords because of their negative experiences with MFA. In general, MFA probably decreases cybersecurity risk in most scenarios. But not all. And any good evaluator of MFA solutions needs to be aware that there are scenarios where MFA might actually *increase* the risk of a successful attack. Many people are shocked to hear this. I, too, was taken aback the first time someone told me that they went back to using logon names and passwords. Now after dozens of people have told me the same thing, I understand that it isn't an uncommon reaction and why they did so.

For example, if an MFA solution is SMS-based, it means that a SIM swap attack or social engineering my phone company's tech support folks may be enough to get around the MFA authentication defenses. SIM swap victims didn't do anything stupid. They relied on the MFA solution to provide them with what they were told was "better" security than what they were previously using—and that reliance ended up hurting them.

If they didn't use SMS-based MFA, maybe they would just use a regular logon name and password. If they use a unique logon name and password for each service, what are the odds that they'll be phished out of it versus a SIM swapping attack happening? That risk comparison needs to be evaluated. And, personally, I trust my ability not to be phished over trusting my authentication to a phone company that hasn't so far proven to be that adept at preventing SIM swap attacks (at least right now). So, I use a logon name and password only to protect some of my most valuable and important resources. And I don't regret it. It's absolutely the right security decision for me, and many others, in some high-risk scenarios.

Of course, I think MFA can provide reduced cybersecurity risk in many or most scenarios. The bigger problem I have is that no single MFA solution works in all my scenarios. That means I have to pick and choose which scenarios I need to protect and decide among the available MFA solutions to protect them. When trying to pick the "best" MFA solution for me or one of my organizations, I use a proven process. It's one you can use, too.

The Process for Selecting the Right MFA Solution

The process for selecting the "right" MFA solution for you and your organization consists of this series of steps:

1. Create a project team.
2. Create a project plan.
3. Educate.
4. Determine what needs to be protected.
5. Choose required and desired features.
6. Research/select vendor solutions.
7. Conduct a pilot project.
8. Select a winner.
9. Deploy to production.

I'll cover each in more detail in the following sections.

Create a Project Team

Picking MFA solutions is best not done by one person, even if you, the main person, are the most knowledgeable computer security and MFA person in your company. Moving from non-MFA solutions to MFA requires senior management support and comments and feedback from the people who will be helping you to decide on the "right" solution. The more people you have involved with the process and supporting the ultimate selection, the more people you have on your side when things start to get a little rough, as they do in most computer security projects. Implementing MFA for the first time is never without at least some minimal operational interruption. Sometimes the issues aren't so small and end up being new learned lessons for your next project. Having more people on your side from the beginning can only help you. And who knows? Maybe you will actually learn something from them that helps you, and the project team, make the right decision and be more successful.

I remember a lesson I learned a long time ago, when I was the regional IT director of a national health-care system. Just before I was hired, they chose a new main computer system to replace the old system. I hated the new system. It looked like a mainframe system, it had to have a lot of expensive customizations, and many of the current users spent their time telling me how the old system was better. And to me, it seemed they were right. I developed a bit of a bad attitude, and I was complaining to the project leader one day about why they picked such an obviously bad system. Upon reflection, I now understand why he didn't take my criticism of the new system so well, especially since he had just led a large team of people over nine months in evaluating different systems before they made their choice. He said something similar to this: "You can say you individually hate the system and perhaps more than a few users do where a few features aren't as good as others they were used to, but we spent nine months evaluating competing systems using a solid, thorough evaluation process and the majority of team members and department end-user representatives selected this system. I'm sure each person involved saw some features they liked and some they thought were better in the old system. But in the end, the majority of the team felt this particular system did best overall for what we needed to do. Every system has warts. You can argue about whether it was the best system for you and some others, but you can't argue with the process." I gotta say, he was right.

Every MFA solution is a trade-off of features, each with its own strengths and weaknesses, advantages and disadvantages. There are going to be people who do not like your MFA solution. So, make sure you put together a good project team and use a good selection process. That's always the right choice.

If you do not have solid project management skills, get a great project manager assigned to your team or gain the necessary skills yourself. Other team members should include the following:

- Senior management sponsor
- Project leader, knowledgeable with computer security, MFA, and other related topics (this should probably be you)
- IT security manager (if not you)

- Technical support representative
- Other IT employees as required
- End-user representative(s), possibly managers and/or stakeholders from different departments and business units
- Communications specialist
- Accounting/budgeting/purchasing

Of course, in small companies, many of these roles may be represented by a single person. You may be the "team." After you have your team, put together a project plan.

Create a Project Plan

Every project leader needs to create a detailed project plan, likely using some project software like Microsoft Project (`products.office.com/en-us/project/project-and-portfoliomanagement-software`) or any one of the other competing good products (for suggestions, see `www.pcmag.com/roundup/260751/the-best-project-management-software`). It's important to figure out and document the key tasks and critical paths. The more detail and estimated timelines, the better. Overall, any project management plan should include the major milestones listed as steps in the process in this chapter.

Create a Timeline

The ultimate objective is to move some or all people of the organization to an MFA solution from what they are using today (i.e., another MFA solution or non-MFA authentication).

Create Project Phase Timeline Estimates

How long will it take you to complete the entire MFA migration project? Estimate how long it will take your organization to move all involved authentication systems to MFA once you start your MFA migration project so that senior management and project members can see likely expectations. The time estimates are unique for every organization and depend on what you have to move, how, and when you are able to move them. In my experience at small to mid-sized companies, the average MFA project takes three to six months from start to finish, including selecting the solution. In large, multistate or global companies, MFA projects start at six months long and can easily last a year or two. Every organization's timeline will be different, but project leaders should start with some basic guesses for each phase of the project. For an example, see Table 23.1.

By assigning some general numbers to these tasks, you can come up with a rough estimate of time needed for the MFA migration project and inform all stakeholders of the tasks and estimated times. Some tasks, such as education, forming a project team and planning, and creating a timeline can be accomplished simultaneously.

Table 23.1: MFA migration phase timeline example estimates

Phase	Estimated time to complete
Put together a project team.	1 day
Create a project plan.	1 week
Educate the project team.	1 week (preparing and teaching)
Research current systems needing protection.	1 month
Select desired features.	2 weeks
Research MFA vendor solutions.	1 month
Select multiple vendors for a pilot program.	1 week
Pilot project	3 months
Select a winning system.	1 week
Performing a full-scale implementation	2 to 6 months

Educate

Start by educating yourself about MFA. You've certainly done at least part of that by reading this book. You are ahead of the curve. Now share some of what you know with your fellow project team members. Everyone needs to have a basic understanding of MFA, the different types and features, and the strengths and weaknesses of each type. The project team should have a common baseline understanding so that they can help with the rest of the project. The actual project team education is likely only to be an hour long or whatever your organization can put aside for such things. I've been teaching computer security topics for over 30 years. Researching and preparing a slide presentation on technical topics lasting an hour for laypeople takes about a week to create and do right in most cases.

After the final MFA solution is selected, you'll need to train users, instructors, department leaders, and help desk support people, although the topic of that education session will be the specific MFA product you selected versus the general education I'm talking about here.

Determine What Needs to Be Protected

No MFA solution can protect everything. That fact is the biggest limitation. So, your first real task is determining what you want your final selected MFA system to protect. Does it involve all users, just administrators, or some other smaller subset of employees? What are the protection scenarios? For a lot of administrators, an MFA solution is used to protect network logons, device logons, server logons, or email. For others, it is used to protect a handful of critical company applications. For others, it is protecting a single high-risk application or project, or a single scenario like building entry or car systems.

For many companies, it's different MFA solutions for different applications, scenarios, and projects. For example, at my last employer, we had a few different MFA solutions for different things with an SSO portal added in so that one of the MFA solutions could handle dozens of our corporate applications that would otherwise not have MFA protection. And we had a few different 1FA/MFA options for other things like building and parking lot entry. The step of defining what needs to be protected is crucial. The performance of this step drives everything else.

Choose Required and Desired Features

The next step is to decide what are the required versus the nice-to-have features.

MFA Requirements

Start with the basic types of MFA, form factors, and other starting decisions, as shown in the main requirements checklist in Table 23.2. You can use this checklist as a starting point during your MFA solution research and evaluation. These questions can be downloaded as a Microsoft Excel spreadsheet from wiley.com/go/hackingmultifactor.

These requirements drive everything else. If an MFA solution you are interested in doesn't support something here, you must drop it from consideration or explain why it's still in contention.

Table 23.2: MFA solution main requirements checklist

MFA solution absolute requirements	Answer
Does the MFA solution support required use cases?	
Does the MFA solution support required platforms? – OS	
Does the MFA solution support required platforms? – Client devices	
Does the MFA solution support required platforms? – Cloud	
Can the solution be cloud-based or must it be on-premises? If cloud-based, can the cloud be multi-tenancy?	
Does the MFA solution support required platforms? – Languages	
Can the MFA solution be used in all required countries?	
Does the MFA solution support required platforms? – Browsers	
Does the MFA solution work with Microsoft Active Directory, Azure AD, or RADIUS (if those are required)?	
Does the MFA solution support security requirements? – Security policies, laws, assurances, certifications, regulations, etc.	
Is any special needs/disabilities support needed?	

NOTE   An interesting website to check out is twofactorauth.org. It lists hundreds of services and the types of MFA they support.

Next, do you have any desired overall MFA solution traits required before evaluation of MFA options, as shown in Table 23.3?

Table 23.3: MFA solution desired main traits

MFA solution desired traits	Answer
Hardware-based vs. software only	
Number of required factors (1, 2, 3, or more)	
Types of factors required/desired (something you know, something you have, something you are, contextual, etc.)	
Should one or more factors be out-of-band?	
Should the MFA solution support one-way or two-way authentication?	
If a hardware token is desired, is there a desired type (dongle, USB, HOTP, TOTP, smart-card, phone, etc.)?	
If a biometric is involved, is there a desired type (fingerprint, face, iris, hand, retina, voice, etc.)?	
Are push messages desired/required?	
If knowledge-based authentication is involved, is there a desired type (password, PIN, graphical solution, personal question, math solution, etc.)?	
Are paper tokens allowed?	
Do you seek wired vs. wireless connection options?	
Are particular types of connections required (USB, micro-USB, USB 3.0, Lightning, USB-C [Thunderbolt], Ethernet, serial, parallel, Wi-Fi, Bluetooth, NFC, RFID, etc.)	
If phone-based, is an SMS-involved solution allowed?	
If phone-based, is a phone app desired/allowed?	
If phone-based, does the solution support required platforms, Android, iPhone, etc., and any other desired phone OS versions?	
Are APIs needed, and if so, are they accessible and compatible?	
Are alternate logon methods allowed/desired once MFA is enabled (knowledge base, SMS, travel/master codes, etc.)?	
Are recovery methods allowed/desired (knowledge-based questions, alternate email, etc.)?	

(Continued)

Table 23.3 MFA solution desired main traits (*Continued*)

MFA solution desired traits	Answer
Is adaptive authentication desired/required?	
Are single-sign-on (SSO) capabilities desired/required or does the MFA solution integrate with your existing SSO solution?	
Does the MFA solution integrate with your privileged account manager (PAM) solution?	
Does the MFA solution work with your VPN solution?	
Does it work with your remote admin tools or remote logon solutions?	
Is a particular type of namespace, directory service, or identity management system support required/desired?	
Does it need to be FIDO compliant?	
Do you need any particular type or level of assurance (for identity, authenticators, federation)? Does the assurance have to be certified?	
Do you have any required regulations or privacy concerns to meet?	

I favor multifactor hardware tokens, phone apps, and smartcards. I avoid 1FA hardware tokens and SMS-based MFA, even though both are very popular. Knowledge-based and biometric factors should be paired with a second different type of factor.

When you are finished, you should have a list of requirements that, if not met, rule out a particular MFA solution as the best answer for your organization. You will have absolute requirements. For example, if your organization uses Chromebooks, does the MFA solution you are interested in work with Chromebooks? You can't buy an MFA solution that doesn't support the operating systems and devices you desire to protect in the first place. You can't skip a requirement. Then there should be a list of nice-to-have features, possibly ranked by importance.

Make Sure the MFA Solution Is Securely Developed

You want your MFA solutions to be securely developed. It's not enough just to ask, "Do you securely develop your MFA solution?" You have to ask specific questions. Table 23.4 lists MFA solution questions about secure development practices. Review Chapter 15, "Buggy Software," for more details.

Cryptography Requirements

An MFA solution must be cryptographically secure. Table 23.5 lists cryptographic requirements and concerns. Review Chapter 3, "Types of Authentication," for more details.

Physical Concerns

A physical MFA solution should be designed to mitigate physical attacks. Table 23.6 lists questions/requirements for physical MFA solutions. Review Chapter 17, "Physical Attacks," for more details.

Table 23.4: MFA solution questions about secure development practices

MFA solution considerations (desired/required/nice-to-have)	Answer
Does the vendor use Security Development Lifecycle (SDL) methodology and tools? If your vendor doesn't understand this question, that is your answer. If they answer yes, then ask how they do it.	
Does the vendor threat-model the MFA solution? If so, are they willing to share the analysis?	
Does the vendor do source code reviews for vulnerabilities?	
Does the vendor do vulnerability testing and pen testing against their product? If so, how often is it done? If so, who does it (internal, external, etc.)? Are they willing to share the reports?	
If vulnerability testing/hunting is done, is it automated using vulnerability scanning software only, human-based, or a combination of both?	
Has the vendor's solution had previous vulnerabilities announced regarding it? If so, can the vendor share details?	
How does the vendor patch their product? If so, how does that occur?	
Does the vendor participate or offer a bug bounty program?	
Does the vendor proactively notify customers of newly discovered critical bugs in a timely manner?	

Table 23.5: Cryptographic requirements and concerns

Cryptographic requirements and concerns	Answer
What cryptography does the MFA solution use (random number generators, hashes, symmetric encryption, asymmetric encryption, key exchange, digital signatures)?	
Does the MFA solution only use known, open, trusted cryptographic algorithms?	
Is any "proprietary" cryptography used? If so, avoid the product.	
What key sizes are used with cryptography? Are they sufficient?	
What is the expiration date/useful life for cryptography implementations used? How are new keys delivered/updated?	
Has cryptography in the device been designed to be resistant to eavesdropping?	
Where are cryptographic secret/private keys stored and how are they protected?	
Is cryptography crypto-agile?	
Does the MFA solution support any post-quantum cryptographic algorithms?	
Is PKI involved, and if so, who manages the PKI?	

Table 23.6: Questions about and requirements for physical devices

Physical questions/requirements	Answer
Does the device seem capable of standing up to normal environmental use and abuse?	
Does the device contain anti-tampering defenses?	
Are all secrets stored in encrypted areas or forms? No leaks into nonsecured areas?	
Has the device been designed and tested to prevent side-channel attacks?	
Is the device designed and protected against side-channel attacks?	
Is the device or its software resistant to cold-boot attacks?	
Does the device have a "viewing disruptor" to prevent easy shoulder surfing?	
If the solution is wireless, are all wireless communications secure by default, using industry-accepted standards, cryptography, and key sizes?	

OTP Questions

If you are considering OTP solutions, the solutions need detailed examination and answers. Table 23.7 lists questions/requirements for OTP devices. Review Chapter 9, "One-Time Password Attacks," for more details.

Table 23.7: Questions for OTP devices

Questions/requirements for OTP devices	Answer
Is the OTP solution event-based or time-based?	
If event-based, what is the event based on?	
Does OTP use open or proprietary methods and algorithms?	
Is the random number generator (RNG) involved NIST-certified or equivalent?	
Does OTP support OATH created standards?	
Does the OTP device support/is compatible with common OTP-device RFCs, such as 2104, 4226 (HOTP), 6234, 6238 (TOTP), FIPS-Pub 198 (or their successors)?	
How many OTP digits are displayed? A smaller number of digits means quicker repeating.	
How often does OTP code change?	
Are static characters or digits required to be entered along with changing OTP code during login?	

(Continued)

Table 23.7 Questions for OTP devices (*Continued*)

Questions/requirements for OTP devices	Answer
Do OTP codes expire in a reasonable period of time?	
Is OTP code replay prevented?	
Is OTP code brute forcing prevented by account lockout or throttling?	
How many bits is the seed value composed of? Anything below 128 bits is considered weak.	
How is/are seed value(s) communicated to the user?	
If any setup codes (numbers, QR codes, etc.) are used for installs, do those codes expire and, if so, when?	
If it's a software-based OTP, can the user have multiple identical instances running at once?	
If it's a software-based OTP, can the user have multiple active instances from separate locations?	
Is Dynamic Symmetric Key Provisioning Protocol (DSKPP) used?	
Where are seed values stored and how are they protected?	

Access Control Token Concerns

Most MFA devices involve access control tokens. Table 23.8 covers some of those concerns. Review Chapter 6, "Access Control Token Tricks," for more details.

Biometric Questions

Table 23.9 lists some additional questions related to biometrics. Refer to Chapter 16, "Attacks Against Biometrics," for more details.

Table 23.8: Questions concerning access control tokens

Access control token questions	Answers
Are access control tokens cryptographically protected?	
Do access control tokens contain unique, randomly generated, unpredictable IDs?	
Can MitM attacks be accomplished between a legitimate client and server? Can access control tokens be intercepted and stolen by an MitM attack?	
Does authentication only work with preregistered sites/services and MFA instances?	
Do tokens expire in a reasonable amount of time?	
Are there anti-reply mechanisms to prevent token replay?	
Are access control tokens tied 1:1 to a specific identity?	

Table 23.9: Additional questions related to biometric MFA solutions

Additional biometric questions	Answer
What biometric traits are used (fingerprint, face, iris, hand, retina, voice, etc.)?	
What anti-spoofing, "liveness detection," technologies are used?	
How are the stored biometric traits protected?	
Where are biometric traits stored: local, network, cloud, etc.?	
What are the Type I errors or false rejection rates (FRRs) and Type II error or false acceptance rates (FARs)?	

Miscellaneous MFA Solution Questions

Table 23.10 lists miscellaneous questions regarding MFA solutions.

Costs

What are the costs of the MFA solution? Table 23.11 covers some common costs.

You don't have to ask a potential MFA vendor all these questions and concerns. You can choose the ones that are important to you and your project team and add your own. Answers can be "yes," "no," "supports," "doesn't support," "partially supports," or whatever the required answer is. Your project requirements determine which features are most important to you.

Table 23.10: List of example miscellaneous questions about MFA

Miscellaneous MFA solution questions	Answer
If transactions are involved, are all critical, relevant details sent to the user for confirmation?	
If SMS codes are used, do the codes expire in 10 minutes or less?	
If SMS is used, are there easy ways for a user to verify the legitimacy of a sent SMS message?	
If recovery/master/travel codes are allowed to be printed, is the full logon information included with the codes?	
If recovery/master/travel codes are allowed, do they expire in a reasonable period of time?	
Does an MFA solution allow geolocation to be used as one of the authenticating factors?	
Is an MFA solution subject to namespace or subject name hijacking?	
Are all authentication factors required to be tied to the same identity?	

(Continued)

Table 23.10 List of example miscellaneous questions about MFA (*Continued*)

Miscellaneous MFA solution questions	Answer
Is channel binding needed/allowed/used?	
If account recovery is allowed, what are the methods allowed?	
Does deployment need to happen automatically and remotely or will physical presence for registration be required?	
Should the solution have a user self-registration portal?	
Should the solution have a user self-help operation?	
Does the MFA solution use or allow split secrets?	
Does the MFA solution support remote decommissioning or remote wipe?	
Does the MFA solution's API, if accessible, require authentication? If so, how is the authentication accomplished?	
What are the usability and operational interruption concerns?	
Does the vendor have alerting for high-risk events?	
What reports does the vendor have?	
Does the vendor have a way of allowing custom reports?	
What TCP/UDP ports must be open on firewalls for the solution to work?	
What components and dependencies are involved?	
Ask the vendor to describe install, deployment, and operational processes.	
Does authentication involve a phone call?	
How are service interruptions handled: fail open or fail closed?	
Is the MFA solution/backend on-premises or accomplished in the cloud (authentication-as-a-service)?	
Who has your user identity information and how well is it protected?	
Does the solution work with common authentication standards such as OAuth, OATH, OpenID Connect, JSON, SAML, etc.?	
Does the MFA provider have many customers at the same size, industry, or complexity as your organization?	
Can the MFA solution provider provide three customer references you can contact?	

Table 23.11: Example common MFA costs

Cost question	Answer
How is licensing done? Per user, device, per instance?	
How much do physical devices cost, if involved?	
Are third-party licenses involved?	
Are solutions per user, per instance, etc.?	
If hardware tokens expire, how long do they typically last (life expectancy), and what is the cost to re-purchase new tokens?	
What is the ongoing, manual maintenance?	
What is the renewal cost?	
Are there activation costs?	
What additional hardware must be purchased?	
Are costs different for different platforms and devices?	

Points Ranking

Many reviewers assign a point system to all the included requirements and desired features, and the MFA system with the most assigned points total wins in the end. Suppose, for example, that all must-have requirements are assigned a maximum value of 10. Then every other individual requirement or feature is assigned a value of 3 to 1. If a vendor's solution meets a requirement or feature completely, it gets the full points for that item. If it only partially meets a requirement or feature, it only gets partial points, however many the team feels is adequate for the partial coverage. In the end, add up all the points, and the top point getter is selected as one of the pilot project contenders or the winner, depending on your haste and project stage.

Research/Select Vendor Solutions

Now that you have your list of requirements and desired MFA features, it's time to begin researching. In the perfect world you would want to review as many MFA solution vendor candidates as possible that would come close to meeting all your needs. But there are literally thousands of possible MFA vendors, and most of them you likely haven't heard of and won't even be able to find (without my help). What you want to do is narrow down all the possible MFA solution vendors to those who could possibly meet your needs and not even have to bother with the rest.

Selected List of MFA Vendors

Once you have your required and nice-to-have set of requirements documented, you can begin looking at vendor choices. Offerings vary widely among MFA solution providers. An MFA vendor can offer everything from stand-alone MFA solutions to integration services so that you can enable your existing (non-MFA) sites and services. Appendix offers over 115 vendor names you can choose among.

You can download an Excel spreadsheet containing those MFA vendor names, websites, and an options matrix indicating which basic features they have or support at `www.wiley.com/go/hacking-multifactor`. You can sort and index the list according to the features that are most important to you.

However, this section of the chapter (versus the appendix) contains a much smaller example of personally selected MFA vendor names (in alphabetical order) and their websites. I list them here because I get asked about them a lot and so they appear to be popular choices to the people who ask and email me. They may or may not be the best MFA solutions for you:

- Authy (`authy.com`)
- Duo Security (`duo.com`)
- FIDO Alliance Certified (`fidoalliance.org/certification/fido-certified-products`)
- Google (`cloud.google.com/titan-security-key`)
- LastPass (`www.lastpass.com`)
- OAuth.io (`oauth.io`)
- Okta (`www.okta.com`)
- OneLogin (`www.onelogin.com/product/multi-factor-authentication`)
- Ping Identity (`www.pingidentity.com`)
- RSA Security (`www.rsa.com`)
- Rublon (`rublon.com`)
- Thales (`www.thalesgroup.com/en/markets/digital-identity-and-security`)
- Trusona (`www.trusona.com`)
- WatchGuard (`www.watchguard.com/wgrd-products/authpoint-multi-factor-authentication`)
- Yubico (`www.yubico.com`)

You should research at least 5 to 10, if not more. The process of looking at more than a few vendors will help educate you about what is out there. If you stop at the first few, there is a chance that you'll fall in love with one, think it's the greatest, and later on learn that a competitor had every feature you wanted for less money. So, research more than a few vendors, but at the same time, know that you can't research them all. There are just too many.

Narrowing Down Your MFA Search

You can start with reading a few recent MFA review articles. They are all over the Internet. Just type **multifactor authentication review** into any search engine. My only caution is not to rely on reviews any more than a few years old. MFA vendors come and go quite quickly, and many others get swallowed up by the big companies. With that said, here are some MFA review articles so you can get a feel for what to expect:

- `themerkle.com/7-best-two-factor-authentication-solutions`
- `www.g2.com/categories/multi-factor-authentication-mfa`

- searchsecurity.techtarget.com/feature/The-top-multifactor-authentication-products
- www.networkworld.com/article/3077997/5-trends-shaking-up-multi-factor-authentication.html

Read MFA Industry Reviews

A great way to narrow down MFA vendor lists is by checking the "official" product reports from the big technology industry researchers, including Gartner (www.gartner.com), IDC (www.idc.com), and Forrester (go.forrester.com/research). Each of these research agencies has decades of experience in reviewing products and industries. Their annual industry reports are some of the most sought-after reading. They usually cover the industry in general, summarize the major players, and pick winners and losers. An MFA vendor has to be around for more than a few years and have a substantial customer base and revenue before they will be listed in a report. The reports will let you know what current customers think about each product and what the strengths and weaknesses of each are. They will also cover the maturation of the industry overall and tell you where it's going. If I had limited time and I wanted to get a quick overview of the top vendors, I'd read one of these reports.

> **NOTE** Many of these review services cater to larger enterprises and the concerns of large enterprises. They may not cover issues that are important to small and medium-sized organizations.

The big negative is that these reports can be expensive to purchase outright (many thousands of dollars), but they are usually worth whatever you might pay. You can sometimes get the reports for free from the vendor winner of these reporting reviews, but that requires that you somehow figure out who the "winners" were and who is willing and able to share their reports. Many times a winner can share how they "placed" in one of the reports but is unable to share that report or review. That's because the industry research group wants to make money selling their report to you. Still, if you have some money to spend, here are some MFA industry reports:

- Gartner MFA reports (www.gartner.com/en/search?keywords=multifactor%20authentication)
- IDC MFA reports (www.idc.com/search/simple/perform_.do?query=multifactor+authentication&page=1&hitsPerPage=25&sortBy=RELEVANCY&lang=English&srchIn=ALLRESEARCH&src=&athrT=10&cmpT=10&pgT=10&trid=76771627&siteContext=IDC)
- Forrester MFA reports (www.forrester.com/search?searchOption=0&tmtxt=multifactor+authentication)

Conduct a Pilot Project

When you've done your research, choose at least two or three MFA solutions for pilot projects. A good pilot project involves the whole team and several user representatives across your organization. Participants should be involved in evaluating all selected MFA solutions so that they can provide comparative feedback. You want to find out how easy the solution is to install, manage, and administer? How easy is it to provision and deprovision users? How well the authentication works?

Are there issues and problems? What's the estimated total cost? Initial purchase, ongoing, and renewal and maintenance?

When you call existing customers who are using the product currently, at the end of your conversation don't forget to ask them, "What would you change about the solution if you could?" You'd be amazed what that one question opens up even from customers who were previously giving you a glowing review.

Select a Winner

You've reached the end of the first part of your long journey. If you are using points scoring, have everyone rank the solutions from best to worst and pick the winner that makes more people happy than all the others. It is good etiquette to let the losing vendors know why they lost. That information can help them improve their solution.

Deploy to Production

Now it's time to roll out the winning solution. I'm a big believer in baby steps, if that is possible. If possible, don't make an implementation plan where one day the old authentication solution is all that can be done and the next only the new method can be used. It's best to do side-by-side runs if possible, opening the new MFA solution to more people and departments as time goes on. If a trickle-in methodology is possible, rarely will you regret it. But I have regretted complete replacement, "go-live" projects where something went wrong that was not detected in the pilot project and other testing and a critical system went down. Save yourself the heartache and frustration. Try to move from one authentication solution to another in stages, increasing the number of people involved and impacted over time.

Be sure to update your policies and training to account for the new MFA solution. Provide training to IT, help desk support staff, train-the-trainers, trainers, and end users. Continue to keep your eyes and ears out for developing MFA trends. MFA is constantly improving. Most MFA solutions end up having significant improvements (or being bought by another company) every few years. Don't be surprised if the MFA solution you select has another name or owner within a few years after you buy it.

Summary

This chapter described how to pick the right MFA solution for your organization and needs. You learned why no MFA solution can cover everything, and we discussed required versus nice-to-have features. This chapter featured dozens of questions over multiple tables related to different MFA features and listed over a dozen MFA vendors to consider. I also pointed readers to Appendix, which lists over 115 MFA solution providers; told you how to download an Excel spreadsheet that contains every question asked and that covers the MFA vendors and their offerings; and provided a summary project plan along with estimated phases and timelines.

Chapter 24, "The Future of Authentication" will cover what I expect the long-term future of digital authentication will look like.

24

The Future of Authentication

Previous chapters covered existing conventional authentication, starting with passwords in Chapter 1, "Logon Problems," and moving progressively forward through traditional, existing forms of MFA. This chapter will discuss what the future of authentication, in the coming years and beyond, might look like.

Cyber Crime Is Here to Stay

Despite the increasing use of MFA and other more sophisticated computer defenses, cybersecurity incidents are here to stay and likely to get worse. I've been a computer security journalist for nearly 30 years and for almost as many years I've been asked, "Do you think we will have fewer attacks next year than this year?" or something similar. People want to know if the increasing sophistication and wider deployment of computer security is finally starting to make digital crime harder to commit. And each year, based on the past 30 years of experience, my reply is "No!"

Every year I say to myself, "Cybercrime is so bad that I can't imagine how it could possible get worse," and then each year it just somehow gets worse. For example, last year ransomware was pretty bad. Ransomware broke in, encrypted data, and brought down businesses (large and small), hospitals, cities, and even law enforcement, all over the world. Ransomware started deleting backups, updating itself ("ransomware-as-a-service"), and asking for a lot more money. I thought to myself, "How could it possible get worse?"

And then ransomware started stealing data and threatening to release it publicly or to other hackers if the ransom wasn't paid. So much for your backup saving you. They stole employees' personal credentials and threatened to reveal them publicly or give them to hackers so that the employees would know if the business owner cared enough about them to pay the ransom. Ransomware started attacking customer accounts of the businesses they invaded, letting those customers know that the only reason they are extorting them individually is that the business they originally invaded didn't want to pay. And just like that, ransomware got much worse.

Every year cybercrime just gets worse. I don't necessarily mean with the number of attacks, but in overall damage and whether or not we can as a society feel generally safer computing this year than last year. The answer each year for three decades has been no. Each year I hope my usual, pessimistic expectations get surprised and that one day, journalists will report that the damage from cybercrime has gone down. But so far, it's always been false hope.

This is unfortunate, because the Internet could be a far safer place for everyone. It doesn't have to be a place where cybercrime is rampant. There are ways to make it a significantly safer place. But it would take international cooperation and a rebuilding of the Internet from a place of pervasive anonymity to a place of default identity and authentication. So far, the appetite for even just good default security doesn't seem to be strong enough for the majority of Internet users to require it. Somehow, no matter how bad the level of cybercrime is, many people treat it as acceptable and don't truly want more security by default.

Perhaps a digital 9/11 event will happen one day, like the Internet or stock market being down for a day or a week, but until then, it's business as usual. And business as usual means increasing crime and damage due to malicious hackers and malware. Even the creation of the best MFA solutions will not change that because many people won't use it.

With all of that said, you and your organization can make your place a safer place to compute. Our overall goal is not to get rid of all cybercrime—we'll never do that anymore than we will get rid of all crime or all sin. Our goal is to make the environment we are tasked with securing a significantly harder place to hack. And using good MFA that is less hackable is a part of how to make a more secure computing environment.

MFA is now in what I would call its 2.0 form and quickly moving into an even more mature 3.0 version. This chapter will cover the traits that the future of authentication and MFA seem to be coalescing around.

Future Attacks

To get a good idea of the future of authentication, you should understand what the attacks of the future will likely look like. It's mostly more of the same, just with more sophisticated examples. Cyberattacks have been with us since nearly the beginning of computers—as soon as they began to be shared by different people with different logons. Cyberattacks, as we think about them today, have been around since at least the 1970s and the invention of digital networking. Early forms of social engineering and malware (e.g., virus, worms, and trojans) started showing up in the 1970s and '80s. By 1990, the personal computer versions of the attacks we know today had already been launched. The first personal computer virus, Elk Cloner, happened in 1982 (en.wikipedia.org/wiki/Elk_Cloner). The first major computer worm that attacked the Internet happened in 1988 (en.wikipedia.org/wiki/Morris_worm). The first ransomware attack, which I remember well, happened in 1989 (en.wikipedia.org/wiki/AIDS_%28Trojan_horse%29). The attacks have become increasingly sophisticated over time, but there aren't many completely new types of attacks.

Most attack types seem to go through a bell curve of where they peak in terms of pure number of attacks, and then the numbers start to go down due to broader implementation of more effective mitigations. But because there are fewer attacks overall, they are often more effective on their chosen targets (i.e., targeted attacks). Here's an article (www.csoonline.com/article/3518864/more-targeted-sophisticated-and-costly-why-ransomware-might-be-your-biggest-threat.html) arguing that ransomware is becoming less prevalent but more targeted and costly. So, future attacks will mostly be more of the same, just more sophisticated and more targeted. That part is probably not that surprising to most readers. I bring it up here because MFA will likely make more everyday types of attacks become more targeted, and successful.

But there are definitely attack traits and trends that we are likely to see more of in the future. Let's look at four.

Increasing Sophisticated Automation

Hackers and malware writers have been using automation for decades to perform their attacks. But the automation actions and the sophistication have been increasing significantly the last few years. For example, ransomware used to exploit a computer, immediately lock it up, and ask for $300 in ransom to decrypt. Now, when a ransomware program breaks into a computer, it "dials home" to let its creator/spreader know that it's in a new victim's environment so that the ransomware gang can investigate further. It usually downloads updated versions of itself or even new malware. As traditional ransomware grew in sophistication, it would look for admin passwords on the first exploited machine and use what it found to break into additional computers within the network. It used to be that the ransomware thugs would remotely access networks and computers and run scripts and other malware programs (like TrickBot) to find additional passwords used by employees and customers. The hackers would disable antimalware defenses, delete backups, and copy data off the network. Now the entire process became part of the ransomware's coding; no human attackers needed to be involved. Why manually do what you can automate instead?

Malware is quickly morphing into "malware-as-a-service," where malicious programs are constantly updating themselves, on the fly, online. Pretty soon a malware program will likely just download the components it needs when it needs them. It will detect that it must bypass a particular antimalware defense and download and use the component it needs to do so. For example, it will detect that it needs to disable User Account Control to get full control of a Microsoft Windows system, and it will download the component to accomplish that. If malware detects that it needs to access data encrypted by Apple's FileVault protection, it will download a module to do that, and so on. Malware will likely become more of a skeleton program to download different offensive modules on the fly when it needs them.

Hackers have been manually doing this since the beginning of hacking. Future malware will just automate the process. Today's malware doesn't have to stretch too hard to get there. There have been multiple exploit hacking frameworks, like Metasploit (www.metasploit.com), that have been modularized and componentized for a long time, split into different exploits and modules for various offensive attacking needs. And there are tools, like Bloodhound (latesthackingnews.com/2018/09/25/bloodhound-a-tool-for-exploring-active-directory-domain-security), that help hackers map networks and vulnerabilities to move from point A to point Z faster by using collected information. I've seen hacking demonstrations that married a vulnerability scanner with Bloodhound and Metasploit, which allowed a hacker to click on a desired target computer on a screen and the automation did everything else. In the demo, seconds after clicking on the victim computer on a screen, the system reported back that remote access had been gained to it, and it opened a remote admin console to the victim computer for the "hacker." If this is being shown to me and others, it's certainly being used by nation-states and well-heeled adversaries.

All the malware or a bot needs to do is detect what offensive capability is needed when it's needed. Detecting what is needed (i.e., fingerprinting) is easier to do than actually defeating something. The bots that gained initial access will detect what defenses are standing in the way of achieving ultimate success, however that is defined, and then download the method or tool required to achieve its goal and use it.

Defenders will be forced to meet the growing threat of malicious automation, and so, computer defenses will evolve in the same way. Proactive defenses will do automated threat hunting and download various defenses on the fly as needed for the different threats that are detected. Vulnerabilities will be patched, firewall rules will be updated, malware will be detected and removed, and indicators of compromise (IoCs) will be updated in the central database. Both sides will use rules-based engines, machine learning (ML), and artificial intelligence (AI). Eventually it will be good bot versus bad bot in a never-ending battle of whose bot and automation is better. I first wrote about this future scenario in 2017: www.infoworld.com/article/3168739/security/prepare-for-the-smart-bot-invasion.html. Humans will only be involved with the computers when the bots think they should be. The Defense Advanced Research Projects Agency (DARPA) even sponsored a machine-versus-machine only cyber hacking and defense contest in 2016 (en.wikipedia.org/wiki/2016_Cyber_Grand_Challenge). DARPA helped invent the Internet as we know it today, so anything they do should be watched.

> **NOTE** For fans of the fictional movie franchise *Terminator* [en.wikipedia.org/wiki/Terminator_(franchise)], yes, when I'm talking good bot versus bad bot, yes, I'm talking about something like Skynet, but I don't believe it will become "self-aware" and turn on humans. Unlike Elon Musk and others, I don't worry about real-world terminators turning on their creators. If you are interested in my reasons, see this article: www.linkedin.com/pulse/5-reasons-why-skynet-ai-kill-us-roger-grimes.

Increased Nation-State Attacks

Ever since Stuxnet was publicly discovered in 2010, many nation-states have been increasingly willing to have their offensive capabilities known and shown to their adversaries. Cyber wars are more popular than kinetic wars (i.e., traditional, physical war) and cold wars. Right now, cyber adversaries can pretty much get away with whatever they can accomplish. Being caught isn't much of deterrent for any side. That isn't a recipe for a decrease in these types of attacks. The worrisome aspect is that more and more nation-states see regular businesses and organizations as legitimate targets. Thousands of nongovernment businesses are targeted by nation-states each year and this number is likely to rise.

Why is this important? Because nation-state attackers are usually among the best funded and organized of attackers and they operate with near immunity. Regular hackers, even if foreign, face the possibility that their actions will be declared illegal one day and get arrested, even in their home countries. It happens all the time.

Nation-state attackers, however, are never arrested in their home countries and even enjoy special protection. The only time a nation-state hacker has to worry is if they venture outside their home country to another country that cooperates with law enforcement from the victim's country and they are actively sought for arrest. This has happened enough that most governments recommend that their nation state hackers only take vacations to other counties that don't cooperate with international arrest warrants.

Cloud-Based Threats

Cloud-based threats, so far, haven't been quite as bad as everyone predicted in the early days. Early on, computer security experts worried about brand-new types of threats from the sharing of Internet-accessible computer resources by multiple, unrelated tenants. And while some early cloud-specific vulnerabilities were discovered, mostly by white-hat researchers, so far most cloud-related attacks have been far more traditional in nature, things that could occur against any type of computer system and not cloud-specific. The most common types of cloud-based attacks are the same ones we had before cloud computing became big: authentication attacks, unpatched software, overly permissive permissions, and so on. Almost none of the real-world attacks have been something that leverage specific cloud features to do their dirty work or only work in clouds.

There is a good chance in the future that true cloud-specific threats and malware will grow in popularity. One major reason is that all computing is increasingly becoming cloud only. On-premises servers and services are quickly dying and being replaced by cloud servers and services, and as the saying goes, "Banks get robbed because there's where the money is." A second major reason is that as malicious bots become increasingly automated and more sophisticated, it will be easier for the bad folks to adopt their bots to the specific peculiarities of cloud computing. In my opinion, it would be almost strange for clouds to become *the* most popular platform for computing and not see malicious hackers concentrate their efforts more there, because if a hacker exploits a cloud mechanism, they get into every hosted tenant at once. I've often thought a cloud-abusing bot or worm would be devastating.

Automated Attacks Against MFA

And yes, I believe attacks against MFA will be increasingly automated. As MFA becomes more popular, so too will attacks against MFA. This means more automation and more victims. It's not like hackers are going to be stymied by MFA while knowing there are potentially dozens and dozens of ways to hack various MFA solutions (as demonstrated by this book alone) and just give up. Past history of cybersecurity shows that after the newness of a particular computer defense is over and starting to be adopted by the majority of defenders, it becomes routinely hacked. It happened with firewalls, access controls, and antivirus programs. Although they provided a ton of protection in their heyday, as they became more popular, they got attacked more successfully. And attackers take the exploit techniques that are working the best and automate them. I don't think MFA will be the ultimate defense that stops all attacks in which the attacker just gives up. And let's not forget that MFA can only try to stop attacks against authentication. There are a lot of different types of hacking and attacks against authentication is just one of them.

In summary, the attacks of the future will likely be mostly the same as today's attacks with four caveats: we are likely to see increasing automation, including good bot versus bad bot competition; an increase in nation-state attacks; an increase in cloud-based threats; and increased attacks targeting MFA.

What Is Likely Staying

There are some clear trends in authentication defense and where it is evolving. But first I want to cover which authentication components are likely staying, at least for the next decade.

Passwords

As explored many times in previous chapters, there simply is no MFA solution that can replace traditional logon name/password combinations as the most prevalent authentication method—at least not yet. Most logons are password logons, and that isn't likely to change any time soon.

Proactive Alerts

It's becoming increasingly common for sites and services using password- or MFA-based authentication to send out warning messages to a user's registered, primary email accounts (see examples in Figures 24.1 and 24.2) to notify them of a different detected authentication trait (device, location, etc.).

Figure 24.1 shows Uber warning me about a logon from what it perceived was a new device. I can't remember if it was because I started using a new laptop or just connected from a new browser. One of the unfortunate false positives of authentication detection is that when I use a new browser or even just get a browser update, the authentication detection heuristics detects my device as a "new" device. It would be great if sites and services could get rid of this false-positive detection. A wide range of factors could be collected and used to determine whether a particular device is new or not, beyond just using "browser agent." But even when I have to confirm a false-positive warning, the worst consequence is that I'm verifying that my valid session was valid. It's a waste of little time, but I'm not losing money because of it. I'd rather my MFA solution err on this side of the equation versus missing a malicious logon from some other person and device.

Figure 24.2 shows an email warning I got from Netflix warning me of a sign-in I did from Melbourne, Australia (which is in the state of Victoria). I had logged on to my Netflix account to start watching movies and shows while traveling and stuck in my hotel room trying to fight off jet lag. Kudos to Netflix for noting my new location and checking with me to make sure I was aware of it.

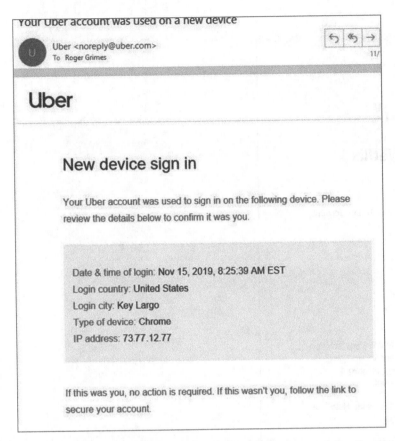

Figure 24.1: Example Uber email warning about a potential authentication issue

I frequently get proactive warnings from many of the websites and services I interact with on a monthly basis. I'm glad for each one. Yes, hackers could possibly capture the notification messages by taking over my primary email account, but unlike recovery emails, receiving a notification message usually would not let them reset my password, bypass my enabled MFA solution, or log on to my account. So, notification messages are all good. All MFA solutions should use these types of proactive messages to users.

Preregistration of Sites and Devices

FIDO and other authentication standards have shown the value in preventing many types of MitM attacks by requiring that sites/services that use MFA be preregistered to the individual MFA solution employed by a user. As covered in previous chapters, the involved site (usually by TLS-protected URL) is registered on the MFA device and the device is registered to the site (by device GUID or some other method). Neither will work with the other unless they have been previously registered with each other. This prevents MitM attacks, as were covered in Chapter 6, "Access Control Token Tricks," from working.

Figure 24.2: Example Netflix email warning about a potential authentication issue

Preregistration MFA solutions to sites, and vice versa, is still not required in the majority of MFA solutions, and it isn't appropriate for many types of MFA. But where preregistration is useful and can be done, it should be required. I expect to see preregistration required more often over time because of its success as a mitigation.

Phones as MFA Devices

Many MFA industry surveys have revealed a sharp uptick in phone-as-a-device MFA solutions, and that is likely to continue to rise in the future. Nearly everyone has a smartphone, and the percentage of people who do not is dropping. Most people have their cell phone with them all the time and each phone has a globally unique GUID, so it's not unexpected that more and more MFA solutions will be using "phone as a token" factors.

Total cost of ownership of hardware MFA tokens is among the highest solutions in the MFA world and often requires additional training beyond a written document or online guide. Phone-based MFA solutions are often easily used and understood by users. There are three basic phone-based MFA models:

- Voice-authentication
- Phone app
- SMS-based

Phone apps are split into OTP methods, traditional MFA phone apps, and phone apps with or without push notification. Phone-based TOTP, like that used with Google Authenticator and Microsoft Authenticator, is very popular, but it is likely to be seriously challenged in popularity by phone apps with push notification over the next few years.

Wireless

Wireless MFA devices are the most common types already and this is not likely to change. MFA solutions requiring a wired connection to work are mostly relegated to legacy products and scenarios.

Changing/Morphing Standards

The authentication standards of my "youth," from 20–30 years ago, are no longer around. Standards are usually a good thing, but they are constantly changing and morphing. They come and go over time. Eventually a new standard comes out that better addresses a growing need, and just like that, today's standard becomes tomorrow's legacy protocol. Expect FIDO, OAuth, OpenID Connect, OATH, SAML, JSON, and all the other standards to be replaced by something else eventually.

The Future

The future of authentication should not be a complete surprise to readers, as I've discussed it in previous chapters: zero trust and continuous, adaptive, risk-based authentication. These methods will be combined with ML/AI to create less user friction. The user will likely be allowed to log on or automatically be logged on simply because the site/service they are accessing is being accessed from a previously user-registered device. Not only is the user's device (be it a phone, computer, car, TV, or other form factor) tied to the user, but the site or service also knows, from past experience, that the device the user is using is the one they usually originate from. The user will likely be allowed to access an involved site/service without having to log on after their logon to their originating device.

This already happens to large user populations today due to browser-saved passwords and phone applications. Most phone apps don't require authentication every time you want to use them. If you've already logged on successfully once, all you have to do each successive time is start the app (as long as it is from the same phone). Even my high-security bank app is fairly frictionless. When I start it, as it's asking for my password or fingerprint, my password manager app comes up and auto-fills in my fingerprint to complete the required logon. The future of authentication is less user friction for most needs.

Zero Trust

Zero trust is the idea that every logon is treated equally with no inherent trust no matter where it originates. Prior to zero trust concepts, connections and logons inside a network were treated as more trusted than those that originated outside a network. I'm not sure that model ever truly represented how risk impacted an organization, but the idea was that firewalls and other access controls made it harder for an outsider to get inside a network, and thus any connection and logon from the inside was highly likely to be a trusted insider and did not undergo as much investigation and control.

The "hard, crunchy outside with a chewy inside" model was shredded the moment we all realized that 99 percent of all successful attacks were client-side attacks. *Client-side attacks* originate on user computers and devices and then move outward over the network to other areas. The original compromise likely occurred because of social engineering or unpatched software. But either way, once an attacker was inside a network, they were fairly free to roam over the network, steal admin credentials, and access other computers and data across the organization. There was (and still is) very little network isolation.

Zero trust was the recognition that the attacker was often already in the organization ("assume breach") and that perimeter defenses were easy to bypass. And so, each connection to any site or service was deemed as untrustworthy as another, whether it was originating from inside or outside the network. Without really announcing it, zero trust turned identity into the verification checkpoint. Identity became the new network isolation point. The reality is it was always this way—identity was always the ultimate isolation point; it just took us a few decades to realize it.

Industry leaders and researchers created zero trust framework models that they themselves followed or promoted. The three most well-known models are:

- Gartner Continuous Adaptive Risk and Trust Assessment (CARTA)
- Forrester's Zero Trust Extended (ZTX)
- Google's BeyondCorp

NOTE You may see also see a reference to the Gartner Trusted Identity Corroboration Model (TICM), which is a subset of CARTA.

Each of these zero trust models encourages continuous, adaptive, risk-based decisions. In the previous world, let's say a user logs on to their network using a local computer or remotely using a virtual private network (VPN) connection. Once they authenticate, however they do it, they are authenticated for a fairly long period of time. They can do whatever their role, permissions, privileges, and group memberships allow them to do. And they have the same access control privileges across the network regardless of what they are doing (although Microsoft User Account Control and Linux `sudo` attempt to control it a bit locally).

This type of access is like a lot of the access in our real lives. We get checked at the door and thereafter we are free to roam throughout most buildings. Even on military bases and at other higher security organizations, this sort of one-time verified trust in real life has been abused by trusted partners or insiders to unleash unexpected, violent, murderous attacks against their fellow workers.

Zero trust networks have the user or device come through a gateway device or software broker program, which authenticates the user or device initially but also continuously thereafter, during the subject's entire experience. Authentication is not checked once or after a set period of time, but continuously, all the time, for every attempted action and movement.

If I compare zero trust with the real-world scenario I described earlier involving the military base, all soldiers would be constantly monitored. If a soldier, who was usually unarmed suddenly picked up a loaded weapon and lots of ammunition, they would be more carefully monitored or perhaps even relieved of their weapon until evaluators determined if the soldier was carrying the weapon and ammunition for a legitimate reason. I'm grossly oversimplifying the problem and solution, but hopefully you get the idea. Everyone's actions and risks are evaluated all the time.

Zero trust networks are likely the future of networking and authentication. According to this article (www.networkworld.com/article/3487720/the-vpn-is-dying-long-live-zero-trust.html), "Gartner predicts that by 2023, 60 percent of enterprises will phase out most of their VPNs in favor of zero trust network access, which can take the form of a gateway or broker that authenticates both device and user before allowing role-based, context-aware access."

It can be difficult to find a lot of free detail on CARTA or ZTX, but Google shares a lot of free information on BeyondCorp (cloud.google.com/beyondcorp). I wouldn't worry about which particular model you follow as long as you understand and focus on the concepts they all share in common, which is continuous, adaptive, and risk-based authentication.

NOTE Another term you will see used to describe this type of authentication is *dynamic authentication*.

Continuous, Adaptive, Risk-Based

Continuous, adaptive, risk-based authentication is absolutely the future of authentication, both on large authentication services (as they are partially deployed today) and what will eventually be deployed on our own organizations' networks. MFA will still play a big part, but how the multifactor components are used and delivered will be the question.

Like passwords, today's traditional MFA solutions will be with us for a long time, a decade more or longer. Moving from the traditional "one-time authentication and you're approved" will not happen overnight. Continuous, adaptive, risk-based authentication will essentially take everything we have learned so far in computer security, every tool we have created, and will put it all together in a real-time, constantly evaluating, automated way.

All of this is also done in a way that requires less user friction for normal, usual, low-risk tasks. Perhaps the way MFA and the new authentication framework meet and meld is that a user is allowed to seamlessly log on to any website and service they like without anything we traditionally think of as authentication being needed. No logon name. No password. No MFA needed. The session originating from the user's normal device, location, and time is all that is needed to gain initial access. Is the user doing their regular tasks in a normal manner? Are they accessing the screens they normally access and in the order they normally access them? Perhaps the user's keyboard and mouse-click activity are evaluated during the rest of the session to determine if the user's actions are normal and natural. And if the user goes to do something of high value or high risk, then maybe they are prompted to use their MFA solution (i.e., step-up authentication).

There are many authentication services (like those at Google and Microsoft) that already look at hundreds of user session traits to determine whether the user is who they say they are and are doing what they legitimately want to do. The future of authentication, regardless of implementation, is likely to look continuously at dozens to hundreds of user session traits, including these:

- User ID
- User logon method (password vs., MFA, etc.)
- Defined role (user vs. admin, etc.)
- User actions (normal, usual, timing, moving around site normally)
- Day/time
- User action vs. user action history
- Device ID (preregistered or familiar devices lower risk)
- Location (physical, IP address, trusted network)
- Behavioral traits
- Contextual clues
- Keyboard/mouse activity analytics

The whole time the authentication system is continuously evaluating the user session's risk score. It adds points for items that increase risk and subtracts points for characteristics that decrease risk. If a user's session exceeds to a particular risk score value, the system can decide between different risk mitigation outcomes, including these:

- Continues to allow access as is
- Continues to allow access as is but increase monitoring
- Prompts user for step-up authentication
- Denies user a specific action they were attempting
- Allows the user action, but an additional system or human is used to confirm validity before potential damage can't be reversed
- Kills action/access or does a forced logout of the user

The whole time you have a threat analytics engine determining how particular traits, characteristics, or actions equate to particular risks. This means the engine has to know the risk from past user actions and traits and newly developing risks and traits that are being learned. For example, a user who is normally logging in from the United States is detected as coming from Romania for this one logon session, and the system has been made aware of a slew of Romanian-based account takeovers that have been detected in the last few hours. This sort of adaptive approach to authentication requires that the system have a set of built-in, updatable rules, and ML or AI to help predict developing threats. Figure 24.3 shows a graphical summary representation of the various main components of a continuous, adaptive, risk-based authentication system.

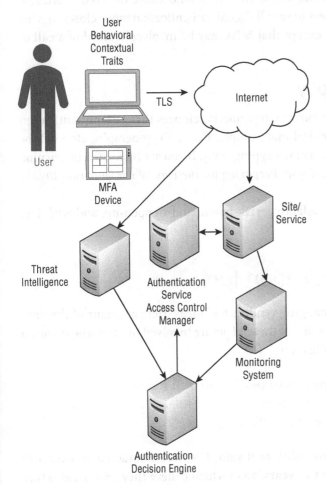

Figure 24.3: The main components of a continuous, adaptive, risk-based authentication system

Many of us are already quite familiar with similar authentication systems today: credit cards. Our credit card vendors allow us to go around the country (and sometimes the world) spending our money to our heart's content. Most of the time we can complete our purchases with little hassle. But sometimes, when the credit card's backend risk analysis engine detects a higher-risk event, your credit card company calls you or sends an SMS message asking you to confirm a particular transaction before they will allow it to proceed. For many people, that additional transaction "friction" happens only once or a few times every few years. Any more than that and your credit card vendor would start to worry that you're going to change credit cards.

Sometimes your credit card vendor detects your card being used in an anomalous way that you are not aware of. Your credit company detects this activity, cancels your card, voids any rogue transactions, and sends you a new card—all before you are aware of any anomalous activity. And sometimes, you detect the anomalous activity before the credit card company does, and you initiate the process. The latter scenario is happening less and less as time goes on because the credit card risk analytics engines are improving so much. Expect to see all digital authentication move closer to what we've already been used to with credit cards, except that MFA may be involved instead of a call or SMS message from the vendor.

Quantum-Resistant Cryptography

I would be remiss if I didn't mention that the current asymmetric ciphers that our authentication systems currently use and rely on (RSA, Diffie–Hellman, Elliptic Curve Cryptography, etc.) will be replaced in the next few years with quantum-resistant cryptography. If you are interested in learning more, check out my book *Cryptography Apocalypse: Preparing for the Day When Quantum Breaks Today's Crypto* (Wiley, 2019).

The future of authentication is continuous, adaptive, risk-based, and stepped-up, and with less user friction.

Interesting Newer Authentication Ideas

The authentication field is full of constantly changing vendors and ideas. Here are some of the ones I've come across recently. Only time will tell if some of these ideas are involved in the authentication of the future, but they are worth a quick investigation:

- Keystroke, mouse, and touchscreen dynamics (intensityanalytics.com)
- Proximity-based hardware tokens (gkaccess.com/products/halberd)
- Proximity-based MFA using phones (www.whitecyber.com)

I've seen some fantastic ideas and solutions. With that said, I've been contacted by over 100 brand-new authentication vendors over the last two years, all of which believe they have an idea that will take the world by storm, if only they can get enough press and publicity. And perhaps that is true. Some of the solutions are very good. But it's very tough to get the computer world to notice your new product. Unfortunately, I don't think a single new vendor that contacted me over the last two years has survived or significantly expanded. The authentication world is super competitive and eats its young.

But hopefully I've covered the traits that I think the future of authentication is going to involve, so if you see an authentication backend solution involving continuous, adaptive, and risk-based authentication, at least you know they are on the right track. And for the next 10 years or more, the MFA I've covered in this book will provide that extra layer of security when it's desired or required.

Summary

This chapter covered how authentication will look in the next 10 years and after. We began by discussing what is staying the same and what is changing regarding cybercrime, and then we did the same for authentication.

Chapter 25, "Takeaway Lessons" will recap the individual and larger lessons learned readers should take away from this book.

25

Takeaway Lessons

This chapter will recap the individual user and developer defenses provided by the various MFA solutions shared in the previous chapters and discuss the lessons readers need to take away from this book. We'll start with the broader lessons first.

Broader Lessons

This section covers some general takeaways from all MFA solutions.

MFA Works

In a book dedicated to hacking MFA, some readers may come away with the idea that MFA is bad or not worth using. Let me be clear: MFA decreases cybersecurity risk in many use cases, especially general account takeover (ATO) scenarios. But there is a difference between MFA decreasing risk in many scenarios and MFA not being hackable.

MFA does stop hacking in many scenarios, especially phishing attacks that ask for the user's passwords and then uses those fraudulently obtained credentials to log on to the victim's legitimate sites and services. If you don't have a password to be stolen because you're using MFA instead, then that type of attack will simply not work against you. MFA also stops many types of traditional attacks against sites and services that require MFA for logon. Unless an intruder finds a way around the MFA requirement in those two scenarios, the MFA solution decreases risk.

Multiple studies have shown that MFA is good at stopping widely broadcasted, general, credential phishing attacks, including these:

- security.googleblog.com/2019/05/new-research-how-effective-is-basic.html
- techcommunity.microsoft.com/t5/Azure-Active-Directory-Identity/Your-Pa-word-doesn-t-matter/ba-p/731984
- docs.microsoft.com/en-us/azure/security/fundamentals/steps-secure-identity

My favorite study is the first one. It shows that even SMS-based MFA—which I, along with many others, am not a fan of—significantly reduces non-targeted attacks. The keyword is non-targeted.

If there is a weakness to MFA, it's targeted attacks. MFA stops or significantly complicates the most popular type of general, widely broadcasted, attacks, where an attacker has nearly zero or zero information about their intended targets. The attackers just use a scattershot approach against a big population of potential victims and hope to get lucky with a few. Most cyberattacks are of this broadcast, scattershot, makeup. And MFA stops most (but not all) of these types of attacks cold. For example, if you are an attacker trying to phish someone out of their Gmail password and the user requires and uses MFA to log on to their Gmail account, that phish is not going to work.

But attackers who spend time learning about specific victims and their related potential attack areas can, with a little creativity, often find a weakness to exploit. Continuing the Gmail scenario, if I know that my victim requires MFA, I have to learn how Gmail MFA works and the methods to get around it. Any MFA method can be hacked, but it takes research and effort, and any increase in effort reduces the number of potential abusers and their chances of success. So, in most logon scenarios, MFA is a good thing to have. But an attacker can easily modify their general, broadcast attack to include MFA scenarios, and by making that one change, bring MFA-using users back into play as potential victims.

MFA Is Not Unhackable

In the same vein, "harder to accomplish" hacking and phishing does not mean impossible. The danger of thinking MFA is unhackable or even *nearly* unhackable can be extraordinarily dangerous, especially if you're a leader or a computer security practitioner. Because if you believe something is unhackable, you probably aren't educating everyone involved with the specific risks they still need to be aware of and defend against.

Anecdotally, most of the general attendees at my Hacking MFA webinars seem shocked to learn that a simple phishing email, like the one shown in Figure 6.4 in Chapter 6, "Access Control Token Tricks," can bypass their favorite MFA solution. Many have been told by their IT people that using an MFA token means they can't be phished and that they don't have to be worried about phishing emails. They have been taught a myth. I can send a regular-looking phishing email and compromise your account even if you are using MFA. That's the reality.

Teaching the wrong advice increases the likelihood of future compromise because the leaders and victims aren't worried and aren't looking out for the signs of a pending attack. It's like someone supposedly saying the *Titanic* was unsinkable. You can't avoid icebergs if you aren't worried about them in the first place. This is the primary lesson of this book — MFA is not unhackable.

Education Is Key

One of the critical recommendations, repeated again and again in this book, in nearly every chapter, is education. Educate your developers about potential attack scenarios so that they can implement mitigations to offset those risks. Educate your MFA users so that they are aware of the risks their MFA solution does and doesn't mitigate. Education and expectations are key to reducing security risk. Hackers are hoping users think they can't be hacked if they are using MFA. Ignorance is bliss and attackers love uneducated users.

In computer security, the field of computer security education is known as *security awareness training*. I used to mock the term the first time I read it in a Gartner report. Now, after thinking about it more, I love the term. It is exactly right. The single best thing you can do for anyone in computer security after implementing the best technical controls possible is to make people aware of the appropriate risks and scams.

For example, someone that doesn't know that Microsoft doesn't proactively call people to warn them that their computer is compromised by malware are far more likely to think the call is legitimate. Craigslist newbies using it for the first time often aren't prepared for all the scammers that will immediately reply to any item the person puts up for sale. They hear from someone who is not only willing to pay them full price, but also pay for delivery and think, "This Craigslist selling is awesome! Why didn't I use it before!" If they don't know about these scams, it makes them far more likely to become a victim. And to prevent a potential victim from becoming a real victim all it takes is a little awareness about the possible scams — security awareness training.

Security Isn't Everything

As covered in Chapter 4, "Usability vs. Security," security isn't everything to everyone. As in the real world, the 100 percent protection of the digital world isn't the primary objective of most users. Users want the least amount of security that allows them to securely carry out their objectives most of the time. What the intersection of security and usability is depends on the use case scenario and needs and wants of the user. For example, in the real world I never want my car's brakes or accelerator to fail. Failure is unacceptable. But I might accept that my radio doesn't always work, and I probably sometimes drive with my windshield wipers in a degraded state longer than I should. Same with computer security. Sometimes I want absolute security or close to it. But most of the time I'm OK with OK security. I don't need 10-factor authentication to protect my Twitter postings.

This lesson is primarily intended for developers so that they will understand that usability and friction are the most important factors in any MFA solution. Make a solution too hard to use and people will use something else. Delivering a very secure solution isn't the only factor buyers consider when selecting an MFA solution.

Every MFA Solution Has Trade-Offs

Every MFA solution has strengths and weaknesses. Different types of solutions have different types of strengths and weaknesses. No solution is perfect. Every solution can be hacked in one or more ways. MFA solution buyers need to find out what those strengths and weaknesses are and then decide which ones they need and which ones they can live without.

Authentication Does Not Exist in a Vacuum

Every MFA solution has a dozen-plus dependencies, many of which are beyond the MFA vendor's control. Every dependency is a potential attack vector. Vendors should threat-model these dependencies and see whether they can mitigate abuses of those dependencies when designing their solutions. Buyers and users must recognize that potential areas of attack exist that an MFA vendor cannot secure.

3×3 Security Pillars

Using MFA as securely as possible goes beyond the MFA device itself. Every defense-in-depth solution is a combination of preventive, detective, and reactive controls as carried out by policy, technical components, and education. I call these controls the 3×3 security pillars, as graphically represented in Figure 25.1. The 3×3 security pillars apply to more than just MFA solutions, but they're useful to consider when deploying your MFA defenses.

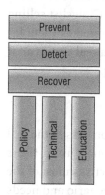

Figure 25.1: The 3×3 security pillars

When I think about computer security defenses, I have three control objectives in my head:

- Prevent
- Detect
- Recover

NOTE The most popular security control framework, the NIST Cybersecurity Framework (www.nist.gov/cyberframework), has five tiers, but I consolidate them into three components.

I want to prevent bad things from happening to an environment I manage. If bad things get past my preventive controls, I want early warning and detection of those things in order to mitigate damage. And I have to recover from the attack and figure out how to prevent it next time. Everything in my planning, including MFA implementations, looks at computer security using these three pillars of security defenses.

When I learn of a risk or threat, I first ask myself, what is the true severity of the risk? One-quarter to one-third of all risks are ranked as high/critical. Considering that we face well over 10,000 different risks each year, that equates to thousands of supposedly high-risk threats we need to respond to. The most likely ones, out of the over 10,000 threats you are told you should fear each year, are the ones you need to mitigate first and best. Most threats (90–98 percent) never occur to the average organization. The trick is to sort out from the much bigger list of threats, the truly important and likely threats versus all the ones you are told you need to prepare for. It can be hard to do without being cognitive of the challenges and plenty of practice.

I'll give you a real example. The Meltdown and Spectre chip vulnerabilities (meltdownattack.com) are likely the most threatening, high-risk, vulnerabilities to be announced in decades. . .certainly in my career. The world's most popular computer CPU chips released since 1990's (i.e., Intel x86, ARM, and IBM Power) had the flaws. Hundreds of millions of computers and devices were susceptible and the vulnerabilities were exploitable no matter which OS you ran and no matter what protection you implemented. And without patching those vulnerabilities, any involved computer would not only fail to stop the attacks, but would not even register an event log record that documented anything had happened, much less, that a successful exploit had occurred. After the announcement of Meltdown and Spectre in 2017, over a hundred demonstration malware programs were created and released to show how easy it would be to "worm" and "weaponize" those vulnerabilities. Years later, there isn't a vulnerability report that won't list devices not patched against Meltdown and Spectre as among the highest risk threats you need to mitigate immediately. You've got to patch, patch, patch against them! Stop what you're doing and patch now!

But there is the very relevant fact that, to my knowledge, there hasn't been a single real-world exploit of Meltdown or Spectre vulnerabilities conducted against a single real-world target by real criminals. That changes the risk calculation immensely. The supposed high-risk threats created by Meltdown and Spectre are really a near-zero risk for most organizations. Until you hear about at least one real world attack, is there really any risk? Perhaps your organization could be the first publicly known victim, but it probably won't be.

There are a lot of things anyone can worry about, but something that hasn't even occurred once in the world probably isn't high on the list. You can worry about a piece of a satellite falling to earth and landing on your building's roof top. It's a possibility. Those sorts of accidents actually do occur, but are extremely rare and even harder to predict. If a satellite piece fell on your roof it would probably cause a lot of damage. But most people don't worry about it or implement mitigations against it because it is such a rare event. Same with Meltdown and Spectre. You can worry about it. The "experts" and every vulnerability scanning software you could run would indicate anything not patched against Meltdown and Spectre is at high risk of being compromised. The world is trying to tell you to worry about it. But no matter what they say, it isn't really a critical risks — at least until the first public attack due to it occurs.

That's what I mean by focusing on preventing and detecting what your biggest and most likely threats really are. Figure out which critical threats you'll likely face in the future and focus on preventing and detecting those things first and best. Most of the things you are told to worry about really aren't high-risk events even if they are labeled as such.

NOTE Another good example of false risks are from the companies that sell the "emergency seatbelt cutters," which are supposed to be used if you are driving a car and happen to find yourself in deep water with a jammed seat belt. A car going into deep water is a fairly rare event. But even if that did happen, why would a person who unbuckles their seat belt every time they drive the car suddenly be unable to unbuckle their seat belt and supposedly be able to find and use some obscure tool they have never used before and use it in an emergency situation? Vendors of useless products love to use fear to sell products.

Prevention of the most likely critical threats is the most important defense anyone can have. It may sound funny that I have to write that sentence, but many of today's conventional computer defenses are based on an "assume breach" mentality, where you either assume your environment is already currently breached or easily could be if someone concentrated on breaking into it. Assume breach essentially focuses on preventing internal spread and detection. That's great. All defenses definitely need a strong set of assume breach defenses. But the primary focus has always been and still needs to be on stopping the badness from being successful in breaking in to an organization in the first place. Accordingly, I'm more of a STOP BREACH mentality.

Efficient threat detection is a matter of figuring out your most likely threats and determining whether you have the appropriate detection capability if they successfully occur against your environment? Take all your potential security logging and alert tools and services and figure out which ones map or don't map to your most likely threats. You'll see a lot of overlap and some weaknesses. Plug the gaps. Recovery is damage control and figuring out what you did wrong in the first two pillars, prevention and detection, so that it won't happen again.

For each of the three security control objectives (prevent, detect, recover) you have to do everything in your power to mitigate the most likely threats. Combine the best defenses you can split out among the three types of controls:

- Policy
- Technical
- Training

Every security control needs policy behind it. Each control needs policy, procedure, guidelines, and education. You must empirically document control expectations to avoid any ambiguity. Everyone needs to understand what the biggest, most likely threats are and how you are mitigating them. Provide expectations, which helps with accountability if someone doesn't do something right. Or perhaps everyone does everything right and when something bad still happens, it means you missed something, and you have to update the controls. Either way, documented and communicated controls help everyone to understand expectations and row in the same direction.

Technical controls are all the mitigations you can implement using software or hardware to enforce a particular input, action, or output. Whenever possible, implement a technical control to mitigate your biggest threats. Such controls help put down the majority of your risks and do so automatically. This is where MFA solutions come into play. If used correctly, they can significantly reduce many types of threats. But any MFA solution cannot do it alone. It takes a complete defense-in-depth strategy with correctly selected and implemented MFA solutions.

Lastly, some amount of badness will always get past your technical controls. I don't care what you implement; technical controls are not perfect, and hackers find ways around them. So, educate yourself, staff, and co-workers on how to spot badness when it gets past existing technical controls and what they should do when they see it (hopefully report and mitigate). Ensure that your MFA solution includes all the necessary components (policy, technical, education) to be as successful as it can be.

There Is No Single Best MFA Solution for Everyone

As covered in Chapter 23, "Selecting the Right MFA Solution," no single MFA solution is best for everyone. No MFA solution works with everything. You must first determine what case scenarios in your organization must be protected by MFA and find the solutions that work with your use cases and applications.

Different people and organizations have different risk scenarios and levels of risk acceptance. What works well with my employers and is seen as "overkill" would probably not be seen as even minimally acceptable at a national research lab or military weapons depot. Follow the concepts in Chapter 23 to help you find the best solution(s) for your organization and personal needs.

There Are Better MFA Solutions

With that said, there are some MFA solutions that are better than others. Those that attempt to mitigate common, large threats are better than those that do not. Those that use mutual authentication are more secure than those that do one-way authentication. MFA solutions that use Security Development Lifecycle (SDL) programming methods and tools and use effective threat modeling to reduce risk are better than those that do not. Phone apps are more secure than SMS-based solutions. Phone apps with push messages are often more secure than those that do not use push messages. OTP tokens that use industry-accepted algorithms are likely stronger than those that do not. MFA solutions that use industry-accepted cryptography and key sizes are stronger than those that do not. Hardware and software multifactor tokens are more secure than single-factor solutions. Solutions that require site preregistration are more secure than those that do not. And so on. Use the methods you've learned in this book to look at different MFA solutions, even of similar types, and pick the best ones. The next section of this chapter will review the individual developer and user recommendations for various types of MFA solutions.

MFA Defensive Recap

This section reviews the individual recommendations for various MFA solution types as covered in previous chapters, split by recommendations for developers and users.

Developer Defense Summary

This is a recap of the main developer defenses discussed in his book:

- All developers should be trained in SDL, in threat modeling, and in the strengths, risks, and types of attacks against the type of MFA solution they are developing (all chapters).
- Developers should threat-model the MFA solutions and implement mitigations against the most likely threats (Chapter 5, "Hacking MFA in General").
- All websites and services should generate random, hard-to-guess session IDs (Chapter 6).
- All MFA solutions should use industry-accepted cryptography and key sizes (Chapter 6 and more).
- Developers should follow secure coding practices (Chapters 6, 15, "Buggy Software," and more).
- Developers should implement secure transmission channels with their MFA solutions (Chapter 6).
- Developers should include authentication timeout protections to prevent malicious token reuse (Chapter 6).
- Developers should tie access tokens to specific devices or sites (Chapter 6).
- Developers should risk-model and secure critical dependencies (Chapters 5, 7, "End-Point Attacks," Chapter 10, "Subject Hijack Attacks," and more).
- MFA solutions should prevent or notify the user of potential unauthorized additional instances (Chapter 7).
- MFA solutions should notify the user of encryption key changes (Chapter 7).
- MFA solutions should use dynamic adaptive authentication for uncharacteristic or high-risk end-user actions (Chapter 7 and others).
- Transaction verification requests must include all critical details (Chapter 7 and others).
- If SMS is involved, MFA solution must use compensating controls to prevent misuse (Chapter 8).
- SMS-using MFA solutions should include a way for the user to verify SMS message legitimacy (Chapter 8, "SMS Attacks").
- SMS-using MFA solutions should expire SMS codes in no more than 10 minutes (Chapter 8).
- For SMS-based MFA solutions, the application or instructions should tell users to put in MFA contact info in their contact list so that SMS message can be verified as coming from predefined vendor phone numbers or code (Chapter 8).
- SMS-based MFA solution developers should prevent suspicious SMS messages from being sent to end users (Chapter 8).
- Developers should use push notifications and apps instead of SMS messages (Chapter 8).

- For OTP-based MFA solutions, developers must use reliable, trusted, and tested OTP algorithms (Chapter 9, "One-Time Password Attacks").
- For OTP-based MFA solutions, OTP setup codes must expire (Chapter 9).
- For OTP-based MFA solutions, OTP result codes must expire (Chapter 9).
- For OTP-based MFA solutions, developers must prevent OTP code replay (Chapter 9).
- Developers should use NIST-certified or quantum random number generators (Chapter 9).
- For OTP-based MFA solutions, developers should increase security by requiring additional entry beyond OTP code (Chapter 9).
- MFA developers must ensure that their MFA solution is not susceptible to brute-forcing attacks (Chapter 9).
- MFA developers need to secure their seed value database (Chapter 9).
- MFA developers need to prevent one-to-many mappings (Chapter 10, "Subject Hjack Attacks").
- MFA developers must lock authentication to predefined authenticated site(s) (Chapter 11, "Fake Authentication Attacks").
- MFA developers should require that users register logon devices (Chapter 11).
- MFA developers should disable legacy protocols and services that can be used to bypass MFA (Chapter 11).
- MFA developers need to use forced logon apps (Chapter 11).
- MFA developers need to provide better/best authentication solutions (Chapter 12, "Social Engineering Attacks").
- MFA solutions must provide contextual information (Chapter 12).
- MFA developers need to expire and anonymize master/bypass/travel codes (Chapter 13, "Downgrade/Recovery Attacks").
- MFA developers should consider requiring a user's acquaintance as a recovery option (Chapter 13).
- If personal knowledge questions are used as a recovery method, developers should use advanced, adaptive personal knowledge questions for recovery (Chapter 13).
- MFA developers need to enforce a maximum number of guesses in a specified time period (Chapter 14, "Brute-Force Attacks").
- MFA developers should rate-limit the number of concurrent logon attempts (Chapter 14).
- MFA developers need to blacklist rogue IP addresses (Chapter 14).
- MFA developers need to increase wait time between each allowed guess (Chapter 14).
- MFA developers should increase the number of possible answers to any guess (Chapter 14).
- MFA developers should enforce answer complexity (Chapter 14).
- MFA developers should send emails to warn end users of elevated risk scenarios, such as logons from new devices or a new location (Chapter 14).
- MFA developers must use secure development tools with secure defaults (Chapter 15).
- MFA developers should do code reviews (Chapter 15).
- MFA developers need to penetration-test their MFA solutions (Chapter 15).
- MFA developers need to enable automate patching of their MFA solution without requiring end-user intervention (Chapter 15).

- Biometric MFA developers should strive for low error rates (Chapter 16, "Attacks Against Biometrics").
- Biometric MFA developers must implement antispoofing measures (Chapter 16).
- Administrators should require MFA with biometric MFA solutions (Chapter 16).
- Vendors should securely protect biometric trait databases and stored data (Chapter 16).
- MFA developers should allow/require split key solutions if possible (Chapter 17, "Physical Attacks").
- Hardware MFA solution developers should implement anti-tampering defenses (Chapter 17).
- MFA solution developers should mitigate side-channel attacks (Chapter 17).
- If practical for the MFA solution type, developers should enable viewing disruptors (Chapter 17).
- MFA solutions should allow easy remote decommissioning (Chapter 17).
- Developers should use default network packet encryption (Chapter 18, "DNS Hijacking").
- Developers should lock down any related DNS registrar records (Chapter 18).
- MFA Developers should enable Send Policy Framework (SPF), Domain Keys Identified Mail (DKIM), and Domain-Based Message Authentication, Reporting & Conformance (DMARC) for emails they send to end users (Chapter 18).
- MFA developers should hard-code values where it makes sense (Chapter 18).
- MFA developers should decrease chances of namespace manipulation (Chapter 18).
- MFA developers should not support Internationalized Domain Names (IDN) or Punycode encoding on any involved URLs (Chapter 18).
- MFA developers should use industry-standard protocols and APIs (Chapter 18).
- MFA developers should limit API attack surfaces (Chapter 19, "API Abuses").
- MFA developers should validate application workflow (Chapter 19).
- MFA developers should lock API keys to locations instead of email addresses (Chapter 19).
- MFA developers should use client-side security enforcements cautiously (Chapter 19).
- MFA solutions should be set to "fail closed" defaults (Chapter 19).
- MFA developers should obscure MFA-related values in URLs (Chapter 19).
- MFA solutions should provide strong reporting and alerting for end users for anomalous events (Chapter 20, "Miscellaneous MFA Attacks").
- Any changes of critical identity information (i.e., email address, phone numbers, etc.) related to an MFA-protected account should be approved by the legitimate account owner using existing contact information prior to being updated to prevent fraudulent changes by attackers.

User Defense Summary

This is a recap of the main user defenses discussed in his book:

- Users should be provided with security awareness training to learn the strengths, weaknesses, and potential threats and exploits of any considered MFA solution (all chapters).
- Users should always have up-to-date endpoint protections (Chapter 7).

- Users should download applications/apps only from official vendors and app stores (Chapter 7).
- Good training should ensure that users do not fall victim to social engineering (Chapter 7).
- Users and admins need to patch security flaws in a timely manner (Chapter 7).
- Users should use split secrets if possible (Chapters 7 and 17).
- Users need to be aware of rogue SMS and email recovery messages (Chapter 8).
- Users need to be wary of SMS recovery PIN scams (Chapter 8).
- Users should try to place a "lock" on their SIM info with their cell phone provider (Chapter 8).
- Uses need to protect their cell phone provider network account logon with MFA (Chapter 8).
- Users should be wary of shortened URL links and expand them before clicking on them (Chapter 8).
- Users should minimize posting their phone numbers online (Chapter 8).
- OTP-based MFA users should make sure they don't get socially engineered out of their OTP code (Chapter 9).
- OTP-based MFA users should delete any OTP setup codes (Chapter 9).
- Hardware-based MFA users should physically protect their OTP device (Chapter 9).
- Users should verify any relied-on URLs (Chapter 11).
- Admins and users should disable legacy protocols and services that can be used to bypass MFA (Chapter 11).
- Users should avoid using basic personal knowledge questions for recovery whenever possible (Chapter 13).
- Users forced to use basic personal knowledge questions should give wrong answers to them whenever possible (Chapter 13).
- MFA users should protect any "master/travel" codes (Chapter 13).
- MFA users should only use MFA solutions with anti–brute force defenses (Chapter 14).
- Users should only use MFA solutions whose developers use Security Development Lifecycle (SDL) practices (Chapter 15).
- Admins should perform vulnerability scans on their MFA solutions on a regular basis, if possible (Chapter 15).
- Admins should not allow biometric authentication in remote/isolated scenarios (Chapter 16).
- Users should protect MFA solutions against physical attacks/theft (Chapter 17).
- Admins or users should replace worn keypad devices showing signs of wear (Chapter 17).
- Users and admins should improve physical safety and awareness (Chapter 17).
- Admins should implement Domain Name System Security Extensions (DNSSEC) (Chapter 18).
- Admins or users should look for, detect, and alert on unauthorized DNS changes (Chapter 18).
- Admins and users should implement secure configuration options (Chapter 19).
- Users should protect any used API keys (Chapter 19).

In summarizing user defenses, all reviewers and buyers need to realize that they have the most chance to influence an MFA vendor and their product before purchasing it. If you note a critical missing feature, your best chance at getting that feature added is to require that the solution have that feature available before you purchase it. Once you have spent money to buy a product, both you and the vendor are locked into each other for the foreseeable future. If the vendor promises to have any particular feature in a future version of their product, get the details documented in writing, along with a penalty of some sort if the vendor cannot meet the promised feature.

I don't make this suggestion for a client to be an adversarial position or assume the vendor is evil. No, quite the contrary; most MFA vendors are doing their best to make the best product they can sell. They want to make customers happy and secure. We are all together in this fight against cyber-security threats. Be a partner with your MFA vendor to help make a better product. Be a good partner. Be patient. But hold vendors accountable to promises for future features. Accountability helps both sides.

In conclusion, identity has always been the true network perimeter, and strong identity requires strong authentication. Any attacker in control of someone's identity can more easily bypass all other defenses. MFA-protected identities prevent many malicious hacking scenarios, sometimes substan-tially so. But that statement isn't the same as saying any MFA solution is unhackable.

MFA buyers should pick the solution that works best for their critical use case scenarios and that fulfills their requirements. Any MFA solution can be hacked, but some solutions are better than others. Anyone wishing to make comments, recommendations, or corrections can contact me at roger@bannertcs.com. Thanks to everyone for reading this book. Now go fight the good fight!

Appendix: List of MFA Vendors

MFA vendors can offer everything from stand-alone MFA solutions to integration services so that you can enable existing (non-MFA) sites and services. This appendix lists more than 115 vendors you can choose among, but it is a partial list. MFA solution providers probably number into the thousands, especially when taking into account small "boutique" firms that cater to particular industries (health care, banking, etc.) and regional firms in particular countries. But this is the most comprehensive list of MFA solution providers I'm aware of, so it's a good starting place. Use the suggestions in Chapter 23, "Selecting the Right MFA Solution" as a way to cull the larger list to a small subset of MFA vendors you're interested in.

You can download an Excel spreadsheet containing these MFA vendor names and websites, including an options matrix indicating which basic features each vendor or solution has or supports, at wiley.com/go/hackingmultifactor. You can sort and index the list according to the features that are most important to you. The spreadsheet is an attempt to do some of the initial research for you.

Acceptto (www.acceptto.com)

Accertify (www.accertify.com)

Accops (www.accops.com)

Arendir (aerendir.info)

Auth2encate (www.authen2cate.com)

Authenticator Plus (www.authenticatorplus.com)

AuthentIQ (www.authentiq.com)

AuthenWare (www.authenware.com/products.php)

AuthLite (www.authlite.com)

AuthPoint (www.watchguard.com/wgrd-products/authpoint-multi-factor-authentication)

Authx (authx.com)

Authy (authy.com)

BankVault (www.bankvault.com)

Bluink (bluink.ca)

Censornet (www.censornet.com)

Centrify (www.centrify.com/tag/mfa)

Cidaas (www.cidaas.com)

Clef WordPress 2FA Plugin (pluginu.com/wpclef)

CryptoPhoto (cryptophoto.com)

Daon (www.daon.com/solutions/multi-factor-authentication)

DualAuth (www.dualauth.com)

Duo Security (duo.com)

Entrust (www.entrustdatacard.com/solutions/two-factor-authentication)

ESET (www.eset.com/us/business/endpoint-security/two-factor-authentication)

Excelsecu (www.excelsecu.com)

Feitian (www.ftsafe.com)

FIDO Alliance Certified (fidoalliance.org/certification/fido-certified-products)

FusionAuth (fusionauth.io)

Google Titan Security Key (cloud.google.com/titan-security-key)

GoTrust (www.gotrustid.com)

Hanko (hanko.io)

HelloID (www.helloid.co.uk)

HID (www.hidglobal.com/authentication-technologies)

Huawei SAASPASS (saaspass.com/sso/huawei-identity-and-access-management-multi-factor-authentication-mfa-single-sign-on-saml)

Hypersecu (hypersecu.com)

HYPR (www.hypr.com)

IBM Cloud App ID (www.ibm.com/cloud/app-id)

ID.me (www.id.me)

Idaptive (www.idaptive.com)

Identité (www.identite.us)

Identity Automation (www.identityautomation.com)

Identy (www.identy.io)

IDEX Biometrics (www.idexbiometrics.com)

Idexbiometrics (www.idexbiometrics.com)

IDmelon (www.idmelon.com)

Infineon (www.infineon.com/cms/en/product/security-smart-card-solutions)

InstaSafe (instasafe.com)

Intensity Analytics (www.intensityanalytics.com)

inWebo (www.myinwebo.com)

iWelcome (www.iwelcome.com)

Kensington VeriMark Fingerprint Key (www.kensington.com/p/products/data-protection/
biometric/verimark-fingerprint-key-fido-u2f-windows-hello-designed-for-surface)

LastPass (www.lastpass.com)

LoginTC (www.logintc.com)

MB Usable Security (mbusecurity.com)

Mi-Token (www.mi-token.com)

Micro Focus NetIQ Advanced Authentication (www.microfocus.com/en-us/products/
netiq-advanced-authentication/overview)

MIRACL (miracl.com)

Movenda (www.movenda.com)

NEC (www.nec.com/en/global/solutions/biometrics/index.html)

Nevis (www.nevis-security.com/en)

Nok Nok (noknok.com)

OAuth.io (oauth.io)

Okta (www.okta.com)

OneLogin (www.onelogin.com/product/multi-factor-authentication)

OneSpan (www.onespan.com)

OnlyKey (onlykey.io)

Optimal IdM (optimalidm.com)

PasswordWrench (www.passwordwrench.com)

Penta Security Systems (www.pentasecurity.com)

Ping Identity (www.pingidentity.com)

PistolStar (www.pistolstar.com)

PixelPin (www.pixelpin.io)

privacyIDEA (www.privacyidea.org)

Protectimus (www.protectimus.com)

PureID (www.pureid.io)

REVE Secure (revesecure.com)

RingCaptcha (ringcaptcha.com)

Rohos (www.rohos.com)

RSA Security (www.rsa.com)

Rublon (rublon.com)

SAASPASS (saaspass.com)

Samsung SDS (www.samsungsds.com/us/en/solutions/bns/ms/mobile_security.html)

Secfense (secfense.com)

Secret Double Octopus (doubleoctopus.com)

SecSign (www.secsign.com)

Secure Metric (www.securemetric.com)

SecureAuth (www.secureauth.com)

SecurEnvoy (www.securenvoy.com)

SECUVE (www.secuve.com/eng/sub03/sub03_0302.php)

Silverfort (www.silverfort.com)

SMSsync (smssync.ushahidi.com)

SolidPass (www.solidpass.com)

SoloKeys (solokeys.com)

Sonavation (www.sonavation.com)

Specops (specopssoft.com)

SSenStone (www.ssenstone.com/eng)

Star Link (www.starlinkindia.com/Products/bio-face-reader)

StrongKey (strongkey.com)

Suprema (www.suprema-id.com)

SurePassID (surepassid.com)

Swivel Secure (swivelsecure.com/authcontrol-sentry-multi-factor-authentication)

SyferLock (www.syferlock.com)

Symantec VIP (vip.symantec.com)

TeleSign (www.telesign.com)

Thales (www.thalesgroup.com/en/markets/digital-identity-and-security)

Thetis (thetis.io)

ThumbSignIn (thumbsignin.com)

Token2 (www.token2.com)

Transakt (gettransakt.com/transakt)

Trusona (www.trusona.com)

TrustKey Solutions (www.trustkeysolutions.com)

Twizo (www.twizo.com)

V-Key (www.v-key.com)

Veridium (veridiumid.com)

Verifyoo (www.verifyoo.com/Verifyoo)

WatchGuard (www.watchguard.com/wgrd-products/authpoint-multi-factor-authentication)

Whykeykey (www.whykeykey.com/en/product/ydentity.html)

WikID Systems (www.wikidsystems.com)

Yubico (www.yubico.com)

ZOLOZ (www.zoloz.com)

Index

Other Wiley Books by Roger Grimes

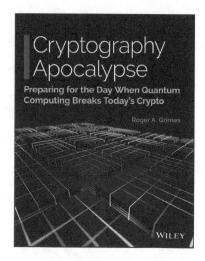

Cryptography Apocalypse: Preparing for the Day When Quantum Computing Breaks Today's Crypto

ISBN: 978-1-119-61819-5; November 2019

Cryptography Apocalypse is a crucial resource for every IT and InfoSec professional for preparing for the coming quantum-computing revolution as unfortunately, many current cryptographic methods will soon be obsolete. The encryption technologies we rely on every day—HTTPS, TLS, WiFi protection, VPNs, cryptocurrencies, PKI, digital certificates, smartcards, and most two-factor authentication—will be virtually useless. . . unless you prepare. Post-quantum crypto algorithms are already a reality, but implementation will take significant time and computing power. This practical guide helps IT leaders and implementers make the appropriate decisions today to meet the challenges of tomorrow.

Hacking the Hacker: Learn From the Experts Who Take Down Hackers

ISBN: 978-1-119-39621-5; May 2017

Hacking the Hacker takes you inside the world of cybersecurity to show you what goes on behind the scenes, and introduces you to the men and women fighting this technological arms race. Twenty-six of the world's top white hat hackers, security researchers, and leaders, describe what they do, with each profile preceded by a no-experience-necessary explanation of the relevant technology. Dorothy Denning discusses advanced persistent threats, Martin Hellman describes how he helped invent public key encryption, Dr. Charlie Miller talks about hacking cars, and other cybersecurity experts from around the world detail the threats, their defenses, tools, and techniques. Light on jargon and heavy on intrigue, this book is designed to be an introduction to the field for aspiring hackers of all ages.

Hacking
Multifactor
Authentication

Roger A. Grimes

WILEY